Human Motivation
Second Edition

Human Motivation
Second Edition

Robert E. Franken

University of Calgary

Brooks/Cole Publishing Company
Pacific Grove, California

Brooks/Cole Publishing Company
A Division of Wadsworth, Inc.

Printed in the United States of America
10   9   8   7   6   5   4   3   2

Library of Congress Cataloging-in-Publication Data
Franken, Robert E., [date]-
   Human motivation.

   Bibliography: p.
   Includes index.
   1. Motivation (Psychology)   I. Title.
BF503.F7   1988   153.8   87-29959
ISBN 0-534-08988-7

Sponsoring Editors: *Phil Curson, C. Deborah Laughton*
Editorial Associate: *Amy Mayfield*
Production Editor: *Phyllis Larimore*
Manuscript Editor: *Barbara Salazar*
Permissions Editor: *Mary Kay Hancharick*
Interior and Cover Design: *Katherine Minerva*
Cover Photo: *John Kelly/The Image Bank West*
Art Coordinator: *Lisa Torri*
Interior Illustration: *Maggie Stevens*
Photo Researcher: *Marquita Flemming*
Typesetting: *Graphic Typesetting Service, Los Angeles, California*
Cover Printing: *Phoenix Color Corp., Long Island City, New York*
Printing and Binding: *The Maple-Vail Book Mfg. Group, York, Pennsylvania*

Credits continue on page 541.

To Helen, Ryan, and Renee

Preface

For centuries scholars have speculated about what motivates humans. In examining the explanations that have been offered, one is immediately struck by their diversity. Certain "bad" behaviors, for example, have been attributed to devils, diseases, evil parents, insanity, inappropriate learning, unhealthy foods, and the positions of the stars, among other things. The growth of empirical research has provided a framework to help us determine the validity of such explanations. Over the years we have ruled out some of them, but a variety of explanations can still be considered good candidates in our quest for an answer to the age-old question of why we do what we do.

In this second edition I have incorporated a great deal of new research while retaining and, I hope, improving on the organization of the first. As in the first edition, I have taken a components approach; that is, I have attempted to identify the various factors that have been found to influence behavior as either biological, learned, or cognitive. The word *component* is meant to imply that each type of factor—biological, learned, or cognitive—contributes to the total event that produces behavior. Each component plays a role, each has an influence, and each is influenced by the others.

As in the first edition, I have organized the research data and theories around practical issues. That does not mean that I have neglected to incorporate animal research. Some of the research that is most helpful to us in our efforts to understand why we do what we do comes from animal models. The focus, nevertheless, is on day-to-day human motivation. Over the years many students have asked a wide variety of questions about why they feel a certain way, why they do certain things, why people they read about or meet tend to think and act in certain ways. Those questions have helped me a great deal to focus on issues that are important to students and people in general. I have been fascinated to find that usually there are research data or theories that can be brought to bear on any question. Even if I can't provide a specific answer, I can at least help students to think about how one might arrive at an answer that is reasonable as well as scientific. It is those questions that have prompted me to write very specific "practical application" boxes, in which I try to show how a body of research and theory can throw light on a fairly specific question. It is very gratifying to me when former students say that they periodically refer back to *Human Motivation* to see if they can answer a question that has recently arisen.

In this edition I have added a new chapter on emotion (Chapter 7). Although I touched on the topic of emotion in the first edition, I see now that I did not give it the emphasis it deserves. As well as dealing with such traditional topics as the theories of emotion, I show that it is possible to understand such common and important emotions as optimism, fear, anxiety, and altruism.

Practically every chapter has been changed to reflect current research and thinking. In Chapter 3, on arousal, for example, I discuss how the concept of arousal can help us understand such syndromes as hyperactivity and autism, and how sensory overload leads not only to high arousal but to altered attention and thinking. I discuss research that shows that a technique called restricted environmental stimulation technique (REST) can help people who are chronically overaroused to react in ways that are more adaptive. I also deal with the everyday problem of vigilance. In Chapter 4, on sleep, I discuss not only some of the current thinking about the various biological rhythms that affect sleep and waking but how these rhythms are involved in such sleep disorders as insomnia and jet lag. In Chapter 5, on hunger and eating, I discuss some of the latest theories on why we tend to overeat and research that shows how our understanding of these mechanisms can be brought to bear on dieting. In Chapter 6, on sex behavior, I deal with the role of hormones not only in sexual development but in a wide range of gender differences that have been identified in recent years. In Chapter 8, on stress and coping, I deal specifically with the role of cognitive factors in stress, such as the role of appraisal.

Chapter 9, on drug use and addiction, incorporates some of the new biochemical findings that explain why various drugs are addictive. In addition I have tried to spell out clearly the role of learning in drug use and addiction. I also discuss the very important role played in the addiction process by beliefs about the effects of drugs. Chapter 10, on aggression, retains most of the material of the first edition, but I have added some material on the factors that link obedience and pornography with aggression. In Chapter 11, on depression, controllability, and assertiveness, I have incorporated some of the new biochemical evidence pertaining not only to the origins of depression but to some of the cognitive/personality factors that make people prone to depression. In Chapter 12, on achievement and power, I have addressed the question of how and why people will or will not accept challenges. The section on power is totally rewritten and updated. Chapter 13, on curiosity, exploratory behavior, and competence, brings together material formerly in other parts of the book to give a more integrated view of these topics. A large section is devoted to sensation seeking, as sensation seekers tend to be motivated by the need for novel experiences—the essence of curiosity and exploratory behavior. Chapter 14, on work motivation, discusses some of the current approaches to management described in such books as *In Search of Excellence.*

Although this book is intended primarily for psychology majors, I have kept in mind that motivation is of interest to just about everyone. Over the years students of business, counseling, education, engineering, nursing, physical education, and social work have said they took my course because they felt that knowing something about human motivation would help them in their chosen professions. Other students in such fields as art, history, and philosophy have said they simply want to know something about their own personal motivation. Because motivation courses often attract a diverse population, I have tried to make the book easily understood by readers with little background in psychology yet challenging to those who are familiar with the subject.

Many people have contributed directly or indirectly to the preparation of this book. Students in my motivation class have given me the inspiration and the feedback that helped shape the book's organization and content. Discussions with colleagues and graduate students have helped sharpen my thinking. To all these people I say thank you.

The four reviewers who offered suggestions for improving this edition and then read the final manuscript deserve a special word of thanks not only for the time they devoted to the task but for their sincere interest in helping me. They are: David Drews, Juniata College; Joan Migdoll, Northwestern University; Ronald Ulm, Salisbury State College; and A. Bond Woodruff, Northern Illinois University.

My former editor, C. Deborah Laughton, has become a good friend over the years. I thank her for her continued support and her thoughtful comments and suggestions. And I also thank Phil Curson, my editor, for his interest and support.

Finally, I thank my wife, Helen, and my children, Ryan and Renee, who have been more than understanding about the many nights and weekends I could not spend with them as I prepared this second edition.

Robert E. Franken

Brief Contents

Contents

SIX   The Sex Motive, Sexual Behavior, and Gender Differences   137

SEVEN   Emotions as Motives: Understanding Optimism, Fear, Anxiety, and Altruism   184

EIGHT   Stress, Distress, and Coping   222

NINE Drug Use and Drug Addiction 264

Human Motivation
Second Edition

Past and Current Issues in Motivation

How did early scholars and thinkers conceptualize motivation in humans and animals?

Why did evolutionary theory change our thinking about motivational processes?

How does a motivational researcher differ from other psychological researchers?

What role do biological structures such as the brain play in producing behavior?

Do past learning and the way we think affect what we do?

What is the current focus of motivational research?

Consider the following event that occurs with persistent regularity. It is a bright, sunny morning, and a young man is walking briskly across the campus, excited by the prospect of a stimulating lecture from his motivation professor. An attractive young woman crosses his path. His interest is suddenly aroused, and he fixes his attention on her. With obvious practice he quickly examines her face and traces the contours of her body. Satisfied that she meets his critera for a good-looking, if not beautiful, woman, he makes a mental note to find out who she is so he can ask her for a date. He again fixes his attention on finding his way to class. Similarly,

The motivations involved in sexual interest are a complex blend of biological, learned, and cognitive factors.

a young woman, also on her way to class, notices a man just ahead of her. He is well dressed and wears a pleasant smile, and she notes that he walks with an air of self-confidence. She quickens her step, hoping he may be going to the same class she is trying to locate.

While these examples appear to have something to do with sexual motivation, there is more to them than first meets the eye. What was it about the young woman that aroused his interest? Why did she want to see more of him? Why didn't each of them merely treat the episode as a pleasant interlude? Is their interest purely sexual? Will they try to arrange an encounter or even a date? To explain such behaviors, we need to know a number of things: We need to know something about the biological factors involved in the sex drive and what sensory factors elicit sexual interest. We need to know how past conditioning affects choice. We need to understand the role of attitudes, beliefs, and self-concept. For example, we need to determine whether the young man or woman is interested in being with this person, being seen with the attractive person, or both.

Through years of research we have come to appreciate that human motivation is complex. It has become clear in recent years that we cannot understand human motivation simply by studying some of the underlying biological mechanisms. Although biological mechanisms are extremely important, the expression of any motive is always due to the interaction of biological, learned, and cognitive factors. It is the purpose of this book to examine how each of these three classes of factors is involved in the expression of a given motive.

What Is the Study of Motivation About?

Texts on motivation typically include discussions of a variety of behaviors because it is thought, for one reason or another, that these behaviors are due to the operation of certain principles of motivation. Inclusion of one topic and exclusion of another therefore implies that there is good agreement on what the term *motivation* means. Unfortunately, there is not. The study of motivation has traditionally been concerned with the arousal, direction, and persistence of behavior. However, the study of arousal, direction, and persistence is not the exclusive domain of motivation theorists. Learning theorists, for example, have also been concerned with what arouses behavior, what gives it direction (choice of one goal object over another or one pattern of behavior over another), and what gives it persistence.

Motivation theorists, in contrast to learning theorists, have been concerned mainly with the question of what arouses and energizes behavior. Therefore, behaviors that most clearly reflect this issue have been of central interest to motivation theorists. For example, sex hormones reduce the threshold for sexual behavior, and therefore sex hormones have become one area of focus for motivational researchers. Similarly, because arousal can increase the intensity of ongoing emotions or reduce the threshold for such behaviors as aggression, factors that produce arousal are of obvious interest to motivation researchers. Because the factors that arouse and energize behavior often give direction to behavior, motivation theorists frequently deal with the question of direction as well. Their main focus, however, is on the dynamic factors that frequently lead to changes in behavior. Learning theorists, in contrast, are generally more concerned with the question of the stability of behavior. What are the factors that ensure that a person or animal will repeat a behavior at different times or under different environmental conditions or even under different motivational conditions? Their concern is more with the permanence of behavior in a variable environment. As it turns out, many of the factors that lead to stability over time can be found in certain past events that somehow altered the individual in a basic and fundamental way.

The term *energize* applies not only to the immediate behavior but to long-term behavior as well. When I persist toward some long-term goal, what is the motivation that maintains that behavior? Most motivation theorists are not satisfied that future goals (and the rewards that presumably will accompany them) are sufficient in and of themselves to maintain behavior over a long period of time. Nor are they willing to accept the idea that such behaviors are simply due to a strong habit. As a consequence, most theorists are interested in identifying the underlying motivational processes they believe are necessary to energize long-term behavior. It has been argued, for example, that the motivational processes underlying the development of competence (or any skill, for that matter) are "feelings of efficacy" (White, 1959) or that what motivates us to develop conceptual systems is the "positive affect" that is associated with the moderate levels of arousal that frequently accompany information processing (Berlyne, 1960). In other words, the motivation theorist is fundamentally concerned with identifying the motivational process that is assumed to be present whenever some behavior occurs.

Most motivation theorists assume that motivation is involved in the performance of all learned responses; that is, a learned behavior will not occur unless it is energized. In other words, although learning can give direction to behavior, a learned behavior will not occur unless there is a motive for engaging in the behavior. Thus, whether events in the environment guide my behavior or I respond out of habit is ultimately linked to the motivational factors. Further, motivation theorists generally assume that motivation affects perception and memory. For example, the motivation theorist is concerned with such questions as whether we are more likely to notice restaurant signs when we are hungry than when we are not and whether we are more likely to remember the name of a person we find stimulating than of someone we regard as boring. In short, do we ever do something that is not in some way tied to our momentary motivational state?

An Example: Analyzing the Flow of Behavior

One topic of particular interest to the motivation theorist is the question of what gives rise to the flow, or stream, of behavior; Sigmund Freud, Abraham Maslow, Kurt Lewin, and Erik Erikson are a few of the motivational theorists who have examined some of the motivational principles that underlie this process. As we observe humans and animals, we quickly note that they shift from one activity to another from time to time, systematically altering the direction of their behavior. People who have succeeded or failed in the pursuit of a goal, for example, frequently alter the direction of their behavior or the amount of effort they are willing to exert. How do we account for this process? There are two important questions that the motivation theorist is inclined to ask. First, are such shifts systematic, and second, are such shifts better explained by principles of motivation or by some other principle (such as learning, personality, or perception)? Most motivation theorists have concluded from controlled experiments that shifts in behavior are usually systematic. They have argued further that such shifts are best explained in motivational terms. Motivation theorists have frequently focused their attention on factors that immediately precede a shift in behavior in order to discover some of the antecedents that may predict the stream, or flow, of behavior (Barker, 1963).

One very common example of the flow of behavior is the tendency for humans to shift their attention from one object to another as they explore a new room, visit an art gallery, or view the scenery while driving. The problem for the motivation theorist is to explain this flow. It has been shown that the shifts in attention are typically systematic (we typically respond sequentially to stimuli of increasing complexity or novelty). Further, motivational indicators often show that as we attend to one object, our interest in that object decreases while our interest in other (more novel) objects increases. Both of these points are good evidence that something dynamic as well as systematic is happening. One theoretical orientation postulates that people are inclined (without the benefit of learning) to respond to increasingly complex or novel events (or stimuli) in the environment. According to this view, whenever we respond to a stimulus, we are inclined to process the information it contains, thereby making the stimulus familiar and less complex. If other, novel stimuli are present, we will be inclined to direct our attention toward them (Dember & Earl, 1957; Walker, 1980). According to this theoretical orientation, the flow of behavior is the result of a dynamic process governed by a principle that ensures that one behavior systematically gives way to another. Over time, this theoretical orientation predicts, we will process all the information in our environment without having to receive any external rewards.

Current Focus of Motivation Research

In recent years there has been growing interest in so-called applied questions. People who are overweight want to know why and what they can do about it. Other people want to know why they sometimes have difficulty sleeping or what it is in their lives that produces stress and how they can deal with that stress. Parents want to know why their children take drugs or why they turn up the volume on their stereo sets. Many people want to know why there is so much aggression in our society. Most of us are concerned with whether we can alter the direction of our behavior. Many of these same questions were of concern to the earliest scholars. Recently more and more research on these and other questions has produced a wealth of facts and principles that give us some insights into why we do what we do in a number of important areas of our lives.

Early Conceptions of Human Motivation

The Greek Philosophers

Some of the first formal attempts to explain the nature of human motivation were undertaken by the Greek philosophers. Epicurus set forth the proposition that we are motivated to seek pleasure and avoid pain. He believed that pleasure was the only thing worth striving for. It is important to note, however, that many of the Greek philosophers realized that immediate pleasure could, in the long run, bring pain. Therefore, they argued that the goodness of a thing could be obtained only if the intellect was fully developed. The development of the intellect allowed the individual to understand the long-term consequences of a given action. It might be necessary to avoid an immediate pleasure that could, sometime in the future, bring pain to the individual. It might also be necessary to endure pain in order to obtain a greater pleasure. The problem for the individual would be to weigh the various alternatives in order to maximize pleasure.

The position of hedonism has persisted in psychology and philosophy. It reached its peak in the thinking of Jeremy Bentham and John Stuart Mill and today is the cornerstone of several theories of motivation. In most current theories, however, the concept of hedonism has a much narrower sense. Typically it refers to the human tendency to enjoy immediate pleasure, often from the stimulation of one or more of the sensory systems.

Although the Greek philosophers clearly recognized the human tendency to seek pleasure and avoid pain, they did not address themselves to the question of exactly how the intellect affected the basic motives, such as hunger, sex, and aggression. It appears that they assumed these motives were ultimately the servants of the intellect. Excesses were simply the results of failure to understand the consequences of one's behavior. It is clear from their writings on ethics that they viewed human conflict as a failure in the development of the intellect. Accordingly, the goal of the individual as well as of the society was to develop the intellects of all. Conflict would then cease. Conflict and aggression, in other words, were simply the results of ignorance, not the expression of some basic biological urge.

The Problem of Analogous Behaviors in Humans and Animals

The observation that animals and humans engaged in a wide variety of similar behaviors (ate, drank, slept, reproduced, fought) interested thinkers and writers from the earliest times. Was this similarity merely a coincidence, or did it reflect something more? Were these systems homologous—meaning they had a common morphology (structure) or a common origin? The possibility that various behaviors in humans and animals were homologous was rejected outright by most early writers. The Greeks, for example, believed that the essence of humanness was the intellect, something they perceived animals lacked. The fact remained, however, that the behavior of humans and animals often had a striking similarity.

The concept of *dualism* was developed in part to deal with this as well as other questions. Thomas Aquinas elaborated the dualistic position of earlier writers to reconcile the view of Aristotle with the dogma of the church. According to Aquinas, humans had a dual nature—physical and nonphysical, or body and soul. Animals, in contrast, were not assumed to have a dual nature. Their behavior was assumed to be the product of physical forces, some external and some internal, acting on the organism. Their behavior, therefore, was assumed to be more or less automatic and mechanical. Although human behavior was also viewed as governed by physical forces, the early position of dualism as advanced by Aquinas did not assume that the laws governing behavior were the same for humans and animals. The reason for this distinction grows out of the position that the behavior of animals was neither good nor bad but that the same behavior in humans could be bad, depending on a variety of things, such as whether it harmed another human or simply whether it was consistent with the will or plan of God.

For example, according to the teachings of the church, the act of reproduction was assumed to be quite different for humans and animals. Animal reproduction was simply a biological or physical act, while human reproduction was assumed to reflect something more. Humans, it was taught, had a soul in addition to their bodies—the soul being put there by God. Because the child's soul was assumed to be immature, it was necessary that someone assume responsibility for its development. Although the church took ultimate responsibility, it delegated part of the duty to the parents, who were joined in marriage—marriage being an act of the church designed to ensure the provision of a family unit in which morality, love, and the will of God would be taught. Not having children ("not being blessed with children") was often believed to represent God's displeasure. Similarly, having children was frequently viewed as a sign that God was pleased. In other words, some people viewed the outcome of the biological act of reproduction as reflecting the direct intervention of God. Such a view was obviously incompatible with the mechanical interpretation of reproduction in animals. Thus, for a period of time people held that the laws governing certain physical functions were quite different for humans and animals.

Instinct Theories

It was from the perspective of dualism that human behavior was seen as due to the existence of a rational soul but animal behavior was not. The need to explain animal behavior led the Stoics to invent the concept of instinct (Wilm, 1925). The Stoics viewed instincts as "purposive activities implanted in the animal by nature or the creator for the guidance of the creature in the attainment of ends useful to it in its own preservation or the preservation of the species, and the avoidance of the contrary" (Wilm, 1925, p. 40). This view of animal behavior persisted for some time. The problem posed by the similarity of the behavior of humans and animals nevertheless continued to interest early philosophers and scientists. Many curious scientists wanted to explore this similarity in greater detail but were forbidden to do so because the church considered any such attempt to be blasphemy. That is, because the church held to the position of dualism, to consider otherwise was impious. René Descartes (1596–1650) is credited with resolving this problem by arguing for a slightly revised version of dualism. Descartes's dualism was based on the assumption that the behavior of the body, below the level of willed action, could be explained mechanically. This idea has been referred to as reflexology. More important behaviors that had to do with such things as moral conduct, however, were thought to be directly under the control of the will. By making this distinction, Descartes opened the door for scientists to study the mechanical side of human behavior. They could do so without infringing on the domain of the church, which considered itself the final authority on such things as the will and the soul. Descartes further assumed that the body and the mind (will, soul) inter-acted, and he suggested that the site of the interaction was the pineal gland. Certain physical acts, then (presumably such things as sexual behavior), were under the control of the individual. Therefore, and most important from the church's viewpoint, people could be held responsible for those actions that involved behav-iors above the level of reflexes. Animals could, of course, be excused for indiscre-tions (such as running around naked and doing the unspeakable in broad daylight) because they lacked reason and self-awareness, the elements assumed to be nec-essary for the existence or the operation of the will.

Descartes's position opened the door for scientists to explore an age-old ques-tion—the similarity in humans' and animals' behavior. Descartes's position also raised an issue with which psychologists have grappled ever since: Exactly how do the biological and cognitive sides of a person interact? Is it true that our cog-nitive side has ultimate control? Are there times when the cognitive side loses control? In criminal proceedings, for example, the question of insanity has very important implications. Similarly, a finding of medical abnormalities can dramat-ically alter the question of whether a person can and should be held responsible for his or her actions.

Although Descartes suggested that humans may share some of the instincts observed in animals, his position clearly argued that we, unlike animals, could control those instincts. It was evolutionary theory that aroused the wrath of the church by suggesting that human behavior was due to the same processes that give rise to animal behavior.

Some Modern Conceptions about Human Motivation

Evolutionary Theory and Charles Darwin

Over the years several theories of evolution have been advanced. All of these theories have maintained, in one way or another, that the biological structure of

Charles Darwin

organisms has changed over time. The most generally accepted current view of evolution is that presented by Julian Huxley (1942). Charles Darwin's contribution was not the discovery of evolution, as people often think; rather, it was the description of the mechanism by which evolution operates. Specifically, Darwin suggested that evolution occurs by means of "natural selection." As a young biologist, Darwin traveled throughout the world, studying a variety of species in a variety of environments. Two important principles emerged from his carefully documented observations. First, he noted that each species seemed particularly adapted to its environment. For example, certain species escaped predators because they blended into their environment. That is, their coloration and its patterning acted as perfect camouflage to permit them to elude predators. Second, he noted that some members of a species differed from other members of the same species if they lived in different environments. He reasoned that at one time the species had been more or less uniform but that each subpopulation had changed over time, adapting to the particular environmental conditions in which it happened to live. Thus Darwin's observations indicated that species do change.

How did these changes come about? Darwin argued that various members of a species differed in ability to adapt to their environment. Those that were most adaptable to their environment survived, while the others did not. Consequently, only some members of a species reproduced, resulting in a gradual change in the genetic structure of the species. Characteristics of the species that had survival value were passed on to succeeding members of the species, while characteristics that did not have survival value were gradually lost. Because the environment determined which members of a species survived, only those characteristics that were compatible with survival in that particular environment were retained. Thus populations of a species were different in different environments, and yet each was totally adapted to its particular environment.

It has been suggested that Darwin's work in particular caused an intellectual revolution about the causes and origins of human behavior. Darwin argued that what he had observed in animals also held true for humans: the principles governing humans and animals were the same. Further, if human behavior was a product of our genetic structure in the same way that animals' behavior was the product of theirs, the route to understanding human behavior lay through observation of humans in relation to their environment. This was a revolutionary concept because human behavior, before that time, had been thought to be largely independent of physical and biological factors. If human behavior is due to the operation of certain biological structures, it can be argued, the concept of dualism is wrong.

Instincts Revised

Darwin's work renewed interest in the biological and physical determinants of human behavior. Much effort was directed toward identifying behaviors in animals and humans that could be considered instinctive (innate). For example, William McDougall insisted that the most important determinants of conduct were instincts and their associated emotions. He rejected the essentially rationalistic assumptions of certain philosophers, such as the British associationists, and instead stated that conduct was the result of irrational forces. The main problem, he argued, was to explain why people behaved in a rational and socially acceptable manner rather than to explain why they behaved irrationally (Boring, 1950).

The list of major instincts postulated by McDougall (1908/1950) consisted of flight, repulsion, curiosity, pugnacity, self-abasement, self-assertion, reproduction, gregariousness, acquisition, and construction. McDougall also postulated seven basic emotions, corresponding to the first seven of these instincts. These emotions were fear; disgust; wonder; anger; negative self-feeling, or subjection; positive self-feeling, or elation; and the tender emotion. The remaining three instincts had no major emotion. McDougall argued that many emotional experiences were simply compounds of the seven basic emotions. In addition he suggested that feelings of pleasure and/or pain as well as excitement and/or depression could enter into and thus modify these compounds. It is clear from McDougall's writings that he viewed behavior not only as largely innate but as impulse-driven, and many historians (for example, Boring) believe that this conception of behavior was the forerunner of such concepts as drive.

While the concepts of impulse and drive lived on in psychology, the concept of instinct did not. A number of psychologists did not like the concept of instinct or innate emotional patterns. John B. Watson, who later formed the school of behaviorism, concluded that there were only three innate emotional reactions—fear, rage, and love (Watson & Morgan, 1917). Evidence of cultural differences led a number of psychologists to conclude that environmental factors could account for many behaviors observed in humans as well as for the differences between cultures (Boring, 1950).

Ethology: The Biology of Behavior

Although the psychologists of Watson's time tended to reject the idea of innate behaviors, ethologists—students of animal behavior—held to the idea that many important behavior patterns were innate. They engaged in extensive research to identify these behaviors. An important idea held by ethologists was that such behavior patterns tended to occur in response to very specific (and specifiable) stimuli in the environment. These specific stimuli or patterns of stimuli, called "releasers," were thought to be capable of releasing certain responses or patterns of responses if the energy associated with such responses was of sufficient strength. For example, when the female stickleback fish becomes laden with eggs, a releasing stimulus for the male, the male stickleback responds by preparing a nest. When the nest is finished, the male suddenly turns bright red. The bright red color, together with a zigzag dance, appears to be the releasing stimulus for the female to enter the male's nest. With very little further stimulation the female deposits her eggs, whereupon the male quickly fertilizes them, and thus the process of reproduction has been ensured.

What is particularly interesting about the ethologists' position, as viewed from a motivational perspective, is their ideas about the source of energy for a particular behavior. Not only do ethologists regard each action as having its own source of energy, they view this energy source as dynamic. Specifically, they suggest that the energy source is analogous to a reservoir that slowly fills. When the animal engages in a behavior specific to that energy source, such as mating or nest building, the reservoir is depleted or diminished. As a consequence the probability of eliciting that behavior will be diminished for some period. It has been argued that the more energy available for a given action, the easier it is to release (trigger) that action. That is, it has been hypothesized that there is an inverse relation between the energy level and the threshold for releasing the action specific to that source of energy (Eibl-Eibesfeldt, 1975).

The current position of ethologists is that, although many responses are prewired, animals are capable of modifying these innate responses in the face of environmental obstacles and can even learn certain new responses. For example, an animal might be prewired to retrieve an egg that has rolled from its nest, but the behavior is not so rigid that the animal cannot adjust it in the face of environmental obstacles—for example, if the egg rolls into an area that is on fire. And it is assumed that animals can learn certain new responses, such as locating food hidden under an object that has identifiable features. In other words, so-called releasers may be acquired under certain conditions.

The ideas of the ethologists have parallels in the motivational research of psychologists. For example, the relation between hormone levels and certain behaviors has been of fundamental interest to psychologists. There is evidence, at least in nonhuman species, that a direct relation exists between sexual motivation and hormone levels. Even in humans, there is good evidence that hormone levels are important in determining the thresholds for sexual stimuli. Such evidence suggests that certain behaviors may have something like their own energy source and, further, that the energy source operates in a fashion analogous to the reservoir concept suggested by the ethologists.

Ethological work has also played an important role in the work of environmental psychologists. More and more psychologists have come to realize that environmental stimuli, often fairly specific, can elicit certain reactions or behaviors. For example, conditions of crowding have been linked to feelings of distress. The question is whether we can specify the exact nature of the environmental stimuli or events that elicit such feelings. In other words, can we find "releasing stimuli" for certain human behaviors?

There is growing interest among psychologists in using ethological methods to study human behavior. Although psychologists who use the methods of the ethologists do not necessarily hold to a biological orientation, those methods have helped identify factors in the natural environment that determine behavior. The operating assumption of people who use these methods is that behavior is often controlled by environmental stimuli (learned or unlearned) and that in order to understand behavior we need to understand what elicits and controls it. Such knowledge might allow us to alter the environment or to help people understand what it is about the environment that determines their behavior. The implicit assumption is that we must understand the environment before we can teach people to cope with it.

Learning Theorists

Inspired by the work of Ivan Pavlov (1927), groups of researchers began to study how it was possible to alter the frequency and direction of behavior by applying certain principles of classical conditioning or a subsequent set of laws that came to be called the principles of instrumental learning, or operant conditioning. Since they could show that it was possible to alter the frequency and direction of behavior by applying these rules, they argued that behavior as we observe it is due largely to our past conditioning—our reinforcement history. That is, we are what we are because our environment shaped us in a particular way. Such a view seemed particularly valid in view of some of the problems with the instinct approach to behavior as outlined by such psychologists as McDougall.

Biological structure, according to the learning theorists, was important because it made learning possible. In addition, it provided the energy base for behavior. The learning theorists did not, however, accept the proposition that biological structures gave behavior direction, nor did they accept the idea that the persistence

Ivan Pavlov

of behavior was due to the operation of biological systems. They argued that direction and persistence were due to the operation of principles of learning. Direction, they maintained, was due to the process of reinforcement, and persistence was due to the scheduling of reinforcement (Skinner, 1938).

For the most part, learning theorists have tended to regard consciousness, thinking, and perceiving as nonessential phenomena that can be explained by principles of learning. In Chapter 2 I discuss in some detail the principles of classical conditioning and instrumental learning.

Although there is an abundance of evidence that learning plays a major role in behavior, at times learning theorists have taken the position that all behavior is learned. For example, they have argued that such things as curiosity are simply the result of learning and that the desire to develop and exercise skills is merely the result of rewards and punishment. We now know that such a view is too narrow. There are biological and cognitive reasons why people explore or develop new skills. Nevertheless, as we shall see, learning does play a very important role in virtually all behavior.

Cognitive Theorists

Cognitive theorists have, in one way or another, been with us from earliest recorded history. The Greek philosophers emphasized the intellect: they viewed humans as essentially cognitive. It was mainly Darwin, the ethologists, and the learning theorists who challenged this view.

Cognitive theories based on scientific principles are fairly recent. For a long time there was little or no good scientific evidence to show that cognitive processes have anything to do with the way we behave. In fact, there was ample evidence that people often give explanations that have nothing to do with their behavior. Further, there is ample evidence that different people often give quite different explanations for the same behavior. Thus, when learning theorists were able to show that certain behaviors are indeed explainable and predictable in terms of the principles of learning, there was good reason to accept the position of the learning theorist—namely, that cognitions do not determine behavior but rather reflect the way different individuals —often inaccurately—explain their own behavior.

To show that cognition is a relevant factor governing behavior and not simply something incidental that happens to be associated with behavior, it is necessary to show that there is a direct link between the way a person interprets or labels an event and a subsequent behavior. Finding a consistency between labels and behavior is not an adequate scientific demonstration. One could argue that the behavior was responsible for the label or interpretation.

In recent years there have been numerous demonstrations that how people interpret or label an event has a great deal to do with the future direction of their behavior. For example, if a person believes that his heart is beating fast because he is angry, he will be inclined to behave in an angry fashion; if he believes that his heart is beating fast because he is excited and happy, he will often behave accordingly (Schachter & Singer, 1962; Valins, 1966). Such important demonstrations have forced psychologists to acknowledge that cognitions do play a role in behavior.

Some cognitive psychologists have taken the position that cognitive processes are the most important in governing behavior. In support of their view, they often point out that numerous examples show that many biological processes can be totally subservient to cognitive processes: the soldiers in combat who feel no pain even though they have lost an arm or a leg; the 100-pound woman who lifts a car off of her child who has been pinned in an accident; the people who are suddenly healed of cancer after a religious experience. All of us can probably think of many more examples.

As we shall see, however, a great deal of evidence shows that cognitions often do not govern behavior. Take neurotic behavior. No matter how irrational we may regard our feelings of guilt or our neurotic fears, we continue to experience these feelings. Often extensive relearning is necessary to free us from these feelings.

Freud

Although Freud is considered one of the most important figures in the history of psychological thought, his ideas have never been prominent in the mainstream of empirical research on motivation. Most of his ideas grew out of a data base that was quite alien to the empirically based psychologist. While Freud made inferences from the reports of his patients (many of whom were supposedly neurotic), the empiricists were carefully designing controlled laboratory studies to identify the antecedents of a given behavior. Nevertheless, it is generally agreed that Freud's ideas have had far more influence than one might infer by counting the times his work has been cited by his empirically based colleagues.

Freud viewed the biological side of humans as providing the energy, or impulse, for behavior (see Freud, 1900/1953, 1911/1949, 1915/1934, 1915/1949, 1923/1947). He posited a group of instincts, each with its own source of energy and its appropriate goal object. Although each of the instincts was hypothesized to have its own source of energy, Freud suggested that they all drew their energy from a general source called *libido*—a term that refers to all life instincts. Unlike the biologists who saw instincts as providing not only the energy but the direction for behavior, Freud viewed instincts as basically an energy source, with the direction of behavior subject to some of the whims of learning and cognition. The process was assumed to work as follows. When the energy associated with one of the instincts built up, it would become a source of tension for the person. To reduce the tension, the person would be inclined to seek out the appropriate goal object. The problem, as Freud conceptualized it, is that in the course of development certain goal objects have been associated with punishment, and therefore, rather than approach the goal object, the person will tend to avoid that goal object. For example, a child who has been taught that sex is "dirty" or "bad" may be inclined to avoid sex as an adult, or a child who has been taught that it is bad to show anger may inhibit her natural tendency to express aggression. Two things can happen when goal objects have been blocked. First, the person can learn to make alternate plans for obtaining those goal objects, a process that leads to development of the ego. However, because it sometimes happens that the ego has not fully developed or the prohibitions associated with the goal object are excessively rigid or strong, the person may redirect the energy along routes that will reduce the tension, even if the appropriate goal object is not attainable by such a path. For example, a person with a strong sex urge may redirect the energy by reading about sex; the person who feels anger toward her boss may redirect that anger by aggressing toward her husband and children. Although redirecting energy in this second way may, for a time, reduce the tension associated with the instinct, Freud argued that, by definition, such methods would never be satisfactory, because he assumed that every instinct had an appropriate goal object. The tension would continue to surface from time to time, in the form of neurotic anxiety. Neurotic people, according to Freud, constantly fear that their instincts will get out of control.

Freud's goal as a therapist was to help people discover why they had redirected

Sigmund Freud

the energy for their instincts—in short, why they felt guilt or fear whenever they considered satisfying their instincts. Freud believed that the instincts were not bad and that the only way to achieve a happy life was to satisfy them. He argued that many young children learn inappropriate ways of dealing with their instincts or learn that the gratification of certain instincts is inherently bad. He believed that people could get rid of the guilt and fear associated with instincts if they gained insight into the conditions surrounding the acquisition of these feelings. Since such feelings were often learned very early in life, it was necessary, Freud argued, for the analyst to help the patient rediscover his or her childhood.

Although Freud believed that insight into the origins of a problem was sufficient to alter the course of behavior, many therapists have concluded that this is often not so. Wolpe (1969), for example, has argued that extensive relearning is often necessary. In other words, Freud's position that cognitions in the form of insights are frequently sufficient for behavioral change has not been corroborated by many therapists.

This is only a brief description of one major part of Freud's theory, but it illustrates how Freud conceptualized the mix of biology, learning, and cognition. We might say that Freud's theory was one of the first interactionist theories. It attempted to explain how certain biological factors interact with principles of learning and cognition to produce behavior.

One of the main problems with Freud's theory has been the difficulty of testing it. In fact, there has been some debate on whether it can be tested, since Freud did not view his theory as predictive (Boring, 1950). He felt that the dynamic nature of motivation, combined with the fact that unknown environmental factors could influence the direction of behavior, meant that the best one could produce was an explanatory theory. Current theorists are interested in designing predictive theories—theories that can be tested in the laboratory or in the field. They do not agree with Freud's pessimistic view that it was virtually impossible to construct a predictive theory.

Humanistic Theories

The humanistic approach was originally proposed by Carl Rogers (1959) and Abraham Maslow (1970). Humanistic psychologists base their theories on the premise that humans are basically good and that they possess an innate tendency to grow and mature. They further believe that each of us is unique. The process of developing or discovering that uniqueness is called self-actualization. To illustrate this approach we will deal briefly with some of the ideas of Carl Rogers. Maslow's theory is discussed in Chapter 14, on work motivation.

Rogers' theory. Rogers' main contribution to humanistic theory is the "self-concept." The self-concept represents the thoughts and perceptions that we all have about ourselves. Rogers assumed that we are innately motivated to develop a positive self-concept. He further assumed that we are motivated to realize our potential. The road to a positive self-concept and to self-actualization, however, is filled with obstacles that block our progress.

A very early experience that often prevents us from developing a positive self-concept is "conditional love." Conditional love is love that is dependent on our acting in an acceptable way. Instead of being loved for who we are or for what we believe, we are loved for what we do. According to Rogers, this kind of love often produces a negative self-image. When parents or other significant people in our lives emphasize the importance of achieving important goals or acting in a certain prescribed way, we develop unrealistic ideas or beliefs about what we must do before we can think positively about ourselves. According to Rogers, if we are to be able to think positively about ourselves, we need to have a sense of worth that is not conditional on a specific behavior. All of us make mistakes; we all fail sometimes. Faced with this reality, we often develop a sense of conditional worth: "When I succeed or when I act in a certain way, I am worthy, but when I don't succeed or act in a certain way, I am not worthy." Conditional worth eventually leads to a negative self-concept. According to Rogers, the realization that I can never achieve certain goals or act in certain ways leads to a sense of futility. I can never be that good person.

Unconditional love, in contrast, leads to a sense of positive self-regard. Since love is not dependent on acting in prescribed ways, it doesn't matter if I sometimes fail or make mistakes. According to Rogers, when mistakes and failures are not linked directly to feelings of worth, they can be viewed in a more realistic and less destructive way. We can view our mistakes simply as part of the process of maturing or as feedback about our progress.

Anxiety is another thing that gets in the way of the development of positive self-regard. Anxiety, Rogers suggested, arises when we behave in a manner that is contrary to our self-concept. If, for example, as a child I lied to my parents about where I had been, I probably experienced anxiety. Anxiety occurs when we attempt to deny an action rather than accept it. The more I try to deny an action that I know was inappropriate, the greater my anxiety. Rogers argued that we need to recognize our faults and learn to accept them. Denial, of course, gets in the way of our acceptance of ourselves. When we experience unconditional love, we can learn to accept our faults and move toward self-fulfillment.

Some Current Issues in Motivation

In recent years there has been a renewed attempt to integrate information about the biological, the learned, and the cognitive sides of human beings. The new theories are more empirically based than Freud's. Starting with existing knowledge about the biological, learned, and cognitive factors that determine our behavior, current theorists are trying to specify exactly how these factors interact. As these new theories have developed, many issues have arisen that need to be carefully understood and, ideally, resolved through controlled studies. Five such issues are fundamental to a number of important topics discussed in this book.

Environmental Stimuli as Sources of Motivational Arousal

There has been growing interest in understanding how the environment affects behavior. How do noise, high population density, the need to use public transit or drive on crowded roads, sharing offices, and any number of other factors in our daily lives affect the way we function? Do such events cause stress or fatigue, and if so, how does that affect our performance? Do such daily experiences change thresholds for aggression? What are the effects of such factors on mental health?

There seems to be little question that the environment does affect behavior in a variety of ways. The motivation theorist tends to view the environment as a source of arousal. The problem for the motivation theorist is to describe and explain how this source of arousal affects behavior: does arousal produced by the environment alter our threshold for experiencing stress, acting aggressively, or feeling helpless?

An issue that is central to this work is whether our responses to these environmental sources of arousal are innate or learned. Do all or most people react similarly to such environmental events in the absence of learning, or are people's reactions the result of learning? Since human behavior is frequently modified as the result of learning or of changing cognitions, another way of stating the issue is to ask: "To what degree are these reactions, if innate, modified by learning or by the way we perceive the situation?" Psychologists interested in helping people cope with their environments are particularly concerned with the second form of the issue. They want to know whether and to what degree people can learn to deal with certain factors in the environment.

Single versus Multiple Determinants of Behavior

Historically, psychologists have tended to look for single causes or antecedents of behavior. It may seem natural to think that a given behavior is due to a single antecedent (or at least to *proceed* on this assumption), but there is no logical reason it should be. For example, it is possible that one person smokes a cigarette to relax while another person smokes a cigarette to experience a "lift." We tend to assume that people smoke cigarettes to get just one thing, the nicotine, and we assume that nicotine has the same effect on all people. It is possible, nevertheless, that people smoke cigarettes for other reasons and that nicotine affects people differently, depending on whether they are experiencing fatigue, stress, or any number of other internal states.

It is becoming increasingly clear that people may engage in the same behavior for different reasons. If several factors can lead to the same behavior, then the important question is whether the probability of observing the behavior will be greater if two or more of these factors (antecedents) are present. For example, is a person who is anxious and experiencing stress more likely to smoke a cigarette than a person who is not anxious but just experiencing stress? This line of argument has become critical in attempts to explain the etiology of alcohol addiction, for example (Sadava, 1978).

Historically, people have argued that the failure to reduce the antecedents of a behavior to a single one simply reflects our failure to go back far enough in the chain of events that determine behavior. That is, if we reconceptualized the antecedents, we would discover that they are merely aspects or dimensions of the same antecedent. For example, stress and anxiety might be viewed as aspects of something more global, such as sensitivity to stimulation. The question of single or multiple antecedents is an important issue in current motivational research. Only history will tell us whether it is necessary to hold that there are multiple determinants of behavior or whether this approach grew out of our inability to perceive or construct appropriate organizing concepts.

Persistence of Behavior over Time

Some time ago Gordon Allport (1937) noted that behavior often continues in the absence of the factors (motives) that initially elicited it. He called this phenomenon "the functional autonomy of behavior." Today the issue is somewhat different. Instead of viewing behavior as occurring in the absence of motivation or simply out of habit, psychologists are assuming that some motivation or other is maintaining the behavior and are asking whether it is the same as the motivation that initially elicited the behavior. In other words, has the motivation shifted over time? For example, can we be satisfied that the motivation that maintains the attachment between a married couple is the same as the motivation that initially led the two persons to be attracted to each other?

There is an appealing simplicity in assuming that a behavior that recurs is due to the operation of the same motivational system, but there is no logical reason to assume so. We may initially go to the theater because we want to circulate with a certain "in-crowd" and then discover to our surprise that we like the experience provided by live performances. This issue is important in drug addiction. There is good evidence that the motivation that initially led someone to try drugs may be quite different from the motivation that maintains such behavior. This issue is by no means limited to addiction. It has been considered by people investigating obesity (Rodin, 1980), altruism (Cialdini & Kenrick, 1976), and aggression (Berkowitz, 1974), among other things.

Just as with the question of single versus multiple antecedents, the fact that the motivation underlying a given behavior appears to shift does not necessarily mean that the behavior has different determinants at different times. Rather, our level of analysis or our understanding of the variables may still be somewhat immature or incomplete. Quite possibly, as we become more sophisticated in our understanding, we will discover that in fact a given behavior is governed by a single underlying motive.

Interaction of Motive Systems

In recent years we have come to realize that the brain and the rest of the central nervous system are not in a constant state of readiness. For example, it has been shown that an area at the top of the spinal column called the reticular activating system can both increase and decrease electrical activity in the cortex. Because we are more likely to detect and process information or respond to events in the environment when the cortex is active, the reticular activating system plays an important role in mediating (controlling) our behavior. Other brain systems have also been implicated in various forms or states of arousal (see Chapter 3 for a more complete discussion). While it is important to know that arousal can facilitate some ongoing activity, it is fascinating to note that these general states of arousal often lower the threshold for other activities. For example, it has been shown that running not only produces arousal but will lower the threshold for provoking an aggressive response from us (for example, Zillmann, Katcher, & Milavsky, 1972). If increased arousal can lower the threshold for other behaviors, and there is ample evidence that it often does, the question arises whether all motive systems may be interdependent. Can we increase our sensitivity to food by engaging in an arousal-producing activity? For example, alcohol in moderate amounts increases arousal. Is that why people often have a cocktail before dinner? Does the arousal produced by alcohol increase our sensitivity to the pleasurable qualities of food? Similarly, why do we like to have company when we eat? Social interactions reliably increase arousal. Does the arousal from such interactions actually make our food taste better?

There is good reason to hypothesize that humans have learned, probably by accident, that combining one activity with another can increase the pleasure of the second activity. Some of us may have come to realize that after a tense (high arousal) day our threshold for loud noises—among other things—is low. Therefore we may warn people that we are not in the mood for certain activities or simply that we are in an irritable mood.

Primacy of Cognitions versus Biological Drives

To what extent is our behavior under cognitive control? The fact that people frequently have difficulty losing weight, stopping smoking, abstaining from the use of a drug such as a tranquilizer or alcohol, and so on, shows that good intentions are often not sufficient to alter the course of behavior. The fact remains, however, that people frequently do lose weight, stop smoking, or abstain from drugs on which they had become dependent. Sometimes such changes are abrupt and dramatic. Further, the fact that people can learn not only to tolerate stress but to find it challenging seems to show that attitudes can change a potentially noxious event into a rewarding one. Therapy that alters people's perceptions of themselves or their environment often produces dramatic long-term behavioral change.

Although evolutionary theory suggests that the biological side of humans should have ultimate control of behavior, it must be remembered that behavior is a product of our interaction with our environment. The environment motivates people to develop the rich repertoire of responses that makes it possible for them to deal effectively with an environment that is not only complex but also changing. The issue remains, nevertheless, whether humans are truly as plastic as we might gather from some of the research on learning and cognition. The important question is whether learning and cognition can produce long-term behavioral change when such change is inconsistent with the biological structure of humans. Can we learn to ignore our hunger drive, our sex drive, or our tendency to retaliate when provoked, or is all learning simply guided by our biological structure? That is, what limitations does our biological structure impose? What are the consequences of overriding these biological tendencies? Is there a price we must pay?

This book takes what I call a "components approach" to motivation. I attempt to point out what we know about several important areas of human motivation. I deal with questions most of us are concerned about at various times in our lives. In the next chapter I will spell out precisely what I mean by a components approach.

Main Points

1. Traditionally, the study of motivation has been concerned with the arousal, direction, and persistence of behavior.
2. Current motivational research is more concerned with the arousal and energizing of behavior. It is also concerned with explaining the stream, or flow, of behavior.
3. Some of the earliest formal attempts to explain human motivation were undertaken by the Greek philosophers, who proposed that the purpose of life was the pursuit of happiness.
4. The route to happiness, according to the Greeks, was the development of the intellect (reason).
5. A recurring problem for early thinkers was the analogous behaviors (and motives) of humans and animals.
6. The position of dualism suggested that humans have a dual nature—physical and nonphysical, or body and soul—and that their behavior is due to nonphysical forces, such as the will, whereas animals' behavior is due to physical forces, such as instincts and reflexes.
7. Descartes modified the original position of dualism, arguing that the behavior of the body, below the level of willed action, could be explained mechanistically (reflexology) while all other behaviors were under the control of the will.
8. Darwin challenged the traditional dualist view when he suggested that human behavior was the product of evolution.
9. Darwin's position encouraged the study of instincts in humans. McDougall's theory is a good example of this approach.
10. Although psychologists rejected the instincts approach to behavior, a form of this position was revived and elaborated by the ethologists.
11. The reservoir model of energy has been of particular interest to psychologists, especially in their interpretation of the relation between hormone levels and behavior.
12. Learning theorists argued, at least for a time, that all behaviors could be explained by the principles of classical and instrumental learning.
13. Freud suggested that the source of all energy was the libido and that the direction of behavior was due to learning and cognition.
14. Freud's goal as a therapist was to help people discover why they had redirected the energy for their instincts in inappropriate ways and to help them feel comfortable with satisfying their natural instincts.

15. Although Freud stressed the idea that people could be "cured" simply by gaining insight into the origins of their problems, other psychologists have argued that often a great deal of relearning is needed in order for people to be "cured."

16. Humanistic theorists start with the position that humans are basically good and possess an innate tendency to grow and mature.

17. Rogers argues that conditional love eventually leads to a negative self-image, whereas unconditional love leads to positive self-regard.

18. Current motivational research is characterized by efforts to resolve several issues. Five of these issues were briefly discussed.

Components
of Motivation

What are the components of motivation?
Why is it necessary to talk in terms of components?
Why have scientists tended to study behavior from a single perspective?
What assumptions are involved when one takes a single perspective?
What are some of the implications of viewing behavior from multiple perspectives?
Why do scientists construct theories and models?
How does a multiple-perspective (components) approach help us understand such things as why people run or why people listen to rock music.

The reason a person might give for engaging in a behavior is often quite different from the reason a scientist might give. Most humans are forced to operate within a very limited framework. They have information about what they think they should do or not do, together with a general theory about why people do certain things but not others. Most do not have access to information about how hormones circulating in their blood predispose them to act in a certain way or about principles of conditioning that in the past increased the probability that they would act in a certain way or about conditions that have altered how the brain filters and organizes information. Motivation, as we shall see, is based on processes that are unavailable to consciousness or to public scrutiny. Only through carefully controlled research is the scientist able to detect the exact nature of these processes and their role in human motivation.

There appear to be at least three types of motivational mechanisms, or processes: biological, learned, and cognitive. I refer to these collectively as the "components" of motivation. Typically all three are involved in varying degrees in any motivated behavior. They somehow interact to produce organized and, ideally, adaptive behavior. Behavior, therefore, is not due solely to a biological, a learned, or a cognitive process but rather to the interaction of the three. (For a more complete discussion of the definition of motivation see Kleinginna & Kleinginna, 1981a.)

An interaction is, by definition, complex. Even though scientists are dedicated to the task of making things simple and understandable, no one has yet been able to account for the complexities of human motivation by a single set of principles, be they principles of biology, learning, or cognition. Nevertheless, our understanding of motivation is growing daily. Slowly the pieces of this complex puzzle are falling into place. It is becoming clear that human motivation is the joint product of these three components working together in a surprisingly smooth fashion. Before examining how these three components work together, we will look at each component separately. As we shall see, each operates according to a quite different set of principles, and each set of principles is based on a quite different set of assumptions.

The Biological Component

The Ethological View
The principles of biology assume that behavior is the product of our genetic structure. We behave as we do because our genetic structure not only sets a behavior in motion but gives direction to that behavior.

The biological position does not necessarily assume that behavior is either stereotyped or totally prewired. Ethologists such as Konrad Lorenz (1969) have acknowledged that learning can play an important role. Nevertheless, he and others have argued that what is learned is guided by the genetic structure of the individual. For example, Lorenz has stated that "all learning is very specifically innately programmed" (1969, p. 21). According to this position, humans (as well as animals) are equipped to take advantage of certain experiences. Several articles and books have clearly shown how the genetic structure we inherit makes it possible for us to learn certain things and not others. The tendency to acquire language appears to be genetically determined (Chomsky, 1972), as does our tendency to form social groups or behave altruistically (Wilson, 1975). Numerous constraints on animal learning have been reported (Hinde & Stevenson-Hinde, 1973), all of which can be readily understood from an evolutionary perspective (Barash, 1977).

Open versus closed programs.   Mayr (1974) has distinguished between open and closed genetic programs. A genetic program that cannot be modified appreciably during its translation into behavior is called a "closed program." For a number of animals, sexual signals serve not only to arouse the partner but to prevent the female from responding to a male of another species. A closed program would achieve this function. A genetic program that allows additional input during the translation of the program into behavior is an open program. If an animal must deal with a varied environment, it may be more adaptive to allow certain forms of learning to modify the program. For example, if the food supply changes because of droughts, fires, or other unpredictable factors, it is adaptive for the eating response to be elicited (released) by stimuli that are not totally innate. Animals can then learn to eat different foods should one of their supplies run out.

Much of human behavior appears to be the product of an open program. Nevertheless, the programs that underlie human behavior vary greatly in degree of openness. The stress reaction, for example, is subject to modification but only within limits. Certain stimulus conditions reliably elicit the stress response in humans without the intervention of learning, but it is possible to condition the response to be elicited by other stimuli as well. In other words, the stress response has characteristics of both an open and a closed program. The fact that all languages have the same underlying grammatical structure (Chomsky, 1972) suggests that language use has characteristics of both an open and a closed program. The structure is programmed, but the program does not specify the sounds used as words.

Reservoir of energy.   Researchers who take a biological perspective have always been very concerned about the question of what arouses and/or energizes behavior. Ethologists, for the most part, have not tried to separate the question of arousal from the question of direction. Their position can readily handle all three traditional questions of motivation: arousal, direction, and persistence of behavior. The concept that behavior is released by a pattern of stimulation (releaser) can account for direction; the concept of an energy pool or reservoir that builds over time accounts for the arousal and the persistence of a response. Lorenz (1966) has used such a conceptual framework in his analysis of aggressive behavior. Lorenz says that one reason humans are so aggressive is that they do not have sufficient outlets for the expression of aggression, and therefore the pool of energy underlying aggressive behavior is not sufficiently drained off. Under such circumstances, he suggests, the threshold for the release of aggressive behavior is lowered. As a consequence, aggressive behavior tends to occur in the absence of a releaser stimulus. Moreover, when a releaser stimulus is present, the intensity of an aggressive behavior will be greater than it would normally be. In other words, he argues that humans have a tendency to exhibit unprovoked aggression. Desmond Morris (1969) has used the concept of releaser stimuli to explain why certain parts of the human anatomy elicit sexual motivation in the other sex. He has argued that the tendency for humans to cover their genitals reflects an attempt to control the instinctive urge to mate. In other words, humans have learned to control their instinctive sexual urges not by blocking them but rather by exhibiting the appropriate sexual signals only at appropriate times.

The Behavioral Neurosciences

Although the ethological position has proved to be a very productive framework for analyzing behavior, there are other ways of viewing the biological system. A more popular view among psychologists is that human evolution favored general activation and reward systems rather than innate responses. According to this view, a behavior is acquired because of a reward mechanism that increases the likelihood of a response. For example, obtaining food for performing a certain response, or eliminating a noxious stimulus by making an avoidance response, is assumed to produce an internal reinforcing event. This reinforcing event is thought to be triggered by some innate reward mechanism or mechanisms. When a reinforcing event occurs it is assumed to have the capacity, according to the principles of learning, to increase the likelihood (probability) of that response occurring again in the future. Since learning is generally assumed to be a gradual process, it is assumed that the reinforcing event must occur several times before learning is complete (before the response will occur with a high probability). In other words, what makes learning possible is the existence of some type of innate reward mechanism or mechanisms.

Reward centers.   A great deal of evidence supports the view that the reward mechanisms that evolved were general rather than specific. Olds (1955, 1956), for example, discovered that animals will learn a wide variety of responses in order to receive electrical stimulation in certain areas of the brain that have come to be called the "reward centers." Such centers also exist in the human brain. The fact that the brain contains structures that are capable of reinforcing a wide range of behaviors raises questions. If all significant behaviors are prewired, as strict biological determinism holds, the existence of these centers is difficult to explain. Why would such centers exist unless they had an adaptive function? The existence of reward centers does not, of course, cause any problems for those who maintain that general reward mechanisms evolved to ensure the survival of organisms. According to this view, such mechanisms serve to reward adaptive behaviors (Glickman & Schiff, 1967). The problem here is to explain what mechanism or structure tells the reward system that an adaptive response has been made. As these reward centers are activated by certain drugs, such as the amphetamines (see Chapter 9), there is good reason to believe that they are indeed very general mechanisms that may not be tied exclusively to adaptive behaviors. They may, in fact, be capable of rewarding maladaptive behaviors.

Reticular activating system.   In 1949 Moruzzi and Magoun discovered that the energy for a wide variety of behaviors came from a general rather than a specific activation system. They found that an area at the top of the brainstem (the reticular formation) is capable of activating the entire cortex. Since then this system has come to be referred to as the reticular activating system. Moruzzi and Magoun's discovery stimulated a great deal of research that suggested not only that humans perform best at moderate levels of activation or arousal (Hebb, 1955) but that they have a preference for moderate levels of activation or arousal (for example, Berlyne, 1960). This finding led a number of theorists to propose that moderate levels of activation or arousal have reinforcing properties. Thus people learn to do things that will raise a low level of arousal and to do other things that will lower a very high level of arousal. As a variety of external stimuli will increase arousal, the existence of such a mechanism can explain why people who are bored (experiencing too little stimulation or too little arousal) may like to travel or to listen to certain types of music. Similarly, the existence of such a mechanism can explain why people will seek out a quiet place when they feel stressed (exposed to too much stimulation or too much arousal) or will learn to avoid certain situations that cause arousal to be uncomfortably high.

Limbic system. The limbic system is a structure deep within the brain which controls many of our emotions, such as fear, love, and anger. We all know from experience that emotions are a source of pleasure as well as pain. For this reason many behavioral neuroscience researchers have proposed that the limbic system is still another area of the brain that is involved not only in the activation of behavior but in its reinforcement.

Constraints Imposed by the Nervous System
These various reward mechanisms do not, however, make human behavior infinitely flexible. They are limited or constrained by a variety of factors. Our ability to activate the brain's reward centers appears to be limited by, among other things, the availability of certain chemicals in the brain, which are released only under certain conditions. There is a great deal of evidence that these chemicals are released only when we find ourselves in a situation that requires us to make an adaptive response. It has been found also that our supply of these chemicals can become depleted. Thus even when the environment provides the appropriate conditions, these structures will not provide the same level of reward as they would had the supply of these chemicals not been depleted.

Similarly, not all stimulation will increase arousal. As we tend to become habituated to stimulation, we often need to find new forms of stimulation to increase our arousal.

The way we express our emotions is determined to a very large degree by the structure of the limbic system. Frustration, for example, is often but not always followed by aggression. According to MacLean (1975), the cortex plays an important role in modifying the expression of emotions. MacLean notes that there are many interconnections between the cortex and such structures as the limbic system. Even the question of whether or not an emotion can be aroused by some specific environmental event is affected by such things as hormones. The sex hormones, for example, play a very important role in determining whether or not an organism will be sexually aroused. When the levels of sex hormones are low, it becomes difficult to arouse sexual motivation. The implications of this finding are far-reaching. If certain drugs suppress the sex hormones, then they will also suppress sexual behavior.

Still other structures in the brain place constraints on the functioning of these reward mechanisms. While the hypothalamus has traditionally been regarded as the energy base for all motivation (Stellar, 1954), more recent researchers (for example, Valenstein, Cox, & Kakolewski, 1970) have argued that the hypothalamus is the locus of species-specific behaviors. This means that, at least to some degree, certain adaptive behaviors are prewired.

While it is not particularly important to remember all these details, as we will be examining many of these concepts more closely later, it is important to remember three things. First, the brain contains general reward mechanisms that make possible great variation in the way we behave. Second, our behavior is nonetheless constrained by the requirement that certain conditions (both physical and psychological) must be met before these reward mechanisms can operate. Chemical or hormonal levels must be right, for example, or the situation might threaten our life. Third, there is evidence that certain behaviors are not governed by these general reward mechanisms. We know, for example, that sleep/wakefulness cycles are controlled by biological rhythms, and that despite our best efforts, we cannot modify them.

Effects of Experience on Biological Structure

There is no question that exposure to certain forms of environmental stimulation is frequently necessary to realize certain biological potentials. For example, exposure to language is typically necessary for language learning in animals that have such a potential. However, exposure to language in animals that do not have this potential is a waste of time. The learning of language in humans does not alter the biological structure; that is, whether the biological potential has or has not been utilized by the parents will have no effect on their offspring. The structure will be passed along to the next generation. If certain environmental conditions exist, the offspring will then be able to realize the potential of that structure (Alcock, 1979). The work of Hubel and Wiesel (1979) provides an excellent example of the role of the environment in realizing the potential of the visual cortex of the brain. Hubel and Wiesel have shown that exposure to certain very specific stimuli (such as lines at various angles) is an important condition for developing the inherent visual capacity of animals. If an animal is deprived of such stimuli when young, the potential of the visual system will not be realized. The resulting defect is due mainly to deterioration of connections that were present at birth (Hubel, 1979).

In general, most biologists hold that it is impossible to talk about the nature of an animal without discussing the environment in which that animal normally lives (Alcock, 1979). If the animal is so constructed that the realization of its structure is dependent on the environment, then trying to study the animal when it has been removed from its environment would be equivalent to studying an animal with part of its brain removed. Neither animal would be normal. This position, often called an "interactionist" position, is gaining support among psychologists (Sadava, 1980). More and more we are seeing that human behavior is influenced by the environment. This position is not to be confused with the position taken by such learning theorists as B. F. Skinner, who try to reduce the environment to rewards and schedules of rewards. It is the structure of the environment that somehow directly or indirectly affects biological systems, which in turn produce behavior.

The question of individual differences. The variations that we frequently observe in behavior could be due to differences in biological structure, differences in the environment, differences in learning, or a combination of these factors. For example, we often observe wide variations in aggressive behavior within a species. At present we cannot be sure whether these differences are due to genetic factors that produce different predispositions toward aggression, to the environment, or to learning. Since we can breed animals for aggressiveness, we must acknowledge that some of the variation we observe among individuals may well be due to biological structure (McLearn, 1969). However, since we can also show that animals frequently learn to be aggressive, we must acknowledge that learning accounts for some of the difference (Moyer, 1976). Finally, because the environment alters the probability of aggression, we must acknowledge that the environment can act as a determinant. The problem for the motivation theorist is to separate these various factors in order to specify the contribution of each.

Enrichment experiments and biological structure.   Several attempts have been made to show that certain environmental conditions will alter biological structure. One type of experiment, the enrichment experiment, has been repeatedly undertaken to determine whether certain types of enrichment will produce a change in behavior that is general as opposed to specific. It has been argued that if certain types of experiences alter an animal's ability to learn new things at some later time, then some general mechanism (or biological structure) has been altered. For example, if certain experiences produce increases in intelligence scores, then somehow the structure or structures underlying intelligence have been modified. Since intelligence tests are based to a large extent on past learning, improvement in the intelligence score of an individual exposed to an enriched environment might be taken as evidence that certain environmental conditions enhance the tendency to learn.

Various experiments have been undertaken to test this hypothesis. Rats exposed to enriched environments have been shown to be intellectually superior to other rats, at least when intellect is measured by how quickly an animal learns the pattern of a maze (Hebb, 1949). These results can be accounted for in ways that do not require one to assume that some fundamental biological structure has changed. The research of Krech, Rosenzweig, and Bennett (1966), however, provides more direct evidence that enriched environments do produce fundamental changes. These researchers found that rats exposed to enriched environments had increased levels of cholinesterase and acetylcholinesterase in the brain. These substances are thought to be involved in transmission of impulses from one neuron to another, thereby facilitating learning. Other experiments have shown that enriched environments affect the growth and development of structures involved in transmission of impulses (for example, Greenough, Volkmar, & Juraska, 1973; Greenough, West, & DeVoogd, 1978) and the synthesis of RNA, an important chemical involved in transmission (for example, Uphouse, 1978; Uphouse & Moore, 1978). It has been argued that these changes reflect the normal realization of function that occurs when animals interact with their natural environment (Uphouse, 1980). That is, the enriched environment simulates the level of stimulation provided by the natural environment of rats in the wild; the standard laboratory environment is deprived by comparison. Thus these changes reflect the fact that the environment is necessary to stimulate the biological structure to develop to its full and natural level of functioning.

Enrichment experiments with humans have not produced consistent or convincing results. The "Early Training Project" (Gray & Klaus, 1965, 1968, 1970) showed that an enriched environment can greatly increase the IQ scores of severely deprived children. Although the initial gains were dramatic, a four-year follow-up indicated that IQ scores were declining. Similar results were obtained with children enrolled in a Head Start program (Wolff & Stein, 1967). When the program ended, the children in it performed better than controls, but six months later they did not. These studies suggest that enrichment can accelerate the natural development of the individual but that in the absence of sustained stimulation other individuals tend to catch up, thereby eliminating any differences that were initially produced by the enriched environment. Further, differences due to enrichment may reflect short-term motivational effects on performance that were somehow induced in the course of providing an enriched environment.

Deprivation experiments and biological structure.   Another type of experiment that has been used to assess the effect of the environment on biological structure is the deprivation or isolation study. In such experiments animals are placed in environments in which stimulation is lacking to various degrees. The argument here is that if lack of certain environmental experiences produces a deficit that cannot be overcome by subsequent exposure to the appropriate environmental stimulation, then biological structure has changed. If motivation and development are dependent in part on the animal's opportunity to interact with the environment that has shaped its biological heritage, then such experiments, it has been argued, tell us very little except that a "normal" environment is important for development (see Alcock, 1979). The failure to develop normally, in other words, simply provides evidence that environment plays a role in the developmental process.

Ingesting Chemicals and Biological Structure

There is growing evidence that the air we breathe, the food we eat, and the chemicals we sometimes use as part of our recreation (for example, alcohol) often alter certain biological systems or functions. Newspapers, radio, and television tell us that various chemicals in our air, food, or water may cause cancer or a variety of other ailments. Most such chemicals do not affect our genes, so that the effects are short-term (that is, limited to one generation). There is concern, however, that some of the chemicals we ingest may in fact alter genetic structure. Swinson and Eaves (1978) indicate that there is some evidence—though it is still meager—that drugs such as LSD may affect genetic structure. Such an effect, of course, would have long-term implications for humans.

Summary

There is ample evidence from a variety of sources that human behavior is not infinitely flexible, as some learning theorists have argued, nor is it totally preprogrammed. The existence of general reward systems and arousal systems suggests that humans are capable of learning a number of new behaviors not specifically dictated by our genetic structure. Not all new behaviors are adaptive. Nevertheless, it can be argued that these behaviors exist because the biological structure of humans allows them to exist and in some instances ensures that they persist. We will examine this point more closely when we look at drug addiction.

Although the environment plays an important role in the full realization of biological structures, there is only modest evidence that these structures are altered to any significant degree by psychological input from the environment. There is evidence, however, that chemicals we ingest can alter these structures. Fortunately, there is very little evidence at this point that such

(continued)

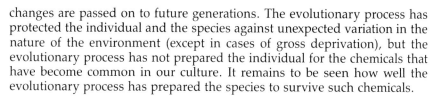

changes are passed on to future generations. The evolutionary process has protected the individual and the species against unexpected variation in the nature of the environment (except in cases of gross deprivation), but the evolutionary process has not prepared the individual for the chemicals that have become common in our culture. It remains to be seen how well the evolutionary process has prepared the species to survive such chemicals.

The Learned Component

Learning plays a very important role in motivated behavior. The term *acquired motives* (or *acquired drives*) is often used to refer to the type of learning that we will be talking about in this book.

Acquired Motives

At birth we have such primary drives or needs as hunger, thirst, sleep, temperature regulation, curiosity, and even tactile stimulation (we need to be held or touched). Certain primary drives are not full-blown at birth but emerge as the organism matures. The sex drive, for example, while present in infants, develops in strength when the sex hormones become more active.

Some drives or motives, however, do not seem to be present at birth or do not seem to be tied directly to any specific biological system. The need to achieve, the need for power, the tendency to take drugs, the tendency to avoid enclosed places (claustrophobia)—all are patterns of behavior that have no specific biological antecedent; that is, no biological state that needs to be satisfied. Hunger is satisfied by food, thirst is satisfied by water, sleepiness is satisfied by sleep, curiosity is satisfied by exploration, and sex is satisfied by engaging in a sexual act that leads to orgasm, usually with a member of the opposite sex.

If there is no specific biological antecedent for such motives as achievement and power, then how do we explain the existence of these motives? What activates the tendency to achieve or the tendency to search for power or the tendency to take drugs? It is important to note that when we talk about acquired motives, we assume that some people will acquire these motives and others will not, and that those who acquire them will do so to varying degrees. The net result is that when we talk about acquired motives, there will often be significant individual differences.

Classical Conditioning

Ivan Pavlov (1927) discovered classical conditioning when he found that dogs could be taught to salivate at the sound of a bell if the bell was rung whenever food was presented. According to Pavlov's analysis, food is an unconditioned stimulus (UC) that naturally leads to the unconditioned response (UR) of salivation. When the bell (which does not naturally elicit salivation) is paired with food (preferably a half second before the food is presented), it acquires the ability to elicit salivation because it is a reliable predictor that food is forthcoming. Pavlov found that after several pairings of bell and food, the bell elicited salivation even when no food was presented. In such circumstances we say that the bell has become a conditioned stimulus (CS). If the bell is repeatedly presented by itself (with no accompanying food), it will lose its ability to elicit salivation.

Fear as a classical conditioned or respondent conditioned motive.   The discovery of classical conditioning was a great help to psychologists in their efforts to understand such things as human fears. Since a variety of common fears—fear of snakes, of heights, of enclosed places, and many other things—are not universal among humans, it has been suggested they are learned. The fear of enclosed places (claustrophobia), it has been suggested, may be the result of some traumatic experience early in life. As a child you may have been locked in a closet as a prank or by accident. While you were in that closet you probably experienced some very negative emotions. You may have thought that whoever locked you in that closet had forgotten about you, and you were doomed to starve to death. Or you may simply have been afraid of the dark, and after a time began to imagine that some monster was surely going to get you. According to the principles of classical conditioning, your emotional state was likely to become conditioned to that closet. Whenever you reentered the closet, you would again experience the same emotion. But that emotional experience would not be limited to that particular closet. Humans are inclined to generalize. That is, we are inclined to react in the same way to any situation we perceive as similar to the one that originally elicited a particular emotion. This tendency serves to explain why a person might exhibit claustrophobia in an elevator, for example, even though that person had never had any aversive experience in one. Fear, according to the theory of classical conditioning, is simply a conditioned emotional response that has generalized to a variety of situations that the individual, for one reason or another, perceives as similar to the original situation that elicited the negative emotional state.

Reversing classical conditioning. It is important to note that, according to the theory of classical conditioning, it doesn't matter if you are aware of the conditions that have led to the conditioning of the aversive emotion. The only way to get rid of your fear is to extinguish the response or to use some kind of counterconditioning procedure. If the response is to be extinguished, the CS must be presented to you repeatedly. This procedure should, according to the theory of classical conditioning, lead to a weakening of the fear response. In many cases it doesn't, for reasons that we needn't go into here. Alternatively, you could condition another response, such as relaxation or feelings of security, to the same conditioned stimulus that elicits the fear response. If the new response is strong enough, it should cancel out or replace the previously acquired response.

Instrumental Learning

A second kind of learning that is often involved in acquired drives or motives is instrumental learning. In instrumental learning a response that occurs at some natural rate (often called the operant rate) can be made to occur at a higher rate if the receipt of a reward is made contingent on a higher rate of responding. If a reward is to work, an appropriate motivational system must be activated. Certain foods can be rewarding (reinforcing) to an animal if it is hungry or if the food stimulates one of the sensory systems associated with food intake. What is particularly interesting about rewarded behavior is that often the behavior will continue at a high rate even if the reward is removed. A nonrewarded response will eventually diminish in rate or strength; this process is called extinction. One way to make a response continue in the absence of reward is to offer partial reinforcement of the behavior. That is, instead of rewarding the behavior on every trial, you reward the behavior on only some of the trials. In Chapter 12 we will discuss why this procedure works.

Achievement as an instrumentally acquired motive.   According to the principles of instrumental learning, the strength of any response can be increased if a reward is made contingent on the occurrence of the response. If a child were to come home with a score of 9 out of 10 on a math quiz, for example, and if her father were to reward her in some way, a likely outcome is that she would strive to do well on other math tests. If her father then rewarded other good outcomes in the same way, she might strive to do well in a variety of other subjects. Over time, the child might develop a tendency to strive to do well in all her school subjects. This tendency might even generalize beyond school and become a much more general characteristic. At this point we might refer to this behavior pattern as achievement motivation.

Secondary rewards and instrumental learning.   If a reward is to be effective, it must be applied as soon as possible after the desired behavior has occurred. While primary reinforcers, such as food, are often very effective as rewards for behavior, especially in the training of animals, primary rewards are not very practical as reinforcers of many human behaviors. It's hard to imagine a university professor offering little pieces of candy to a student each time the student does well on a test. It has been shown that symbolic rewards, such as "Very good" or a big "A" on a paper, are often even more effective than primary rewards. The question is why these symbolic rewards actually work. There are at least two lines of thinking. One is that various forms of praise acquire reward value because they have been associated with the presentation of a primary reward. When your dog sits up and you give him a little piece of meat, for example, you are likely to say something like "Good dog." After a time the phrase "Good dog" acquires reinforcing properties, through the principles of classical conditioning, because it has been paired with the presentation of the primary reward. When you were a child, your parents did the same thing when they fed you. As a result, when they express praise for you now, it makes you feel good, just as the food you ate as a child made you feel good. The second line of argument is simply that since humans can think and reason, you know that "Very good" or an "A" at the top of your paper means that you are acquiring a skill that has value. This skill can be used to earn money or simply to earn the love and respect you want from people who matter to you.

Intrinsic versus extrinsic rewards.   A distinction is often made between intrinsic and extrinsic rewards. When the activity itself provides the reward, we say that the activity is intrinsically rewarding; when an activity is done in order to obtain a reward that is unrelated to it, then we say that the activity is extrinsically rewarding. A child who does well in school simply to gain approval from his parents or to acquire a skill that he can then use to earn money or acquire fame is engaging in the activity for extrinsic reasons (rewards). If, however, he finds the activity motivating even in the absence of approval or some other form of gain, then we say that he is engaging in the activity for intrinsic reasons (rewards). Some people have argued that one reason people become strongly achievement-oriented is not to obtain extrinsic rewards (as I suggested above) but rather because achievement motivation is linked to more intrinsic forms of motivation. Robert White (1959), for example, has suggested that achievement or mastery is linked to what he calls "effectance motivation," whereas David McClelland (1985) has argued that it grows out of curiosity or exploratory motivation; both are viewed as intrinsic forms of motivation. We will talk more about such motivation in Chapter 13.

Both intrinsic and extrinsic rewards play an important role in shaping such complex motives as the need for achievement. The rewards and punishments that we experience modify not only the strength but the direction of the initial motivation on which complex motives are built. Throughout this book we will examine how both intrinsic and extrinsic rewards affect the way motives are shaped and expressed. Sometimes we may start to do something for extrinsic reasons and end up doing them for intrinsic reasons. At other times we start to do something for intrinsic reasons and end up doing them for extrinsic reasons.

The Opponent Process Model of Acquired Drives

Richard Solomon (Solomon, 1980; Solomon & Corbit, 1974) has advanced a very different kind of model to account for such acquired drives as fear, achievement, power, drug taking, and other complex motives. According to the opponent process model, reinforcers are viewed as affective states (ranging from positive to negative feelings) that are aroused or elicited by stimuli in the environment. Jumping off a high building, for example, typically produces negative affect (fear). Taking drugs produces positive or negative affect (euphoria), depending on the drug. The appearance of an attractive person of the opposite sex elicits positive affect (attraction and arousal). In other words, according to Solomon's model, every event naturally elicits some state that may range from very satisfying (positively reinforcing) to very aversive (negatively reinforcing).

We all know, however, that events that elicit positive affect typically lose their power over time. For example, after repeated exposure to a song that we initially found very exhilarating, we tend to lose interest in it. Similarly, events that produce negative affect can also lose their power over time. We may find it very aversive to drive in heavy traffic, for example, but after a time we grow accustomed to it if we have to do it every day.

We also know from experience that ongoing affective states not only diminish in strength but may actually undergo quite dramatic changes. A sexual encounter may at first elicit great joy, but when we say good night, we experience great loneliness. For some reason, that delightful experience does not stay with us in its original form; it undergoes a transformation to something we find aversive.

In order to account for the fact that events lose their ability to reinforce us and that affective states often undergo some sort of change, Solomon has proposed a two-process model called the opponent process theory. Initially, an environmental event arouses or elicits a process that is experienced as an affective reaction. According to the theory, process a automatically elicits process b, an affective reaction that is opposite in direction to process a. Process b, the opponent process, counteracts process a and brings the organism back to its normal operating state.

While process a is always the same, process b changes as the result of experience. With repeated exposure to process a, process b begins earlier, has greater magnitude, and lasts longer. People who parachute from a plane for the first time typically experience fear and then relief when they hit the ground. After many jumps the fear gets weaker and the relief is experienced as joy or exhilaration, which often lasts for a considerable period of time. According to Solomon's theory, process b has strengthened and become long-lasting. Experienced parachutists typically report that they experience great exhilaration during their descent. According to the theory, process b has started to occur earlier.

Solomon's theory is a very powerful one because it can explain why some activity that is initially aversive can come to motivate behavior. It seems to make little sense, for example, that people get hooked on something like work, yet we know that many people do. According to Solomon's theory, work, often a boring or even painful experience, is capable of triggering an opponent process that is experienced as joy and even exhilaration. I will discuss Solomon's theory in more detail in Chapter 9, when I talk about drug addiction.

Summary
Acquired motives or drives are often linked in some very basic way to the biological side of human behavior. Fears, for example, are thought to be linked in some way to unlearned reactions, such as those that occur when we are presented with a painful stimulus, such as a loud noise or an enclosed space, which may seem to threaten our survival. Similarly, achievement motivation may be linked in some fundamental way to such basic biological drives as the need to be loved or simply the need to accommodate the environment. According to the opponent process model, some underlying biological mechanism gives rise to the opponent process.

Even though these new motives or drives may be linked to some underlying biological need, these motives differ from the original motive that gave rise to them. In many cases they seem to have become autonomous. That is, they seem to have their own source of energy. Even though we may not always be able to specify what that new source of energy is, it is important to recognize that without the occurrence of learning, that new drive or motive would not exist. What makes the opponent process theory so attractive is that it spells out where the new energy comes from.

The Cognitive Component

Psychologists use the term *cognitive* to refer to processes that have to do with knowing. Cognition, therefore, involves thinking, perceiving, abstracting, synthesizing, organizing, or any other process that allows the individual to conceptualize the nature of the external world and the nature of self, or that thing called "person."

Cognitive Dissonance Research
Leon Festinger's work on cognitive dissonance had an enormous impact on how psychologists have come to think about certain cognitive processes. In a variety of experiments and situations, Festinger and others have shown that people are inclined, at least under certain conditions, to make their cognitions consistent with their behavior. For example in one experiment male students were asked to perform a very boring task. After doing this for about a half hour, each subject was told by the experimenter that his assistant would not be able to come in and that he would pay them either $1 or $20 (depending on the group to which each was randomly assigned) to act as his assistant for the next subject. Among other things the job of the assistant was to tell the subject that the task was interesting and enjoyable. According to dissonance theory, since the task was boring, saying that the task was interesting would create dissonance. Further, according to dissonance theory, if you were paid only $1 you would experience more dissonance than if you were paid $20. The argument is that when you are paid $20 you have a reason

for "lying" but when you are paid only $1 you do not have a "good" reason; that is, while it may be worth $20 to lie, is it worth $1 to lie? After the subjects had served as the assistant, they were then asked such questions as how enjoyable they had found the task, how much they had learned, whether they would like to participate again, and if they thought the experiment was important. The subjects who had been paid $1 (versus those given $20 and those that did not participate in this part of the experiment but who had done the boring task) were more inclined to say that they found the experiment enjoyable, that they thought the experiment was important, and that they would be willing to participate again (Festinger & Carlsmith, 1959). What this indicates, according to Festinger, is that when people do things that are not consistent with their cognitive attitudes they experience dissonance. When they experience dissonance, according to Festinger, they are motivated to make their attitudes consistent with their behavior. The reason they change their attitudes or beliefs is that they cannot change what they have already done.

Practical significance.   Why is this theory so important? We know that attitudes often direct behavior and, therefore, when people change their attitudes we know that future behavior will also change. Since people often do things they do not intend to do, there is the real possibility that they may come to accept that behavior as characteristic of themselves. For example, a person who puts on weight might think, "The reason I am fat is that I must be one of those fat people." As a result of adopting that label the person might begin to act like a "fat person." People who suddenly realize they have been drinking too much might suddenly think, "Since I am drinking so much, I must be an alcoholic." As a consequence of this label a person might abandon any attempt to control his or her drinking.

Social psychologists argue that one of the best ways to produce changes in peoples' behavior is to "trick" them, or somehow persuade them to behave in a way that is consistent with what they (or you) want them to eventually do. If you want somebody to join your political party you might start by asking them to do you a little favor such as stuffing envelopes containing political propaganda. After that you may ask them to do something a little more demanding such as delivering the envelopes. Eventually, people will ask themselves "Why am I doing this if I'm not getting paid to do this?" According to dissonance theory, under these conditions they will be inclined to bring their beliefs and attitudes in line with their behavior. In short, they will say are doing the work because they believe in the political party they have been working for. In the next section I talk about people who have belief systems that can be labeled internal or external.

Internal and External Causes

Heider (1958) proposed that ordinary people, in their concern with knowing the causes of behavior, differentiate between two types of causes: internal and external. One difference between external and internal determinants of behavior is that only sources of action attributed to the person (internal) can be labeled "intentional." For example, if someone were to step on your toe, you might arrive at two different conclusions: that she did it intentionally (internal) or that it was an accident (external). How you assess the situation will, of course, affect how you will respond to the situation. "Should I ignore the fact that she stepped on my toe, or should I retaliate?" Interestingly, some people are more likely to use an external frame of reference to label an event, and other people are more likely to use an internal frame of reference. Because of this difference, "internals" often react somewhat differently than "externals" to the same environmental event. We will return to this difference later. For the moment it is sufficient to note that humans are inclined to look for causes and in the process often label events in some systematic fashion.

Labels and Categories

Labels and categories reflect our cognitive structure. If I didn't have the category of "clumsy," I might be forced to conclude that the behavior of someone who stepped on my toe was aggressive. (Indeed, some guard dogs, lacking categories, cannot distinguish a friend from an enemy, and it is necessary to warn visitors of this fact.) We have cognitive structures that not only affect the way we interpret the external world but tell us how we should react to it. For example, if I were to perceive and label the behavior of another person as more selfish than altruistic, I might be more inclined to provide a poor job recommendation for that person, especially if the job involved helping handicapped children. If that same person were applying for a job as a construction worker, however, my perception of the person as more selfish than altruistic might have no effect on my recommendation. Labels are closely linked to belief systems. Because people's belief systems vary widely, their behavior can vary greatly as well, in accordance with their belief systems. The way we label an event often reflects something about the nature of our belief systems, including our beliefs about the causes of behavior.

Attribution Theory

In recent years a great deal of research has been done on the question of how humans come to perceive the causes of behavior. This issue falls under the heading of "attribution theory." To what cause does a person attribute a given behavior? How does he account for the fact that he failed? How does he account for the fact that he succeeded? When a person notices her heart is beating faster, how does she account for this fact? Will her interpretation affect her subsequent behavior? If someone's perceptions (interpretations) about the cause of behavior affect subsequent behavior, then we have good evidence that cognitive factors are not just secondary or incidental but are in fact fundamental to behavior itself. That is, cognitive factors play a fundamental role in the arousal, direction, and persistence of behavior.

An experiment by Nisbett and Schachter (1966) illustrates how cognitive factors can affect behavior. Nisbett and Schachter showed that humans could be made to tolerate high levels of shock by persuading them that their autonomic responses, such as fast heart rate, were due not to the shock but rather to a pill they had taken. In their experiment Nisbett and Schachter asked subjects to take a series of electric shocks of steadily increasing intensity, telling them to indicate (1) when the shocks became painful and (2) when the shocks became too painful to tolerate. Before receiving the shocks, the subjects were given a pill. Some were told that the pill would produce hand tremors, palpitations, and other autonomic responses. Others were told that the pill would produce a variety of symptoms that were not autonomic. Actually, the pill was a placebo (it had no physiological effects).

If attribution theory is correct (that people are inclined to look for reasonable explanations for their behavior, including autonomic responses), then the subjects who thought the pill would increase autonomic activity would be inclined to attribute their autonomic responses to the pill, while the other subjects would be inclined to attribute their autonomic responses to the shock. Subjects who do not perceive their autonomic responses as due to a shock should not be as sensitive to it. As a result, they should be willing to tolerate higher levels of shock. Nisbett and Schachter found that, indeed, subjects who were told the pill would produce autonomic responses tolerated shock levels four times as great as the other subjects. These results indicate that cognitive factors play an important role even in something as basic as the perception of pain.

Cognitions and Emotions

Schachter and Singer (1962) have shown that the perceived intensity of an emotion is often due to cognitive factors. They have noted that humans are inclined to perceive arousal as related to ongoing emotions. Thus they suggest that humans are inclined to interpret high arousal levels as meaning that they are experiencing an intense emotion and low arousal levels as meaning that they are experiencing a less intense emotion. For example, feelings of pleasure or of anger would be greater under high arousal. Several ingenious experiments, examined later in more detail, have confirmed their view.

Will the intensity of an emotion also be increased if subjects are merely *convinced* that they are experiencing high levels of arousal? In other words, can cognitive factors alone produce the effect observed by Schachter and Singer? Valins (1966) studied this question by asking male students to rate pictures of seminude women for attractiveness while he ostensibly monitored their heart rate. In fact, he used a recording and arranged the experimental situation so that the subjects could overhear what they thought was their own heartbeat. The heartbeat recording was programmed in such a way that the subject's heart seemed to beat faster in response to some pictures than to others. If Schachter and Singer are correct in asserting that subjects are inclined to make inferences about emotions from arousal (as signaled by heart rate), the subjects should conclude that certain pictures are more pleasing or arousing than other pictures. This is, in fact, what Valins found. Not only did the subjects indicate that the pictures associated with the faster heart rate were more appealing, but when given the opportunity to select one of the pictures to take with them, they selected a picture that had been associated with the fast heart rate. This experiment provides clear evidence that subjects are inclined to use information related to autonomic responses to evaluate the intensity of their feelings. Further, since the heart-rate information was fraudulent, this experiment provides evidence that the processes underlying this outcome were cognitive. A replication and extension of this study confirmed Valins's conclusion that subjects use heart rate to infer affect (Kerber & Coles, 1978).

Cognitions and Pathology

These and other experiments raise the possibility that certain types of emotional disorder may result from a wrong inference, a process called "misattribution." If a man interpreted arousal as anxiety, for example, he might believe that women caused him anxiety. This belief might inhibit him from asking women out on dates even though he found himself attracted to women. Valins and Nisbett (1972) have reviewed some of the evidence for this possibility, together with some of the techniques that have been developed to redirect the attribution process. In general, they conclude that certain emotional disorders can be caused by misattribution and that emotional stability can often be reestablished by redirecting the attribution process.

Summary

Humans are inclined to look for causes of behavior, whether their own or someone else's. The labels people use frequently provide a clue to the way they interpret, perceive, or think about the cause of an event. Research has shown that the way we label an event—be it an internal event, such as a change in arousal level, or an external event, such as having someone step on our toe—can affect not only how we feel but how we react. Valins's study showed, for example, that humans are inclined to interpret increased autonomic activity (arousal) as an increase in the intensity of an ongoing emotion. This effect occurred even though the autonomic activity was fraudulent, a finding that attests to the importance of cognitive factors in mediating the intensity of emotional reactions. The study by Nisbett and Schachter illustrated this same point in a slightly different way. They showed that misattribution (mislabeling) of the source of increased autonomic activity was sufficient to decrease a person's sensitivity to pain. Subjects who thought that their elevated arousal level was due to a placebo pill, not to the shock itself, tolerated shock levels four times as high as other subjects. Because there is evidence that the process of misattribution can alter emotional reactions, it has been suggested that certain emotional disorders may be caused by misattribution. If this is true, it should be possible to cure such disorders by redirecting the attribution process.

The Nature of Theories and Models

The Search for Critical Variables That Govern Behavior

In the past, psychologists have tended to construct models and theories of motivation that are based solely on principles of biology, principles of learning, or principles of cognition. Often these models can explain a limited body of facts but are unable to explain other facts. In short, these models are useful but limited in scope.

Exactly why scientists have tended to base their theories and models exclusively on biological, learning, or cognitive principles is not altogether clear. One reason may be that it is difficult to integrate principles derived from different approaches. The language and assumptions of biology, learning, and cognition are quite different. For example, biological principles typically assume that the reason for a behavior is laid down in the genetic structure. Thus a person behaves aggressively because his or her genetic structure determines which responses will be made. Learning theory, in contrast, tends to view aggressive behavior as a learned pattern. Sometime in the person's past, he or she was rewarded for behaving aggressively. Cognitive theory might view aggression as a means of regaining control over the environment or exercising power. Therefore, a person behaves aggressively to avoid losing everything he or she has worked so hard to get or simply because exercising power is satisfying. It would be difficult for any theorist to reconcile these differences by means of a single set of assumptions.

Another possible reason theorists have tended to explain behavior according to a single set of principles is that one of the goals of science is to simplify—to use the fewest number of concepts or assumptions required to account for phenomena. One obvious way of attaining this goal is to adopt only a single set of principles and stretch these principles rather than add new ones.

Still another reason may be that the nature of scientific analysis leads scientists to study very limited phenomena. That is, since it is necessary to control all variables in a scientific study, the scientist is forced to deal with only parts or aspects of a larger problem. It follows that scientists tend to select those parts of problems that they are most competent to analyze. The biologically oriented psychologist will focus on behaviors that appear to be determined biologically; the learning theorist will tend to focus on those that appear to be the result of learning. Thus, although all are working on the same global problem, the behaviors they select are quite different. A problem arises, therefore, when the theorist attempts to construct general principles on the basis of a limited set of observations. A biologically oriented psychologist interested in understanding aggression, for example, might focus her research on the relation between hormone levels and aggression, while a learning theorist might focus on the repetition of aggression following rewards and no rewards. The biologically oriented psychologist would discover, as we shall see, that hormones do affect aggressive behavior; the learning-oriented psychologist would discover, as we shall also see, that rewards also affect it. If each of these scientists were to construct a theory on the basis of his or her limited set of observations, we would have two very different theories about aggression.

In recent years more and more attempts have been made to integrate divergent data and principles under a single theory. Pribram (1976), for example, has integrated both learning and cognitive principles into his basically biological view of human behavior. This approach appears to have its origin in a productive interaction of three men who initially came together with somewhat divergent views of human beings (Miller, Galanter, & Pribram, 1960).

Testing the Generality of Theories
The goal of science is to find general principles rather than specific ones. The discovery of general principles permits a wide variety of specific facts to be organized and understood. Often quite diverse facts can be integrated by certain general (typically abstract) principles. When a theory has been formulated, usually on a limited set of observations, the next step is to see how general the theory is. Can it predict a variety of behaviors other than those on which it is based? If it can, then it is assumed that the principles discovered from a limited set of observations are general principles. Darwin's theory of evolution is a theory that grew out of a limited set of observations. When Darwin applied his ideas to a wide variety of species, he concluded that the idea of natural selection was a general idea that could explain the changes in all species.

Although it is desirable to see whether a theory is generally applicable, the tendency to generalize must be treated with caution. For example, there is considerable evidence that many behaviors are learned, but there is also considerable evidence that learning is constrained by the structure of the nervous system. Accordingly, before we try to use principles of learning, often derived from research with animals, to modify human behavior, we need to consider carefully such things as the structure of the human nervous system and the way humans interpret events. Although there are many similarities between the nervous systems of humans and animals, there are also differences. There also appear to be major differences in the cognitive structures of humans and animals. The exact implications of this fact are still not totally understood. Nevertheless, we must constantly remind ourselves that these differences are probably not an evolutionary accident: they presumably arose for a very good reason. Humans are different from other animals, and it is our job to understand the exact nature of the differences.

Current Focus of Motivation Theory: Individual Differences

The main problem with most of the early theories of motivation was their failure to account for individual differences. Many of the theories of the 1950s were about so-called average humans. (A notable exception was Atkinson's theory of achievement motivation, to be discussed in Chapter 12.) Data averaged from random samples of rats, pigeons, and humans were used to tell us how the average person learned. Since then we have come to realize that most of us don't behave in this way. Humans differ because of sex, age, temperament, past conditioning, cognitive structures, momentary stress, goals, and recent failures and successes. Each of these factors can cause us to respond in distinctive ways to our environment. It is these often-dynamic factors that we need to understand if we are to explain why different humans do quite different things under the same environmental conditions.

Current studies of motivation are trying to come to grips with the question of individual differences. Why is it that some people become obese while others do not? Why do some people take drugs while others do not? Why do some people like to jump from planes while others do not?

At one time psychologists operated on the assumption that all motivational systems (hunger, thirst, sex, and so on) could be described by the same set of general laws, but there is now good reason to believe that each system is more or less unique, being both similar and dissimilar to other systems. Further, there is reason to believe that a given system (such as hunger) is not the same in all people. That is, basic individual differences are associated with each system. Therefore, the current focus is on explaining how different people will react when a given motivational system is activated. If these systems are more or less unique, are they also independent? There is good reason to believe they do interact. The question then arises of what happens when two or more systems are activated simultaneously. Do they tend to compete for control of behavior, or is the person so constructed that one system always takes precedence over another? What are the implications of having different motive systems that need to be satisfied? Does this ever lead to stress and unhappiness? What role do our cognitions play in controlling the simultaneous activation of different motive systems?

Although explanations of individual differences are important, any theory worth its salt should be able to predict individual behavior patterns. At least, that is our goal. As we all know, it is easy to explain at the end of a game why a team won or lost. It is far more difficult to predict ahead of time whether it is going to win or lose. If we know the critical variables, we should be able to predict. Therefore, the best criterion for determining whether we have identified the important variables—the best criterion for a good theory—is to take some behavior we think we understand and predict whether it will occur given that certain variables are present, absent, or combined in certain amounts. In short, good explanations of behavior are based on studies that have shown that certain variables are truly antecedents of a given behavior.

Summary

In their attempts to account for behavior, scientists have based their approaches on different sets of assumptions, all of which have proved partly true. The biologically oriented researcher found there was evidence for a genetic basis to behavior. The learning theorist was able to demonstrate that learning is important. The cognitive psychologist has been able to demonstrate that cognitions are important. Today we realize that evidence that supports one set

(continued)

of assumptions does not invalidate the others. Most psychologists accept the position that each of these approaches can tell us something about why we do what we do. The present goal, therefore, is to understand the nature of the interaction of biological, learned, and cognitive factors. In accepting the idea that behavior may be the product of an interaction, we have also had to accept the possibility that the nature of the interaction may vary from person to person. We have had to recognize that important individual differences exist, be they biological, learned, or cognitive.

Some Examples of a Components Approach

I started this chapter by arguing that it is necessary to adopt what I call a components approach to the analysis of motivation. To illustrate this approach, I have selected two common behaviors to analyze, to see whether we can devise some hypotheses about why people engage in them. These hypotheses (as opposed to explanations) are based on the assumption that behavior is the product of biological, learned, or cognitive factors or of some combination of these three basic classes of behavioral determinants. Let us start by examining the current craze for running.

Motivation for Running

On the surface, running appears to be a straightforward activity. People state that they decide to run in order to "get into shape," to "lose weight," or to "improve their health." No doubt these are some of the reasons that people initially run. There are less obvious reasons. Some people run, they confess, in order to get away from their spouses or to avoid having lunch with their colleagues or to escape from the close confines of their office or house. So far, all the explanations I have listed are couched in avoidance terms. People run to escape from "being fat," "a noxious spouse," "an unpleasant environment," or something else. What are some of the positive reasons? The positive reasons for running often emerge when people have engaged in running for a while. It is hard for most people to see that puffing and sweating on a hot day or freezing on a cold day can be pleasant. It is only when they have had a chance to experience the effects of running that they honestly say they do it because it makes them feel good or look good or because the act of running is itself pleasant and satisfying. The immediate question is how an activity that appears to demand so much effort (and sometimes pain) can be pleasant.

Before we try to answer this question, we need to understand that why people initially do something and why they continue to do it may be unrelated. This simple fact is very important. Most of us are aware that we often have good intentions that somehow fail to get translated into long-term behavioral change. I call this "the New Year's resolution phenomenon." People often change their behavior for a day, a week, sometimes even a month, but more often than not the change turns out to be transitory. Once the initial motivation fades, there is nothing to maintain the behavior.

What, then, is the motivation that maintains running, as distinct from the motivation for taking up running? We should start by noting that not all people who try running continue. Some, however, develop signs of being addicted. If they stop running for a few days, they experience a negative physiological or psychological state that is analogous to withdrawal from a drug. In short, they have a compulsion to engage in the activity on a regular basis, just as a drug addict feels

What keeps runners dedicated after the initial motivation fades?

a compulsion to take a drug regularly. The obvious question that needs to be answered is whether running produces in this group of people some kind of chemical output that has motivating and possibly addicting properties.

The answer is a qualified yes. It appears that running (and aerobic exercise in general, such as swimming, cycling, walking, rowing, jogging, and cross-country skiing) does stimulate the output of several chemicals. Norepinephrine, for example, will increase to as much as 4½ times normal (Davis, 1973; Howley, 1976). Since increased norepinephrine levels have been implicated in feelings of elation and euphoria whereas low levels have been implicated in feelings of depression (Post et al., 1978; Schildkraut & Kety, 1967), there is reason to argue that people may run in order to experience increased outputs of this or related chemicals. Can people become addicted to norepinephrine? Again, the answer is a qualified yes. Addiction to amphetamines, which produce arousal and euphoria, has been documented for some time. Among other effects, amphetamines stimulate the output of norepinephrine and dopamine. It has been hypothesized that people take amphetamines to stimulate the output of norepinephrine or dopamine. It makes sense, therefore, that people will continue to perform a response, such as running, that stimulates the output of one of these rewarding chemicals.

A number of studies have shown that aerobic exercise alleviates anxiety (for example, Morgan & Horstman, 1976) and depression (Greist et al., 1979). Although these studies must be considered preliminary because several alternative explanations have not been completely ruled out, the results are consistent with a number of other physiological findings (Ledwidge, 1980). Concerning anxiety, exercise has been shown to be a muscle relaxant (Baekeland, 1970; Baekeland & Lasky, 1966) and to reduce lactate, an acid that has been found to play a key role in anxiety symptoms (Clarke, 1975; Larson & Michelman, 1973; Pitts, 1969). In fact, there is evidence that aerobic exercise produces a general decrease in the adrenocortical response to stress (Tharp, 1975; White, Ismail, & Bottoms, 1976). This means that a person who engages in aerobic exercise will experience a less severe reaction to physical stress. Concerning depression, we have the evidence already discussed above implicating norepinephrine in depressive disorders. The fact that running increases norepinephrine output offers a compelling argument that exercise can alleviate feelings of depression. Further, there is evidence that chronic fatigue, a common complaint of depressives, is alleviated by aerobic exercise (Kraines, 1957). The fact that depressives exhibit less slow-wave sleep (Gresham, Agnew, & Williams, 1965), together with the fact that aerobic exercise increases slow-wave sleep (Griffin & Trinder, 1978), suggests another important link between exercise and depression (Ledwidge, 1980).

It is frequently observed that people who run tend to increase the amount they run. Returning to the analogy between running and drug addiction, we might say that these people are showing a tolerance effect. That is, they are increasing their dosage level in order to experience the same effect. If people run to experience the effects of norepinephrine or some other chemical, it makes good sense that they should tend to increase the amount of time they devote to running, for two reasons. First, as their bodies become conditioned, it is likely that they will have to run longer to get the same output of norepinephrine and dopamine. Second, and not unrelated to the first, human motivation appears to have the character of an "opponent process" (Solomon & Corbit, 1974). For every process set in motion, as we have seen, the body develops an opposing process to return itself to its original state. Thus, when a drug stimulates one type of reaction, the body initiates another reaction that opposes the action of the drug. Norepinephrine and dopamine appear to produce arousal and euphoria; the opposing process of the body would be one that reduced arousal and counteracted euphoria. People who take amphetamines often experience fatigue some time after they have taken the drug. According to the opponent process model of drug addiction, this reaction is due in part to the operation of the opponent process. It is assumed that the opponent process occurs more quickly and becomes stronger each time it is activated as the result of taking a drug, and a person would need to take larger doses of the drug to override this opponent process. In other words, because the opponent process becomes stronger each time it is activated, the person develops a tolerance for the drug. Using the same line of reasoning, we could argue that the body develops a tolerance for the chemicals produced by running, and so a runner needs to run more to get the same reaction.

If running is analogous to an addictive drug, why doesn't everybody who tries running become addicted to it? The most plausible explanation is that not everybody finds the chemical changes reinforcing. According to Schildkraut and Kety (1967), some people (such as those who experience depression) have a deficit of norepinephrine. Such people, according to their hypothesis, would be inclined to find running rewarding. Hans Eysenck (1967) has argued that certain people (extraverts) tend to have subnormal arousal levels and that these people are more inclined to pick out situations or take drugs that increase their arousal level. Thus the failure of some people to become addicted is not altogether unexpected.

Our explanation of why people run is, at this point, a hypothesis. Further research is needed to verify all facets of this explanation. Moreover, even if some people run for the reasons given above, it does not mean that all do. Psychologists have been inclined to assume that there is one and only one reason for a given behavior. It may well be that some people run simply to lose weight and do not find running rewarding, aside from its results. I have talked to many people who run. Most of them say they enjoy the activity, but a number state that they do not and that they do it only for extrinsic reasons. They say that their doctor told them they must exercise to control their blood pressure or that they want to get in shape for another sport, such as skiing or racquetball. If it is true that some people do not find the activity intrinsically rewarding while others do, it may well be that these two groups differ in resting arousal levels, resting norepinephrine levels, or even something else that has not yet been suggested as a mechanism that mediates the rewards associated with running.

When people say they run because they want to lose weight or because their doctor told them to, we label such motivation as cognitive. Remember that I suggested that all motives probably reflect the interaction of biological, learned, and cognitive components. It seems quite possible that people run not only because it makes them feel good but because they enjoy the attention they get when they look younger and sexier and can wear more stylish clothes. Also, people sometimes feel virtuous when they have done something they perceive required effort, discipline, and determination. These would be cognitive factors. What about learning? If a person performs a response, such as running, at the same time each day, time of day could become a sufficient cue to elicit that response. Learning theorists have shown that once a response has become a habit (usually because it has been rewarded for a period of time), that response will often be emitted for some time in the absence of a reward. Even if it is rewarded only occasionally, it will often continue at a steady and predictable rate for long periods. Therefore, it seems reasonable to suggest that sometimes a person runs out of habit. A person might run also because other rewards, not directly linked to running, are contingent on it. The opportunity to enjoy the company of friends might induce some people either to run in the first place or to continue running. Because the activity of running itself would then not be providing the reward but would only be instrumental in its acquisition, the behavior would be viewed as being governed by the principles of learning.

It should also be noted that the rewards for a given behavior may shift over time. It is quite possible, for example, that after a runner has become trim and sexy, or when tolerance has increased until the activity provides little biological reward, other rewards come to maintain the behavior. Enjoying the company of other runners could, for example, come to act as the primary source of motivation for this activity. As such, running would be viewed as occurring for learned rather than cognitive or biological reasons.

Before we leave the topic of running, it should be mentioned that there is a great deal of concern about the high rate of divorce and marital problems among runners (Lowther, 1979). Some therapists have noted that running often leads to a change in personality, which may contribute to marital breakdown. For example, people who take up running often gain self-confidence. Such a change might motivate someone to extricate himself or herself from an already unhappy relationship. Why self-confidence should increase as a result of running is not altogether clear. It could be due to chemical changes or to changes in one's self-image. There are several other reasons that running might lead to marital breakdown. The addictive properties of running might leave one spouse alone and neglected for long periods. Or it may be that a person took up running to escape his or her spouse. Thus the marital breakdown might have begun long before the running, so that running was the result, not the cause, of a marital problem.

Although this discussion is interesting in itself, it was included here to make several points. First, what appears to be a simple behavior may be due to a complex set of processes working together. Second, the reason someone initially engages in a behavior may be quite different from the reason he or she continues the behavior. For example, we noted that a person may initiate a behavior for cognitive reasons (doctors' recommendations), come to do it for biological reasons (norepinephrine and/or dopamine output) or psychological reasons (to reduce anxiety and/or depression), and finally maintain it out of habit or learning (to be with friends). In the final analysis, probably all three components are jointly responsible for maintaining the response over a long period. People run for a variety of reasons. The same person may run for different reasons at different times. One cannot infer motivation from simply seeing the behavior. The reasons that each individual runs can be uncovered only when we understand the individual.

Although running may be maintained to a large degree by chemical outputs, it must be emphasized again that this is a hypothesis. It is a good hypothesis because the converging data all seem to point to chemicals (such as norepinephrine) as a possible common mediating variable. That is, we can explain the relation between certain events because we have identified an underlying common variable. Frequently in the field of psychology, converging data are used to formulate possible explanations about behavior. When more and more data point to the same mediating variable (such as norepinephrine), we tend to view that variable as a good candidate to explain the behavior. An important question for the motivation theorist is whether such common mediating variables are motivational. That is, can they be considered important in the arousal, energization, and persistence of behavior?

Motivation for Listening to Rock Music

Presumably we come to appreciate music, at least in part, because of cognitive processes. We listen to new records because they have different words, different melodies, and different combinations of notes and instruments. Hunt (1963) has argued that we are motivated by newness or incongruity—that is, the difference that exists between what we already know and what we have just experienced or are about to experience. Walker (1974) has suggested that a new piece of music can provide the psychological complexity that we seek after we have become familiar with other pieces. Most of us eventually grow tired of a piece of music and put it aside, at least for a time. At such times we seek out music that has new dimensions or qualities, something that is capable of stimulating our interest.

In addition to the motivating properties arising from cognitive variables, there are motivating properties that come as a result of previous learning. We may like a piece of music because it stimulates pleasant memories or evokes pleasant fantasies. The voices of certain rock singers appear to be able to conjure up images of a romance or just plain sex. Under certain conditions a piece of music could conceivably evoke feelings of well-being or even self-confidence if in the past the music had been associated with this psychological state. All of us have probably at one time or another suddenly remembered a pleasant experience that was associated with a particular piece of music. We may even deliberately play a piece of music in order to evoke the pleasurable state that it elicits.

For a number of people, mainly adolescents, rock music is best appreciated when it is played loud. What makes loudness an integral quality of rock music for some people? We know from several sources that sounds over a certain loudness level (approximately 80 decibels, abbreviated dB) tend to produce certain reliable physiological changes. Live rock music is often played at well over 100 dB in a closed room. If you happen to sit near a speaker, it may be as high as 120–140 dB—a

When rock music becomes painful

level that can produce permanent hearing loss (see Dey, 1970; Fern, 1976; Mills, 1975, 1978). The main physiological change produced by high noise levels is increased arousal. As we have already noted, arousal has to do with the level of activity in the central nervous system. A structure in the brain, the reticular activating system, appears to govern arousal levels. As sensory input bombards the arousal system, the system responds by activating the brain. From a motivational point of view, moderate levels of arousal are experienced as pleasurable. In fact, humans will often seek out stimulation in order to experience moderate to high levels of arousal. We might ask, therefore, whether listening to rock music is motivated, at least in part, by the desire to experience increases in arousal.

Given what we know about the relations among noise, arousal, and pleasure, this explanation of why people like to listen to loud music seems to be grounded in basic science. A problem arises, however, if we try to explain why people often like to listen to loud rock music with friends as well as to dance to rock music. The problem comes from the knowledge that social interactions and exercise also produce arousal. If a person is listening to rock music to experience moderate arousal, then dancing and social interactions will increase arousal beyond a moderate level. Since high levels of arousal have been hypothesized to be aversive (Hebb, 1955), why do people seem to enjoy listening to rock music while dancing and socializing? Why do some people, in fact, seek out such situations? Perhaps adolescents need a great deal of stimulation in order to experience moderate arousal, or it may be that there are times when very high levels of arousal can result in pleasure (Berlyne, 1960). Schachter and Singer (1962) have shown that relatively high levels of arousal can intensify an already pleasurable reaction. If a person is already enjoying the company of friends, rock music together with dancing may enhance this already pleasurable state. Music and dancing are often an integral part of festivals and celebrations and have been so for thousands of years. Obviously there is something about music and dancing that makes one feel good or possibly enhances an already festive mood.

Like running, the activity of listening to rock music demonstrates that a common behavior can have several components that vary from time to time. Research clearly indicates that some type of biological factor is involved in listening to rock music played at noise levels above 80 dB. The fact that people listen to rock music when they could more readily obtain the same arousal level by running around the block indicates that something more is involved. Obviously, the structure of the music and the associations it elicits are important factors in the total reaction to it. Somehow all these factors interact to produce a particular sensation.

Given that all these factors may contribute to the final motivation, can we ever know exactly which factors are involved in a particular person's motivation, and in what proportions? Is it possible that one person is motivated mainly by biological components, another mainly by cognitive components, and yet another mainly by learned components? The answer is yes. It is possible, within limits, to determine whether one of these factors is more important for one person than for another. We could make this determination by designing a series of controlled experiments to compare the reactions of several people. It would be a good exercise for the student in experimental psychology to design just such an experiment. Whether it would be worth the time and the effort required to carry it out is another question.

Before leaving this example, let me summarize why I included it. Like the previous example, it demonstrates that motivation, even esthetic appreciation, involves the interaction of three basic components. In addition, the example demonstrates that the motivation for a particular activity may be enhanced or even changed by other activities that also have motivational properties. Specifically, rock music is often used in social situations that themselves are arousal-producing. Further, people often dance to music in social situations, and dancing has been implicated not only in arousal but in the output of norepinephrine. The joining together—or, more precisely, the pooling—of motivation is a fascinating thing to note about human behavior. It is a phenomenon that characterizes much of daily human motivation. Rarely does one motive arise in isolation from other motives. For that reason, we need to understand not only what components are involved in each motive system but how different motive systems interact.

Summary

The two examples discussed in this section—the motivation for running and the motivation for listening to rock music—illustrate why it is necessary to consider biological, learned, and cognitive factors when we try to explain a particular behavior. Although most, if not all, behaviors have a biological component, biological factors can never be viewed as the sole determinants of human behavior. Humans are subjected to a wide variety of external rewards, which we know have a profound effect in modifying the direction of their behavior. Further, we must recognize that biological factors frequently find their expression because humans have learned a response that stimulates a biological mechanism. This pattern appears to reflect the fact that many human responses are not prewired but can be acquired because we possess general reward mechanisms. People who run, it can be argued, have learned to perform a response in order to experience a feeling of euphoria—a feeling that all people are inherently capable of experiencing, provided they find a means

(continued)

of tapping that system by making a response that will activate it. Cognitions, too, play a profound role in human behavior. Our ability to appreciate music, for example, appears to be mediated to a very large degree by our ability to respond to the pattern of stimulation music provides.

Main Points

1. This book takes a components approach to the study of human motivation.
2. Three basic components are involved in all motivational systems: a biological component, a learned component, and a cognitive component.
3. The biological approach to motivation has traditionally assumed that behavior is ultimately tied to the genetic structure.
4. Open and closed programs have been proposed as a means of accounting for the varying amounts of learning that are involved in the development of a behavior.
5. Some chemicals may alter the genetic structure of individuals, but psychological input does not. Environmental input may be important, however, for the realization of a genetic structure.
6. The learning approach to motivation has traditionally assumed that behavior is the result of a person's reinforcement history and is governed by principles of conditioning.
7. The cognitive approach has traditionally assumed that the way a person interprets, labels, and classifies an event determines how he or she will behave.
8. The idea that all motivational systems can be explained by a single set of principles based on a single set of assumptions has, to this point, failed. An abundance of research shows that each system operates according to somewhat distinctive principles.
9. Theorists are now being forced to account for the interaction of the three components—a task that has forced them to question some of the early ideals that guided theory construction.
10. Current motivation theorists are concerned with the question of individual differences.
11. No matter how well a theory can explain behavior after the fact, the most important criterion of a good theory is its predictive ability.
12. Analysis of why people run and why they listen to rock music indicates that all three components—biological, learned, and cognitive—can be important in motivating a behavior.

T H R E E

Arousal,
Performance,
and Attention

Why do we suddenly get a burst of energy when we are faced with an emergency?

Why do even little changes in the environment sometimes make us feel alert and energetic?

Why can we sustain our alertness for long periods of time when we become intellectually involved in something?

Why are we more efficient at some times than at others?

Why do we feel stressed and tend to make mistakes when we become flooded with information?

How can we learn to maintain our attention to boring tasks?

Why do we like our environment to be sometimes very stimulating and at other times more monotonous and restful?

When we are suddenly confronted by an emergency, such as a car accident, our whole body prepares itself to deal with that event. Mentally, we attempt to make sense of the situation. Is anybody in danger? Is there anything we can do? What alternatives are available to us? At the same time that our mind is attempting to grasp what has happened, our body is preparing to expend enormous amounts of physical energy. When people are confronted by emergencies, they often do things that they never thought they were capable of doing—lift enormous weights or swim several miles, for example. People who have never before delivered a baby will undertake this formidable task. People who normally feel faint at the sight of blood will administer first aid to a bleeding victim.

Not all emergencies are matters of life and death, but the body responds as though they were. The mind becomes active while the body prepares for the increased demand for energy. When we compete in a sports event, for example, our mind searches for things we can do to beat our competitor. At the same time our body prepares to deal with the energy requirements of the competition. Our heart rate speeds up, we breathe more quickly, and we begin to sweat. Even the prospect of having to give a speech can increase our heart rate and breathing and make our palms sweat.

What we are experiencing under such conditions is an increase in arousal. As we shall see, arousal involves physiological as well as psychological changes. The interaction between them is fairly complex. On the one hand, the physiological changes produce psychological changes. When arousal increases, we think differently, process information differently, and act differently. Some of these psychological changes we cannot control. That is, certain changes in the way we think, process information, and act are often automatic.

But this is a two-way street. The way we think, process information, and act can and often does produce physiological changes. In other words, just as the body influences the mind, the mind influences the body. In the course of adapting to a new situation, a kind of back-and-forth process produces changes in the way we think and act and alters certain brain chemicals and body secretions. These changes further alter the way we think and act. In this chapter we examine some of these interactions between the mind and the body. (In Chapter 7, we will look at this question again as it pertains to the emotions.) We will start by examining one of the most basic physiological reactions, the arousal response.

Definition of Arousal

Arousal is the activation of the brain and the body. When we are aroused, the brain and the body are in a state of readiness, preparing us to engage in adaptive behaviors. Electrical activity in the brain increases, the heart beats more rapidly, and blood is redirected to the brain and muscles. Muscle tonus increases in preparation for quick and efficient response. The activation or arousal of the brain and the body can be viewed as a state of energization. When we are aroused, the brain and the body are prepared to make use of various chemicals (stored in various places in the body) that facilitate the processing of information, planning, and the expenditure of physical energy.

Biological Mechanisms of Arousal

We generally speak of two primary mechanisms of arousal: the reticular activating system (RAS) and the autonomic nervous system. As we shall see, these two systems are not the only ones involved in arousal, but they are the two primary ones.

The Reticular Activating System (RAS)

Each of the various sensory receptors (visual, auditory, tactile, and so on) is connected to a sensory area in the brain via an afferent nerve pathway that ascends to the cortex via a specific projection system. Fibers branching from these pathways ascend to the reticular formation (Figure 3-1). Until 1949, it was assumed that the reticular formation was simply some type of relay station for the many sensory signals. In 1949 Moruzzi and Magoun found that if they directly stimulated the upper part of the reticular activating system with a mild electrical current when

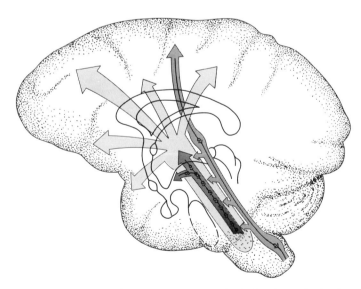

Figure 3-1. Ascending reticular activating system (reticular formation) schematically projected on a monkey brain (Lindsley, 1960)

an animal was asleep, the entire cortex would suddenly become active (aroused). Simultaneously, the animal showed all the normal signs of awakening from sleep, such as opening its eyes and stretching. On the basis of their work, Moruzzi and Magoun decided that the reticular formation acted as a center for arousing the cortex and therefore named it the "reticular activating system" (RAS). They suggested that the incoming sensory signals activate the reticular activating system, which in turn activates the cortex.

The nature and measurement of cortical activity. The brain is composed of many interconnecting nerve pathways. Electrical impulses are generated by chemical processes and travel along these pathways. There are many gaps in these nerve pathways, called "synapses." In order for an electrical impulse to move from one part of the brain to another, it must cross several synapses. One of the main chemicals that facilitates passage of nerve impulses across synapses is norepinephrine (von Euler, 1956). When norepinephrine is secreted at various sites in the brain, movement of electrical impulses across synapses in those sites is facilitated. Because generation of electrical impulses and movement of these impulses are governed by chemical processes, it has been suggested that the brain can most accurately be characterized in terms of the various chemical reactions that occur within it.

The electroencephalogram (EEG) was designed to amplify these impulses so that a permanent record could be made of the activity of various brain structures. It is technically possible to obtain records of activity in any brain structure, but EEG recordings on humans are typically taken from the structures on the outer perimeter of the brain. Surface recordings can be made by means of electrodes attached to various locations on the skull with a high-conductance glue. These electrodes can measure the activity of the visual cortex, auditory cortex, motor cortex, or other areas near the surface of the brain, depending on the location of the electrodes. Since the electrodes cannot readily measure the activity of deeper brain structures, such as the hypothalamus, it is often necessary to use animals in order to learn about these deeper structures. In general, therefore, when we talk about EEG activity in humans, we are talking about the activity of the cortex. The cortex, the outer layer of the brain, mediates, at least in part, our ability to see, hear, smell, taste, experience tactile stimulation, and perform a wide variety of motor responses, including speech. We say the cortex is involved "in part" in these activities because other brain structures also play a fundamental role in these functions. Whatever the exact role of the cortex, we know it plays some role in the processing of sensory information so that the external world appears to be organized and predictable.

EEG readings have shown that changes in brain activity are characterized by abrupt rather than gradual changes in the amplitude and frequency of the impulses ("brain waves"). In general, as a particular brain structure becomes more active, the amplitude (height of a wave) decreases and the frequency (number of peaks per second) increases. Figure 3-2 shows some examples of cortical activity corresponding to various behavioral and mental states.

The Autonomic Nervous System

Although cortical activity has frequently been used as a measure of arousal, many other physiological changes occur when a person is in a state of arousal.

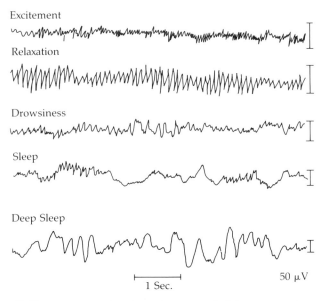

Excitement

Relaxation

Drowsiness

Sleep

Deep Sleep

1 Sec.

50 μV

Figure 3-2.   EEG patterns ranging from sleep to wakefulness to excitement (Jasper, 1941)

The autonomic nervous system is responsible for these changes. A wide array of stimuli trigger activity in the autonomic nervous system. For example, physical exertion, exposure to a loud noise or novel stimulus, injury to the body, anxiety, apprehension, or certain drugs will elicit a rather predictable pattern of responses. Heart rate increases and blood vessels constrict. Together these two reactions produce an increase in the flow of blood. The liver releases glucose for immediate energy, and the spleen releases red corpuscles, which are important for carrying oxygen. Digestion halts; however, fats are released into the bloodstream for conversion to energy. Perspiration increases, which is important for cooling when the person is expending great amounts of energy. Secretion of saliva and mucus decreases, giving the "dry mouth" feeling. The muscles tense, the pupils dilate, and the senses are improved. This pattern of responses is generally accompanied by increased cortical activity.

This pattern of responses is due mainly to the action of the hypothalamus, which triggers two parallel and complementary reactions: it stimulates activity in the autonomic nervous system and in the endocrine (glandular) system (Levine, 1960). Figure 3-3 shows the pathways in the sympathetic nervous system, a division of the autonomic nervous system. Most of the physiological changes noted above can be traced to the activity of the sympathetic nervous system. In addition to producing these changes, the autonomic nervous system stimulates the adrenal medulla, which then secretes various amounts of epinephrine or norepinephrine.

Both epinephrine and norepinephrine are involved in a number of physical and psychological reactions. They both produce RAS arousal. RAS activity is often associated with general arousal, which mediates sensory thresholds, muscle tonus, and the other responses mentioned above. It has been suggested that the release

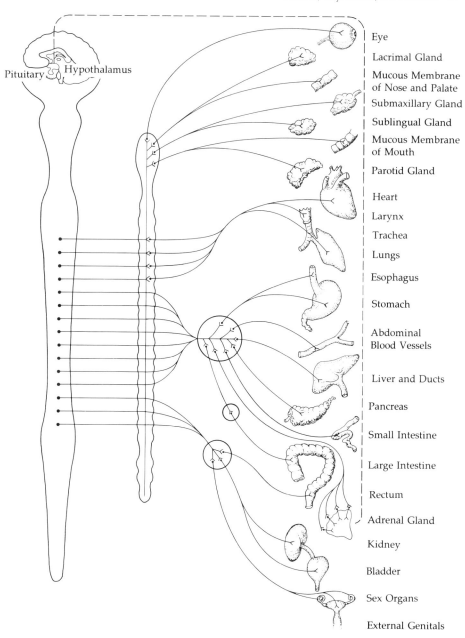

Eye

Lacrimal Gland

Mucous Membrane
of Nose and Palate

Submaxillary Gland

Sublingual Gland

Mucous Membrane
of Mouth

Parotid Gland

Heart

Larynx

Trachea

Lungs

Esophagus

Stomach

Abdominal
Blood Vessels

Liver and Ducts

Pancreas

Small Intestine

Large Intestine

Rectum

Adrenal Gland

Kidney

Bladder

Sex Organs

External Genitals

Figure 3-3.   Schematic diagram of the sympathetic nervous system (solid lines) and
the action of the pituitary on the adrenals via the bloodstream (dashed line) (Levine,
1966)

of epinephrine and norepinephrine provides a long-lasting chemical backup for
the immediate action of the sympathetic nervous system. Epinephrine and nor-
epinephrine have also been implicated in human emotional reactions.

Other Mechanisms of Arousal

Routtenberg's model of two arousal systems.   Routtenberg (1968) noted that often there is a lack of correlation among behavioral arousal, EEG activity, and RAS activity. This fact immediately raised the question whether the RAS is the sole brain structure responsible for cortical and behavioral arousal. Routtenberg found that when lesions are made in the RAS, EEG desynchronization will still occur. (The term *desynchronization* is typically used when the normal alpha rhythm changes abruptly into an activation pattern—a phenomenon that happens, for example, when a new or novel stimulus is presented.) However, no EEG desynchronization occurs if lesions are also made in the limbic system (a complex system of the brain that involves certain subcortical structures, the hypothalamus, and part of the cerebral cortex, which has been implicated in emotion and related activities). Thus it appears that the limbic system can, under certain conditions, take over for the RAS when it has been damaged. This finding seems to provide evidence that the RAS is not the sole structure responsible for cortical arousal. Routtenberg has argued that this fact, along with a number of others, can be explained by the assumption that the RAS is arousal system I and the limbic system is arousal system II.

Why two systems? Routtenberg has suggested, following the lead of others, that the RAS is concerned mainly with the neuronal organization involved in responding whereas the limbic system is concerned mainly with rewards. There is ample evidence that when the limbic system is active, a person is more likely to repeat a response; this does not appear to be the case when the reticular system is moderately active. There is also ample evidence that responses are better organized when the RAS is moderately active; this does not appear to be the case when the limbic system is active. Thus the evidence seems to indicate that the two systems serve different functions.

Origins of Arousal

Arousal is produced by three basic phenomena: (1) stimulation of the sensory system, (2) biological rhythms, and (3) our interpretation of an event.

Stimulation of the Sensory Systems

Stimulation of any of the sensory systems (visual, auditory, olfactory, tactile) is accompanied by an increase in arousal. From the point of view of survival, it is important that the individual be prepared to deal with any sudden change in the environment. Often an increase in sensory input from the environment requires the individual to make some adaptive responses, and quickly. We obviously make our best adaptive responses when we are functioning at some optimal level, that is, when the brain is fully active and the body is prepared to deal with enormous energy demands. Since an adaptive response to change involves the entire body, it is important that the entire brain become active, not just that area of the brain that must process the incoming stimulation. Similarly, it is important that the body be put into a state of readiness so that no matter what the demand on it, it will be ready to respond. If we hear a window break in the middle of the night, for example, it is important that the entire brain should become active, not just that area of the brain that processes auditory stimulation. If the window has been broken by an intruder, all our senses must be prepared to deal with the event.

Rhythmic Activity of the Nervous System

Arousal, especially cortical arousal, is also under the control of certain biological rhythms. Michel Jouvet's (1967) work suggests that the alternating activity of the raphe nuclei (which secrete serotonin) and the locus coeruleus (which secretes norepinephrine) governs arousal and alertness in humans. Jouvet found that serotonin is associated with reduced cortical activity (reduced arousal) while norepinephrine is associated with increased cortical activity (increased arousal). All of us are more alert at some times than at others. Not only do all normal people experience these involuntary changes in arousal (alertness), but they often experience them at certain predictable times of the day. So-called morning people, for example, experience greater alertness in the mornings, while night people experience greater alertness in the evenings. Still others have a mixed pattern—they experience a period of alertness in the morning followed at midday by a drop in alertness, which is followed in turn by another period of increased alertness. Not surprisingly, such people are more likely than others to take a nap.

Cognitive Interpretation

Anticipatory bodily preparation.   The third major source of arousal is our interpretation of the environment. Whenever we interpret an event as threatening or potentially exciting, we are likely to experience an increase in arousal, both cortical and autonomic. When we are threatened, it is important that the body be prepared to deal with that threat, both mentally and physically. Similarly, when we select some activity that is capable of providing excitement, the body must be prepared for that event. If we are going to engage in some sport such as scuba diving, for example, we need to be both physically and mentally prepared for it. An increase in arousal, in other words, is associated with a wide variety of activities.

The important point to remember about this kind of arousal is that it is anticipatory. That is, the arousal typically occurs before some event or anticipated event takes place. Because it is based on our cognitive interpretation, it may be inappropriate. I may anticipate that I am going to be fired, for example, when in fact nothing of the sort is about to happen. Sometimes it is the magnitude of the arousal we experience that is not appropriate. While I may have good reason to experience a very high level of arousal if I am asked to address a large audience, it would be inappropriate to experience that same high level of arousal if I were asked to introduce a friend to someone else I know.

Cognitive dissonance.   When people behave in ways that are not consistent with their beliefs, they frequently experience what is called cognitive dissonance. That is, they experience a discrepancy between what they believe and what they have done. Laboratory research has repeatedly shown that people tend to reduce such dissonance by changing their attitudes in the direction of their behavior. There is evidence that cognitive dissonance tends to produce increases in arousal. Robert Croyle and Joel Cooper (1983) induced cognitive dissonance by asking students who had previously indicated their disagreement with the statement "Alcohol use should be totally banned from the Princeton campus and eating clubs" to write forceful arguments in support of a ban on alcohol. Their findings indicate that cognitive dissonance indeed produces increases in arousal. Their research also indicates that arousal often provides the motivation that leads to attitude change. The point I want to emphasize here is that cognitive factors can and often do lead to increases in arousal.

Summary

Arousal is the activation or energization of the brain and the body. Arousal has two primary mechanisms: the reticular activating system (RAS) and the autonomic nervous system. The RAS, located at the top of the brainstem, is primarily responsible for the activation of the brain. Studies focusing on the electroencephalograph (EEG), a recording device designed to measure and record brain activity, have shown that changes in brain activity are abrupt rather than gradual. The autonomic nervous system produces a number of bodily changes that prepare the individual to expend great amounts of energy. Most of the bodily changes are produced by a branch of the autonomic nervous system called the sympathetic nervous system. The adrenal glands are activated by the pituitary. The chemicals secreted by the adrenal glands, epinephrine and norepinephrine, provide the long-term backup for the more immediate action of the sympathetic nervous system. There are three basic phenomena that elicit arousal: stimulation of the various sense systems, rhythmical activity of the nervous system (alternating activity of the raphe nuclei and locus coeruleus), and cognitive interpretation.

Performance and Arousal

Research on the RAS has shown that unless the cortex is aroused, sensory signals going to the cortex will not be recognized or processed. If the cortex is optimally aroused, it will quickly recognize signals and efficiently process incoming information. In one study (Fuster, 1958), rhesus monkeys were required to learn to discriminate between two objects (learn which object had a food reward hidden under it) when the objects were presented tachistoscopically (that is, for a fraction of a second at a time). In the experimental condition, the animals were electrically stimulated in the RAS through a permanently implanted electrode. Control animals received no stimulation. Not only did the experimental animals learn faster, but they had faster reaction times.

The RAS also has a descending tract, which influences motor functions. Since reactions are faster and more finely coordinated under higher levels of arousal, there is good reason to believe that the descending tract of the RAS may be in part responsible for this improvement.

Table 3-1 summarizes some of the data relating psychological states, EEG, and behavioral efficiency. Note that behavior is most efficient not when arousal is at its highest level but when it is more moderate.

Hebb's Model of Arousal, Attention, and Performance

After reviewing all the data relating behavioral efficiency to arousal, Donald Hebb (1955) proposed that the relation between arousal and performance could be represented by an inverted-U-shaped function (Figure 3-4).

Following Hebb's lead, other investigators began to examine in some detail just what happens when arousal increases. In order to study the relationship between arousal and performance, they began to manipulate arousal systematically. While it is possible to manipulate arousal by means of drugs, the ethical considerations associated with the use of drugs caused investigators to look for other ways to achieve the effects they sought. Noise increases autonomic arousal, and many investigators began to use noise in laboratory studies. The results of these studies clearly showed that as autonomic arousal increases with noise level, performance increases (Takasawa, 1978). Up to a point, then, there is a direct relationship between

Table 3-1. Psychological states and their EEG, conscious, and behavioral correlates (Lindsley, 1952)

Behavioral Continuum	Electroencephalogram	State of Awareness	Behavioral Efficiency
Strong, excited emotion (fear, rage, anxiety)	Desynchronized: low to moderate amplitude; fast, mixed frequencies	Restricted awareness; divided attention; diffuse, hazy; confusion	Poor (lack of control, freezing up, disorganization)
Alert attentiveness	Partially synchronized: mainly fast, low-amplitude waves	Selective attention, but may vary or shift; concentration, anticipation, "set"	Good (efficient, selective, quick reactions); organized for serial responses
Relaxed wakefulness	Synchronized: optimal alpha rhythm	Attention wanders— not forced; favors free association	Good (routine reactions and creative thought)
Drowsiness	Reduced alpha and occasional low-amplitude slow waves	Borderline, partial awareness; imagery and reverie; dreamlike states	Poor (uncoordinated, sporadic, lacking sequential timing)
Light sleep	Spindle bursts and slow waves (larger); loss of alphas	Markedly reduced consciousness (loss of consciousness); dream state	Absent
Deep sleep	Large and very slow waves (synchrony but on slow time base); random, irregular pattern	Complete loss of awareness (no memory for stimulation or for dreams)	Absent
Coma	Isoelectric to irregular large slow waves	Complete loss of consciousness (little or no response to stimulation); amnesia	Absent
Death	Isoelectric: gradual and permanent disappearance of all electrical activity	Complete loss of awareness as death ensues	Absent

noise and arousal. As autonomic arousal increases beyond some point, however, performance tends to fail (Kahneman, 1973) or responsivity may simply decline (Alexander and Epstein, 1978). The problem is to account for such failures and loss of responsivity. What are the mechanisms by which increases in arousal produce these effects?

Performance and Sensory Overload

It makes a great deal of sense that performance should increase as arousal increases. When the brain is more active, it should be able to process information better; similarly, when the body is in a state of readiness, it should be able to execute responses better. But why should performance decrease when the brain and body still have not reached their peak of arousal? It has been proposed that even though the body appears to be attaining ever greater levels of preparedness, something limits the individual's ability to respond with greater efficiency. G. A. Miller (1956) suggested that the body is able to handle only a limited amount of

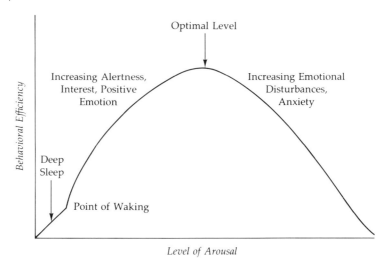

Figure 3-4.   Hypothetical relation between behavioral efficiency and level of arousal (Hebb, 1955)

information input. Thus whenever a given amount of information input is exceeded, the individual becomes overloaded and the orderly processing of information simply breaks down. Various people have suggested that in conditions of overload the RAS may limit information input by blocking certain sensory signals or by reorganizing the incoming stimulation in some way (Easterbrook, 1959; Lacey & Lacey, 1978; Pribram & McGuinness, 1975). According to this view, the RAS is more than a simple activating system. It is, in a very basic sense, an executive that controls not only how much but what we see in the environment.

Biological Mechanisms That Reduce Sensory Overload

Lacey and Lacey's attention/rejection model.   Beatrice and John Lacey (1970, 1978) have proposed a model that suggests that the heart acts as the mediator for controlling excessive stimulation (sensory overload). For many years they have been interested in the fact that about a third of the nerve pathways connecting the reticular system and the heart are feedback pathways. Until this discovery by the Laceys, it was assumed that all the nerve pathways merely carried information from the reticular system to the heart; that is, the pathways existed so that the reticular system could instruct the heart to beat faster or slower. The Laceys' discovery suggested that the heart provided information to the reticular system. The question was, why? When the Laceys began to study the relationships between the activity of the heart and the activity of the reticular system, they found that there is a correlation between acceleration of the heart and inhibition of the RAS and, conversely, between deceleration of the heart and excitation of the RAS. Because acceleration of the heart produces pressure on the receptors in the heart (in the carotid sinus and aortic arch) and this pressure has been shown to reduce RAS activity (Bonvallet & Allen, 1963), Lacey and Lacey have suggested that changes in heart rate determine reticular activity, at least in part. Their position is quite different from that of most arousal theorists. Most theorists have proposed that the RAS controls heart rate, not the reverse.

Lacey and Lacey have suggested that such a feedback system has important psychological significance. The reduced activity of the RAS resulting from heart-rate acceleration would, according to their model, block a certain portion of the incoming stimulation and thereby reduce cognitive overload. Similarly, when the person was not working to capacity, the RAS, signaled by deceleration of the heart, would allow an increase in the amount of incoming stimulation.

In one test of Lacey and Lacey's model, subjects had to do three tasks (Lacey et al., 1963). In one task the subjects had to pay close attention to external stimulation. In another they had to do mental problem solving that presumably would be disturbed by external stimulation. The third task involved both internal and external stimulation. The results showed that when the task called for careful attention to external stimulation, the heart decelerated, and when the task called for the momentary rejection of external stimulation, the heart accelerated. In the combined task, there was no change. The Laceys and their colleagues argued that when the subject had to concentrate on both external and internal information simultaneously, there was a conflict, which would, of course, have resulted in no change.

Further evidence consistent with the Laceys' view comes from the work of Nancy Israel (1969). It has been known for some time that people's responses to external stimulation vary. Some people, called "levelers," tend to respond to the overall organization of the external environment, ignoring detail or differences between situations. "Sharpeners," in contrast, seem to focus on detail, readily noting differences between situations. According to Lacey and Lacey's model, since sharpeners are more open to and accepting of external stimulation, they should show greater cardiac deceleration than levelers in response to new situations that involve the processing of information about the external environment. This is, in fact, what Israel found. Thus it appears that different people may have different cognitive styles that are mediated by the heart.

There are several questions that Lacey and Lacey's model does not answer. For example, what signals the heart to accelerate or decelerate? Does cognitive overload stimulate the heart directly, or do people learn to accelerate the heart in response to overload? Further, what gives rise to different cognitive styles? Is it because people differ in their ability to process information that they adopt different cognitive styles, or are cognitive styles learned and then generalized to a wide variety of situations? As we shall see, there is evidence that people can learn to control input and that fundamental differences in cognitive style do affect arousal levels.

Pribram and McGuinness' model of cortical control.   Karl Pribram and Diane McGuinness (1975) have also argued that cortical activity changes in relation to levels of incoming stimulation. They have suggested, however, that the control is exercised by two subcortical systems of the brain. (*Subcortical* means that the systems lie deeper inside the brain than the cortex.) One system acts as a "stop" system, the second as a "go" system. These systems, they suggest, monitor momentary stimulation and adjust cortical arousal accordingly.

Pribram and McGuinness' model is not necessarily incompatible with Lacey and Lacey's. There are probably several monitoring systems that inform the reticular activating system, or some other system responsible for cortical arousal, about the level or intensity of incoming stimulation. The reticular system or some other system can then adjust cortical arousal so that the individual can deal effectively with that stimulation.

Learned Ways of Dealing with Sensory Overload

Young children have a very easy way of dealing with sensory overload; they simply cover their eyes or their ears with their hands. As adults we learn similar ways of dealing with sensory overload. We seek out a nice quiet place or we put on some soothing music. Realizing that many people often arrive for work already too highly aroused to work efficiently, some companies have instituted brief periods of relaxation at the beginning of the day. Coffee breaks often serve a similar function.

In Chapter 8 we will deal with a variety of procedures, such as biofeedback, relaxation, and meditation, that are very effective in reducing arousal. One such technique is restricted environmental stimulation technique (REST).

Restricted environmental stimulation technique (REST).   It has been suggested that many people in our society suffer from excessive environmental stimulation. When environmental stimulation is excessive on a regular basis, it can produce physical as well as psychological disorders (Suedfeld, 1975; Suedfeld & Kristeller, 1982). Because excessive environmental stimulation increases arousal, it can lead to hypertension (high blood pressure), for example. And because people are inclined to avoid excessive stimulation, exposure to it may lead to withdrawal (one of the symptoms of autism), which in turn can lead to loneliness and other psychological problems.

One technique that has been devised to deal directly with problems that seem to be related to excessive environmental stimulation is the restricted environmental stimulation technique (REST). Two basic methods have been used in the REST research. One method involves secluded bed rest in a completely dark, sound-proofed room for 24 hours. A second method is to have the individual float for approximately an hour in a shallow tank filled with a solution of Epsom salts and water.

The REST technique can increase the power of more standard stress-management techniques, such as biofeedback (Plotkin, 1978). When REST was used as a component in the treatment of essential hypertension, clinically significant drops in systolic and diastolic blood pressure were found (see Suedfeld & Kristeller, 1982). REST has also been used successfully to help people stop smoking, to lose weight, and to reduce drug dependency.

Why does REST work? Studies have shown that REST has not only an immediate but a long-term effect. Peter Suedfeld and Jean Kristeller (1982) have suggested that REST may help people to shift their attention away from external cues to internal cues. High arousal, as we shall see shortly, often directs attention to survival-related cues. As survival-related cues are often external (because our survival is typically threatened by things outside ourselves), it follows that people exposed to excessive environmental stimulation may acquire the habitual tendency to attend to the external environment. REST may help such people to shift their attention to internal cues. As a result, they tend not only to monitor those cues more closely but to deal with them before they produce serious health problems.

Cognitive Ways of Dealing with Sensory Overload

As humans are capable of anticipating events, they often experience a form of anticipatory arousal (Spinks, Blowers, & Shek, 1985). Anticipatory arousal is simply the arousal that will be required to deal with some forthcoming event. If, on a particular day, we realize that we have a great deal to accomplish and little time, we may experience anticipatory arousal that exceeds some optimal level. One way of reducing this kind of arousal is to break down the tasks that face us into manageable units and then proceed to deal with each unit without thinking about the others (Horowitz, 1979). The idea is to prevent the system from becoming overloaded. When we fail to break down activities into manageable units, we experience anticipatory sensory overload.

Optimal Stimulation, Hyperactivity, and Autism

Two syndromes, hyperactivity and autism, can be accounted for by optimal stimulation theory (see Zentall & Zentall, 1983, for a review of the literature). The syndrome called hyperactivity consists of excessive displays of a variety of related behaviors that include high general activity, impulsivity, short attention span, aggression, and variability (Davids, 1971). According to optimal arousal theory, hyperactivity results from a chronic state of underarousal. In order to experience optimal arousal, hyperactive children engage in activities that will increase momentary arousal. Motor activity is a very good way of increasing momentary arousal. Motor activity stimulates arousal not only of the autonomic nervous system but of the cortex. Feedback from the muscles stimulates the RAS, which in turn activates the cortex. The impulsivity and short attention span that characterize hyperactive children are also believed to result from the tendency of such children to seek out new and different experiences. When we are confronted by new stimuli or new information, the brain automatically becomes aroused in order to process it. Once the information has been processed, the brain can then relax. Therefore, in order to maintain momentary arousal at an optimal level, the hyperactive child must continually seek out new stimulation. Consistent with this interpretation, it has been shown that hyperactive children become habituated very rapidly to novel stimuli (see Rosenthal & Allen, 1978, for a review). The aggression and variability of hyperactive children seems to be characteristic of a delinquent antisocial behavior pattern. It has been suggested that both delinquency and antisocial behavior grow out of a tendency to seek stimulation (Quay, 1977).

Autism is a syndrome characterized by stereotyped movements, gaze avoidance, echolalia (repetition of words or phrases), lack of responsiveness to sound, minimal variation in facial expression, withdrawal, resistance to change, fears, inappropriate social behavior, and inability to play (Wing, 1971). According to optimal arousal theory, autistic children are in a state of chronic overarousal. Since any form of environmental stimulation would produce further increases in arousal, the autistic child is motivated to keep environmental stimulation to a minimum. As social interactions, change, play, and sound reliably lead to increases in arousal, these things must be avoided. Repetition is the opposite of change. It seems to make sense, therefore, that these children should be inclined to engage in stereotyped movements and to repeat things they have heard (echolalia).

Why are hyperactive children chronically underaroused and autistic children chronically overaroused? It has been shown that levels of blood serotonin are abnormally low in hyperactive children (Coleman, 1971) and abnormally high in autistic children (Geller et al., 1982). Serotonin is a central nervous system neurotransmitter. High levels of this neurotransmitter could account for the chronically high arousal of autistics and the chronically low arousal of hyperactives.

Summary

Hebb has concluded that humans process information best when arousal is moderate, so that the relation between arousal and performance can be best represented by an inverted-U-shaped function. Various researchers have argued

(continued)

that when humans experience sensory overload, arousal levels can be adjusted to deal with this problem. Lacey and Lacey have argued that the heart can act as a mediator when there is sensory overload. This suggestion is based on the fact that when the heart accelerates, the activity level of the RAS is reduced, whereas when the heart decelerates, the activity level of the RAS increases. Further support for Lacey and Lacey's position comes from the finding that "sharpeners" show greater cardiac deceleration than "levelers" in response to new situations. Pribram and McGuinness have argued that sensory overload is controlled by subcortical brain systems that adjust cortical arousal.

The restricted environmental stimulation technique (REST) is one way to help people learn to deal with the effects of excessive environmental stimulation. REST has been successful in helping people to reduce hypertension, stop smoking, lose weight, and reduce drug dependency, among other things. According to one theory, REST teaches people to switch their attention from external to internal cues. Cognitive approaches to the management of sensory overload suggest that people can reduce overload by breaking down incoming information into manageable units. According to the theory of optimal stimulation, hyperactive children are chronically underaroused while autistic children are chronically overaroused.

Arousal and Selective Attention

Selective attention is a tendency to orient oneself toward, attend to, or process information from one part of the environment to the exclusion of others. There is an abundance of evidence that selective attention is governed, at least in part, by arousal level. One of the persistent questions is whether the shifts in attention that accompany changes in the arousal level are automatic (you don't have to plan them or think about them) or purposeful (you must engage in some active planning or thought process in order to decide your best course of action). The general consensus seems to be that these changes are more or less automatic. That does not mean that rational thought plays no part in the process, only that much of it occurs in the absence of active or purposeful thought. Are these so-called automatic processes learned or innate? Some researchers (Hamilton, Hockey, & Rejman, 1977) view the link between arousal and attention as learned (people learn to use the most optimal set of cognitive operations for a given level of arousal); others have argued that shifts in attention need not be learned but may be innate. The tendency of birds to avoid gardens in which there are snakes, for example, is assumed to be an unlearned or innate response. On the other hand, the tendency of a soldier to pick up a gun when he hears some noise in the adjacent undercover would be regarded as mainly learned. Both responses, nevertheless, can be automatic.

Arousal and the Reorganization of Attention

James Easterbrook (1959) hypothesized some time ago that high arousal tends to make one concentrate on the dominant aspect of the stimulus or on cues closely related to survival. Let me relate a personal experience to illustrate this point.

Several years ago I was attending a convention in a large city in the United States. My parents were in the same city, staying at the apartment of some friends who were away on vacation. I wanted to join them for dinner and decided to use the subway to get there. As I was unfamiliar with the routes, I bought a map of the subway system and proceeded to locate what I thought was the right train. As the train proceeded I kept track of the street numbers that periodically appeared in the stations that we passed. When I arrived at a station that corresponded to the approximate street I wanted, I got off the train and proceeded up the stairs to find myself in a very rough area of the city. After consulting my map again, I realized I had taken the wrong train. As I was already late, I didn't want to return to the city center, so I decided I could walk the few blocks to get to the address I wanted. After all, I thought, it would take at least another hour to go back down-town. After I had walked a little more than a block, it began to dawn on me that not only did I look very much out of place but people were watching me very closely. I could feel my heart begin to pound. I accelerated my pace. I wanted to walk fast enough so that I would know if anybody was following me but I didn't want to run because I thought that might betray my fear. At this point I found my attention beginning to shift. I remember looking for safety signs, such as a police car, another person who looked like me, or simply a reassuring smile from some-one. I remember thinking about how I should respond if someone blocked my path. Would I defend myself? Would I run? If I ran, how far could I get? Could I climb that chain-link fence that I saw in the distance? When I did get to that chain-link fence, I found a hole in it and proceeded up a steep bank to a very different-looking neighborhood. I had made it without incident. A wonderful feeling of relief came over me and I continued to do what I normally do when I go for a walk. I looked at the architecture, I thought about what I would like to eat that night and what I would do the next day.

What caused my attention to shift? Laboratory research provides considerable evidence that such shifts in attention are governed by arousal. In the laboratory it is possible to manipulate arousal and then study what happens to attention. Such studies provide evidence that changes in arousal are sufficient to produce changes in attention.

The Interaction of Arousal and Selective Attention
Daniel Kahneman (1973) has suggested that Easterbrook's hypothesis can account for the failure of experimental subjects to perform well on certain tasks that demand fine discriminations or response to less dominant cues. In a more elaborate devel-opment of such an idea, Peter Hamilton, Bob Hockey, and Mike Rejman (1977) have argued that arousal alters the "control hierarchy." They suggest that our cognitive operations are affected directly by our arousal state. According to their model, we may learn to use one set of cognitive operations at one arousal level and another set of cognitive operations at another arousal level. They maintain that attention is systematically redirected to achieve the goals that are associated with each specific arousal level. In this sense, arousal serves an executive function.

In the example I provided above, I pointed out that when I entered a rough neighborhood my arousal level increased (I became fearful for my safety), and when that happened my attention shifted (I began to search for safety cues). In that sense, arousal served the executive role of directing my attention toward safety cues.

Nonspecific Arousal
According to various models of selective attention, arousal that has not been elicited by the situation (nonspecific arousal) can come to influence our attention in that situation. If I happen to be more aroused than you because of a drug I

Practical Application 3-1
Arousal and the Detection of Deception

In recent years there has been a great deal of interest in using indicators of arousal to determine whether or not people are lying. One device that is currently being used to detect lying is the polygraph. The polygraph provides continuous print-outs of three indicators of arousal: the electrodermal response (EDR), blood pressure (BP), and respiration (R). When people are aroused they tend to perspire. Perspiration increases the electrical conductivity of the skin (EDR), the heart beats faster and the blood vessels constrict (BP), and the breathing deepens in preparation for greater oxygen exchange (R).

It has repeatedly been demonstrated in the laboratory that the polygraph can detect deception. In one demonstration, people were given a deck of eight cards and asked to pick one card from the deck. Next they were told to deny that they had seen any of the cards, including the one they had just picked. Polygraph recordings showed clearly that when the people denied seeing a card, they did show a distinct change in arousal (see Waid & Orne, 1982). While it can be shown that the polygraph is capable of detecting deception, that does not mean that it can necessarily be used to determine whether someone is deliberately lying.

Field studies have also shown that the polygraph is capable of detecting deception. In one such study, the police who administered the polygraph tests (they were not trained to make quantitative measurements), identified approximately 75% of the deceptive subjects. They also, however, identified as deceptive 49% of the truthful subjects (Horvath, 1977). What does this mean? Let's say that you are the boss of a government agency that is responsible for maintaining some top secrets. You discover that some of the secrets have fallen into the hands of the enemy. You ask all your employees if they have been selling secrets and of course they all deny they have ever done so. You decide to identify the culprit or culprits and give all eight of your employees polygraph tests. The polygraph identifies five people as lying. If four of your employees have in fact sold secrets to the enemy, did you get all of them? The answer, of course, is no. You got three of the four who were guilty and two of those who were not guilty. In another field study 98% of the deceptive subjects were identified, but again at the expense of identifying 50% of the truthful subjects (Barland & Raskin, 1973). The big problem with the use of the polygraph to establish guilt or innocence revolves around the fact that the polygraph does not show guilt or innocence, it merely shows arousal. The

(continued)

recently took or because of some immediately preceding event or simply because I tend to have a higher base-line level of arousal, I will attend to different cues than you will. One implication of this idea is that I may overreact. That is, I may attend to safety cues when in fact the situation does not call for such a reaction. People frequently behave inappropriately when they enter new situations, probably because new situations tend to be highly arousing, and the resultant high level of arousal makes them involuntarily attend to cues they would otherwise ignore. Some people have suggested that we attend to survival cues when we are highly aroused. Such a tendency would of course be highly adaptive. It can at the same time be very maladaptive.

question then is why arousal often increases when we lie. More important from a practical point of view is why some people do not show the arousal pattern when they deceive and why some people who have nothing to hide do show the arousal pattern.

The general conclusion that has been reached (for example, Waid and Orne, 1982) is that the arousal pattern observed by means of the polygraph is due to increased attention. When attention goes up, so does arousal and so does learning. Data from a wide variety of sources support this theory. For example, when people are asked a number of questions while their EDRs are being measured and then are later asked to recall as many of the questions as possible, they tend to recall those questions that originally elicited large EDRs. As we have already noted, learning tends to be most efficient when arousal is optimal. Another line of evidence shows that when people are distracted from attending to the questions being asked by the examiner, it is more difficult to identify deceivers. One method that has been used to distract people is to instruct them to count backward by 7s when they hear a question. When they count backward by 7s, not only is it harder to differentiate polygraph responses to target, control, and irrelevant questions but it can be shown that the amount of attention directed to the question is directly related to their ability to recall the item.

If the polygraph is measuring arousal, then it follows that if a person uses a drug that is designed to reduce the arousal response (such as a tranquilizer), it will be more difficult to identify when and if that person is being deceptive. Indeed, this is the case. Hypnosis and biofeedback training have also been shown to increase the ability to deceive. This makes sense, since both hypnosis training and biofeedback training involve learning how to relax.

A number of social variables also affect the possibility of detecting deception. One of the most interesting social factors is degree of socialization. Deception may be easier to detect in more socialized people, it has been hypothesized, than in less socialized people. The idea behind this hypothesis is that when people are highly socialized, questions pertaining to lying, stealing, and other activities that bear on socialization have greater attention value (as a result of past learning or conditioning), and therefore are likely to lead to greater arousal. Consistent with this idea is the finding that deception is easier to detect in firstborns than in people of higher birth order. It has been suggested that this finding may be related to the socialization process, which makes firstborns more dependent and more conforming (Waid & Orne, 1982).

It should be noted that people who work on problems in selective attention often do not distinguish between attention and responding. Attention is often not directly accessible to observation but responses are. When a bird avoids a garden with snakes, we typically cannot measure the bird's attention, but we can see it make an avoidance response. Nevertheless, we have good reason to believe that the avoidance response can be traced to selective attention.

The Orientation Reaction and Selective Attention
Novel stimuli typically elicit a pattern of physiological responses that has been called the "orientation reaction." These responses include EEG desynchronization,

autonomic arousal (sympathetic-nervous-system activity), increased galvanic skin response, and dilation of the pupils (Lynn, 1966). Of particular interest to psychologists is the fact that the orientation response habituates—it diminishes with repeated presentation of a novel stimulus. Because altering a stimulus in certain ways will typically reelicit the orientation reaction, we can be fairly certain that the person continues to monitor that stimulus. It would appear, however, that the stimulus no longer has the same motivational qualities. That is, it is no longer capable of holding the person's attention.

The fact that the orientation reaction can be elicited by a new or novel stimulus, or when the person is deliberately searching for a significant stimulus from some stimulus array, suggests that the orientation reaction is intimately tied up with selective attention (Bernstein, 1973, 1979; Bernstein, Taylor, & Weinstein, 1975; Maltzman, 1979). Specifically, it appears that the orientation reaction occurs whenever we are confronted with new or unassimilated information or whenever we happen to locate an important stimulus in our environment. We have all experienced the phenomenon of seeing something new in our environment. Such an event may simply grab our attention for a brief moment or literally stop us in our tracks. Similarly, we have all experienced the effect of spotting someone we know in a crowd. Typically our scanning stops, at least momentarily, as we fixate the person carefully as though to confirm our initial detection.

The fact that the orientation response tends to habituate to a stimulus suggests that attention is no longer being focused on that stimulus. It has been suggested that the habituation of the orientation response is a type of gating mechanism that underlies selective attention. That is, habituation serves to shift our attention (Waters, McDonald, & Koresko, 1977). It can be argued that once we have processed the necessary information a stimulus contains, we no longer need to continue focusing our attention on that stimulus. We are free, so to speak, to turn to new stimuli or to process other information in our environment. In this sense it can be argued that arousal in general and the orientation response in particular in some way control the processing of all the information in our environment.

Vigilance: The Ability to Maintain Attention for Long Periods of Time

It is extremely difficult for humans to maintain their attention in a situation that involves little change. It has been found, for example, that the performance of people who must attend to a radar screen and identify certain signals (such as the appearance of a blip that signifies an enemy aircraft) declines significantly after as little as 30 minutes (Mackworth, 1948). Since many jobs require people to maintain attention under similar conditions, it is important that we understand not only the source of the decline in performance but how we might reverse this decline.

What is it that makes it difficult for people to maintain their attention? Part of the problem appears to be linked to the lack of change or the absence of complexity. Repetition and monotony lead to a reduction in arousal. People whose vigilance declines often show signs of low arousal, such as low levels of adrenaline in the urine and blood and brain wave patterns that signify sleepiness (Warm & Dember, 1986). What can be done to restore vigilance? Several strategies have been devised.

Increasing arousal or taking advantage of rhythmical arousal levels.   Since arousal tends to be subject to rhythmical fluctuation, we can take advantage of those periods of the day when arousal is highest. If this suggestion proves impractical, we can turn to mild physical exercise and other forms of sensory stimulation, such as music, which can stimulate arousal and therefore help us to remain attentive. Even the stress that comes from working in an uncomfortably warm environment can help people remain attentive. Students who study for long periods might be well advised to take a walk or change the background stimulation in order to increase their arousal. Since social interactions can increase arousal, brief social encounters (provided they do not become too distracting) can be a useful means to maintain attention. Coffee breaks have long been regarded as a very practical means of helping people maintain attention.

Characteristics of the task. Not surpisingly, the task itself is an important source of arousal. Tasks that are too repetitive or boring tend to result in reduced vigilance. On the other hand, tasks that are too complex or demanding can also lead to reduced arousal and attention. One study showed that a reduction in the rate at which bottles passed before inspectors improved their performance (see Warm & Dember, 1986). Obviously, excessive demands produce sensory overload. Again, students may be well advised to gauge their reading rate to match the difficulty of the material they are trying to digest.

Feedback about performance. Providing people with immediate feedback about their performance has been shown to be a very effective procedure for maintaining performance. In one study people were asked to watch lines that appeared on a video screen and indicate the lines they thought were longer. Some people heard a tone when they were correct (hits), some when they were wrong (misses), and still others when they said they saw a long line when the line was in fact short (false alarm). Feedback about hits and false alarms improved performance, whereas feedback about misses did not (Warm & Dember, 1986). One practical application of this research would be the practice of programming into a boring or repetitious task the opportunity to receive feedback on hits and false alarms.

How might students make use of this information to improve their efficiency in studying? I remember hearing many years ago that it was a good idea to spend time periodically reciting the ideas that one has just read. When you do that, your memory of the material typically improves. Your recitation gives you immediate feedback about whether or not you have actually processed the material.

Summary
Work on the orientation reaction indicates that when we are exposed to new or novel stimulation, we respond with increased arousal together with a tendency to orient our sense receptors toward the source of that stimulation. After repeated exposure to the new or novel source of stimulation, we tend to become habituated to it. Individual differences in autonomic arousal affect such things as rate of habituation. Several theorists have argued that arousal serves an executive function in that it often redirects or reorganizes attention. According to one theory, arousal alters the "control hierarchy."

One of the basic problems associated with attention is that of maintaining attention (vigilance), especially in situations that involve repetition. Research has identified several things that tend to maintain arousal and thereby help to maintain attention under boring and repetitive conditions.

Individual Differences

Individual Differences in Autonomic Arousal and Performance

Numerous studies have shown not only that humans have different character-istic arousal levels but that they tend to perform differently as a function of their habitual arousal level. In general, high arousal is associated with alertness and clear thinking (Schubert, 1977). In addition, people who are characterized by high arousal as measured by the galvanic skin response are easier to condition and show greater resistance to extinction (for example, Hugdahl, Fredrikson, & Öhman, 1977). Further, people who are characterized by high arousal as measured by heart rate tend to habituate more slowly to a tone (for example, Gatchel et al., 1977; Goldwater & Lewis, 1978). The failure to habituate can be viewed as either desirable or undesirable, depending on other needs of the person. Ability to persist at a task may be facilitated by slow habituation. However, the failure to habituate might lead to a form of behavioral rigidity. Habituation may be an important process underlying the tendency for people to tolerate isolation or to become sensation seekers (Zuckerman, 1978b). An obvious (and trite) conclusion is that some people are better suited than others to certain activities.

Eysenck's Theory

Do people differ in their levels of motivation? The obvious answer is yes. Given that they do differ, how can this difference be explained? Eysenck (1963, 1967) believes that the difference can be traced to the biological roots of personality. He has attempted to explain why most experimental approaches to the study of per-sonality have found that there is an underlying factor, or continuum of factors, on which a population of people can be reliably differentiated. Specifically, he has suggested that the main continuum on which people can be differentiated is that of arousal, or activation. Some people, he has suggested, have an arousal level that is relatively low (extraverts), while others have an arousal level that is mod-erate to high (introverts).

Extraverts.   The key to understanding the difference between extraverts and introverts, according to Eysenck, is to understand how these two types of people maintain optimal stimulation. Eysenck assumes that people are motivated to main-tain an optimal level of arousal. Since extraverts require external stimulation in order to raise their normally low arousal to an optimum level, they fill their lives with behaviors designed to increase arousal. For example, the highly social nature of extraverts can be understood if it is recognized that social situations typically produce increases in arousal. Similarly, the impulsive nature of extraverts, their tendency to do new and different things, can be understood if it is recognized that behaviors directed toward producing change increase arousal. Even behaviors such as drug use can, according to Eysenck, be explained, at least in part, by the struc-ture of personality. Since nicotine is a stimulant, it is not surprising that extraverts are more likely to smoke than introverts (Eysenck, 1973).

Introverts.   Because introverts tend to have a moderate to high arousal level, they are motivated either to maintain existing arousal levels or to reduce arousal levels. Therefore, in contrast to extraverts, who seek out social stimulation, intro-verts tend to avoid social contacts in order to prevent any further increase in arousal. Similarly, since sudden changes would increase arousal, introverts main-tain more orderly, less impulsive lives. Even the kinds of drugs and how they are

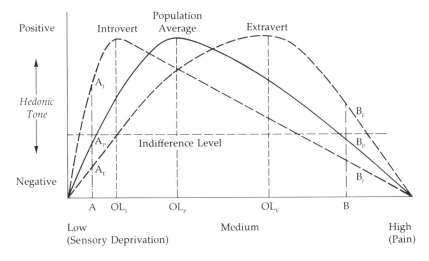

Figure 3-5. Relation between level of sensory input and hedonic tone as a function of personality (Eysenck, 1963)

used should be different for the introvert. Introverts should use drugs for sedation rather than stimulation. Thus the introvert should tend to use barbiturates (tranquilizers) rather than stimulants.

Figure 3-5 shows the relation between level of sensory input and hedonic tone (affect) as a function of personality. The optimum level of sensory input for the introvert (OL_I) is toward the left of the continuum called "level of stimulation." The optimum level of stimulation for the extravert (OL_E) is to the right. The optimum level for the combined groups (the average, OL_P) lies in the middle. When we compare points A and B, we see that low levels of sensory input (A) produce positive hedonic tone (are pleasurable) for the introvert and produce negative hedonic tone (are unpleasurable) for the extravert, whereas high levels of sensory input (B) produce positive hedonic tone for the extravert but negative hedonic tone for the introvert.

Over a period spanning three decades Eysenck and his colleagues have collected a vast amount of data to support his theory. The general research strategy has been more or less the same. A population (such as a group of university students) is administered the Eysenck extraversion/introversion scale. This scale simply has people report their preferences among a variety of activities (for example, would they rather go to a party or read a book) and their characteristic way of responding to the environment (for example, impulsive versus orderly). Their answers are scored according to a standard procedure. These people are then required, for example, to answer questions about their sexual practices or to perform a mental or physical task that tests their skills or to serve in an experiment involving their physiological responses to a standard set of test stimuli. The theory makes rather precise predictions about the way extraverts and introverts will respond, and the object of the research is to determine whether behavior can be predicted from extraversion/introversion scores. This strategy has proved very successful. For example, Eysenck has been able to show that extraversion/introversion scores can predict EEG activity, at least in part (Eysenck, 1967; Gale, Coles, & Blaydon, 1969), performance and learning under the influence of certain drugs (Eysenck, 1963), and sexual practices and preferences (Eysenck, 1976).

According to Eysenck, humans are motivated to find pleasure and avoid pain. They are hedonists who are tied to their biological roots even when engaged in complex mental activities.

Background stimulation.   Since extraverts prefer more stimulation than intro-verts, one implication of Eysenck's theory is that extraverts may tend to select environments with greater background stimulation. Various tests of this idea have demonstrated that extraverts do indeed prefer environments that provide greater background stimulation. In one study extraverts and introverts were asked to select a level of noise that they preferred for a paired-associates learning task. Extraverts selected a higher level of noise than introverts (Geen, 1984). Another study showed that extraverts are more inclined to select a location for studying which provides for greater external stimulation. Not only do extraverts prefer higher noise levels but they like environments that provide a greater opportunity to socialize (Campbell & Hawley, 1982). Both noise and social interactions are excellent sources of arousal.

Reversal Theory: An Alternative Way of Viewing Optimal Stimulation
Reversal theory assumes that rather than preferring some moderate level of arousal, people sometimes prefer high arousal and at other times they prefer low arousal. That is, sometimes people like to experience excitement and at other times they like to relax. According to this theory, people tend to swing back and forth between these two states. Even though all people are assumed to swing back and forth, some people are assumed to be dominated by the high arousal state while others are dominated by the low arousal state (Apter, 1982).

People also shift between two other motives. At certain times the individual is motivated by a desire to achieve goals (telic goals). They not only carefully plan their activities but tend to complete those activities in order to receive the satis-faction that comes from achieving a goal. Their behavior is marked by efficiency rather than pleasure. In this state they are serious-minded and future-oriented; they plan. At other times the same individuals are motivated by a desire to expe-rience pleasure in the here and now (paratelic goals). They are inclined to prolong activities as long as they are producing high levels of pleasure. They tend to be playful and spontaneous (Svebak & Murgatroyd, 1985).

The crux of the theory is that the hedonic tone associated with arousal can shift abruptly, depending on which of the two motives is currently active. In other words, satisfaction comes not from high or low arousal but from the interaction of these two motives with the appropriate level of arousal (see Figure 3-6). When we are in the achievement state, low arousal can be pleasant; we call it "relaxation." When we are in the pleasure-seeking state, we call the same low level of arousal "boredom." Similarly, high arousal can be very unpleasant ("anxiety") in the achievement state and very pleasant ("excitement") in the pleasure-seeking state.

Since preference for arousal shifts with the motivational state, it follows that the individual may at one time want to increase arousal (arousal-seeking state) and at another time may want to decrease arousal (arousal-avoidance state). In one test of this theory, subjects were asked to indicate their preference for certain colors under various motivational states (such as states corresponding to achievement versus pleasure-seeking). Colors that are more arousing (red, yellow) were selected more often in the pleasure-seeking state, whereas less arousing colors (green, blue)

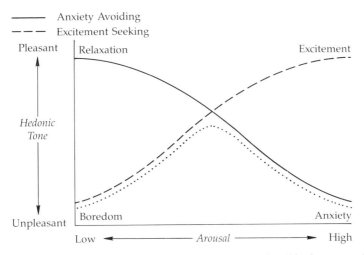

Figure 3-6. The hypothesized relationship between arousal and hedonic tone for the anxiety-avoidance and the excitement-seeking systems (Apter, 1982)

were selected more often in the achievement state. The study also showed that within a given experimental session subjects tended to shift between the achievement and pleasure-seeking states (Walters, Apter, & Svebak, 1982).

Practical implications of reversal theory. To the degree that we can recognize which state we are in (achievement or pleasure-seeking), we should be able to manipulate the pleasure we are experiencing (hedonic tone) by manipulating our arousal. Since social interactions tend to increase arousal, we might increase our feelings of pleasure when we are in the pleasure-seeking state by increasing our social interactions. When we are in the achievement state, on the other hand, we may want to decrease social interactions because they lead to feelings of anxiety. Trying to maintain low arousal by avoiding other people when we are in the pleasure-seeking state might, on the other hand, lead to feelings of boredom. If we are in the achievement state, however, maintaining low arousal by avoiding other people could give us increased feelings of pleasure.

Summary
Eysenck hypothesizes that some people have a chronically low level of arousal (extraverts) while others have a chronically high level of arousal (introverts). In order to produce an optimal level of arousal, extraverts seek out stimulation in an effort to increase their arousal level whereas introverts seek out a nonchanging environment in an attempt to avoid being flooded with more stimulation than they want. Reversal theory, in contrast, suggests that people sometimes like high levels of arousal and at other times like low levels of arousal. Some people, according to this theory, are dominated by the high arousal state while others are dominated by the low arousal state. Whether or not people enjoy high or low arousal depends, however, on which of two other motive states is active: the achievement motive or the pleasure-seeking motive. According to this theory, the hedonic tone we experience (positive or negative) depends on the interaction of the appropriate arousal level with one of the two motive states.

Main Points

1. Arousal is the activation or energization of the brain and the body.
2. Arousal is produced by two primary mechanisms: the reticular activating system (RAS) and the autonomic nervous system.
3. Chemicals secreted by the adrenal glands, epinephrine and norepinephrine, provide the long-term backup for the more immediate action of the sympathetic nervous system.
4. Three basic phenomena elicit arousal: stimulation of the various sense systems, rhythmical activity of the nervous system, and cognitive interpretation of events in the environment.
5. The relationship between arousal and performance appears to be best described as an inverted-U-shaped function.
6. According to Lacey and Lacey's attention/rejection model of sensory overload, the heart provides feedback that affects activity in the reticular activating system (RAS).
7. Pribram and McGuinness have argued that cortical activity is regulated by two subcortical systems, one acting as a "stop" system and one as a "go" system.
8. Restricted environmental stimulation technique (REST) has proved to be a useful way of helping people deal with excessive environmental stimulation. It is hypothesized to work by helping people to focus their attention on internal rather than external cues.
9. People can also deal with excessive environmental stimulation by breaking information down into manageable units.
10. According to optimal arousal theory, hyperactivity results from a chronic state of underarousal, whereas autism results from a chronic state of overarousal.
11. Both hyperactivity and autism may be linked to abnormal levels of serotonin.
12. It has been proposed that arousal may automatically control or direct the attention process. Under higher levels of arousal, our attention tends to shift to cues that have to do with our safety, whereas under low levels of arousal, our attention shifts to facilitate the processing of new information.
13. Studies of the orientation response have provided evidence that new or novel stimuli elicit arousal.
14. People become habituated to new or novel stimuli more slowly at high levels of arousal than at low levels of arousal.
15. Vigilance is the ability to maintain attention for long periods of time.
16. It is very difficult for people to maintain their attention in a situation that involves little change.
17. Feedback is a very good procedure for maintaining arousal during vigilance tasks.
18. Eysenck's theory to account for individual differences is based on the concept that different people have different arousal levels. The low arousal level that presumably characterizes extraverts motivates them to seek out stimulation, including social situations. The moderate arousal level that presumably characterizes introverts motivates them to keep external stimulation to a minimum.
19. Reversal theory assumes that rather than preferring some moderate level of arousal, people sometimes prefer high arousal and at other times prefer low arousal.
20. Also according to reversal theory, people are sometimes motivated by a desire

to achieve goals (telic goals) and at other times they are motivated by a desire to experience pleasure in the here and now (paratelic goals).

21. Measures of arousal have been used in the detection of deception.

22. Increases in arousal that are associated with deception appear to be linked to attention: when attention increases, so does arousal.

Wakefulness, Alertness, Sleep, and Dreaming

Why do we fall asleep?

Why do we wake up?

Why isn't it possible for us to fall asleep any time we want to?

Why do we have difficulty falling asleep when we are under pressure or when we are excited?

How should people deal with jet lag when they fly long distances?

Why can't people learn to do without sleep?

Why do we dream?

What is the significance of dreams?

What causes insomnia?

Why do we feel tired and drowsy at some times but rested and alert at others? We all know from experience that these states are related, at least in part, to how long ago and how well we slept. As our normal sleep time approaches, we typically feel somewhat tired. Usually, shortly after waking we feel rested and alert (sometimes with the aid of a cup of coffee) unless, of course, we did not sleep well. We also know from experience, however, that feelings of drowsiness and alertness can be somewhat independent of how long and how well we slept. We sometimes feel drowsy even though we have slept recently, and we sometimes feel alert even though it is well past our normal sleep time. We also know from experience that it is difficult to shift our normal sleep pattern. Anyone who has tried to get up earlier than usual can attest to the fact that such a shift requires more than just going to bed earlier. People who cross several time zones in their travels often have difficulty adjusting to a new clock time. Such experiences seem to suggest that humans have an internal clock that can be reset only with some difficulty. There is also the question of dreams. What is the function of dreams? Are they important for mental health, processing information, or what?

Years of controlled laboratory research have begun to provide answers to these and other fascinating questions about wakefulness and sleep. As we shall see, wakefulness and sleep involve physiological and psychological mechanisms that work together in a complex manner. The states of wakefulness and sleep are not so distinct as one might think. Yet we cross a very important line when we pass from wakefulness to sleep: we lose consciousness—awareness of the external environment. Typically, loss of consciousness is fairly abrupt, although at times we seem to enter a detached intermediate state that may reflect what Gerald Vogel (1978) calls "sleep-onset mentation."

Wakefulness, Sleep, and EEG Activity

Correlates of Sleep and Wakefulness

The best index of wakefulness, drowsiness, and sleep in humans is cortical activity (Webb, 1975). Figure 4-1 shows EEG activity during the various stages of sleep. A typical night of sleep consists of gradual progress from stage 0 (wakefulness) through stages 1, 2, 3, and 4 and then backward through stages 3, 2, and 1 into what is called stage 1–REM. This cycle, which takes about 90 to 120 minutes, then repeats itself. In the course of seven to eight hours of sleep we go through this cycle about five times. The regularity of the pattern I have described comes from the averaging of EEG data from several individuals. It is typically not quite

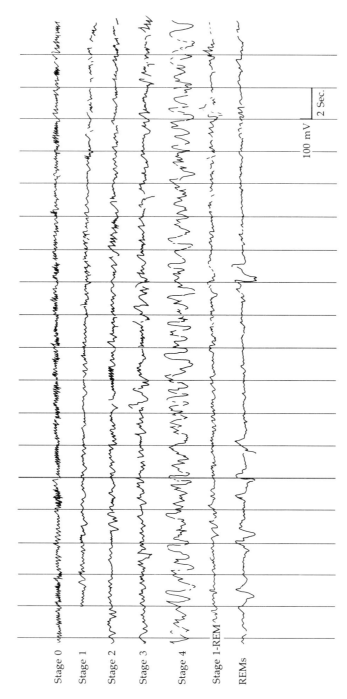

Figure 4-1. EEG tracings of the sleep stages. Stage 0 is wakefulness (Webb, 1975).

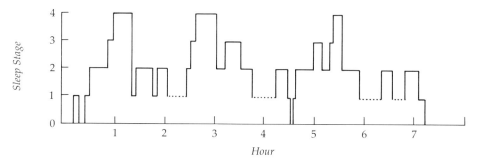

Figure 4-2. Stages of sleep during a night. Dotted lines identify periods of stage 1–REM (Webb, 1968).

this regular for a given individual. Figure 4-2 shows the EEG pattern of a typical individual. The important thing to note is that while an individual may bypass certain stages from time to time, a rhythm (pattern) can nevertheless clearly be observed.

REM is an acronym for rapid eye movement. In studying electrical recordings of eye movements, Eugene Aserinsky and Nathaniel Kleitman (1953) found that rapid eye movements occurred in conjunction with low-voltage mixed brain-wave frequencies, and that when people were awakened on such occasions they regularly reported vivid dreams. Since then it has been common to refer to this pattern as REM sleep and to all other patterns as NREM ("non-rem") sleep. The dotted lines in Figure 4-2 identify periods of REM sleep. Although it was initially thought that REM sleep was synonymous with dreaming, it has since been shown that humans dream during the other stages of sleep as well. For example, dreaming often occurs at the onset of sleep, in the absence of REM (Vogel, 1978).

Periods of REM typically occur in conjunction with stage 1 sleep. REM—or REM bursts, as they are sometimes called—occur about 90 minutes after one goes to sleep and then recur on an average of every 90 minutes (the time varies between 70 and 110 minutes). Interestingly, REM sleep tends to lengthen as the night progresses until it lasts as long as an hour at a time. As a result, an adult who sleeps 7.5 hours generally experiences 1.5 to 2 hours of REM sleep (Dement, 1972).

Jouvet's Model of Sleep

Why do EEG patterns fluctuate during sleep? Probably the most widely held view is that EEG activity during the sleep state is governed by the RAS. Michel Jouvet (1967) has shown that changes in EEG activity during sleep are due to alternating activity of two sites in the RAS. The raphe nuclei, which secrete serotonin when active, have been shown to increase NREM sleep in cats (sleep characterized by low levels of EEG activity). Jouvet has suggested that the onset of sleep is due to the increased activity of the raphe nuclei. The locus coeruleus, which secretes norepinephrine when active, has been shown to increase REM sleep. Since increased EEG activity during REM sleep is typically associated with dreaming in humans, Jouvet has suggested that the onset of dreams is due to increased activity of the locus coeruleus. Because the activity of these two sites tends to alternate, Jouvet's model can readily account for the rhythmic nature of sleep—its fluctuation between deep and light sleep. Exactly why these two sites alternate in activity is not altogether clear. One good possibility is that the activity in one center, after a period of time, stimulates activity in the other center, producing the alternating pattern (see also Siegel, 1979). Morgane and Stern (1975) agree that serotonin and norepinephrine play a role in the generation and maintenance of sleep. They suggest, however, that these biogenic amines only trigger processes that actually control the onset of waking or the onset of sleeping. That is, other chemical circuits may actually induce sleep or waking.

Jouvet's model can account for fluctuations in EEG activity at night (and possibly during the day). It is not altogether clear, however, why a given center should become active at a particular time. Specifically, why do people wake up at a given hour, and why is it difficult to shift periods of wakefulness and sleep?

Paralysis during REM

Since the brain and the entire central nervous system tend to become very active during REM, the question is why people don't walk, talk, and engage in other motor responses when they begin to dream. The answer is very simple. In each period of REM sleep the action of the motor neurons of the spinal cord that cause skeletal muscles to contract is inhibited. As a result, the muscles are atonic (without tone): they are paralyzed. The mechanisms that control this inhibition and the release from it are located in the reticular formation (Morrison, 1983). One reason researchers have been so interested in understanding these mechanisms is that some people experience a condition called narcolepsy, which causes them suddenly and unexpectedly to pass from wakefulness to REM sleep without losing consciousness. This condition typically is not only stressful but dangerous, for a narcoleptic who suddenly slips into REM sleep could, for example, topple over and be injured by the fall.

Sleep and Attention

Sleep, it has been suggested, can be considered a state of extremely low attention (Glaubman et al., 1979). When we are asleep, our threshold for detecting incoming stimulation is very high, and as a result information input is low. It has been suggested that some type of filter allows only intense or specific forms of stimulation (such as a baby's cry) to reach the brain. This filter may be very important for maintaining the sleep state; without it we might tend to awaken periodically.

Since the learning of new material involves the ability to process information, it is not surprising that people show little if any new learning when they are asleep (Aarons, 1976). This does not mean that during sleep we may not be able to engage in important cognitive activities that involve information we processed when we were awake. As we shall see later in this chapter, it appears that we in fact do just that.

Why We Fall Asleep and Why We Wake Up

At least three sets of factors determine when we fall asleep and when we wake up. As we shall see, each set of factors interacts with the others.

Circadian rhythm.   One of the prime factors that determines when we fall asleep is our circadian rhythm. The word *circadian* comes from the Latin *circa diem*, "about a day." People who have been left to establish their own routine in caves, bunkers, or specially designed laboratories tend to adopt a 25-hour cycle as opposed to the 24-hour circadian rhythm (Aschoff, 1965). It appears that the tendency to follow a 24-hour cycle is due largely to the synchronizing effects of events in our environment. Because we generally have regular times for eating, watching TV, going to bed, and so on, we tend constantly to reset our biological clock so that it is attuned to the 24-hour day. When we free ourselves from the normal synchronizing effects of the environment, as on a weekend or vacation or when we stay up late, "sleep in," and eat when we like, we often experience great difficulty getting back into our normal routine. The Monday-morning blues may be a direct result of letting ourselves shift to our natural 25-hour biological rhythm. Even after only two days we can experience a marked delay in awakening and becoming alert. Wilse Webb and H. W. Agnew (1975a) have argued that our society may produce a state of chronic sleep deprivation because we sleep according to clock time rather than according to our need for sleep. They found that subjects who were allowed to awaken spontaneously after three nights of controlled sleep (11 P.M. to 7 A.M.) slept an additional 126 minutes, on the average.

What produces this rhythm? There is evidence that not only the time we fall asleep but the soundness of our sleep and the length of time we sleep are linked to the output of adrenaline (also called epinephrine) by the adrenal glands. When the epinephrine level declines, we tend to fall asleep, and when it rises, we tend to wake up (Nishihara et al., 1985). Going back one further step, researchers have suggested that the rhythm of the adrenal glands is controlled by the hypothalamus. Ultimately, in other words, the circadian rhythm is due to some rhythmical activity of the hypothalamus.

It should also be noted here that there is a correlation between body temperature and sleep. Our temperature tends to fluctuate one to two degrees in the course of a day. When we fall asleep, our temperature drops rather suddenly. The lowering of body temperature may be an important factor that not only induces sleep but helps to maintain it. Anybody who has tried to stay up late to study or work on a project can attest to the feelings of coldness that often occur during those prolonged vigils. During the course of the night our temperature tends to rise gradually. It has been suggested that the rise in temperature (which is linked to our daily arousal rhythm) may signal us to wake up (Gillberg & Åkerstedt, 1982). Our inability to maintain sleep during the day may simply be due to the fact that our underlying arousal level (presumably due to the secretion of the adrenal glands) maintains our temperature at a level that is inconsistent with sleep. Several studies have confirmed that there is a positive relation not only between temperature and wakefulness but between temperature and performance on a vigilance (attention-demanding) task (Moses et al., 1978; Taub, 1977). P. L. Parmeggiani (1977) has suggested that the link between temperature and sleep is governed directly by the hypothalamus. His reasoning is based largely on research showing that the hypothalamus appears to govern the link between temperature, sleep, and conservation of energy in hibernating animals.

Environmental arousal.   When we are under stress, our body moves into a state of high arousal. Under these conditions we often find that we cannot go to sleep or that we have trouble staying asleep. Drugs that increase arousal, such as stimulants, also disturb sleep onset and interfere with the ability to stay asleep. An exciting event can and often does produce increases in arousal. Not surprisingly, therefore, exciting events often tend to interfere with sleep onset and good sleep. Since environmental arousal is situational, sleep disturbance due to environmental arousal tends to disappear when the event that produces the arousal disappears or is removed.

Sleep deprivation.   One of the important factors that determines if and when we go to sleep is the length of time that has passed since we last slept. When people are deprived of a night's sleep, they tend to go to sleep sooner and to stay asleep longer, even if they have recently experienced environmentally induced arousal. We will return to this topic shortly.

Individual Differences in Sleep Cycles
There is evidence that personality variables may predict the rhythm of daily patterns. Extraversion and introversion measures, for example, may predict fluctuations not only in body temperature but in performance on vigilance tasks (Taub, Hawkins, & Van de Castle, 1978). Extraversion is associated with higher body temperature and better performance in the evening, introversion with higher body temperature and performance in the morning.

Why We Periodically Feel Drowsy or Find Our Attention Shifting: Other Rhythms

The 12.5-hour ultradian rhythm.   Studies have shown that when subjects are first deprived of sleep and then allowed to sleep for an extended period of time, there is a significant return of SWS (slow-wave sleep) after 12.5 hours of sleep (Gagnon, De Koninck, & Broughton, 1985). These findings are consistent with the observation that people tend to become not only less alert but sleepy around noon (Richardson et al., 1982). In many cultures it is the norm to take an afternoon siesta. The phenomenon of afternoon napping, according to Pierre Gagnon and his colleagues, "may reflect a biological propensity to re-enter the psychological state that accompanies SWS" (1985, p. 127) (also called stage 4 sleep).

The 90-minute ultradian rhythm.   There is a basic rest/activity cycle (BRAC) that lasts about 90 to 120 minutes. This cycle has been found in such waking activities as performance on various sensory tasks, vigilance tasks, and fantasy tasks. The ability to fall asleep during the day is determined by this cycle. That is, it is easier to fall asleep when we are in the rest part of the cycle.
The regularity of REM sleep every 90 minutes raises the interesting possibility that REM is somehow controlled by BRAC. It has been shown, for example, that people tend to dream at the same time every night (McPartland & Kupfer, 1978). Some researchers have supplied evidence that seems to contradict this conclusion. They have shown, for example, that REM tends to occur 90 minutes after sleep onset (McPartland & Kupfer, 1978; Moses, Naitoh, & Johnson, 1978). If sleep onset controls REM, then it cannot be controlled by some natural BRAC rhythm that is independent of sleep onset. This apparent inconsistency disappears when we recognize that people often don't go to sleep until they are in a certain phase of their BRAC. In other words, not only our overall circadian rhythm but our BRAC rhythm affects our inclination to go to sleep.

BRAC, waking mentation, and dreams.   The brain has two hemispheres, each of which performs slightly different functions. The right hemisphere tends to be involved in fantasy and intuitive thought, while the left hemisphere tends to be involved in verbal and intellectual thought. What is fascinating is that each hemisphere has a 90- to 100-minute cycle that is 180 degrees out of phase with the other hemisphere. Thus we tend to swing back and forth between fantasy-intuitive thought and verbal-intellectual thought (Klein & Armitage, 1979). REM dreams tend to be more fantasy/intuitive in character whereas NREM dreams tend to be more verbal and intellectual. It may well be that before I can have REM dreams or NREM dreams I need to be in the right mental state—that state being determined by my BRAC.

How Much Sleep Do We Need?

The fact that some people seem to need very little sleep has intrigued both the layperson who would like to get along on less sleep and the scientist who is interested in the function of sleep. In a study of long and short sleepers, it was observed that short sleepers tended, on the whole, to deny personal or interpersonal problems, to have a greater need to be accepted, and to be more socially skilled and more socially dominant. Long sleepers tended to be more shy, more depressed or anxious, and more inhibited sexually and in expressing aggression (Hartmann, Baekeland, & Zwilling, 1972). In a similar study Webb and Friel (1971) found no differences; these results may be due to differences in sampling techniques. A more recent approach to the question of whether length of sleep is related to personality functioning has been to expose people to gradual sleep reduction to see what, if any, effects are observed.

Voluntary sleep reduction to 4.5–5.5 hours a night has not been shown to reduce performance or to produce significant personality changes, but it tends to produce persistent feelings of fatigue (Friedman et al., 1977). As sleep time is reduced, the pattern of sleep undergoes several changes. Although there is no reduction in the amount of stages 3 and 4 sleep (see Figure 4-1), there is a significant reduction in REM and stage 2 sleep (Mullaney et al., 1977; Webb & Agnew, 1975a). When the regimen of partial sleep deprivation is maintained, it appears that REM sleep begins to occur earlier in the sleep period, thus attenuating the REM deficit. It rarely, however, replaces stage 4 in the order of appearance, and it never achieves normal levels.

The fact that people tend to make up for certain types of sleep when their sleep time is curtailed is probably one of the important reasons that lack of sleep does not have a greater impact on their normal functioning. As we shall discuss in more detail shortly, stage 4 and REM sleep seem to serve specific functions that help to maintain physiological and psychological integrity. If they are important, it would make sense for the system responsible for sleep to give priority to them when total sleep time is reduced. As a result of this priority design, humans are able to function when sleep is shortened, even if that functioning may be less than optimal. Since shortened sleep regimens tend to lead to persistent fatigue, it appears that some mechanism tells us to return to more normal sleep patterns.

Interestingly, subjects who voluntarily reduced their total sleep time for experimental purposes maintained their total sleep time 1–2.5 hours below baseline. The fact that none of the subjects ever went below 4.5 hours of sleep per night while on this voluntary program suggests that there may be biological limits to sleep reduction (Mullaney et al., 1977).

Altering Sleep/Wakefulness Cycles

If we assume for the moment that adults need about 7 to 8 hours of sleep each 24-hour period, the question arises whether we can redistribute our sleeping time in some way. Studies of this question have found that adjustment to new schedules is possible but difficult. Since the best predictor of sleep onset is elapsed time since last sleep, and since the best predictor of sleep termination is how long we have slept, it is not surprising to find that people tend to lose sleep in new schedules because they have difficulty getting to sleep or wake up too soon. Finally, circadian rhythms make it difficult to adapt to schedules that do not follow the approximately 24- to 25-hour cycle (Webb & Agnew, 1975b).

What Is the Best Way to Adjust to Jet Lag?

Let's say you left New York on a plane bound for Paris at 6 P.M. eastern standard time. Flight time is about eight hours. Therefore, when you arrive in Paris it's 10 A.M. Paris time, but your circadian clock is telling you it's 2 A.M. (two hours past your bedtime). What should you do—take a nap or stay up till midnight Paris time? The answer depends on whether you want to see Paris nightlife or be a "regular tourist." If you go to your hotel and sleep, you're likely to sleep for seven to eight hours, so you will wake up at 6 P.M. That will give you plenty of time to have a leisurely dinner, close down the last nightclub, and sip a brandy with or after breakfast before retiring for eight hours. But, if you want to be a regular tourist, then you should stay up until midnight. By midnight you will be experiencing the effects of sleep deprivation and you should have little or no difficulty getting to sleep and sleeping most of the night, even though you are not synchronized with your circadian rhythm. A night's sleep will help to reset your circadian rhythm. Remember that one of the factors that determines when you will next be sleepy is the time that has elapsed since you last slept. Even a short nap is not a good idea because it will reduce some of the effects normally associated with sleep deprivation, and as a result you will not be able to sleep as long when you do go to sleep.

The Effects of Sleep Reduction

Sleep reduction and feelings of sleepiness and fatigue.   Lack of sleep often produces feelings of sleepiness and fatigue. We use *sleepiness* to indicate a craving or desire for sleep, while *fatigue* refers to a general lack of motivation or energy. Sleepiness is generally viewed as the converse of alertness (Dement & Carskadon, 1982). While the belief is widespread that sleepiness (lack of alertness) will impair performance, it has sometimes been hard to document this effect in the laboratory by means of various psychomotor and intellectual tests (see Dement & Carskadon, 1982). There is also little evidence that sleepiness resulting from a reduced sleep regimen produces any physiological abnormalities (see Hartse, Roth, & Zorick, 1982). After several days of sleep reduction, most people show full recovery after a single night of sleep (Carskadon & Dement, 1981). It appears that REM sleep is more important than NREM as far as reversing sleepiness is concerned (Carskadon & Dement, 1977).

Sleep reduction and performance.   Despite the fact that lack of sleep does not seem to do any harm, people report difficulty in performing when they feel sleepy. Field studies have shown that people who work at night not only complain of sleepiness but perform more poorly than they do when they work during the day (Åkerstedt, Torsvall, & Gillberg, 1982). In general, it appears that sleep loss can produce fairly marked deficits in performance when tasks require persistent attention, whereas the deficits are comparatively mild when tasks require precision and cognitive processing (see Webb, 1985). Interestingly, older subjects seem to be affected more by sleep loss than younger ones (Webb & Levy, 1982).

Probably the reason it is more difficult to demonstrate an association between sleepiness and poor performance in the field than in the laboratory is that humans are capable of "rising to the occasion" for short periods when the situation requires them to do so. The implication is that while we may perform more poorly following reduced sleep, probably because of lack of motivation, we can nevertheless perform well if we have to.

Sleep reduction and fragmented sleep. It should be noted that the loss of one night of sleep not only can produce sleepiness but can impair performance as well. Recently it was shown that when people were repeatedly waked in the course of a night's sleep (after every minute of sleep), the severe reduction in SWS and REM led to a decline in performance and indexes of sleepiness equivalent to those found after a loss of 40 to 64 hours of sleep, even though the subjects had been sleeping a great deal of the time (Bonnet, 1985). Later we shall see why the loss of SWS and REM is believed to be so devastating. As I have already mentioned, when people go on reduced sleep regimens, they typically compensate for the loss of sleep by increasing REM and SWS at the expense of other states of sleep.

Sleep Deprivation and Mood
Roth and his colleagues (Roth, Kramer, & Lutz, 1976) found that sleep deprivation adversely affects certain moods (friendliness and aggression) but not others. In a carefully controlled study David Cohen (1979) tried to determine whether REM deprivation was particularly important in the control of mood. All he could find is that when people are awakened during either REM or NREM, they experience increases in aggression and decreases in friendliness.

Studies conducted in clinical laboratories suggest that mild to moderate antidepressant effects can follow just one night of sleep deprivation in 30 to 60% of endogenously depressed individuals (those whose depression cannot be linked to a specific life event) (Gerner et al., 1979). It has been suggested that the neurophysiological effects of sleep deprivation are similar to those produced by antidepressant medication (Buchsbaum, Gerner, & Post, 1981).

Summary
EEG activity has a rhythmical pattern during sleep. Jouvet has suggested that these rhythms are controlled by the RAS. But why do people fall asleep in the first place? Various biological rhythms (circadian, 12.5-hour cycle, and BRAC) play important roles in our sleep patterns. In addition, the time that has elapsed since we last slept and the level of our arousal at the time we try to go to sleep are further determining factors in our ability to sleep. Why do we wake up? Rhythmic increases in temperature and arousal seem to be the main reason. While it is possible to get along with as little as 4.5 to 5 hours of sleep, reduced sleep produces feelings of sleepiness and fatigue. Performance of some tasks is affected by sleep reduction, but not all—only those tasks that require sustained interest and attention. While people can learn to get along on reduced sleep, it is important that their bodies maintain a certain minimal level of SWS and REM.

This research emphasizes what sleep consultants have said for some time: In order to go to sleep, maintain sleep, and have quality sleep, it is important

(continued)

to have a routine. Routines not only synchronize our biological rhythms with our daily performance demands but allow us to have reasonably continuous sleep. A routine is important even when sleep must be reduced because it enables SWS and REM to occur soon after we fall asleep, thereby ensuring that we will get enough SWS and REM in the course of a night's sleep.

Arousal, EEG Activity, and the Quality of Sleep

A common explanation of why people cannot get to sleep or stay asleep or simply do not benefit from sleep is that some arousal-producing event interfered with the normal tendency to sleep. For example, people say they were too excited, were currently experiencing stress, were feeling anxious about some impending stressful event, or found that they were unable to relax. Because arousal in some form is common to all these events, the question arises whether increases in arousal are sufficient to interfere with good sleep patterns.

Muscle Tonus
It has been assumed for some time that people need to relax in order to sleep (for example, Luce, 1969). Sleep clinics frequently teach people to relax in order to overcome a variety of sleep disorders. The reasoning is based on sound psychological principles. Increased muscle tonus (tension) leads to increased cortical activity, which is incompatible with the slow-wave activity that characterizes much of sleep. It follows that increases in muscle tonus not only delay sleep onset but can disrupt the course of sleep. The fact that anxious people frequently report sleep disorders, together with the fact that they typically have higher frontalis-muscle tension (R. P. Smith, 1973), seems to provide prima facie evidence for the validity of this line of argument. (The frontalis muscle is the muscle of the forehead.)

A direct test of this hypothesis, however, has failed to substantiate the argument. Good (1975) was unable to find a positive correlation between frontalis-muscle tonus and sleep onset. Surprised and puzzled by this finding, Good suggested that perhaps other muscles should be monitored to determine whether their tonus correlates with delayed sleep onset. In a study comparing progressive muscle relaxation with exercise and a boring, monotonous vigilance task, it was found that sleep onset was delayed least by relaxation and most by exercise (Brownman & Tepas, 1976). Since exercise just before sleep would increase arousal, it is not surprising that exercise delayed sleep onset. Although variations were found in the onset of sleep as a function of presleep activities, the quality of sleep was not affected by these manipulations.

Exercise
In view of the failure to find a relation between muscle tonus and sleep, the question arises whether exercise has any relation to sleep. Although the immediate effects of exercise are increased muscle tension together with increased autonomic arousal, there is considerable evidence that regular exercise has many long-term effects, including reduction of sensitivity to a variety of stressors, of anxiety, and of depression. Therefore, it is not immediately obvious whether one should expect people who exercise to have better or poorer sleep. For the most part, research on the relation between exercise and sleep has yielded equivocal results. Most of this research has been designed to determine whether exercise increases the time spent in stage 4 sleep, also called "slow-wave sleep" (SWS), as it has been argued that

SWS has a bodily restorative function (Hartmann, 1973). In assessing the contradictory findings, Griffin and Trinder (1978) noted that most studies had failed to control for the physical fitness of the participants. Therefore, they decided to examine SWS in fit and unfit subjects. They found that fit subjects spent more time in SWS and, further, that exercise increased SWS in fit but not unfit subjects. Unfortunately, this finding did not hold for a slightly older sample (Trinder et al., 1982). In order to assess whether aerobic fitness per se is the main factor and not some other set of characteristics associated with being an "athlete," another study was done to compare fit and unfit athletes with a comparable group of fit and unfit nonathletes. The athletes, fit and unfit, tended to sleep longer and have more elevated SWS than the nonathletes, an indication that variations in sleep are attributable not to fitness but to some other characteristic associated with athleticism. (Paxton, Trinder, & Montgomery, 1983). (For a complete review of this topic, see Horne, 1981.)

Stress

Intuitively, it seems that an activity such as skydiving could have dramatic effects not only on sleep onset but on the nature and quality of sleep itself. To test this hypothesis, experienced and novice parachutists were studied in the sleep laboratory for four nights before and one night after a scheduled jump. Comparison with a group of control subjects revealed no significant differences in any of the measures, including delay of sleep onset (Beaumaster, Knowles, & MacLean, 1978). The failure to find any differences is surprising in view of the commonly held belief that stress interferes with the onset and quality of sleep. As the authors themselves note, it may be important to consider differences in the characteristic attitudes of people who voluntarily select a stressful event and those who are simply exposed to such an event.

Baekeland, Koulack, and Lasky (1968) showed subjects a purportedly anxiety-causing film before sleep. They found that viewing the film produced significant increases in both the number of REM awakenings and REM density (number of eye movements per REM period). Since REM density has been shown to be positively correlated with the affective content of dreams (anxiety, bizarreness, vividness, intensity, emotionality), it seems that the stress did affect the quality of sleep. A similar study (Goodenough et al., 1975) failed to show that a stressful film increased REM density. The investigators suggest that individual differences may modify the way people respond to stress. That is, the way people react to stress may be determined not by arousal but by some sort of cognitive event. Our perception of an event as controllable or uncontrollable, for example, may significantly affect our reactions to it.

Noise

Noise has been found reliably to increase arousal levels in humans. The question arises, therefore, whether noise disrupts sleep. In one study of motor activity during sleep, subjects were exposed to noise during all stages of sleep. It was found that subjects changed body positions 22% more often than controls. There were more spontaneous awakenings and a general increase in spontaneous muscular twitches (Goebel & Jovanovic, 1977). It can be concluded that noise impairs human sleep. The fact that humans do learn to sleep under conditions of noise does, however, raise an interesting question about the adequacy of the design of this study. To adequately test whether noise is disruptive, it would be necessary to allow the subjects time to habituate. There is evidence that sleeping subjects will habituate to auditory signals. For example, it has been shown that the heart-rate response to an auditory signal will habituate during certain phases of sleep even though the EEG responses do not (Johnson, Townsend, & Wilson, 1975).

Attention and Arousal

Mental activity is one of the many factors that increase arousal (Berlyne, 1960). People often talk about a "stimulating" conversation or a project that made them feel "high." It is fairly common for people to link such activities to poor sleep, especially when the activity occurred just before normal sleep onset. Can mental activity in fact be linked to alterations in sleep?

In general, research seems to suggest that mental activities, if they occur just before sleep, can have a modest effect. For example, one study found that listening to music before sleep increased REM sleep, while listening to verbal material had the reverse effect (Cartwright et al., 1977). In another study, subjects were required to perform several tasks just before sleep. Sleep was lengthened, and there was a dramatic increase in REM sleep (Glaubman et al., 1979). In contrast, when subjects were given fairly extensive visual stimulation during the day but not before sleep onset, no effects on REM sleep were observed. There was, however, an increase in slow-wave sleep for the subjects who had received extensive visual stimulation together with a fairly demanding decision task (Horne & Walmsley, 1976). The increase in REM sleep, as we will discuss shortly, has been hypothesized to reflect some type of memory consolidation. That is, if subjects have not had a chance to consolidate information in memory before sleep, they may do so during REM sleep. Increased REM sleep, according to this hypothesis, reflects an increase in time made available for memory consolidation. According to this hypothesis, it makes sense that REM sleep would increase if a subject had been exposed to some mental task just before sleep.

Probably the best way to determine whether arousal affects sleep is to increase arousal directly. DeGroen (1979) administered an electrical current to the brain by means of widely spaced electrodes outside the skull—a technique called "diffuse brain stimulation." This technique, DeGroen argues, stimulates activity mainly in the ascending reticular activating system. When subjects were stimulated in this way for 20 minutes just before sleep, the first sleep cycle was significantly altered. It was longer, REM sleep increased, and there was a shift from deep to more superficial NREM sleep. It is interesting that REM sleep increased even though mental activity itself had not been manipulated. This fact suggests that arousal may mediate increases in REM sleep. We will return to this possibility when we discuss the results related to the hypothesis that REM sleep facilitates memory consolidation.

Summary

There is little evidence that increases in arousal sometime before sleep affect sleep onset or the pattern of sleep, but there is good evidence that increases in arousal just before sleep can delay sleep onset or disrupt the sleep pattern. The main change in the pattern of sleep resulting from increased arousal is an increase in REM sleep. For the most part, this appears to be confined to the first cycle or first few cycles of sleep. Both the changes in REM sleep that follow mental activity just before sleep and the changes that follow the viewing of a stressful film can be explained by the memory-consolidation hypoth-

(continued)

esis of REM sleep. Diffuse brain stimulation, which appears directly to affect the ascending reticular activating system, leads to increased REM sleep, suggesting that increases in REM sleep may be mediated by arousal.

The Psychological Functions of Sleep

By continuously monitoring the EEG of a sleeping person and waking that person whenever a particular sleep pattern appears, it is possible to study the effects of certain types of sleep deprivation on various activities. To date, the majority of studies have focused on REM sleep deprivation; however, there is a growing interest in other types of sleep deprivation (Webb, 1979). We will begin by examining some of the effects of REM sleep deprivation.

The REM Rebound Effect

Early studies of REM deprivation showed that people who are deprived of REM sleep for one or more nights show what is called REM rebound. That is, when people are allowed to sleep without interruption for a whole night following at least one night of deprivation, they spend more total time in REM sleep than they normally do. This observation led people to conclude that REM must indeed be important for normal functioning. This finding is consistent with the study of Carskadon and Dement (1977), who studied the sleep patterns of subjects who were permitted to sleep for 30-minute periods separated by 60 minutes of forced wakefulness. Sleep-onset REM periods occurred frequently during the 30 minutes of sleep, an indication that although REM sleep may be subject to some biological clock that normally programs REM to begin 90 minutes after sleep onset, the lack of REM for any significant period will trigger some other mechanism to override the first in order to ensure that the body gets adequate REM sleep.

REM Sleep Deprivation and Psychological Health

Early work. Probably the main reason people have focused on REM sleep deprivation grew out of the reports of Dement (1960). He noted not only that people who were awakened from REM sleep reported vivid dream content but that interruptions of REM sleep (REM deprivation) produced anxiety, irritability, and difficulty in concentrating. People have for some time been interested in the function or purpose of dreams, and Dement's findings suggested that the REM deprivation technique might uncover their function. As we have noted, people later realized that dreams also occur in other stages of sleep (Foulkes, 1962; Foulkes & Vogel, 1965). Nevertheless, the impetus for REM deprivation studies had been well established by that time.

Vogel's research on depression. Following Dement's initial reports of the effects of REM deprivation, people freely speculated on the relation between the absence of REM sleep and psychological health. It was suggested that absence of REM sleep could produce such disturbances as schizophrenia and depression (Fisher & Dement, 1962; Snyder et al., 1968). These speculations, it turns out, were not well founded. Vogel (1975) has deprived people of REM sleep for up to three weeks without serious side effects. In fact, he has shown that REM deprivation can be beneficial in depressives. He has offered a motivational theory of REM deprivation that not only can account for this effect but has some important implications for understanding the function of REM sleep.

Vogel's theory.　Vogel (1979) has suggested that neural activity is heightened during REM sleep and prevented or inhibited by REM deprivation. As a result, REM deprivation leads to greater neural activity or excitability during the waking state. (Neural excitability is a hypothesized state of neural readiness necessary for efficient and effective response to events in the environment. It is generally assumed to be due to some chemical process that readies the cells to fire.) Because there is evidence that greater neural excitability increases such drive-motivated behaviors as sex, aggression, pleasure seeking, food seeking, and grooming, Vogel argues that under certain conditions REM sleep can have a detrimental effect on certain waking behaviors. It is possible, Vogel argues, that depression results from excessive neural disinhibition during REM sleep. That is, REM sleep dissipates too much accumulated neural excitability. As a result, depressives lose interest in or fail to engage in those activities that provide the positive rewards that normally accompany "healthy" behavior. According to this view, it is easy to understand why REM deprivation would lead to improved mood in depressed persons. Since such deprivation would prevent the discharge of neural excitability, depressed persons would again become more sensitive to their drive states. As a result, they would engage in behaviors that produced rewards associated with these drive states. In short, they would experience the positive affect that typically flows from adaptive behaviors.

It should be noted that Vogel's theory of depression is essentially a theory of endogenous, rather than reactive, depression. Endogenous depression is depression that occurs for unknown reasons, whereas reactive depression is typically precipitated by some traumatic event, such as the loss of a spouse, a child, or a job. According to Vogel's theory, endogenous depression occurs when, for still-unknown reasons, there is excessive neural disinhibition during REM sleep. Normally, he argues, neural activity is not allowed to dissipate completely. He believes that some inhibitory mechanism exists to prevent complete discharge and serves an important survival function by ensuring that the person is in a stage of readiness to respond to drive stimuli.

Vogel (1975) has reviewed some of the research showing that drugs can frequently alleviate symptoms of depression. The most effective drugs, he notes, are those that produce a dramatic and sustained reduction of REM sleep—the major antidepressants (monoamine oxidase inhibitors and the tricyclics). In other words, he maintains, these drugs work because they block REM sleep, which is assumed to be responsible for the dissipation of neural excitability.

REM Sleep, Learning, and Adaptation

REM sleep and the consolidation hypothesis.　One of the most actively pursued hypotheses concerning sleep is that REM sleep is important for the consolidation of memory. According to the consolidation theory, it takes time for recently learned material to be transferred from immediate or short-term memory to long-term memory. The question is whether the REM state facilitates the transfer. There is indeed very good evidence that REM does facilitate the consolidation of memory (see McGrath & Cohen, 1978; Grosvenor & Lack, 1984). There is further evidence that REM may be involved not simply in the consolidation of memory but in the active integration of complex information (Scrima, 1982). The emphasis here is on *active.* Apparently previously acquired information or knowledge is somehow involved in the consolidation process to ensure that the newly acquired material is integrated with material that has already been learned.

Type of task.   While REM sleep seems to facilitate most kinds of learning, it is most beneficial for certain kinds of tasks. In general, the REM deprivation literature shows consistent benefits from REM sleep on the learning and retention of more complex and/or emotionally loaded tasks. In one study that demonstrated beneficial effects of REM sleep (Cartwright et al., 1975), subjects were required to Q-sort adjectives as descriptive of themselves and of their ideal selves and then tested for immediate and delayed (seven hours) recall of the words. A Q-sort task requires the subject to place cards bearing descriptive words into stacks corresponding to how well they describe the thing specified. In this case, subjects were required to order the items in accordance with how well they described their actual and ideal selves. During the retention interval, subjects were treated in one of four ways: (1) were maintained awake day or night, (2) were allowed undisturbed sleep, (3) were allowed to sleep but were REM-deprived, or (4) had their REM sleep reduced by 25%. After the retention intervals, subjects were asked to recall as many of the adjectives as they could. For our purposes, there were two important results: the REM-deprived subjects tended to recall more self-affirming items, whereas the normal-sleep subjects tended to recall more items indicating personal dissatisfaction. That is, REM sleep facilitated memory for items related to personal dissatisfaction. In contrast to this study, subjects have also been asked to learn to associate two neutral words (paired-associate learning). Such studies have consistently failed to show that one or two nights of REM deprivation affect retention of paired associates (for example, Castaldo, Krynicki, & Goldstein, 1974).

Adaptation to stress.   That REM sleep can increase adaptation to a stressful or noxious stimulus has been clearly demonstrated by Greenberg, Pillard, and Pearlman (1972). They exposed subjects to a stressful film and then allowed the subjects (1) undisturbed sleep or (2) REM-deprived sleep or (3) NREM-deprived sleep. After sleep the subjects were shown the film again and their reactions to it were assessed. REM-deprived subjects showed the greatest anxiety, suggesting that the opportunity to experience REM sleep had produced some adaptation to the stressful events in the film.

Timing of REM sleep.   The research on REM deprivation does not show that REM sleep is necessary for good processing or storage of information, only that if a person must sleep, REM is the best form of sleep. Whether it is better to sleep or stay awake during the retention interval is another question (McGrath & Cohen, 1978, fn. 2). Studies on this question suggest that it is better to stay asleep, presumably because when awake we learn new material that interferes with our ability to recall the target material. It should be noted in this regard that the benefits of REM sleep are directly proportional to its proximity to learning. That is, deprivation of early REM (that which occurs closest to sleep onset disrupts retention of the target material more than deprivation of late REM (that which occurs some time after sleep onset) (Hockey, Davies, & Gray, 1972).

REM Sleep and Divergent (Creative) Thinking
If REM sleep facilitates the processing of information, especially information that must be integrated with existing information, the mental activity of REM sleep should be consistent with such a task. Indeed, there is evidence for such a position. Lewin and Glaubman (1975) have found that REM sleep is characterized by extremely flexible and divergent thinking. They have argued that mental activity during REM sleep is not integrative and consolidating but rather divergent and exploratory;

however, this does not rule out the possibility that the flexible and divergent aspects of REM mental activity are involved in the integration of new, complex, emotional, or unusual information. In fact, it could be argued that such divergent mental activity during REM sleep would facilitate the integration of such information. In a replication of Lewin and Glaubman's original study with somewhat different procedures, it was again shown that REM sleep does indeed facilitate divergent thinking (Glaubman et al., 1978). Subjects were assigned a divergent-thinking task in the evening and told they would have to perform the task in the morning. The task required them to tell what the consequences would be "if gravity disappeared," for example, or "if all people went blind." During the night, subjects were deprived of either REM or NREM sleep. NREM-deprived subjects gave not only more original responses but numerically more responses (both are indexes of degree of divergent thinking). Interestingly, the NREM-deprived subjects gave more positive consequences than the REM-deprived. For example, to the question "if all people went blind" they were more likely to say "Wars would be abolished" than "All people would die."

Individual Differences in the Need for REM Sleep

Do all people need the same amount of REM sleep? If amount of REM sleep under nondeprivation conditions is used as a measure, then there is only meager evidence that different people have different needs. Although most studies have found equivocal results, it has been shown that retardates with lower IQ scores need less REM sleep (for example, Castaldo & Krynicki, 1973) and that elderly people with lower IQ scores also need less (Feinberg et al., 1973). Because of the samples, these results must be treated with caution.

It should also be noted here that schizophrenics show little or no increase in REM sleep following REM deprivation (for example, Gillin & Wyatt, 1975). Because schizophrenia is a complex topic and because there is some question about whether this lack of REM rebound is well established (Vogel, 1975), I will not speculate on the significance of this phenomenon.

Field dependence and field independence.   If increased REM sleep following REM deprivation (REM rebound) is used as a measure of need, then there is good evidence for individual differences. For example, it has been shown that field-independent people exhibit greater REM rebound than field-dependent people (Cartwright, Monroe, & Palmer, 1967). Field dependence/independence is an aspect of cognitive style. Field-independent people tend to use an internal frame of reference in organizing incoming information. This means the person is inclined to relate information to the self, and this style is therefore regarded as a very active form of information processing. Field-dependent people, in contrast, tend to use external frames of reference. This means they are not likely to involve the self and thus take a more passive approach to information processing (Goodenough, 1978).

That field-independent people require more REM sleep fits with the consolidation hypothesis of learning—the hypothesis that it takes a period of time for information initially stored in some type of temporary memory storage system to be transferred into a more long-term storage system. Dealing actively with information (organizing it according to some internal scheme) would be not only a more difficult or complex task but one that would take more time. As a consequence, field-independent subjects would tend to need more REM sleep.

Ego threat.   Greiser, Greenberg, and Harrison (1972) showed that ego-threatening manipulations affect memory. In their study subjects were given anagrams preselected to ensure that about half of them could be solved in the allotted time. To threaten the subjects' concept of themselves (ego), they were told that the task was a measure of intelligence. The subjects were then exposed to sleep manipulation. The results showed that REM sleep deprivation (compared with NREM sleep deprivation) disrupted recall of failed anagrams but did not affect recall of solved anagrams. These results suggest that REM sleep facilitates the processing of material that draws one's self-concept into question or material that is inconsistent with one's self-concept.

Why would a person be inclined to have better recall of material inconsistent with or threatening to his or her self-concept? One obvious explanation is that the person is motivated to resolve the discrepancy. We know from other work that this form of dissonance (discrepancy or conflict) tends to produce arousal and that people are motivated to reduce such dissonance (Kiesler & Pallak, 1976). If a person fails to reduce the dissonance before sleep onset, REM sleep may offer an opportunity to accomplish this task.

Other researchers have threatened the egos of subjects by giving them a difficult test (they intimated that it measured intelligence) that could not be completed in the allotted time. Control subjects were given an easier version of the test that they could complete in the time allowed. The study found that ego threat did produce stress and that one night of uninterrupted sleep resulted in significant adaptation to the stress (Koulack, Prevost, & De Koninck, 1985). Further, subjects who recalled more of the presleep stressful event in their dreams showed less adaptation upon awakening. These findings suggest that the adaptive value of sleep is the resolution or partial resolution of the stressful presleep event (ego threat). When subjects did not resolve the stressful event, as indicated by their failure to show the same adaptive effects as other subjects, they continued to have elements of the presleep stressful event represented in their (REM-state) dreams.

Neuroticism.   People who score high on neuroticism (sensitizers) show less REM rebound following deprivation than low-neuroticism people (repressors) (see, for example, Nakazawa et al., 1975). The terms *sensitizer* and *repressor* are used in connection with the neuroticism scale to differentiate the general way these two groups of people deal with threat. The person who tries to deny or minimize a threat or avoids thinking about its consequences is called a "repressor." The person who tries to control the danger by dwelling on its potential consequences is called a "sensitizer" (Bell & Byrne, 1978). In one study, subjects were deprived of either REM or NREM sleep early in the sleep period to determine the effects on REM episodes later in the period (Pivik & Foulkes, 1966). Repressors showed increased dreamlike fantasy during these later REM periods, while sensitizers did not. Finally, consistent with these results, Cohen (1977) showed that repressors have a greater need for REM sleep.

Why the greater need for REM by repressors? A repressor tends to deal with threat by denying it. A great deal of cognitive activity will be required to resolve the dissonance associated with such a strategy. In that sense the repressor may be behaving like Greiser's subjects (Greiser et al., 1972) who were subjected to ego-threatening manipulations.

Greenberg and Pearlman have suggested that REM sleep is necessary for the consolidation of learning that involves the "assimilation of unusual information" (1974, p. 516). Such a view explains why personality interacts with the nature of the task. Remember that the field-independent person tries to organize all incoming information in terms of an internal (and personal) frame of reference. Understanding how all external information relates to this frame of reference may require the testing of several hypotheses. The repressor has a different problem: how to rationalize the fact that he or she is denying the existence of a threatening event. A good or adequate solution may involve the generation of hypotheses. The need to generate hypotheses would, of course, require divergent thinking.

Other Types of Sleep Deprivation

As we noted in connection with the question of how much sleep we need, reduction of total sleep produces a proportional increase in stage 4 sleep but not in REM sleep. Studies that have combined total sleep deprivation with selective deprivation of stage 4 and REM indicate that deprivation of stage 4 produces stage 4 rebound, just as REM deprivation produces REM rebound. Further, it appears that stage 4 sleep takes precedence over REM sleep. That is, any lack of stage 4 sleep will always be satisfied before a lack of REM sleep is made up (Moses et al., 1975). It has also been shown that when sleep regimens are varied in length, stage 4 and REM are maintained (Webb & Agnew, 1977). In a review of the research on sleep requirements and stages, Hartmann (1974) has concluded that there are two separate requirements for sleep—for slow-wave and desynchronized sleep (such as REM)—and that the need for slow-wave sleep is more constant than the need for desynchronized sleep. Andrew Tilley (1985) has suggested that "obtaining a daily stage 4 quota acts as the primary drive mechanism of the sleep system" (p. 129).

Summary

Although some early studies found that deprivation of REM sleep produced anxiety, irritability, and difficulty in concentrating, more recent studies have failed to replicate these findings. In fact, Vogel has found that REM deprivation often alleviates symptoms of endogenous depression. Although lack of REM sleep may not drive a person insane, it frequently leads to feelings of sleepiness and affects certain moods, such as friendliness and aggression. Considerable evidence indicates that REM sleep facilitates learning, especially learning that is complex or emotionally loaded. There is also evidence that REM sleep increases adaptation to stressful and noxious events. The timing of REM has been found to be important in this regard. REM sleep has been characterized as extremely flexible and divergent, qualities that would facilitate storage of complex and emotionally loaded material. Greenberg and Pearlman (1974) have argued that REM sleep is necessary for the consolidation of learning that involves the "assimilation of unusual information" (p. 576).

Not all people have the same need for REM sleep. Field-independent people, people who are ego-threatened, and repressors tend to need more. These findings are consistent with the hypothesis that certain cognitive styles or certain habitual ways of dealing with problems or events require a divergent approach that can be augmented through REM sleep.

Dreaming

When Do We Dream?

If people are awakened during REM sleep, they report a dream about 83% of the time (Dement, 1972); during NREM sleep, anywhere from 24 to 74% of the time (Vogel, 1978); and during the four transition stages between wakefulness and sleep, the following frequencies have been found: alpha REM, 31%; alpha SEM, 43%; descending stage 1, 76%; and descending stage 2, 71% (Vogel, 1978). The four transition stages as defined by Vogel can be identified through a combination of EEG measures, measures of rapid eye movement, and measures of muscle tonus. Thus alpha REM is characterized by continuous alpha EEG activity together with one or more rapid eye movements, and alpha SEM by alpha with slow eye movements. Descending stages 1 and 2 are defined mainly by EEG activity, although there are differences in the eye-movement and muscle-tonus measures as well.

It is not particularly important to remember the exact definition of each of the stages of sleep that contain dreams or the exact amount of dreaming associated with each stage. What is important to remember is that a great deal of dreaming occurs during REM and NREM and during sleep onset. In view of the fact that the electrical activity associated with these dream states is quite different, the most immediate questions are whether the dreams associated with each of the stages are the same as REM dreams and whether they serve the same function as REM dreams.

Mental and Emotional Content of Dreams

REM versus NREM dreams. In many ways REM and NREM dreams are the same. They tend to be of similar lengths, occur throughout the sleep period, and be equally identified as having dreamlike qualities (Cohen, 1979; Foulkes, 1966). Nevertheless, they do differ in some basic ways. NREM dreams tend to reflect greater conceptual thinking. Their content is often a re-creation of some recent psychologically important event. In contrast, REM dreams are more perceptual and emotional. Unrelated scenes and people are frequently brought together. Strong feelings often accompany these dreams, such as feelings of anxiety, hostility, and violence (Foulkes, 1966). It has been suggested that in Freudian terms REM dreams are more like primary-process thinking, which is frequently unrealistic and emotional, whereas NREM dreams are more like secondary-process thinking, which is more realistic (Vogel, 1978).

An interesting property of REM dreams is that they tend to become more intense throughout the sleep period (Czaya, Kramer, & Roth, 1973; Kramer et al., 1974); NREM dreams apparently do not (Tracy & Tracy, 1974). For example, Czaya's subjects rated 12 aspects of their dreams on a 5-point scale: recall, activity, emotion, anxiety, clarity, pleasantness, violence, hostility, degree of distortion, how frightening, how related to personal life, and sensibleness. Of these, emotion, recall, anxiety, and pleasantness showed a significant linear increase throughout the sleep period. What does this mean? In Freudian terms, it might mean that the subjects were giving greater expression to primary-process thinking. To the degree that there is a need for this type of mental/emotional activity, it might be argued that people tend to satisfy this need more in later than in earlier sleep cycles. It might be hypothesized, for example, that some kind of inhibitory mechanism, such as that proposed by Vogel, is more operative in the early stages of the sleep period and that with time the inhibition on this type of mental activity is reduced, leading to increases in the length and intensity of REM sleep. This idea is consistent with the finding that as a person is deprived of REM sleep, attempts to compensate for it increase. Presumably, as the need for REM increases, the mechanism that inhibits this type of activity finds it more and more difficult to block the activity.

Sleep-onset dreams.   Some people are more inclined to dream at sleep onset than others (Vogel, 1978). The dreams of these people, sleep-onset (SO) dreamers, tend to resemble waking fantasy. To understand why certain people are more likely to dream at sleep onset, Foulkes, Spear, and Symonds (1966) gave a variety of psychological tests to SO dreamers and SO nondreamers. From tests they were able to identify profiles of these two types. SO dreamers, they found, were more self-accepting, less rigidly conforming to social standards, and more socially poised. SO nondreamers were more rigid, intolerant, and conformist.

Since some people do not tend to dream at sleep onset, it is not surprising that studies of the relation between REM dreams and SO dreams have found no correlation (Foulkes et al., 1966). For this reason, Vogel (1978) has argued that the mechanisms responsible for REM dreams and for SO dreams differ. In effect, this means the two kinds of dreams have different functions. Vogel (1978) has offered a psychoanalytic interpretation of the difference between SO dreams and REM dreams. According to Vogel, REM dreams reflect the operation of the subconscious as directed by the id. SO dreams, in contrast, reflect the operation of more volitional processes as directed by the ego. According to this explanation, SO dreams are more controllable than REM dreams.

Equivalence of REM dreams, NREM dreams, and waking mentation. Different kinds of dreams probably satisfy different needs. This conclusion is based on the fact that depriving people of one type of dream (such as that associated with REM sleep) does not increase the frequency or length of other types, nor does it change the nature of dream mentation (Arkin et al., 1978). There is some evidence, however, that depriving people of REM sleep does affect waking mentation. The extent to which REM deprivation affects waking mentation appears to be related to individual differences. Cartwright and her associates initially found that REM-deprived subjects, when given the opportunity for REM rebound, show one of three basic response patterns: "disruption," "compensation," or "substitution." In subjects showing the disruption pattern, stage 2 intrusions occur during REM sleep. In the compensation pattern, REM time increases, and the first REM period after REM deprivation begins sooner after sleep onset than usual. In the substitution pattern, subjects do not show the normal REM rebound effect that characterizes the compensation pattern (Cartwright, Monroe, & Palmer, 1967). In a later study, Cartwright and Ratzel (1972) found that substituters were more likely than compensators to have dreamlike fantasies while awake. They interpret this finding to mean that for substituters, dreamlike fantasy can take the place of a dream during sleep, thus removing the need to make up for REM deprivation. The lack of this tendency or ability in compensators means that the compensator will have to make up for lost REM sleep through increased REM sleep (REM rebound). Responses to tests both before and after REM deprivation were consistent with the idea that REM deprivation affects mental activity during the waking state.

The work of Cartwright and her associates suggests that one reason some people can get along with less sleep is that they are able to compensate in some way through waking activity for the lack of REM sleep that typically occurs when sleep is restricted. To test this explanation, it is necessary to analyze waking activity more thoroughly in order to assess the relation between waking and sleeping mental activity (Hoyt & Singer, 1978). Since people on restricted sleep regimens tend to compensate for lack of sleep by increased stage 4 sleep, there is a good possibility that stage 4 sleep may not be related to waking behaviors in the same way that REM seems to be. Future research will undoubtedly answer this question.

Hartmann's Theory of Sleep

The function of REM and NREM sleep.   Ernest Hartmann (1973) has offered a theory of sleep that suggests that REM sleep and NREM sleep serve two distinct and important functions. He proposes that NREM sleep serves a general phys-iological restorative function and REM sleep serves a more specialized "repro-gramming" function. Because of the complexity of our daily lives, he argues, we have much unfinished business, such as stress, conflict, and unorganized infor-mation. REM not only helps deal with this unfinished business but plays a general role in maintaining the systems that underpin the processes of alertness and attention.

Synchronous versus asynchronous electrical activity during REM and SWS.   In a study involving patients with implanted electrodes that monitored the activity of 13 deep subcortical structures, it was found that changes in electrical activity in the various areas were asynchronous (not related to activity in other areas) during SWS (NREM) sleep but were highly synchronous during REM (Moiseeva, 1979). This finding is consistent with Hartmann's theory that during SWS each of the various areas of the brain is undergoing "repair," whereas during REM the various areas work together to reprogram the individual so that the individual will be prepared for the following day.

REM sleep restores catecholamines.   Hartmann has specifically argued that information processing depletes catecholamines and that REM sleep serves to replenish them. According to his theory, when we are awake we are able to main-tain our attention because of subtle feedback systems that allow us to block out irrelevant information or focus on relations that make the situation meaningful. These feedback-modulated guidance systems weaken with extended use (because of catecholamine depletion), and REM sleep restores these systems to their proper level. In effect, Hartmann argues that these systems are bypassed while they are under repair. From this perspective, he argues, we can understand the nature of dreams. During dreams, he notes, we often are unable to focus attention; we simply experience a pattern of environmental events that sometimes may even violate laws of time and space. That is, we sometimes put two things together that normally don't go together, or we perceive two events occurring simultaneously when in fact they occurred at different times. For example, we may dream of two persons who have never met (but whom we happen to know) talking to each other as though they were old acquaintances. It is because the feedback systems are not operative that this can happen.

In a test of this theory, Hartmann and Stern (1972) deprived rats of desynchro-nized (REM) sleep, thus producing a decrement in acquisition of an avoidance task. When the rats were then injected with a drug that increased the availability of catecholamines, this deficit was reversed. That is, the rats learned normally when the catecholamine level was raised.

Summary

Most dreaming occurs during REM sleep, but dreams also occur during NREM sleep. Although REM and NREM dreams have many similarities (length, dreamlike qualities, periodic occurrence), their contents differ. NREM dreams tend to reflect greater conceptual thinking, whereas REM dreams are more perceptual and emotional. Further, REM dreams become more vivid as the sleep period goes on; NREM dreams do not. A separate class of dreams, called sleep-onset (SO) dreams, have been found to occur more for some people (SO dreamers) than others (SO nondreamers). Vogel has suggested that REM dreams reflect the operation of the id, SO dreams the operation of the ego. Research on the question of equivalence of REM dreams, NREM dreams, and waking mentation has led to the conclusion that lack of REM sleep affects waking mentation. The extent of this effect is affected, however, by individual differences. Hartmann has proposed that REM and NREM sleep serve two distinct functions, a "reprogramming" function and a restorative function, respectively.

Sleep Disorders

The best way to determine the exact nature of a sleep disorder is to take EEG measures during one or more nights of sleep in a sleep clinic. Often people who complain of a sleep disorder are unable to explain its exact nature, or they perceive a problem that in fact doesn't exist. With objective data, it is possible to chart a course of action that may alleviate the problem (Dement, 1972).

Insomnia

One of the most common categories of sleep disorders is insomnia. Insomnia is any failure of sleep. It may involve inability to get to sleep, inability to stay asleep, periodic awakenings, or "light sleep," a condition in which the person has difficulty staying asleep and tends to have a high proportion of stage 1 sleep and a low proportion of stage 4 sleep (Webb & Agnew, 1975b). Large-scale surveys have found that about 14% of the population feel they have some difficulty with sleep. These studies indicate that difficulties with sleep are independent of racial origin, socioeconomic status, and nationality (Webb & Agnew, 1975b). Age, however, has been found to be a major predictor. Up to half of the older people questioned indicated they experienced troubled sleep from time to time.

Drug-related insomnias.   One of the most common treatments for insomnia has been barbiturates. Although barbiturates will initially increase sleep time, larger and larger doses are typically required to maintain this pattern. Eventually most people who use barbiturates develop a very disturbed sleep pattern. They can initially go to sleep (with the aid of barbiturates), but they have difficulty staying asleep. The reason has become clear. Initially barbiturates suppress REM sleep. In larger and larger doses, barbiturates suppress not only REM sleep but stages 3 and 4 sleep. Because the absence of REM and stage 4 sleep produces deficits that need to be made up, people who take barbiturates are put into a state of continuous REM and stage 4 sleep deprivation. The many bursts of cortical arousal observed among barbiturate users during sleep can be interpreted as attempts to enter stage 3, 4, or REM sleep (Dement & Villablanca, 1974).

The effects of alcohol on sleep are similar in many respects to those of barbiturates. In single doses alcohol reduces REM sleep while sometimes slightly increasing slow-wave sleep. Chronic alcohol use typically produces fragmented sleep characterized by a reduction of REM and slow-wave sleep. Withdrawal of alcohol following chronic use often results in hallucinations. It has been suggested that delirium tremens ("DTs") may result when REM sleep breaks into the waking state (Webb & Agnew, 1975b).

Mild stimulants such as caffeine (found, for example, in coffee, tea, some soft drinks, and NoDoz) produce a mild disruption of sleep. The equivalent of three to four cups of coffee before retiring lengthens the time it takes to get to sleep, produces more awakenings, and generally leads to the subjective evaluation of "poor sleep." Strong stimulants such as the amphetamines have a much more pronounced effect. They not only increase the time it takes to get to sleep and the number of awakenings but reduce REM and slow-wave sleep. Withdrawal from chronic use results in REM rebound and associated nightmares.

Antidepressants and some tranquilizers also decrease REM sleep, as do some nonprescription sleeping pills. The ultimate benefit of these drugs as far as sleep is concerned is therefore questionable.

Non-drug-related insomnias.   Webb and Agnew (1975b) have suggested that there are basically five categories of non-drug-related insomnias: situational, benign, arrhythmic, sleep anomalies, and secondary sleep disorders.

Situational insomnias are those produced by a response to some event in the waking world. Excitement about a new business opportunity or a new love, the death of a loved one, guilt, or failure may all create a temporary sleep disorder. Often the passage of time will solve a situationally induced sleep disorder.

Benign insomnias are those in which people perceive they have "poor sleep" although in fact their sleep patterns are well within normal limits. For example, the person who feels she is not sleeping enough or has difficulty trying to get to sleep may not need to sleep as long as she thinks she should. Such a person may simply need to be made aware that there are great variations not only in the length of sleep but in its timing.

Arrhythmic insomnias are those caused by irregular sleep patterns. Going to bed or getting up at irregular hours eliminates some of the cues that normally control sleep. As a consequence, a person may have difficulty going to sleep or may not get enough sleep because of the tendency to wake up early. Following a regular sleep pattern will usually control if not eliminate such forms of insomnia.

There are several types of *sleep anomaly*. One kind involves the intrusion of sleep into the waking state (narcolepsy and hypersomnia). These disorders are frequently disruptive but can be treated by sleep clinics. A second kind involves the presence of wakelike behaviors during sleep (sleepwalking, night terrors, nightmares, enuresis). These sleep disorders are age-related. Typically they disappear by middle childhood.

Sometimes sleep disorders occur because of some form of pathology. Treatment requires an attack on the primary cause. Once the primary pathology has been removed, sleep typically returns to normal—hence the term *secondary sleep disorder.* For example, a person who has difficulty sleeping because of feelings of guilt must learn how to deal with the guilt before normal sleep can be achieved.

Sleep Apnea

A person who suffers from sleep apnea stops breathing for about ten seconds 30 or more times during the course of one night. Some sufferers stop breathing as often as 500 times a night. While this condition is reasonably rare (Bixler et al.,

Practical Application 4-1
Some Common Reasons for Insomnia

Many of us suffer from insomnia from time to time. There are at least four common reasons for difficulty in going to sleep.

Sleeping In

If we have stayed up late or if we have not been getting enough sleep, we are often inclined to sleep in. Also, since the duration of our circadian rhythm tends to be 25 hours rather than 24 hours, we have a natural tendency to go to bed later on succeeding nights and so to get up later and later in the morning. According to Kleitman, the grandfather of sleep research, one of the best predictors of the time we will go to sleep is the length of time we have been awake, because the body tends to alternate between sleep and wakefulness in a very orderly fashion. Because our circadian rhythm lasts 25 hours, the body will quickly adjust to any new pattern that puts us to bed later and gets us up later. In order to maintain a 24-hour rhythm, we must constantly reset the cycle by getting up at the same time each day. When we interrupt the pattern by sleeping in, our body adopts a new arousal (alertness) pattern that finds us staying alert longer in the evening and being less alert in the morning. Alertness (arousal) in the evening makes it very difficult to get to sleep. The Monday-morning blues that many people experience may simply be the result of having let their bodies get out of synchrony with the 24-hour world in which they live. When they try to get to sleep on Sunday night, they discover that they cannot readily fall asleep. When they finally do fall asleep, they simply do not have enough time to get the necessary amount of REM and stage 4 sleep. And since they have not reset their alertness cycle, they tend to be out of synchrony with the 24-hour working day.

Engaging in an Activity That Produces High Arousal before Sleep

I find that if I lecture for three hours in the evening, say from 7:00 to 10:00 P.M., I have a great deal of difficulty getting to sleep. The reason is fairly simple. In order to sleep, our arousal level needs to decline to a level that makes sleep possible. Certain activities, such as lecturing for three hours, tend to produce a fairly high level of arousal (at least for me), which takes time to diminish. The bottom line is that even moderately high levels of arousal are incompatible with sleep. That is why people who win lotteries or suffer the death of a loved one typically

(continued)

1982), it nevertheless is considered life-threatening because it can cause severe hypoxia (deficiency of oxygen in the body tissues), and cardiac arrhythmias (irregular heartbeat). Although it has been considered a common cause of insomnia in adults, controlled laboratory studies have not confirmed this belief (Kales et al., 1982). Insomnia occurs for a wide variety of reasons other than sleep apnea. Because cessation of breathing typically causes one to awaken, such people tend to suffer fragmented sleep, which typically leads to daytime sleepiness (Stepanski et al., 1984; see also the earlier section on fragmented sleep). The mechanism by which this disorder is produced is not completely understood. The condition has been cannot sleep. Students who must take an exam the following day often have difficulty sleeping. When we think about some forthcoming activity, especially one that is challenging, we often experience fairly high levels of arousal.

Irregular Bedtime
People who do not go to bed at the same time each night often experience insomnia, especially on a night when they try to go to bed early. The reason is linked to the fact that while we can get along with less than eight hours of sleep, we tend to thrive on regularity. That is, our body attempts to synchronize itself with certain demands or expectations that we place on it. When we stay up late, our body attempts to accommodate that demand. When we suddenly go to bed early expecting to sleep, we find that our body is still operating at a higher level of arousal than is compatible with sleep. The net effect is that we lie awake waiting for our body to shut down.

It should be noted that while our body tends to respond to internal clocks (rhythms), we can reset those clocks by adopting a new pattern of waking and sleeping. While some people can adjust their rhythms quickly, others find the task difficult. Most researchers agree that the best way to produce a good internal rhythm is to adopt a set schedule. When you do not stick to a schedule, the body fails to develop a consistent rhythm. As a result, you are likely to have occasional difficulty getting to sleep.

Napping
Since the ability to fall asleep is determined to a very large degree by the time that has passed since you last slept, an afternoon nap can make it very difficult for you to fall asleep at your regular bedtime. People who are inclined to nap in the evening can also suffer a form of insomnia. Sometimes naps in the evening are treated by the body as part of the sleep cycle. Since awakening is determined to a very large degree by the length of time we have slept, people who nap in the evening tend to wake up very early. Not surprisingly, they then have difficulty getting back to sleep. The best way to cure this problem is to discontinue the evening naps. This is often very difficult to do because people who are in the habit of taking such naps often fall asleep involuntarily while they are reading or watching television. A nap serves to maintain the pattern they have established: early to sleep and much too early to wake. Not all people have trouble with naps. The body can learn to accommodate naps in the daily waking/sleeping cycle. This fact indicates that the sleep-wakefulness pattern can to some degree be trained.

successfully eliminated by plastic surgery. Consumption of alcohol before bedtime can increase sleep apnea (Scrima et al., 1982).

Summary
One of the most common sleep disorders is insomnia. A wide variety of chemicals including barbiturates, alcohol, and caffeine, can produce this condition. Insomnia can also be produced by environmental conditions. In some cases the person believes he or she is suffering from insomnia but is not—a
(continued)

condition called "benign insomnia." Sleep apnea, characterized by cessation of breathing, is a life-threatening disorder. There are several kinds of sleep anomaly, such as intrusion of sleep into waking state or the presence of wakelike behaviors during sleep. Though disruptive, many of these disorders can be treated.

Main Points

1. The best index of wakefulness, drowsiness, sleep, and dreams is cortical EEG activity.
2. In the course of a night an individual goes through approximately five sleep cycles, involving four states of sleep plus what is called stage 1–REM.
3. Sleep has been divided into two general categories called REM and NREM.
4. Dreaming is typically associated with REM sleep.
5. REM sleep episodes lengthen as the sleep period continues; the total is about 1.5–2.0 hours of REM sleep a night.
6. According to Jouvet's model of sleep, serotonin controls the onset of sleep and norepinephrine produces REM sleep.
7. Paralysis experienced during REM sleep is controlled by mechanisms in the RAS.
8. Sleep can be considered a state of extremely low attention in which the individual's threshold for detecting stimulation is high.
9. If people are left to establish their own sleep/wakefulness cycles (circadian rhythm), they tend to adopt a 25-hour cycle.
10. We tend to have more difficulty going to sleep when we have been aroused by some environmental event.
11. One of the factors that most strongly determines the time we go to sleep is the length of time that has elapsed since we last slept.
12. It has been shown that we have a 12.5-hour rhythm, which explains why many people like to nap in the afternoon.
13. The basic rest/activity cycle (BRAC) lasts from 90 to 120 minutes.
14. The tendency to shift from fantasy and intuitive thought to verbal and intellectual thought and back again follows a 90-minute cycle.
15. People who reduce the total time they sleep to 4.5–5.5 hours experience less REM and stage 2 sleep than normal but the same amount of stages 3 and 4 sleep.
16. Typically people experience difficulty alternating their sleep/wakefulness cycle.
17. Although reduced sleep may lead to feelings of sleepiness and fatigue, it does not seem to produce any serious psychological disturbances.
18. Typically people fully recover from sleep deprivation after a full night of sleep.
19. Sleep reduction tends to reduce performance in tasks that demand persistence and attention but not in tasks that demand precision and cognitive functioning.
20. Fragmented sleep, defined as sleep from which the individual is awakened repeatedly, can produce deficits similar to those that accompany total deprivation of sleep.
21. Loss of sleep reduces friendliness and increases aggression.
22. There is some evidence that muscle relaxation facilitates the onset of sleep.
23. Athletes, whether fit or unfit, have better slow-wave sleep (SWS) than non-athletes. SWS is associated with quality sleep.

24. Stress itself does not appear to affect the onset of quality sleep, but attitude toward stress may be a critical factor.
25. Noise to which one has not been habituated can interfere with normal sleep.
26. Increased attention demands just before sleep can delay the onset of sleep and increase REM sleep.
27. Increases in arousal produced by diffuse brain stimulation are sufficient to increase REM sleep.
28. Lack of REM sleep typically leads to REM rebound.
29. There has been some controversy as to whether lack of REM sleep produces serious psychological disturbances.
30. Vogel has provided evidence that REM deprivation may in fact benefit people experiencing endogenous depression.
31. Vogel's theory is that too much REM sleep leads to too much dissipation of neural energy.
32. There is convincing evidence that REM sleep is involved in the consolidation of memory.
33. Further, REM may be involved in the integration of recently learned material with previously learned material.
34. There is evidence that REM facilitates the learning not only of complex tasks but of emotionally loaded ones.
35. REM sleep appears to play a particularly important role in dealing with material that is threatening to the ego.
36. Field-independent people and repressors have a greater need for REM sleep.
37. REM sleep has been characterized as a form of divergent thinking.
38. Deprivation of stage 4 sleep reliably produces stage 4 rebound.
39. It appears that people need a daily quota of stage 4 sleep.
40. People dream during several stages of sleep, but the dreams differ in nature in the various stages.
41. NREM dreams tend to be conceptual and logical; REM dreams tend to be perceptual and emotional.
42. Sleep-onset dreams are similar to waking fantasy.
43. Because REM dreams and NREM dreams differ somewhat in content, it has been suggested that they have different functions.
44. Hartmann has suggested that NREM sleep has a restorative function and that REM sleep has a reprogramming function.
45. Up to 14% of the population suffers from insomnia.
46. One major cause of insomnia is the use of drugs, including sleeping pills.
47. There are three categories of insomnia in addition to the kind related to drugs: situational, benign, and arrhythmic insomnia.
48. Sleep apnea is characterized by the cessation of breathing.
49. There are numerous sleep disorders. Two common types are narcolepsy and hypersomnia.

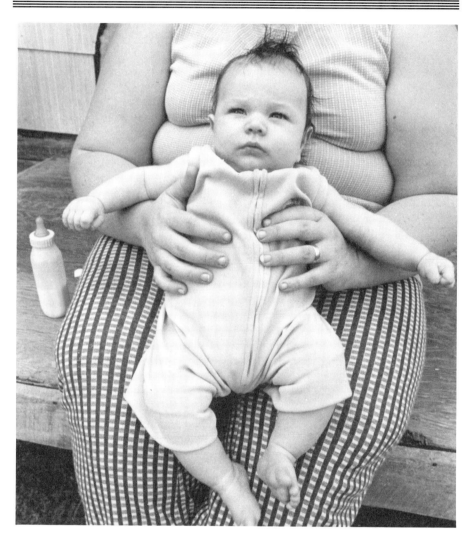

Hunger
and Eating

What makes us feel hungry?

What makes us feel satisfied or full after we eat?

Why are certain foods more appealing to us than others?

Are people biologically equipped to select foods that are good for them and to avoid foods that are bad for them?

What factors are involved in the rate of energy use?

Why do so many people tend to become obese?

Why do people who have become overweight have difficulty shedding those extra pounds?

Why do some people binge?

Why do some people starve themselves to the point of emaciation?

Why is it so important for women in our society to be thin?

Thousands of articles have been written about various aspects of hunger and eating and about the relation between them. The abundance of articles and research reflects the difficulty that has been encountered in giving a clear picture of the mechanisms involved in hunger and eating. Several persistent issues have stimulated research in this field. We will be dealing with five of the more important issues.

Five Important Issues

What psychological mechanism produces hunger? From a biological perspective, it seems that we should eat when we need to replenish depleted metabolic fuels, just as we fill the gas tank of a car when the gauge nears the empty mark. Humans and animals store two types of fuel—food in the gastrointestinal tract (which is immediately available) and reserves of fat. The problem is that we often feel hunger even though we have ample fat reserves (Friedman & Stricker, 1976). Researchers have therefore focused on the glucose level in the bloodstream. It has been found, however, that overall blood glucose levels do not correlate with reports of hunger (Mayer, 1955), even though glucose injections inhibit eating (Mook, 1963) and even though injections of insulin, which lower glucose levels, lead to reported feelings of hunger as well as stomach contractions (Goodner & Russell, 1965). Therefore, the reason that people report they are hungry must be more complex. In this chapter we will examine other data that suggest exactly what stimulus conditions give rise to hunger.

Why do humans have a propensity to obesity? An abundance of anecdotal and experimental data indicate that organisms (humans in particular) often eat too much. The by-product of overeating is overweight. The extra food is simply converted to fat. The fact that obesity can be induced in the laboratory by lesions in certain areas of the brain (parts of the hypothalamus) has led to the idea that naturally occurring obesity is due to some failure in a "satiety center." Current research has tended to rule out such a simple explanation. The reasons for obesity, as we shall discover, are very complex. Several biological systems in addition to the hypothalamus are involved in hunger and eating. Learned habits and cognitions have also been clearly identified as part of the obesity syndrome. We must consider all of these factors together if we are to account for obesity.

Why do humans have difficulty getting rid of unwanted fat?   People who are obese often wish they were not. As a consequence, many of them pursue some form of dieting. The fact that people often have difficulty in curbing the amount they eat has provided us with a wealth of data about the role of learning and cognition in hunger and eating.

What produces anorexia nervosa?   Although the number of people who fail to eat enough to maintain a normal weight is small compared with the number who overeat, the phenomenon is so dramatic that it has aroused wide attention. Why do some people restrict their food intake to such a degree that they become emaciated? Is there a biological explanation, or is this disorder psychological?

What produces bulimia?   Bulimia involves binge-eating followed by purging. It is typically a very secretive activity. Bulimics tend to plan their binges carefully so that no one will know what they are doing. After they have binged, bulimics deliberately vomit the food they have eaten to avoid gaining weight. Why are some people so unable to control their eating that they must resort to purging to control their weight?

Biological and Learning Factors in Hunger and Eating

Food, Metabolism, and Energy

Manufacturing glucose.   When carbohydrates, fats, and proteins are ingested in the form of food, they initially enter the stomach and then pass into the gastrointestinal (GI) tract, where they are converted into glucose, a more usable form of energy. One of the main chemicals that is secreted when we eat is insulin, secreted by the pancreas. Insulin plays an important role in the metabolism process. It is involved in the conversion of food into energy. Once the food is converted into glucose, it passes through the liver into the bloodstream. The circulatory system distributes that fuel or energy to all parts of the body. The GI tract, it should be noted, is an excellent storehouse of energy. After a big meal it typically takes several hours for all the food in the digestive tract to be digested (converted into glucose). Our blood, then, should be rich in glucose for several hours after we have eaten (Friedman & Stricker, 1976). If we do not use all the glucose that is generated by the digestive process, the liver converts some of it to fat, which is then stored in our fat cells, or adipose tissue.

It should be noted that proteins are converted not only into glucose but also into amino acid. Amino acid is important for rebuilding muscles and manufacturing a number of important chemicals that the body needs, such as the neurotransmitters in the brain (Wurtman, 1982).

Quick energy.   It is widely believed that a candy bar is a source of quick energy. While you may feel a spurt of energy after you have eaten one, it probably does not come from your actual digestion of the candy bar. It takes 20 minutes or more for the body to convert such things as sugar (which is a carbohydrate), chocolate, and nuts into glucose. The quick energy you experience is probably attributable to the secretion of insulin, triggered by the candy bar. There is ample evidence that the mere sight or smell of food can trigger this reaction (for example, Woods et al., 1977; Rodin, Slochower, & Fleming, 1977). Insulin has been shown to be important in transporting glucose, especially to or in the cerebral tissue (for example, Hertz et al., 1981). The insulin that is triggered by a candy bar acts on glucose in the bloodstream and transports it to various areas of the body. The effect is short-lived. Not surprisingly, people often feel more hungry after eating a candy bar than they did before. In the next few paragraphs we will see why.

The glucose theory of hunger.   Since we tend to get hungry when the food in our intestinal tract is depleted, it seems to follow that the reason we eat is that our blood glucose level is low. Indeed, early research on this topic provided good support for this idea. Researchers manipulated the level of available energy by transfusing blood from a starved dog to a satisfied dog and vice versa. They found that a recently fed dog had stomach contractions when it received blood from a starving one (Luckhardt & Carlson, 1915; Tschukitschew, cited in Templeton & Quigley, 1930). Similarly, a transfusion of blood from a recently fed dog to a starving dog terminated stomach contractions (Bash, 1939). It has been suggested that the stomach, liver, and hypothalamus contain glucoreceptors that provide feedback on the available glucose in the system (Russek, 1963).

The fatty acid theory of hunger.   When we have used up the food in our GI tract and depleted the glucose that is circulating in our blood, our body will begin to release fatty acids and glycerol from the adipose (fat) tissue. Because these free fatty acids are deposited in the bloodstream, the level of free fatty acids should be closely related to hunger. Various researchers have proposed that the body may have receptors that are designed to detect an increase in the level of fatty acids, and that their activation triggers the subjective feeling we call hunger (Dole, 1956; Klein et al., 1960).

The insulin theory of hunger.   In general, the correlation between hunger and low blood glucose levels has not been very close. For this reason researchers have continued to search for other explanations for hunger. Another theory is that insulin plays an important if not the primary role in producing feelings of hunger. Since food (in and out of the GI tract) stimulates the secretion of insulin, the level of insulin is highly correlated with the level of glucose: either both are high or both are low. In other words, it could be insulin rather than glucose that actually triggers those feelings of hunger. In order to find out which is more important, the levels of glucose and insulin have to be manipulated independently. Researchers inserted catheters into a vein so that they could administer insulin and glucose directly into the blood. They found that insulin was a better predictor than glucose not only of hunger and eating but of the pleasure people derived from sweet-tasting foods (Rodin et al., 1985).

The insulin theory is attractive because it can explain phenomena that are hard to explain by other theories. It can, for example, explain why people who are overweight have higher basal levels of insulin than people of normal weight (Rabinowitz & Zierler, 1962). It can also explain the frequent finding that insulin administered to human and other animals leads to overweight. While the insulin theory is appealing, it should be pointed out that there is other evidence that high levels of circulating insulin may result in decreased food intake (see Rodin et al., 1985).

The heat-production theory of hunger.   John Brobeck (1960) has suggested that a drop in body and blood temperature, as sensed by brain cells, will lead to feelings of hunger, while a rise in body and blood temperature will lead to decreased feelings of hunger. This theory, too, can explain findings that pose difficulties for other theories. Since one of the by-products of activity is heat production, it can explain why various activities lead to a decline in hunger. It can also explain why we feel hungrier in a cold environment than in a warm one.

Brain receptors for hunger and satiety.   Amphetamines have been used for some time to control appetite. Apparently amphetamines and their derivatives work by binding to receptors in the brain. This finding has led to speculation that the body must produce its own "amphetamines" that normally control appetite. Tricyclic antidepressants, on the other hand, increase appetite. Tricyclic antidepressants increase the level of norepinephrine, a neurotransmitter that is produced and stored in the brain. Taken together, these findings suggest that the mechanisms for the control of appetite (both hunger and satiety) have a biological basis. What this research fails to tell us is why these mechanisms fail to control weight in some people (Kolata, 1982).

Signals from the gastrointestinal tract.   Apparently more than one mechanism tells the body when to start eating and when to stop. It has been shown, for example, that glucose leads to a decline in eating when it is injected slowly into the gastrointestinal tract (the duodenum) but can actually increase eating when it is injected quickly (Geiselman & Novin, 1982). The implication is that one could decrease feelings of hunger by slowing the rate at which food arrives at the duodenum. Henry Koopmans (1985) has provided evidence of the existence of satiety signals from the stomach that control short-term eating and other satiety signals from the lower small intestine that appear to be involved in the control of long-term eating. How can we make use of these mechanisms to control eating in people who are obese? Would it be possible, for example, to devise harmless pills that would stimulate these receptors?

Can Humans Select a Balanced Diet?

Do we instinctively know what foods we should eat in order to meet our nutritional needs? From time to time it has been suggested that humans are indeed born with this capacity. A now-classic and often-quoted study (Davis, 1928) showed that young children presented with an array of food items will, over a period of time, select a nutritionally balanced diet. If humans can in fact perform this remarkable feat, a point we will consider in some detail, then the problem is to explain how we manage to do it. One mechanism that seems capable of providing the necessary feedback is taste.

Although we have evidence to suggest that humans may select balanced diets under certain conditions, we also have an abundance of evidence to the contrary. In many isolated instances people both individually and in groups have developed food preferences that have led to various forms of malnutrition, even when nutritious foods have been readily available. Our own society seems to be enamored of the so-called junk foods, which have an appealing taste but are low in essential nutrients.

There is evidence that people at the lower socioeconomic levels of American society eat foods with less nutritional value than people at the upper socioeconomic levels (Adelson, 1968). Some people have erroneously argued that this difference simply reflects the fact that poor people cannot afford nutritious foods. A more careful analysis has shown that people at the lower socioeconomic levels buy more prepared foods and more snack foods, both of which tend to be low in nutritional value. Interestingly, these foods are generally more expensive. Therefore, although such people spend more money on food, they select foods that are not so good for them. It has been suggested that the reasons people at the upper socioeconomic levels of society tend to buy more nutritious foods are that they are more knowledgeable about the nutritional value of food and more willing to spend time preparing them.

Specific hungers?   A great deal of controlled laboratory work has addressed the question whether animals can detect the absence of a vital nutrient in their system and can select a diet that will make up for that lack (for example, Bare, 1949). The general procedure has been first to create a deficiency by giving the animal a diet lacking in a particular nutrient, such as vitamin A or sodium. Once the deficiency has been established, the animal is then typically allowed to choose among diets that either contain or lack the absent nutrient. If the animal is able to identify by taste the nutrient that is absent, it should immediately select the diet that contains that nutrient. The results of such studies (for example, Rodgers, 1967; Rozin, 1965, 1967) indicate that although animals develop an aversion to the diet lacking in the deficient nutrient, they do not, under most conditions, immediately select the diet with the vital nutrient. Over a period of time, however, they do come to select the correct diet. How do we explain these results?

It appears that absence of a vital nutrient from the diet produces a general state of malaise (sickness) that is aversive or noxious. As a result, the animal learns to avoid that diet. The mechanism, as we shall discuss later, can under certain conditions be taste. Because this general malaise might be produced by the lack of one among many nutrients or a combination, the animal must, through principles of learning, come to identify the diet that will reduce and then eliminate the malaise. The reason it takes some time for this association to be established is probably that it usually takes some time for nutrients to produce a physiological change of detectable magnitude. Thus the feedback is relatively slow. According to the principles of learning, any delay in feedback or reinforcement usually slows learning.

The general conclusion that can be drawn from this work is that animals do not appear to have "specific hungers" per se. Rather, the absence of certain vital nutrients appears to cause a general malaise. Fortuitously, animals may select the correct diet to reduce that malaise. If they do, they can learn to select a diet that will replenish the depleted nutrients.

The critical factor that is necessary in order to learn to choose the correct diet is the sampling of a variety of foods. What happens if the organism has preferences that discourage it from sampling foods other than the preferred one? Animals that learned to prefer a sugar solution to a salt solution before adrenalectomy, an operation that made them deficient in salt, continued to prefer the sugar solution after adrenalectomy. As a result of their continued preference for sugar, the animals all suffered severe weight loss, and several died (Harriman, 1955). Similar results have been found when animals were maintained on a protein-free diet. If these animals had previously come to prefer a sucrose solution, they failed to select a diet that would have given them the required protein (Young & Chaplin, 1945).

Sickness and taste.   Much evidence indicates that animals will learn to avoid any food with a certain taste if it is followed by sickness. If a poison is injected into a rat after it has eaten a food with a certain flavor, it will form an aversion to that flavor, even if the poison was injected six to eight hours later (Nachman, 1970). It is interesting and important to note that rats do not learn to avoid a food on the basis of visual cues, such as color (Wilcoxin, Dragoin, & Kral, 1971), nor do they learn to avoid a particular flavor that is associated with shock (Garcia & Koelling, 1966; Garcia et al., 1968). It can be argued that organisms either are structured in a certain way or come to learn that certain cues or classes of cues are reliably associated with other classes of cues. Thus, since taste is associated with states of the stomach, it seems reasonable to expect that animals would associate taste with sickness. Similarly, if certain cues or classes of cues are randomly paired, animals could not normally come to associate them. Since taste is not normally a reliable predictor of pain to the external receptors (as in shock), it is not surprising that animals do not come to associate taste with shock. Similarly, it is not surprising that they do not learn to associate color with sickness, because the eyes are often stimulated quite independent of food intake whereas taste is not.

The foregoing research indicates that animals learn to associate a taste cue with the reduction of malaise. Therefore, animals should be able to maintain a balanced diet by selecting a food with a given taste. Animals can be readily fooled, however, if the taste cue is switched to a food deficient in a vital nutrient. Even though the animal may eventually die, it will persist in eating the food with a given taste. From this finding we can conclude that the mechanisms involved in preventing malnutrition are very fragile. It would appear that they were not designed for a 20th-century world of chemicals and junk food.

Implications for food selection and malnutrition.   The foregoing research has important implications for understanding food selection and malnutrition. For some time now the food industry has been able to produce artificial flavors (and odors) that are almost exact duplicates of naturally occurring flavors. Many such flavors have been added to foods that have little if any nutritional value. Consequently, even if we had learned early in life to use taste as a cue for eating a nutritionally balanced diet, we could readily be fooled into selecting products that might eventually result in malnutrition. The food industry has also become aware that visual and textural properties of food are important in determining food-selection behavior. As a result, it has created products with such appeal. As a result, many products on the market are very appealing to the senses but have minimal nutritional value.

It is difficult to put the blame on the individual for selecting foods poor in nutritional value in view of the fact that we are constantly being seduced through the very senses that may normally help us select a balanced diet.

Summary

When food is eaten, it initially enters the gastrointestinal tract, where it is converted into glucose. Glucose that is not converted into energy is further converted into fat. Several theories of hunger have been proposed. One is that low levels of glucose trigger the hunger mechanism. Another theory is that the release of fatty acids from adipose tissue is somehow the event that triggers hunger. It has also been shown that an increased level of insulin in the blood is linked to hunger. Since various drugs, such as the amphetamines, reduce feelings of hunger, it has been suggested that the body produces its own "amphetamines" to control hunger. Finally, the gastrointestinal tract apparently has receptors that tell us when we have eaten enough. The question of how people manage to select a balanced diet has led researchers
(continued)

to examine the relation between taste and food selection. This research suggests that human and other animals learn to select balanced diets. Because taste is frequently the primary cue associated with "good" and "bad" foods, it is possible to lead people to eat nonnutritious food by giving that food a taste that is associated with a nutritious food. It is also possible to get people to eat nonnutritious foods by making the foods appeal to the senses.

Factors That Affect the Rate of Energy Use

The Three Components

Energy expenditure has three main components: basal metabolism rate (BMR), physical activity, and specific dynamic action (SDA) of food. About one-third of our energy use is attributable to exercise and about two-thirds to our BMR (Rodin, 1981). SDR is the increase in energy expenditure following the ingestion of food. SDR can increase the BMR by up to 20% for a few hours after a meal. Certain foods, such as proteins, produce the greatest increase (Powers, 1982). The actual proportions of energy expended in exercise and metabolism obviously depend on individual exercise patterns. The basal metabolism rate is the amount of energy we use in a given period of time in relation to our body size. Specifically, it is measured as the number of calories we burn per square meter of body surface in an hour when we are resting. What is interesting about basal metabolism is that it changes with age, varies markedly from individual to individual, and is affected by how large we are, what we eat, and how long we have gone without food.

Age. From birth to about age 18–20 in females and a little later in males, the metabolism rate declines rapidly. As Figure 5-1 shows, at about age 20 the rate levels out, and from then on it declines much more slowly. This means that the amount of food we need to function at resting levels, in proportion to body size, declines rather sharply, starting shortly after birth, until age 20 or so. From then on we need approximately the same amount of energy to operate on a day-to-day basis. There is a sharp increase in food intake around puberty because food is needed to build bones and muscles that are developing rapidly at that time as well as to supply the energy for the high level of activity that frequently occurs then.

Although obesity can occur at any age, humans often first encounter problems of overweight around age 20 or shortly thereafter. If the amount we eat is controlled more or less by habit, it is not surprising that overweight first shows itself at this age. First, because we have stopped growing, we no longer require as much food. Second, the reduction in metabolism rate means our bodies burn up fuel more slowly. The extra food will be converted to fat. Finally, any reduction in exercise would further make us prone to overweight. The slow but continuous decline in basal metabolism rate with increasing age and the tendency to exercise less with increasing age are important factors in the tendency for humans to become overweight in their later years.

Individual factors. There are large individual differences in basal metabolism rates. In one study, subjects who had wide differences in caloric intake were matched for height, weight, and level of activity. Even though their weights did not change over a period of weeks, it was often found that one member of the matched pair ate twice as much as the other (Rose & Williams, 1961). Such differences in basal

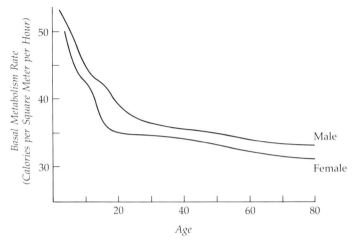

Figure 5-1.   Changes in basal metabolism rates with age (Stuart & Davis, 1972)

metabolism rate obviously play an important role in determining who will be prone to obesity and who will have difficulty dieting.

Diets and dieting.   Interestingly, our basal metabolism rate depends on the type of food we eat. When our diet includes an excess of carbohydrates in proportion to saturated fats, our basal metabolism is higher (Goldman et al., 1975). Thus the popular low-carbohydrate diets actually reduce the metabolism rate. Further, because over time the metabolism rate tends to stabilize at a lower level, the person on a low-carbohydrate diet is almost certain to gain weight after terminating the diet (Beller, 1978). Relatively long periods of food deprivation also lower the basal metabolism rate (Wooley, Wooley, & Dyrenforth, 1979). Therefore, trying to lose weight by selecting a low-carbohydrate diet or by dieting can eventually be counterproductive (Rodin, 1981).

Summary

Energy expenditure has three main components: basal metabolism rate (BMR), physical activity, and specific dynamic action (SDA). Our basal metabolism rate, which accounts for about two-thirds of our energy expenditure, decreases as we age. It slows fairly abruptly at around age 20. This change can explain why some people tend to put on weight around that age. BMR varies widely among individuals so that some people can eat considerably more than others without putting on weight. Eating certain foods can reduce the metabolism rate. A reduction of food intake, as by dieting, can also reduce the metabolism rate.

Obesity

If we continue to eat after we have ingested sufficient food to last us until our next meal, the extra food will be stored as fat in the adipose tissue. This is as certain as that the sun rises. Should we repeat this practice regularly, we not only will tend to gain weight but eventually will become obese (severely overweight). The question is why many people eat more than they need. As we shall see, there are several possibilities. At least three of the explanations assume some abnormality in the biological structure of obese people.

Defining Obesity

Who are the obese? Unfortunately, there is no easy way to define *obesity*. The term has been used to refer to people who have a very moderate amount of fat and to those who are grossly overweight. In many of the studies I will be discussing, *obese* is defined simply as exceeding the average weight for one's height, build, age, and sex by a given percentage, for example 20% or 30%. This means that a person who should weigh 150 pounds would be classified as obese if he or she weighed 180 pounds. Thus we are not talking about the fat lady at the circus sideshow but about people with whom we interact daily. Many of us have experienced or will experience excessive weight gain sometime in our lives. Therefore, within many of us there lives the potential obese person, ready to emerge if given half a chance.

Obesity as Preparation for Famine

David Margules (1979) argues that obesity can be understood as an adaptive mechanism gone astray because we are no longer faced with periodic food shortages. He theorizes that the adipose tissue evolved to protect humans against food shortages, and now that such shortages are rare, we tend to continue adding to an already adequate reserve. In short, people are inclined to progress from a comfortable reserve to a state of obesity.

Some people, David Margules argues, may be more inclined to overeat than others because of elevated beta-endorphin levels. Elevated beta-endorphin levels may be due to a number of factors, including genetics. In one study it was found that genetically obese mice and rats had elevated beta-endorphin levels (Margules et al., 1978). Beta-endorphin, it has been shown, is closely linked to the conservation and expenditure of energy. For example, beta-endorphin (as well as enkephalin) has antisympathetic properties that attenuate the arousal-producing potential of various stimuli, thus reducing the use of energy. The fact that the individual can conserve energy makes hibernation possible. Margules points out that obese people are sometimes characterized as lethargic. Lethargy may be a direct behavioral outcome of elevated beta-endorphin levels. In other words, beta-endorphin simultaneously stimulates eating and causes the conservation of energy.

According to Margules's theory, beta-endorphin is responsible for such things as insulin output or its lack. In short, Margules is suggesting that beta-endorphin is a more basic mechanism than insulin. The question we need to answer next is why some people have elevated levels of beta-endorphin. Is this a purely genetic matter, or does learning play some role in it?

Obesity and Anorexia as Malfunctions of the Hypothalamus

Two areas of the hypothalamus have been linked to the two behavioral phenomena of overeating and failure to eat. Lesions of the ventromedial nuclei of the hypothalamus produce overeating, which leads to obesity (see Teitelbaum, 1961), and lesions of the lateral hypothalamus lead to a failure to eat, a state called "anorexia."

Lesions of the ventromedial nuclei.   Philip Teitelbaum (1961) noted that animals with lesions of the ventromedial nuclei (VMN) show the following characteristics.

1. They are unresponsive to normal satiety cues that are presumably mediated by glucose.
2. They will not work as hard as normal animals to obtain food.
3. They will stop eating "adulterated" foods (such as food laced with quinine) sooner than normal animals.
4. They will eat large amounts of highly palatable foods.

Lesions of the lateral hypothalamus.   Lesions of the lateral hypothalamus (LH) have been shown to produce an effect analogous but complementary to those in the VMN. Specifically, it has been shown that lesions of the LH result initially in the cessation of eating. After such animals have lost considerable body weight, they begin to eat again, but at a much reduced rate. This reduced rate of eating tends to be very stable. While palatable foods tend to result in increased eating and weight gain, just as they do in normal and obese animals, animals lesioned in the LH continue to maintain their weight well below the normal level. The degree of anorexia that the animals display is related to the size of the lesion (Keesy & Powley, 1975).

What is the exact mechanism?   Does the hypothalamus simply regulate the amount we eat or does it act as a monitor of, say, the level of body fat? The most widely held view is that the hypothalamus is involved in monitoring the store of adipose tissue. There is considerable evidence that VMN lesions produce a disruption in fat metabolism, which increases the amount of glucose that is converted to lipids, which are then transferred to adipose tissue for storage (Frohman, Goldman, & Bernardis, 1972; Goldman et al., 1970, 1972a, 1972b; Haessler & Crawford, 1967). It could be argued that the obesity resulting from the VMN lesion is due to the disruption of the normal metabolism process—that is, the lesion produces overeating because of the abnormally low glucose level that results from this disruption.

Set-Point Theory

Richard Keesy and Terry Powley (1975) have proposed that the findings of studies of the hypothalamus provide evidence for a set-point theory of weight level. Specifically, they have proposed that the hypothalamus sets our weight. Some of us will have normal weight, some of us will tend toward obesity, and still others will tend toward anorexia. This hypothesis is summarized in Figure 5-2.

Keesy and Powley argue that their theory of weight level can readily account for the tendency of people who are inclined to overweight to fall off their diets. According to set-point theory, they would be expected to do so. Only by deliberately restraining their eating would they be able to keep their weight down. Any failure to restrain their eating would immediately result in a tendency to increase the quantity eaten.

Boundary Theory of Hunger, Eating, and Obesity

Janet Polivy and Peter Herman (1983; Herman & Polivy, 1984) have proposed a boundary model of hunger and eating. According to this model, two separate mechanisms control hunger and eating, one for hunger and one for satiety (see Figure 5-3a). Both mechanisms are assumed to have a physiological basis. Following the lead of other theorists, Polivy and Herman assume that if we fail to eat or if we eat too much, we will experience an aversive state. Between these two boundary points is a range that is not under direct physiological control. Once we become

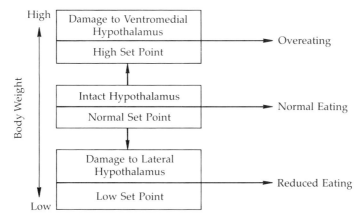

Figure 5-2. Damage (or lesions) to the ventromedial hypothalamus raises the set point, while damage (or lesions) to the lateral hypothalamus lowers the set point.

hungry and begin to eat, the amount we eat will be controlled by such factors as social expectations and the taste and texture of the food. They argue that within these boundaries eating is under cognitive rather than biological control.

They further suggest that the upper and lower boundaries vary from person to person. The lower hunger boundary is lower in dieters than in nondieters, they suggest, and the upper satiety boundary is higher (compare Figures 5-3*a* and *b*). They further argue that because dieters want to control their weight, they impose on themselves an upper boundary that is well below the biological satiety boundary. This is purely a cognitive boundary. This particular idea is an outgrowth of work on dieters and nondieters, which led Polivy and Herman to distinguish between restrained and unrestrained eaters.

Restrained and unrestrained eaters. Dieters, Polivy and Herman have found, tend to be restrained eaters. That is, while they often feel hungry, think a great deal about food, and are readily tempted by the sight and smell of food, they consciously attempt to control their impulse to eat, and if they do overeat or eat high-calorie foods (a no-no for dieters), they feel guilty. Nondieters, in contrast, tend to be unrestrained eaters. They do not experience persistent feelings of hunger, do not think about food as much as restrained eaters, and are not so readily tempted by the sight and smell of food. More important, as far as this distinction

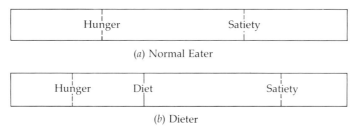

Figure 5-3. Hunger and satiety boundaries of normal eaters and dieters. (The diet boundary is purely cognitive.) (Herman & Polivy, 1984)

is concerned, they are not constantly trying to control their food intake, nor do they feel guilty when they do overeat.

Polivy and Herman have developed a scale to determine whether or not people are restrained or unrestrained (normal) eaters. They argue that the ideal of normal weight, as prescribed by society, is often below the lower limit of a person's natural range. If such people are to achieve this "ideal" weight they must constantly restrain themselves from giving in to their natural urges. In other words, the problem for the restrained eater is the need to deal more or less constantly with hunger and attraction to food. To see if you are a restrained eater, take the test in Table 5-1. The higher your score, the more restrained an eater you are.

The preloading studies.   One of the most convincing lines of evidence for Polivy and Herman's theory comes from studies that I will simply refer to as the "preloading" studies. They gave dieters and nondieters either one or two milk-shakes (preloading) and then asked them to judge the tastes of three varieties of ice cream; some subjects got no milkshake. The subjects were told that the purpose of the "preloading" was to determine how a previous taste affected subsequent taste perception, but the real purpose was to determine if preloading would affect the amount of ice cream that dieters and nondieters would eat. As dieters are restrained eaters who avoid such foods as ice cream, would they feel guilty and consequently make fewer taste tests (that is, eat less) than nondieters? The initial study showed that as the size of the preload increased, the amount of ice cream the dieters ate in the course of the taste test also increased (Herman & Mack, 1975; see Figure 5-4). In a subsequent study subjects were told that the caloric content was high or low. When they were told that the caloric content was high, the effect was even greater (Polivy, 1976). That is, contrary to what one might intuitively expect, dieters ate more than nondieters.

Table 5-1.   Eating restraint scale (Polivy & Herman, 1983)

1. How often are you dieting? Never; rarely; sometimes; often; always. (Scored 0–4)

2. What is the maximum amount of weight (in pounds) that you have ever lost within one month? 0–4; 5–9; 10–14; 15–19; 20 + . (Scored 0–4)

3. What is your maximum weight gain within a week? 0–1; 1.1–2; 2.1–3; 3.1–5; 5.1 + . (Scored 0–4)

4. In a typical week, how much does your weight fluctuate? 0–1; 1.1–2; 2.1–3; 3.1–5; 5.1 + . (Scored 0–4)

5. Would a weight fluctuation of 5 pounds affect the way you live your life? Not at all; slightly; moderately; very much. (Scored 0–3)

6. Do you eat sensibly in front of others and splurge alone? Never; rarely; often; always. (Scored 0–3)

7. Do you give too much time and thought to food? Never; rarely; often; always. (Scored 0–3)

8. Do you have feelings of guilt after overeating? Never; rarely; often; always. (Scored 0–3)

9. How conscious are you of what you are eating? Not at all; slightly; moderately; extremely. (Scored 0–3)

10. How many pounds over your desired weight were you at your maximum weight? 0–1; 2–5; 6–10; 11–20; 21 + . (Scored 0–4)

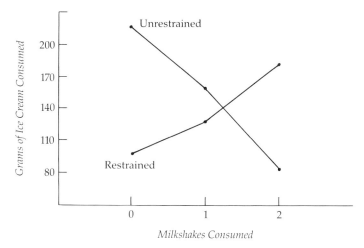

Figure 5-4. Unrestrained eaters, having consumed one or two milkshakes, show appropriate compensation when asked to taste and rate the flavors of three kinds of ice cream. Restrained eaters, however, eat more ice cream the more milkshakes they have already consumed. Herman and Polivy (1984) hypothesize that the suspension of their self-imposed restraint (in this case, in the form of the milkshakes) causes dieters to capitulate to internal (hunger) and external (taste) cues.

The disinhibited eater. Herman and Polivy have suggested that when dieters fail to restrain their eating (in this case because they had agreed to serve in an experiment that required them to break their normal strict rules), they adopt a what-the-hell attitude. That is, they say to themselves, "As long as I've already lost control, I might as well eat as much as I want." What has happened, Herman and Polivy suggest, is that, having for the moment abandoned their diet boundary, they are left with only their biological satiety boundary, which is higher than the nondieter's. The fact that the effect increases when they are told that the preload is high in calories provides compelling evidence that the diet boundary is indeed cognitive rather than biological. How long does the dieter remain in this disinhibited (what-the-hell) state? Many dieters consider the next day a new beginning and restrained eating is again the rule. It has also been shown, however, that the what-the-hell effect can be markedly reduced if their attention is called to their behavior (either by themselves or by someone else) (Polivy et al., 1986).

While the boundary theory appears to be able to explain the behavior of dieters (especially the characteristic disinhibition effect) and of bingers as well, it has been criticized on the grounds that it fails to contribute to a better understanding of why people actually become obese (Ruderman, 1986).

Binge eating and anorexia. Herman and Polivy's theory can also account for binge eating and anorexia. Figure 5-5 depicts these two types. Note that the binge eater is not responding to the satiety boundary (or the satiety boundary is inoperative) whereas the anorexic is not responding to the hunger boundary (or the hunger boundary is inoperative).

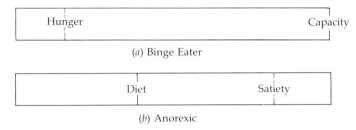

(a) Binge Eater

(b) Anorexic

Figure 5-5.   Failure of satiety and hunger boundaries in binge eaters and anorexics. (The diet boundary is purely cognitive.) (Herman & Polivy, 1984)

Internal-External Theory

Some people seem to eat in response to external cues, such as the sight and smell of food and the time of day; other people do not. Since some people do not respond to external cues, it has been suggested that their eating may be governed by internal cues, such as stomach contractions, glucose levels, and fat levels. When people first made this observation, obese people appeared to be the ones who ate in response to external cues, while the nonobese seemed to respond to internal cues.

Stomach contractions and hunger.   One of the first systematic demonstrations that obese and nonobese people respond to different cues was made by Albert Stunkard (1959). He arranged for both obese and nonobese subjects to enter the laboratory at 9:00 in the morning, having gone overnight without food. Each volunteer was asked to swallow a gastric balloon (filled with water) that was attached to a mechanical device to record stomach contractions. Every 15 minutes for 4 hours, the volunteers were asked to report whether they were hungry. It was found that the nonobese were more likely to report hunger when the stomach was active than the obese. This finding suggests that feelings of hunger are associated with internal stimuli for the nonobese but not for the obese. Since we would expect hunger to be associated with internal cues, the question is why the obese fail to respond to these cues. If they are not responding to internal cues, what cues are eliciting their reports of hunger?

Stanley Schachter (1971a) demonstrated that whereas the nonobese person tends to respond to internal cues, such as stomach motility or hypoglycemia (low blood glucose level), the obese person does tend to respond more to external cues. An obese person who is accustomed to eating at a certain time, for example, will feel hungry when the clock indicates mealtime. The nonobese person will be less influenced by the time on the clock unless it happens to coincide with his or her internal cues or biological clock. To test this prediction, Schachter had volunteers come to the laboratory under the pretense of studying "the relation between physiological reactions and psychological characteristics which require base level measurements of heart and sweat gland activity" (Schachter & Gross, 1968, p. 99). Electrodes were attached, presumably to measure heart rate and galvanic skin response. Half the obese and half the nonobese subjects were then left for a period of time (presumably to establish a baseline) with a rigged clock that over 50 minutes would be 15 minutes slow. The other half were left for the same period with a rigged clock that would be 30 minutes fast. The first group finished this phase of the study when their clock said 5:20 P.M., the second when theirs said 6:05 P.M.

Table 5-2. Amount of crackers eaten (in grams) by Schachter's subjects in four conditions (Schachter, 1971a)

	Time	
Weight	Slow	Fast
Obese	19.9	37.6
Normal	41.5	16.0

The experimenter returned at this point with a box of crackers from which he was snacking and offered some to the volunteer. The experimenter also asked the subject to fill out an irrelevant questionnaire. If the obese person is more affected by clock time than real time, he should eat more in the "fast clock time" condition than in the "slow clock time" condition, since in the fast-time condition the apparent time was either near or past his normal eating time. The results (Table 5-2) supported the hypothesis. On the average, obese subjects ate more crackers in the fast-time condition than in the slow-time condition—just the reverse of the non-obese subjects, who ate more in the slow-time condition. Why was there a reversal for the nonobese? Schachter notes that when the nonobese in the fast-time condition refused crackers, they said, "No, thanks, I don't want to spoil my dinner." Apparently cognitive factors were responsible for the tendency to eat less in this condition.

The Air France study. These findings are consistent with those obtained by more naturalistic methods (Goldman, Jaffa, & Schachter, 1968). An airplane crosses several time zones when it flies from Paris to New York, so that a passenger's internal cues will fail to correspond with clock time after a flight. Because obese people respond to clock time rather than internal cues, they should adjust quickly to the local eating time; the nonobese, in contrast, should find it much more difficult to adjust their eating habits to local time. Interviews with Air France personnel assigned to transatlantic flights indicated that those who were overweight had less trouble adjusting to local eating time than those who were average in weight (Figure 5-6).

Fear, stomach contractions, and hunger. To determine more precisely whether nonobese people respond to an internal state—namely, stomach motility—a study was designed in which stomach cues would be suppressed or eliminated (Schachter, Goldman, & Gordon, 1968). Because it has been found that fear will suppress gastric movement, and because researchers find it easy to manipulate fear by informing subjects that they will receive a shock, it was relatively easy to design a study in which nonobese subjects would experience little or no gastric movement. Subjects were told that the purpose of the experiment was to evaluate the effects of tactile stimulation on taste and that electrical stimulation would be used to stimulate the skin receptors. In the low-fear condition, subjects were told the electrical stimulation would produce a mild tingling sensation; in the high-fear condition, subjects were told the shocks would be painful but would cause no permanent damage. They were further instructed that the experimenters wanted to get measures of taste before and during tactile stimulation. Hence the subjects started the tasting part of the experiment with the belief that they would shortly be experiencing shock in the next phase of the study. Actual shock was not given;

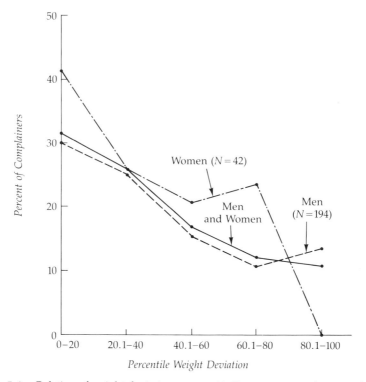

Figure 5-6. Relation of weight deviation among Air France personnel to complaining about the effect of time-zone changes on eating (Schachter, 1971a)

the instructions were used merely to induce fear. The tasting task involved judging some crackers in terms of several dimensions (salty, cheesy, garlicky, and so on). However, the actual behavior of interest was the number of crackers obese and nonobese volunteers ate. Subjects were told they could eat as many crackers as they wanted in order to make their judgments. If the fear manipulation worked and if it is true that nonobese subjects' tendency to eat is determined by gastric motility, the nonobese volunteers should have eaten less under the high-fear than the low-fear condition. This was, in fact, what was found (Figure 5-7). The obese volunteers were not sensitive to the fear manipulation: they ate almost equal amounts under high- and low-fear conditions. This finding is consistent with the view that obese people are insensitive to internal cues.

Sensory cues and the obese. As we noted earlier, oral cues are a very important factor governing whether an animal will eat. The fact that the obese person seems to ignore stomach or gut cues does not necessarily imply that he or she will ignore all internal cues. The data indicate quite clearly that the obese are very sensitive to sensory cues. In fact, they appear to be more sensitive to sensory cues than the nonobese.

Before trying to resolve this question, we need to examine some of the research on the effects of sensory cues on amount eaten. Probably one of the most dramatic demonstrations that the obese person's eating is highly dependent on sensory cues is a study that compared grossly obese men and women with nonobese

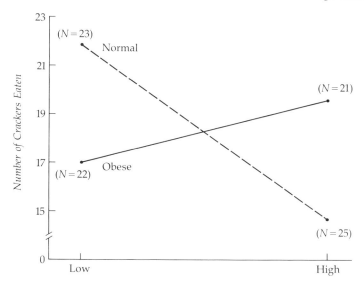

Figure 5-7.   Effects of fear on number of crackers eaten by normal and obese subjects in Schachter, Goldman, and Gordon's study (Schachter, 1971a)

controls (Hashim & Van Itallie, 1965). The researchers prepared a bland, homogenized liquid diet similar in taste and composition to the vanilla flavors of such commercial preparations as Nutrament and Metrecal. The subjects (who were confined to a hospital) were allowed to eat as much of this diet as they wanted, but consumption was in a situation totally devoid of any social trappings. Normals continued to consume their daily average of about 2400 calories, but obese subjects diminished their intake to 500 calories a day, about 3000 calories less than their daily average before admission to the hospital (Figure 5-8).

Although other studies have not shown so dramatic an effect, the general finding seems to hold even in very tightly controlled studies. In an experiment that asked subjects to evaluate taste (Nisbett, 1968), for example, obese subjects ate significantly less ice cream if its flavor had been doctored somewhat with a bitter-tasting chemical, while normal-weight subjects were less influenced by the taste and ate about the same amounts of the bitter and normal-tasting ice cream (Figure 5-9). Similar results have been obtained with cake and milk (cited in Schachter, 1971b).

Externality and the nonobese.   One might conclude from Schachter's work on the relation between obesity and externality that only obese people are sensitive to cues in the environment that are associated with eating. Some recent work by Judith Rodin and her colleagues indicates that this is not true. They have shown that many nonobese people are sensitive to such environmental cues and that many obese people are not (for example, Rodin, 1981; Rodin & Slochower, 1976). Further, they have shown that losing weight is not accompanied by a decrease in responsiveness to those cues (Rodin, Slochower, & Fleming, 1977). If a steak made an obese person's mouth water when she was obese, it would also make her mouth water after she had lost considerable weight. Rodin's work indicates that although externality may be associated with the motivation to eat, there is no one-to-one correspondence between that motivation and a person's weight. This lack of cor-

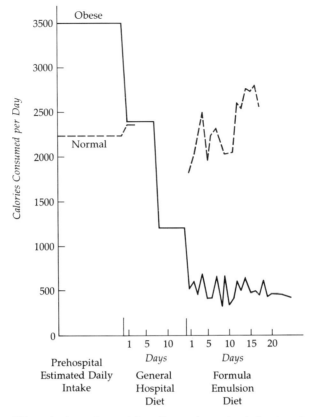

Figure 5-8. Effect of a formula emulsion diet on the eating behavior of an obese and a normal subject (Schachter, 1971a)

respondence is undoubtedly due to three factors: differences in metabolic rates, differences in self-control, and differences in availability of food, especially palatable foods.

Sensory cues, externality, and the insulin response. In a series of studies, Rodin (1981) has explored the hypothesis that such sensory cues as taste and smell are sufficient to stimulate the release of insulin in "externals." As we noted earlier, Rodin has argued that an elevated insulin level produces feelings of hunger. If, indeed, sensory cues are capable of triggering the release of insulin in externally responsive people but not in internally responsive people, then we have a mechanism that can explain why externals tend to become obese. In order to determine whether this hypothesis was correct, Rodin first determined subjects' degree of externality by using a battery of noneating measures. Next she asked the subjects not to eat anything for a period of 18 hours. When they arrived at the laboratory at noon, having eaten nothing since the previous night, a steak was in the process of being grilled. They could see it, smell it, hear the crackling sound of it. At the same time a blood sample was drawn in order to measure their insulin level. The externally responsive subjects, whether they were of normal weight or overweight, showed the greatest insulin response to the sight, smell, and sound of the grilling

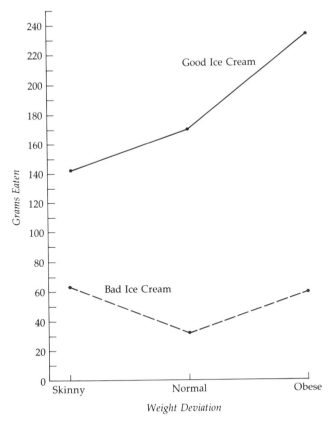

Figure 5-9. Amount of good-tasting and bad-tasting ice cream eaten by subjects of different weights (Schachter, 1971a)

steak. In another study Rodin examined whether the insulin response would increase as a function of palatability. As expected, the insulin response was greater in externally responsive subjects.

Summary
Obesity is commonly defined as weight in excess of some norm, usually by approximately 25% or more. There are several theories as to why humans tend to be overweight. Margules has argued that obesity is an adaptive mechanism gone astray: we prepare for a famine that never comes. Set-point theory suggests that we have a set point that governs our weight. This theory grows out of research that has shown that lesions in the hypothalamus can produce obesity and anorexia in animals. Boundary theory proposes that we have two boundaries, one for hunger and one for satiety. Polivy and Herman suggest that restrained eaters are people who have a very high satiety boundary and as a result tend to overeat. In order to maintain their weight, they set a cognitive boundary. If circumstances should induce them to exceed their cognitive boundary, they tend to become disinhibited eaters for a time, usually the remainder of the day. Boundary theory can also account for binge
(continued)

eating and anorexia. Internal-external theory grew out of the observation that obese people often eat in response to external cues whereas nonobese people eat in response to internal cues. Several studies have been done to show that obese people do indeed tend to respond to such things as time of day, palatability of food, and other external cues, whereas the nonobese tend to respond to internal cues. In a fascinating study, Judith Rodin has shown that the insulin response to the sight and smell of food is greater in externally responsive people than in internally responsive people.

Origins of Obesity

The inheritance factor.   In order to separate what is inherited from what is acquired through experience, it is necessary to control for either the environment or our genes. Since it is often difficult to control the environment, scientists have traditionally liked to study adopted versus natural children and identical versus fraternal twins. These studies have shown that adopted children tend to resemble their biological parents in weight far more than they resemble their adoptive parents (Stunkard et al., 1985) and that identical twins, even when reared apart, are more similar in weight than are fraternal twins or other siblings (for example, Stunkard, Foch, & Hrubec, 1985). One of the things that may be inherited is metabolism rate. A person who has a high metabolism rate tends not to become obese.

The resemblance of children to their parents in weight may be due to factors other than metabolism rate. In one study it was found that children of overweight parents not only preferred sweeter solutions but were more responsive to external cues in their environment (Milstein, 1980). In other words, they were externals.

The environmental factor.   Statistics indicate that overweight children are likely to have overweight parents (Garn & Clark, 1976). Further, there is evidence that overweight children tend to become overweight adults (Eden, 1975; Hirsch, Knittle, & Salans, 1966). Although these findings provide support for the idea that obesity may be genetically determined, there are reasons for questioning this conclusion. First, if a separate correlation is calculated between the child's weight and the weight of each parent, the child's weight tends to be more highly correlated with the mother's weight than with the father's (Garn & Clark, 1976). If the cause were purely genetic, the correlations should be equal. Second, the resemblance in weight of siblings, even identical twins, decreases in later life. The decreasing resemblance suggests that factors other than genetics must be responsible for weight patterns.

How, then, do we account for these findings? The fact that the child's weight tends to be correlated with the mother's can be accounted for by the likelihood that the mother controls to a large degree the eating behavior of her children or simply the availability of food. Because of her own tendency to overeat, for example, the mother may fill her children's plates with more food than they require or simply make food available. If they are encouraged to eat all the food on their plates or to snack, they will eventually convert the extra food into fat. If this tendency to take more food than is needed becomes a habit, it could help to explain their tendency to overeat in later life.

Another possibility is that fat mothers like to prepare appealing foods. Children who learn to eat such foods when they are hungry may learn to associate eating with certain cues. Thus foods that had a particular taste, texture, or smell would tend to elicit the eating response. The presence or availability of such foods would determine whether such a person became obese. If in later life he found himself in an environment where such foods were readily available, he would be likely to overeat.

Number of fat cells and obesity. Since the number of fat cells we have can increase but can never decrease, overeating, for whatever reason, can lead to an increase in the total number of fat cells, and the condition will stay with us throughout life. Further, since the number of fat cells a person has is a good predictor of whether or not that person will put on weight, people have concluded that the more fat cells one has, the more likely one is to become obese. In other words, we are faced with a vicious cycle: more fat cells lead to more eating and more eating leads to an increase in the number of fat cells. Until recently it was thought that fat cells multiplied only during the first few years of life. Now there is good evidence that significant weight gains in later life can also cause the number of fat cells to increase (Sjöstrom, 1980).

It follows that a child who is overfed not only will become a fat child, but will develop a propensity to become obese in later life. Of course, overfeeding in childhood is not the only factor that influences us to overeat. Rodin (1981) has pointed out, for example, that as people who are externally responsive are more likely to overeat, they therefore are more likely to develop greater numbers of fat cells. It is also possible that certain drugs that lead to overeating, such as tricyclic antidepressants, can push some people toward obesity. Even something as simple as two weeks of overeating on a cruise ship could be an important contributing factor. The point is that the effect of overeating can be irreversible if the overeating is of sufficient magnitude to stimulate the fat cells to divide. We are not yet certain of the exact conditions that cause the fat cells to divide. It appears that we can tolerate weight gains within limits. It remains to be seen what those limits are for most people.

Emotional disorders and obesity. Do we eat more when we are depressed, anxious, or stressed? At present no direct link has been established between emotional disorders and overeating. Typically depression is characterized by weight loss rather than overeating. It has been shown, however, that when a depressed state had been induced in subjects high in self-restraint, they ate significantly more than similarly depressed subjects who were low in self-restraint (Frost et al., 1982). This finding makes a great deal of sense if we assume that the ability to control eating is greater in people who have more self-control. One of the things that happens when people become depressed is that they feel they have lost control over their lives.

It has periodically been suggested that the reason some people, but not all, tend to eat more when they are emotionally upset or when they are experiencing stress is that they have been taught to eat under these conditions. If a mother tries to comfort her children with food when they are upset, for example, the child may learn to eat under these conditions. Later in life, such people turn to food just as they turned to mother in the past.

Obstacles to Dieting: Why People Can't or Won't Lose Weight

Anabolism ("caloric thrift") and catabolism ("caloric waste"). The metabolism rate tends to slow down during food deprivation (Apfelbaum, 1975; Garrow, 1978).

The deceleration of metabolism is referred to as anabolism or "caloric thrift." This mechanism is generally viewed as adaptive. If people begin to run out of food, one good way of conserving energy is to reduce one's metabolism. A large weight gain, on the other hand, is often accompanied by an acceleration of metabolism, which is referred to as catabolism or "caloric waste." In this state energy is spent more freely (Polivy and Herman, 1983). Further, overweight people tend to have higher levels of insulin than people of normal weight, a condition referred to as hyperinsulinemia (Rabinowitz & Zierler, 1962). In this condition fat storage is enhanced because insulin accelerates the conversion of sugar into fat. As we noted earlier, an excess of insulin tends to increase feelings of hunger (for example, Williams, 1960). The net effect is that fat people tend to get fatter.

While caloric thrift may be adaptive in a world where food is scarce, it comes to haunt the overweight person who decides it is time to diet. When the overweight person begins to cut down on food, the body responds with a reduced metabolism rate, thus frustrating the dieter's attempt to lose weight. To overcome this counterregulatory mechanism, the dieter must cut down still further. And again the body responds by further reducing the metabolism rate.

Increased preference for restricted or forbidden foods.   One way to make a diet more efficient is to stop eating foods high in calories. The problem with this strategy is that the more one restricts one's intake of these restricted or forbidden foods, the more one craves them (Striegel-Moore, Silberstein, & Rodin, 1986). Why should an individual have an increased desire for sweets? Polivy and Herman (1983) have suggested that the body has a memory of the amount of food it normally gets. When an individual begins to eat fewer calories, the body responds by signaling the need for more food, especially foods high in calories, which would bring the caloric intake back to normal.

Dealing with new expectations.   Some fat people acquire a variety of behaviors that center on their fatness—spending a great deal of time cooking and preparing foods, reading cookbooks, hunting out good restaurants. At the same time, they shun sports and avoid thinking or worrying about fashion; they may even take on the stereotyped "jolly fat person" style. The problem for the obese person who does lose weight is to find new activities that will help maintain the weight loss. Such people have to learn to redirect some of their energy toward things other than food. Another problem is learning how to deal with other people's assumptions that a loss of weight indicates a change in character. Since it is common in our society to view fatness as a sign of self-indulgence and inability to control oneself, people who do lose weight often find that people begin to treat them as having suddenly acquired willpower and the ability to control events. As a result they expect more of the formerly fat person—more achievement, more success, more drive. This is a tall order. Perhaps a more serious problem is the need to deal realistically with one's own expectations. Fat people tend to feel that if only they were thin, all their problems would disappear. They would be admired and respected and sought-after. They would get the job, get the raise, get the guy or the girl. When at last they really are thin and find that they still have problems—other problems, perhaps, but still problems—they wonder if a fashionable figure is worth the self-control that they did in fact exert and are still exerting. Some people decide it's easier to be fat. It has even been suggested that some people become fat in order to solve problems. A woman who finds sex distasteful, for example, may become overweight in order to avoid it. Unless this problem is treated first, it would be pointless to urge her to go on a diet.

Is There Hope for the Dieter?

In view of the many factors that work to make us gain weight and the equally numerous obstacles to losing it, is there any room for optimism? Most people working on the problem believe that the average person can be optimistic. First, there is good evidence that many of the regulatory mechanisms do work reasonably well in most individuals. In a classic study short-term obesity was induced in 15 volunteers who came close to the goal of a 25% weight increase by eating high-calorie diets. At the termination of the study all but two had returned to control values within a few weeks (Sims et al., 1968). These results, however, do not tell us how obese people can achieve normal weight; they only tell us that short-term weight gains are normally not a problem.

Behavior modification. The most popular and probably the most successful approach to weight control for the average person has been the application of the principles of learning. According to this approach, the main problem for the overweight person is to learn new patterns of eating that not only will lead to an immediate weight loss but will maintain the new weight. Many diets can result in weight loss; the problem is to keep from gaining the weight back again. "Weight Watchers," probably the most famous behavioral program, was developed out of the belief that the best way to treat overweight is to teach people new eating habits.

To illustrate this approach I have constructed a series of rules that a person in such a program might be required to follow. The rules in Practical Application 5-1 are merely logical extrapolations from the research literature on hunger and eating and are similar in some respects to rules that can be found in books on how to alter eating habits (for example, Jeffrey & Katz, 1977; Mahoney & Mahoney, 1976; Stuart, 1978). I have briefly summarized the reasons that these rules not only should lead to weight loss but should, over time, lead to a new set of eating habits that will maintain that weight loss. There is nothing magical about these rules; they simply show how we may use our current knowledge base to keep our weight under control. I should caution the reader, however, that our knowledge about dieting and weight control is still incomplete. Not all overweight people are overweight for the same reason, a point that Rodin (1981) and others have repeatedly emphasized. Nevertheless, there is a great deal of agreement that whatever the exact cause of the problem, it is important for overweight people to learn to reorganize their lives if they are to lose their unwanted weight and keep it off.

Natural Weight Control

Can people control their weight and not feel hungry by carefully selecting the foods they eat? Many people find that the effort to maintain some desired weight level is a constant battle. Not only do they feel hungry most of the time (they are restrained eaters) but they find they must avoid exposing themselves to food cues because they are prone to eat whenever they are exposed to food, especially very palatable foods. For these people life is very unnatural.

Very encouraging research suggests that it may be possible to control one's weight by carefully selecting the foods one eats at various times of the day. In a study by Spitzer (cited in Rodin, 1984) subjects were asked to drink lemon-flavored water that contained either fructose, glucose, or glucose that was made to taste as

Practical Application 5-1
Some Rules for Dieting

Rule 1: Eat in only one place and at regular times
This rule is intended to help you stop snacking by limiting the number of places where you eat and ensuring that you eat at appropriate intervals rather than by impulse. Remember that people are typically not good at monitoring their food intake and that many overweight people have become overweight because they snack. If you eat at regular times, your body will have the necessary calories and nutrients to keep you going. Eat *nothing* between meals.

Rule 2: Use small plates
Overweight people tend not only to fill their plates but to eat what is on them. Therefore, when you use a smaller plate, you tend to eat less.

Rule 3: Eat slowly
You should accomplish three things by eating slowly. First, the pleasure you get from eating will be maximized. Second, since the mouth provides feedback about the amount we have eaten, we can signal the brain that we have eaten a great deal by carefully chewing our food and making the eating process last as long as possible. Third, when we eat slowly, our digestive system has time to absorb some of the food, and this process should help to stimulate our satiety mechanism. I call this the "fondue phenomenon." A meat fondue is made at the dining table, not in the kitchen. Each diner immerses little pieces of meat, one at a time, in a pot of near-boiling oil. When one piece is eaten, another goes into the pot. The process often takes a couple of hours. People often report that they feel full long before all the meat is gone, even when the quantity of food eaten is quite small.

Rule 4: Eat in the company of others
People tend to eat slowly and to eat less when they are in the company of others. Besides, conversation tends to extend the eating time, an important factor in reducing food intake (see rule 3).

Rule 5: If you eat alone, don't read or watch television
The purpose of this rule is to help you learn to respond to internal cues as well as to help you monitor what and how much you are eating. When you are doing something else, you not only fail to monitor your intake but tend to eat quickly.
(continued)

sweet as fructose. Two and one-quarter hours later subjects were presented with a buffet containing a very large variety of foods and asked to eat whatever they liked until they were comfortably full. Subjects in both glucose conditions ate significantly more than subjects in the fructose condition. Extrapolating to what might happen if subjects ate as they had done during the experiment over the course of a year, Rodin calculated that a given individual would gain (or lose) up to 50 pounds. What mechanism is involved here? Since fructose triggers the release of much less insulin than glucose does, Rodin suggests that this may be the mech-

Rule 6: Limit the availability of fattening foods
If you can't resist cookies, candy, cake, and other high-calorie foods, limit the amounts that are available. Remember that overweight people are often externals, and the mere sight of such food can stimulate the output of insulin.

Rule 7: Allow for variety
When we eliminate from our diet certain foods that we normally eat, we often develop a craving for those foods. When the craving becomes strong, we have a tendency to eat large quantities of those foods if they are available. So if you are accustomed to eating pastas, for example, don't try to eliminate them altogether, just cut down.

Rule 8: Don't try to lose weight too fast
When we try to lose weight too fast, our body often responds with a reduced metabolism rate. This response not only interferes with our ability to lose weight but may cause problems for us when we have reached our ideal weight. Another problem with trying to lose weight very quickly is that when we fail to meet our short-term goal, we tend to give up.

Rule 9: Eat a balanced diet
The goal of dieting should be not only to lose weight but to keep that weight off. Sometimes you can lose weight very rapidly by following a diet that requires you to eliminate certain types of food. Not only do such diets often precipitate health problems but they fail to teach us how we should eat after we have reached our desired weight. The goal of dieting is simply learning to eat less while staying healthy.

Rule 10: Combine your diet with exercise
Since basal metabolism can account for two thirds of our energy expenditure, and exercise increases the BMR, exercise is useful not only for getting rid of excess fat but for maintaining our desired weight. The most effective program calls for at least 20 minutes of exercise three times a week and involves an activity that uses 300 calories and raises the heart rate to 60 or 70% of its maximum (Thompson et al., 1982). Ideal activities are running, swimming, bicycling, walking upstairs, or any other aerobic activity that induces us to take in large amounts of oxygen (oxygen is required for the "burning" of calories).

anism. Remember that there is good evidence that an elevated insulin level is associated with increased feelings of hunger. Therefore, if we are offered food when our insulin level is still relatively high, we will tend to eat more simply because our feelings of hunger are more intense at the time.

Other Approaches to Weight Control
Several other approaches to the treatment of obesity are currently being taken (Leon, 1976). Various forms of psychotherapy, including group therapy, have been

devised on the assumption that the problem has a psychological origin. Drugs, wiring the mouth shut, surgery to remove fat, and bypass surgery have also been used. Despite all these techniques, however, dieting is the most commonly accepted approach to the problem of obesity.

Summary
There is good evidence that the tendency to obesity is at least partly inherited. Twin studies show that adopted children are more likely to resemble their biological parents in weight than their adoptive parents. Since a child's weight is more likely to resemble her mother's weight than her father's, it has been argued that fat mothers probably have fat children because in a variety of ways they encourage their children not only to eat but to eat foods high in calories. There is also the question of the number of fat cells in the body. Until recently it was thought that fat cells multiplied only during the first few years of life, but it is now believed that they can multiply (within limits) at any time. The more fat cells you have, the more you tend to eat; the more you eat, the more fat cells you will have.

There are several obstacles to dieting. First, the metabolism rate tends to slow down when the body is deprived of food, thereby frustrating the dieter's attempt to lose weight. Second, dieting often produces a craving for restricted foods, often high-calorie foods. Third, dieting is often accompanied by a set of new expectations, both the dieter's own and those of other people.

Despite all the obstacles, there is hope for the dieter. One of the most successful approaches to weight loss, behavior modification, has grown out of learning theory. Also, there is growing evidence that as we learn more about the characteristics of certain foods, we can learn to control our weight "naturally" by carefully selecting what we eat. Foods that do not produce a high insulin response, such as fruits, may reduce the constant feelings of hunger that some dieters experience.

Disturbed Eating Patterns

Binging
Binging is a session of extreme overeating in which the individual typically eats until the stomach can tolerate no more food. It is a fairly prevalent syndrome that occurs among the overweight, the underweight, and people of normal weight (Crowther, Lingswiler, & Stephens, 1984). Typically a binge episode lasts less than two hours, according to the third edition of the *Diagnostic and Statistical Manual* (*DSM-III*, 1980) of the American Psychiatric Association. Surveys of college populations have found self-reported binging to be quite high, with incidence levels ranging from 13% to 67% (Halmi, Falk, & Schwartz, 1981; Hawkins & Clements, 1980; Olmstead & Garner, 1982). The reason for the great variability in the rates found is probably that what some people consider a binge, others call simply pigging out.

Obesity, dieting, and binging.   Overweight people tend to binge (Loro & Orleans, 1981). The question is why they have this tendency. Is it something they are born with, such as a faulty satiety mechanism, or is it acquired? There is considerable evidence that the tendency is acquired. It has been shown, for example, that rats who have been deprived of food develop a tendency to overeat, especially if they are presented with palatable foods (Coscina & Dixon, 1983). Another piece of compelling evidence comes from the work of Ancel Keys and his associates (1950). During World War II a group of conscientious objectors volunteered to serve in an experiment on the effects of semistarvation on behavior. These men starved themselves down to 74% of their original body weight. When unlimited food was later made available, they exhibited a tendency to binge.

Polivy and Herman (1985) have argued that dieting may indeed be one of the factors that leads to binging. The tendency to binge, they suggest, may represent the body's attempt to restore one's weight to a level that is more biologically appropriate. If there is a set point for weight, as Nisbett (1972) and others have argued, then even people whose weight is well above normal may tend to binge when their weight drops below set point as the result of dieting. As Polivy and Herman (1985) point out, the precise mechanism for this tendency has not yet been identified. Perhaps, as they suggest, chemical changes in the body result in increased hunger, increased sensitivity to food, and/or lowered inhibitions. Polivy and Herman favor the interpretation that overeating is linked to lowered inhibitions. As we noted earlier, their research has suggested that when dieters (restrained eaters) exceed their cognitive boundary, they tend to overeat.

Bulimia

Definition and prevalence. Bulimia is often referred to as the binge-purge syndrome. People who are bulimic periodically eat so much that they experience abdominal pain. Then they force themselves to vomit or take a laxative to rid themselves of the food; after it is gone, they often sleep (Schlesier-Stropp, 1984). Bulimia has been referred to as the "secretive syndrome." People who are bulimic tend to plan these episodes to ensure that they will not be discovered and rarely share their secret with other people (Herzog, 1982a). Bulimics tend to be preoccupied with food and the urge to eat. At the same time, they are concerned with their weight and often alternate between dieting and gorging (Schlesier-Stropp, 1984).

While binging may be fairly prevalent, bulimia, as defined by *DSM-III*, is not. Stangler and Printz (1980) found that 3.8% of a sample of 500 students could be considered bulimics by *DSM-III* criteria. Since this study represented only individuals who had sought treatment for an eating disorder, the researchers concluded that their estimate was very conservative. Another survey of 355 students found that 13% met the criteria of bulimia (Halmi, Falk, & Schwartz, 1981). The diagnostic criteria for bulimia are presented in Table 5-3.

Table 5-3. Criteria for a diagnosis of bulimia

Recurrent episodes of binge eating

At least three of the following:
  Consumption of high-caloric, easily ingested food during a binge
  Termination of binge by abdominal pain, sleep, or self-induced vomiting
  Inconspicuous eating during binge
  Repeated attempts to lose weight
  Frequent weight fluctuation greater than 10 pounds

Awareness of abnormal eating pattern and fear of not being able to stop eating voluntarily

Depressed mood after binges

Cause not anorexia nervosa or any physical disorder

Adapted from *DSM-III.*

Sex, age, race, and family history.   It seems fairly clear that bulimia is a woman's disease. It has been suggested that about 90% of all bulimics are women (see Striegel-Moore, Silberstein, & Rodin, 1986). Most studies have found bulimics to be in their 20s—the mean age is between 21 and 25.3—and white (Schlesier-Stropp, 1984). Self-report data indicate that bulimics' families have a high incidence of alcoholism and weight problems (for example, Herzog, 1982b).

Psychological factors.   Bulimics tend to be characterized by depression and anxiety (Fairborn & Cooper, 1982; Herzog, 1982b), which may be linked to their perceived lack of control in regulating their food intake. It has been suggested, for example, that eating, especially binge eating, elicits anxiety and that vomiting reduces it (Rosen & Leitenberg, 1982). (In Chapter 11 we will examine in more detail the link between feelings of lack of control and depression.) Further, it appears that bulimics tend to suffer a great deal of guilt, shame, and self-contempt following a binge (see Schlesier-Stropp, 1984). If the bulimic, having binged, is prevented from vomiting by an unexpected interruption, she feels extreme anxiety together with overwhelming guilt and self-contempt. Purging may be a kind of safety valve that helps the bulimic to deal with her tendency to binge (her lack of self-control).

Treatment.   The most appropriate treatment for the bulimic is still an open question. Since cognitions appear to play an important role in this disorder (bulimics are obsessed with thoughts of weight, food, eating, and ridding themselves of food they have eaten), cognitive therapy seems an obvious treatment model. Cognitive therapy attempts to change the bulimic's maladaptive thoughts about such things as ideal body image and self-control without focusing on the vomiting. The need to vomit, it is assumed, will diminish once the individual has gained control of the eating process (Fairborn, 1980, 1981). Behavior therapy has focused more on breaking the link between the anxiety produced by eating and the need to vomit (Rosen & Leitenberg, 1982). The data available are still insufficient to permit evaluation of the adequacy of this approach.

Anorexia Nervosa

Anorexia is typically considered an eating disorder. It has been argued, however, that the drive to be thinner is secondary to a need for control and/or fears about the consequences of achieving a mature shape. The individual pursues thinness in order to feel a sense of mastery over his or her body (Garfinkel & Garner, 1982). Paul Garfinkel and David Garner have suggested that the most appropriate clinical diagnostic criteria for anorexia nervosa are those arrived at by the Pathology of Eating Group (Garrow et al., 1975). These criteria, presented in Table 5-4, require not only that the individual show signs of significant weight loss but other symptoms as well.

The second main symptom after weight loss is amenorrhea (absence of menstruation) in women and loss of sex drive in males. Amenorrhea is very closely linked to anorexia. In fact, 100% incidences have been found in a number of studies in which amenorrhea was not a requirement for diagnosis of anorexia (for example, Berkman, 1948; Bruch, 1973; Warren & Vandewiele, 1973). Since amenorrhea may precede visible weight loss by several years, it seems unlikely that this symptom is due to weight loss or to any associated state of malnutrition (Danowski et al., 1972).

Table 5-4. Criteria for a diagnosis of anorexia nervosa (Garfinkel & Garner, 1982)

Self-inflicted severe loss of weight, using one or more of the following devices:
  Avoidance of foods considered to be "fattening" (especially carbohydrate-containing foods)
  Self-induced vomiting
  Abuse of purgatives
  Excessive exercise

A secondary endocrine disorder of the hypothalamic anterior pituitary gonadal axis manifest in the female as amenorrhea and in the male by a diminution of sexual interest and activity

A psychological disorder that has as its central theme a morbid fear of being unable to control eating and hence becoming too fat

---

The third symptom is the presence of a psychological disorder characterized by fear of losing control and becoming fat. While all of us from time to time may be concerned about losing control, such as when we "pig out," anorexics are obsessed with this fear and spend a great deal of time and effort controlling anything related to eating. They are inclined, for example, to use appetite suppressants, such as amphetamines and other diet pills, or drink large quantities of fluid in order to feel full (Garfinkel & Garner, 1982).

Biological and emotional factors.   Several researchers have found links between anorexia and disturbances in the endocrine system (such as Brown, 1983; Gardiner, Martin, & Jukier, 1983). It has been suggested that the origins of these disorders may be linked to disturbances in the hypothalamic–pituitary–adrenal axis. It has been shown, for example, that the hypothalamic–pituitary–adrenal axis is activated for anorexia and that anorexics' adrenals are unusually responsive (Weiner & Katz, 1983). Why this is true is still not known.

In order to better understand the biological side of anorexia, various researchers have used animals to explore some of the possible biological mechanisms. The animal research has shown, among other things, that there are several regulatory mechanisms in the brain for food intake. Further, such research has shown that food deprivation has dramatic effects on neurochemical processes, specifically noradrenergic activity. The implication is that when people begin to deprive themselves of food, such as when they diet, they may produce a disturbance in certain neurochemical processes that are important in maintaining normal patterns of eating. The disturbance may then set in motion the oscillatory feeding pattern that characterizes anorexics and bulimics (Leibowitz, 1983). In other words, normal eating depends on the complementary activity of different systems in the brain. When one or more of those systems is disturbed various abnormal patterns of eating result.

Inasmuch as adrenal activity was found to be considerably higher in a group of anorexia nervosa patients than in a group of control subjects, it has been suggested that anorexia may be an affective disorder (Walsh et al., 1978). In another study (Cantwell et al., 1977), not only were depressive symptoms evident before and after recovery, but a history of affective disorders was common in mothers of anorexia nervosa patients. Further, levels of MHPG (3-methoxy-4-hydroxyphenylglycol), a major metabolite (metabolic product) of brain norepinephrine, were found to be significantly lower in anorexia nervosa patients than in controls (Halmi et al., 1978). An increase in urinary MHPG concentration after treatment was correlated with a decrease in depressive symptoms even though the patients did not carry a primary diagnosis of depression. It is not clear whether anorexia nervosa was caused by the lowered catecholamine level or whether anorexia produced this lowered level. It is only because Dennis Cantwell and his colleagues (1977) found some evidence of a family history of affective disorders that there is reason to argue that anorexia nervosa may be an affective disorder resulting from differences in the standing levels of certain catecholamines.

Learned factors.   It has been suggested that the North American preoccupation with slimness may be a cause of anorexia nervosa, at least in its milder forms (Bliss & Branch, 1960; Bruch, 1973). According to this view, *any* fat may be perceived as excessive, and this perception may lead to a pattern of constant and excessive dieting. The incidence of anorexia nervosa tends to be greater in middle and upper socioeconomic groups (for example, Bruch, 1973; Dally, 1969) and in college and university populations (Bemis, 1978). Because such groups are typically concerned with slimness, the learned origin of anorexia nervosa is a tenable position. The best evidence to support the learning model, however, comes from research showing that behavior modification techniques can produce substantial weight gains (for example, Bhanji & Thompson, 1974; Halmi, Powers, & Cunningham, 1975). Bruch, however, has argued that although behavior modification techniques may produce gains, such techniques often fail to get at the primary cause. In a follow-up study of anorexia nervosa patients who had been "successfully" treated by behavior modification, Bruch (1975) found that some of them had undergone physical and emotional deterioration that sometimes included suicidal behavior. Thus there is evidence that learning alone is not responsible for anorexia nervosa.

Cognitive factors.   Anorexia nervosa patients almost always have distorted body images: they tend to overestimate their weight even when they have become extremely emaciated (for example, Askevold, 1975; Ben-Tovim, Whitehead, & Crisp, 1979; Crisp & Kalucy, 1974; Garfinkel et al., 1978; Gomez & Dally, 1980; Slade & Russell, 1973). Their failure to recognize their emaciation is difficult to explain in view of the fact that the patients have frequent opportunities to see their own reflections and the reactions of other people to them. Despite an abundance of evidence to the contrary, they continue to maintain that they are either normal or overweight. Such irrational behavior has led many people to conclude that these patients are suffering from a profound psychological disturbance.

Considerable evidence indicates that anorexia nervosa may be due, at least in part, to disturbed family relationships. Numerous reports depict mothers of anorexics as dominant and intrusive (for example, Bruch, 1973; Goodsitt, 1974; Katz, 1975). These and other observations have led to the argument that the disorder grows out of a desperate struggle for self-determination. According to this view, the anorexic's refusal to eat is her means of asserting control over one important area of her life (Bruch, 1973, 1975). Consistent with this view is the finding that the ego strength of anorexics is low (Wingate & Christie, 1978). Salvador Minuchin and his colleagues have observed that families of children who suffer from anorexia nervosa, and other psychosomatic disorders as well, share a general pattern of interaction characterized by overinvolvement, overprotectiveness, rigidity, and poor conflict resolution (Rosman, Minuchin, & Liebman, 1975). Such observations have led these researchers to view anorexia nervosa as an interpersonal problem rather than an individual problem (Minuchin et al., 1978). They have suggested that the reason anorexia nervosa develops when family relationships are disturbed is that the family comes together as a unit primarily at mealtimes. For this reason these researchers have proposed a technique called the "family therapy lunch session" to help restructure the interactions that tend to occur when the family members sit down together for meals (for example, Liebman, Minuchin, & Baker, 1974; Minuchin, 1974; Minuchin et al., 1978; Rosman, Minuchin, & Liebman, 1975).

Not all researchers agree that the problem arises from a dominant mother or a pathological family organization (for example, Katz, 1975; Sours, 1974), and some have argued that no consistent pattern is to be found among the families of anorexics (for example, Bliss & Branch, 1960; Dally, 1969).

Prognosis.   Whatever the exact origins of anorexia nervosa, the prognosis for complete recovery is not good. It is likely, according to some authors' estimates, that 25 to 50% of patients will experience a recurrence of the symptoms after successful treatment (Moldofsky & Garfinkel, 1974) and as many as 38% will require readmission for anorexia nervosa within two years (Dally, 1969). These figures emphasize the chronic nature of the disease.

Sociocultural Variables in Bulimia and Anorexia Nervosa

Throughout our society women are told that thin is in. Fashion magazines link beauty with thinness. Studies of bulimics and anorexics yield an abundance of evidence that they are motivated to diet by the belief that fat is ugly and must be gotten rid of. One study found that by age 13, 80% of girls (but only 10% of boys) have already been on weight-loss diets (Hawkins, Turell, & Jackson, 1983).

Slenderness is also linked to femininity. Several studies have supported the observation that physically attractive women tend to be perceived as more feminine than unattractive women (for example, Unger, 1985; Heilman & Saruwatari, 1979). And what does that ideal woman look like? She is a thin, nonathletic type (Guy, Rankin, & Norvell, 1980). The ideal man, in contrast, is muscular and athletic. In view of such widely held perceptions, it is not surprising that many women become obsessed by thinness.

To be feminine is to behave in certain stereotyped ways. Feminine women are presumed to eat sparingly. When they eat heartily, others see their behavior as masculine (Chaiken & Pliner, 1984). But not all women ascribe to the stereotyped view of women. Are these women just as vulnerable? Various people have suggested that being a feminist or simply being ambitious does not free the average woman from pursuit of a thin figure. An image of femininity may give a woman a competitive edge (Brownmiller, 1984). Also, as we have noted, failure to control one's weight is often viewed as indicating a lack of control or willpower. It is not to the advantage of the ambitious woman to be viewed as weak-willed and self-indulgent. It has been suggested that weight loss in our society is often viewed as a sign of maturity (Steele, 1980), and therefore a concern with dieting may be a symbol both to oneself and to others that one is indeed mature. Finally, there is growing evidence that self-esteem is linked to body image. Because society says that women should be thin, the achievement of thinness can be a source of self-esteem.

It is not easy, however, to achieve the level of thinness that fashion magazines set as the standard if one has a set point well above the level that permits a person to be naturally thin. The consequences may be binging or obesity. On the other hand, an attempt to achieve acceptance, maturity, and femininity by becoming thin may result in anorexia nervosa.

What is the solution? Since bulimia and anorexia nervosa seem to be related to our cultural values or practices, the real solution lies in a swing of the cultural pendulum. Values change. People not yet old can remember when women as thin as today's ideal were spurned as "too skinny." Such women tried as desperately to gain weight as contemporary women try to lose it. The pendulum will swing back one day. It always does.

Summary

Binging, or periodic bouts of overeating, is a fairly prevalent syndrome that occurs among people who are overweight, underweight, and of normal weight. There is considerable evidence that binging is an acquired syndrome. One of the antecedents of binging is prior deprivation. Polivy and Herman suggest that it may represent the body's attempt to restore weight to a point that is more biologically appropriate. Bulimia, a condition characterized by episodes of binging followed by purging, is now considered to be a clinical eating disorder. There is good evidence that it is an acquired syndrome. It is found predominantly in young white women whose families have a history of alcoholism and weight disorders. Bulimics tend to experience both anxiety and depression. Cognitive therapy has proved to be effective with some bulimics.

A weight loss of about 25% is one of the primary criteria for a diagnosis of anorexia nervosa. The disorder occurs mainly in adolescent girls and is often accompanied by amenorrhea (absence of menstruation). It has been suggested that the symptoms may be due to a malfunction of the hypothalamus or a below-normal level of catecholamines. Because anorexia nervosa is more common among middle and upper socioeconomic groups, there is good reason to believe that the disorder has a learned component. The fact that anorexics almost always have a disturbed body image has led to the belief that such patients are suffering from a cognitive disorder. One group of researchers has argued that the disorder is the result of disturbed family relationships.

In view of the fact that our society tends to equate thinness with beauty and femininity, it is not surprising that many women strive to achieve a thin figure. Given that there are serious consequences associated with trying to be thin, the question is whether or not the best solution might be to change society's attitudes.

Main Points

1. The carbohydrates, fats, and proteins in foods are converted into glucose, a more usable form of energy.
2. Insulin, secreted by the pancreas, plays an important role in the conversion of glucose into energy.
3. Unused glucose is converted into fat and stored in the adipose tissues.
4. Some of the proteins are converted into amino acid, which is important in the rebuilding of muscle and the manufacture of essential chemicals.
5. According to the glucose theory of hunger, hunger is due to lowered glucose levels.
6. According to the fatty acid theory of hunger, when we begin to make use of stored fat, we become hungry.
7. It has been suggested that we become hungry when the blood and body temperatures begin to fall.
8. Receptors in the brain and the gastrointestinal tract provide feedback about when to stop eating.

9. There is no evidence that humans are equipped at birth to select a balanced diet.
10. Animals and humans tend to avoid foods that have made them sick.
11. About two-thirds of our energy expenditure is due to basal metabolism rate and one-third to exercise.
12. Basal metabolism rate decreases from birth until about age 20, when it tends to level off.
13. There are large individual differences in basal metabolism rate.
14. Certain foods, as well as dieting, can lower the metabolism rate.
15. Obesity is defined as weight about 25% or more in excess of normal.
16. According to Margules, the tendency to store fat is an adaptive mechanism that evolved to prepare us for periodic famines. Obesity, therefore, follows from the fact that we no longer have to endure famines.
17. Lesions in the ventromedial nuclei of the hypothalamus lead to overeating, which leads to obesity.
18. Lesions in the lateral hypothalamus cause the individual to reduce food intake.
19. Set-point theory suggests that the hypothalamus sets our weight.
20. Boundary theory proposes that two separate mechanisms control our eating, one for hunger and one for satiety.
21. Dieters tend to be restrained eaters; people who often feel hungry think a great deal about food and find it necessary constantly (and consciously) to control their food intake. It has been suggested that in order to control their weight, they set a "cognitive boundary."
22. Preloading studies have shown that when this "cognitive boundary" has been overstepped, restrained eaters tend to become disinhibited eaters.
23. Internal-external theory suggests that one of the reasons people become overweight is that their food intake is controlled by external cues, such as the sight and smell of food, rather than by internal cues, such as stomach contractions, the glucose level, or other internal mechanisms.
24. Externals show an increase in insulin output when palatable foods are available.
25. Twin studies indicate that genetics plays an important role in overweight.
26. Environmental factors also play an important role in overweight.
27. A child's weight tends to be correlated more highly with the weight of the mother than with that of the father. This asymmetrical correlation, combined with the fact that the mother tends to be the person who controls the availability of food, has led to the assertion that obesity may be due in part to the availability of food.
28. The number of fat cells is a good predictor of whether or not a person will put on weight.
29. Metabolism tends to slow down during deprivation (anabolism).
30. Metabolism tends to increase after weight gain (catabolism).
31. Increased desire for forbidden or restricted foods often accompanies weight loss.
32. People often spontaneously develop new expectations in regard to people who are successful at dieting, as do the dieters themselves.
33. Behavior modification has been used to help people lose weight. This approach focuses on helping people to modify their eating habits.
34. There is some evidence that careful selection of the foods one eats can result in "natural" weight control.
35. While binging is fairly prevalent in our society, the condition of bulimia (binging and purging) is less so.

36. Anorexia nervosa is primarily a disorder of young white women.
37. In addition to weight loss of at least 25%, amenorrhea (absence of menstruation) is a major criterion for a diagnosis of anorexia nervosa.
38. The profound distortion of body image that accompanies anorexia nervosa has led people to argue that this disorder reflects a psychological disturbance of some magnitude.
39. There is considerable evidence that the family relations of anorexia nervosa patients are disturbed.
40. The prognosis for permanent cure of anorexia is poor.
41. North America's preoccupation with thinness has been suggested as a major determining factor in both bulimia and anorexia nervosa.

The Sex Motive, Sexual Behavior, and Gender Differences

Why is sex not confined to periods of female fertility in humans, as it is in other animals?

Do men have a stronger sex drive than women?

What is it about a new female that arouses the male sex drive?

How do males and females of all species signal each other that they are interested in sex?

What role do sex hormones play in arousing and directing sexual behavior?

What role does learning play in sexual behavior?

Why are some people more interested in sex than others? Do they enjoy sex more? If so, why?

What leads people to fall in love suddenly or gradually?

How do men and women differ in such things as abilities, interests, and self-esteem?

Where do these differences come from? Are they learned or are they by-products of the sex hormones?

Sex from an Evolutionary Perspective: Did Sex Evolve Only for Reproduction?

From a purely biological point of view, the sex drive serves to ensure that a species will reproduce and therefore survive. For most species, sexual behavior is confined to those relatively brief periods when it is likely to result in fertilization of the egg. The female rat or dog, for example, will accept the advances of the male only when she is in estrus (heat). The male rat or dog appears to be interested in sex only when the female is in estrus; during estrus the female emits a particular odor that is a releasing stimulus for male sexual behavior. Consequently, sexual behavior occurs only at certain times that coincide with fertility in the female.

Although most animals' sexual behavior coincides with the female's fertility, humans engage in sexual intercourse at times when it is unlikely to result in fertilization. Exactly why humans are so different from other animals is not altogether clear. Desmond Morris (1969) has argued that human sexual behavior not only serves to ensure the survival of the species but helps maintain "pair bonding" (attachment between a couple). He argues that pair bonding emerged in humans for two basic reasons. First, it allowed the male to leave the female (to obtain food) without having to fear that he would lose her to another male. Second, the pair bond is important for rearing offspring. Because the human is very dependent and not fully developed at birth, both parents are required to share in the rearing process. Morris argues that if the pair bond is to be maintained, it must entail a very strong motive or reward. He proposes that the sexual responses have emerged in humans to maintain the pair bond. The sensory experience of humans, unlike that of other species, is not confined to the period of fertility. This factor is important because it increases the frequency of reward and thereby increases the likelihood that the pair bond will be maintained.

Even if Morris's reasons are not altogether correct, an abundance of data show that sexual behavior is a highly rewarding, shared sensory experience for humans. William Masters and Virginia Johnson (1975) have called it "the pleasure bond." As we discuss the nature of the sensory system associated with sexual behavior, it will become clear why sexual behavior is one of the most intense and satisfying sensory experiences known and, further, why it is a shared sensory experience.

The Question of the Female Orgasm

While the male members of many species have orgasms, it has been suggested that only the human female has orgasms (Symons, 1979), although some data indicate that the females of some of the higher primate species may occasionally have orgasms as well (Goldfoot et al., 1980). Once again the question arises as to why this difference between humans and other species arose. Perhaps, as Desmond Morris has noted, it serves to promote pair bonding.

It is interesting to note that it is only fairly recently (during the last 30 to 40 years or so) that the scientific community has agreed that women do indeed have orgasms. The reason it has taken so long for some people to recognize what may seem obvious may be related to the great variability of orgasm in the human female. Some women (20–40%) indicate that they "always" experience orgasm during intercourse, while some (5–10%) indicate they never do (Masters & Johnson, 1966; Symons, 1979). Those who occasionally experience orgasm during intercourse indicate they do so only if their partner stimulates their clitoris. Not surprisingly, it has been found that masturbation is a more reliable technique for producing orgasm than any other sexual behavior.

Morgan's theory.   If the orgasm evolved for the purpose of enhancing pair bonding, then why is it so unreliable? Elaine Morgan (1972) has argued that the female anatomy evolved to be stimulated when the penis entered from the rear. In the course of evolution, humans assumed an upright position that eventually led to the front-entry sex position. In this position the woman no longer experienced vaginal orgasm on a regular basis, and the ability to experience vaginal orgasm began to atrophy. To compensate for this loss, women began to develop clitoral orgasm. As this transition is still in progress, women may now experience both types of orgasm. (Note that there is a distinction between vaginal orgasm and clitoral orgasm.)

Symons's theory.   Symons (1979) has argued that the female orgasm is simply a by-product of the male orgasm. That is, as the male orgasm evolved to ensure the continuation of the species, it came to be manifested in both sexes. Because of their anatomical differences, however, the orgasm tends to be more reliable in men than in women.

Do Men Have a Stronger Sex Drive Than Women?

Various people have argued that men have a stronger sex drive than women (Hoyenga & Hoyenga, 1979). Evidence offered in support of this assertion comes from analysis of such things as the frequency and variety of male versus female sexual behavior (Green, 1980; Hoyenga & Hoyenga, 1979; Money, 1980). Such analyses have indicated that men are more sexually active than women, engage in more premarital sex, have more sexual partners, have more extramarital affairs, and tend to engage in more varied forms of sexual behavior. Why is this true?

The sociobiological view.   According to the sociobiologists, all species are motivated to ensure the survival of their genes in future generations (Barash, 1977; Freedman, 1979; Wilson, 1975). The best strategy for males, according to the sociobiologists, is to produce as many offspring as possible. It follows that any receptive female will stimulate the male to engage in intercourse. The human female has a more difficult task. As she is the one left with the responsibility of raising the offspring, her investment in a sexual encounter is greater than the male's. It is to her advantage, according to the sociobiologists, to be more selective. Rather than mate with any male, she gains an advantage by selecting one who is likely to produce strong and healthy offspring and to stay with her to help raise them. From the sociobiological perspective, it is important to remember that if one's genes are to live on in future generations, the offspring must survive and reproduce in their turn. A male could simply leave this responsibility to the female (confident that she will do her best to ensure that the offspring will reach maturity and reproduce so that her own genes will survive) or participate in the raising of the offspring. While a monogamous relationship can help to ensure the survival of the offspring, the question is whether this is an optimal strategy for the male. From a sociobiological point of view, it generally is not. One solution is for the male to have concurrent polygamous relationships (with multiple wives, concubines, or occasional extramarital partners). Another solution is to have serial monogamous relationships (that is, divorce and remarriage). Both of these solutions can also benefit the female. It is interesting to note that about 75% of human societies, past and present, have been polygamous (Symons, 1979; Lovejoy, 1981).

The Coolidge effect.   After a male has engaged in intercourse with a female, a substantial period of latency generally follows, during which he is not interested in initiating intercourse with the same female again. If, however, a new female is introduced, the period of latency is relatively short (Bermant & Davidson, 1974). This and similar observations have led to the suggestion that sexual motivation can be restored in the male simply by the introduction of a new or novel female. The reason for calling this the "Coolidge effect" grows out of a story attributed to Calvin Coolidge. It seems that President Coolidge and his wife were being escorted separately on a tour of an experimental farm. Mrs. Coolidge was astonished to learn that though the henhouse held dozens of hens, there was only one rooster. "One is all we need," her guide assured her. "He can keep going all day." Mrs. Coolidge, a glint in her eye, said to an aide, "Go tell the president about that rooster." The aide did as she asked. The president thought a moment, then said, "He doesn't have the same hen every time, does he?" No, the aide agreed, he had dozens. "Tell that to Mrs. Coolidge," said the president.

The Coolidge effect is consistent with sociobiologists' view of male behavior. In order to ensure that his genes will be carried on in future generations, a male should engage in intercourse with as many females as possible. He should not, according to the sociobiological view, pass up any opportunity to fulfill that biological imperative. There is little point, on the other hand, of having sex with a female with whom he has very recently mated, as she is either already pregnant or unable to conceive at the moment.

It has been noted that the human penis is large in relation to the size of the body, at least in comparison with the chimpanzee (Short, 1980). It has been suggested that the large penis evolved to increase the male's attractiveness to the female. C. Owen Lovejoy has gone so far as to suggest that such distinctive features as penile development, head and facial hair, and other striking differences in the appearance of males and females make the human male the most "adorned" primate (Lovejoy, 1981).

Signals for sexual behavior.   Many species respond to a very specific stimulus that acts as a signal for sexual behavior. For rats, dogs, and a number of other animals, an odor given off by the female is the primary signal that she is receptive. Males become aroused by this odor and initiate a sexual approach to the female. A wide variety of male birds show special behavior patterns to attract the female, such as displaying their feathers or hanging upside down from a tree (Eibl-Eibesfeldt, 1975). Some male fish carry releaser stimuli—usually color patches—on their fins and display them by spreading these fins (Eibl-Eibesfeldt, 1975). The female primate will indicate receptivity by displaying her genitals to the male while standing in a sexually receptive position.

The fact that a specific stimulus often elicits sexual behavior in animals seems to indicate that the behavior is more or less prewired. It should be noted, however, that although the sexual behavior of some animals is triggered at certain times by specific (releasing) stimuli, the sexual behavior of other animals is not tied so closely to such stimuli.

The ethological position of Desmond Morris.   Morris (1969) has taken the ethological position that human sexual behavior, too, is released by certain stimuli. He suggests that humans, like other primates, are particularly aroused by the genitals of the opposite sex. Curiously, he notes, humans feel compelled to hide their genitals from all members of the other sex except their sex partners. Morris suggests that this almost universal practice among humans reflects an attempt to avoid arousing any member of the other sex except the pair-bond partner, and thereby to preserve the pair bonding that is such an important part of human evolution.

The female breasts appear to be another primary sex signal. Morris (1969) notes that the breast as sex signal is unique to the human species. The breasts of most mammals are virtually nonexistent except when the female is lactating (which is a poor time to emit sex signals, as conception is unlikely). Even during lactation, the breasts of most primates do not take on the rounded shape of the human female breast. Morris argues that the protruding breasts have emerged as a sex signal in the human female because the upright posture of humans tends to obscure the female genitals. Thus, in order to attract males, the female had to develop a more prominent sex signal that could readily be displayed in the upright posture. To this end the breast emerged as a signal.

The female breast has, of course, become highly commercialized in our society. Magazines and films have presented the female breasts in a wide variety of ways in order to sell magazines and films. Women seem to be well aware that their breasts are important and often go to great lengths to display them, pad them, or flatten them, depending on whether they want to entice men, excite them, or avoid their advances.

Elaine Morgan's position.   Morgan (1972) has challenged Morris's argument about the female breasts. She argues that it is equally plausible to assume that the shape of women's breasts serves a function in the feeding of infants: the protruding breast came about because, at one point in our evolutionary history (when we were water mammals), this shape helped the infant to find its food supply. Although she apologizes for the analogy, she notes that the breast of the sea cow has a similar protruding shape, which she argues helps the infant to feed.

Although it could be argued that current research on pornography tends to support Morris, an abundance of research suggests that his argument is too simplistic. It is not that Morris is necessarily wrong, simply that the human sexual response encompasses much more than his hypothesis can explain.

Summary

While the males of many species have orgasms, among females the orgasm is unique to humans and possibly a few of the primates. Morris and Morgan have argued that the female orgasm has evolved to facilitate pair bonding. Symons has argued that it is simply a by-product of the male orgasm.

Various researchers have pointed to the greater promiscuity of males as evidence that males have a stronger sex drive than females. According to the sociobiologists, it is important for the male to impregnate as many females as possible. Experimental evidence in regard to the Coolidge effect is consistent with the sociobiological view. According to the ethologists, sexual behavior in humans and other species is "released" by species-specific releasing stimuli. In the case of humans, the strongest of those releasers is the sight of the genitals of the opposite sex.

The Biological Component

The Sex Hormones

The most important thing to consider in regard to the sex motive is the sex hormones. Sex hormones play an important role not only in the development of the sex organs but in motivating and organizing adult sexual behavior.

Three major categories.   The major category of hormones that govern male sexual behavior consists of androgens. The most important of the androgens is testosterone. The two main categories of hormones that govern female sexual behavior consist of estrogens and progestins. The major estrogen is estradiol and the major progestin is progesterone. Though we speak of androgens as a "male" sex hormone, and of estrogens and progestins as "female" sex hormones, this distinction is not entirely accurate. Androgens can be converted into estrogens and progestins, just as progestins can be converted into androgens. Estrogens and progestins, then, circulate in the blood of men as well as women, and androgens circulate in the blood of women (Hoyenga & Hoyenga, 1979). Estrogen levels in males have been found to range from 2% to 30% of the level found in females, while the androgen levels in females has been found to range from 6% to 30% of the level found in males (Money, 1980). The main difference between the sexes, therefore, is simply the degrees of concentration of these hormones. One reason that the range is so large is the fact that the levels of all hormones change constantly. As we shall see, both internal and external factors can dramatically alter their levels.

Origins of the sex hormones.   The sex hormones are produced by the adrenal glands and the gonads. The male gonads are the testes and the female gonads are the ovaries. The male gonads produce mainly androgens, whereas the ovaries produce mainly estrogens and progestins. The adrenal glands produce mainly androgen. It has been estimated that about half of the androgen found in females is produced by the adrenal glands and about half by the ovaries.

The amount of each sex hormone that is present at any given moment is governed by the pituitary gland, which is ultimately controlled by the hypothalamus. The pituitary releases as many as ten hormones that act in various ways to excite, inhibit, and generally modulate the complex patterns involved in the arousal and direction of the sexual response (Whalen, 1976). Most research has focused on the two gonadotropic hormones: FSH (follicle-stimulating hormone), which induces maturation of the ovarian follicles in the female and stimulates production of sperm in the male, and LH (luteinizing hormone), which induces ovulation in the female and stimulates the output of androgen by the testes of the male. Androgen influences the mating response of male animals and is generally regarded as one of the hormones that governs the arousal of sexual interest in the human male.

Androgen is produced more or less continuously in males. The amount produced increases suddenly in early adolescence (thus accounting to a large degree for the sudden awakening of sexual interest in adolescent boys) and declines gradually through adulthood and old age.

The female hormones, in contrast, are produced in accordance with a 28-day cycle that is linked to the production of the egg. It should be noted that the ovaries have a dual function: they produce both egg cells and hormones. The beginning of a cycle is initiated by an anterior-pituitary hormone, follicle-stimulating hormone, which stimulates an ovarian follicle—an ovum and the surrounding cells— to grow. This growth continues for half the cycle. Because it is the follicle cells that secrete the hormone estrogen, the amount of estrogen produced increases with the growth of the follicle. About halfway through the cycle, the ovum breaks through the wall of the follicle and the ovary. This phenomenon is called "ovulation," and the few days surrounding it are the period of the cycle when the female is fertile (that is, the ovum is capable of being fertilized by the male spermatozoa). In many lower animals, the female is at her peak of receptivity at this time, and therefore copulation generally occurs at the point in the cycle when conception is most likely. It appears on the basis of research in which estrogen has been injected at various times in the cycle that estrogen is responsible for female receptivity. Since the production of estrogen corresponds to the development of the ovum, it is no accident that the female is receptive when conception is most likely. Once the ovum breaks through the wall of the follicle and the ovary, estrogen production diminishes quickly, but it continues to circulate in the bloodstream for some time.

In humans, ovulation ceases between ages 40 and 50, on the average. Simultaneously, of course, estrogen production dwindles. This change in physiological functioning is called "menopause." Although estrogen is closely tied to receptivity in lower animals, it does not appear to be tied to receptivity in humans. Many women do report a decline in sexual interest at 40–50 years, but just as many report no decline or even an increase.

The menstrual cycle and sexual activity/interest in women. If sexual interest is measured by frequency of intercourse, no relation is typically found between ovulation periods and sexual interest. The problem with using intercourse as a measure of a woman's sexual interest is that it is frequently initiated by the man. To control for this factor, one study had women record the timing of their sexual interest as well as when they initiated sexual activity. When this was done, it was found that female interest peaks at the time of ovulation (Adams, Gold, & Burt, 1978). In other words, women exhibit peaks in sexual interest that are analogous to the sexual receptivity of animals in estrus.

Rhythms in male sexual activity.   Several predictable patterns in male sexual activity have been found. One study found that male sexual activity was greatest in the fall and that plasma testosterone was highest about that time. This finding seems to show that sexual activity in males, as in females, is governed to some degree by hormone rhythms (Reinberg & Lagoguey, 1978). One must be careful, however, not to assume a simple cause/effect relation. It has also been shown that psychological sexual arousal can change hormone levels. For example, a group of men who watched a sexually arousing film showed increases in two sex hormones, luteinizing hormone (LH) and follicle-stimulating hormone (FSH). Interestingly, the levels were substantially higher when anxiety was low (LaFerla, Anderson, & Schalch, 1978). Like other studies, this one seems to show that the anterior-pituitary hormones are responsive to (their secretion is elicited by) psychological states.

In order to demonstrate that male sexual activity is governed by internal rhythms, it would be necessary to control for environmental events that might stimulate or depress pituitary activity. Since this is virtually impossible, it may be impossible to establish whether male sexual activity is rhythmic.

The monitoring function of the hypothalamus.   The hypothalamus is generally conceptualized as having both a directing and a monitoring function. Hormones that are released by the gonads are "analyzed" by the hypothalamus, and on the basis of this analysis the hypothalamus directs the pituitary to release varying amounts of the ten or more hormones under its control. The result is a well-coordinated sexual response that involves several different but related activities.

Other brain systems.   The temporal lobes of the brain have also been shown to be related to sexual behavior. Lesions of the temporal lobes of rhesus monkeys produce hypersexuality (Klüver & Bucy, 1939). Since the original demonstration by Klüver and Bucy, it has been shown that the same effect can be produced in a wide variety of species, including humans (Whalen, 1976). It has been suggested that the temporal cortex may have an inhibiting or directing function, and therefore when the temporal cortex fails to function, inappropriate sexual responses are made to a variety of objects. After lesions in the temporal cortex, animals will often make sexual responses to a wide variety of nonsexual stimuli. This bizarre behavior pattern reflects sexual arousal that is at best unorganized or inappropriate. In general, it can be shown that the neocortex plays an organizing role, ensuring that the behavior that occurs in response to sexual arousal is appropriate (Whalen, 1976).

Hormones and sexual behavior.   To study the role of hormones, it is necessary to observe behavior with and without hormones present in the animal. Because the sex hormones are secreted directly into the bloodstream by the gonads of both males and females, the only way to eliminate sex hormones is to remove the organs that manufacture them—castration in the male, ovariectomy in the female. Both estrogen and androgen have been isolated chemically, and it is possible to inject the appropriate sex hormone into animals that now lack it. In this way it is possible to determine clearly whether a behavioral change is due to the absence of a particular hormone or is a more general result of removal of the gonads or simply of the stress caused by surgery. Some of the early studies on the role of sex hormones in sexual behavior produced some rather unexpected and difficult-to-explain results. As the research continued, however, many of the early puzzles were at least partly solved. Although there are still many unanswered questions, a fairly clear picture has emerged.

Castration and ovariectomy studies. One early group of studies with rats involved either castration or ovariectomy either before or after puberty. The purpose of these studies was to determine whether sex hormones were responsible only for sexual maturation (that is, development of secondary sexual characteristics) or whether the hormones also directed sexual behavior. (In humans secondary sex characteristics include the growth of body hair and beard, voice changes, and increases in the size of the genitals or the development of the breasts.) The results of these studies indicated several things. First, it was found that the sex hormones are responsible for sexual maturation; that is, animals whose testes or ovaries were removed before puberty failed to show the same sexual maturation as their counterparts whose gonads were not removed. Second, it was found that male rats castrated before puberty never develop sexual behaviors. When sexually experienced rats are castrated, they show a considerable loss of sexual interest in an estrous female and a corresponding decline in copulatory behavior (Beach, 1958). Ovariectomy in the female rat has an even more pronounced effect: ovariectomy either before or after puberty produces a total lack of receptivity. Not only is the female rat not responsive, but she fails to elicit any sexual excitement in normal male rats (Beach, 1958). To determine whether androgen and estrogen would reinstate normal sexual behavior, gonadectomized male and female rats were injected with their respective sex hormones. Both sexes immediately showed sexual responsiveness (Beach, 1947, 1958). Furthermore, it has been shown that the increase in copulatory behavior in the male rat is directly related to the amount of androgen administered (Beach & Fowler, 1959).

Similar studies with other species have somewhat different results. Ovariectomy in the female dog abolishes sexual receptivity promptly and permanently, as it does in the rat. The results of castration in the male dog, however, depend on the dog's age and prior experience with mating. Dogs castrated before puberty never copulate successfully, even after hormones are injected. Rats, in contrast, copulate successfully if given hormone injections even if castrated before puberty. Mature, experienced male dogs that are castrated show either no loss of copulatory ability or a gradual decline that is readily reversed by an injection of the male sex hormone. This result is in sharp contrast to that for the rat, which shows a marked decline after castration. There are few studies with primates, but the scattered reports indicate that the female ape whose ovaries have been removed behaves very much like the female ape who is not in estrus. That is, she is generally not receptive but occasionally will permit copulation. Male apes castrated in infancy become very sexually active, and castrated adults remain sexually active, even though neither animal is capable of ejaculation or orgasm (Beach, 1969).

Sex differences and species differences in the control of sexual behavior. The difference in results obtained with animals at different points on the evolutionary scale suggests two things. First, as one moves up the evolutionary scale, sexual behavior is less controlled by hormones. Second, male sexual behavior is less dependent on hormones than female sexual behavior is, at least among subhumans. A question then arises: If hormones do not energize and direct sexual behavior, what does?

Frank Beach, who has worked extensively on the hormonal control of sexual behavior, has suggested that lack of dependence on the hormonal system in the higher primates, including humans, is a direct consequence of the tendency of this group to depend on the complex and intricately organized neocortex (Beach, 1956, 1965, 1967, 1969). He notes, for example, that fish and amphibians have no neocortex; reptiles and birds have only a rudimentary one; rats have a well-developed but small cortex; primates have not only a well-developed but a large, specialized cortex; and, finally, the human cortex constitutes 90% of the volume of the brain. The great adaptability of humans to various environmental conditions and our higher position on the evolutionary scale correspond to our highly developed cortex.

Beach has suggested that the reason the male's sexual response is less influenced than the female's by the presence or absence of hormones is that male sexual behavior is more dependent on the cortex, perhaps because the male sexual responses are quite complex and therefore require more participation of the cortex for their control. For example, the male rat must respond to several sensory cues, both visual and olfactory. The female, in contrast, need only respond to the tactile stimulation of the male's clasp. If Beach is correct, one would expect the male sexual response to suffer more loss if the cortex were extensively damaged. Further, the loss should be greater for animals higher on the evolutionary scale. Research on cortical damage is clearly in line with Beach's view. Female rats and dogs submit to copulation after extensive brain damage, although their responses are not so well integrated as those of normal animals. Male rats and dogs, however, immediately become sexually inactive if the cortex is removed. It appears, in other words, that females do not require a cortex for sexual behavior, and males do.

Hormones and sexual attraction.   If sexual behavior is released by stimuli, as a great deal of evidence (at least from animal studies) suggests, do hormones mediate this effect? This is a particularly interesting question from a motivational perspective because one of our primary concerns is what controls the arousal of behavior.

There is good evidence that when the testosterone level is elevated in the male, the threshold for arousal is lowered. That is, male sexual behavior can be more readily elicited when the testosterone level is high. For example, castrated rats are insensitive to the odor or taste of the female's secretions when she is in estrus (receptive); injections of testosterone will restore that sensitivity, thereby eliciting sexual interest. Similarly, it has been shown that a female rat is not aroused by the male unless she is in estrus.

Beach (1976) has argued that hormones can induce temporary changes in brain functions. In other words, the brain becomes primed to respond to certain types of stimuli relevant to its motivational (hormonal) state. Acknowledging that many sex-related behaviors are learned, Beach suggests that they too could become activated under certain hormonal states. Thus sexual arousal in animals is frequently due to the interaction of hormones and appropriate releasing stimuli. For example, although sexual behavior in the female dog is governed in large part by hormones, female dogs do show preferences for certain males (Beach & LeBoeuf, 1967). When hormone levels are in a state of readiness, the animal is prepared to be aroused; however, arousal is more likely in the presence of appropriate releasing (arousing) stimuli.

Human Sex Hormones, Sexual Motivation, and Sexual Performance

The male sexual response.   For obvious reasons it is impossible to do with humans the kind of studies that can be done with animals. Nevertheless, data from clinical sources and studies involving the analysis of hormone concentration levels give us a relatively clear picture about the role of hormones in humans. Sometimes gonadectomies are performed on human males to treat cancer and other diseases. Studies of such cases have shown that after gonadectomy sexual motivation (ability to be sexually aroused) decreases, as does the capacity for ejaculation (Bancroft, 1980; Money, 1980). It has also been shown that the stimuli that normally can elicit an erection tend to lose their capacity to do so following gonadectomy. Sexual fantasies, for example, may no longer be able to elicit an erection, although stronger stimuli such as erotica can. Androgen replacement therapy is often used to restore sexual motivation in gonadectomized patients. Administration of androgens has been shown to restore sexual interest and sexual capability to preoperative levels.

Another way of determining the role of hormones is to study the relationship of the level of sex hormones and certain indicators of sexual performance. Again the data are quite clear: the length of time between erections in the human male is positively related to the concentration of testosterone (Lange et al., 1980). The spontaneous erections frequently experienced by adolescent boys have been attributed to their high levels of testosterone. When the testosterone level is very high, the threshold for arousal tends to be very low. Since the testosterone level tends to decline as we age, it is not surprising that older men sometimes have more difficulty achieving an erection than they once did. These and other studies show that male sexual performance is indeed closely linked to hormone levels.

In recent years it has been shown that a variety of factors can disrupt the male sexual response. One such factor is drugs. Alcohol, for example, has been repeatedly linked to impaired sexual functioning in men. Many of the so-called recreational drugs, such as cocaine, heroin, and marijuana, have also been implicated. Drugs prescribed to regulate the heart and blood pressure can lead not only to a loss of sexual motivation but to impotence. Another factor that has been linked to decreased sexual motivation and performance is stress. One reason that stress leads to reduced sexual functioning is that it reduces the concentration of testosterone. Anxiety can also disrupt the male sexual response. The "need to perform," then, can actually interfere with the ability to achieve an erection or to ejaculate.

The female sexual response.   Removal of the ovaries appears to have no effect on the sexual motivation of the human female, and neither does the onset of menopause (Money, 1980; Short, 1980). It has been shown, on the other hand, that injections of androgens will increase her sexual motivation. This finding is consistent with the finding that removal of the adrenal glands leads to a decline in sexual motivation (Gray & Gorzalka, 1980). Remember that most of the human female's androgen comes from the adrenal glands.

One study found that the frequency of intercourse among a group of married women was directly related to their testosterone levels. Interestingly, the wife's sexual activity was also found to be related to her husband's testosterone level (Persky et al., 1978). We cannot conclude from this finding that the husband's testosterone level somehow influences his wife's behavior; it probably means that people who have strong sexual motivation marry people who also have strong sexual motivation.

The female sexual response, like that of the male, may be disrupted by a variety of factors. One of those factors is a reduced level of testosterone. Clinical studies of frigidity have found that injections of testosterone, in combination with counseling, can increase a woman's desire for sexual activity (Bancroft & Skakkebaek, 1979; Carney, Bancroft, & Mathews, 1978).

Summary

There are three major classes of sex hormones: androgens ("male"), the most important being testosterone; estrogen ("female"), the main one being estradiol; and progestins ("female"), the main one being progesterone. The practice of labeling these hormones as male and female is not altogether correct because androgens can be converted to estrogen and progestins can be converted to androgens, with the result that each sex has the hormones associated with the other. It has been shown that sexual interest in both males and females is rhythmical and can be linked to the release of various hormones. These rhythms do not, however, account for all human sexual activity. Environmental factors seem to play an important role in it as well.

Castration and ovariectomy studies have shown that the sexual motivation of lower animals is much more dependent on hormones than that of animals higher on the phylogenetic scale, and that the sexual behavior of females is more dependent on hormones than that of males. Beach has suggested that the cortex plays a more important role in male sexual behavior than it does in female sexual behavior.

There is a great deal of evidence, nevertheless, that testosterone plays a very important role in both male and female sexual motivation. Beach has suggested that testosterone primes the male brain, lowering the threshold for stimuli that can release or arouse sexual motivation. A lowered hormone level not only reduces motivation in humans but interferes with the male's sexual response.

Sex Hormones, Sex Differentiation, and Adult Sexual Behavior

Sex hormones and development of male and female physical characteristics. For about one month after the egg has been fertilized, the male and female embryos cannot be differentiated. In the second month sex differences begin to appear. If the egg has been fertilized with an XX chromosome, the gonads (the two collections of germ cells) begin to develop into ovaries. As the male ducts disintegrate the female ducts thicken and become the womb, the fallopian tubes, and the upper two-thirds of the vagina.

If the egg has been fertilized with an XY chromosome, the process of development moves in a very different direction during the second month. H-Y antigens, believed to be produced by the XY chromosome, change the ovaries into testicles. The testicles produce various hormones: one that absorbs the female parts, such as the womb; testosterone, which thickens the spermatic cord; and still another, dihydrotestosterone, which promotes the formation of the external male genitals (Goy & McEwen, 1980; Haseltine & Ohno, 1981; Wilson et al., 1981; see also Durden-Smith & de Simone, 1983, for a very readable coverage of the material presented in this section).

To demonstrate that hormones are indeed responsible for the development of sex organs, female rats have been injected with the male hormone testosterone. Their female offspring are then found to be modified in several ways. They are born with an external vagina, often have a penis, and exhibit few mating responses in adulthood (see Beach 1976).

It is obviously impossible to perform such manipulations with humans, but a great many data indicate that the human hormones do work in the same way. One line of evidence comes from observations of people who have undergone a voluntary sex change. Candidates for sex-change operations are injected with either testosterone (for a female-to-male change) or estrogen (for a male-to-female change). A male transsexual who receives estrogen (the family of hormones related to estradiol) can expect to grow breasts and add fat at the hips and thighs. Conversely, if androgen (the family of hormones related to testosterone) is given to a female transsexual, she develops an enlarged clitoris and grows facial hair; her voice deepens and her musculature becomes more masculine (Rubin, Reinisch, & Haskett, 1981; Ciba Foundation Symposium, 1979).

Sex hormones and the hypothalamus.   The sex hormones that are produced by the developing embryo alter the development of the brain some time before birth. It has been shown, for example, that certain nuclei in the hypothalamus of the rat are larger if the animal (male or female) has received injections of the male sex hormone before birth. Normally these nuclei are five to seven times larger in the male than in the female. When male embryos were castrated, the animals were born with much smaller nuclei. Apparently there is a critical period during which the size of these nuclei may be altered; it is not possible to alter them in adulthood (see Haseltine & Ohno, 1981; Wilson et al., 1981).

Sex hormones and the cortex.   There is considerable evidence that the sex hormones alter the development of the cortex. One series of studies found that the surface of the female rat's left hemisphere is slightly thicker than the male's, while the back of the male's right hemisphere is thicker than the female's (Diamond, Dowling, & Johnson, 1981). That finding fits with what we know about certain human skills. We know, for example, that females have greater language skills, a function that is performed mainly by the left hemisphere of the brain. Similarly, we know that males have greater visual and spatial abilities, a function that is performed by the back of the right hemisphere of the brain. We know that these differences are, at least in part, due to sex hormones because it is possible to produce these differences artificially by an injection of testosterone in the female infant at a critical stage, usually around birth or shortly thereafter, or by castration of the male infant at the time of birth (see Beach, 1976; Haseltine & Ohno, 1981; Wilson et al., 1981).

Sex hormones and adult sexual behavior.   A great deal of research indicates that adult sexual behavior in animals (such as the rat) is dependent on the balance of sex hormones during brain differentiation (that period of time during which various areas of the brain are developing specific functions, such as speech and spatial ability). If male rats are castrated the day they are born, for example, they tend to show what Günter Dörner (1983) calls heterotypical behavior; that is, these animals show "a significant preference of sexual responsiveness to male partners, following estrogen or even androgen treatment in adulthood" (p. 205). The higher the androgen level during brain differentiation, the stronger the male and the weaker the female sexual behavior in adulthood, irrespective of sex. Even complete sexual inversion (male sexual behavior in place of female sexual behavior or vice versa) has been observed when androgen has been deficient in the male and in excess in the female. In other words, it can be shown that early alterations in the hormone levels will create a predisposition for lowered sexual motivation, bisexuality, and homosexuality (see Dörner, 1983).

The mechanism of male and female brain differentiation.   Dörner (1983) and other researchers (see McEwen, 1981) have argued that the sex hormones produce different patterns of sexual and other behavior by somehow affecting neurotransmitter activity in the brain. Neurotransmitters are important in the execution of various behaviors and in the processing of information. In short, neurotransmitters are involved not only in learning but in unlearned responses. This line of research may ultimately tell us why and how an alteration in hormone levels produces those behaviors that are commonly considered to be specific to a particular sex. Perhaps they facilitate the acquisition of certain behavior patterns or simply inhibit others. It has been shown, for example, that hormone levels determine whether or not a male canary can sing. Normally it is only the male that does sing. This ability is learned, and the learning is an activity primarily of the left hemisphere. When females were injected with testosterone, they started to sing, though somewhat falteringly (Nottebohm & Arnold, 1976).

Sex hormones and sex-typed behaviors.   Sex hormones play an important role in a wide variety of sex-related behaviors. Work at the University of Wisconsin indicates that the style of play adopted by males and females is linked to the sex hormones. Robert Goy has noted that the behavior of young male rhesus monkeys differs from that of females in four ways: they initiate play more often, they roughhouse more often, they mount their peers of both sexes more often, and they mount their mothers more often. When pregnant mothers were given injections of testosterone for various periods of time during the critical period of fetal development, their female offspring not only had masculinized genitalia but adopted a male style of play. Goy and McEwen also observed that male rhesus monkeys usually occupy the dominant position in a mixed-sex troop. When pregnant female monkeys were given injections of testosterone, they were more likely than other females to assume the dominant position in mixed-sex troops (see Goy & McEwen, 1980).

Animal research yields extensive evidence that androgens play an important role in the emergence of aggressive behavior (Brain, 1977). As it is not possible to inject pregnant women with testosterone, the evidence for a link between human aggression and sex is less clear. Though we have reason to argue that human aggression is affected by environmental factors, human studies also suggest an association with testosterone. It has been shown, for example, that hockey players who respond aggressively to threats tend to have higher levels of testosterone than those who do not (Scaramella & Brown, 1978); and that violent criminals tend to have significantly higher levels of testosterone than the average man (Kreuz & Rose, 1972; Ehrenkranz, Bliss, & Sheard, 1974; Rada, Laws, & Kellner, 1976).

In order to show that aggressive behavior is somehow linked to high levels of sex hormones during brain differentiation, it is necessary to study women who have been exposed to high levels of androgens (testosterone) during pregnancy and then compare the behavior of their offspring with other children (Hines, 1982). Researchers have identified two categories of such women: those who have produced abnormally high levels of one of the sex hormones (endogenous types) and those who have been treated with one of the sex hormones (exogenous types).

Congenital adrenal hyperphasia (CAH).   Women with congenital adrenal hyperphasia, CAH, have a cortisol deficiency that results in high levels of adrenocorticotropic hormone and androgens (especially testosterone and dihydrotestosterone). Their sons tend to have precocious puberty (about age 2 or 3); the daughters tend not only to have masculinized genitalia but to be tomboyish and athletic, to prefer boys as playmates, and to join in organized competitive sports. There is also evidence that CAH girls prefer toy guns and cars to dolls, prefer functional clothing to more feminine clothing, would rather play cowboys and Indians than house, and prefer career-rehearsal games over fantasizing about marriage and the care of infants. There is further evidence that in later life they tend to become attracted to other women, just as a man might be attracted to a woman. The incidence of bisexuality and homosexuality is higher among such women than among women in general (see Ehrhardt & Meyer-Bahlburg, 1981; Money & Ehrhardt, 1972).

While such findings seem to support the idea that prenatal sex hormones can influence such things as sexual orientation, these studies have been criticized on the grounds their findings can be accounted for in other ways (for example, Hines, 1982). The parents of a girl who had masculinized genitalia might tend to treat her more as a boy, thus encouraging the tomboyishness, the tendency to play with toy weapons, the interest in functional clothing, and the other behaviors noted by the researchers. Further, if the male sex hormone enlarged the girl's muscles, heart, and lungs, she might reasonably be expected to be attracted to sports and so to have boys as playmates. Though the evidence is not unequivocal, the findings of many studies tend to support the idea that sex hormones play an important role in human sexual behavior, in human sex-typed behaviors (behaviors usually associated with male and female), and in the complementary abilities of men and women (Hines, 1982).

The question of defeminization. Are women who have been exposed to increased levels of testosterone less feminine than other women? The general consensus seems to be no, they have not been defeminized. Goy points out, for example, that he has not been able to identify any feminine traits that are suppressed by exposure to male hormones. In other words, while women can be masculinized by exposure to extraordinary levels of testosterone, they are not defeminized. They have gained something they might not otherwise have had; they have lost nothing in the process.

Hormones to maintain pregnancy. Various hormones have been administered to pregnant women to help maintain pregnancy. Progesterone and chemicals closely related to it seem to have a slight demasculinizing effect on their children. Boys who have been exposed to them before birth tend to be less aggressive and assertive than their peers. They also show poorer athletic coordination and what has been referred to as lessened "masculine interests" (see Meyer-Bahlburg & Ehrhardt, 1982). In the case of a boy, then, we talk about demasculinization as a result of some process by which the testosterone level is lowered. In order to understand this idea better, we need to look at the way sex hormones affect brain differentiation.

Sex hormones and brain reorganization. In general, it is believed that the brains of male and female fetuses would undergo a very similar (homogeneous) pattern of differentiation if it were not for the presence of testosterone. Both human and animal studies make it very clear that testosterone dramatically affects the brain differentiation process. It affects not only the sexual behavior of organisms but the behaviors we normally associate with male and female—the so-called sex-typed behaviors. Women are generally considered to be more verbal-serial, men more visual-spatial.

If we assume that the pattern of brain differentiation depends on the level of testosterone, how do we account for the fact that female behavior varies so widely? In order to answer this question we need one important piece of information: that the ovaries produce small amounts of testosterone. Since the amount of testosterone they produce varies from mother to mother (and from fetus to fetus), women vary in the way they characteristically interact with the environment, the way they think, the way they process information, and so forth. Since the levels of testosterone tend to be much higher in male offspring, the difference between males and females will be fairly large in comparison with the differences among females. As the amount of testosterone produced in males also varies, their behavior, too, will vary. On the average, however, males will interact with the environment, think, and process information in ways that can be contrasted with those characteristic of females.

When, under unusual conditions, male fetuses have very low levels of testosterone during brain differentiation and female fetuses have very high levels, certain very predictable things should happen. A low level of testosterone in a boy should result in brain differentiation that produces behaviors generally associated with girls; a high level of testosterone in a girl should produce behaviors generally associated with boys.

Günter Dörner's Theory of Homosexuality

Günter Dörner (1980a, 1980b, 1981, 1983) has argued that male homosexuality can result from a low level of testosterone during a critical stage of brain differentiation, while female homosexuality (lesbianism) can result from an elevated level of testosterone during a critical stage of brain differentiation. He is convinced that particularly in the case of male primary homosexuality (homosexuality in an individual who has had no heterosexual experience and does not respond to aversion therapy), the individual's sexual orientation was shaped in the womb by a deficiency in testosterone.

Many animal studies indicate that deprivation of the male hormone testosterone during a critical period of brain differentiation will result in a female pattern of sexually dimorphic behavior (Beach, 1975, 1976). The evidence in regard to humans is less clear. Later we will consider the importance of learning. Perhaps, as various people have suggested, a low or high level of testosterone merely primes the individual to move in one direction rather than another, and the critical role is played by learning.

Given the large number of homosexuals in the general population (somewhere around 10 to 15% of the male population) and the relatively few cases of endogenously and exogenously induced low levels of testosterone, how can Dörner's theory account for homosexuality? He has argued that the level of testosterone in the fetus can be lowered by stress experienced by the mother. Stress causes the adrenal glands to depress the testosterone level. Animal research has shown that when a pregnant female rat experiences stress, the level of circulating testosterone declines (Ward, 1977), and that the effects of stress can be reversed by injections of androgen (Dörner, Götz, & Docke, 1982). Since it is unethical to induce stress in humans, the ability to verify this part of the theory is much more difficult. One study identified 794 German homosexuals who had been born during or shortly after World War II. It was hypothesized that stressful war or postwar experiences may have affected the brain differentiation of these men. The results showed that significantly more homosexuals were born during the stressful war and early post-

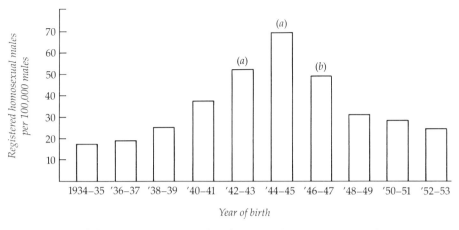

(a) $P < 0.001$ and (b) $P < 0.01$ as compared to the years of birth 1934–1939 and 1948–1953

Figure 6-1.   Relative frequency of homosexual males born in Germany (or GDR) before, during, and after World War II ($n = 794$) (Dörner et al., 1980)

war years between 1942 and 1947 (Dörner et al., 1982). These findings are seen in Figure 6-1.

Other evidence that might be considered consistent with Dörner's view comes from the work of researchers at the Kinsey Institute for Sex Research. After interviewing 979 homosexuals and 477 heterosexuals, they announced that they could find no psychological or environmental variable that accounted for either male or female homosexuality (Bell, Weinberg, & Hammersmith, 1981).

Other important research has shown that both sons and daughters of prenatally stressed mothers have altered levels of neurotransmitters (Herrenkohl, 1979; Moyers, 1978). Remember that the neurotransmitters have been hypothesized to be the mechanism by which the sex hormones achieve brain differentiation.

More recently, John Money (1987) has argued that although prenatal brain hormonalization does not directly cause sexual orientation, it certainly plays a role. Specifically, prenatal hormonalization interacts with socialization processes to determine whether a person becomes heterosexual, homosexual, or bisexual.

Summary

If the egg is fertilized with an XX chromosome, the gonads develop into ovaries; if the egg is fertilized with an XY chromosome, the H-Y antigens change the ovaries into testicles. The testicles produce testosterone, a hormone that is critical for the development of the penis and the male brain. Among other functions, testosterone alters the size of certain nuclei in the hypothalamus and thus differentiates the male's brain from that of the female. They differ not only in anatomy but in functioning. Research has shown that the male and female sex hormones are responsible, at least in many animals, for the sexual behavior of the adult. It has also been shown that the sex hormones are responsible for such sex-typed behaviors as the rough-and-tumble play characteristic of many male animals. Clinical data have shown that exposure to elevated levels of testosterone not only alters female genitalia but produces play behaviors normally associated with males. Similarly, pro-

(continued)

gesterone (a hormone that seems to suppress the action of testosterone) can produce in males behaviors normally associated with females. As females also produce testosterone, though in smaller quantities, behavioral differences among females may be traceable to differences in the levels of testosterone produced by their mothers or by themselves as fetuses. Günter Dörner has proposed that male homosexuality may be produced, at least in large part, by a low level of testosterone during a critical stage of development. He has suggested that since stress can reduce the testosterone level, homosexuality may result if a mother experiences stress during pregnancy.

The Nature of Human Sexual Arousal

It was not until the pioneering work of Masters and Johnson in their book *Human Sexual Response* (1966) that we had any solid scientific information about the nature of human sexual arousal. This seems an extraordinary fact in view of the vast number of books and articles that had been and were being published purporting to inform the professional and the layperson about human sexual motivation. For example, a leading medical text stated unequivocally that not only were women nonorgasmic, but they rarely, if ever, had sexual feelings and certainly had little sexual interest. Two books by Alfred Kinsey and his associates, *Sexual Behavior in the Human Male* (1948) and *Sexual Behavior in the Human Female* (1953), caused a storm of controversy. In these books Kinsey objectively reported the results of interviews he and his associates had had with male and female volunteers. Kinsey's books indicated not only that women enjoy sex (as do men) but that both sexes seem to enjoy a wide variety of sexual practices. Many people regarded as perverse the whole idea of variation in the sexual response. Kinsey was attacked for the procedures he followed to obtain his sample. The basic argument was that his volunteers were not representative of the general population, as evidenced by their willingness to talk to a stranger about their sexual practices. Although there were problems with Kinsey's sampling procedures, time has more or less vindicated him. People are no longer arguing about whether his figures are correct. Current information about human sexual practices clearly supports his findings. Not only do humans enjoy sex, but a large number of them enjoy variations in their sexual behavior. There is, in fact, a growing tendency to regard anybody who does not engage in a variety of sexual positions as abnormal. This tendency appears to be traceable to the abundance of books that have appeared in recent years advocating diversity. The person who wants diversity finds no lack of material providing step-by-step instructions. A quick inspection of these books indicates that in many cases great athletic skills appear to be required. The number of positions the human body can assume with any degree of comfort is limited. People who have no wish to develop their athletic skills may be quite satisfied with less diversity and more comfort.

Sensory and Arousal Factors

The consensus that has emerged from the work of Masters and Johnson is that human sexual behavior occurs in stages. The two major stages consist of a nontactile stage followed typically by a tactile stage. First, the person becomes interested in a member of the opposite sex because of visual, auditory, olfactory, or even cognitive cues. A woman, for example, may arouse the interest of a man by the shape of her body, her clothes, the way she smiles, the quality of her voice, the way she smells, or what she says. If she in turn finds the man attractive, she may agree to spend some time in close proximity to him. They may go to a movie, have dinner together, walk together, and so on. If this first stage of close proximity is satisfying for both, they move on to the second stage, which involves tactile stimulation. It usually begins with touching or holding hands and proceeds to petting, gradually becoming more intimate provided that there are no inhibitions to prevent the natural progression. Those areas of the body that not only are highly sensitive to touch but are regarded as belonging to the sexual response will become involved in a mutual attempt to bring pleasure to the other person. The eventual aim is usually to have intercourse with accompanying orgasm.

Masters and Johnson focused their research on the stages that characterize the tactile phase of sexual behavior. In general, they hold that human sexual behavior can be described as a sensory event. To understand the nature of the sexual system, therefore, it is critical to understand exactly how this system is designed to provide the sensory events that are assumed to be the reason we, as humans, engage in sexual behavior.

The Female Sexual Response

There are a number of misconceptions about the female sexual response. One is that women do not experience any pleasurable sensation from sex. Another is that they do not experience orgasm. Masters and Johnson (1966) have found not only that women experience a variety of pleasurable sensations but that they experience orgasm. In fact, they have never found a case in which a woman who was properly stimulated did not experience an orgasm. It is likely that some of the misconceptions about female sexual responses have resulted from men's tendency to compare the female sexual response with their own. There are some differences, but the differences do not necessarily make a woman's response less intense or less satisfying than her partner's.

Masters and Johnson have divided the female sexual response into four stages in order to describe the patterning of physiological and psychological responses. These stages, or phases, are called (1) the excitement phase, (2) the plateau phase, (3) the orgasmic phase, and (4) the resolution phase.

The female sexual response involves physiological changes that can be classified roughly under three headings: (1) those that are outside the genital area, (2) those that are specific to the clitoris, and (3) those that occur in the vagina. Figure 6-2 is a schematic representation of the female pelvic area and should be used as a reference in the following discussion.

It is beyond the scope of this chapter to describe all the varieties of stimulation that will produce a female orgasm; it should simply be noted that the most effective stimulation for most women is some form of tactile stimulation in the genital area. Some women can be brought to orgasm by stimulation of the breasts, abdomen, or buttocks, but these women do not represent the norm. Masters and Johnson have identified three women who can fantasize themselves into orgasms, but most women's imaginations are not quite so vivid.

Stimulation of the female genital area produces a more or less uniform pattern of physiological and psychological responses. The three major classes of reaction (extragenital, clitoral, and vaginal) will be described separately for the excitement, plateau, orgasmic, and resolution phases. Table 6-1 summarizes the reactions in a form that makes it possible to compare those associated with the various phases.

The four extragenital changes that take place during the excitement phase are nipple erection, enlargement of the breasts, sex flush (of the breasts), and involuntary contraction of muscles. Breast enlargement and the sex flush (a type of

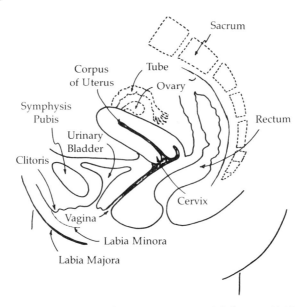

Figure 6-2.   Female pelvis: normal anatomy (Masters & Johnson, 1966)

rash) are the direct results of increases in the blood supply to certain blood vessels. Such increases are called "vasocongestion." Vasocongestion is a very important part of the sexual response. Its increase is correlated with sexual excitement, and the relief from sexual tension following orgasm is correlated with its dispersion.

As the woman progresses into the plateau phase, the sex flush may spread to the lower abdomen, thighs, and buttocks, and the breasts may enlarge further. Toward the end of the plateau phase, hyperventilation (rapid breathing) tends to occur, accompanied by increases in heart rate and blood pressure.

The reactions that occur toward the end of the plateau phase tend to peak in the orgasmic phase. Once orgasm has been attained, there is a decline in reactions, and a filmy sheen of perspiration may appear on the back, thighs, and chest.

Some of these reactions are produced by sexually arousing symbolic stimulation as well as by tactile stimulation. One study found that sexually arousing videotapes increased vaginal blood flow, skin conductance, systolic and diastolic blood pressure, and forehead temperature (Hoon, Wincze, & Hoon, 1976). Even though such forms of erotic stimulation can increase arousal, there is little evidence that such stimulation by itself will produce an orgasm in most women. Rather, it appears that such stimulation may reduce the threshold for arousal in response to subsequent sexual stimulation, including tactile stimulation (Hoon, Wincze, & Hoon, 1977).

The clitoris.   According to Masters and Johnson (1966), the clitoris is unique among organs in the human body in that its only function is pleasure. They argue that it exists solely for the purpose of receiving and transforming sensual information. Although no one denies that stimulation of the clitoris produces pleasure, some have argued that it is analogous to the penis (for example, Morris, 1969). Masters and Johnson maintain that it is unique because it has nothing to do with reproduction and may not be necessary for orgasm, although it obviously plays some role in the pleasure associated with sex and is usually involved in orgasm.

Table 6-1.   The human female sexual response (Masters & Johnson, 1966)

Phase	Site of reaction		
	Extragenital	*Clitoris*	*Vagina*
Excitement	Nipple erection Enlargement of breasts Sex flush (breasts) Involuntary muscle contractions Contraction of rectal sphincter	Size of clitoris increases (wide variation among individuals)	Vaginal lubrication Lengthening and distention of vagina Retraction of cervix and corpus of uterus into false pelvis
Plateau	Nipple erection continues Breasts enlarged Sex flush may spread to lower abdomen, thighs, buttocks Involuntary muscle contractions (hands and feet) Hyperventilation Increased heart rate Increased blood pressure	Entire clitoris retracts from normal overhang position	Marked vasocongestion near vaginal opening
Orgasm	Nipple erection continues Breast enlargement continues Sex flush terminates abruptly Involuntary muscle contractions Continued hyperventilation Peaking of heart-rate increase Peaking of blood-pressure increase	Clitoris remains in retracted position	Rhythmic contractions near vaginal opening (area of vasocongestion)
Resolution	Decrease in all the above; also perspiratory reaction	Clitoris returns to normal overhang position	Rapid dispersal of vasocongestion Relaxation of vagina

During the early stages of the excitement phase, the clitoris increases in size because of a small but reliable vasocongestive reaction. As excitement builds, the clitoris retracts from its normal protruding position into the surrounding tissue, and during the later part of the plateau phase and during the entire orgasmic phase it remains retracted. Only after the orgasmic phase does the clitoris return to its normal position. (Direct stimulation of the clitoris produces retraction early in the plateau phase.)

The fact that the clitoris retracts before orgasm not only illustrates the lack of parallels between the clitoris and the penis but raises the important question of what role the clitoris plays in the total sexual response. Masters and Johnson have suggested that the clitoris should be viewed not only as a receptor but as a focus for other forms of sensual stimulation. Clinical evidence indicates that during heightened sexual arousal, direct stimulation of the clitoris may actually be irritating or painful. In many instances women have indicated that stimulation of the area surrounding the clitoris may be more satisfying than stimulation of the clitoris itself. Thus, although the clitoris may be the site of greatest sensitivity, direct stimulation may not be the best way of producing optimal stimulation. The fact that the clitoris tends to retract early in the plateau phase when directly stimulated suggests that the retracting response may be an adaptive means for lowering the level of stimulation. Even in the retracted position, the clitoris is capable of receiving stimulation, though less so than in the extended position. Marriage manuals that stress that the man should keep in contact with the clitoris in order to promote sexual satisfaction in his partner may in fact be giving poor advice. Attempts to continuously stimulate the clitoris may actually prove irritating to her, whereas general stimulation to the genital area may be very satisfying.

The vagina.   The first physiological evidence of the human female's response to any form of sexual stimulation is the production of vaginal lubricant. This response has an obvious function in preparation for the act of intercourse. As sexual excitement develops, the vagina lengthens and distends. The cervix and corpus (body) of the uterus retract into what is called the false pelvis (the upper part of the pelvis). Again, this response has an obvious preparatory function. Toward the end of the excitement phase, there is marked vasocongestion in the outer third of the vagina. This vasocongestion reaches a peak in orgasm, which is characterized by recurring contractions. After orgasm, the vasocongestion in the outer third of the vagina is lost rapidly in the resolution phase. Once the penis is withdrawn, the vagina returns to its unstimulated state.

Female orgasm.   Masters and Johnson have identified at least three stages in the female orgasm. In stage I there is a sensation of intense sensual awareness, clitorally focused but radiating upward into the pelvis. Stage II is characterized by a sensation of "suffusion of warmth," specifically in the pelvic area but spreading throughout the body. Finally, in stage III there is a sensation of "pelvic throbbing," a sensation of involuntary contraction with specific focus in the vagina and lower pelvis. For the female, the orgasm is a state in which there is a heightened awareness of the senses, especially those that relate to sexual stimulation.

The Male Sexual Response
The sexual responses of males and females are very similar. Figure 6-3 shows a lateral view of the male anatomy; Table 6-2 summarizes the male's reactions at various stages.

Extragenital reactions.   Like the female, the majority of males (60%) in Masters and Johnson's research have shown nipple erection during the excitement, plateau, and orgasmic phases of the sexual response. Although there was wide variation, many males also showed the sex-flush reaction. Involuntary muscle contractions of the hands, feet, and rectal sphincter were found to occur in a pattern almost identical to that observed in the female. Males, like females, hyperventilated, experienced an increase in heart rate and blood pressure late in the plateau phase,

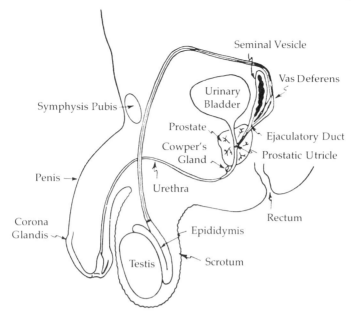

Figure 6-3.   Male pelvis: normal anatomy (Masters & Johnson, 1966)

which carried over into the orgasmic phase, and finally tended to have a perspiratory reaction in the resolution phase closely paralleling that of the female.

The penis.   As already noted, the penis is not an organ totally parallel to the clitoris, although both serve as important receptor systems for sensual stimulation. The penis is also an integral organ for reproduction; the clitoris, as we have noted, is not necessary for reproduction. Further, the penis serves an important role in stimulating the female, while the clitoris has no similar role in stimulating the male.

One of the first signs of sexual arousal in the male is penile erection, which results from vasocongestion in the penis. The tissue structure of the penis is such that the increased supply of blood results in elongation and distention of the penis. Continued stimulation of the penis typically produces ejaculation, an involuntary response that is composed of two parallel and complementary processes. First, there are the rhythmic muscle contractions associated with the penis, and, second, the rhythmic muscle contractions associated with expulsion of the seminal fluid from the seminal duct system (which terminates in the penile urethra). Although the two muscle systems are distinct, they act in a more or less parallel fashion. From the point of view of reproduction, the ejaculatory response maximizes the likelihood of fertilization.

The scrotum and testes.   A number of changes occur in the scrotum and testes as sexual excitement increases. There are a thickening of the scrotal skin surrounding the testes and a simultaneous elevation of the testes. In addition, there is some localized vasocongestion. As sexual excitement reaches the plateau phase, the testes are drawn up tightly, and they increase markedly in size. Although the exact reasons for this reaction are not altogether clear, it appears that the reaction is a

Table 6-2.   The human male sexual response (Masters & Johnson, 1966)

Phase	Extragenital	Penis	Scrotum and testes
		Site of reaction	
Excitement	Nipple erection (60% of males) Some sex flush Involuntary muscle contraction Involuntary contraction of rectal sphincter	Penile erection (vasocongestion) Urethra lengthens	Localized vasocongestion Contraction of smooth-muscle fibers Thickening of scrotal skin Testicular elevation
Plateau	Nipple erection Greater sex flush (25% of males) Involuntary muscle contraction Involuntary contraction of rectal sphincter Hyperventilation Increased heart rate Increased blood pressure	Vasocongestive increase in penile diameter Penile urethral bulb enlarges	Continues as above, plus greater elevation of testes and increase in testicular size
Orgasm	Continued nipple erection Continued sex flush Involuntary contraction of rectal sphincter Hyperventilation Increased heart rate Increased blood pressure	Ejaculatory reaction (regular contractions of muscles) Seminal fluid expelled through involuntary muscle contractions Urethra contracts in rhythm	Continues as above
Resolution	Very gradual retraction of nipples Rapid disappearance of sex flush Perspiratory reaction	Penile detumescence (two stages): rapid decrease in vasocongestion followed by slow decrease in vasocongestion	Either rapid or delayed return to normal state

necessary prerequisite to the ejaculatory response. After ejaculation the scrotum and testes rapidly return to the normal unstimulated state, depending on individual differences or the length of the plateau phase.

Male orgasm.   The male orgasm is synonymous with the ejaculatory response. Masters and Johnson have indicated that there are two stages. First, there is a sensation of ejaculatory inevitability accompanied by the initial muscle contractions. Next, there are the sensations associated with the propulsion of seminal fluid through the urethra and its expulsion. Many males report that a sexual response is more satisfying if greater amounts of seminal fluid are expelled. Thus, experiencing only the first stage does not produce as satisfying an orgasm as experiencing both stages.

Catecholamines and Sexual Activity

Although, as Masters and Johnson have noted, sexual activity is pleasurable because stimulation of the sex organs produces a rewarding sensation, sexual pleasure may involve something more. Specifically, sexual activity may stimulate the output of certain catecholamines, which, as we have seen, have been implicated in various affective reactions. For example, there is evidence not only that norepinephrine is greatly elevated during male sexual activity (100% to 1,200%) but that it is closely correlated with amount of activity and degree of erection (Wiedeking et al., 1977). Dopamine was not found to be highly correlated with sexual activity. Animal research provides evidence that norepinephrine and dopamine levels may be related to fluctuations in ovulation and therefore to mating behavior in female animals (Crowley, O'Donohue, & Jacobowitz, 1978).

Summary

It seems intuitively obvious that sexual arousal can be evoked, at least in part, by a member of the opposite sex. Exactly what cues evoke this arousal, however, has been a matter of some dispute. One thing we do know is that the ability to evoke sexual arousal is governed in part by hormone levels. Increases in androgen levels in men and estrogen levels in women appear to lower the threshold for eliciting sexual interest and sexual behavior in humans.

The pioneering work of Masters and Johnson has provided us with a scientific description of the physiological events that result from sexual stimulation. The sexual response of both females and males can be divided into four phases: excitement, plateau, orgasm, and resolution. We have known for some time that there are important differences in the reactions of females and males. The work of Masters and Johnson has shown that there are many similarities. Most important, perhaps, is the finding that women are just as capable of having an orgasm as men are—a finding that has made it necessary to rewrite many of the authoritative medical books.

Masters and Johnson acknowledge that pleasurable sex can occur without love and that a person can enjoy love without sex. They take the position that one of the best ways to achieve pleasurable sex is to have the right nerve receptors stimulated. In short, sex is rewarding because sex stimulates certain receptors that provide pleasurable sensory stimulation. Recently it has been shown that sexual intercourse will increase the output of norepinephrine by as much as 1,200%. Because running increases norepinephrine by only 300–400%, we may have an explanation of why some people prefer sex to running.

Learned Factors

Earlier in this chapter I noted several lines of evidence that suggest that the role played by learning in sexual behavior tends to increase in proportion to the species' cortical area. If this principle is correct, we should find that human sexual behavior is far more dependent on learned factors than the sexual behavior of animals lower on the phylogenetic scale. Unfortunately, research on learned factors in humans is somewhat meager for a number of reasons. First, it is difficult to delineate clearly the role of learning in humans because of the difficulty of doing the kinds of studies that would be scientifically sound. For example, to conclude that a particular behavior or pattern of behaviors is the result of learning, we must show that a particular set of experiences produced normal sexual behavior in one group of individuals and the absence of the same experiences resulted in the absence of normal sexual behavior in another group. Only in this way can we be sure that the pattern of behavior we observed was not due to other factors, such as hormones or innate tendencies. Second, there is the problem of not knowing exactly what types of experiences are likely to be important. Unless we have a specific idea about what might be important, we are faced with the task of trying to examine all experiences. Freud, for example, suggested that many experiences early in childhood are important. Others have suggested that experiences at puberty are important. Thus the impracticality of doing research with humans is even greater because we don't know exactly what we should study. Third, and most important, is the problem of ethics. If we deprive a person of certain experiences and thereby produce less-than-normal sexual behavior, we cannot be sure we can reverse the process. We may, in fact, produce irreversible damage. We have good evidence from studies with primates that this is probably the case.

If one is interested in learned factors, it is necessary to do research with animals. There is good justification for this approach because we have, on a number of occasions, found that certain principles established by animal research can be readily generalized to humans. One must, of course, always be cautious because generalization is never complete.

Harlow's Research

It was somewhat by accident that Harry Harlow, of the University of Wisconsin, became involved in research on the role of learning in the sexual behavior of primates. Harlow had been investigating the effects of mothering on primate development. To understand more precisely the role mothers play in primate development, he compared monkeys raised with their mothers and monkeys raised without their mothers. The latter monkeys were raised in more or less deprived environments that lacked not only the stimulation that might be provided by their mothers but the stimulation and the normal socialization that result when young primates play with other young primates. To Harlow's surprise, the monkeys that were raised under these rather deprived conditions failed to display normal mature sexual behavior (that is, correct approach and posturing) when they were adults, although they did appear to be interested in members of the opposite sex (Harlow, 1962). Apparently the deprived environments had not provided the basic experiences that lead to mature heterosexual behavior. This fact interested Harlow, and he designed a series of experiments to identify exactly what experiences were necessary to produce mature heterosexual behavior. To determine what experiences were important, Harlow compared monkeys raised under a variety of conditions that ranged from ones that approximated the monkeys' natural environment to one that provided little or no opportunity for normal socialization. In their natural environment, monkeys tend to live in large groups, or colonies. In such groups, the young monkey typically spends a great deal of time exploring and playing with other monkeys of the same age (its peers). To simulate this situation in the laboratory, a large play area was constructed where monkeys were allowed, in certain conditions, to play with their peers.

Harlow studied the effects of four basic conditions on monkeys' sexual behavior as adults. In one condition monkeys were raised by their mothers and were allowed to play in a playpen or playroom with their peers. In a second condition, infant monkeys were separated from their mothers and housed with peers in a playpen. In a third condition, monkeys were raised with their mothers but were not given the opportunity to play with peers. In a fourth condition, monkeys were raised alone. It did not seem to matter whether the infant monkey was raised with the mother so long as the monkey had the opportunity to play with peers. If the monkey was raised by the mother but without peers, it showed an almost total absence of sexual behavior, similar to that found for monkeys raised in isolation. Thus, although the mother may be important for acquiring a variety of behaviors, she does not appear to be important for acquiring mature sexual behavior (Harlow & Harlow, 1962, 1969).

Exactly why play with peers promotes sexual behavior is not altogether clear. Harlow has noted that it is in the process of playing together that monkeys begin to display sexual posturing. During the first six months such behavior is immature and fleeting. However, by the end of the first year it is more frequent and adult in form. It may well be that sexual posturing is more or less innate but that the social/play experience is necessary for eliciting or realizing that tendency. Apparently the failure to elicit or nurture such behaviors when the monkey is developing results in a more or less permanent loss. Hence monkeys that have never had the social/play experiences show hopelessly inadequate sexual behavior as adults.

Peers and Human Sexual Behavior

To what degree are peers important in the development of a mature sexual response in humans? Simon and Gagnon (1970) have concluded that the peer group is the most important factor in sex education. They point out that early peer relationships allow both boys and girls to compare their feelings—something that adults do less often. The peer group not only is important for acquiring information but plays a fundamental role in shaping a person's sex-role identity (Kagan, 1976). A boy who is clumsy on the playing field in a neighborhood devoted to athletics or a boy who is not successful in establishing heterosexual relations may question his sex-role identity. These and other examples have been used to argue that the peer group is indeed important in shaping a person's sex-role identity. It remains to be demonstrated, however, whether peer interactions are as important for human sexual development as they appear to be for the sexual development of certain monkeys.

There is a growing tendency to treat the human sexual response as a complex behavior pattern that has biological, learned, cognitive, and social components. Within this context, Masters and Johnson, among others, regard sexual problems as requiring a careful analysis of all the components. They are particularly sensitive to the social context. Their position is that many sexual problems are due to deficits in the social relations between the partners. In their book *Human Sexual Inadequacy* (Masters & Johnson, 1970) they emphasize the need to treat both partners, since the problem is usually not due to just one partner. In many cases, they note, the partners are lacking in basic skills of arousing each other. As a consequence sexual satisfaction is less than complete. Although there is a great deal of evidence that being properly stimulated is important for sexual satisfaction, cognitive factors must also be considered.

Summary

Much has been written suggesting that learning plays an important role in human sexual behavior, but there is little in the way of scientific data that can be put forth as evidence supporting this position. Harlow's work with monkeys provides good evidence that learning does play an important role in the

(continued)

development of sexual adequacy in certain monkeys. Because one can show that peers often do play an important role in adolescent development, it is tempting to argue, by analogy, that Harlow's findings probably apply to humans. In support of Harlow's position, one can point to the work of Masters and Johnson, who take the position that sexually inadequate behavior can often be corrected by teaching the techniques for arousing one's sexual partner.

Cognitive/Personality Factors

Research from a variety of sources indicates that cognitive factors are important in determining not only the frequency and variety of sexual behavior but the satisfaction that is derived from the sexual response.

Introverts and Extraverts

As already noted, Eysenck has delineated two major types of people, labeled introverts and extraverts. Extraverts are characterized by a high degree of sociability, impulsiveness, physical activity, liveliness, and changeability. Introverts tend to be less sociable, less impulsive, less active, and more stable in their responses to the external environment, and they can generally be characterized as more fear/anxiety-prone.

Questionnaires administered to introverts and extraverts have found several differences in the sexual behavior of these two types of people. For example, Giese and Schmidt (1968), in a study of German students, found that extraverts petted more and had intercourse more often, while introverts tended to masturbate somewhat more often. Eysenck's study of English students (1976) produced similar findings. He found in addition that extraverts tended to engage in a greater variety of sexual behaviors (such as cunnilingus, fellatio, and varied coital positions). A summary of these findings, broken down for males and females, is presented in Table 6-3. Probably the most important finding from both Eysenck's study and Giese and Schmidt's is that extraverts tend to express more satisfaction with their sexual behavior. In fact, Eysenck reports that introverts are dissatisfied with their patterns of sexual behavior. Eysenck has suggested that this dissatisfaction results from inhibitions, worries, and guilt feelings that prevent introverts from fulfilling

Table 6-3. Sexual practices of extraverts and introverts among unmarried German students (Eysenck, 1971)

Practice	Males		Females	
	Extraverts	Introverts	Extraverts	Introverts
Masturbation at present	72%	86%	39%	47%
Petting	78	57	76	62
Coitus	77	47	71	42
Long precoital sex play	28	21	18	21
Cunnilingus	64	52	69	58
Fellatio	69	53	61	53
More than three different coital positions	26	10	13	12

their desires. The introvert, Eysenck notes, tends to endorse the orthodox Christian approach to sex, in which virginity and fidelity are emphasized while the sensory aspects of sex are downplayed. The extravert, in sharp contrast, endorses the unorthodox permissive and promiscuous approach, in which frequency of sex and different partners are important to sexual satisfaction. Similar results were obtained in a study of Canadian college students (Barnes, Malamuth, & Check, 1984).

Unrestricted Orientation versus Restricted Orientation to Sex

People whose orientation to sex is considered to be unrestricted indicate that they have had many sex partners and plan to have many more, have had one-night stands, and endorse casual sex as a comfortable experience. In contrast, people whose view of sex is considered to be restricted indicate that they have had few sex partners, anticipate having few in the future, do not have one-night stands, and endorse the idea that commitment is a necessary prerequisite for sex. It has also been found that an unrestricted view is more prevalent among men than among women (Snyder, Simpson, & Gangestad, 1986).

What produces this difference? A person who holds an unrestricted orientation is a personality type that has been called a high self-monitor, while a person who has a restricted orientation is a personality type that has been referred to as a low self-monitor. Low self-monitors are people whose actions are based on underlying dispositions and attitudes. High self-monitors tend to be responsive to the social and interpersonal cues of the situation in which they find themselves; that is, these people make decisions on the basis of their personal analysis of situational variables, and so their behavior tends to vary with the situation to which they are responding. While we do not know the precise factors that cause variations in self-monitoring, it seems clear that the degree of promiscuity displayed by an individual is related to relatively stable personality factors (Snyder, Simpson, & Gangestad, 1986).

It appears that low self-monitors tend to associate sex not only with love and romance but with commitment to a long-term attachment. High self-monitors, in contrast, tend to view sex as a romantic encounter that does not necessarily imply any long-term commitment. If one associates intimacy with long-term commitment, then high self-monitors are the people who form truly intimate relationships.

Summary

The fact that the sexual practice of extraverts differs from that of introverts indicates that cognitive factors play a basic role in sexual behavior. The finding that extraverts petted more, had intercourse more often, and tended to engage in a wider variety of sexual behaviors is consistent not only with Eysenck's theory but with the position of Masters and Johnson. According to Masters and Johnson, sex can be viewed as a sensory experience. According to Eysenck, extraverts tend to seek out more stimulation than introverts, a theory that would explain why they tend to have sex more frequently and to engage in more varied practices. It is interesting that people who tend to let the situation determine their behavior (high self-monitors) are more likely to hold an unrestricted view of sex, whereas people who tend to let their beliefs and attitudes govern their behavior (low self-monitors) hold a more restricted view of sex. These findings seem to indicate that low self-monitors are the more inhibited.

Studies of Arousal and Attraction

The Question of Attraction

What is it that makes a person of the opposite sex attractive? For that matter, what is it that makes a person of the same sex attractive? If attraction were simply governed by releaser stimuli, as Desmond Morris has suggested it is, the question of attraction would simply be a question of finding what size and shape of the female breast were most effective or finding the size or shape of the penis that most readily elicited sexual interest. The question is obviously more complex. The fact that there are cultural preferences in such things as height, weight, skin color, facial features, and cognitive style, to mention only a few, suggests that learning plays an important role. Given that individual and cultural differences exist, what type of model will account for the attraction that one person feels for another?

Falling in Love

The phrase *falling in love* is frequently used in our society to describe the emotional attachment that members of the opposite (or sometimes same) sex develop toward each other. "Falling in love" can be fairly sudden or gradual. Can we identify some of the factors that contribute to two persons' falling in love? Everyone, of course, seems to look for certain physical and psychological variables in a mate. Nevertheless, it has been found that we frequently fall in love with somebody other than our ideal. In one study, only 40% of the subjects reported that their most intense experience of love was with a person close to their ideal (Averill & Boothroyd, 1977). In other words, falling in love depends on factors other than those we think we are looking for.

Certain common elements are associated with the process of falling in love. Thoughts about the other person and dating frequency seem to be important factors (Kleck & Rubenstein, 1975; Tesser & Paulhus, 1976). Obviously, if one person is attracted to another, thinking about and wanting to be with that person would be normal and expected. Interestingly, chance meeting appears to be among the conditions most conducive to falling in love (Averill & Boothroyd, 1977). There is also good evidence that attraction is enhanced in aversive situations (see Kenrick & Cialdini, 1977; Kenrick & Johnson, 1979). The question is how to explain this interesting phenomenon.

Theoretical Models of Situationally Induced Attraction

Two quite different models have been suggested to account for the fact that as the aversiveness of a situation increases, so does attraction. Since arousal tends to increase as aversiveness increases, the misattribution model suggests, the person is faced with the task of accounting for his or her arousal. Although Schachter (1964) has argued simply that people tend to account for arousal in terms of the emotion they happen to feel at the time, there is good reason to argue that the way a subject interprets an event can affect the emotion that is experienced. According to the misattribution model, meeting a stranger can have romantic overtones. In our culture we frequently hear about people suddenly and unexpectedly meeting their "true love." Alternatively, a stranger might be viewed as a potential sexual encounter. Whatever the reason, there may be some justification for arguing that strangers are sometimes viewed as potential lovers. According to the misattribution model, if a person should view a stranger in this way, increased arousal associated with increased aversiveness could be interpreted as increased attraction. In other words, attributing the arousal to the wrong cause could lead to increased feelings of attraction (Dutton & Aron, 1974). This model has a certain appeal. However, Kenrick and Johnson (1979) argue that the same findings can be explained by a reinforcement model. According to this model, the aversiveness of a situation is often reduced whenever another person is present. The other person, consequently, is viewed as a potential reducer of aversive arousal and therefore is perceived as attractive. This interpretation is consistent with the generally held view that we tend to become attracted to people associated with positive affect (for example, Clore & Byrne, 1974).

Attraction and Difficulty of Attainment

Are so-called easy-to-get women as attractive as hard-to-get women? Recent work on this age-old question indicates that neither easy-to-get nor hard-to-get women are as attractive as women who are moderately hard to get. Apparently when a woman is perceived as hard to get, men simply feel that the possible reward is not worth the time or the effort required to pursue it. In other words, they fail to become motivationally aroused. Easy-to-get women, it appears, also fail to arouse motivation. Very simply, it is not necessary to be highly motivated to win the easy-to-get woman. Moderately difficult-to-get women, on the other hand, are perceived as potentially attainable goals if a reasonable amount of time and effort are devoted to the pursuit. Under these conditions, men appear to experience a high level of arousal, a condition that is assumed to enhance the attractiveness of the goal (Wright, Toi, & Brehm, 1984).

Why are goals that require some effort to attain more attractive to us than those we can have for the asking? There is no obvious answer. Apparently the process of working toward a goal can be just as important as the goal itself, perhaps even more so. The opportunity to experience a high level of arousal, as we have seen, can be reinforcing. One reason the romance goes out of marriage may be that the element of pursuit is lost.

Summary

Although individual preferences in physical and psychological characteristics may account in part for romantic attraction, situational factors apparently do play a significant role. Aversive situations, it seems, can increase the attractiveness of another person. Whether this effect is due to the interaction of arousal and an emotion, as Schachter has proposed, or to the principles of generalized reinforcement remains an unanswered question. The fact that the attractiveness of another person is related to the perceived difficulty of being with that person further points to the need to consider situational or task-related factors in conjunction with the person's physical and psychological attributes.

The Study of Erotica and Pornography

Psychologists have been particularly interested in studying erotica and pornography because such material provides an excellent framework for testing several hypotheses about the motivation underlying human sexual behavior. For example, if seeing the genitals is sexually arousing, as the ethologists have suggested, then all humans should be aroused by viewing the genitals of the opposite sex. Are they? A related question is what mediates this effect. If it is possible to arouse humans in this way, does the cognitive/symbolic activity stimulate the output of hormones, which in turn leads to sexual arousal? Still another question concerns the effect of guilt and anxiety on sexual arousal. If it is true that cultural taboos modify sexual arousal, can it be shown that people who experience guilt about sex are less aroused by this type of stimulation?

One reason psychologists found it difficult to study sexual arousal until recently was that they had no objective measure of sexual arousal. Ever since Kinsey reported his findings, there have been strong objections to reliance on verbal reports. Verbal reports, it can be shown, are sensitive to both conscious and unconscious desires to put oneself in a favorable light. For example, people may deny sexual arousal because of religious training or cultural expectations, or they may exaggerate sexual arousal because of a desire to appear sexually sophisticated or desirable. After Masters and Johnson showed that a reliable set of physiological changes was associated with sexual arousal, the door was opened to measurement of arousal independent of verbal reports. Sexual arousal might vary from person to person depending on attitudes and beliefs, but there is good reason to believe that physiological measures are not affected by the desire to appear in a favorable light.

In recent years many studies have been published in which some form of sexually arousing material was presented while a variety of devices monitored the physiological activity of various organs of the body. In general, these studies have found a relatively strong correlation between physiological measures of sexual arousal and subjective reports of arousal in volunteer subjects. As a result, many studies have used only subjective reports. In order to answer the three questions posed above, we will draw on studies of both types.

What Is Sexually Arousing to Humans?

Pictures of nude members of the opposite sex can elicit sexual arousal. However, pictures that show a member of the opposite sex in a state of sexual arousal or two persons engaged in sexual acts appear to be more potent elicitors of sexual arousal (for example, Griffitt, May, & Veitch, 1974; Mosher & Abramson, 1977). Several studies have shown that the stimulus material does not have to be in pictorial form. Verbal descriptions of sexual behavior are sufficient to elicit sexual arousal in the majority of volunteer subjects (for example, Heiman, 1977). The ability to fantasize may be an important mediator of this phenomenon, because subjects can become sexually aroused through fantasy (for example, Heiman, 1975, 1977; Masters & Johnson, 1966). Fantasy-prone people as well as those with greater sexual experience find it easy to produce sexual fantasies (Carlson & Coleman, 1977). In other words, there may be some validity to the ethologists' suggestion that animals (including humans) are frequently sexually aroused by certain stimuli in the environment; however, it appears that the effect in humans is mediated by cognitive factors.

Romantic themes and lust themes apparently produce the same amount of arousal (for example, Fisher & Byrne, 1978; Heiman, 1977; Osborn & Pollack, 1977). It has long been held that women are not aroused by explicit erotic material whereas men are (for example, Abelson et al., 1971). It has further been suggested that women are more sexually aroused by romantic themes. The failure to find evidence for this generally held opinion may be accounted for by the cultural expectations for women with respect to pornography. It appears that women are not expected to be aroused by pornography, and as a result they have been reluctant to say they are (Gebhard, 1973).

Although romantic and lustful themes have not produced differences in sexual arousal, the theme of chance encounter appears to increase sexual arousal in response to pornographic material. This finding is consistent with the literature on romantic attraction. Remember that one of the conditions that increase romantic attraction is chance meeting. Sociobiologists might say that the evolutionary value of "romantic stranger" attraction is to encourage outbreeding or formation of alliances between different populations.

Interaction of Cognitive, Hormonal, and Physiological Events

Evidence from a variety of sources suggests that cognitive states have a more or less direct effect on the output of sex hormones and on autonomic arousal as well as on sexual arousal. For example, an erotic or pornographic stimulus has been shown to increase the output of luteinizing hormone and follicle-stimulating hormone (LaFerla, Anderson, & Schalch, 1978) and to increase autonomic arousal and sexual arousal (for example, Hoon, Wincze, & Hoon, 1976). Hormones, of course, sensitize humans to sexual stimuli (for example, Money, 1961). One particularly interesting finding is that autonomic arousal augments sexual arousal. Subjects in one study (Cantor, Zillmann, & Bryant, 1975) were shown an erotic film in each of three phases of recovery from exercise. Subjects who viewed the film during the second recovery phase (while they still showed signs of autonomic arousal as detected by physiological measures but no longer reported subjective feelings of arousal) were more sexually aroused by the film. This finding is consistent with Schachter's (1964) dual-process theory, which suggests that unexplained autonomic arousal will add to the intensity of an ongoing emotion.

While there is ample evidence that cognitive states or activities affect hormonal output and physiological activity, what about the effects of hormone levels and arousal on cognitive states? Do we fantasize more when we are sexually aroused? Do people to whom we find ourselves attracted become even more attractive? A study by Dermer and Pyszczynski (1978) suggests that sexual arousal does alter cognitive processes. Dermer and Pyszczynski had subjects describe their "loved one" after being exposed to either an erotic or a control procedure. They found that viewing erotic material increased subjects' ratings of attraction to their "loved one" and increased their feeling of love for that person. This finding suggests that erotic material may enhance pair bonding rather than weaken it. If the pair bond is important for human survival, it makes a great deal of sense that the various components of that bond should reinforce each other.

How Do Sex-Guilt Feelings Affect Responses to Erotica?

Although erotica and pornography can elicit sexual arousal, there are wide individual differences in people's descriptions of their feelings when they view such material, ranging from excited and entertained to disgusted, nauseated, and depressed (see Byrne et al., 1974). One obvious hypothesis is that some people have come to associate feelings of guilt with sexual arousal (Mosher, 1965). As a result they will experience negative affect, which might be labeled disgust or nausea.

In one study to test this hypothesis (Griffitt & Kaiser, 1978), subjects were divided into two groups, high sex guilt and low sex guilt, on the basis of their responses to Mosher's (1966) forced-choice measure of sex guilt. Some subjects were then shown an erotic slide after each correct choice in a discrimination task and a nonerotic slide after each incorrect choice; others were shown nonerotic slides after all choices. The results showed that high-sex-guilt subjects made fewer choices leading to erotica than low-sex-guilt subjects. Further, subjects who experienced positive affect when viewing erotic slides were likely to make more choices that led to erotic slides. In other words, erotic slides acted as reinforcers for low-sex-guilt subjects and punishers for high-sex-guilt subjects. Mosher and Abramson (1977) obtained similar results using films of masturbation. If subjects had a negative attitude (guilt) about masturbation, they experienced negative affect; if they did not have a negative attitude, they experienced arousal. In a study by Fehr and Schulman (1978), the heart rate of subjects was monitored as a sexually pleasurable and a sexually aversive passage were read to them. During the sexually pleasurable passage, the subjects showed heart-rate deceleration. Fehr and Schulman argue that the pattern of results fits with Lacey and Lacey's attention/rejection model (see Chapter 3).

Summary

Psychologists have used erotic material to manipulate sexual arousal. The ability to manipulate arousal has made it possible to increase our understanding of some of the cognitive, physiological, and hormonal factors that mediate sexual arousal. Studies indicate that most people are sexually aroused by erotic material whether it is visual or verbal in form. Failure to become aroused seems to be due to the feelings of guilt that people have come to associate with erotic or pornographic materials for one reason or another. People who are characterized as high in sex guilt tend to experience negative affect when presented with erotic materials; low-guilt subjects tend to experience positive affect.

Variety and Change in the Human Sexual Response

In many animal species the sexual response is stereotyped and occurs only when the female is receptive (fertile). In humans the sexual response not only varies but occurs when the female is not fertile. From time to time it has been suggested that excessive variation in the response or frequent intercourse may be abnormal or perverse. The conclusion one draws depends to a large extent on whether one views sexual behavior simply as a reproductive act or as a sensory experience. Masters and Johnson have taken the point of view that sexual behavior in humans is a sensory experience. In their book *The Pleasure Bond* (1975), they discuss how this sensory experience may be enhanced for the satisfaction of both partners. Variety and change may be important for some couples but not for others. It depends on whether variety and change enhance the sensory experience.

For most sensory experiences, a certain amount of change is necessary to maintain the same level of affect. In the absence of change, habituation or adaptation typically occurs, with a resulting loss of affect. For example, it has been shown that repeated presentation of pornography can result in habituation unless the pornography is new (Schaefer & Colgan, 1977). It can be argued, therefore, that to maintain a high level of sexual arousal, either one needs a new partner periodically or some variety must be introduced into the sex act itself.

In recent years it has become increasingly common for marriage counselors and sex therapists to instruct their clients on how to introduce variety into sexual encounters. Many books have been published depicting different sexual positions that are intended to produce somewhat different sets of sensual experiences. The idea behind these books is that if a person can introduce variety into a sexual encounter, the desire to change partners will be reduced, or the person will simply come to enjoy sex more with any partner, or both.

Summary

There is considerable agreement among marriage counselors that pair bonding often weakens if intercourse is not satisfactory to both partners. For this reason, considerable attention has been directed toward devising ways of helping people obtain more enjoyment from sex.

Homosexuality

Because heterosexuals and homosexuals often engage in similar sexual behaviors, the main distinguishing difference between heterosexuals and homosexuals seems to be the sex of the partner. In an extensive study comparing homosexuals and heterosexuals, Masters and Johnson (1979) report not only that homosexuals and heterosexuals show similar physiological responses during sexual arousal but that they are aroused by the same forms of tactile stimulation. In view of the fact that homosexual behavior often leads to social rejection or punishment, the question arises why a certain portion of humans, irrespective of culture, select a member of the same sex as a sex partner.

The Mental Illness Hypothesis

One explanation that has been prevalent until recently is that homosexuality is due to some type of mental disturbance. In a classic study, Evelyn Hooker (1957) examined the disease hypothesis. She found 30 homosexual men, not in treatment, whom she felt to be reasonably well adjusted. She then matched 30 heterosexual men with the homosexuals for age, education, and IQ. Hooker gave these 60 men a battery of psychological tests and obtained material on their life histories. She then had several clinical colleagues try to determine which of the men were homosexuals. They were unable to distinguish between the two groups. There was no evidence that the homosexuals had a higher degree of pathology than the heterosexuals. Hooker concluded: "Homosexuality as a clinical entity does not exist. Its forms are as varied as those of heterosexuality. Homosexuality may be a deviation in sexual pattern that is in the normal range, psychologically" (p. 30). As a result of this and other studies, the American Medical Association and the American Psychological Association no longer list homosexuality as a mental disease.

The Hormone Hypothesis

Another hypothesis that has been advanced is that homosexuality is due to a hormonal imbalance. Specifically, it has been hypothesized that male homosexuality is due either to low levels of androgen (or some other male hormone) or to high levels of estrogen (or some other female hormone) and that female homosexuality is due to just the reverse. Indeed, several studies have found differences in the testosterone levels of male homosexuals and heterosexuals (for example, Rohde, Stahl, & Dörner, 1977; Starká, Šipová, & Hynie, 1975). However, other studies have failed to find such differences (Doerr et al., 1976; Friedman & Frantz, 1977). One study even reported the opposite relation: testosterone levels were higher in homosexual males than in heterosexual males (Gartrell, Loriaux, & Chase, 1977). In reviewing these studies, both Masters and Johnson (1979) and Meyer-Bahlburg (1977) have concluded that what we can infer from many of the studies is limited because of the methodology. Nevertheless, both reviewers acknowledge that hormones may interact with principles of learning to produce a homosexual orientation.

In some of the original studies of the relation between hormones and homosexual behavior, homosexual men were given injections of androgen. Rather than producing heterosexual behavior, such injections merely increased homosexual behavior (Ford & Beach, 1951). There is good reason to argue that androgen may energize behavior but does not, by itself, seem to give direction to behavior.

The Genetic Hypothesis

Still another hypothesis that has been advanced is that homosexuality is due to some genetic factor. In a study by Kallmann (1952), the twin brothers of 85 predominantly or exclusively homosexual men were investigated. All 40 pairs of monozygotic (identical) twins were concordant as to overt practice; that is, among the identical twins, all the brothers practiced homosexuality. In the dizygotic (fraternal) pairs, fewer than half of the brothers showed signs of overt homosexuality. Hoffman (1976) suggests that this study needs to be replicated before we draw any conclusions. At this point he suggests that we should conclude merely that genetic factors *may* play a role.

The Chance-Learning Hypothesis

From time to time it has been argued that homosexuality is due to chance learning. According to this hypothesis, if a young person were seduced by someone of the same sex, he or she would learn to associate the pleasures of sex with the gender of the seducer. No solid evidence has ever been put forth to support this hypothesis. Male homosexuality is fairly common in jails and prisons; however, upon release most men return to a heterosexual way of life. If homosexuality is as rewarding as the chance-learning hypothesis suggests (that is, if one homosexual experience is sufficient to produce a lifetime commitment to homosexuality), then why would men who have repeatedly engaged in homosexual activity during their terms in prison abruptly return to heterosexual relationships on their release? Masters and Johnson (1979) failed to find good evidence to support the chance-learning position, although in some cases there was reason to believe that seduction was a contributing factor. The problem, of course, is to determine who seduced whom. Did the seduced person have homosexual leanings before the actual event? Such a question is very difficult to answer.

The Multiple-Determinants Hypothesis

Masters and Johnson (1979) have suggested that there probably is no one cause of homosexuality, just as there is no one cause of heterosexuality. A combination of factors may somehow produce the homosexual orientation. For example, it may be a combination of certain hormone levels and learning, or it may be a combination of negative feelings toward members of the opposite sex and a satisfying same-sex relationship. One can think of many possibilities that might aim a person in one direction rather than another. Masters and Johnson point out that homosexuals often report a more satisfying sex life than heterosexuals do. They suggest that the homosexual might be more sensitive to the partner's needs because he or she is more knowledgeable about what it is that sexually arouses and fulfills a person of the same sex.

Summary

Over the years four main hypotheses have been advanced to account for homosexuality: mental illness, hormonal imbalance, genetics, and chance learning. In reviewing the evidence, Masters and Johnson have concluded that none of these hypotheses is sufficient to explain homosexuality. They argue that the evidence suggests that homosexuality occurs for a variety of reasons.

Gender Differences

Personality Differences

The words used to describe men and boys tend to differ from those used to describe women and girls. They have always differed, from the time of the earliest known writings (see Bakan, 1966). Men and boys tend to be described as active, aggressive, independent, competitive, rough, confident, persistent; women and girls tend to be described as passive, emotional, sensitive to the feelings of others, kind, gentle, understanding, and helpful. While it might be argued that these ways of describing the two sexes are simply holdovers from a time when we had different ideas about the roles of men and women, the attitudes they reflect have by no means disappeared. When men and women are asked to characterize themselves, men typically ascribe to themselves those qualities traditionally associated with male behavior and women typically describe themselves as having traditionally feminine qualities (Spence & Helmreich, 1978).

What is the major difference between the two sexes? It has been suggested that men tend to be more self-assertive and instrumental whereas women tend to be interpersonal and expressive (Locksley & Colten, 1979; Siem & Spence, 1986). In terms of actual behaviors, "instrumental" has to do with setting goals and accomplishing goals; expressiveness has less to do with action than with gaining understanding. The question that we will address in the following sections is whether or not the differences we see today are the products of our genes, of an environment that treats males and females differentially, or of the interaction of genetic and environmental factors.

Differences in Abilities

The kinds of abilities typically evinced by males and females tend to differ. Visual-spatial skills are more pronounced in men. Such skills enable them to locate things in space (find their way from one place to another, for example) and to rotate things in space (a skill that is important for visualizing an object from different perspectives, even when only one aspect of the object is in view). Women, in contrast, tend to have superior language skills (fluency, verbal reasoning, writing, and reading). It seems obvious that language skills are important in communication. In addition, it has been found that women tend to have a better sense of touch and better finger dexterity. In Japan and elsewhere, women are generally selected over men to assemble miniature parts for such things as computers because women are more adept at such tasks (Maccoby & Jacklin, 1974; Nash, 1979; Signorella & Jamison, 1986).

Hemispheric localization of cognitive abilities. There is a great deal of evidence that visual-spatial skills are located in the right hemisphere, whereas language skills are located mainly in the left hemisphere. Apparently, then, the differences noted in men's and women's abilities simply reflect this fact. But why should one hemisphere be dominant in men and the other in women? As we have noted, there is a great deal of evidence from work with humans and other animals that these differences can be traced to testosterone. What happens, it has been suggested, is that testosterone slows the growth of the left hemisphere, so that the right hemisphere becomes dominant in males.

Cognitive differences and evolution.   One interpretation as to why these differences emerged in the first place comes from an analysis of our evolutionary past. It has been suggested that these differences emerged when we were hunters and gatherers. In order to succeed as a hunter, an individual had to have certain physical characteristics (such as strength and a highly developed respiratory system) and the ability to track an animal and find the way home again. The hunter, in other words, needed to have visual-spatial abilities. The female, according to this analysis, was also involved in obtaining food. She, it is argued, gathered fruits, seeds, nuts, roots, and any other foods that were available. She also devised the baskets and other containers that held the food she gathered. For these important tasks she needed finger dexterity.

The female also, of course, had the task of caring for her children. It is likely that the females of the group cooperated in their tasks. The group, it is argued, developed ways of dividing the work among themselves. In order for this division of labor to work successfully, it was necessary for females to develop rather sophisticated communication abilities, which also served an important function in the teaching of the young. In other words, the greater language abilities of the female were important for the successful functioning of the group.

The evolutionary explanation can also account for some of the personality differences. The hunter, it is argued, needed to be active, aggressive, and independent. Hunting with primitive weapons is a dangerous activity and required the individual hunter to take care of himself for his own good and for the good of the group. While cooperation probably played a role in the pursuit of the food source, when the time came to kill, there was each man for himself. Kill or be killed was the only way to survive. (It should be noted here that aggression is linked to testosterone.) Females, in contrast, needed quite different characteristics to survive. As it would have been dangerous for a female burdened with young to leave the protection of the group, a greater degree of passivity and compliance may have served her well. Further, since it was the existence of the group that provided for her protection and protection of the offspring, it was important that irritants be removed before they could threaten the existence of the group. It was critical from her point of view that the group not become divided. Further, in order to maintain the division of labor (which permitted the females to keep their children close to the relative safety of the homeplace), it was necessary for the various members of the group to be sensitive to the needs of the other members. Being helpful would be a very good way of setting the stage for some system for the exchange of services.

Paying the price for being different.   Biologists have argued that a species has to pay the price for any evolutionary change that gives them some kind of advantage. That is, to gain one thing, you have to give up something else. What price do males and females pay for their differences? There is a great deal of evidence that males pay one kind of price and females another. Males tend to be more susceptible than females to such developmental disorders as dyslexia and stuttering (McGuinness, 1985). This makes a great deal of sense: when the right hemisphere of the male brain became dominant, the language skills governed by the left hemisphere suffered. The price females pay for being different, among other things, is reduced strength and lowered visual-spatial ability. It has been suggested that precise movements (manual dexterity) are more difficult when a person has the bulky muscles that give greater strength. Since we do not fully understand the role of visual-spatial abilities in daily functioning (except, perhaps, as this ability pertains to helping us find our way home in an unmarked environment) it is not yet clear whether this difference constitutes a serious handicap for females.

The Question of Handedness

The right side of the human brain controls the left side of the body and the left side of the brain controls the right side of the body. If the right hemisphere of the male brain is dominant, why aren't all males left-handed? The answer to that question apparently lies in what we do with the dominant arm and hand. We define dominance in terms of certain kinds of activities, such as picking things up and throwing things. There is a great deal of evidence that activities of that kind are best performed by persons whose left hemisphere is in control, since the left hemisphere is good at serial movements—the sort of movements involved in picking things up and throwing things. If, however, a very high level of testosterone should make an individual's right hemisphere extraordinarily dominant, then he might well be left-handed. In that case, there should be more left-handed males than left-handed females. About 10% of males are left-handed whereas 6% of females are left-handed. More important, it has been found that whereas 10% of left-handed people have such developmental disorders as dyslexia and stuttering, only 1% of the right-handed have such disorders. Another finding is that 11% of the left-handed have immunity disorders while only 4% of the right-handed do. What makes this finding so important is that immunity disorders (autoimmunity) can be linked to a high level of testosterone. Testosterone reduces the size of the thymus gland, an organ that enables the body to distinguish its own tissues from transplants. Without cells that can distinguish foreign tissues from one's own, the body tends to attack its own tissues (Geschwind & Behan, 1982).

The Concept of Androgyny

When we are born, we have (with few exceptions) male or female sex organs. The existence of these sex organs determines whether we are of the male gender or the female gender. Our gender, however, does not perfectly predict our sex orientation. As we have already noted, being born with male sex organs does not guarantee that we will be attracted to females or vice versa. While gender and sex orientation are highly correlated, approximately 10–15% of the population has a homosexual orientation whereas about 90% has a heterosexual or bisexual orientation. Neither our gender nor our sex orientation predicts a third thing about us: whether we will have a personality associated with the male gender or with the female gender. One of the most widely held current conceptions is that we all have characteristics associated with both. That is, we are all, to greater or lesser degree, androgynous—both masculine and feminine. This is called the dualistic view.

Two inventories have been constructed to assess the degree of masculinity, femininity, and androgyny in any individual: the Bem Sex-Role Inventory (BSRI) and the Personal Attributes Questionnaire (PAQ) (see Bem, 1974; Spence & Helmreich, 1978; Spence, 1984). The most frequent interpretation of these instruments is that the M (masculine) scale measures instrumentality and the F (feminine) scale measures expressivity (Locksley & Colten, 1979). Androgyny is reflected in equal measures of masculine and feminine traits. Figure 6-4 shows that people can be placed in four categories on the basis of high and low scores on the masculine and feminine scales.

Origins of Masculine and Feminine

There is a great deal of controversy concerning whether the traits that are referred to as masculine and those referred to as feminine are due to biological factors, to environmental factors, or to the complex interaction of the two.

The biological model. Researchers who stress the biological factors argue that masculine and feminine traits result from large concentrations of either testosterone or estrogen during certain critical stages of brain differentiation. According to this view, androgyny results when neither the right nor the left side of the brain is dominant. We have already considered some of the data that support the view that behaviors associated with masculinity and femininity are traceable to the early influences of hormones. Further support comes from a study of women that related sex-role identity to testosterone level as determined by saliva samples (Baucom, Besch, & Callahan, 1985). The researchers found that women of a masculine type (those with androgynous and masculine sex-role identities) had somewhat higher levels of testosterone than women with feminine sex-role identities. They also found that women with high testosterone concentrations perceived themselves to be more self-directed, action-oriented, and resourceful individuals, whereas women with lower testosterone concentrations viewed themselves as more conventional, socialized, and caring.

The environmental position. The environmental view is that behaviors that are referred to as masculine and feminine are traceable to sex-role stereotyping. A boy who is told, either overtly or covertly, that he must "behave like a man" will tend to imitate the kind of men who have been held up as good examples. Similarly, a girl who is encouraged to "act like a lady" will tend to imitate the kind of women who appear to be appropriate models. If no particular model is suggested, it is assumed that the child will tend to imitate the parent of the same sex. As the parents have been socialized in the male and female sex roles of their

	Masculine Scale: High	Masculine Scale: Low
Feminine Scale: High	Androgynous	Feminine
Feminine Scale: Low	Masculine	Undifferentiated

Figure 6-4. People who score high on both the masculine and feminine scales are androgynous types; people who score high on the masculine scale but low on the feminine scale are masculine types; people who score high on the feminine scale but low on the masculine scale are feminine types; and people who score low on both scales are undifferentiated types.

culture, the child adopts the stereotyped sex role of the society in which he or she lives. As no person is culture-free, this position is hard to either prove or disprove. It is clear that learning (modeling) indeed plays an important part in the formation of sex-role behaviors. Whether learning (stereotyping) has greater influence than biological factors continues to be debated.

The interaction of hormonal and learned factors.   Probably the most realistic position to take at this time is that biological and environmental factors are of equal importance. It may well be that hormones point us in a particular direction and that the development of certain traits depends on experience. For example, a girl may develop masculine traits provided that her brain is masculinized and that she is exposed to masculine people of either sex who reward her for masculine behavior. Similarly, feminine qualities in a boy may require a brain that is not overly masculinized and role models of either sex who reward the behaviors normally associated with girls.

Studies Involving Masculinity and Femininity

M-F and homosexuality.   In view of Dörner's hypothesis, one might expect that homosexual men would be more feminine than heterosexual men and that lesbians would be more masculine than heterosexual women. That is exactly what was found in a study of gay men and women. Gay men, it turned out, scored significantly lower than a heterosexual control group on the masculine and androgynous scales and higher on the feminine scale of the PAQ, whereas lesbians scored higher than a control group on the masculine and androgyny scales and lower on the feminine scale. Gay women scored higher on the masculine and androgyny scales than gay men; both groups scored the same on the feminine scale. The male homosexuals did not differ significantly from the male controls on a measure of self-esteem, but the lesbians scored significantly higher than the female controls (Spence, Helmreich, & Stapp, 1975).

M-F, love, and sex.   Are macho men and feminine women better lovers than people with less conventional sex-role identities? One prevailing cultural belief is that men are more concerned with sexual activity and work whereas women are more concerned with romance and love (Walster & Walster, 1978). While some research provides support for this widespread belief, in a number of instances just the opposite has been found—that men are more romantic lovers than women (see Coleman & Ganong, 1985). In a study of university students who identified themselves as being in a love relationship, it was found that androgynous individuals were more aware of feelings of love, more willing to express those feelings, and more tolerant of the loved one's faults than either masculine or feminine types. These findings indicate that it is not the macho man or the feminine woman that is the best lover. It appears that in order to experience and express love, one must have both instrumental and expressive qualities. That, of course, makes a great deal of intuitive sense.

M-F and self-esteem.   For some time psychologists have held the view that happiness and success are directly linked to self-esteem. When we feel good about ourselves, we tend to be not only happier but more successful. We tend to set more difficult goals for ourselves and to work harder to achieve those goals. While some studies have found that people who are classified as androgynous tend to have the greatest self-esteem (followed by people who are classified as masculine, followed next by people who are classified as feminine; bringing up the rear are people classified as undifferentiated; see Figure 6-4) (Helmreich, Stapp, & Ervin, 1974). Other studies have found that masculinity is the main component of self-esteem. When these studies are considered together, the weight of the evidence seems to favor the conclusion that self-esteem is linked to masculinity in both sexes rather than to androgyny (Whitley, 1983). Remember that the masculine scale tends to measure instrumentality whereas the feminine scale tends to measure expressivity. Remember also that our society tends to value people who achieve goals. From this perspective, it makes a great deal of sense that self-esteem is more closely linked to masculinity than to femininity.

M-F and achievement.   A study of high school and college students found that in general males tended to have higher educational aspirations than females, and that educational aspirations tended to rise with rising socioeconomic status. These findings are neither new nor unexpected. It is interesting to note, however, that educational aspirations can also be predicted by the traits of masculinity and femininity. It was found that males who were classified as androgynous and masculine had higher educational aspirations than those who were classified as feminine or undifferentiated; females who were classified as masculine also had higher educational aspirations, followed by women who were classified as androgynous, feminine, and undifferentiated. Achievement tests administered to the same sample indicated that in general, androgynous individuals had the highest motivation, followed by masculine, feminine, and undifferentiated individuals. Specifically, it was found that people who have higher aspirations tend to score higher on scales that measure work, mastery, and effort (Spence & Helmreich, 1978).

M-F and creativity.   There is evidence that creativity, at least as measured by empirical tests, is correlated with masculinity (Harrington & Andersen, 1981). What are the origins of this relationship? Why is it that androgynous people are not more creative than masculine people? It has been suggested that creativity is linked to the right hemisphere, and since masculinity also tends to be linked to the right hemisphere, people in whom the right hemisphere is dominant will be more creative. There is also evidence, however, that creative men have been raised by relatively androgynous parents—that is, relatively masculine mothers (Domino, 1969) and relatively feminine fathers (Grant & Domino, 1976). If it is true, as some people have asserted (Heilbrun, 1976), that creative men tend to identify more with their mothers than with their fathers, it can be argued that the mother played an important role in nurturing this behavior. Parallel evidence indicates that creative women also had relatively masculine mothers (Helson, 1966). In some cases it has been shown that creative women have identified with their fathers (for example, Anastasi & Schaefer, 1969; Helson, 1971, 1978). All of this evidence seems to suggest that the development of creativity may depend to a very large degree on having a parent or parents who possess masculine characteristics. That is, even if you have a biological predisposition toward creativity, it is important to interact with a parent who has masculine characteristics.

M-F and helping.   In the first study to assess whether men or women were more likely to help a victim, no sex differences were found (Darley & Latané, 1968). Subsequent studies varied the number of bystanders. As the number of bystanders rose, helping was significantly reduced by women but not by men (Schwartz & Clausen, 1970). The reduced helping in these and later studies has been attributed to "diffusion of responsibility"; that is, when other people are present, each individual feels proportionately less responsibility for helping a victim and less need to take decisive action. It has been suggested that the reason the men in the Schwartz and Clausen study did not show this effect was that some of the bystanders were women, and their presence induced the men to assume a male behavior pattern: they took charge. One obvious question is whether this behavior is due to the trait of masculinity rather than to maleness per se. In a study designed to address this question, an experiment was conducted in which the "victim" choked on food. It was found, as expected, that more men than women helped, that helping was reduced when others were present, and that more androgynous than sex-typed individuals helped. This last finding seems to make a great deal of sense if one assumes that the motivation to help involves two complementary but related processes. First, one must be able to empathize, a quality assumed to be feminine; and second, one must be able to act (be instrumental) on the basis of that empathy, presumably a masculine quality (Senneker & Hendrick, 1983).

Since then, however, others have found that men high in masculinity (instrumentality) and high in femininity (expressivity) are less likely to respond than men who score low in both qualities. Women who are high in both, on the other hand, are likely to help (e.g., Siem & Spence, 1986). It has been suggested that one of the moderating factors for men may be the fear of appearing foolish or gullible. That is, men who score high in both masculinity and femininity may want to intervene on behalf of a victim but are deterred by the fear of looking ridiculous.

Parental Antecedents of Masculinity and Femininity

A variety of factors appear to influence the tendency to be androgynous, masculine, or feminine. Research on parental antecedents indicates how a person may be nudged in one direction or another.

Some empirical findings. Probably the most general finding is that androgynous individuals tend to have parents who encourage cognitive independence, curiosity, and competence (Spence & Helmreich, 1978). Other studies have found other factors that may be involved. One study found that androgynous men tend to have parents who are both warm and accepting. Undifferentiated men, in contrast, seem to have parents lacking in these qualities. Further, androgynous men tend to be more involved with their fathers, whereas feminine men tend to be more involved with their mothers. Feminine men had warmer and more accepting parents than masculine men and tended to conform more to their fathers (Spence & Helmreich, 1978). These findings suggest that warmth and acceptance by both parents play important roles in the development of the androgynous individual. It appears that involvement with the father (rather than conformity to him) is another important factor. One particularly interesting finding was that undifferentiated men received relatively little encouragement in independence, curiosity, and competence.

Androgynous women were involved with both their mothers and fathers, although they tended more than masculine women to be involved with their mothers. The mothers of androgynous women encouraged their daughters' curiosity more than the mothers of the masculine group. Interestingly, the masculine women received greater encouragement in cognitive competence and curiosity from their fathers. The undifferentiated women, like men in the same category, received less cognitive encouragement from their parents than the other groups. The undifferentiated also were less involved with their mothers (Spence & Helmreich, 1978). An important factor that emerged from this study related to strictness of discipline: masculine women were treated more strictly by their fathers than were the androgynous women; the undifferentiated women experienced more strict discipline from their mothers than the others. Again, parental involvement seems to play a role. In addition, strictness of discipline seems to be a moderating factor.

Since such traits as cognitive independence, curiosity, and competence tend to be viewed as natural tendencies that will emerge more or less on their own given the right environment, the question is how the behavior of the parents interacts with the behavior of the child to produce the kind of results I have just reported.

The nature of the parent–child interaction.　It is important to remember that the way parents treat their children is often determined to a very large degree by the child (see Bell & Harper, 1977). A child who tends to be competitive, for example, may receive more encouragement for such behavior than a child who does not. Similarly, a child who tends to be expressive may be more encouraged for such behaviors than a child who does not. In other words, the child can shape the parent.

Parents, however, are not unbiased onlookers. Since men tend to value competition, they are more likely to reward competitive behavior in their children. Women, in contrast, tend to value such things as expressiveness, and so they are likely to reward such behavior. If a daughter shows signs of competitiveness, her inclinations may be encouraged by her father rather than her mother. Similarly, the mother will be the main source of encouragement of any expressiveness she sees in her son. With these things in mind, it becomes much easier to understand why we obtain some of the results that I reported above. Parents who exhibit warmth accept their children for what they are. Under those conditions we would expect such natural tendencies as cognitive independence, curiosity, and competence to emerge. If you are going to be a balanced (androgynous) person, you need to receive warmth and encouragement from both parents. If you receive such encouragement from only one parent, you will tend to develop the psychological characteristics of that parent. You may want to go back and reread some of the findings I reported above in the light of these remarks, using the framework of parent–child interaction to help organize your thinking.

Misdirected parents.　Unfortunately, we know that some parents do not encourage the development of certain natural tendencies, and may even discourage them. A father who wants to protect his daughter, for example, may disencourage her natural curiosity, which he considers a male characteristic. As a result, the daughter is unlikely to develop this tendency. Parents often fail to realize that such natural tendencies as the urge to explore are linked to a wide variety of behaviors in later life. Curiosity, for example, may play an important role in developing the ability to synthesize new information. In the course of exploring the immediate environment, one learns to identify each new thing as it is encountered, and a mass of information is reduced to manageable levels. Repeated explorations add new information that combines with the old to deepen one's understanding of one's world. A father who fails to understand the importance of the drive to satisfy one's curiosity may focus on the harm that might come to his daughter if she wandered away from the house. This well-intentioned father could inadvertently impair the child's capacity to synthesize new information. A child thus handicapped is unlikely to become a creative adult. Go back to the section headed "M-F and Creativity" and reflect from this perspective on the finding that women score less well than men on tests of creativity.

Summary

It has been suggested that men tend to be more self-assertive and instrumental, whereas women tend to be more interpersonal and expressive. Women tend to have superior language skills (fluency, verbal reasoning, writing, and reading) whereas men tend to have better visual-spatial skills (locating things in space and rotating things). There is evidence that visual-spatial skills are located in the right hemisphere whereas language skills are located in the left hemisphere. In other words, there is some evidence that the differences between males and females may be linked, at least in part, to biological differences. According to an evolutionary analysis, the better visual-spatial abilities of the male (as well as other characteristics) may have evolved in order to equip him to be a superior hunter. Similarly, it has been suggested that the better language abilities of the female may have equipped her to be a superior communicator, a trait that some biologists have argued is important if your survival depends on harmonious group interactions. It has been suggested that both males and females have paid a price for their differences.

Regardless of your gender, having a personality more like a male than a female would make you a masculine type, whereas having a personality more like a female than a male would make you a feminine type. If you have personality traits that are both masculine and feminine, you would be an androgynous type. Not having the major personality traits of either males or females would make you an undifferentiated type. Research has shown that gay men tend to be more feminine than heterosexual men and that gay females tend to be more masculine; that androgynous types are better lovers; and that masculine types tend to have greater self-esteem, higher achievement aspirations, and tend to be more creative. Whereas androgynous types are sometimes more inclined to help, there is evidence that rating high on the masculine scale for a male may interfere with helping.

There is a great deal of evidence that parents play an important role in nurturing those qualities that are associated with masculinity and femininity. The most general finding is that androgynous individuals tend to have parents who encourage cognitive independence, curiosity, and competence.

Main Points

1. Unlike other animals, humans engage in intercourse even when the female is not fertile.
2. The human female is almost unique in experiencing orgasm. It has been suggested that the orgasm has evolved to enhance pair bonding.
3. Evidence from a variety of sources suggests that males may have a stronger sex drive than females.
4. About 75% of human societies, both past and present, have been polygamous.
5. The Coolidge effect is the tendency of a satiated male to show reduced latency for sexual activity (intercourse) when a new or different female is made available.
6. In many animal species, sexual behavior is "released" when certain (often very specific) cues are present.

7. According to Desmond Morris's position, the sight of the genitals is the main releasing stimulus for human sexual behavior. Morris has also suggested that the female breasts act as a "releaser"; this point has been disputed by Elaine Morgan.
8. There are three main categories of sex hormones: androgens (mainly male), estrogens (mainly female), and progestins (mainly female).
9. Both males and females produce hormones associated primarily with the other sex; thus their behavior is governed by the joint action of male and female hormones.
10. Two important gonadotropic hormones are luteinizing hormone and follicle-stimulating hormone.
11. The hypothalamus exerts control over sexual behavior by affecting the endocrine glands, especially the pituitary, which secretes at least ten hormones.
12. While females' sexual behavior is not tied directly to periods of fertility, their sexual interest peaks at the time of ovulation.
13. While there is some evidence that male sexual activity is linked to changes in hormone levels, there is also evidence that environmental factors exert an important influence.
14. The temporal lobes of the brain play an important role in inhibiting and directing sexual behavior.
15. Studies of castration and ovariectomy have shown that the role played by the hormones declines as one moves up the evolutionary scale, and that male sexual behavior is less dependent on hormones than female sexual behavior.
16. Hormones appear to mediate sexual attraction in animals by sensitizing the animal to sexual cues in animals of the opposite sex.
17. Testosterone plays a very important role in the erection and ejaculation responses of the human male.
18. Human female sex motivation has been linked to androgens.
19. If an egg has been fertilized by an XY chromosome, H-Y antigens change the embryo's ovaries into testicles.
20. Testosterone, produced by the testicles, produces a variety of changes in the embryo, including the development of the penis.
21. The sex hormones play an important role in the development of the hypothalamus, the cortex, and appropriate sexual behavior in animals.
22. There is evidence that the hormones produced during early stages of development are associated with certain sex-typed behaviors. Human evidence for this influence is linked to such clinical syndromes as congenital adrenal hyperphasia (CAH).
23. According to Dörner's theory, homosexuality in both sexes is linked to abnormalities in hormone levels during critical stages of brain differentiation.
24. Masters and Johnson have identified four more or less distinct phases in the sexual response of males and females.
25. Masters and Johnson suggest that the main motivation governing human sexual behavior is the pleasure derived from various forms of tactile stimulation.
26. Harlow's research suggests that peers are crucial in the development of the human sexual response.
27. Extraverts tend to pet more and have intercourse more often than introverts.
28. Chance meetings and difficulty of attainment appear to increase sexual attraction.
29. The study of erotica and pornography has shown that humans tend to be aroused by pictures and descriptions of humans involved in sexual behavior.

30. Guilt feelings can reduce the arousal typically produced by erotic or pornographic material.
31. Variety and change tend to enhance sexual arousal.
32. Masters and Johnson conclude that homosexuality has multiple determinants.
33. Males and females tend to have somewhat different abilities, which have been linked to differences in hemispheric dominance. Various evolutionary explanations have been offered for the origins of these differences.
34. According to the concept of androgyny, humans of each sex have characteristics of the other.
35. Studies comparing masculine, feminine, androgynous, and undifferentiated types have led to the conclusion that degrees of masculine and feminine qualities are linked to such things as the ability to love, self-esteem, achievement, and helping.
36. There is evidence that the environment plays an important role in nurturing the attributes of masculinity and femininity.

Emotions as Motives: Understanding Optimism, Fear, Anxiety, and Altruism

What do optimism, fear, anxiety, and altruism have in common?

Are emotions simply a state of mind, or do they have a neurological and chemical basis?

What is the evolutionary significance of such emotions as optimism, fear, anxiety, and altruism?

Can people learn to do things that will make them feel euphoric or optimistic?

Can people learn to do things that will lead to a reduction in fear and anxiety?

What is the difference between fear and anxiety?

Why are some people more fearful and anxious than others?

Why is it that people sometimes help and at other times look the other way?

Why do people tend to blame victims for their misfortunes rather than empathize with them?

What Do Emotions Have in Common?

Dimensions of emotions. If you ask people to characterize various emotions—fear, anger, sadness, happiness, disgust—they typically use three basic dimensions: (*a*) pleasant/unpleasant, (*b*) active/passive, and (*c*) intense/not intense (Daly, Lancee, & Polivy, 1983). The emotion of sadness is typically characterized as unpleasant and passive. The intensity of sadness varies with the situation, from extreme to slight. Sadness is usually experienced as a very intense emotion if it has been precipitated by the death of a loved one. Sadness is typically viewed as a passive emotion because there often is little one can do about the situation. Besides, when people are sad, they often lack the motivation to do anything. The emotion of happiness, on the other hand, is characterized as pleasant and active. If we are very happy, as we might be if we won a lottery, we are likely to be very active. We might, for example, want to have a party. While various researchers agree that emotions can be described in terms of a limited number of dimensions, they have reached no consensus on the names or numbers of those dimensions (for example, Russell & Steiger, 1982).

Circular ordering of emotions. A slightly different way of approaching the emotions is to consider how they relate to one another. It has been proposed, for example, that emotions can be ordered in a circular fashion. Figure 7-1 shows such a circular model of emotions (Fromme & O'Brien, 1982). The four dimensions of this model are dominance/submission, pleasure/pain, approach/avoidance, and parasympathetic arousal/sympathetic arousal. A good exercise is to think of various emotions and attempt to locate them on Figure 7-1.

Definition of emotion. Probably because emotions are so complex, a wide variety of definitions have been proposed over the years. In an attempt to arrive at a consensual definition, Paul Kleinginna and Anne Kleinginna (1981b) examined the definitions then in use and proposed a definition that incorporated the key elements of existing definitions. According to this consensual definition, emotions occur as a result of an interaction between subjective factors, environmental factors, and neural/hormonal processes. In support of this definition they point out

Figure 7-1. The circular structure of the emotions and associated behavior (Fromme & O'Brien, 1982)

that emotions (*a*) give rise to affective experiences (such as pleasure or displeasure), (*b*) stimulate the individual to generate cognitive explanations (to attribute the cause to oneself or to the environment, for example), (*c*) trigger a variety of internal adjustments (such as increased heart rate), and (*d*) elicit behaviors that are often, but not always, expressive (laughing or crying), goal-directed (helping or avoiding), and adaptive (removal of something that may threaten the individual's survival).

One very important additional function of emotions is to reward and punish behavior. When people experience a very positive emotion, they are likely to engage in behaviors that will produce that emotion again. Similarly, when people experience a very negative emotion, they will avoid behaviors that will cause them to feel that emotion again.

Emotions obviously play an important role in motivating behavior. In this chapter we will examine a few of the more basic emotions—optimism, fear, anxiety, and altruism—and discuss how these emotions motivate various kinds of behavior, such as risk taking on the one hand and helping, on the other. As in regard to the other factors in human motivation, we will examine emotions in terms of their three basic components: the biological, learned, and cognitive factors.

Summary
When people are asked to characterize emotions, they tend to view them in terms of three dimensions: pleasant/unpleasant, active/passive, and intense/not intense. Another way to view emotions is in terms of how they relate to one another. According to this approach, emotions have four dimensions: dominance/submission, pleasure/pain, approach/avoidance, and parasympathetic arousal/sympathetic arousal. It has been suggested that emotions give rise to affective experiences, stimulate the individual to generate cognitive explanations, trigger a variety of internal adjustments, and elicit expressive, goal-directed, and adaptive behaviors.

The Emotion of Optimism

Probably no emotion is of more interest to humans than the emotion of optimism. Optimism is an emotion that is very pleasant and active and often very intense.

The Biological Component

Reward pathways in the brain.   More than 30 years ago James Olds discovered that rats with electrodes implanted in certain areas of the brain would learn to press a bar in order to receive electrical stimulation that activated those areas (Olds, 1956; Olds & Milner, 1954). He confirmed that laboratory animals stimulated themselves in this way only when the stimulation activated particular brain areas. It should be noted that self-reward systems have also been found in humans (Heath, 1963). The reward systems of the human brain are seen in Figure 7-2.

If these areas of the brain are able to provide very powerful and satisfying feelings, as various people have proposed, the question is how people manage to activate these areas of the brain. For many years no one was quite sure how to activate them short of implanting an electrode in someone's brain. In recent years, however, we have come a lot closer to understanding how various behaviors lead to the activation of these reward centers.

One way of activating those areas of the brain is apparently to take drugs. Aryeh Routtenberg (1978) has demonstrated that the amphetamines facilitate self-stimulation, whereas chlorpromazine reduces self-stimulation. The amphetamines do not themselves activate the reward centers but rather stimulate the output of two brain chemicals, dopamine and norepinephrine. Routtenberg (1978) has argued that dopamine plays a more important role than norepinephrine, but Larry Stein

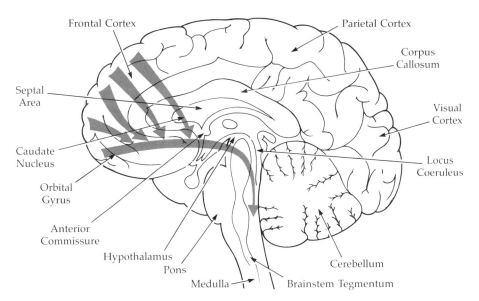

Figure 7-2.   The reward system of the human brain has been roughly localized in the shaded regions. These areas correspond to the parts of the rat brain that support self-stimulation behavior (Routtenberg, 1978).

(1980) has argued that it is impossible to determine whether dopamine or norepinephrine is more important, as the two systems appear to act jointly.

Are there other ways of activating these reward centers? The implication of Routtenberg's work is that any activity that triggers the release of dopamine and norepinephrine will produce the positive feelings associated with these centers. Let us examine some of the data relevant to this idea.

Norepinephrine and affect.   Both dopamine and norepinephrine are neurotransmitters: they conduct messages across the synapses in the brain (gaps between adjacent neurons). Without neurotransmitters, messages cannot pass from one area of the brain to another. When there is a high concentration of a neurotransmitter such as norepinephrine at a synapse, signals pass freely and rapidly across it (von Euler, 1956). When norepinephrine is present in abundance, then, we are good at processing information.

Norepinephrine also plays a very primary role in determining our emotions. It has been found that when concentrations of norepinephrine are high at the synapses, we tend to feel euphoric. Apparently the reason cocaine produces feelings of euphoria is that it increases the concentrations of norepinephrine at the synapses. (The effects of cocaine are discussed in greater detail in Chapter 9.) When concentrations of norepinephrine are low, we tend to feel depressed (Schildkraut & Kety, 1967). (We will address the question of depression in Chapter 11.)

The brain has many storage sites for norepinephrine. We know that large amounts of norepinephrine can also be found outside the brain. The norepinephrine produced by the adrenal cortex plays an important role in energy metabolism. As we noted earlier in connection with running, the level of norepinephrine in the blood rises quite markedly when we run. The important point here is that we know norepinephrine is often readily available at various sites in the brain. We also have good evidence, however, that the level of norepinephrine available can decline quite dramatically under certain conditions. Apparently the synapses absorb and then destroy the norepinephrine that is released at the synapses. The net effect is that, at least for a time, the norepinephrine stores are depleted. When this happens, our mood shifts from positive to negative and our ability to process information declines. Normally the stores of norepinephrine will be replenished in due course. According to one theory (Hartmann, 1973), sleep plays an important role in ensuring that these stores of norepinephrine are replenished. Rest, proper diet, and even exercise may be important in this regard.

The Learned Component

The work of Brady and associates.   Since we can experience a very positive emotional state by stimulating the release of norepinephrine, the question is how we can do this without resorting to drugs. A growing body of data indicates that we can tap these emotions by exercising certain adaptive responses. A series of studies by Joseph Brady (Brady, 1967, 1975) clearly illustrate this point (see also Mason, 1975; Mason, Brady, & Tolson, 1966). Brady and his colleagues measured epinephrine and norepinephrine output in monkeys during a shock-avoidance task. In such a task the monkey is presented with a signal (such as a horn) which is followed several seconds later by shock. The point of the task is for the monkey to learn that it can avoid the shock by making some adaptive response, such as pressing a lever. When the monkey makes that response, the shock does not occur. Being fairly intelligent animals, monkeys quickly learn what they must do to avoid the shock. In order to determine whether the levels of these two catecholamines change as the result of learning, the investigators measured the levels of these two chemicals before the monkeys had learned to avoid the shock and then again after they had learned to do so. As the first two panels in Figure 7-3 reveal, the levels of both epinephrine and norepinephrine were quite low before learning had occurred when either the horn or the shock was presented alone. After learning, however, norepinephrine levels rose quite dramatically when the horn was sounded.

It should be noted that when the monkeys made an avoidance response (exercised a well-practiced adaptive response), the level of plasma 17-OH-CS (17 hydroxycorticosteroids) declined. Because 17-OH-CS has been associated with anxiety, the decline in 17-OH-CS suggests that the ability to make an adaptive response reduces anxiety (Brady, 1967, 1975). This finding, of course, is consistent with our general impression that when we gain control over events in our lives, anxiety is lessened. Further evidence in support of Brady's position comes from the work of Jay Weiss and his colleagues (Weiss, Stone, & Harrell, 1970). They subjected rats to shock under conditions in which it was possible to escape and avoid the shock and under conditions in which it was not. Animals that could escape showed a significant elevation in brain norepinephrine, whereas animals in the "inescapable" condition showed a significant decrease in brain norepinephrine. What this and other studies show is that norepinephrine levels are elevated when the situation is predictable and controllable.

Responding to an unpredictable event.   Not all situations are completely predictable. How might subjects respond to situations that are only partly predictable and therefore only partly controllable? To examine this question, Mason, Brady, and Tolson (1966) introduced random shocks in a shock-avoidance task, using monkeys as subjects. They found that both epinephrine and norepinephrine levels

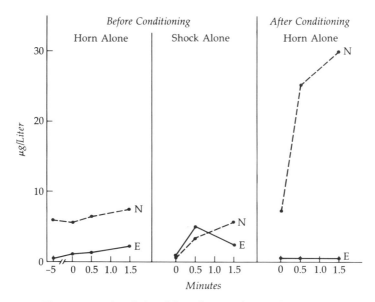

Figure 7-3.   Plasma norepinephrine (N) and epinephrine (E) responses in monkeys before and after shock-avoidance conditioning (Mason, Brady, & Tolson, 1966)

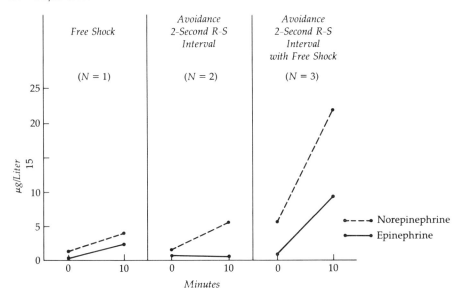

Figure 7-4.   Plasma epinephrine and norepinephrine responses to "free shock" alone, "regular" nondiscriminated avoidance, and avoidance with "free shock." *N* = number of animals in sample (Mason, Brady, & Tolson, 1966).

were elevated (see Figure 7-4). These and other findings indicate that epinephrine may be elevated when the situation becomes somewhat ambiguous. After examining this and other experimental evidence, Schildkraut and Kety suggested that

> increased epinephrine (adrenaline) excretion seems to occur in states of anxiety or in threatening situations of uncertain or unpredictable nature in which active coping may be required but has not been achieved. In contrast, norepinephrine (noradrenaline) excretion may occur in states of anger or aggression or in situations which are challenging but predictable and which allow active and appropriate behavioral responses to the challenge. Under various conditions increase of either epinephrine or norepinephrine or of both of these catecholamines may represent specific adaptive responses [1967, p. 23].

Why the increase in norepinephrine levels shown in Figure 7-4? It may be that ambiguous situations not only give rise to anxiety but challenge the subject to intensify adaptive efforts. Sensation-seeking often involves activities that have a certain amount of ambiguity or unpredictability associated with them. If people are motivated to engage in activities that increase norepinephrine levels, it follows that they might select activities that contain some degree of ambiguity or unpredictability. It may well be that sensation-seeking activities, such as skydiving or racing cars, attract people because such activities produce higher levels of norepinephrine than more predictable and controllable situations do. I will examine this hypothesis further when I discuss sensation-seeking behaviors (Chapter 13).

The incentive to have impact.   David McClelland (1985) has argued that the natural incentive to have an impact is served by the release of catecholamine neurotransmitters in the brain. He suggests that the desire to have an impact is unlearned, and that a variety of behaviors—those directed toward competence, mastery, and self-determination, for example—are derived from it. He has suggested further that assertiveness and aggression too may flow from a desire to have impact. Finally, he argues that the need to control can be viewed as a derivative of the need to have impact. The implication is that when we strive for competence or mastery and simply try to gain control of our situation, such catecholamines as norepinephrine and dopamine are released, which lead to a positive mood.

It is interesting to note that men respond to such diverse things as injections, the threat of an examination (Frankenhaeuser, Dunne, & Lundberg, 1976), and the prospect of jumping from a mock training tower (Hansen et al., 1978) by releasing more norepinephrine and epinephrine as measured by levels in the urine. As we shall see in more detail shortly, the ability to face a difficult or threatening task demands optimism, a sense that all will be well in the end. There is good reason to believe that the optimism we feel in such situations is not simply a positive attitude but rather a neural/hormonal response that is triggered when we engage in some adaptive behavior or anticipate making an adaptive response.

The Cognitive Component

It is important to recognize that the way one appraises a threat or a challenge plays an important role in determining how one will deal with that event. Three basic theories of emotion have emerged, all of which have addressed the question of the relation of cognitions to various neural/hormonal events.

The James-Lange theory.   William James (1884) and Carl Lange (1885/1922) first questioned the traditional assumption that affect was cognitive. They independently suggested that the basis of emotional experience was to be found in peripheral physiological sensations, such as those resulting from increased heart rate and blood pressure and from contractions of visceral and skeletal muscles. For example, a man who runs at the sight of a bear will experience a number of sensations resulting from running, and those sensations will serve as the basis for the emotion called fear. Why does the man run from the bear? He runs, according to the James-Lange theory, because it is adaptive for humans to engage in some kind of "flight or fight" response when confronted with an event that threatens their survival. This reaction, according to James and Lange, occurs not because of an emotion but rather because it is necessary to react appropriately to a wide variety of stimulus events. Different events might require slightly different responses. Emotions, they believed, are synonymous with the physiological changes that accompany each of these different reactions. If there were no physiological changes, there would be no emotions. It should be noted, however, that it is not necessary to have an overt reaction before one feels an emotion. Physiological changes may occur without any overt response. Just before we engage in a flight response, for example, a number of physiological changes occur to prepare us for this reaction. Clearly, we experience an emotion under such conditions.

Cannon's theory.   William Cannon (1927) criticized the James-Lange theory on the basis of a series of experiments showing that visceral changes are nonspecific reactions that accompany diverse emotions. If visceral changes are nonspecific, Cannon argued, they cannot provide the basis for different emotions. Therefore, the diverse emotions we experience must be cognitive. Some theorists have argued that certain motivational systems (for example, eating, aggression, and sex), together with their accompanying affects, have their bases in more primitive parts of the brain (Arnold, 1960, 1970); however, the importance of the cerebral cortex in directing the behaviors associated with these systems has repeatedly been emphasized (for example, Hebb, 1949). That is, in the final analysis, the label we give to an emotion is determined by the way we perceive the event that prompts it.

Schachter and Singer's theory.   According to Schachter and Singer (1962), emotions are essentially cognitive; however, since emotions are accompanied by physiological responses, such as rapid heart rate and a flushed face, the person is confronted with the task of accounting for these physiological responses. They assume that the person will interpret the physiological reactions in such a way as to be consistent with his or her cognitive appraisal of the stimulus events evoking the physiological responses. If a person has already labeled a situation as producing a particular emotion, such as euphoria, anger, or fear, then how should the person account for differences in arousal? Because emotions are perceived to vary in intensity, it seems reasonable to hypothesize, as Schachter and Singer do, that the person will infer that differences in physiological activity accompanying a particular emotion reflect differences in intensity. Thus, the greater the magnitude of the physiological activity, the greater the intensity of the emotion.

To test their theory experimentally, Schachter and Singer manipulated physiological responses by using epinephrine under the guise of studying how vitamin supplements affect vision. Epinephrine, of course, produces autonomic arousal, whose symptoms include increased heart rate, hand tremors, and flushing of the face. To evaluate the joint effects of autonomic arousal and cognitive activities, Schachter and Singer used four conditions, of which three are of interest here. In one condition, participants were given injections of epinephrine but were told it was a vitamin compound that could be expected to produce some side effects—heart palpitations, tremors, and so on. This was the "epinephrine informed" group. In a second condition ("epinephrine ignorant"), subjects were also given injections of epinephrine and told it was a vitamin compound, which most subjects would not associate with symptoms of autonomic arousal; they were not informed of any side effects. A third group ("placebo") were given injections of saline solution, an inert substance that does not produce autonomic arousal. (In the fourth condition, subjects were given epinephrine and misinformed about its side effects—they were told it would cause numbness and itching.)

Since the subjects in the epinephrine-ignorant condition were not told about the side effects of epinephrine, they would experience physiological changes for which they had no explanation. Subjects who were informed about the side effects would experience the same physiological responses but would have an explanation for them. Schachter and Singer's theory predicts that the participants who were not informed would be motivated to find an explanation for these reactions, while the informed participants would not.

In a clever design to test whether unexplained physiological reactions contribute to the intensity of a cognitively manipulated emotion, Schachter and Singer exposed the subjects to a variety of situations that were designed to elicit particular emotions. For example, they exposed some subjects to a situation involving some tomfoolery by a euphoric confederate in order to elicit euphoria. They insulted other subjects in order to elicit anger. According to their theory, subjects who had not been informed about the side effects of their injections would experience more intense emotions than subjects who had been informed, regardless of the type of emotion aroused.

Observations of the participants and data obtained with a questionnaire supported Schachter and Singer's hypothesis. As predicted, the uninformed participants were angrier in the anger-inducing situation and more euphoric in the euphoria-inducing situation than either the informed group or the placebo group. These findings support Schachter and Singer's theory that physiological reactions contribute to the magnitude of the emotion under conditions in which such reactions are unlabeled. The fact that arousal level, when labeled, does not contribute to the intensity of the emotion is consistent with their view that both the direction and the intensity of an emotion are mediated by cognitive factors.

In a later experiment, Schachter and Wheeler (1962) demonstrated the generality of the previous findings. Participants were injected with epinephrine, a placebo, or chlorpromazine (a drug that inhibits autonomic arousal). Then they were shown a brief comedy film. Observations of their reactions to the film indicated that level of expressed amusement was greatest under epinephrine and lowest under chlorpromazine.

Recently several attempts have been made to replicate Schachter and Singer's work. Erdmann and Janke (1978) obtained results that are consistent with those originally reported by Schachter and Singer (1962). That is, they found that epinephrine enhanced happiness and anger. Two other papers, however, have reported failures to replicate (Marshall & Zimbardo, 1979; Maslach, 1979). Whether these are truly failures to replicate remains unanswered at this point, because there are several important procedural differences between these studies and Schachter and Singer's. Schachter and Singer (1979) argue that these differences are critical and therefore it is impossible to compare the two sets of experiments. Rainer Reisenzein (1983) has reviewed the research evidence relevant to Schachter's theory of emotion and has concluded there is good support for the idea that misattributed arousal intensifies emotions.

What about individual differences? Do all people attempt to account for physiological arousal? The answer is no. It appears that people who are more "unemotional" do not respond the same way as people who are "emotional" (Valins, 1967). In a study already described in Chapter 2, Valins (1967) gave fraudulent heart-rate feedback to men while they were shown pictures of seminude women. He found that the feedback had a greater effect on emotional than unemotional men. It may be that the reason some people are more "unemotional" is that they have, for whatever reason, become insensitive to their own physiological reactions. Possibly through such mechanisms as denial (see Lazarus, 1966), they have come to ignore this source of information. Failure to consider this information would, according to Valins, result in a lowered emotional reaction. Hirschman and Hawk (1978) and Liebhart (1977), using aversive slides and fraudulent heart-rate feedback, found results similar to those reported by Valins. Hirschman and Hawk found, in addition, that resting autonomic levels affect reactivity: people with higher resting autonomic levels showed larger electrodermal responses (increases in electrical conductivity of the skin, typically accompanying increases in autonomic arousal) to the heart-rate-feedback/slide combination and reported the experience to be more unpleasant. This finding suggests that emotional reactivity is not just a cognitive event but is mediated as well by resting physiological activity.

What do these theories tell us about optimism? The Schachter-Singer theory suggests that the degree or intensity of our optimism at any given moment will be related to the level of arousal we are experiencing at that moment. If optimism is somehow linked to adaptive responses, then it follows that the harder a person works, the more optimistic he or she will feel. In other words, optimism leads to effort, which leads in turn to feelings of optimism. Does this make sense? In the next section I will review Tiger's theory of the evolutionary origins of optimism. According to his theory, optimism not only leads people to put forth effort (provides the motivation for acting) but is the mechanism for ensuring that certain adaptive behaviors will be repeated in the future (acts as a reward for adaptive behaviors).

Optimism from an Evolutionary Perspective

In *Optimism: The Biology of Hope*, Lionel Tiger (1979) argues that when our ancestors left the forest and became plains animals, they were faced with the task of having to obtain food by killing other animals. In the course of hunting, he argues, they doubtless experienced many adverse circumstances. Many of them must have suffered a variety of injuries. The principles of learning tell us that humans tend to abandon tasks that are associated with negative consequences. So why did hunters carry on in the face of such adverse conditions? Tiger argues that it was biologically adaptive for our ancestors to develop a sense of optimism. Optimism would carry them through adverse circumstances, even injury.

By what mechanism or mechanisms did optimism develop? Tiger suggests that one of the mechanisms that evolved consisted of endorphins. The word *endorphins* was coined from *endogenous morphine*, which refers to the fact that our bodies produce their own morphine-like substance. When we are injured, our bodies typically release endorphins. Endorphins have at least two important qualities. First, they have analgesic properties (they have the ability to reduce pain). Second, they produce feelings of euphoria. Sometimes people talk about their ability to reduce feelings of fatigue. Tiger argues that it was adaptive for our hunting ancestors to experience a positive rather than a negative emotion when they were injured because it would reinforce rather than punish their tendency to hunt in the future. It would have been disastrous, he argues, if our ancestors had abandoned the tendency to hunt.

Tiger points out that it is important to have a sense of optimism in general. When things go wrong, it is important not to give up. He points out that optimism is not only a very positive emotion but a very active one as well. Optimism makes us look to our environment with the view that it can provide us with the resources we need. Such an attitude, he argues, was very important for our ancestors' survival, especially in the face of hardships and setbacks.

Summary

Self-stimulation studies have provided evidence that feelings of euphoria (and optimism) are linked to reward pathways in the brain. These reward pathways are activated by the release of dopamine and norepinephrine. The work of Brady and his associates indicates that when organisms make an adaptive response, norepinephrine is released. These studies suggest that we may be able to learn responses that lead to the release of norepinephrine, a chemical that has been implicated in feelings of euphoria. It is interesting to note that when events are made unpredictable, the chemical released is epinephrine, which has been linked to feelings of anxiety. McClelland has argued that the release of norepinephrine is linked to the "impact incentive."

According to the James-Lange theory, emotions are intimately linked to peripheral physiological sensations. Cannon's position, in contrast, is that

(continued)

emotions are purely cognitive. Schachter and Singer have argued that while emotions are essentially cognitive, the intensity of emotions is determined to a very large degree by the feedback that comes from our peripheral physiological responses, such as heart rate and breathing. According to the Schachter-Singer theory, optimism is increased when an individual engages in adaptive behavior. According to Tiger, optimism not only provides the motivation for acting (engaging in adaptive behavior) but rewards behaviors that have an adaptive function.

Fear and Anxiety

Distinguishing between fear and anxiety.   It is not altogether clear that we should make a distinction between fear and anxiety. Some theorists have suggested that the two are basically the same (Izard & Tomkins, 1966); others have suggested that the goal object of fear is fairly specific while the goal object of anxiety is more vague or ambiguous (Miller, 1951). For example, we may fear snakes or high places or failing a test. Anxiety, on the other hand, is an emotion that we experience when it is not possible to specify the exact reason. We might, for example, experience anxiety in connection with the prospect of giving a speech. While we have no good reason to think that anything will go wrong, we nevertheless have a feeling that something terrible may happen. Images flit through our mind: we open our mouth to speak and nothing comes out; or we speak all too clearly and everyone laughs at us.

Some theorists have suggested that anxiety is a more powerful emotion than fear. When we are afraid, we know what is causing our emotion. When we are anxious, however, the emotion is so unfocused that we have difficulty dealing with it (see Epstein, 1972).

Definition of anxiety.   Rollo May (1983) has proposed the following definition of anxiety:

> Anxiety is the apprehension cued off by a threat to some value that the individual holds essential to his existence as a personality. The threat may be physical (the threat of death), or to psychological existence (the loss of freedom, meaninglessness). Or, the threat may be to some other value that one identifies with one's existence: patriotism, the love of another person, "success," etc. [p. 205].

Antecedents of anxiety.   Seymour Epstein (1972) has argued that three primary conditions elicit anxiety: (1) overstimulation, (2) cognitive incongruity, and (3) response unavailability. These three conditions produce not only feelings of anxiety (apprehension) but high arousal as well. When we are anxious we may experience such physical symptoms as an increased heart rate, flushed skin, and a general state of muscle tension. Mentally, we may feel confused and unable to deal with the environment around us. In the following sections we will be dealing with these and other conditions that elicit anxiety.

The Biological Component

Our knowledge about the biological bases of fear and anxiety is sketchy at best. One way to understand fear and anxiety is to examine the workings of various drugs that reduce these feelings. Among the drugs frequently prescribed to reduce

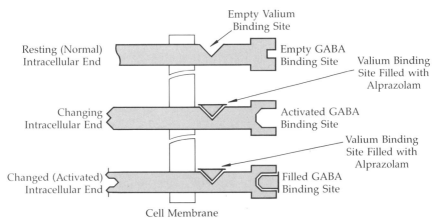

Figure 7-5. Valium/GABA receptor. This simplified schematic drawing shows three stages in activation of the receptor complex: (1) The receptor, lodged in a cell membrane, has unfilled binding sites for GABA and a benzodiazepine (Valium, alprazolam, etc.) molecule. (2) When alprazolam binds to its site, like a key in a lock, it may open (activate) the GABA site, allowing it to bind a GABA molecule. (3) Once both alprazolam and GABA are bound and active, the intracellular end of the receptor may change its shape, setting off a "chemical domino effect" that can transmit a message inside the cell (Fishman & Sheehan, 1985).

feelings of anxiety are the benzodiazepines. These drugs (Valium, Librium, alprazolam) seem to work by making it possible for GABA (gamma-amino butyric acid) to perform one of its functions. GABA may be thought of as a naturally occurring transmitter inhibitor (Cooper, Bloom, & Roth, 1982; Tallman et al., 1980). That means that GABA somehow reduces the flow of neural transmission.

The way such benzodiazepines as Valium work is depicted in Figure 7-5. The drug "binds" to a chemical receptor that is shaped to receive and use just such a drug. The fact that there are receptors for such drugs suggests that the body probably produces its own benzodiazepines, though naturally produced benzodiazepines have not yet been isolated. When Valium binds to its site (like a key in a lock), it opens the GABA site, thereby making it possible for a GABA molecule to bind to that site. When a GABA molecule is in place, the biochemistry of the cell changes. The net effect is that people experience less anxiety (Fishman & Sheehan, 1985).

From a subjective point of view, when we are flooded with stimulation or information (experience overstimulation) or when we have difficulty reconciling some event, such as the loss of a loved one, with a deeply felt belief in a just world (cognitive incongruity), or when we simply do not know how to handle a difficult situation, such as meeting new people (response unavailability), we often experience anxiety together with high arousal. People who parachute for the first time often report anxiety attacks that some people describe as pure panic. The reason we think that people who are new to parachuting experience anxiety attacks is that the first time they jump they are suddenly faced with a totally new event that requires them not only to process information but to make decisions. They find themselves overloaded (or "overwhelmed"). There are simply too many demands being placed on the system, and the novice skydiver responds subjectively with feelings of anxiety.

What we think the antianxiety drugs do in such situations is regulate neural transmission. There is considerable evidence that when some optimal level of stimulation or arousal is exceeded, we not only experience anxiety but lose a large measure of our ability to think, act, and perform (Hebb, 1955). GABA appears to be one of those substances in the body that helps to maintain an optimal flow of stimulation or information. But as we have noted, GABA may perform this function only in association with another substance, such as benzodiazepine. Perhaps people who experience more anxiety than others fail to produce or release either the benzodiazepines that are necessary to keep anxiety under control or the amount of GABA needed to regulate neural transmission.

The Learned Component

Fear and anxiety as conditioned pain.   According to such neobehaviorists as Neal Miller (1951) and O. H. Mowrer (1939), fear is a conditioned response to pain. If a person experiences pain in a specific situation, the stimuli associated with that situation will acquire the ability to elicit the same emotional reaction that the pain originally elicited. According to Miller, the main difference between fear and anxiety is whether the stimuli eliciting the fear are identifiable or vague.

Many of the early studies of fear and anxiety involved the use of pain. In the avoidance-learning paradigm used in these studies, the animals, often rats or dogs, were administered a painful shock to the feet in an enclosure called a shuttle box. The long, rectangular shuttle box is divided into two compartments by a low wall that the animal can jump over. The shock is administered through a grid floor on either side. The animal can escape the shock by jumping over the low wall. The procedure can then be repeated in reverse: the side of the box that was safe is now electrified and vice versa. In the course of several trials the animal jumps back and forth; thus the name "shuttle box." In the experimental setup a signal (often a noise or bright light) is presented a few seconds before the shock is administered. Because a signal precedes the shock, the animals can learn to avoid the shock by jumping over the low wall when the signal is presented. Typically animals learn this task fairly quickly.

It is important to note that in the course of learning, the animals show a great deal of emotionality. Rats, for example, urinate and defecate. Dogs often yelp or whine. As learning progresses, however, these signs of emotionality decrease (Amsel, 1962).

Why does the avoidance response occur progressively earlier?   A number of important things have been learned from such experiments (Solomon & Wynne, 1954). First, with experience the animals learn to respond progressively earlier, until they are responding as soon as the signal is presented. As their response time shortens, the emotionality associated with this kind of learning decreases. The behavior, in fact, looks quite routine after extensive training. What we believe is happening is that the signal triggers the emotional response, which would normally increase in strength as time passes. The animal learns that it can reduce the aversive emotion triggered by the signal by making a quick response. One piece of important evidence that provides converging evidence for this interpretation is the fact that when animals are prevented from making that response quickly, they show a great deal of emotionality. Humans react in much the same way. When we have to wait for an hour in a dentist's reception room, we tend to experience more anxiety than we do when we are ushered immediately into the chair. Performers often say that having to wait to go onstage is one of the things that causes them the most anxiety.

Why does the avoidance response persist over time?   The second thing that we have learned from the avoidance-conditioning studies is that the avoidance response tends to persist for a long time in the absence of any reinforcement. Normally, a learned response will diminish in strength with time. The explanation that has been offered is that when the response is made early, any anxiety that occurs is immediately reduced. The reduction in anxiety comes to act as a reinforcer for the avoidance response. Thus the avoidance response is being continually reinforced. This finding is consistent with the clinical observation that certain kinds of anxiety reactions (especially phobic reactions) persist and even become stronger despite the absence of any recent experience that would explain why someone would continue to maintain that response.

Principles of desensitization.   Further evidence in support of this explanation comes from work pertaining to the elimination of fear and anxiety. Two procedures have been successfully used to reduce fear and anxiety. The first procedure is called desensitization. Since humans show less fear in response to symbolic forms of the fear stimulus than to the actual object of fear, it is possible to rank-order stimuli along a continuum ranging from those that elicit only mild fear (usually symbolic stimuli) to those that elicit extreme fear (usually concrete stimuli). People who are afraid of spiders, for example, usually respond with only mild fear to the word *spider,* with greater fear to pictures of spiders, and with intense fear to an actual spider. In desensitization training the therapist starts by presenting a stimulus that elicits only mild fear under conditions in which the client feels relaxed and in control. Under these conditions, the mild fear stimulus often loses its ability to elicit the fear reaction. The therapist then moves to a stronger stimulus and repeats the procedure. Eventually the therapist moves to the strongest stimulus. The idea behind this procedure is that some kind of counterconditioning is occurring. That is, the client is conditioning a feeling of elation/control to the stimulus or stimuli that originally elicited fear.

Flooding.   A second procedure that has been successful in reducing the fear response is called flooding (Kazdin, 1978). In this procedure the individual is typically presented with a fear-producing stimulus and the full emotional reaction is allowed to run its course. The key to success with this procedure is to make sure the client remains in the presence of the eliciting stimulus. This is a sink-or-swim procedure. The explanation for its effectiveness is again counterconditioning. When the emotional reaction subsides, a new reduced emotional response is conditioned to the stimulus. Over repeated experiences, that emotional response dwindles away.

The important thing about both procedures is that the client is not allowed to make an avoidance response. The fact that an avoidance response interferes with the effectiveness of the treatment lends additional support to the idea that persistence of the avoidance response is linked in some way to the anxiety reduction that accompanies it.

The Cognitive Component

Cognitive factors play an important role in the fear/anxiety response. We will limit our discussion to a few of the major cognitive components.

Loss of control.   Losing control, or simply the fear of losing control, often leads to feelings of anxiety. Martin Seligman (1975) has suggested that when events are unpredictable, we develop feelings of helplessness. Feelings of helplessness are sufficient, it is argued, to produce not only anxiety but depression. One of the reasons people experience anxiety in connection with having to give a talk, for example, is the fear that they may lose control. Uncertainty and unpredictability are associated with such a task, and it is the unpredictability that makes people anxious.

Inability to make a coping response.   Various theorists have argued that the inability (or the perceived inability) to make an adaptive response to a threatening event, or the fact (or perception) that no such response is available, will lead to feelings of anxiety (for example, Epstein, 1972; Richard Lazarus, 1966). Lazarus points out that ambiguity is the key consideration here, because it prevents the elaboration of clear action patterns (coping strategies) that would allow the individual to deal with the threat.

It has been suggested that transforming anxiety into fear might be a useful way of getting people to cope with a threat. The reason is that when we know what it is that is threatening us, we can devise a pattern of action to deal with it. When we don't know what the threat is, we are left in limbo, experiencing anxiety but not knowing what to do about it.

State versus Trait Anxiety

Is anxiety caused by events in the environment or is it a characteristic of the individual? There is no question that certain events in the environment are a source of threat. Venturing into a rough neighborhood or being caught in a snowstorm while driving on the highway may cause us to fear for our personal safety. But should we experience a threat to our personal safety when we are sitting at home on a nice sunny day or simply driving down the highway? Some people feel much more threatened than others. Some people spend considerable time making sure the doors are locked and making sure they have enough food in the house in case of a snowstorm.

Anxiety that occurs in response to some threat posed by the environment, such as a rough neighborhood, is called *state anxiety*. It occurs in response to something specific. There is typically good reason to be afraid. But not everybody responds the same. Some people simply feel more anxiety in all situations. Because they feel more anxiety in all situations, we assume that they bring that anxiety with them to the situation. This type of anxiety is called *trait anxiety*. It is a characteristic of the individual.

Where do these two kinds of anxiety come from? State anxiety is usually learned, but sometimes not. Humans have a natural fear of heights, and as a result most people show a healthy fear of high places. Other kinds of fear are learned. Through experience we learn that a certain situation, such as being in a rough neighborhood, increases the likelihood of being mugged. The origins of trait anxiety are less clear. Like state anxiety, trait anxiety may be learned or innate. People who are born with higher arousal levels may be more sensitive to all forms of environmental stimulation and as a result respond to any threat with heightened anxiety. There is also evidence that people may develop cognitive styles that lead them to interpret events in distinctive ways. Differences in cognitive styles have already been mentioned briefly in Chapter 3, where we noted the distinction between sensitizers and repressors.

Sensitizers and repressors.   Sensitizers are people who dwell on the potential consequences of a threat; repressors avoid thinking about the consequences. Sensitizers, not surprisingly, tend to experience more anxiety than repressors. Yet, while repressors may experience less stress in a moment of threat, there is some question as to whether this is truly an adaptive way of dealing with a threat. Generally we believe it is more adaptive to deal objectively with a threat. Most psychologists would probably agree that dwelling on a threat is not adaptive, either.

If you tend to experience stress in certain social situations, such as meeting new people, it probably would not be a good idea to dwell on what might go wrong. Such thoughts are likely to increase your natural tendency to avoid social situations in which you would have to meet new people. On the other hand, avoiding thinking about those situations might not be adaptive either. A more adaptive approach might be to recognize that you do indeed have a problem and then think of ways you might improve your ability to handle those situations.

The disposition to experience aversive emotional states.   A wide variety of personality scales that purport to measure trait anxiety, neuroticism, repression-sensitization, ego strength, and general maladjustment appear to measure the same underlying personality trait—a trait that has been called a disposition toward negative affectivity (Watson & Clark, 1984). People who score high on these measures of negative affectivity are likely to experience discomfort at all times and in all situations. They tend to be introspective, to dwell on the negative side of themselves and of the world, and to have low self-esteem. At the cognitive level it might be said that people who have a disposition toward negative affectivity view the world as antagonistic. In view of the fact that this disposition seems to be chronic rather than situational, the question arises: What is the origin of this disposition? Is it due to some biological state, is it learned, or does it represent a certain cognitive orientation? Further research is needed to answer this question.

Summary

It has been suggested that the goal object of fear is fairly specific, while the goal object of anxiety is more vague or ambiguous. It has been suggested that three basic conditions elicit anxiety: overstimulation, cognitive incongruity, and response unavailability. Current knowledge suggests that GABA normally controls anxiety by reducing the flow of neural transmission. The benzodiazepine family of drugs (antianxiety drugs) is believed to help reduce anxiety by assisting GABA to perform its function.

According to the neobehaviorists, fear and anxiety are conditioned responses to pain, and the only difference between them is the stimulus to which they respond: an identifiable stimulus elicits fear, an ambiguous one anxiety. Two important things happen in the course of learning to avoid an aversive stimulus: first, the avoidance response tends to occur progressively earlier, and second, it tends to persist over time. Desensitization and flooding are two

(continued)

treatment techniques that can reduce fear and anxiety. Both procedures are assumed to work according to principles of counterconditioning.

Loss of control and the inability to make a coping response are two very important cognitive antecedents of fear and anxiety.

Individuals vary widely with respect to the amount of anxiety they experience. State anxiety is thought usually to be learned; the origin of trait anxiety is less clear. It may result from a low threshold of arousal, which makes people unusually responsive to all forms of stimulation, or it may result from the way one has learned to view the world. Some people, for example, tend to dwell on the consequences of a threat (sensitizers), while others tend to avoid thinking about such consequences (repressors). It has been suggested that trait anxiety reflects a general disposition toward negative affectivity.

Risk Taking (Thrill Seeking):
The Interaction of Optimism and Fear

Many people like to take voluntary risks by engaging in such activities as parachuting, hang gliding, mountain climbing, and deep-sea diving. When you ask them why they take such risks, they often say they do it to get a "high." Do they experience fear and anxiety when they take these risks? Often they do.

It appears that risk taking involves the interaction of two basic emotions, optimism and fear. How does this interaction work? S. Z. Klausner suggests that as one begins to exercise one's skills, fear gives way to optimism or enthusiasm. He writes (Klausner, 1968, p. 153):

> My study of sport parachutists provides an example of the challenging appraisal of emotion as the succession of acts constituting the parachute jump are executed. Self-reports were used to assess the quality and the intensity of emotion experienced by sport parachutists at various points during the jump. As they prepare for the jump, board the plane, and ascend to jump altitude, the level of arousal increases. During this preparatory phase the arousal is experienced primarily as fear. The level of arousal remains relatively stationary while the jumper prepares for exit. However, the feeling of fear decreases while the feeling of enthusiasm correspondingly increases during this time. After exiting there is a sharp decrease in fear and a corresponding sharp increase in enthusiasm. Just before the parachute opens, fear increases and enthusiasm decreases. After opening, with the level of arousal still remaining about the same, enthusiasm increases again. Fear displaces enthusiasm just before landing; upon landing, enthusiasm becomes dominant again.

Subjective Appraisal of Arousal and Enthusiasm

What is particularly interesting about these parachutists is the point at which their fear is replaced by enthusiasm—not after they have landed safely on the ground but during the activity itself. Clearly, the enthusiasm is not simply the relief that might follow the termination of a stressful event but has something to do with the jumper's appraisal of his or her role in relation to the risks involved in the task. Klausner points out further:

> At any given point during the jump phase, fear and enthusiasm are negatively correlated. The peak level of fear, which is experienced at the inception of the jump run, is positively correlated with the level of enthusiasm at subsequent

points. The more frightened the skydivers are at the start of the jump run, the more enthusiastic they become later. Since the level of arousal is fairly constant throughout, it is the jumper's appraisal of the situation and of the task remaining before him that changes from point to point [p. 153].

Klausner's observations indicate that the positive emotions felt during sensation-seeking activity are associated with one's adaptive responses to the stress or to one's appraisal that one is able to handle the stress. (Note that these results are consistent with the idea that when a person can engage in adaptive responses, norepinephrine is released.) But what happens when someone has not fully developed a set of adaptive responses to deal with the activity? Klausner's view suggests that the person who is deficient in adaptive responses will not experience the same degree of positive affect as someone who is experienced. The work of Fenz and Epstein (1969) bears on this question.

Fenz and Epstein had experienced and novice parachutists rate their fear at 14 points in time before, during, and after a jump. Figure 7-6 summarizes their findings. Clearly, experienced and novice parachutists have quite different patterns of fear and fear reduction. If engaging in adaptive behaviors reduces fear, then part of the results can be readily understood. The experienced parachutist shows a systematic decrease in fear until the time of actually jumping. This makes sense because the parachutist has many things to do in preparation for a jump. For example, the equipment must be carefully checked. The novice parachutist, however, may not have sufficient experience to make these checks of the equipment. The novice depends to a great extent on the experienced parachutist for such checks. Consequently, while the experienced parachutist is engaging in adaptive behaviors, the novice is simply waiting. At the point of the "ready" signal, the novice has to initiate adaptive responses, and hence fear will decrease. But why do experienced parachutists show an increase in fear just after the jump, while novices do not? It may well be, as Fenz and Epstein have noted, that experienced parachutists are more aware of the uncertainty that follows the jump. They know that there are factors over which they have no control. Novices, in contrast, may

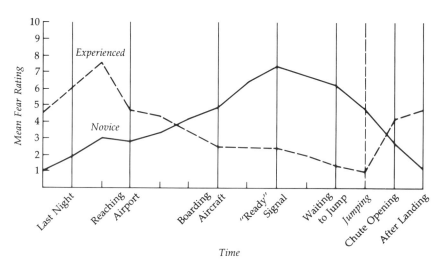

Figure 7-6.   Fear responses of experienced and novice skydivers (Fenz & Epstein, 1969)

have been led to believe that once they jump, the outcome is cut and dried as long as they engage in a series of adaptive responses. Performing these adaptive responses will therefore reduce their fear. If Klausner is correct in noting that fear is inversely related to enthusiasm, then we may infer that Fenz and Epstein's parachutists were experiencing their greatest enthusiasm or elation when fear was lowest.

Many activities produce high arousal, which is experienced in various combinations of fear, anxiety, enthusiasm, and elation. Entertainers frequently report that before a performance they are extremely anxious but that this anxiety typically decreases once they begin their performance. Public speakers and teachers report a similar pattern (Taggart, Carruthers, & Somerville, 1973). Mountain climbers often experience extreme fear and elation in the course of climbing a mountain (Lester, 1969).

Why take risks? Since norepinephrine levels are elevated under a variety of situations that don't involve obvious high risks, such as running or public speaking, why do some people like to engage in activities that put their very lives at stake? Klausner's research suggests that fear is a necessary ingredient in the high that comes from sensation seeking. Klausner found that the greater the initial level of fear among parachutists, the greater their subsequent enthusiasm. If fear is necessary for high levels of enthusiasm, it follows that sensation seekers would deliberately expose themselves to risks in order to increase the subsequent elation. It would be important, of course, not to increase the risk level beyond one's ability to exercise an adaptive response. Increasing the level beyond that point would decrease the probability of obtaining any positive affect.

There is a more basic way of looking at this same relationship. Earlier we noted (Figure 7-4) that norepinephrine levels are elevated when "free" (random) shocks are introduced into a shock-avoidance task. This effect provides a ready explanation for the apparent need to take risks in order to get the kind of high reported by sensation seekers. If humans engage in sensation seeking to get high, then they need to select situations that provide the ingredients for this high. Situations that are basically controllable but also have an ambiguous or unpredictable quality appear to be the kind that elicit high levels of norepinephrine. Figure 7-4 also showed that epinephrine levels increase when free shocks are introduced. If epinephrine adds to the intensity of an emotion, we can readily understand why people experience intense fear and anxiety in certain situations that are risky, ambiguous, or unpredictable. The point to remember, however, is that norepinephrine levels are also increased in ambiguous or unpredictable situations. If norepinephrine is one of the chemicals that provide the high that risk takers are after, then it is important to seek out tasks that are essentially controllable but have an unpredictable quality. The fact that epinephrine levels are also high may simply be an unfortunate by-product of sensation seeking; or, if Schachter and Singer are correct, high levels of epinephrine may in fact contribute to the intensity of the high experienced by sensation seekers.

Increasing the Level of Risk

Once a person has mastered the adaptive responses associated with a particular type of stress, he or she tends to increase the risk level. This tendency cannot be readily handled by traditional drive-reduction theory. Rewards, in traditional drive-reduction theory, result in a stereotyped response to a given set of stimulus events. Thus the theory does not predict a shift in the level of risk. Berlyne's concept of arousal jag could handle this phenomenon. Berlyne (1960) assumes that people will seek out greater arousal as they adapt to current levels of arousal. If it is assumed that acquiring skills reduces the unpredictability of a situation, then as skills increase, the person will seek what would be, for the novice, a higher level of risk. For the skier this may involve tackling more difficult slopes; for the mountain climber, climbing a more difficult mountain; for the race-car driver, driving a faster car.

Is Risk Taking Adaptive?

It may well be that risk takers have learned how to tap mechanisms that evolved to reward adaptive behaviors. In selecting tasks that not only are risky but require an adaptive response, they are able to get the high feeling that evolved to reward adaptive behaviors. Richard Lazarus and Raymond Launier (1978) have noted that some people treat *threats* as *challenges*, thus causing negative affect to shift to more positive affect. Hans Selye (1974) has argued that attitudes do indeed alter the subjective experience of stress. A positive attitude, Selye argues, can reduce the distressful feeling that often accompanies the stress reaction. Sazanne Kobasa (1979a) has found that executives who experience high stress but do not tend to become ill have a clearer sense of their values, goals, and capabilities than their stressed colleagues who are more susceptible to illness, and have a strong tendency toward active involvement in their activities. When faced with challenge, they tend to react positively and adaptively. Such findings seem to indicate that positive emotions have a basic survival function, promoting both psychological and physical well-being.

Summary

It appears that risk taking often involves two complementary emotions, optimism and fear. Why do people like situations that elicit these two complementary emotions? One explanation is that if humans seek situations that will give them a high, one of the best situations for that purpose is one that is basically controllable but has an element of unpredictability. In such situations norepinephrine levels tend to be highest. Also, an unpredictable element elicits high levels of epinephrine, a chemical that has been shown to increase arousal. As long as the individual is in control, a high level of epinephrine can increase the intensity of an already pleasant emotion. The reason it is often necessary to increase the level of risk is that as one's skills improve, the unpredictability of the situation decreases.

Altruism

When a baby cries, a mother often listens attentively before she goes to the child. She listens to the cries in order to determine how badly the child needs or wants her to come. Psychologists have argued for some time that going to the aid of another person is more than just a learned response; to a very large degree, the tendency is innate. In other words, there is a strong biological basis for the feelings that well up inside us when we hear the cries of a baby or the pleas of a person who is in danger and needs our help. We also know, however, that many people will ignore the cries of a baby or of other people who are asking for help. What makes it possible for us to turn off this response if, as psychologists have argued, it is innate?

Altruism is defined as the tendency to give of one's time, resources, or energy in order to help another person. The phenomenon of altruism has intrigued not only social scientists but biologists. Why do parents devote years of effort to the care of their children? Why will a person help her sister or neighbor or a stranger with a flat tire? Why does a driver give a hitchhiker a ride? The reason that both psychologists and biologists are intrigued by altruism is that they tend to assume that people are basically selfish. If that is the case, why do we ever offer our help and why do we feel good after we have done so? Obviously many factors influence the tendency to help or not to help. We will begin by examining some of the biological factors that seem to play an important role in altruism.

Biological Factors

Sociobiology. Sociobiology is concerned with explaining the biological bases of behavior within an evolutionary framework (Barash, 1977). It is assumed that altruistic behaviors evolved because they served an adaptive function that has helped the species to survive. The problem for the biologist, therefore, is to explain how altruism is adaptive for the individual. How does giving more than one gets benefit the individual? This question is central to any analysis that holds to an evolutionary framework, because within the evolutionary framework it is necessary for the individual to survive in order that he or she can reproduce. Being selfish, therefore, would serve not only the individual but the species. The fact remains, however, that people sometimes act altruistically. The problem, therefore, is to account for this fact.

Group selection. A model that has come to be called "group selection" was originally developed by V. C. Wynne-Edwards (1962) to account for the tendency of animals to control overpopulation. It is paradoxical within an evolutionary framework that animals tend to restrain their natural tendency to reproduce. Yet this seems to be what happens when a population begins to exceed the available food supply. Wynne-Edwards suggested that at least some members of a species have genes that somehow sensitize them to indications that overpopulation is imminent. Thus, on behalf of the group, certain animals are genetically prepared to control their tendency to reproduce.

In genetic terms, there are several problems with this model. Animals that carried such altruistic genes would tend to become extinct. If they were not to become extinct, they would have to reproduce at the same rate as the other animals. And if they did, there would be no reduction in the population. Therefore, the model, even with all its appeal and explanatory power, had to be abandoned.

Kin selection. The production and care of offspring involve an enormous investment of time and energy. If individuals tend to act only in their own self-interest, why are they willing to make this investment (Barash, 1977)? What's in it for them? Why not take the course of least resistance and avoid the whole process? The sociobiological answer to this seeming paradox has its origins in the work of William Hamilton (1964), who noted that the tendency of parents to show care and concern for infants is a special case of a more general tendency to show care and concern for those with whom the individual shares genes through common descent. Expanding on these observations, J. Maynard-Smith (1964) suggested that an individual's behavior in such circumstances is governed by a tendency to maximize his or her genes in succeeding generations. The best way of doing this, of course, is first to reproduce and then to protect the offspring in order to ensure that they too will reproduce. Because relatives other than one's children also carry some of one's genes, one could also maximize one's genes in succeeding generations by protecting and caring for one's relatives. Our children share more genes with us than an uncle, however, and the theory therefore predicts that the degree of care and concern we give our children will be greater than that given our uncle.

The kin-selection theory not only has proved to have a great deal of explanatory power but tends to predict, at least in animals, the quality of care and attention an individual will receive from various members of its social group. One fascinating example of the explanatory power of the kin-selection theory involves the infanticide behavior of langur monkeys in India. Female monkeys live in a harem group controlled by a single male monkey who does most of the breeding. Periodically, nonbreeding males from peripheral bachelor groups attempt to overthrow the harem master. If one of these monkeys succeeds, the new harem master proceeds to kill all the infants in his newly acquired harem (Sugiyama, 1967). We may find such behavior reprehensible, but it can readily be explained by the kin-selection theory. Because nursing females do not ovulate, removal of the infants serves the function of making the females receptive. In this way the new male increases the number of females available for reproduction and thereby increases the number of his offspring, thus maximizing his genes in succeeding generations (provided he can maintain control long enough).

Kin-selection theory can account for a wide range of human altruistic behaviors, especially those directed toward relatives. The theory also offers an explanation of why the human female engages in sex even when she is not in estrus. Barash (1977) points out that although the mother knows that half of the infant's genes are hers, the father can never be sure. Therefore, staying with the mother and helping her raise the infant does not necessarily ensure that he will maximize his genes. An alternative strategy would be to find other available females and impregnate them. Because the human infant needs a great deal of care, it is desirable from the female's point of view to have the assistance of the male in this endeavor. One way of keeping him around for such purposes would be to provide him with sex on a regular basis while rejecting other males. In this way she would not only behaviorally assure her mate that the infant was his but enlist the male's help in raising the infant. Barash admits that this scenario is pure speculation; however, it does provide an explanation for the phenomenon, unique to humans, of female receptivity outside estrus.

Kin-selection theory is not without problems. How, for example, does the theory account for the fact that humans will adopt and care for children who do not share their genes? Why would someone help a stranger fix a flat tire? In short, how do we account for any act of altruism that is not directed to a genetic relative? For that matter, why will people help elderly relatives who are no longer expected to reproduce?

Reciprocity theory.   An obvious alternative mechanism that would not demand genetic relatedness is reciprocity. A person might be willing to expend effort and time on behalf of someone else, or even to take a risk, if the person felt there was a good chance that such an act of altruism would be returned sometime. The crux of the theory is the question of who is likely to reciprocate. One could optimistically hope that any act of altruism would eventually find its way back to the originator. On practical grounds, however, it would make much more sense to act altruistically only toward a person who is in a position to reciprocate. Altruistic acts should therefore be more common toward those with whom one interacts often. This pattern would also help ensure against cheaters in the system, because one could simply monitor the frequency with which an altruistic act was reciprocated. Obviously, as Barash points out, this mechanism for altruism is most likely to evolve in animals that are highly intelligent. To make or plan an exchange of altruistic acts would require the ability not only to remember that one has a debt to a certain person but to evaluate the magnitude of that debt.

Although reciprocity should occur more often between familiar persons, there is no reason, according to reciprocity theory, that a person might not periodically direct acts of altruism to strangers, especially if the person had been the recipient of an act of altruism from a stranger. It is possible within the framework of reciprocity theory to assume that we may simply tend to reciprocate altruistic acts in like kind. From a genetic point of view, this assumption is somewhat difficult to handle because it is necessary to account for the origins of altruism, not merely for the reciprocal nature of altruism. Because evolutionary change is typically very slow, it is likely that the behaviors we observe now are quite different from those that occurred at the beginning of the move toward altruism. It is possible that altruism was initially directed only toward relatives, but that sometime during the evolutionary process this mechanism became more general and took on qualities of reciprocity.

It is also possible that altruism was never restricted specifically to relatives but rather was restricted to the group to which one belonged. Primates, it should be noted, live in groups. This arrangement serves several functions, one being that the group provides protection for the individual. In such an arrangement, it would make sense for altruism to be directed to all members of the group, not just to one's relatives.

Hormones and altruism.   There is good evidence that the tendency for adults to help children may be mediated by hormones. For example, certain hormonal events seem to sensitize the female to respond to stimuli associated with nurturant caregiving, and other hormonal events may raise the threshold of sensitivity to these same stimuli (Money & Ehrhardt, 1972). Specifically, it has been suggested that the hormonal changes associated with pregnancy increase sensitivity (for example, Klopfer, 1971; Moltz, 1974). There is evidence that this sensitivity is established shortly after fertilization. As we noted in Chapter 6, sex hormones secreted by the fetus produce different patterns of brain differentiation in males and females. Females who are exposed to the male sex hormone during this phase of differentiation are less sensitive to infants when they are adults (Money & Ehrhardt, 1972), suggesting that female sensitivity is established very early in life. Further, there is evidence that it is between the ages of 12 and 14 (that is, at puberty) that females come to prefer pictures of infants, whereas it is in adulthood that males come to prefer pictures of infants. The difference that occurs at puberty may be mediated by the rise in estrogen that is associated with the onset of puberty. Why males should come to prefer pictures of infants as adults is not clear. What is clear is that hormones appear to play an important role in making females sensitive to infants.

Summary

Although altruism is important for the smooth functioning of society, the motivation for altruism is not immediately obvious. Sociobiologists have offered at least three explanations of altruistic behavior. The group-selection model
(continued)

suggests that at least some animals have genes that make them sensitive to overpopulation. The kin-selection model suggests that an individual's behavior in such circumstances is governed by a tendency to maximize his or her genes in succeeding generations. Finally, the reciprocity model suggests that the individual is willing to expend effort on behalf of others if there is a good chance that such an act of altruism will be returned at some later time. The fact that hormones have been linked to the sensitivity of females toward infants indicates that the care of infants has not been left to chance. Whether hormones mediate other forms of altruism remains to be shown.

Learned Factors

The infant cry and altruism.   Hormones may sensitize the female toward caregiving, but exactly what are the signals that elicit such behavior? Eibl-Eibesfeldt (1975) has suggested that the infant cry may be a signal (innate releaser) that elicits this particular kind of altruism. Indeed, a large body of data suggests that the infant cry is a compelling sound that elicits actions of nurturance (Murray, 1979). Paradoxically, at least according to Eibl-Eibesfeldt's view, crying has also been linked to various forms of child abuse (Murray, 1979). For example, in one study of "infant battering," 80% of the parents indicated that excessive crying had been the main precipitating event (Weston, 1968). How is it possible to account for the paradoxical finding that the infant cry elicits both nurturant and nonnurturant behavior?

One model designed to resolve this paradox assumes that the cry does not simply release an innate behavior, as Eibl-Eibesfeldt would argue, but rather that the cry is a noxious stimulus (Ostwald, 1963, 1972). According to this model, the parent engages in nurturant behavior in order to reduce the distress caused in himself or herself by the cry. Thus the motivation for responding to a cry is not altruistic but rather self-serving. The adult feels compelled to respond to the infant's cry because it produces feelings of distress. According to this model, an adult might use nurturant or nonnurturant means to reduce the distress caused by the infant's cry. The problem with this model is that it fails to explain why nurturant caregiving is the typical response to crying whereas a nonnurturant reaction (beating the child) tends to occur only when the crying does not stop.

To deal with this problem, Martin L. Hoffman (1975) has introduced a cognitive component that is assumed to interact with the affective (noxious) component of the infant's cry. Hoffman has suggested that as the child develops, he or she gains a sense of "other" as distinct from "self." As a result the person is able to experience empathetic distress, which Hoffman defines as "the involuntary forceful experiencing of another person's painful emotional state" (p. 613). It is from this ability to experience empathetic distress that the person comes to develop a general conception about the welfare of a victim. When this happens, it can be argued, the person is no longer responding in a self-serving manner but rather is responding more altruistically.

If, according to Hoffman, children tend to develop altruism as a result of their (cognitive) ability to experience empathetic distress, why is it that adults will sometimes engage in punitive rather than altruistic behaviors when exposed to a noxious stimulus for long periods of time? The answer seems to lie in the nature of the interaction between the affective and cognitive components. Specifically, it appears that the ability of the cognitive side of humans to override the affective side in the presence of a noxious stimulus is limited. Very simply, continued exposure to a noxious stimulus may overtax a person's ability to tolerate the noxious stimulus, producing a shift in motivation from altruistic to egotistic (see Murray, 1979).

Such a view fits nicely with Paul D. MacLean's (1973) conceptualization of the relation between the limbic system and the neocortex. Because there is evidence from a wide variety of sources that affective speech and soundmaking (such as crying) are mediated by the limbic system (for example, Chauchard, 1963; Myers, 1968), there is good reason to believe that the empathetic-distress response has a biological basis. Further, since there are interconnections between the limbic system and the neocortex in primates, there is also good reason to believe that the cognitive and biological systems in humans can influence each other. MacLean has argued that such interconnections make possible empathy, in the form of both shared affect and shared cognitive understanding. According to MacLean's view, cognitive understanding could, as Hoffman has argued, affect the expression of a biologically based emotion. It may be, therefore, that shifts from altruistic to self-serving responding in the face of prolonged exposure to a noxious stimulus reflect a breakdown in the ability of the cognitive side of an emotion to influence (suppress) the biological side. As a result, a cry that initially elicited a helping response can come to elicit an abusive response.

Social learning theory and altruism.   Social learning theory has argued that we come to behave as we do in social settings because of the rewards and punishments we receive from others (Aronfreed, 1968). It is assumed, according to this approach, that the rewards and punishments become internalized, so that when we behave according to the norms and rules of society, we feel pride (internalized praise from others), and when we violate those norms and rules, we feel shame or guilt (internalized rejection or punishment from others). A person often has to expend effort or give up some personal goal to help others (or to engage in any prosocial behavior). Whether a person helps another person is assumed to be determined by an algebraic summation of the positive and negative rewards associated with helping. For example, if helping means that an important personal goal must be relinquished, the tendency to help will be reduced. If a person has, in the past, been severely reprimanded (punished) for his failure to follow the accepted norms of society—and if he has internalized this punishment—he will be more inclined to help. Very simply, the failure to help will produce severe guilt feelings—a negative psychological state that it is assumed humans are motivated to avoid.

Leonard Berkowitz (1972, 1973) and his students have developed a norm-based approach for prosocial behaviors that has been subjected to a number of experimental tests. In one of their typical studies, a student was informed that another student's supervisory-capacity rating as well as his opportunity to earn a reward was dependent on the subject's carrying out a simple task, such as making envelopes out of sheets of paper. The supervisor was, in actuality, nonexistent. The subject was simply led to believe, through instructions provided by the experimenter, that the other student's welfare depended on him. The results of these studies have, on the whole, provided rather convincing evidence consistent with the position of social learning theory. For example, when the supervisor was dependent on the student/worker for obtaining success (such as winning a prize or receiving a good rating), the student/worker tended to exert more effort (Berkowitz & Daniels, 1964) even though the student/worker was not rewarded for his efforts. Such results provide good support for the idea that the norm for helping has become internalized and therefore does not depend on some immediate gratification in the form of an external reward.

Mood and altruism.   Long before Hoffman spelled out his model of altruism, there was considerable interest in the relation between mood and altruism. Dennis Krebs (1970), for example, in reviewing the literature on altruism, cited 16 experiments examining this relation. Since then there have been many more studies. Several studies have shown that positive mood leads to greater helping than negative mood (for example, Berkowitz & Conner, 1966; Cunningham, 1979; Isen, 1970; Isen, Horn, & Rosenhan, 1973; Moore, Underwood, & Rosenhan, 1973). In these studies the researchers induced positive mood by manipulating the success/failure rate of subjects. Subjects who succeeded were more inclined to behave altruistically than those who failed. These results have been generally interpreted as providing evidence that subjects hold to some type of "norm of deserving." That is, when they succeed, they feel others should succeed, and therefore they are more likely to share under these conditions.

Several studies have also shown that negative mood leads to increased altruism (for example, Aderman & Berkowitz, 1970; Cialdini, Darby, & Vincent, 1973; Cialdini & Kenrick, 1976; Filter & Gross, 1975; Kenrick, Baumann, & Cialdini, 1979; Kidd & Berkowitz, 1976). Cialdini and Kenrick (1976) have suggested a negative-state-relief model to account for these findings. They argue that in most societies the recipient of aid learns that he or she has an obligation to return it. Humans thus come to expect a reward for behaving altruistically. As a consequence, they argue, engaging in altruistic behaviors is "self-gratifying." In short, it provides an immediate reward. Assuming that this is true, why are negative-mood subjects more likely to act altruistically? Cialdini and Kenrick argue that they behave altruistically in order to reduce negative affect, which is aversive.

What makes Cialdini and Kenrick's research particularly interesting is their finding that the relation between negative mood and altruism increases with age. In their study they gave subjects the opportunity to share coupons with nonparticipating students. Their findings are shown in Figure 7-7. The fact that the older participants shared more coupons indicates, Cialdini and Kenrick argue, that the tendency to be altruistic is not innate. If it were, the youngest participants should have been just as altruistic as the oldest. Instead, they argue, the results suggest that altruism is learned. Specifically, altruism is essentially a form of hedonism. Humans learn that altruistic behaviors are often rewarded, and because of this learning, humans come to behave in an altruistic manner.

In a follow-up study with children, Kenrick, Baumann, and Cialdini (1979) obtained further evidence not only that negative mood leads to increased helping but that the tendency to help under conditions of negative mood is learned. They suggest a three-step model to account for the development of altruism. Initially, helpful behavior is rarely performed by an unsocialized person. From the child's perspective, helping is not a means of producing rewards. In fact, it is viewed as just the opposite. In the second step, the child begins to acquire norms for prosocial behavior. He or she begins to learn that prosocial behaviors lead to systematic social reinforcement. At this point the child will help publicly to reduce negative mood. However, he or she will tend to be less helpful under anonymous conditions. It is in the third stage that charitable behaviors begin to become self-reinforcing. That is, after sufficient experience with external rewards, acting charitably takes on the quality of a secondary reinforcer. At this point a person in a negative mood will engage in charitable behaviors, presumably because such behavior reduces

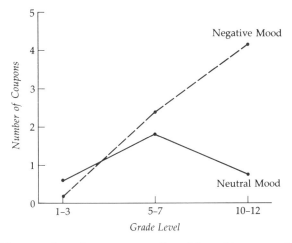

Figure 7-7. Mean number of coupons contributed by subjects at each grade level. (Numbers of subjects for neutral and negative mood, respectively, were as follows: grades 1–3, 28, 25; grades 5–7, 17, 16; grades 10–12, 7, 7.) (Cialdini & Kenrick, 1976)

the negative mood. In other words, charitable behaviors are no longer tied to external rewards; they occur because they are self-gratifying.

Michael Carlson and Norman Miller (1987) have concluded from their research that negative mood, per se, does not affect helping, but that negative mood alters certain psychological (cognitive/attentional) processes that can lead to increased helping. They found, for example, that negative mood increases the likelihood of people perceiving they are responsible for causing some negative event and that negative mood tends to engender a sense of self-awareness. They argue that these two changes in the focus of one's attention can lead to increased helping, provided the situation calls for prosocial behavior. That is, if people perceive that they should help or that they would receive approval for helping, they are more likely to actually help when they experience negative mood. These results are consistent with the position that a key element of altruism is not only learning what constitutes prosocial behavior but actually experiencing a sense of reward for engaging in prosocial behavior. The negative mood simply alters attention in such a way as to facilitate that underlying tendency to help, a tendency that must be aroused or made salient for that specific situation.

Altruism as power in disguise. It has been suggested that sometimes people exercise power through acts of altruism (Winter, 1973). That is, people exercise power on behalf of other people. According to this interpretation, altruistic acts are self-serving. They provide the person with the opportunity to exercise power for the reward that comes from exercising power. It might be argued that the behavior of politicians offers an example of this type of altruism. We frequently read or hear about politicians seeking political office (and the power associated with such office) using themes of justice, fair treatment, and human rights as part of their election platform. Such politicians frequently argue that, unlike their opponent, they are not seeking political office for selfish reasons. Rather, they are motivated by a deep desire to help people. In other words, they want to have power so they can exercise it on behalf of other people. Although many politicians may be motivated by a sense of justice, they may also be motivated by the desire of what McClelland (1975) calls s-Power (socialized power) and p-Power (personalized power). While s-Power may be a commendable motive, McClelland's work suggests that if inhibitions are removed, s-Power can turn into p-Power. A politician who feels secure in her position may begin to punish those people whom she disagrees with or cannot control.

Kenneth Clark (1980), in discussing the question of empathy, has argued that power drives tend to block empathy. The person loses the ability to feel the experiences, joys, anxieties, hurt, or hunger of others as though they were his or her own. This, Clark argues, is the basis of social tensions, conflicts, violence, terrorism, and war. He maintains that humans can be trained to become more empathetic. Such training, he suggests, will tend to counteract the mere animalistic determinants of behavior, such as the tendency to dominate and control people. In short, he is arguing that we need to increase s-Power and in doing so decrease p-Power.

Summary

Although there is good evidence that an infant's cry is a compelling sound that elicits actions of nurturance, there is also evidence that it sometimes elicits child abuse. According to Hoffman's theory, humans find the infant cry noxious and engage in acts of altruism to eliminate the noxious stimulus. However, if the crying continues, humans may find it impossible to tolerate, and under these conditions they tend to act more egotistically. MacLean's view of the brain is consistent with Hoffman's theory. According to social learning theory, people behave altruistically because of the rewards and punishments they receive. Berkowitz and his students have obtained data consistent with the view that humans indeed tend to behave according to the standards society has established. Mood has been linked to altruism; however, there is some debate as to whether positive or negative moods are more likely to elicit acts of altruism. Finally, it has been suggested that some acts of altruism are simply acts of power in disguise.

Cognitive Factors

The justice motive and altruism.   In recent years there has been growing interest in the question of why a person will at one time exhibit deep compassion for someone who is suffering and at another time will be indifferent to equal or greater suffering (Lerner, 1977). One of the themes that has emerged is that people perceive that certain forms of suffering are deserved and others are not. This "deserving," or "just world," hypothesis suggests that people are, under certain conditions, responsible for their own fate. To the degree that a person is capable of bettering his or her current state, he or she is expected to do so. At a more abstract level, it has been suggested that our culture gives us a sense of "entitlement" (Rosenhan, 1972). According to this view, a person's goals are based on his or her concept of entitlement. The question that arises is why a person should become committed to such a concept. What is the motivation that would give rise to this "personal contract"?

Melvin Lerner (1977) suggests that the underlying motivation "is probably to maximize payoffs over a longer time perspective" (p. 7). People accept the concept of entitlement because they perceive that such a system will in fact give them what they are entitled to. For example, we learn to let others have their turn because in doing so we are assured that we will also get our turn. Note that the justice motive is basically a self-serving motive: "I make sure others get what they deserve so that I will get what I deserve." The assumptions underlying this position are virtually the opposite of those on which the social learning approach is based. According to social learning theory, we learn to behave altruistically in order to obtain a reward (or avoid a punishment) from a source external to us. According to justice theory, we learn to behave altruistically in order to ensure that our selfish desires will be satisfied within the larger social context with which we must come to terms.

One situation in which people have strong feelings about getting what they deserve is the situation in which they have agreed to perform some task for a specified payment. If people are not paid the amount they were promised, they typically object. An interesting question, therefore, is what happens when people are overpaid. Do they keep the money or are they more likely to share it? Justice theory predicts that they should be more inclined (because of the concept of entitlement) to share their unearned good fortune with others. Self-serving theories suggest they would be inclined to keep it. In one experiment designed to test this idea, it was found that overrewarded children were more inclined to help a child in need (Braband & Lerner, 1975).

The justice motive and suffering.   If people have a need to believe that they live in a world where people generally get what they deserve, how will they respond to other people's suffering? The justness of any person's fate has implications for one's own fate. If other people can suffer undeservedly, then the possibility arises that I too can suffer undeservedly. One way of dealing with this problem is to compensate the victim. Another way is to convince oneself that the victim deserves to suffer (Lerner, 1970). Even though we may believe in a just society, we generally acknowledge that there are exceptions. A person can have a "bad character" or can make a mistake. As a consequence, the suffering he or she might experience would simply be due to factors that lie outside the realm of justice.

Extensive research has been carried out to examine how people respond to the suffering of another person (see Lerner & Miller, 1978). In the original study, Lerner and Simmons (1966) had subjects view a videotape of a person showing pain who they were led to believe was being shocked for making errors. In one condition (compensated condition) subjects could compensate the person by reassigning her to a condition in which she would receive money instead of shocks. In another condition (uncompensated condition) they were simply informed the shocks would continue. In a third condition (martyr condition) they were told she had allowed herself to be talked into being shocked. When the subjects were asked to rate the person, they tended to rate the compensated subject as most attractive and the martyr subject as least attractive. According to justice theory, the reason a person tends to degrade a victim who is suffering is the person's need to reassure himself or herself that the world is just. Unattractive people can be considered to have brought on their own problem. Therefore, if a person is suffering, he or she is perceived to be unattractive.

Several conditions modify the tendency to degrade a victim (Lerner & Miller, 1978). First, if the victim can be viewed as behaviorally causing his or her suffering (making a mistake, exercising poor judgment), there is not the same tendency to derogate the victim. In other words, no injustice has occurred. Second, if the victim is highly attractive or enjoys high status, there is a greater tendency to find fault with the victim's actions rather than derogate the victim's character. Third, if the observer expects to be in a situation similar to that of the victim, the tendency to derogate the victim is decreased. Empathy appears to emerge under this condition. Fourth, if the victim was in a situation in which the chances of escaping were equal for two persons, the tendency to derogate is also decreased. Apparently the observer feels that someone had to be the victim, and since self-interest prevailed, the victim's suffering was not his or her fault. This is related to the third condition, in which the prospect of being a victim tends to elicit empathy.

Justice theory and individual differences.   Not all people are equally committed to the concept of entitlement. For example, children who have not been repeatedly and consistently exposed to this idea may not have developed a clear concept of entitlement. In addition, children raised in an unstable environment may have discovered that behaving according to the entitlement principle does not pay off, because other people do not consistently follow this principle. Although it is logical to expect such individual differences to exist, the problem is how to measure them.

In a study designed to look at the question of individual differences, Long and Lerner (1974) used Mischel's (1973) scale to measure willingness to defer immediate gratification. Mischel has shown that some children are more willing to delay immediate gratification in order to obtain a larger reward later. Such children, it could be argued, are committed to the concepts of entitlement. That is, they believe that the world is sufficiently stable that it is possible to give up something now for future gains. A child who does not believe the environment is sufficiently stable would be more inclined to take his or her reward immediately rather than risk losing everything.

Again using the manipulation of "overpayment" versus "proper payment," Long and Lerner found that children who, by Mischel's scale, were more inclined to delay gratification tended to donate more money to poor children when they were overpaid (compared with children who were less inclined to delay gratification) but were less inclined to give money to poor children when they were properly paid (again compared with children who were less inclined to delay gratification). Clearly, these results show that some people have a fairly clear idea about what they should receive for their efforts. When they receive more than what they feel they are entitled to, they are quite willing to share; however, when they feel they have received exactly what they are due, they are not inclined to be altruistic.

If a person is committed to the concept of entitlement, does this mean that he or she will try to help each and every victim he or she encounters? Will such a person feel responsible for the plight of all victims? D. T. Miller (1977) argues that because it is impossible for a person committed to the concept of entitlement to help all victims, he or she develops a symbolic approach to the problem. Rather than helping every victim directly, the person reasons that the appropriate way of helping is through agencies that have been created to deal with victims. For example, he or she reasons that paying taxes, contributing to charities, and patronizing businesses that help those who have not received what they deserve are better ways of dealing with the problem of entitlement than intervening directly on behalf of victims he or she might encounter. Thus paying taxes and similar activities are perceived as the appropriate vehicles for ensuring that the concept of entitlement is preserved.

Miller further argues that if a person does, for whatever reason, decide to respond directly to the plight of a particular victim, the person will tend to use a scheme by which his or her actions are consistent with the more general (abstract) system discussed above. For example, instead of giving money directly to a hungry beggar, the person might create a job so the beggar could earn the money, or the person might agree to buy pencils or light bulbs from a handicapped person when he or she was unwilling to donate money directly. In this way people maintain the more abstract system they normally use to support their commitment to their concept of entitlement while still allowing themselves to indulge periodically in a specific act of altruism. Miller argues that, in general, people are not inclined to engage in direct acts of altruism. To do so on a consistent basis would symbolize to the person that he or she was directly responsible for the plight of other people. Because this would be an overwhelming responsibility, the person tries to ensure that his or her periodic acts of altruism are made not directly to an individual but to the organization or group of which the individual is a member. In this way, the person shifts direct responsibility to the group. Such an approach would be consistent with his or her view that the appropriate way to preserve the concept of entitlement is to support those agencies whose responsibility it is to take care of people who have, for one reason or another, not obtained a fair share.

Lerner (1977) reports an interesting experiment (Holmes, Miller, & Lerner, 1974) that illustrates the tendency for people to behave in this fashion in real life. The researchers had people sell candles for a suggested donation of $3. Half the sales were made in the name of a group of perceptually handicapped children who had difficulty with normal activities; the other half were made on behalf of a children's softball team that needed uniforms. The average money collected on behalf of the perceptually handicapped victims was about $1.75; the money collected for the softball team was only 30 cents. These results are consistent with the idea that people tend to help victims if their helping is disguised as a business transaction. An additional condition of the experiment lends further credence to this interpretation. Instead of selling candles, direct solicitations were made to another (similar) group of people. Under this condition similar "good citizens" were not inclined to donate money. They gave only about 55 cents, on the average, for the handicapped children. What is particularly interesting is that, on the average, people also gave about 55 cents to buy uniforms for the children's softball team. In other words, when confronted with a direct request for help, people showed no tendency to favor the victim over the able-bodied.

These results suggest that people are inclined to help the individual victim but will do so only if the helping can be disguised as a normal business transaction. In one condition of the candle-selling experiment, the researchers checked to see what would happen if the people from whom they were soliciting money felt they were being overcharged. They found that when buyers of candles felt they were being overcharged (with the extra money going to the handicapped), their giving dropped, on the average, from $1.75 to $1.20—a significant decrease. This finding further demonstrates that people are less inclined to help victims through a business transaction if that transaction violates the concept of fair profit. It follows that if a person is being overcharged on behalf of a victim, he or she would tend to perceive the extra money as a direct (unearned) donation. This extra donation, according to Miller, would constitute an act of helping an individual victim. Because people tend to guard against responding to individual appeals because this would open the door to all (individual) victims, Miller argues, it is necessary for the person to ensure that any act of helping is consistent with the normal rules of fair business practices. Thus, only when one is presented with a fair business deal will one be inclined to help.

Attributional analysis of helping behavior.   Ickes and Kidd (1976) have argued that the tendency to help is governed not just by the need for aid but also by whether the victim could have controlled the outcome. For example, one study found that people are more likely to help an ill person than a drunk (Piliavin, Rodin, & Piliavin, 1969). According to these researchers, drunkenness is perceived by most people as being under volitional control, while illness is not. They suggest that the normal tendency to help is mediated by the perception of whether the victim could have done something to avoid his or her plight. If the victim could have exercised control but didn't, help is withheld; if control was external to the victim, people are more willing to help. According to this model, the tendency to help, whatever its origins, is under cognitive control. Specifically, the tendency to help is withheld under certain specifiable conditions.

Bernard Weiner (1980), examining the attributional model of helping within a classroom context, asked students whether they would be willing to lend their notes to a (hypothetical) classmate who had failed to take notes. Several explanations were provided for why the student had failed to take notes: he didn't try, and/or he was unable to take notes because of something about himself, and/or he was unable to because the professor did not give good lectures. Failure to take notes because of something about himself or something about the ability or performance of the professor reflects an internal/external dimension. Not trying or not being able to take good notes reflects the dimension of controllable/uncontrollable. In addition, Weiner provided the option that the student was consistent in his behavior or not consistent—that is, sometimes he took notes and sometimes he didn't. This element was designed to determine whether the dimension of stable/unstable mediates the tendency to help in such situations.

Students were asked to respond to a series of causal statements by rating the likelihood of lending their notes on a 10-point scale anchored at the extremes with "definitely would lend my notes" and "definitely would not lend my notes." The dimension of stable/unstable was not found to have any effect and as a result was not included in the analysis. The results, presented in Table 7-1, show that the tendency to help is markedly reduced when the cause is internal and controllable. That is, if the student did not try to take good notes, there was a strong tendency to withhold help. Similar results were obtained with an employer/employee theme, indicating that these findings are not unique to note-lending behavior.

Weiner's research suggests that people are considered responsible for things over which they can exercise control. It makes sense that if people have a strong need to control events in their own lives, they would tend to perceive such control as a relevant factor in other people's behavior.

Summary

The "deserving" or "just world" hypothesis suggests that people are, under certain conditions, responsible for their fate. It has also been suggested that people develop a sense of entitlement. Expanding on these themes, Miller has proposed that people tend to believe in a just world, a belief he calls the "justice motive." Within this framework it is possible to explain why people sometimes derogate victims and at other times do not. Not all people are equally committed to the concept of entitlement. Those who are often perceive that the best way to preserve this concept is to support those social agencies whose mandate is to help victims or simply to help those who, for whatever reason, have not received their fair share. If, for some reason, a

(continued)

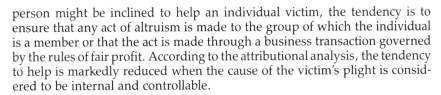

person might be inclined to help an individual victim, the tendency is to ensure that any act of altruism is made to the group of which the individual is a member or that the act is made through a business transaction governed by the rules of fair profit. According to the attributional analysis, the tendency to help is markedly reduced when the cause of the victim's plight is considered to be internal and controllable.

The Interactionist Position

The question of bystander intervention.   How willing are people to intervene on behalf of the victim of a physical attack, to help someone who has had an accident, or to respond to a request for help? These questions are of importance to all of us, especially in view of stories we hear or read about people being beaten or killed while bystanders looked on or about an accident victim who was left unattended even though people had perceived there was an emergency. Are these isolated instances, or do they represent, as Rosenthal (1964) suggested, a fundamental indifference? We also hear about instances in which people do intervene. Why will bystanders sometimes intervene and sometimes not? Are there conditions under which people are inclined not to help? What about personality differences? Do they play a role in whether a person will intervene?

In recent years research has focused on the interaction of the person and the environment to answer the question of why people will sometimes intervene and sometimes not. Not surprisingly, many variables affect whether a person is likely to help a victim. As we shall see, physical characteristics of the situation, cognitive factors, and personality qualities influence the inclination to intervene (Schwartz, 1977; Staub, 1978).

Costs of intervention.   Intervening on behalf of a victim entails potential costs (Piliavin & Piliavin, 1972). First, there is simply the question of effort: it takes time and energy to intervene. A person may have to interrupt his or her own goal-directed behavior to help a victim. That not only is inconvenient but could entangle the person in a long-term commitment. Intervening in a crime might mean he or she would have to give evidence in court; helping an accident victim might mean having to agree to interviews with insurance agents, police officers, or any number of other people concerned about the cause of the accident. There is also the question of personal risk. Intervening on behalf of a crime victim could bring physical retaliation, and intervening on behalf of an accident victim could result in a court action claiming the intervener was liable, in part, for the injury.

People are also reluctant to react if they think their behavior may be inappropriate. Can one be sure the perceived victim did not in fact provoke the action? In other words, in a fight, can one be sure who is the victim (Simons & Piliavin, 1972)? Should one intervene on behalf of an accident victim, or should one wait

Table 7-1.   Mean likelihood of helping as a function of perceived locus of causality and controllability (Weiner, 1980)

Locus of causality	Controllable	Uncontrollable
Internal	3.13	6.74
External	7.35	6.98

Note: Higher numbers indicate greater likelihood of note lending.

for expert help? What exactly is the best procedure to follow when one encounters an accident?

There is also the cost of not responding. Guilt or self-blame for the fate of a victim might spur a person to action. Further, the fear of social ostracism for not responding could be a factor, especially if prosocial behaviors are highly rewarded.

Berkowitz (1973) has suggested that people are generally reluctant to help others because intervention represents a threat to their own freedom. Therefore, people tend to weigh the costs. If the costs are not great, they will be inclined to intervene. Not surprisingly, therefore, it is found that the tendency to intervene is greater when people are not pressured by other concerns. For example, if they are in a good mood or have time to spare, they will be more inclined to help. Conversely, if they perceive the request for help as unwarranted or a threat to their own independence, they will not be inclined to help (Berkowitz, 1973).

Group size and bystander intervention.   Although the presence of others has been shown to facilitate certain prosocial behaviors, the presence of others tends to reduce helping behavior when helping is the appropriate response to a crime, accident, or other emergency. Bibb Latané and John Darley (1968) have suggested that the reduced tendency to help when others are present is due to two factors. First, the presence of others may lead the person to perceive that the responsibility is shared ("diffusion of responsibility") and therefore that it is not his or her responsibility to initiate some helping action. Second, the failure to see others respond may lead the individual to underestimate the seriousness of the situation, thus again reducing the tendency to initiate a helping action.

Latané and Darley's study suggests that a person needing help becomes increasingly likely to get it as the number of bystanders declines, but this idea was not supported in a study by Irving Piliavin and his colleagues (1969). They found no significant differences by group size. Latané and Dabbs (1975), using an experimental situation in which anyone could help even if others were already helping, found that the probability of helping does change with group size. It should be noted that these two studies have looked at slightly different aspects of the problem. Latané and Dabbs looked at individual probabilities, whereas Piliavin looked at whether a group would contain at least one person who was willing to intervene. In an attempt to resolve this issue, Charles Morgan (1978) manipulated cost as well as group size. When the cost of intervening increased, response latency was found to increase with increases in group size. That is, the more people present, the longer it took before anyone intervened. This finding indicates that the diffusion effect increases with cost. In other words, a bystander is more likely to shift the responsibility to others when his or her personal cost is high.

Magnitude of harm, sex differences, and bystander intervention.   Another study (Austin, 1979) examined whether magnitude of harm to the victim played a significant role in bystander intervention. Subjects were observed to see whether they would intervene to stop the theft of personal belongings left in their trust. High harm (greater value of the belongings) produced a higher rate of intervention. Interestingly, women tended to intervene in both high- and low-harm situations, whereas men intervened only in high-harm situations. This greater tendency of women to intervene irrespective of harm level is due mainly to the fact that they were simply more likely to help other women (80.7%) than men were likely to help women (51.1%). That is, men were less inclined to intervene on behalf of a woman if the harm was low. Austin suggests that women value future interpersonal relations more than men, and therefore even when the harm is low they are more likely to intervene. A study of bystander intervention in emergencies has shown that the degree of harm that is caused by waiting (not intervening) is also a determining factor in intervention in emergencies (Shotland & Huston, 1979).

Interaction of helper and victim.   It has been noted from time to time that the tendency to intervene on someone's behalf requires that the victim indicate in some way that he or she needs help. Verbal requests are one obvious way of indicating help is needed. What other cues do bystanders use to determine that the victim wants or needs help? One obvious way of communicating a need for help is by means of the eyes. Indeed, eye contact does facilitate bystander intervention (Shotland & Johnson, 1978). In commenting on their findings, these researchers suggest that eye contact not only can serve as a plea for help but forces responsibility on the bystander. In effect, the bystander is "trapped" because the eye contact signals recognition of the victim's state, thus forcing the bystander to behave according to social norms.

The Individual, Society, and Altruism

As most current theorists seem to recognize, altruistic acts are not in one's immediate self-interest (for example, Kanfer, 1979). It is therefore not always easy to teach people to be altruistic, even though many might agree on the need for greater altruism in our society. Frederick H. Kanfer (1979) nevertheless argues that we have the knowledge to train and maintain prosocial behaviors. First, he notes that we must acknowledge that prosocial behavior will fluctuate as any of its determinants fluctuates. That is, biological, learned, or cognitive factors may vary from time to time in their contribution to altruistic behavior. Having recognized this fact, we need to train the person to exercise greater prosocial behavior. In the beginning this may require external rewards. Over time, however, this pattern of behavior should become more habitual. As it becomes more habitual, Kanfer argues, people will come to recognize that they have gained control over a behavior pattern and take satisfaction from this fact. Further, they will come to recognize that this new pattern of behavior brings benefits not only for themselves but for others important to them. It is within this context that people will spontaneously initiate altruistic acts and gain satisfaction from such acts. Kanfer's main theme is that it is important to take what is essentially a selfish motive (the need for control) and use that motive to develop altruistic behaviors.

Summary

Intervention on behalf of a victim has obvious costs that can either increase or decrease the tendency to intervene. Effort, personal risk, and fear of behaving inappropriately can reduce the tendency to intervene; guilt, self-blame for harm to the victim, or fear of social ostracism can increase the tendency to intervene. Work on group size and bystander intervention indicates that humans are quite willing to shift responsibility to others, especially when intervention carries more personal cost. Nevertheless, people do appear to be inclined to intervene, especially if the potential harm to the victim is great. It appears that two important variables governing intervention are whether the victim communicates in some way his or her need for help and whether the bystander recognizes that he or she is the object of that communication.

(continued)

The bystander who recognizes a request for help, through verbal messages or eye contact, is obliged to follow the socially prescribed norms for dealing with such requests.

Main Points

1. People characterize emotions in terms of three basic dimensions: pleasant/ unpleasant, active/passive, and intense/not intense.
2. Emotions give rise to affective experiences, stimulate the individual to generate cognitive explanations, trigger a variety of internal responses, and elicit behaviors that are expressive, goal-directed, and adaptive.
3. Reward pathways are activated by the release of norepinephrine and (probably) dopamine.
4. The release of norepinephrine, a chemical important in rewarded behavior, has been linked to the exercise of adaptive responses.
5. The release of epinephrine has been linked to unpredictability and uncertainty.
6. McClelland has argued that the natural incentive to have impact leads to the release of catecholamine transmitters in the brain.
7. The James-Lange theory of emotions suggests that emotions depend on peripheral physiological sensation; Cannon's theory suggests that emotions are purely cognitive; the Schachter-Singer theory suggests that only the intensity of the emotion is dependent on physiological response.
8. Tiger has argued that optimism not only provides the motivation to act but rewards adaptive behaviors.
9. According to the neobehaviorists, the goal object of fear tends to be fairly specific, whereas the goal object of anxiety tends to be vague.
10. GABA appears to be one of those substances in the body that helps to maintain an optimal flow of stimulation.
11. Benzodiazepines help reduce anxiety by either stimulating GABA output or making it possible for GABA to do its job.
12. Neobehaviorists have argued that both fear and anxiety are conditioned pain.
13. Two important things take place in avoidance learning: the response occurs progressively earlier and tends to persist.
14. Feelings of loss of control, unpredictability, and the inability to make a coping response can give rise to feelings of anxiety.
15. State anxiety is specific to a given situation, whereas trait anxiety is not situation-specific.
16. Sensitizers dwell on the consequences of a threat, whereas repressors tend to avoid thinking about the threat.
17. In the course of engaging in such risky sports as parachuting, fear tends to give way to enthusiasm when the individual begins to exercise skills or make adaptive responses.
18. One reason people may engage in risky sports is that such sports provide the optimal combination of neural/hormonal reactions that are necessary for a "high." They provide the opportunity to exercise a skill (make an adaptive response) in a situation that poses a threat to one's very life or safety (unpredictability).
19. The theory of group selection is that certain individuals carry genes that make them sensitive to overpopulation and that such individuals restrain reproduction for the good of the group.

20. According to the kin-selection theory, the behavior of animals is governed by a tendency to maximize their genes in succeeding generations.
21. The kin-selection theory suggests that acts of altruism will be directed mainly, if not exclusively, to relatives.
22. Reciprocity theory proposes that all acts of altruism are governed by the rules of reciprocity.
23. Hormonal changes associated with puberty and with pregnancy sensitize females toward nurturant caregiving to infants.
24. The infant cry is aversive to most humans of all ages and can either lead to nurturant caregiving or precipitate child abuse.
25. Hoffman has argued that humans have a basic tendency toward altruism but that altruistic acts depend on cognitive development.
26. MacLean has noted that since there are interconnections between the limbic system and the neocortex in primates, the cognitive and biological systems in humans may influence each other in making empathy possible.
27. Social learning theory suggests that acts of altruism are governed by social norms that have been internalized through rewards and punishment.
28. A number of studies have shown that positive mood leads to increased helping.
29. A number of studies have also shown that negative mood leads to increased helping. These results can be explained by a learning model of the development of altruism.
30. Recent findings indicate negative mood does not directly cause helping but rather increases the perception that the mood caused some negative event, thus engendering a sense of self-awareness.
31. It has been suggested that some forms of altruism are tied to the power motive.
32. According to the view that a "justice motive" influences altruism, people have a need to believe they live in a world where people get what they deserve.
33. The tendency to derogate the character of victims can be explained by the justice-motive theory. That is, people have a need to believe that people deserve what they get.
34. Failure to derogate a victim's character occurs when the victim is attractive, when the victim can be viewed as having done something that brought on his or her own suffering, when the person believes he or she might be in a similar situation, and in situations in which the chances of two persons' escaping were equal.
35. People committed to the concept of entitlement (the idea that one should get what one deserves) are more likely to behave altruistically.
36. Attributional analyses of helping have shown that the tendency to help is reduced when the cause of the victim's plight is perceived as internal and controllable.
37. Perceived costs associated with intervention on behalf of a victim can increase or decrease the tendency toward altruism.
38. Humans are inclined to shift (diffuse) responsibility when others are present, especially if the costs of intervention are high.
39. The tendency to intervene is greater when the potential harm to the victim is more severe.
40. Eye contact increases a bystander's tendency to intervene on a victim's behalf.
41. Kanfer has outlined a method for using the selfish motive of a need for control to increase acts of altruism in society.

Stress,
Distress, and Coping

What causes stress?

Why is stress often referred to as the fight/flight response?

How are arousal and the stress reaction related?

What chemicals are released when we are under stress and what do these chemicals do?

Is it true that our learning is altered when we are experiencing stress?

Why do people often fail to experience pain when they are injured?

Why does stress often lead to disease?

Are some people constitutionally better able to deal with stress than other people?

What are some of the things that give rise to stress in humans?

Why are people doing research on stress so interested in the Type A personality?

What are some of the moderators of stress?

What can people do to cope with stress?

We often use the term *stress* in our daily lives in connection with a variety of events, including taking examinations, the breakup of a marriage or other close relationship, the difficulty involved in not having enough money to pay our bills, the annoyance and frustration of having to drive on congested roads, the conflict that occurs when we have to deal with someone we dislike or disagree with. In general, the layperson has come to use the word to describe a set of negative feelings and reactions. Failing an examination is experienced as a highly aversive event that can lead to feelings of humiliation and shame. The breakup of a close relationship may lead to a deep sense of loss and remorse. Not being able to pay our bills can be frustrating and irritating. Driving on a crowded road may produce both frustration and anger. Interpersonal relationships that are marked by conflict can lead to contempt and disgust. These feelings are often accompanied by a set of physiological responses that include anything from increased heart rate to rumblings in the stomach.

The layperson, then, generally uses the term *stress* to describe negative feelings. But the scientist uses it somewhat differently. Stress is generally viewed as a set of neurological/physiological reactions that serve some ultimate adaptive purpose. How the individual responds to those reactions determines whether they are *distressful* (as the layperson typically uses the term) or produce *eustress* (a positive feeling that accompanies successful coping with stress).

Hans Selye, the person who has had the greatest impact on our understanding of stress, published an article in 1936 suggesting that a wide variety of diseases are associated with a common reaction that has come to be called the stress reaction or the general adaptation syndrome (G.A.S.). This general reaction was and is viewed as a set of reactions that mobilize the person's resources to deal with an impending threat. Over the years Selye has published many articles and books arguing that this general reaction is produced not only by diseases but by a wide variety of psychological situations as well (see Selye, 1974, 1976). He has argued that people need not experience distress whenever they experience a stress reaction. Feelings of distress or eustress are, to a large degree, results of people's attitudes toward events and/or their own physiological responses (Selye, 1978). Before we examine this point in detail, we need to understand exactly what we mean by the stress reaction, or, as Selye likes to call it, the G.A.S.

Conceptualizing Stress as a Fight/Flight Response

When people talk about the stress reaction, they frequently refer to it as the fight/ flight response. This label grows out of an evolutionary analysis of the origins of the stress response. Animals have two basic ways of dealing with threats: they fight or they flee. A rabbit depends on its ability to flee in order to stay alive. A lion, in contrast, depends on its ability to fight to stay alive as well as to obtain the food supply that it requires. Whether one fights or flees, certain basic requirements must be met. First, one needs to expend a great deal of energy. Second, one has to keep one's head. Third, one frequently has to deal with injury. Stress can be viewed as a reaction that maximizes the expenditure of energy. Blood rushes to the sites where it is needed (the muscles and brain), fats are released into the bloodstream, we perspire to cool ourselves, and so forth. The high level of arousal we experience helps us to focus our attention on survival cues. Our blood thickens, and chemicals are released that will enable our body to deal with injury, should it happen.

From a stress-management point of view, the problem is that we live in a world where we do not have to expend the same amount of physical energy as our foraging ancestors did, nor are we normally threatened with injury when we experience stress. We no longer need to have so much fat released in our blood, we do not need to perspire, it is not necessary for our blood pressure to skyrocket, it is not necessary for our blood to thicken to guard against an injury, we do not need to have chemicals circulating in our blood ready to attack some foreign body that might enter our system. Even though it is not necessary for any of these things to happen, each time we experience stress our body prepares itself as though we were still living as our ancestors lived.

The Biological Component

Distinguishing between the Sympathetic/Adrenal and the Pituitary/Adrenal Responses

When people are challenged, they tend to mobilize a great deal of effort in order to deal with that event. Similarly, when people lose control, they may try to reassert their control. Under these conditions the body makes what is called a sympathetic/adrenal response. The sympathetic system allows us to respond to the immediate demands of the situation by activating the body. Our heart rate accelerates, our blood pressure rises, we become more alert, and so forth. In short, we become aroused (see Chapter 3). Two main chemicals, epinephrine and norepinephrine, are released by the adrenal glands to provide a chemical backup to the immediate action of the sympathetic system. These two chemicals are released from the adrenal medulla (the inner part of the gland). Epinephrine and norepinephrine are also referred to respectively as adrenaline and noradrenaline, especially when those chemicals are released to the periphery of the system rather than to the brain. As this distinction is often ignored, however, we will call them by the names most commonly given them: epinephrine and norepinephrine.

The pituitary/adrenal system is more closely associated with what is traditionally called the stress response. The adrenal cortex (the outer part of the gland) secretes two main hormones, mineralocorticoids and glucocorticoids. It is important to understand that the release of these two hormones is linked to the release of other chemicals. I will discuss this pattern of responses shortly. The point I want to make here is simply that when people are faced with stress, they often engage in behaviors that are designed to eliminate or control the stress. Thus the sympathetic/ adrenal and the pituitary/adrenal responses typically occur together. These two systems, however, can and frequently do operate separately, generally when an individual gains control over stress by engaging in some kind of adaptive behavior. As one gains control, the cortisol level frequently drops while the epinephrine level remains high (Frankenhaeuser, Lundberg, & Forsman, 1980). Cortisol is frequently used as a measure of the action of the pituitary/adrenal system, whereas urinary epinephrine is a measure of the activity of the sympathetic/adrenal system. As we have already explored the nature of the sympathetic/adrenal system in Chapter 3, let us turn now to the pituitary/adrenal system.

The Pituitary/Adrenal Response

Figure 8-1 is a schematic representation of the pituitary/adrenal system. The hypothalamus initiates activity in the endocrine system by secreting corticotropin-releasing factor (CRF), which stimulates the pituitary. The pituitary, in turn, secretes adrenocorticotropic hormone (ACTH), whose effects are shown in Table 8-1. Experimental findings suggest that ACTH plays a central role in our ability to respond to threatening stimuli. Curiously, ACTH stimulates another hormonal reaction that is responsible for terminating the secretion of further ACTH. Specifically, ACTH stimulates the adrenal cortex, which then secretes glucocorticoids. When the glucocorticoid level is elevated, the central nervous system shuts down the processes that lead to the secretion of the stimulating hormone ACTH (de Wied, 1967, 1980; Vernikos-Danellis & Heybach, 1980).

Increased circulatory level of adrenocorticotropic hormone leads to increased autonomic arousal, a topic discussed in some detail in Chapter 3 (Mason, 1959; Mason, Brady, & Sidman, 1957). While increased arousal will affect the way a person reacts to the environment, secretion of ACTH has some important specific effects that mediate our reactions to a stressful event. It is important, therefore, that we understand these effects (Makara, Palkovits, & Szentagothai, 1980).

Animal research indicates that ACTH is released approximately 10 seconds after a stressful event. The slowness of this reaction in comparison with the immediate action of the central nervous system suggests that the endocrine system is probably not responsible for the immediate survival responses of fight and flight but is probably involved in longer-term survival reactions. For example, ACTH stimulates the release of fatty acids and the utilization of glucose, which provide the energy to deal with a threat (White, Handler, & Smith, 1964). It takes between 15 minutes and 1 hour before glucocorticoids are elevated to a level sufficient to terminate secretion of ACTH (Vernikos-Danellis & Heybach, 1980). Thus, once the stress reaction has been set in motion, it continues for a time. The glucocorticoids remain active much longer than ACTH. It has been suggested that the continued presence of glucocorticoids in the blood accounts for some poststress reactions, such as weight loss, changes in body temperature, and increased secretion of stomach acid (Weiss, 1968).

A somewhat different pattern of events occurs when a stressor is present for a long time. It appears that prolonged stress results in a breakdown of the adrenal system, making the person susceptible to a wide variety of diseases. This question will be dealt with a little later under the heading "Stress and Disease."

Epinephrine and Affect

One of the consistent findings is that the epinephrine level rises in response to a wide variety of both pleasant and unpleasant psychosocial stimuli (Franken-

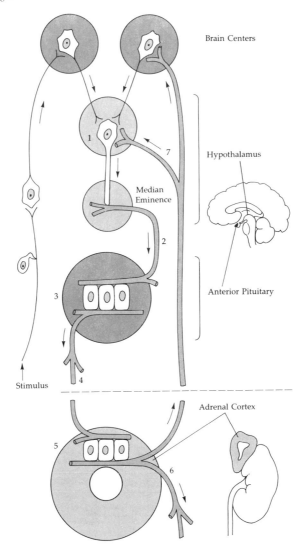

Figure 8-1. The pituitary/adrenal system, which involves nerve cells and hormones in a feedback loop. A stress stimulus reaching neurosecretory cells of the hypothalamus in the base of the brain (1) stimulates them to release corticotropin-releasing factor (CRF), which moves through short blood vessels (2) to the anterior lobe of the pituitary gland (3). Pituitary cells thereupon release adrenocorticotropic hormone (ACTH) into the circulatory system (4). The ACTH stimulates cells of the adrenal cortex (5) to secrete glucocorticoid hormones (primarily hydrocortisone in humans) into the circulatory system (6). When glucocorticoids reach neurosecretory cells or other brain cells (it is not clear which), they modulate CRF production (7) (Levine, 1971).

haeuser, 1975, 1980). Levi and Kagan (1980) have pointed out that epinephrine level is high when stimuli produce either pleasant or unpleasant feelings. The level is lower when feelings are neutral. They describe this relation as a U-shaped function.

Table 8-1. Principal physiological and pharmacological effects of norepinephrine, epinephrine, ACTH, and adrenal steroids (DiGuisto, Cairncross, & King, 1971)

Substance	Effects	General adaptive functions
Central norepinephrine	Drug-induced decreased and increased levels associated with sedation and excitement, respectively, in humans and animals	Influences alertness and behavioral arousal in a relatively nonspecific manner
Peripheral norepinephrine	Transmitter substance in postganglionic sympathetic nerve endings; maintains blood pressure; produces RAS arousal	Maintains reflex excitability of sympathetic portion of autonomic nervous system; protects organism from acute effects of hemorrhage
Central epinephrine	Not synthesized centrally in significant quantities	
Peripheral epinephrine	Produces RAS arousal; promotes sweating; moves blood from skin to muscles; raises free fatty acid level and mobilizes blood glucose; inhibits muscular activity in abdominal viscera and increases output of heart	Makes skin more difficult to penetrate; decreases bleeding and allows greater muscle output; (quick) energy factor
Central ACTH	ACTH and other pituitary peptides present in hypothalamus, but their function is unknown	
Peripheral ACTH	Stimulates fatty acid release by adipose tissue and glucose utilization	Energy factor
Central steroids	Adrenal steroids not synthesized centrally	
Peripheral steroids	These may be divided into mineralocorticoids and glucocorticoids	
	The major mineralocorticoid is aldosterone, which controls electrolyte and water metabolism; the major glucocorticoids are corticosterone and hydrocortisone, which control carbohydrate and protein metabolism	Relatively slow-acting, long-term energy factors, especially as regards muscular energy
	Glucocorticoids must be present for the catecholamines to exert their calorigenic action and their vascular effects	Adrenal steroids are critical for life maintenance and somatic resistance to stress

The Stress Reaction and Learning

A considerable amount of research has been conducted to examine how various biochemical reactions influence adaptation to stress. Because one of the most effective ways of reducing or eliminating the effects of stress is to avoid the stressor, much research has focused on the effects of biochemical reactions on avoidance learning (Levine, 1971). Shock has been commonly used as a stressor in this research because its intensity is easily varied and it is reliable in producing the stress reaction. In the avoidance-learning paradigm, the stressor is preceded by a signal, such as a tone or light. The subject can avoid the stressor by learning to make a response that will prevent the onset of shock.

In the typical avoidance-learning experiment with animals, the animal initially learns to reduce the duration of the shock by making what is called an escape response. In the shuttle box, as shown in Figure 8-2, the animal merely has to learn to run to the other side of the box in order to escape the shock. After a number of trials the animal typically makes this response to the signal that precedes the onset of shock. If the animal makes the response without receiving shock, the response is called an avoidance response.

A great deal of research has focused on the question of whether the stress reaction facilitates avoidance learning. If the stress reaction evolved as a mechanism for ensuring survival, then it follows that this reaction should help the individual in dealing with not only the physical but also the psychological aspects of stress. Although we are still a long way from understanding all the factors involved, a relatively clear pattern has begun to emerge.

There is evidence that activation of the sympathetic nervous system facilitates the learning of an avoidance response (DiGuisto et al., 1971; Moyer & Brunell, 1958). This makes good sense: the sympathetic nervous system is faster-acting than the endocrine system and therefore is likely to be involved in acquisition of an adaptive response. Because epinephrine and norepinephrine are arousal-producing chemicals, it has been suggested that these agents facilitate avoidance learning by increasing the arousal level. As we noted in Chapter 3, the relation between arousal and performance can be described as an inverted-U-shaped function.

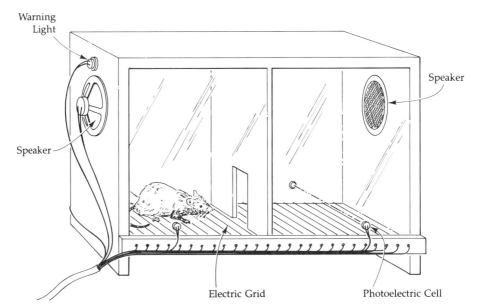

Figure 8-2. The shuttle box used for studying avoidance behavior, a two-compartment cage. The floor can be electrically charged. A shock is delivered on the side occupied by the rat (detected by the photocell). The rat can avoid the shock by learning to respond to the conditioned stimulus, a light or noise (or both) delivered briefly before the shock. The avoidance response, once learned, is slowly extinguished if the conditioned stimulus is no longer accompanied by a shock (Levine, 1971).

According to Hebb (1955), the reason performance is better when arousal is moderate is that moderate arousal tends to direct the individual's attention to the important, or dominant, cues. Therefore, it can be argued that learning is faster because norepinephrine and epinephrine increase arousal to some moderate level.

There is little evidence that ACTH facilitates acquisition of an avoidance response but considerable evidence that ACTH prevents extinction of a learned avoidance response (see de Wied, 1980). Further, there is evidence that destruction of the sympathetic nervous system will retard the acquisition of both escape and avoidance learning (Wynne & Solomon, 1955) but that once an avoidance response has been established, destruction of the sympathetic nervous system does not affect avoidance performance (Moyer & Korn, 1965). These findings indicate that the mechanism responsible for the acquisition of an avoidance response is different from the mechanism that maintains that response.

It is important, of course, not only that an individual quickly learn an avoidance response when threatened but that such a response be maintained as long as it is adaptive. It appears that the sympathetic nervous system is involved in acquisition of an avoidance response whereas the endocrine system is involved in maintenance of that response. This is consistent with the idea that the sympathetic nervous system is responsible for the individual's initial reaction to stress and the endocrine system is involved in long-term reactions to stress.

Although it is important that an adaptive response be maintained as long as it is required, it is also important that the response be eliminated when it has outlived its usefulness. There is considerable evidence that glucocorticoids facilitate extinction of a learned response (de Wied, 1966, 1967). As we noted above, glucocorticoids block the action of ACTH. It appears, therefore, that the function of glucocorticoids is to shut down the stress reaction and, in doing so, to return the individual to a normal state of learning in which nonadaptive responses are systematically eliminated.

Adaptive Behaviors and the Reduction of Stress

There is considerable evidence that when an organism engages in an adaptive behavior, the stress response is reduced. It has been shown, for example, that corticosterone levels in the rat progressively decline during the course of shuttle-box avoidance training (Ursin et al., 1975). Humans exposed to highly stressful occupational tasks that they can control show a reduction in cortisol (another indicator of stress). It has been shown that such behaviors as eating, drinking, fighting, and escape also inhibit the pituitary/adrenal system (Coover, Ursin, & Levine, 1973). If ACTH and related peptides (hormone fragments) help prepare the organism to make an adaptive response, then once that response has been made, it would make a great deal of sense for that response to shut down. Engaging in adaptive behavior, in other words, appears to be one of the events that tells the body to shut down the stress reaction.

Endorphins and Stress

The brain contains significant amounts of endorphins. The term *endorphin* was derived from the words *endo*genous and mor*phine* because of the similarity of effect of morphine and these naturally occurring peptides. That is, like morphine, endorphins have strong analgesic (pain-reducing) properties. The endorphin that has received the most study, both because of the amount found in the brain and because its action is similar to that of morphine, is beta-endorphin.

It has been observed that beta-endorphin is mobilized from the pituitary during stress in approximately the same quantities as ACTH (Rossier, Bloom, & Guillemin, 1980). The main significance of this fact may be its ability to explain why stress tends to induce analgesia (Akil et al., 1976). In addition, it has been shown that endorphins produce feelings of euphoria. It appears that endorphins produce these feelings by altering concentrations of neurotransmitters that activate the reward pathways in the brain (J. E. Smith et al., 1980).

Laboratory studies of endorphins indicate that the endorphin response can be triggered not only by physical stressors, such as shock, but by fear (see Bolles & Fanselow, 1982). This finding may explain why people frequently expose themselves to situations that elicit fear, such as parachuting and mountain climbing.

As I pointed out in Chapter 7, Tiger (1979) has argued that endorphins evolved in order to facilitate hunting behavior in our ancestors. Tiger argues that in order to be a good hunter it is important not to be afraid in the face of danger, and that if one should happen to be injured, it would be highly adaptive not to experience pain, at least for a time. Pain would reduce the hunter's ability to deal with the immediate situation and could negatively reinforce him not to hunt in the future.

Stress and Disease

Although the stress response is very important for mobilizing the organism's defensive reactions to deal with such threats as diseases, there is considerable evidence that the stress reaction can precipitate diseases. Hans Selye has spent a lifetime analyzing this paradox. His work seems to indicate that the negative side of stress occurs only when stress is prolonged.

Selye (1974) has noted that a person who is subjected to prolonged stress goes through three phases. The first stage is the *alarm reaction*. I have already discussed the various physiological and psychological responses that occur when a person is initially confronted with a stressor. When the stressor continues, the person enters what Selye has called the *stage of resistance*. A number of important physiological reactions characterize this phase. The pituitary secretes ACTH, which is mainly responsible for energy metabolism and also stimulates the adrenal cortex. The adrenal cortex secretes glucocorticoids, which are important for resistance to stress. The two most important glucocorticoids are cortisone, which inhibits tissue inflammation, and mineralocorticoids, which promote inflammation. As Selye notes, "These hormones allow the body to defend its tissues by inflammation or to surrender them by inhibiting inflammation" (1969, p. 26). There is evidence from animal research that the adrenal glands actually increase in size during the resistance stage, presumably a reflection of their increased activity. If the stress is prolonged, the adrenal glands stop functioning or collapse. The collapse of the adrenal glands is often the precursor to death and is called the *exhaustion stage*.

Selye has noted that many of the diseases precipitated or caused by stress occur in the resistance stage. These "diseases of adaptation" seem to be due to some form of derangement in the secretion of the adaptive hormones. For example, Selye notes that excessive production of a proinflammatory hormone in response to some local irritation could damage organs in other parts of the body. Many "diseases of adaptation" have been identified, including emotional disturbances, headaches, insomnia, sinus attacks, high blood pressure, gastric and duodenal ulcers, certain somatic or allergic afflictions, and cardiovascular and kidney diseases (Selye, 1974).

Although Selye's *generality model* has dominated thinking about the relation between stress and disease, evidence is growing in support of a *specificity model*. There is increasing evidence that different physical stressors produce different hormonal profiles—a finding that is inconsistent with Selye's "general adaptation syndrome" theory (Mason et al., 1976). The amount of norepinephrine and epinephrine secreted, for example, as we saw in Chapter 7, typically varies with the degree of control one has over an aversive event.

Unpredictability, stress, and disease. While aversive events can elicit the stress reaction, it is important to distinguish between events that are predictable and those that are not. It has been shown repeatedly that exposure to aversive events is much more likely to produce stress and disease if the events are unpredictable than if they can be foreseen. In comparison with predictable stress, unpredictable stress produces higher levels of corticosterone (Weiss, 1970, 1971a), more severe stomach ulceration (Caul, Buchanan, & Hays, 1972; Weiss, 1971a), greater weight loss (Weiss, 1970), alterations in levels of glucose and free fatty acids (Quirce, Odio, & Solano, 1981), and myocardial dysfunction (Miller et al., 1978). Thus it is not the experience of an aversive event per se that causes stress and disease. As we shall see, when people know an aversive event is coming or when they can make some kind of coping response, stress and the diseases that accompany it are often dramatically reduced.

Genetics and Constitutional Differences in the Stress Reaction

Evidence from a wide variety of sources indicates that there are large individual differences in people's reactions to stressors. As we shall see shortly, some of these differences are due to learned and cognitive factors. There are also constitutional differences, which can be traced to at least two sources: genetics and early stimulation.

For some time now it has been known that it is possible to breed animals for emotionality (for example, Broadhurst, 1957b). When the more emotional animal is exposed to tasks varying in difficulty, it tends to show signs of stimulus overload at much lower levels of stimulation than the less emotional animal (Broadhurst, 1957a). Research with human subjects has produced similar findings. People who secrete more epinephrine tend to perform better on a monotonous task than low-epinephrine subjects; however, on a task that is more demanding, high-epinephrine subjects tend to do worse than low-epinephrine subjects (Frankenhaeuser & Andersson, 1974; Frankenhaeuser et al., 1971). Because it would require a selective breeding program to prove that these differences are due to genetic factors, we can only surmise, on the basis of our knowledge of heritability, that they are, at least in part.

Early Stimulation and Constitutional Differences

Extensive research on early stimulation with animals as well as humans suggests that some of the individual differences are due to long-term effects of early stimulation (Levine, 1960). In these studies, infant rats and mice were subjected to various forms of stimulation that would produce a stress reaction. One of the most extensively used stressors in these studies was "handling." Infant mice and rats were picked up and stroked briefly and then returned to their nests. This procedure was repeated for several days. Administering mild shock to the feet, dropping the infant a short distance, and brushing the animal were some of the other stressors used. After a brief period of stress in infancy, the animals were allowed to develop without further interference. When these animals were adults, they were subjected to a wide variety of stressors to determine whether the early stress had altered their ability to resist stress. The results were dramatic. Animals that had been subjected to stress early in life showed a greater ability to tolerate stress than animals that had not. For example, they could better withstand cold and electrical shock (Levine, 1960, 1971).

It has been suggested that early stimulation accelerates maturation of the central nervous system. There is evidence, for example, that handled animals have higher cholesterol levels in the brain, open their eyes earlier, achieve motor coordination sooner, gain weight faster, and grow body hair sooner. Analysis of the hormonal output in reaction to stressful stimuli indicates not only that the stress reaction is initiated sooner after a stressful stimulus in animals that received early stimulation but that the stress reaction ends sooner after the termination of a stressful event (Levine, 1960, 1971). It is adaptive, of course, to react quickly to the presence of a stressor. It is also important that the stress reaction shut down quickly after the stressful event is over; otherwise, the stress reaction itself becomes an enemy and may be responsible for what Selye has called "diseases of adaptation." Figure 8-3 shows hormonal reactions of stimulated and nonstimulated animals to electrical shock. Note the sluggishness of the reaction in nonstimulated animals.

Early stimulation also affects an individual's psychological reactions to its environment. Animals that have received some form of early stimulation typically explore more than animals that have not. It has been suggested that differential exploratory behavior can be explained by the differences in the emotional reactivity of stimulated and nonstimulated animals. It has been noted that rats not stimulated in infancy are more emotionally reactive to novel stimuli (Denenberg, 1967). This finding parallels the observation that stimulated animals are more resistant to such stressors as cold and shock. Presumably the greater hormonal output of the non-

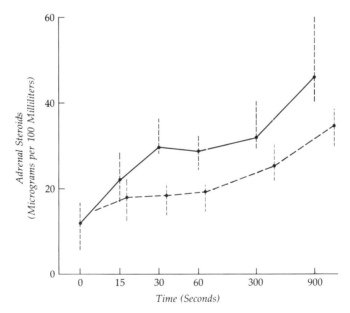

Figure 8-3. Concentration of circulating steroid hormones in response to electrical shock in rats receiving early stimulation (solid line) and nonstimulated rats (dashed line). Sluggish response to shock is indicated by the slow rise in hormone concentration in previously nonstimulated rats. In the stimulated animals, the level increases rapidly for about 15 minutes. The points on the curve indicate the average level and the broken vertical lines the range of values (Levine, 1971).

stimulated animals leads to a reaction that inhibits exploratory behavior. It is likely that the presentation of a novel stimulus leads to the output of epinephrine, which somehow reduces exploration.

According to arousal theory, individuals explore in order to increase arousal to some optimal level. It is assumed that exploration is one way of increasing the level of incoming stimulation. Thus, according to the theory, if an individual is already at some optimal level, it will not engage in exploratory behavior. If non-stimulated animals are more emotionally reactive to new stimuli, it follows that they should explore less, because their arousal level will be nearer their optimal level. In one study (Franken & Strain, 1974), it was shown that experimentally increasing an animal's arousal level by injecting the animal with an arousal-producing drug resulted in decreased exploratory behavior, a finding that provides direct support for such an interpretation. As noted earlier, extraverts tend to show lower cortical arousal than introverts and tend to explore more than introverts, a finding that is consistent with Eysenck's position that differences between extraverts and introverts are mediated by arousal.

There is a growing body of evidence that early stimulation has a similar effect in humans. Tactile and kinesthetic stimulation of low-birth-weight infants, for example, has improved performance on various developmental tests (Powell, 1974; Rice, 1977; Scarr-Salapatek & Williams, 1973). Further, certain forms of early stimulation may increase exploratory behavior (Rubenstein, 1967; Yarrow et al., 1972).

What the research on early stimulation shows is that early stimulation modifies the action of the adrenal/pituitary system. Specifically, it appears that the adrenal/pituitary system reacts more quickly to the presence of a stressor and, as a consequence, helps the organism deal more effectively with it. Data show that novel stimuli will elicit the stress response, and it is not surprising to find that early stimulation not only increases tolerance to such physical stressors as cold and shock but reduces the aversive (stress-producing) aspects of novelty. Reduction of the aversive qualities of novelty would, of course, be associated with an increase in the tendency to explore, especially if the increased efficiency of the adrenal/pituitary system produced corresponding increases in ability to process incoming stimulation.

The fact that early stimulation can increase ability to tolerate stress opens the door to the question whether it is possible to alter an adult's ability to tolerate stress. The research on early stimulation has far from ruled out this possibility. All the research has shown so far is that it is relatively easy to modify the stress reaction at certain critical stages of development.

Summary

When an individual is threatened physically or psychologically, a characteristic pattern of responses called the stress reaction occurs. A series of chemical reactions set in motion by the hypothalamus alter, in a predictable way, an individual's response to events in the environment. Secretion of epinephrine and norepinephrine facilitates acquisition of an avoidance response, while secretion of ACTH tends to prevent extinction of an avoidance response. These two complementary reactions, it has been argued, serve to ensure that the individual learns and maintains responses that are adaptive in dealing with stress.

Selye has identified three stages of the stress reaction: the alarm reaction, the stage of resistance, and the exhaustion stage. In animals subjected to
(continued)

prolonged stress, the adrenal cortex increases in size during the stage of resistance but eventually collapses. The collapse is typically the precursor to death.

Although the stress response is important in mobilizing the organism's defensive reactions to deal with threats, Selye has shown that stress itself can precipitate diseases. This outcome tends to occur in the second stage of the stress reaction, when stress is prolonged. Specifically, it appears that the glucocorticoids begin to attack the very system they initially were mobilized to protect.

Aversive events that are unpredictable result in greater stress and disease than aversive events that are predictable. An adaptive response has been shown to reduce greatly the magnitude of the stress response.

There are wide individual differences in the magnitude of the stress reaction. Both animal and human research suggests that early stimulation can modify the stress reaction in two ways: it can improve the individual's ability to cope with a threat and reduce the likelihood that the stress reaction, once elicited, will become an enemy of the system.

Learned Factors

The nature and the magnitude of the stress reaction are also affected by factors that relate to principles of learning. In at least four areas, learning affects either the magnitude and nature of the stress reaction or the ability to function under stress. Much of the work on this topic comes from the laboratory of Neal Miller (see Miller, 1980).

Discrimination

If an organism experiences intermittent stress, knowing when that stress will come could be important in helping the organism to prepare for the stress just before onset and to relax after the stress has ended. The problem for the organism, therefore, is to learn to discriminate the cues that predict the onset of stress. Laboratory research has shown that, indeed, this is an important factor. In one study (Weiss, 1970) rats were given a warning signal that they were about to receive a tail shock. A yoked control group received the same duration and pattern of shocks but without a warning signal. Intermittent shocks produce not only a reliable stress reaction but lesions in the stomach (thought to be a precursor to ulcers). The question was whether signaled or unsignaled shock would produce more lesions. The results are shown in Figure 8-4. Clearly, unsignaled shocks are more stressful than signaled shocks. The analogy with humans is obvious. Scheduled tests are difficult enough at the best of times. Unscheduled tests are even more stressful because they do not allow the person to relax.

Several studies have failed to show that signaled shock leads to less stress (see Averill, 1973). Commenting on these studies, Averill notes that signaled shock seems to work only if the signal tells the subject not only when shock will come but also when the subject can relax. The key, in other words, is knowing when to relax.

Learning a Coping Response

As we noted in Chapter 3, monkeys in a shock-avoidance situation showed somewhat different patterns of catecholamine output when they could and could

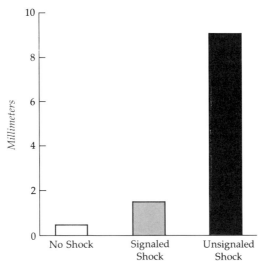

Figure 8-4. Total length of stomach lesions produced by shocks that are signaled so that rats can learn a discrimination and shocks that are unsignaled so that no discrimination is possible (Weiss, 1970)

not avoid the shock. Weiss (1968, 1971a) found that animals that learn an avoidance response not only experience less lesioning of the stomach but show less stress (as measured by level of plasma corticosterone) than yoked control subjects that do not have the opportunity to make an avoidance response. Exactly why coping responses reduce stress is not altogether clear. Studies have ruled out the possibility that their effectiveness is due to the greater activity (exercise) that accompanies active avoidance (Weiss, Glazer, & Pohorecky, 1976). As we shall see in the next section, there is good evidence that the effect is, at least in part, cognitively mediated.

The coping response must be fairly easy as well as free of conflict if it is to be effective. In one study rats had to perform either an easy coping response (a single bar press) or a more difficult response (several bar presses) to avoid shock. Animals with an easy response had fewer stomach lesions than their yoked partners (Tsuda & Hirai, 1975). In another experiment rats had to experience a brief shock while making an avoidance response that prevented a longer train of shocks. In this situation, the coping group developed more stomach lesions than the yoked control subjects (Weiss, 1971b). These latter results are presented in Figure 8-5, together with the results for a no-conflict control condition.

Training the Stress Response

Various studies have shown that an acute stress reaction depletes norepinephrine (see N. E. Miller, 1980). Animals are slow to learn after an acute stress reaction, and it has been hypothesized that the failure to learn is due to the depletion of norepinephrine. The problem, therefore, is to find some way of replenishing norepinephrine. The question is whether it can be replenished through some kind of training procedure. If the failure to replenish norepinephrine is due to some inhibitory mechanism, for example, can a training regimen be devised to reduce this

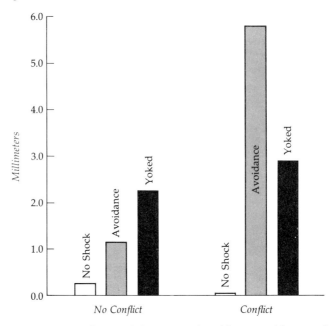

Figure 8-5.   Total length of stomach lesions produced by an avoidance task when the avoidance response involves conflict and when it does not. The "executive" rat that learned the avoidance (coping) response suffered fewer stomach lesions than yoked control subjects when the task was simple and clear-cut but considerably more when the task involved conflict (Weiss, 1971).

inhibitory effect (Miller, 1980)? One obvious procedure would be to expose the individual to acute stress repeatedly in the hope that a tolerance to stress would build up.

In one study designed to test this possibility, rats were exposed to acute stress for 15 consecutive days. Control rats were exposed to acute stress on only one day, with no prior exposure. The rats were then sacrificed in order to examine the effects of the experimental manipulations on norepinephrine metabolism in the brain. The prior-exposure animals had higher levels of enzymes involved in norepinephrine synthesis than the no-exposure animals (Weiss et al., 1975). In a follow-up experiment, performance in a shuttle box was substituted for the test of brain norepinephrine metabolism. Rats trained to endure stress learned faster after exposure to acute stress (shock) than animals not previously trained but exposed to the same acute stress. In other words, the training, or "toughening up," procedure helps protect the rats from the adverse effects of exposure to acute stress.

Marianne Frankenhaeuser (1980) has argued that repeated exposure to a stressor will reduce the stress reaction (particularly the activity of the adrenal medulla) only if there is a decrease in psychological involvement. For example, she notes that parachute jumping never becomes routine. Catecholamine secretion during jump periods tends to remain high even after several jumps (Bloom, von Euler, & Frankenhaeuser, 1963). Probably the reason is that parachute jumping demands constant attention and concentration. In other words, when a high degree of readiness is required for psychological reasons, the stress reaction remains high.

Prior exposure is often used as a training procedure to help people in a variety of situations come to deal more effectively with certain forms of stressful stimulation. Training soldiers for combat typically involves exposing them to acute stress over a period of time prior to any combat duty. Mountain climbers train extensively, exposing themselves to as many as possible of the conditions that they will encounter in an important climb, such as cold, rain, wind, and simply physical exertion. Pilots are trained in simulators to react to a wide variety of emergencies. In all these situations, the goal is not only to train the stress reaction but to teach the person to evaluate correctly the nature of the stimulus that is a potential stressor. Certain patterns of stimulation should elicit the stress reaction and others should not.

Learning to Perform under Stress

Human performance often deteriorates under stress. Most theorists hold to a position similar to that proposed by Hebb (1955). That is, as stress (or arousal) increases up to some optimal level, performance will be facilitated. However, further increases in stress (or arousal) will impair performance. The exact reason for this pattern has been the object of much speculation. Many theorists attribute it to alterations in attention (for example, Easterbrook, 1959). The question arises whether it is possible for a person to maintain certain behaviors when the level of stress increases. Any coach knows that the stress of competition can affect an athlete's performance. It can improve performance, but it can also disrupt performance. Often an athlete's performance is disrupted in those situations in which performance should be at its peak. It has often been argued that the poor performance is due to stress.

Laboratory research has shown that it is possible to maintain good performance under conditions of considerable stress. The procedure that has proved most successful involves gradually increasing stress while the individual executes a response. In one study Neal Miller (1960) trained rats to run down an alleyway by rewarding them with food. After they had learned this response, one group of rats was given a mild shock after reaching the end of the alleyway. Because they were still rewarded, they learned to run in spite of the shock. On subsequent trials the shock was gradually increased. At the end of training, the rats were tested under high levels of shock, as were control rats that had received food at the end of the alleyway but no shock. Rats given the gradual increase in shock continued to perform under high levels of shock; the majority of control rats did not.

Similar results have been obtained with humans. University students who were required to solve arithmetic problems under stress showed decreased heart rate and better performance in a test phase with a new stressor (Vossel & Laux, 1978). Because the subjects trained under stress did better when they were required to perform under different conditions of stress, it seems not only that stress resistance can be trained but that such training generalizes to new stressors, causing them to be experienced as less stressful.

Summary

Both the nature of the stress reaction and the way a person or animal tends to respond under stress can be modified by learning. Learning to predict when a stressor will come allows the individual to relax when the stressor is absent. Short periods of relaxation appear to help ward off the effects of
(continued)

stress. Learning a coping response seems to reduce some of the adverse effects of stress, such as ulcers. Training a response under stress seems to mobilize the body to provide the necessary physiological base for good performance. Finally, learning to perform under stress can be facilitated by gradual increases in the intensity of the stressor.

Cognitive Factors

Lazarus's Theory

One of the most comprehensive theories about the role of cognitive factors in stress has been developed by Richard Lazarus and several of his colleagues (Coyne & Lazarus, 1980; Folkman, 1984; Folkman et al., 1986; Folkman, Schaefer, & Lazarus, 1979; Lazarus, 1981; Lazarus & Launier, 1978). According to this theory, the way an individual appraises an event plays a fundamental role in determining not only the magnitude of the stress response but the kind of coping strategies that the individual may employ in efforts to deal with the stress.

Primary Appraisal

According to this theoretical formulation, a stressful event may be appraised as representing either harm/loss, threat, or challenge. *Harm/loss* refers to injury or damage that has already taken place, such as loss of a limb, loss of a job, or simply loss of self-esteem. *Threat* refers to something that could produce harm or loss. *Challenge* refers to the potential for growth, mastery, or some form of gain. As we shall see, a variety of factors, both personal and situational, are involved in an individual's appraisal of a situation. From this perspective, we cannot assess the origins of stress by looking solely at the nature of the environmental event that precipitates it. Rather, stress is a process that involves the interaction of the individual with the environment.

Secondary Appraisal

After assessing a stressful event as a situation of harm/loss, threat, or challenge, we evaluate our coping resources and options. We ask "What can I do?" The coping resources available to any individual are classified as physical, social, psychological, and material resources. Physical resources include such things as health and energy; social resources include family and friends; psychological resources are such things as self-esteem and problem-solving abilities; and material resources include such things as money and equipment.

Problem-Focused versus Emotion-Focused Coping

According to the theory, "coping refers to cognitive and behavioral efforts to master, reduce, or tolerate the internal and/or external demands that are created by the stressful transaction" (Folkman, 1984, p. 843). One of the important things to note about this definition is that *coping* refers to efforts to manage rather than the outcome of those efforts per se. In other words, having or developing a positive attitude is a form of coping even if that positive attitude ultimately fails to resolve the situation.

The theory makes an important distinction between two ways of reducing stress. One way, termed *problem-focused coping*, is to engage in some kind of problem-solving behavior designed to resolve the stressful transaction. If an individual is experiencing stress on the job because of another person, for example, it may be possible to reduce that stress by asking to be transferred to another department, arranging for the other person to be transferred, or devising some strategy to change the other person's behavior. Another way of reducing stress, termed *emotion-focused coping*, is to focus on controlling the symptoms of stress. If it is impossible to avoid the other person, for example, one might deliberately take time out after every encounter to relax and think about the positive aspects of the job or to talk with some other person who might provide sympathy.

Situational Factors and Personal Control

Whether an individual tends to focus on the problem or on the emotion in an attempt to reduce stress depends to a very large degree on whether the individual appraises the situation as controllable and on whether the situation is in fact controllable. Some situations are basically uncontrollable—living near a nuclear reactor, perhaps, or working as a police officer, or having a friend who is dying of cancer. Other situations are subject to control—having an examination scheduled next week, perhaps, or having a tire on your car that has a slow leak, or having no money but having a job that permits you to work overtime. I say "perhaps" because circumstances may make what appears to be an uncontrollable situation controllable and vice versa. But more important for our present purposes, people sometimes appraise as uncontrollable a situation that is really under their control and may perceive themselves to have control when they do not.

Potentially controllable situations.   When people are faced with a forthcoming examination, they tend to appraise that event as both challenging and threatening (Folkman & Lazarus, 1985). When people appraise an event as challenging, two things typically happen. First, they engage in problem-solving behaviors. Second, they develop a positive emotion (excitement, eagerness, hopefulness) that acts as a motivational support for their problem-solving behavior. In other words, two complementary processes emerge that lead to effort. When people appraise an event as threatening, however, something quite different happens. It is important to note that people tend to appraise a situation as threatening when they perceive that it may not be altogether controllable. A negative emotion typically accompanies this kind of appraisal. Negative emotions typically are indicators that something is wrong; at least, that is the traditional way of viewing negative emotions. Whatever the exact reason, it appears that humans experiencing a negative emotion tend to focus on that emotion. The time and effort devoted to coping with the negative emotion distract the individual from activities better calculated to solve the problem.

Getting a promotion or simply having a high-level job can be perceived as both challenging and threatening. What makes a promotion threatening is the possibility that one may not succeed in the new job. As long as the job is perceived as challenging, the individual is likely to handle it effectively. When feelings of threat arise, however, the individual is likely to spend a great deal of time and effort coping with those feelings. Management systems that use threats to motivate people obviously undermine the motivation of those people.

Situations unlikely to be controllable.   When people are faced with events over which they are unlikely to gain much control, it may be prudent to accept this fact rather than treat the situation as potentially controllable. Inasmuch as viewing a situation as a challenge leads to such a positive psychological state, this may seem like bad advice. But what happens when people make repeated attempts to control a situation that in fact is not controllable? A study of residents of Three

Mile Island, the site of a nuclear accident (Collins, Baum, & Singer, 1983), suggests that people who engage in problem-focused coping to deal with such an uncontrollable situation develop more psychological symptoms than people who rely on more emotion-focused coping. When we are faced with a problem that is truly beyond our control, it seems to make more sense simply to deal with our emotions.

The Theory of Cognitive Adaptation for Severe Personal Tragedy

Sometimes stress results not from a passing event but from a situation that alters one's life permanently and dramatically. How do people deal with such events? In an attempt to integrate some of the experimental findings, Shelley Taylor (1983) has proposed a theory that involves three basic processes. She argues that adjusting to a threatening event, such as receiving a diagnosis of cancer, involves three related processes. First, the individual searches for meaning in the experience. Since, in the case of cancer, the cause is not known, the individual may search for meaning by examining the role played by such things as heredity, diet, and environmental pollution. Second, the individual attempts to gain a sense of mastery over the event. Some cancer patients attempt to maintain a positive mental state, in the belief that one can control the disease by one's attitude. Alternatively, the individual may seek out additional medical help. Third, the individual attempts to enhance the self and restore self-esteem, which often drops dramatically when one is threatened, even when the threat is completely beyond one's control. Social comparison appears to be a very effective means of enhancing self-esteem. People feel much better about themselves when they focus on someone who seems to be worse off than they are. This theory emphasizes that adjustment depends to a very large degree on the ability to sustain and modify illusions that buffer one not only against the present threat but against possible future setbacks.

Rising to the Challenge

Frequently we are presented with new challenges in the form of increasing demands. More often than not, we rise to the challenge rather than let it pass. One important consequence of this tendency is increased stress, or, as Selye (1974) has called it, "raising the body's thermostat of defense." Frankenhaeuser and Johansson (1976) confronted subjects with a challenge in the form of cards bearing the name of a color—printed in a different color. Whether subjects were asked to read the word or to name the color, they experienced a conflict between the semantic and perceptual properties of the stimulus. To increase the demands of the task, one group was subjected to auditory interference. The results showed that subjects not only responded positively to the added demands but secreted more epinephrine. In a further study, the demands of the task were increased by additional noise. Again subjects not only increased their efforts but showed increased output of epinephrine, norepinephrine, and cortisol.

Why do people increase their efforts in response to increased demands? One reason is that humans are inclined to maintain their self-esteem. If they view themselves as competent and dependable, they will work to maintain that perception. Thus, even though rising to the demands may increase stress, they tend to work harder. It should be noted that rising to the challenge does not necessarily lead to feelings of distress. In fact, the resultant feelings may be positive. Moreover, increases in stress should not be viewed as necessarily bad. Some stress is necessary to maintain the integrity of the system (Selye, 1974). In other words, rising to the challenge may be both personally rewarding and good for the system.

Rising to the challenge and controllability.   If one is to deal with a challenge, the positive and negative aspects of stress (challenge and threat, in Lazarus's theory) must be in balance. Frankenhaeuser (1983) has found that one of the things that mediates the balance is controllability. Frankenhaeuser found that under conditions of low control, both catecholamines and cortisol were elevated. Catecholamines are a good indicator of sympathetic arousal, and a rise in their output is virtually always found when an individual rises to a challenge or puts forth effort. Cortisol, on the other hand, is an indicator of the amount of stress the individual is experiencing. Under conditions of high control, cortisol output fell nearly to baseline level. This finding suggests that rising to a challenge is a negative experience when ambiguity or uncertainty is associated with the task. When the individual gains control, the challenge assumes a positive aspect.

Controllability and longevity.   Apparently, perceived controllability even promotes longevity. In a long-term study of a group of institutionalized aged, Rodin and Langer (1977) studied the effects of giving people more options for control and responsibility. They found that those given more control not only became more active but reported being happier. Reduced levels of corticosteroids provided further empirical data suggesting that these subjects were experiencing less stress. After two years, this group was significantly more healthy than a comparison group. A dramatic finding was that half as many people died in this group as in a comparison group.

Summary

Primary appraisal, according to Lazarus's theory, involves classifying or labeling a stressful event as representing either harm/loss, threat, or challenge. Secondary appraisal involves the evaluation of the coping resources and options available, given the initial labeling of the event. In general, coping strategies are either problem-focused or emotion-focused. According to Lazarus's theory, whether an individual tends to use problem-focused or emotion-focused coping depends on two additional factors: whether the threat is potentially controllable and, if it is, whether the individual perceives that he or she has the skills to deal with it.

In an attempt to account for the way people deal with severe tragedy in their lives, Taylor has proposed the operation of three related processes: the individual first searches for meaning, then attempts to gain mastery, and then attempts to enhance or restore self-esteem.

Since the human tendency to "rise to the challenge" tends also to produce a stress response, the question is what mediates this effect. The evidence seems to suggest that people rise to the challenge in order to maintain their self-esteem. Once they have gained control, the stress response tends to diminish. Controllability has also been shown to promote longevity.

Stressors of Everyday Life

The stress reaction is elicited by a wide variety of psychosocial stimuli—stimuli associated with our jobs, our residences, our social interactions, the activities we engage in. Because they are part of our daily lives, they can elicit a prolonged stress reaction, which may precipitate a variety of "adaptive diseases." Research is just beginning to show why many psychosocial stimuli are experienced as stressors and therefore why they frequently lead to illness.

Examination Stress

Appraisal and coping strategies. A forthcoming examination is typically a source of stress. As we have noted, students tend to respond to the prospect of an exam with feelings of threat and challenge. How do students deal with this threat? Typically they use a combination of problem-focused and emotion-focused coping strategies. During the anticipatory stage they tend to prepare for the examination. During this stage of problem-focused coping they experience positive emotions, such as hopefulness. Just before the exam, during the final waiting stage, their emotions begin to turn negative. Having reviewed the material to be covered by the exam, they are no longer actively preparing (at least to the same degree as before) and they have time to appraise the adequacy of their efforts (Folkman & Lazarus, 1985).

It is important to note that there are large individual differences in the amount of stress experienced. This is not surprising, as the outcome has different implications (stakes) for different individuals. Students who need a certain grade to get into graduate school, for example, may perceive the stakes as very high indeed. Individuals differ, too, in the amount of control they feel as they prepare for the exam, wait for the day to arrive, and finally take the exam. Their perceptions of the exam's difficulty vary as well. We will look at the effects of perceived difficulty in Chapter 12.

Stress, anxiety, and test taking. For some time now we have had evidence that stress and anxiety tend to interfere with the ability to perform on tests. Why should this be the case? Sarason (1984) has argued that the problem with stress and anxiety is, to a very large degree, a problem of "self-preoccupying intrusive thinking" (p. 929). A preoccupation with one's own thoughts interferes with task-focused thinking. What kind of thoughts? They seem to fall into a general category of responses that arise from a self-assessment of personal deficits in the face of certain situational demands. Can an individual learn to reduce the interference that comes from such thoughts? Sarason has shown that self-preoccupying intrusive thinking is reduced when one focuses on the task. He argues that helping people to focus on the task is a much better way of helping them to deal with this type of situational stress than simply attempting to reassure them. In other words, problem-focused coping is a better way of dealing with this kind of stress than emotion-focused coping.

Physiological changes. A variety of physiological changes have been shown to take place as one prepares for and takes an examination. It has been shown, for example, that glucose levels rise before an exam and decline significantly over the course of the exam. Lactic acid, too, was found to be elevated before an exam, but unlike glucose, it continued to increase during the course of the exam (Hall & Brown, 1979); both of these responses are indicative of the stress level. It has also been shown that norepinephrine levels rise while immunoglobin A levels (a measure of B-cell immune function) decline, especially in people with a strong power motive (McClelland, Ross, & Patel, 1985). McClelland has argued that the power motive reflects, among other things, the need to control. People with a strong power motive tend to be most highly aroused by situations in which they fear loss of control, such as examinations. Following an examination (or loss of control), this research suggests, an individual might be more susceptible to various kinds of infection.

Sex differences. While the epinephrine response to mental stress has been found to be weaker in women than in men, this finding may be due to the fact that many studies that have compared male and female responses have not matched men and women in terms of achievement orientation. Men, for reasons that are still debated, tend to have a higher need for achievement than women. When a man and a woman were studied in a situation that involved equal challenge in an achievement-oriented situation (public oral defense of a Ph.D. thesis), no differences were found between them in the epinephrine response: both subjects showed a threefold increase (Johansson, Collins, & Collins, 1983). The male subject showed a marked increase in urinary cortisol, confirming that the situation was indeed stressful. The problem remains, however, to explain why men tend to have a greater achievement orientation than women.

The Job

A commonly held view is that jobs that involve decision making are more stressful than jobs that do not. To prove their point, people often cite the high rate of ulcers among executives. But are there any empirical data to support the view that executives have more ulcers than the rest of us? Not only are good data lacking, some data indicate that this view is probably incorrect. One study compared executives, foremen, and craftsmen in the same company. The highest rate of ulcers was among the foremen, and the lowest was among the executives (Lobb, cited in Tanner, 1976).

Researchers who studied the relation between the ambiguity of the job and various emotional reactions found that tension was highest when the situation was ambiguous (Kahn et al., 1964). Both job satisfaction and self-confidence were found to be significantly lower when the job was ambiguous. Finally, people in ambiguous situations perceived their attempts to cope with the environment as futile. These findings are summarized in Table 8-2. Since a foreman must deal with the demands of management as well as the demands of the workers, his job may well have all the qualities that produce ambiguity. As we saw in Chapter 3, ambiguous situations tend to lead to greater production of epinephrine than of norepinephrine.

There is evidence that peptic ulcers are negatively related to self-esteem. The lower the self-esteem, the more likely the person is to have ulcers (Kahn, 1969). Although a person's self-esteem tends to be relatively stable over time, there is evidence that self-esteem on the job is affected by people's perceptions of their role in the organizational structure. If they perceive themselves as occupying an

Table 8-2. Correlations between measures of experienced ambiguity and various emotional reactions in 53 subjects (Kahn et al., 1964)

	Experienced-ambiguity measures		
Emotional reaction	Ambiguity index	Role expectations	Evaluations
Tension	.51*	.44*	.40*
Job satisfaction	−.32[+]	−.33[+]	−.17
Futility	.41*	.34[+]	.20
Self-confidence	−.27[+]	−.20	−.44*

*$p < 0.01$.
[+]$p < 0.05$.

important role (more responsibilities, more subordinates, higher pay), they tend to experience good self-esteem. If they do not perceive themselves as occupying an important role, they tend to suffer from low self-esteem.

The feedback people receive on how well they are doing their job also affects self-esteem. Negative job appraisal not only lowers self-esteem but leads to a lower level of performance. Positive job appraisal leads to improved self-esteem and a corresponding output in performance (French & Meyer, cited in Tanner, 1976).

Air-traffic controllers seem to experience not only high stress but a high incidence of ulcers. The question asked in one study (Cobb & Rose, 1973) was whether they have a higher rate of ulcers (as well as high blood pressure and diabetes) than pilots. The study showed that air-traffic controllers had a significantly higher incidence of ulcers, diabetes, and high blood pressure than pilots. This result parallels the finding that foremen have a higher incidence of ulcers than executives. What mechanism is responsible for the higher ulcer rate? Epinephrine has been implicated in ulceration in rats (Phillip & Boone, 1968); however, whether epinephrine is responsible for ulceration in humans remains to be demonstrated. As I have already noted, epinephrine tends to be secreted when the organism is unable to make an adaptive response. It is interesting to note that most experiments on stress-induced ulceration have used situations that prevent active coping (Weiss, 1968).

It is likely that the reason pilots and executives experience less stress than some other people who work at related jobs has to do with the availability of coping responses. The foreman's job is particularly difficult because he is caught between an executive whom he cannot afford to offend and workers for whom he must assume responsibility. Similarly, the air-traffic controller must assume responsibility for the safe landing of an aircraft he is not flying.

Crowding

One of the by-products of modern society is crowding in large urban centers. People are faced with crowding when they travel to and from work, when they shop, when they ride elevators. Because there is much evidence that crowding, at least under certain conditions, is stressful, a great deal of research has focused on the effects of crowding. For some time biologists have been intrigued by the observation that animals tend to maintain a population level that is consistent with the carrying capacity of their territory. In their research they discovered that one of the mechanisms behind this tendency is the stress reaction. For example, in one study it was observed that a rapid expansion of a herd of deer was followed by a rapid reduction. Autopsies revealed enlarged adrenal glands and signs of chronic kidney disease—both signs of stress (Christian, Flyger, & Davis, 1960). Controlled laboratory research with mice has produced similar results (Brian & Nowell, 1971; Christian, 1955). The controlled laboratory research indicates that the amount of space available is almost irrelevant. For example, when ten rats were put into a cage 3 feet by 3 feet, their adrenal glands became larger than those of a rat that was caged by itself in a cage 1 foot by 1 foot, even though the rats in the two conditions had about the same space (1 square foot per rat). Even when the cage containing the ten animals was made 32 times as large, their adrenal glands were larger than those of the rat confined to the small cage (Rodgers & Thiessen, 1964). Evidently it is not the amount of space per animal that produces increased adrenal activity but rather having to interact with other animals. This makes a great deal of sense, because interaction with other animals would produce higher levels of stimulation than would occur when the animal was caged alone. It is clear from other work that stress is probably not the sole factor responsible for the deaths and decline in population growth associated with crowding. Laboratory work has indicated that one of the main factors responsible for the decline in population growth is the high infant mortality rates that often result from high density (Calhoun, 1962). Nevertheless, stress appears to be a reliable by-product of crowding.

Research with humans poses a number of problems. One cannot, for example, simply compare people who live in cities with people who live in the country. People who live in cities may not only be more crowded but have jobs that are more demanding or be more concerned about personal security. The fact that over the years there has been a tendency for people to move to cities, combined with the fact that many people report they enjoy living and working in the city, seems to suggest that high density itself is not necessarily stressful. In many circumstances, the heightened stimulation produced by crowding can contribute to the pleasure of an event. Spectators at a sporting event do not seem to be bothered by the density. In fact, a filled stadium often seems to provide a more intense crowd reaction, which people often find both exciting and pleasurable.

The question, therefore, is "Do humans find crowds stressful?" The data suggest a qualified yes. Jonathan Freedman (1975) argues that it is not density itself that produces stress in humans but a loss of control. He suggests that people do not even become aware of density or feel they are being crowded until the situation begins to restrict their options or interfere with their aims and objectives. A number of studies clearly demonstrate this point. In one study designed to examine the relation between heart disease and stress (cited in Tanner, 1976, p. 50), executives were fitted with pulse counters to determine when they experienced the greatest stress during a working day. One executive was surprised to discover that the greatest stress occurred as he drove to and from work in heavy traffic that required him to dodge cars, wait, and drive bumper-to-bumper. In another experiment (Lundberg, 1976; Singer, Lundberg, & Frankenhaeuser, 1978), commuter passengers were divided into two groups: those who boarded the train at the beginning of the line and those who boarded it midway. On arriving at their destination, the commuters were interviewed, and urine samples were collected to measure epinephrine levels. Unexpectedly, it was found that the commuters who had boarded the train midway had higher epinephrine levels than those who had boarded at the beginning. Intuitively, it would seem that those who had been on the train longer would have experienced more stress and therefore would have higher epinephrine levels. The interviews indicated, however, that commuters who boarded the train at the beginning of its run felt they had more control. They were able to choose which seats to take, whom to sit with, where to put their coats and parcels. Those who boarded midway, however, had little or no choice, because the train was almost full when they got on. Work has also been done to determine whether some living arrangements in prisons produce more stress than others. A positive relation was found between degree of crowding and blood pressure (D'Atri, 1976).

There is evidence that the need to interact with other people is one of the main factors that gives rise to the feeling of being crowded. In one study participants were presented with scaled-down rooms and human figures and asked to place as many people as possible in the rooms without overcrowding them. The results exactly parallel the results obtained with animals. "Being crowded" is determined by the amount of social stimulation, not the amount of space (Desor, 1972). Manipulating both density and physical interaction, Heller, Groff, and Solomon (1977) concluded that the presence of other people places additional demands on attentional (cognitive) mechanisms and often interferes with goal attainment. In an attempt to handle these and similar findings, Schmidt and Keating (1979) have offered a control/attribution model of crowding. According to their model, behavioral constraints and cognitive overload lead the person to evaluate the environment as uncontrollable. This perceived decrement in control is assumed to produce arousal, a condition that the person needs to explain (Schachter & Singer, 1962). Schmidt and Keating suggest that the person will attribute the arousal to density if there is sufficient density to make this a reasonable explanation. In other words, they argue that people are inclined to attribute arousal to density when density is a salient factor. Presumably this tendency is an acquired one and has developed because people have noted that arousal increases when density increases.

Life Stressors

Many events, of course, are stressful, particularly those that require adaptation to change in one's life. The person may perceive such events as positive (marriage, a raise, personal achievement) or negative (death in the family, divorce, separation, being fired). Studies have related such life changes to a wide variety of diseases (Wyler, Masuda, & Holmes, 1971).

To determine whether certain life changes are consistently more stressful than others, Holmes and Rahe (1967) developed the Social Readjustment Rating Scale. Using people from different cultures and different age groups, they showed that there is considerable agreement about the seriousness of certain life changes (Harmon, Masuda, & Holmes, 1970; Ruch & Holmes, 1971). The ratings from Ruch and Holmes's study are presented in Table 8-3. Each respondent was required to give each item a number to express the amount of life change involved, with "Death of spouse" arbitrarily set at 100. The item scale score is the average of the numbers respondents gave. Research based on this scale has shown that people are more likely to develop one or more of a wide variety of illnesses in the year following a life change and, further, that the greater the life change (as measured on the 100-point scale used in Table 8-3), the more serious the illness (Rahe, McKean, & Arthur, 1967; Wyler, Masuda, & Holmes, 1971).

In a recent examination of this scale, Masuda and Holmes (1978) found great variability among various groups of people in what they regard as a significant life event and the occurrence of such events. They found significant differences among age groups, between single and married people, between males and females, and among different socioeconomic groups. In short, their work indicates that different people appraise the same event differently, thus producing differences in the magnitude of subjective stress.

Theoretical models of life stressors.   One of the main theoretical explanations that have been offered of why people experience stress from serious life events is based on the idea that people need to be in control of events in their lives (Geer, Davison, & Gatchel, 1970; Krantz & Schulz, 1980). If this explanation is correct, it follows that internals and externals might differ greatly in their reactions. This idea was tested by Johnson and Sarason (1978). They found that externals experienced greater depression and anxiety than internals. It can be argued that the reason externals experience greater stress is that they depend on their environment for assurances that things are fine. When an unexpected event occurs (over which they have no control), the source of that assurance is questioned. Internals, in

Table 8-3.   Ranking and item scale scores of the total adult and adolescent sample on the social readjustment rating scale (Ruch & Holmes, 1971)

Life event	Adult group		Adolescent group	
	Rank of arithmetic mean value	*Arithmetic mean value*	*Rank of arithmetic mean value*	*Arithmetic mean value*
Death of spouse	1	100	1	69
Divorce	2	73	2	60
Marital separation	3	65	3	55
Jail term	4	63	8	50
Death of a close family member	5	63	4	50
Major personal injury or illness	6	53	6	50
Marriage	7	50	9	50
Fired from work	8	47	7	50
Marital reconciliation	9	45	10	47
Retirement	10	45	11	46
Major change in health of family member	11	44	16	44
Pregnancy	12	40	13	45
Sex difficulties	13	39	5	51
Gain of a new family member	14	39	17	43
Business readjustment	15	39	15	44
Change in financial state	16	38	14	44
Death of a close friend	17	37	12	46
Change to a different line of work	18	36	21	38
Change in number of arguments with spouse	19	35	19	41
Mortgage over $10,000	20	31	18	41
Foreclosure of mortgage or loan	21	30	23	36
Change in responsibilities at work	22	29	20	38
Son or daughter leaving home	23	29	25	34
Trouble with in-laws	24	29	22	36
Outstanding personal achievement	25	28	28	31
Wife begins or stops work	26	26	27	32
Begin or end school	27	26	26	34
Change in living conditions	28	25	24	35
Revision of personal habits	29	24	35	26
Trouble with boss	30	23	33	26
Change in work hours or conditions	31	20	29	30
Change in residence	32	20	30	28
Change in schools	33	20	34	26
Change in recreation	34	19	36	26
Change in church activities	35	19	38	21
Change in social activities	36	18	32	28
Mortgage or loan less than $10,000	37	17	31	28
Change in sleeping habits	38	16	41	18
Change in number of family get-togethers	39	15	37	22
Change in eating habits	40	15	40	18
Vacation	41	13	39	19
Christmas	42	12	42	16
Minor violations of the law	43	11	43	12

contrast, engage in coping responses. Such responses may be sufficient to ward off depression or to lessen its severity.

Horowitz (1979) has offered an explanation of the types of coping responses an internal person might use. He argues that in order to deal with life stressors, the person must avoid becoming overwhelmed. To do this, the person engages in a variety of control operations that allow him or her to keep the stress within bounds. For example, a person might use denial in order to regain composure or might break up the stressful information into a series of micro-intervals to reduce its impact or might focus on only one aspect of the event. Horowitz uses the term *micro-interval* to capture the idea that information can be broken down into a series of units. The size of the unit (or the interval containing that unit) would be determined by the person's ability to deal with that information. In this way the person would be able to master a stressful event by sequentially attacking each of its parts, or units. Failure to put the stressful information under tight control, Horowitz says, might lead to information overload, which could precipitate a total breakdown. In computer language, we might say the system would crash.

Daily hassles, uplifts, and major life events.   While life events have been linked to stress and the development of illness, the relationship is not strong. Various researchers have argued that a more important source of stress and illness is the chronic strains of everyday life (DeLongis et al., 1982; Zika & Chamberlain, 1987). In an effort to assess the effect of everyday hassles on health, the Hassles Scale, the Uplift Scale, the Life Event Questionnaire, and the Health Status Questionnaire were administered to a sample of 109 people aged 45 to 64. The Hassles Scale is a 117-item questionnaire that asks questions related to work (e.g., don't like work duties), family (e.g., don't have enough time for family), social activities (e.g., unexpected company), the environment (e.g, pollution), practical considerations (e.g., misplacing or losing things), finances (e.g., someone owes you money), and health (e.g., not getting enough rest). The Uplift Scale is a 135-item scale that measures comparable things: work (e.g., using skills well at work), family (e.g., children's accomplishments), the environment (e.g., weather), practical considerations (e.g., car running well), finances (e.g., saving money), and health (e.g., getting enough rest).

The findings indicate that while daily uplift contributed little to health, daily hassles were a major source of somatic health problems. Statistical analyses of the data indicated that daily hassles were a more important source of health problems than were major life events. These findings emphasize the importance of learning to manage our daily lives in such a way as to minimize the irritations that we tend to characterize as "minor" but that have major repercussions on our well-being.

Age-Related Stress: The Seasons of Life

The process of getting older places different demands on humans at various stages in their lives. An ambitious study by Levinson and his colleagues have given us a glimpse into the types of stress that males experience at various stages, or "seasons," of life. Levinson (1978) has suggested that males experience increased stress at four transition periods: early-childhood transition (ages 0–3), early-adult transition (ages 17–22), midlife transition (ages 40–45), and late-adult transition (ages 60–65).

Levinson's study focuses mainly on the early-adult and midlife transitions, although he has briefly discussed the other two. We will briefly look at the last three transitions.

Early-adult transition. The early-adult transition involves separating oneself from the security of the childhood world while simultaneously establishing oneself as an independent adult—separating oneself from parents and their influence and establishing oneself as an independent and responsible adult living apart from one's parents. Levinson suggests that this period is characterized by several tentative steps, all of which help the young man select a future lifestyle. One of the tentative steps is to examine various work possibilities. He might, for example, try out various jobs, engage in some further education such as university or trade school, or become an apprentice. Another of the tentative steps involves establishing new friendships with both sexes. He may join new social groups that involve activities quite different from any that he has previously encountered—a ski club, a theater group, a discussion group, even the regulars at a local bar.

The conflicts experienced during this transition typically involve the family or community from which the young man is trying to separate himself. The tendency during this period to question religious and political values often results in conflicts with parents. The tendency to question and sometimes violate the values of society may result in conflicts with authority figures and even with the law. Once the man has explored these alternatives and is ready to settle down, he typically forms a game plan, often vague in outline, which provides stability for the next several years. Levinson calls this game plan the "Dream." The man selects a job, a wife, and friends and settles into a relatively predictable pattern of behavior that for the most part is free of major conflicts.

Midlife transition. The midlife crisis, as it has come to be called, involves a second major period of questioning. During this time the man is faced with the critical question "Is my Dream coming true?" That is, did I make the right choices, and are my efforts paying off? Because for many people the Dream was an idealized goal that was virtually impossible to realize, the Dream could not realistically come true. The scientist may realize that he will never win a Nobel prize, the executive that he will never be president, the laborer that he will never own his own business. When a man has managed to attain his occupational goal, he has done so at the expense of other parts of his life. He may realize that his marriage is faltering, his health is failing, he doesn't know his children, he never took time to learn to ski or play tennis. One of the factors that make these questions critical is the perception, whether correct or incorrect, that he has very little time left to change the course of his life. In short, he realizes that youth is rapidly disappearing and that death is inevitable.

This preoccupation with the loss of youth (and opportunities) and the inevitability of death leads the man at 40 to question every aspect of his life. Does my job make me happy? Do my wife and children give me what I want from life? Would I be happier if I changed jobs or found a new lover? Have I made the best use of my talents? Is there something I should try before it is too late? How do I justify having failed some people and hurt others? Have I neglected my children? Did I hurt my parents?

The midlife crisis is characterized by a preoccupation with lost opportunities. The man makes a last desperate attempt to do all those things he has failed to do. He may change jobs, have an affair, take up a new hobby. The transition requires him to see that the future still holds a promise of pleasure and satisfaction. Life is not over, and there is time to learn new things, develop new skills, and build a happy and satisfying marriage.

Late-adult transition.   Although Levinson did not study the late-adult transition in detail, he notes that this appears to be an important stage in development. At this time a man must wrap up those activities started in middle adulthood and plan for the last years of his life. Again he is faced with the task of making life meaningful by engaging in satisfying activities. Friendships and the marital relationship often intensify as the person realizes that other people play a significant role in making life meaningful and pleasurable.

Summary

Students tend to appraise a forthcoming exam as both threatening and challenging, and they respond with both emotion-focused and problem-focused coping. Positive emotions tend to be associated with problem-focused coping. It has been argued that the reason anxiety tends to interfere with performance on exams is that anxiety produces self-preoccupying intrusive thinking. Problem-focused coping can reduce the negative effects of anxiety on test performance. It has been shown that the stress associated with taking an exam can produce a reduction in immunoglobin A. While most research to date has shown that women show a weak epinephrine response to mental stress, this finding may result from comparisons of men and women who are unequal in achievement motivation.

A job can be a significant source of stress, especially if it is characterized by ambiguity or if it fails to provide self-esteem. Perceived control also affects whether a job will produce stress.

A third major class of events that can produce stress is crowding. Research has found that in animals there is frequently a direct link between high density and a variety of disorders, including an increase in the size of the adrenal glands, but that in humans density per se is not a cause of stress. Whether one has to interact with other people is a major variable mediating stress in high-density situations. Freedman has argued that loss of control is the major cause of stress in humans. Substantial data have been collected to support this idea. Schmidt and Keating have offered a control/attribution model of crowding. They argue that crowding frequently elicits arousal and that people tend to attribute this arousal to density only if the situation does not allow them to attribute it to other factors and if density seems to be a reasonable and sufficient explanation.

One major class of events that elicit stress is events that require adaptation to changes in one's life, such as the death of a family member, divorce, being fired, and retirement. Interestingly, externals tend to experience greater stress from such events than internals. Even more important than life events, as far as health is concerned, are daily hassles. At least four age-related life stages have been identified as stressful: early-childhood transition, early-adult transition, midlife transition, and late-adult transition.

The Type A Personality, Stress, and Heart Attacks

The Type A Personality and Heart Attacks

Friedman and Rosenman (1974) have found that a certain type of personality syndrome, called Type A, is related to heart attacks. The Type A person is characterized by three qualities: a competitive striving for achievement, an exaggerated sense of time urgency, and a tendency toward aggressiveness and hostility in interpersonal behaviors. The Type B person is less competitive and more easy-going but not necessarily less effective. The Western Collaborative Group Study, a study of men in the San Francisco area, found that the Type A person was three times as likely to have a heart attack as the Type B person (Rosenman et al., 1966, 1970, 1975).

In recent years many studies have been conducted in an effort to ascertain the factors that mediate Type A behavior. Is the behavior pattern learned? Does it represent the end product of a heightened arousal level? Is it due to a particular way of viewing the world? In a series of studies of the Type A, David Glass (1976, 1977a, 1977b) tried to answer some of these questions. We will examine some of these findings and then suggest some possible links between these factors and the tendency for Type A's to have a higher incidence of coronary diseases.

Nature of the Type A

Rising to a challenge. Given that Type A's are characterized by competitive striving toward achievement, it follows that they would tend to work hard at a task that challenged them. Glass (1977a) found that Type A's indeed tend to respond to a challenge. They not only work at the upper levels of endurance longer but suppress feelings of fatigue. In one task, when there was unwanted noise, they waited longer to terminate the noise. Although Glass has not found reliable differences in arousal between Type A's and other people (Type B's) when challenged by a difficult task, other researchers have. When subjects were challenged by a difficult cognitive task, for example, Type A's showed a significantly greater increase in systolic blood pressure than Type B's (Manuck, Craft, & Gold, 1978).

Although the Type A appears motivated to achieve, it should be noted that the motive is somewhat different from that seen in a person who is achievement-oriented. Studies of the relation between Type A and achievement motivation have found that these two types are highly related. They overlap, but they also differ (Matthews & Saal, 1978).

Time urgency. Although Type A's and Type B's do not seem to differ greatly in their perception of time, they do differ greatly when they are interrupted in the middle of an ongoing activity: Type A's show greater impatience and irritation than Type B's (Burnam, Pennebaker, & Glass, 1975). When Type A's are interrupted, they show many outward signs of annoyance and impatience, such as frowns and grimaces (Glass, 1977a). Not surprising, perhaps, is the finding that Type A's are challenged by tasks that require rapid responses. Not only do they work hard on reaction-time tasks, but they show significantly higher levels of systolic blood pressure than do Type B's in such a task (Dembroski, MacDougall, & Shields, 1977).

Aggression and hostility. To study aggression and hostility, Glass and his associates (Glass, 1977a) used an experimental design in which a confederate of the experimenter makes degrading comments about the performance of the experimental subject on a skill task. In a second phase of the study, the subject is given the opportunity to shock the confederate in a so-called teacher/learner situation. The subject is told that he is the teacher and the confederate is the learner and that, as the teacher, he can select different levels of shock to provide feedback to the learner. In this setup the subject now has the opportunity to retaliate for the confederate's previous indiscretions by selecting high levels of shock. Are Type A's likely to select higher levels of shock than Type B's? That is, do they have a greater tendency to retaliate after being provoked? If Type A's are more prone to be aggressive, it follows that they would be more inclined to use higher levels of shock. This is, in fact, what was found. It is important to note that the aggression was provoked. It is not surprising that the Type A would show greater retaliation in view of the fact that Type A's tend to maximize their output when given a challenging task. To put it another way, if I were a Type B and hadn't put forth maximum effort, I wouldn't be quite so upset if someone told me what I already knew—that I wasn't putting forth maximum effort.

What Mediates Type A Behavior?

Uncontrollability.   The studies by Glass and his associates help us understand the nature of Type A's, but they do not tell us what mediates this behavior pattern. Hypothesizing, from a wide array of evidence, that A's and B's may differ in their need to control their environment, Glass and his associates conducted a series of experiments to examine this question.

One common way to study the question of whether a person has a need to control is to present the person with a controllable or an uncontrollable event and then observe his or her behavior (this issue is dealt with in more detail in Chapter 11). In a series of experiments Glass and his associates used noise as an aversive and stressful stimulus. Some subjects could control the noise by engaging in some instrumental response, such as pushing a button; other subjects were unable to control the noise. In general, the results indicate that Type A's are more motivated by the uncontrollable condition. For example, when Type A's were unable to control a loud noise, they worked harder than Type B's. This finding, suggesting that Type A's are more motivated than Type B's to master a task, is consistent with the earlier findings that Type A's tend to rise to a challenge, work hard at tasks when time is important, are upset when they are interrupted while working at such tasks, and tend to retaliate against people who degrade their efforts.

Extended uncontrollability.   If Type A's are motivated by a desire to master activities that challenge their abilities, will they continue to respond in the face of considerable feedback indicating their effort has not paid off? In view of the fact that mastery is adaptive, would it be maladaptive to continue to work at a task that gave every indication of being uncontrollable? Glass and his associates found that Type A's do not continue to work indefinitely. In fact, they come to recognize sooner than Type B's that certain tasks are uncontrollable. This was especially true when the cues indicating uncontrollability were made more salient. Making the cues more salient would, of course, facilitate processing of information. Such an effect is consistent with the view that higher motivation levels facilitate the processing of more dominant, or salient, cues. In other words, it could be argued that this effect is mediated by arousal.

Relinquishing control.   Recently it has been shown that Type A's are more reluctant than Type B's to relinquish control to another person even when it seems fairly clear that the other person is better at the task. If, for example, a Type A has a partner who is performing better and the outcome depends on their combined performance, Type A's will often fail to relinquish control to their partner (Miller, Lack, & Asroff, 1985; Strube & Werner, 1985). This finding has important implications for the work setting where it is often important to delegate jobs. One way of handling the situation is to make sure the Type A's are aware of the fact that someone else is more effective before any suggestion is made that they relinquish control (Strube, Berry, & Moergen, 1985). It appears that Type A's often are fully aware of the advantage of relinquishing control but fail to do so because they do not believe that their partner's ability is greater than their own. Once they have decided not to relinquish control, they tend to stick with that decision mindlessly. A Type A in this situation is likely to have to work longer and harder. It is interesting to note that women are quicker to relinquish control than men. This characteristic may actually help to moderate stress in women (Miller, Lack, & Asroff, 1985). That is, if they can relinquish control, they will feel less pressure of work, and so may avoid the negative health implications associated with overwork.

There is reason to argue that Type A's process task-relevant information differently than Type B's (Matthews & Brunson, 1979). It has been shown that Type A's tend to focus their attention more on high-frequency attributes (Humphries, Carver, & Neumann, 1983). When given a task that required them to recognize sequences of letters, Type A's were more certain they had seen stimuli composed of frequently occurring letters and were more certain they had not seen stimuli composed of rarely seen letters. These results provide direct support for the hypothesis that Type A's tend to focus their attention on events that are central or important and actively inhibit attention being directed to tasks or events portrayed as more peripheral. This finding could help to explain why Type A's tend not to relinquish control unless the relevant information is made explicitly clear to them.

Type A Behavior and Coronary Disease
What is the link between Type A behavior and coronary disease? At this point we can only suggest some possible links. Further research is needed before these possibilities can be either confirmed or rejected.

Catecholamines and blood platelets. The greater norepinephrine output by Type A's has been suggested as one reason the Type A pattern leads to increased coronary disease (for example, Friedman et al., 1975). The greater norepinephrine levels of Type A's are not surprising in view of the fact that attempts to control have often been linked to increased norepinephrine output (see Chapter 3). The problem, therefore, is to find some link between norepinephrine and coronary disease. Since norepinephrine enhances platelet aggregation, which has been implicated in coronary disease, there is reason to hypothesize that norepinephrine may be the culprit mediating increased coronary problems for the Type A (Carruthers, 1974; Simpson et al., 1974). There are other links, such as the fact that norepinephrine stimulates the release of fats. For example, Taggart and Carruthers (1971) found that not only do race-car drivers show large increases in norepinephrine when racing but their blood becomes saturated with fat. Doctors have been concerned for some time about high levels of fat in the blood because this condition may be linked to cholesterol buildup on artery walls.

The existing data seem to indicate that the reason Type A's are more prone to heart attacks than Type B's is that Type A's are more inclined to rise to a challenge. When people rise to a challenge, they tend to put forth maximum effort. Effort is associated with high outputs of norepinephrine and other chemicals. When the body is subject to a high level of norepinephrine over a long period, blood platelets should have a tendency to aggregate. It is interesting to note that Type A's are aroused by any task, whether difficult or easy, whereas Type B's are aroused only by difficult tasks (Gastof, 1981). This inappropriate activation of the stress response would, of course, lead Type A's to experience more stress than Type B's in the course of a day.

Coronary disease and hypertension.   As hypertension is linked to coronary disease, the question arises whether the Type A syndrome somehow produces hypertension. The evidence suggests that the Type A syndrome may indeed be a contributing factor. Anger and hostility, for example, have been found to play an important role in the development of hypertension (Diamond, 1982), and numerous studies have demonstrated that Type A's display significantly more hostile aggression than Type B's (for example, Strube et al., 1984). It has also been found that Type A's have a greater tendency to deny their irritation or anger, and such denial enhances cardiovascular responsivity (Smith, Houston, & Stucky, 1984). One important point to keep in mind is that the critical factor in coronary disease is probably not reactivity per se (becoming physiologically aroused under stress) but whether the stress response is chronic (Krantz & Manuck, 1984). There is considerable evidence that Type A's react to the environment with almost chronic stress that grows out of their high need to achieve and their almost compulsive tendency to do everything themselves.

Stress and the Immune System
In recent years a direct link has been found between stress and the immune system. It has been argued that under increased stress the immune system loses its ability to deal effectively with infectious and noninfectious diseases, from the common cold to cancer. Research has shown that the psychological factors that help an individual to maintain control also alleviate stress and so make people more healthy. This research lends increased emphasis to the importance of controlling or managing stress if we want to remain healthy. In reducing stress, we reduce disease (Maier & Laudenslager, 1985).

Heritability of Type A Personality
There is growing evidence that the Type A pattern may be inherited. A study of 93 monozygotic and 97 dizygotic middle aged male twins provided evidence for a heritability factor in Type A behavior (Rahe, Hervig, & Rosenman, 1978). Glass (1977a) has also reported some evidence for the heritability of the Type A pattern. There is, nevertheless, reason to be cautious at this time, as the relation is not strong.

Modifying the Type A Response
Given that Type A people are prone to heart attacks, can the Type A pattern be modified? Richard Suinn (1975, 1976) has outlined a program that involves two factors. The Type A person is taught first how to control the stress reaction, then how to reorganize his or her life so as to reduce the incidence of stress. In a test of his program, Suinn, Brock, and Edie (1975) were able to show that it lowered cholesterol levels. Thus, even though it may be difficult to effect a total change in a Type A person's response style, it is possible to modify the style to some degree. The fact that the pattern is hard to modify is not surprising in view of the fact that it is established early in life (Matthews, 1982). As such, it has become a pervasive feature of the person's approach to the world.

Glass and Carver (1980) have noted that some of the techniques for modifying the Type A response may lead to passivity and feelings of helplessness. Although telling someone that it is not important to finish a job appears to be a helpful way of getting the person to slow down, it could lead the person to experience even more stress because it is inconsistent with his or her response style. Obviously, one needs to consider why the Type A behaves as he or she does, not simply the fact that he or she is working too hard. Since there appears to be some overlap between the motivation for control and self-esteem enhancement (Rodin, Rennert, & Solomon, 1980), it is essential to know exactly why someone adopts the Type A pattern before deciding how to modify it. A tendency toward the Type A pattern may, as Averill (1973) has pointed out, be a deep-seated motivational variable that is based in either biology or the person's early development. Therefore, learning to relax may be more effective than attempting to modify the Type A pattern (Glass & Carver, 1980).

Summary

Friedman and Rosenman (1974) have found that a Type A personality is related to heart attacks. The Type A personality is characterized by a competitive striving for achievement, an exaggerated sense of time urgency, and a tendency toward aggressiveness and hostility. The Type A person is inclined to rise to a challenge, to experience annoyance and impatience when interrupted, and to retaliate when provoked. The Type A has a stronger need to control the environment than others (Type B's). There is evidence that differences in arousal levels elicited by differences in the need to control may mediate the behavior patterns of Type A's and B's.

There are several possible reasons that the Type A personality is linked to coronary disease. The greater norepinephrine output of Type A's has been hypothesized to be a link because norepinephrine has been shown to enhance platelet aggregation as well as to stimulate the output of fats that are carried in the blood.

The reason that Type A's tend to experience more heart attacks than Type B's is probably that they have a greater tendency to rise to a challenge. One consequence of putting forth maximum effort, even in simple tasks, is that the body is subjected to a high level of arousal and stress for long periods of time.

Links have also been found between hypertension and coronary heart disease. Anger and hostility have been implicated in hypertension. Both are characteristic of the Type A personality.

There has been some controversy over whether it is possible to modify the Type A pattern. The fact that the pattern may be inherited suggests that it may not be modifiable. Some researchers have shown, however, that it can be modified, at least in some people. Attempts to modify the pattern without understanding the motivation underlying the behavior could be highly disruptive and not in the best interest of the Type A person.

Moderators of Stress: Social and Personality Factors

Social Support

One factor that has consistently emerged as a moderator of life stress is social support—the sympathy and help provided by one's family and friends, particularly in times of trouble (Johnson & Sarason, 1979). Three dimensions of social support have been identified: emotional support (intimacy and reassurance), tangible support (the provision of aid and service), and informational support (advice and feedback) (Schaefer, Coyne, & Lazarus, 1981).

The Hardy Personality

It has been suggested that the personality profile of people who remain healthy after experiencing high degrees of life stress differs from that of people who sicken under stress. This sort of personality, which has been referred to as the hardy personality, is distinguished by three main characteristics: control, commitment, and challenge (Kobasa, 1979a, 1979b, 1982; Kobasa, Maddi, & Kahn, 1982). *Control* refers to the belief that it is possible to influence the course of life events; *commitment* refers to the belief that life is meaningful and has a purpose; and *challenge* refers to the attitude that difficult or onerous events are normal and can provide an opportunity for mastery and development. It has been suggested that the concept of hardiness may account for other moderators of stress, such as the internal/external dimension and sensation-seeking (Kobasa & Puccetti, 1983). Sazanne Kobasa has shown that people who have a hardy personality profile are less likely than others to become ill after experiencing stress. It is important to note that while the concepts of social support and hardiness sound different, they are highly correlated and may be two sides of a single coin (see Ganellen & Blaney, 1984).

Internals and Externals

Internals' belief that the environment is essentially controllable has been shown to be an important factor in the reduction of stress (Lefcourt et al., 1981). But what happens when an event is in fact not controllable? Lundberg and Frankenhaeuser (1978) have shown that internals give evidence of greater stress when in such situations than they do when a task is controllable, whereas externals show less stress when the situation is uncontrollable than when it is controllable. In other words, stress is related to the consistency of one's cognitive orientation with the outcome of one's effort to control the stressor. Inconsistency leads to greater stress.

One particularly interesting finding is that internals derive greater benefits from social support than those who have a more external orientation (Lefcourt, Martin, & Saleh, 1984). This finding may help to clarify why some studies have not been able to demonstrate that an internal orientation does not always lead to the amelioration of stress. Apparently the internal orientation interacts with such variables as social support and cognitive appraisal. One study demonstrated that internals appraise situations in a more adaptive fashion than externals (Parkes, 1984).

A Sense of Humor

It has been shown that a sense of humor helps to reduce stress (Martin & Lefcourt, 1983). Why this should be so is not altogether clear. One possible interpretation is that people with a sense of humor appraise stressful situations differently than people who do not. Another possibility is that a sense of humor leads to responses that are incompatible with the stress reaction. It has been shown, for example, that putting on a happy face is sufficient to produce the changes in heart rate and other physiological reactions that would be expected if one were actually experiencing a happy mood. Even thinking about an emotion produces the reactions that accompany the emotion when it is actually being felt (Ekman, Levenson, & Friesen, 1983). This research strongly suggests that some sort of feedback mechanism helps to reduce stress. Whatever the exact mechanism, it seems to make a lot of intuitive sense that humor should be an effective means of reducing stress.

Emotion-Focused Coping Strategies

A wide variety of strategies have been advocated to deal with stress. They include exercise, relaxation, meditation, and even biofeedback training. In recent years much research has been done on some of these techniques in an effort to assess their ability to reduce stress. We shall briefly examine a portion of that research.

Meditation. Transcendental meditation (TM) was introduced to North America by Maharishi Mahesh Yogi in the 1960s. Over half a million people have already been trained, and their numbers still grow. There has been a virtual explosion of books and articles advocating the use of meditation to overcome stress and "increase inner energy" (for example, Bloomfield et al., 1975; Schwartz, 1974).

There are several techniques for meditation. All seem to be equally effective in lowering anxiety and countering the effects of stress (Goleman, 1976). According to Daniel Goleman, who has compared several techniques, each retrains attention in some way. Goleman (1976, p. 84) has offered the following brief procedure that anyone can follow to learn to meditate:

> Find a quiet place with a straight-back chair. Sit in any comfortable position with your back straight. Close your eyes. Bring your full attention to the movement of your breath as it enters and leaves your nostrils. Don't follow the breath into your lungs or out into the air. Keep your focus at the nostrils, noting the full passage of each in- and out-breath, from its beginning to its end. Each time your mind wanders to other thoughts, or is caught by background noises, bring your attention back to the easy, natural rhythm of your breathing. Don't try to control the breath; simply be aware of it. Fast or slow, shallow or deep, the nature of the breath does not matter; your total attention to it is what counts. If you have trouble keeping your mind on your breath, count each inhalation and exhalation up to 10, then start over again. Meditate for 20 minutes; set a timer, or peek at your watch occasionally. Doing so won't break your concentration. For the best results, meditate regularly, twice a day, in the same time and place.*

The evidence showing that meditation does reduce the stress reaction is fairly impressive. It has been shown, for example, that meditation will reduce high blood pressure (Benson & Wallace, 1972) as well as the frequency of such complaints as headaches, colds, and insomnia (Wallace, Benson, & Wilson, 1971). One series of studies showed that transcendental meditation practiced by volunteer subjects produced a decrease in oxygen consumption (Wallace & Benson, 1972). These results are presented in Figure 8-6. This study is particularly impressive because oxygen consumption reflects metabolism rate—a physiological response that cannot be altered through voluntary efforts. Of particular interest is the question whether meditators can reduce the activity of the adrenal cortex. In general, there is evidence that meditation does reduce adrenocortical activity, as indicated by reduced cortisol levels (Jevning, Wilson, & Davidson, 1978).

To discover why people who meditate are better able to handle stress than people who do not, Goleman (1976) compared the reactions of experienced med-

*From "Meditation Helps Break the Stress Spiral," by D. Goleman. In *Psychology Today*, February, 1976, 9, 82–86. Copyright © 1976 American Psychological Association. Reprinted by permission.

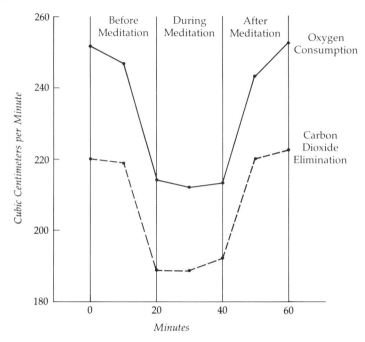

Figure 8-6.   Effect of meditation on subjects' oxygen consumption (solid line) and carbon dioxide elimination (dashed line), recorded in 20 and 15 cases, respectively. After the subjects were invited to meditate, both rates decreased markedly. Consumption and elimination returned to the premeditation level soon after the subjects stopped meditating (Wallace & Benson, 1972).

itators with those of a group of people who were interested in meditating but had not begun to do so. While recording their heart rates, Goleman showed the two groups of subjects a film that depicted a workshop accident. He observed that just as the accident was about to happen, the meditators' heart rates increased more than the nonmeditators'. After the accident, the meditators recovered faster than the nonmeditators. It is interesting to note that the meditators' response pattern is similar to that found in rats that had experienced early stimulation (Levine, 1960). It appears, on the basis of Goleman's work, that humans can acquire this adaptive pattern late in life.

Goleman has noted that rapid recovery from stress is a typical trait of meditators. He has suggested that this fact is the key to understanding why meditators are successful in resisting the effects of stress. If a person can relax after each stressful event, the aversive effects associated with stress are kept to a minimum, so that the person will have greater reserves of energy to deal with future stressful events. Rather than letting each stressful event add to the previous one, the person treats each event more or less separately. As we have noted, stress seems to have a damaging effect only if that stress is prolonged. It appears that the meditator's rapid recovery from stress serves to circumvent this possibility.

Relaxation.   Researchers have attempted to determine whether relaxation is as effective as meditation. The hypothesis guiding this research is that the beneficial effects of meditation are due to the increased relaxation produced in the course of

meditation—in other words, that there is nothing mystical or unique about meditation. Indeed, several lines of research have shown that relaxation is just as effective as meditation (Beary, Benson, & Klemchuk, 1974; Cauthen & Prymak, 1977; Fenwick et al., 1977; Holmes, 1984; Morse et al., 1977). Several studies have shown that relaxation is effective in reducing both systolic and diastolic blood pressure (for example, Fey & Lindholm, 1978; Mount et al., 1978). In his book *The Relaxation Response* Herbert Benson (1975) tells how relaxation can be readily learned and used.

Exercise.   The effects of exercise have been examined mainly in connection with anxiety. As anxiety is often associated with stress, however, the results of this research are highly relevant. A study comparing the effects of exercise and meditation found that although exercise reduced certain somatic aspects of anxiety, it did not necessarily reduce the cognitive aspects (Schwartz, Davidson, & Goleman, 1978). These researchers argue that exercise has a more specific effect. If exercise were combined with relaxation, exercise could enhance the beneficial effects of relaxation. In other words, exercise cannot be substituted for relaxation.

Biofeedback.   Ever since it was first shown that "involuntary" responses mediated by the autonomic nervous system can be altered through operant conditioning procedures, there has been a great deal of interest in using these procedures to reduce the stress reaction. After reviewing the research on this question, Tarler-Benlolo (1978) concluded that there is no evidence that biofeedback is better than relaxation for dealing with a variety of stress-induced disorders, including migraine headaches and elevated blood pressure. Each of these two techniques may be particularly suited to certain people or certain disorders, but as yet there is no clear indication which technique is preferable for particular persons or ailments. There may, in fact, be reason to use both techniques at the same time (Cuthbert et al., 1981; Fey & Lindholm, 1978).

All of us at one time or another will be troubled by stress. Practical Application 8-1 summarizes some of the things we can do to reduce it.

Summary

One of the most fundamental moderators of life stress is social support. Another moderator of life stress is the hardy personality, characterized by control, commitment, and challenge. The belief that things are controllable is also important. It has been shown that internals are more stressed by uncontrollable situations whereas externals are more stressed by situations they feel they can control. Not surprisingly, it has been demonstrated that a sense of humor can reduce stress. Even putting on a happy face can be an effective way of reducing stress.

Several approaches have been suggested to help people deal with stress. Transcendental meditation has been shown to be effective; however, researchers such as Goleman have concluded that all forms of meditation are equally effective. It appears that meditation teaches people to relax following a stressful event. Relaxation is important in reducing the adverse effects that often accompany a prolonged stress reaction. Some researchers have suggested that meditation is not a necessary condition to obtain the effects of relaxation. Relaxation can be taught directly. Exercise has also been advocated as a way of reducing stress. Although exercise reduces certain somatic components, it

(continued on page 262)

Practical Application 8-1
Some Rules for Dealing with Stress

A wide variety of organizations, agencies, and educational institutions are offering courses or seminars designed to help people deal with unwanted stress. Some of the courses and seminars teach methods for reducing the magnitude of the stress reaction. Meditation, relaxation, exercise, and biofeedback are some of the more commonly used methods. Other courses and seminars help people plan their lives so that they either encounter fewer stressors or arrange for the stressors to come at times when they are both physically and psychologically prepared to deal with them. Below are five rules that one may follow to deal with unwanted stress.

1. Plan Activities to Reduce or Eliminate Stressors

The daily routine of many people exposes them to a wide variety of events that produce stress. Traffic snarls on the way to and from work, periodic interruptions, noise, the need to make quick decisions, requests for assistance in areas that are not one's responsibility, criticisms relating to quality or quantity of work, and involvement in hostile exchanges are some of the events that can increase stress. Although some of these events are unavoidable, it is often possible to reduce the number or magnitude of such stressors. Arranging to go to work earlier and leaving earlier could, for example, allow one to avoid traffic snarls, work at least for a period of time without interruptions, experience less noise, reduce the opportunity for people to make unwarranted requests, and reduce hostile exchanges. If it is possible to do at least part of one's job before the rest of the employees arrive, there may be more time to make decisions and to respond tactfully to criticisms and requests. The resulting reduction in stress may decrease irritability and arousal and thus make one less sensitive to potential stressors. Finally, the overall reduction in stress could lead to improved performance, which not only would reduce criticism (another potential source of stress) but could lead to rewards and promotions.

2. Plan Activities So That Stressors Come at Times When They Are Psychologically Easier to Handle or Tolerate

An event can induce a more intense stress reaction if it occurs at certain times rather than others. For example, one of the most common sources of stress for many people is interruptions that occur when they are trying to complete a task—a ringing telephone, a person dropping by to ask questions or simply to chat, certain unexpected or distracting noises. It is often possible to reduce or eliminate this source of stress by some planning. Turning off the telephone bell, telling one's secretary that one will return the call, putting up a "Do not disturb" sign, and moving to a location where such interruptions are unlikely are some possible solutions. People often find that after an important task is completed, such events are less stressful or possibly not stressful at all. Alternatively, one might take care of details early in the day so that a block of time will be available later in the day to work at certain tasks.

(continued)

3. Learn to Relax between Activities

Stress-resistant people tend to experience less stress in the course of a demanding or rigorous schedule than certain other people. Although constitutional differences may account for some of this difference, there is evidence that the difference is due in part to the way people pace themselves. Shutting down the stress reaction periodically by relaxing appears to be one way to keep the stress reaction under control. Research from a variety of sources suggests that stress becomes distressful when it is allowed to become intense. When a person fails to shut down the stress reaction periodically, the stress of one activity tends to add to the stress of another. At some point stress becomes the person's enemy. It is likely to have an adverse affect not only on one's health but on one's performance. Intense stress, therefore, not only can interfere with one's ability to cope but can become an additional source of stress. If one can learn to relax between activities, there is much less chance that stress will either become distressful or adversely affect health and performance.

It has also been suggested that it may be easier to reduce a little stress than a lot. When the stress reaction becomes very intense, it frequently provokes a psychological state of helplessness. That is, one perceives that one no longer has control over the events that are capable of inducing stress. Such a feeling can, of course, act as a primary source of stress. Because stress can interfere with a person's ability to cope, which would remove this state of helplessness, the person is caught in a vicious circle in which the experience of stress becomes a stimulus for further stress.

4. Learn to Recognize the Early Signs of Stress

Because humans are dynamic, their reactions to events are always affected by previous activities and events. This means that at certain times an event may cause only mild stress but at other times it may cause intense stress. Since there is reason to believe that we need to gain control of the stress reaction before it becomes too intense, we must be able to recognize when stress is starting to exceed some "safe limit." For many people this is not an easy task. Many people can recognize stress only when it has reached a high level of intensity. Biofeedback training can help such people to understand the nature of the stress reaction and teach them how to intervene when it starts to exceed some safe limit.

5. Learn to Treat Stress as a Challenge

Stressful events often demand that we react. We can react with fear and helplessness, or we can rise to the challenge. If we treat a stressor as a challenge and attempt to control it, we will create norepinephrine. Norepinephrine not only helps supply us with energy but provides us with positive affect. In other words, it appears that norepinephrine has evolved to help us cope with stress. To tap that adaptive chemical, we must rise to the challenge. We must view stress as an opportunity to exercise our adaptive responses or to develop such responses. Failure to rise to the challenge will only undermine our self-concept and our natural tendency to control stressful events in our environment.

does not appear to be a substitute for relaxation. Biofeedback has also been used. It is effective, but it appears to be no better than relaxation. Exactly why relaxation is so effective is not altogether clear. Research is needed to determine whether relaxation affects only bodily reactions or whether it also affects cognitive reactions.

Main Points

1. Stress is frequently called the fight/flight response.
2. Stress can be elicited by a variety of physical and psychological stimuli, called "stressors."
3. Two separate systems, the sympathetic/adrenal and the pituitary/adrenal, are involved in the stress response.
4. The sympathetic system is a fast-acting system that produces, among other things, a general increase in arousal.
5. In the case of the pituitary/adrenal response, the hypothalamus initiates activity in the endocrine system by stimulating the pituitary, which secretes ACTH (adrenocorticotropic hormone).
6. Activation of the sympathetic nervous system facilitates avoidance learning while inhibiting exploratory behavior.
7. The secretion of ACTH does not facilitate avoidance learning but does prevent the extinction of a learned avoidance response.
8. Glucocorticoids facilitate the extinction of a learned response.
9. Engaging in adaptive behavior reduces the stress response.
10. Endorphins are mobilized from the pituitary and are important for their analgesic properties.
11. Stress itself does not cause diseases but rather makes the person more susceptible to diseases.
12. The "general adaptation syndrome," as Selye calls it, is characterized by three stages: alarm reaction, resistance, and exhaustion.
13. It is during the resistance stage that the adrenal glands first increase and then decrease in size. When the adrenal glands lose their capacity to resist, the individual becomes susceptible to disease.
14. Generally, unpredictable events are more likely than predictable events to elicit the stress response.
15. Constitutional differences in the stress reaction may be due in part to genetics and/or early exposure to mild or moderate levels of shock.
16. Early stimulation not only facilitates the ability to react to stress but helps shut down the stress response sooner.
17. Being able to discriminate (predict) the onset of stress can reduce the magnitude of the stress response.
18. Coping can reduce the stress response.
19. Under certain conditions the stress response can be trained to react more adaptively to meet impending threats.
20. Stress can alter certain attentional processes, thus undermining performance. However, training methods can teach the organism to resist these effects.
21. There are three types of primary appraisal: harm/loss, threat, and challenge.
22. Secondary appraisal involves the evaluation of coping resources and options and may be either problem-focused or emotion-focused.

23. The tendency to use a problem-focused or an emotion-focused approach depends on whether the situation is perceived to be controllable and whether one feels one has the ability to control the event.
24. Adjustment to severe personal tragedy involves three related processes: a search for meaning, an attempt to gain mastery, and an attempt to restore self-esteem.
25. The tendency to rise to the challenge often results in increased stress.
26. Many psychosocial events—problems in one's job, crowding, death, divorce, or any events that require us to adapt—can be sources of stress.
27. Students facing an examination typically use both problem-focused and emotion-focused strategies.
28. It has been argued that the stress and anxiety associated with taking a test produces "self-preoccupying intrusive thinking."
29. Job-related stress is greatest when the job situation is characterized by ambiguity. Job satisfaction is lowest when ambiguity is high.
30. The ability of crowding to induce stress is moderated to a large degree by the degree of one's feeling of personal control.
31. It appears that people can reduce the stress associated with a serious life change by controlling information input or by delaying their analysis of that information.
32. Four transition periods in a person's life demand changes that are frequently stressful.
33. The Type A person is prone to heart attacks.
34. Type A's are sensitive to loss of control, which may account for their increased susceptibility to coronary disease.
35. The level of catecholamine output associated with the Type A behavior pattern may mediate coronary disease. It has been argued that sustained effort may be the main factor that accounts for the tendency of Type A's to develop coronary disease.
36. Although it may be difficult to modify the Type A pattern, people can reduce stress by learning to relax and to restructure their environment.
37. The hardy personality is characterized by control, commitment, and challenge.
38. Internals show more stress than externals in uncontrollable situations.
39. A sense of humor has been shown to be an important moderator of stress.
40. Meditation, relaxation, and biofeedback have all proved effective ways to reduce the stress response.

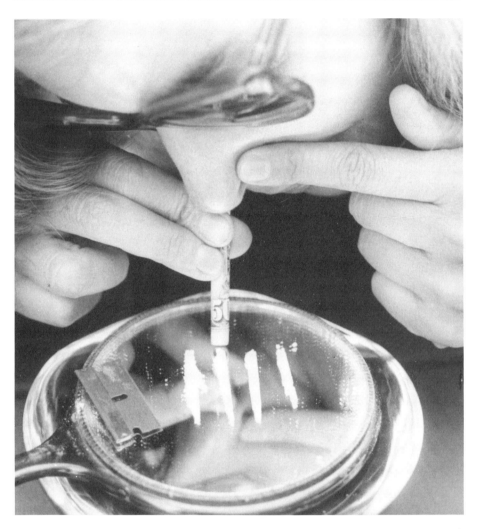

Drug Use and Drug Addiction

What is drug addiction?
What is the difference between drug abuse and drug addiction?
What are some of the biochemical explanations of the effects of nicotine,
    alcohol, cannabis, LSD, cocaine, amphetamines, heroin, and barbiturates?
What is the disease explanation of addiction?
What role does learning play in the addictive process?
What role do cognitive processes play in addiction?
Is there an addictive personality?
Does the environment play an important role in the addictive process?
Is abstinence the only cure for addiction, or can people who have become
    addicted learn to use drugs responsibly?
Does alcohol increase sexual arousal?
Is having a couple of drinks a good way to relax?

Although the term *addiction* is typically used in connection with the use and abuse of drugs—alcohol, barbiturates, stimulants, heroin, marijuana, nicotine, even caffeine—there is a growing tendency to extend the term to such activities as meditation, running, and work (Glasser, 1976). In this chapter I will focus my attention on the use and abuse of drugs. I will try to answer a number of questions, such as "Why are people more likely to become addicted to some drugs than others?" "Why is it that some people become addicted and others do not?" "Can the addiction process be reversed? If so, how?" As we shall see, the answers to these questions are complex. There is no single determinant of drug addiction, nor is there a single route to drug addiction. Nevertheless, certain principles appear to describe the process, at least in part.

Current Focus

World Health Organization Definition
The World Health Organization has defined drug addiction as "a state of periodic or chronic intoxication produced by repeated consumption of a drug" (Swinson & Eaves, 1978, p. 56). Characteristics of drug addiction described by the World Health Organization are presented in Figure 9-1.

The World Health Organization has recognized that there are many problems with this definition and as a result has suggested that the term may be counterproductive and should be dropped (Worick & Schaller, 1977). The term has gained such wide currency, however, that it is unlikely to fade from use.

The main problem with this definition is that it identifies only the final stages of addiction. Often in the final stages, such as confirmed alcoholism, serious health problems have set in, making it virtually impossible to reverse the process. Further, serious psychological dependency on the drug often exists in the final stages. Years of use can dramatically alter a person's ability to cope with the real world: years of failing to exercise normal coping responses can leave the person without any. In short, the drug may have changed the person both physically and psychologically. To understand drug addiction, we need to know the motivation for drug use, not just its effects. What we need to know is why people initially take drugs and, further, why they continue to take drugs. What roles are played by biological factors, the environment, and personality?

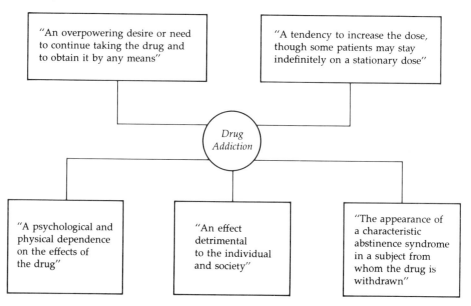

Figure 9-1. Characteristics of drug addiction as defined by the World Health Organization (Swinson & Eaves, 1978)

Drug Abuse

The one common factor in most, if not all, instances of drug addiction is drug abuse (Worick & Schaller, 1977). *Drug abuse* refers to the tendency to use a drug to excess, either more than was prescribed by a doctor or more than the person can handle without physical and psychological ill effects. It also refers to any tendency to use a drug indiscriminately without regard for one's need to function as a member of society. The question that we need to answer, therefore, is why some people are able to use a drug in moderation so that it does not markedly affect their health, their performance, or their interpersonal relationships while other people use the drug to excess so that it causes problems in these areas of their lives.

Summary

The term *addiction* is typically used in connection with the abuse of such drugs as alcohol, barbiturates, stimulants, heroin, marijuana, nicotine, and even caffeine. In recent years research has focused on attempts to determine what motivates people to use drugs rather than merely on the effects of drugs. This shift in emphasis grows out of the perception that it makes more sense to prevent addiction than to devise methods for treating it.

Drugs and Health Disorders

Many of the commonly used drugs can produce a variety of health-related disorders. Some of the disorders are mild and transient, others debilitating and chronic. Generally, the more often a drug is used, the more likely it is to cause some health problem. Similarly, the larger the dose, the more likely it is to lead to a health disorder. Although drugs can be linked to health disorders, this is by no means a one-to-one relation. Many people use drugs over long periods and show no serious health disorders. They may suffer from sleep disturbance or other transient effects, but such effects often disappear if they stop taking the drug. The potential, however, is always there for a health disorder. Alcoholism, for example, can lead to serious health problems, including heart problems, cirrhosis of the liver, and even malnutrition. Cigarette smoking has been linked to increased probability of lung cancer and related disorders. Marijuana may also increase lung disorders. And so the list grows. There are many good health reasons for not using drugs. It should be noted, however, that there are also good reasons for not eating a variety of foods that contain preservatives, have been sprayed with insecticides, or have been artificially colored. Nevertheless, given that there are serious risks, why do people use drugs?

In addition to physical health problems, there is the risk of psychological problems. Alcohol can lead to hallucinations and feelings of paranoia. Marijuana can alter perceptions of time and space. Such alterations in perception can have serious implications for a person driving a car, conducting business, or mediating a dispute. Why, then, do people use drugs under such conditions?

We will not be dealing with health problems in this chapter. Our interest is in understanding why people take drugs in full awareness of the risks involved. Further, why do people take drugs that have annoying side effects, such as the smoker's cough? Why would a person like to alter his or her perceptions of the world? What is it about the real world that the person dislikes—or, conversely, what is it about the altered state that is so rewarding? We will start our analysis by examining some commonly held views that, as we shall see, have turned out to be too simplistic to explain drug addiction. We will then turn to a more detailed analysis of some of the factors that have been found to account, at least in part, for drug addiction.

Summary

Many of the commonly used drugs have been linked to a variety of health disorders. Although people often are aware of this fact, they continue to use drugs. This fact raises the important question of what it is about their lives that motivates them to take these risks or, alternatively, what the drug does that makes it such a powerful reinforcer.

Some Traditional Views of Drug Addiction

"Addiction Is Inevitable When People Use Drugs"

Dependency. It can readily be shown that most drugs produce a variety of physiological and chemical changes in the body. It is assumed or can be shown that a drug that produces addiction has altered normal body functions to such a degree that further doses of the drug are required to maintain a state of normal well-being. This state of drug dependency is generally assumed to be physiological even though the main symptoms associated with the absence of the drug are often psychological. For example, a drug may produce a very pronounced feeling of euphoria or general well-being. Once a dose of the drug has run its course, the person may suffer intense depression or anxiety. Because more of the drug is required to return the person to a normal psychological state, let alone a state of euphoria, the person is regarded as having a physical dependency on the drug even though the main indicator is psychological.

Tolerance.   The term *tolerance* is typically used in the drug literature to refer to the fact that people often need to use increasing amounts of a particular drug in order to obtain the same psychological effects. There is evidence that tolerance to many if not all drugs is due to the physiological changes they produce. Solomon and Corbit (1974) have argued that tolerance is due to the development of an "opponent process" that tends to return the organism to its normal resting or operational level (the model is described in detail later in this chapter under "Biological Theories of Drug Addiction"). According to their model, the person needs to take increasingly larger amounts of the drug to overcome the sluggish but powerful opponent process. Whatever the exact mechanism, the fact that people tend to develop a tolerance for drugs has been taken as clear evidence that drug addiction is due to physiological changes that result from repeated use of a drug.

Failure to become addicted.   Curiously, many people who use drugs on a regular basis fail to develop the tolerance effect that characterizes the addict, especially if they use the drug intermittently. Others who develop a tolerance fail to show a dependency effect. For example, many people use cannabis (marijuana or hashish), alcohol, tranquilizers, even heroin without developing a dependency. That is, they do not feel compelled to obtain the drug at any cost, they do not tend to increase the level of intake, they do not develop a full-blown abstinence syndrome, and the detrimental effects to themselves and society are either minimal or nonexistent. In fact, some people seem to function better as a result of their habitual use of a drug—for example, a tranquilizer (Swinson & Eaves, 1978).

There are several possible explanations for this phenomenon. In this chapter we will explore several of these possibilities. It is because addiction is not inevitable that the motivation theorist has become interested in the question of addiction. What factors account for these individual differences? Are they differences in biological structures, processes of learning, ways of thinking, personality, or what?

"Addiction to Hard Drugs Is Inevitable"

It has often been assumed that it takes longer to develop an addiction to weaker drugs, such as cannabis, than to stronger drugs, such as heroin, because the body is capable of countering the action of the weaker drugs through opposing metabolic processes. Further, it is sometimes assumed that the addiction process to either a weaker or a stronger drug can be delayed or avoided altogether if the drug is used in moderation. That is, if the drug is used intermittently and in low doses, the person will be able to resist its physiological and psychological effects. It is generally assumed that stronger drugs are harder to resist, and as a result such drugs will produce addiction at a faster rate. It was predicted, therefore, that when soldiers in Vietnam began to use heroin extensively, there would be a generation of war-veteran heroin addicts. To the surprise of many people, this turned out not to be the case. Many soldiers who had used heroin regularly while in Vietnam resumed normal lives when they returned home (Davis, Goodwin, & Robins, 1975; Robins, Davis, & Goodwin, 1974). Conversely, it has been assumed that many drugs, such as tranquilizers, do not lead to addiction. As a consequence, doctors have for years freely prescribed tranquilizers. One of these, regarded as a particularly good tranquilizer, is Valium. Recent statistics indicate that about 15% of the United States population is addicted to Valium (Ledwidge, 1980).

Although animals are sometimes used to study addiction, Vincent Dole (1980) states that "it is noteworthy that most animals cannot be made into addicts" (p. 142). This fact suggests that it is not the drug itself that is the cause of an addiction.

Indeed, it is important to note that often special conditions need to be met in order to produce addiction in animals. For example, in one study it was necessary to use isolation in order to produce a preference for morphine (Hadaway et al., 1979).

"Hard Drugs Are More Likely to Produce Health Disorders"

Hard drugs have often been linked to serious physical and psychological health disorders. Many heroin users, for example, suffer from serious malnutrition (together with all the implications of malnutrition) as well as psychological disturbances. Does this mean heroin produced these disorders? A careful analysis has led a number of investigators to reject this conclusion. In many cases the psychological disorder was present before heroin was used. There is good reason to conclude that the psychological disorder was responsible for the addiction, not the reverse (Nichols, 1972). Why malnutrition? A person taking heroin might develop malnutrition for several reasons that are only indirectly related to the drug. Lack of money, for example, might be responsible for failure to eat, or the action of the drug itself might lead to poor eating habits. Malnutrition, in other words, is due to poor eating habits, not to the action of heroin itself. In fact, people who have studied heroin and marijuana users have concluded that neither heroin nor marijuana is closely linked with major health disorders (Swinson & Eaves, 1978). This is not to say that drugs do not affect the person in a variety of important ways. Rather, many of the health disorders that often afflict street addicts are not due to the drug itself but rather happen to be among a number of things that characterize street addicts. Our interest is in examining how drugs may contribute to these problems indirectly, by modifying some motivational process underlying normal adaptive mechanisms.

"The Environment Produces Addiction"

From time to time it has been suggested that the environment is the main variable responsible for drug addiction. The frustrations produced by our modern society, the stress associated with our jobs, the availability of drugs, and society's tendency to condone the use of drugs provide a constellation of factors that could account for addiction. Indeed, there is good evidence that conflicts facilitate the development of a preference for alcohol in cats (for example, Masserman & Yum, 1946) or that isolation produces a preference for morphine in rats (Hadaway et al., 1979). The problem is to explain why some people who live in our modern society come to use drugs while others do not. For that matter, why do people who live in the less technologically developed societies often use drugs if it is assumed that drug use is due to the stresses produced by modern technology?

"Only People with Psychological Problems Use Drugs— Especially Hard Drugs"

Although it is possible to determine who uses certain prescribed drugs, it is another matter to determine who uses nonprescribed drugs, such as heroin, marijuana, cocaine, and LSD. It is not likely that a door-to-door survey would produce an accurate estimate, because people know the use of such drugs is illegal and are not inclined to volunteer such information. (Pushers tend not to be good sources, either.) Where, then, does one get such information? One approach has been to check police or hospital records. Police records tell us who got caught; hospital records tell us those times a doctor has said the reason for admission was related to drug use. Not surprisingly, police and hospital records isolate a certain class of users, commonly called the "street user." Street users obviously are more likely to be identified by the police and more likely, because of their habits (and lack of a family doctor), to be admitted to hospitals as drug users (for instance, after an overdose). While such drug users may have psychological problems, do they represent the population of drug users at large? The answer is clearly no (see Kolb, 1962; Sadava, 1975). There is growing evidence that quite a few people of otherwise normal habits, both workers and professionals, use such drugs as heroin either intermittently or regularly. Psychological health among this group of users is typically indistinguishable from that of a randomly selected group of nonusers (Swinson & Eaves, 1978). Thus there is no evidence that a unique set of personality factors is associated with drug use. There may, as I will discuss later, be a set of predisposing factors that, when combined with other factors, tend to lead to addiction.

Summary

One of the traditional views of drug addiction is that it is inevitable if people use drugs, at least certain drugs. The fact that some people become dependent or show a tolerance effect has been offered as evidence. The paradox is that some people who show a tolerance effect do not become addicted. Two other traditional views are that so-called hard drugs are more likely to lead to addiction and are more likely to lead to health disorders. There is no good evidence to support either of these positions. Another traditional view is that the environment is responsible for addiction. Although it may play a contributory role, the environment, by itself, does not appear to cause addiction. Finally, it has been argued that drug use reflects the existence of a psychological disorder. Psychological disorders may be a contributory factor, but they are not the sole or possibly even the main reason that people use drugs.

Models of Drug Addiction

Most current models of drug addiction reject the idea that biochemical, environmental, or personality factors are sufficient by themselves to produce addiction. Rather, most current models suggest that addiction is the result of some complex interaction of several factors (Ausubel, 1958; Sadava, 1978). Obviously, drugs are potent reinforcers. Their reinforcing properties, however, can be shown to be mediated by both environmental and personality factors (Endler & Magnusson, 1976a, 1976b). If society tends to punish drug use, the reinforcing effects are likely to be reduced, or a person who is anxious may fail to find a particular drug reinforcing. Principles of reinforcement tell us that our behavior can come to be controlled by both internal and external cues. What happens if we take a drug repeatedly in the presence of these cues? What role does availability of the drug play in this process? Exactly how do parental attitudes affect our tendency to use drugs? What about peer pressure? How does our self-concept affect our behavior? Current models adopt the idea that all these factors may play a role. The problem is to determine which combinations are likely to lead to addiction and which are not. In other words, current models accept the possibility that there are several routes to the same addiction.

This chapter will examine the biological, learned, and cognitive factors that contribute to drug abuse. Our focus on abuse rather than addiction per se reflects an interest in the motivational antecedents of addiction. If abuse leads to addiction, then we must ask what leads to abuse. Abuse can have many antecedents. We want to find out what they are and then see whether we can determine how they interact.

Motivation theorists have become interested not just in drug abuse but in the very basic question of why people use drugs (for example, Eysenck, 1963; McClelland et al., 1972). Is the drug used to reduce boredom? To ward off fatigue? To facilitate social contacts? To gain a sense of power and well-being? To provide altered sensory input? To escape from painful experiences? As a substitute for love, sex, feelings of adequacy? There is growing evidence that the motivation to use alcohol, for example, plays a very significant role in determining whether a person will become addicted (Nathan & Lisman, 1976). Addiction is more likely when a drug is used as a crutch than when it is used merely for entertainment. This suggestion is consistent with Kolb's (1962) finding that there are two more or less distinct types of people who take drugs. On the one hand is the hedonist, who takes drugs to obtain a euphoric effect; on the other hand is the psychoneurotic, who takes drugs to obtain relief from anxiety. Clearly, a person who uses a drug to obtain relief from anxiety is using the drug as a crutch. Such a person, according to Nathan and Lisman (1976), is therefore more likely to become addicted.

Summary

The main model that has emerged to account for drug addiction is the interaction model. This position assumes that several factors play a role in the addiction process. The problem is to understand the way these factors interact to produce drug addiction.

Biological (Biochemical) Factors in Addiction

This section will describe psychological and biochemical reactions to many of the commonly used drugs, summarizing some of the facts that indicate that these drugs produce positive reinforcement in humans. Some drugs are capable of reducing or eliminating negative psychological states; others seem to produce mainly positive psychological states. Still others do both. Drugs in this last group tend, as a consequence, to be used by different people for different reasons.

Alcohol

In low doses, alcohol stimulates the central nervous system. In moderate doses, it excites the brain by direct action on the brain. The heart rate rises with moderate doses, and the mechanical efficiency of the heart as a pump is reduced. In large doses alcohol temporarily increases the level of blood glucose. Later, the blood glucose level falls, often to disastrously low levels. Alcohol tends to decrease the formation of glucose in the liver and accelerates the deposition of fat in the liver, a condition giving rise to cirrhosis of the liver. Large amounts of alcohol affect the cerebellum, producing the motor impairment typically associated with large alcohol intake (Swinson & Eaves, 1978). Because one of the main functions of the cortex is to inhibit behavior (Eysenck, 1973), the depressant action of alcohol on the cortex (and the reticular activating system) produces a state of disinhibition. That is, behaviors that are normally inhibited are freely expressed under the influence of alcohol. There have been several demonstrations of this phenomenon. It was first shown by Masserman and Yum (1946). Cats that showed no inclination to drink alcohol were trained to obtain food from a closed feeding box. Once this habit was well learned, the cats were given an air blast when they opened the box.

This noxious stimulus not only disrupted the cats' normal feeding pattern but produced a number of emotional responses that Masserman and Yum labeled "experimental neurosis." When the cats were given alcohol, they approached the food box and persisted in spite of the noxious air blast. Many of these cats came to prefer a milk/alcohol mixture over plain milk. Other work has confirmed that alcohol tends to reduce anxiety in the type of situation that Masserman and Yum created (Smart, 1965).

Since Masserman and Yum's situation is a classic approach/avoidance conflict, Conger (1956) decided to determine whether alcohol was increasing the tendency to approach or decreasing the tendency to avoid. Conger first taught rats to eat at a particular location and then introduced shock at the feeding site. After measuring the rats' tendency to approach the food site under normal and alcoholic states, Conger concluded that alcohol reduced the avoidance gradient. His findings can be summarized in the form of a general model that includes approach and avoidance gradients (Figure 9-2). It has not always been possible to confirm these findings (for example, M. Weiss, 1958). There is considerable evidence, nevertheless, that alcohol does reduce emotional reactivity in frustrating situations and does lead to a greater persistence of goal-directed behavior in such situations (Barry, Wagner, & Miller, 1962).

In addition to the direct action of alcohol on the central nervous system, including the brain, alcohol stimulates the adrenal cortex (Goldfarb & Berman, 1949). This fact probably helps to account for the rise in blood sugar levels and for the arousal response, such as increased heart rate and skin conductance (Carpenter, 1957; Lienert & Traxel, 1959). As we have noted, increased arousal is often associated with strong emotions but does not in itself seem to produce a particular emotion. It is not surprising, therefore, that people report rather diverse feelings when they are intoxicated. Evidence from a variety of sources indicates that the mood change associated with alcohol may be due largely to social expectations

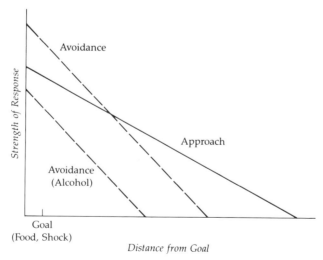

Figure 9-2.   Approach and avoidance gradients for appetitive and aversive goal stimuli. Alcohol produces a general reduction in the tendency to avoid while leaving the tendency to approach unaffected.

rather than to specific actions of the drug (MacAndrew & Edgerton, 1970). Thus, if people expect to have a good time, they probably will.

Alcohol is frequently used in connection with sex. In small amounts, alcohol seems to facilitate sexual interest and performance. This effect presumably is due to the fact that many people experience inhibitions in connection with sex, which are reduced when alcohol is consumed. In large amounts, alcohol lowers testosterone output in males, thus often reducing sexual interest or performance or both (Farkas & Rosen, 1976).

Endorphin hypothesis of alcohol addiction.   There is a considerable evidence that alcohol increases endorphin activity (Blum, Hamilton, & Wallace, 1977; Davis & Walsh, 1970; Vereby & Blum, 1979), the body's own way of producing morphine. The body also has receptors that are sensitive to the presence of morphine. When these receptors are stimulated, humans not only experience analgesia (a lowered pain threshold), but also a sense of euphoria. Since alcohol stimulates endorphin activity, this can provide a ready explanation for the sense of euphoria that drinkers often experience. This finding also offers an explanation as to why people become addicted to alcohol. If alcohol can stimulate endorphin output, it could eventually produce a marked reduction in the concentration of endorphins circulating in the body. When this happens a person experiences a negative mood state together with other symptoms of withdrawal. Through the learning process, a person would learn to drink alcohol in order to further stimulate endorphin activity. In other words, the person would become addicted to alcohol.

What is not clear from this explanation is how alcohol can stimulate endorphin activity if the stores of endorphin are depleted or markedly reduced. It may be that alcohol produces metabolites that can stimulate the receptors directly, thereby acting as a substitute for endorphin, that alcohol somehow increases the opiate receptors' sensitivity to endorphins, or that when the stores are reduced alcohol is still capable of triggering the output of still more endorphins. For a discussion of the evidence related to these hypotheses see a review by Joseph Volpicelli (1987).

Nicotine

It appears that heavy smokers smoke in order to obtain the effects of nicotine. In a carefully controlled study, Stanley Schachter (1977) showed that when nicotine levels are varied, smokers tend to adjust the number of cigarettes they smoke in order to maintain a constant (preferred) nicotine level. It is not clear at this time whether people smoke cigars and pipes for the same reason. Probably many do.

Nicotine produces a number of physiological changes. One of the primary effects is arousal (Eysenck, 1973). In small doses, nicotine increases arousal, but in larger doses it paradoxically decreases arousal (Armitage, Hall, & Sellers, 1969; Gilbert, 1979). The arousal elicited by nicotine appears to be very similar to the arousal elicited by a variety of agents, such as amphetamines, caffeine, and LSD (Eysenck, 1973). Unlike other stimulants, however, nicotine produces arousal that is of short duration and is followed by three distinct phases: "a period of EEG alternations between sedation and excitation, a period of behavioral and EEG sedation and sleep, and, finally, a frequent occurrence of paradoxical or activated sleep" (Eysenck, 1973, p. 123). In other words, the effect of cigarettes varies with time after intake.

There is good evidence that urinary acidity mediates the tendency to smoke. As urinary acidity increases, so does the tendency to smoke (Schachter, Kozlowski, & Silverstein, 1977; Schachter et al., 1977). Since people often smoke more in a variety of situations, including stress, the question is whether these situations produce greater urinary acidity. The answer is yes. In one study, urinary pH was found to be significantly lower (more acid) for college students assigned to give reports that day than for students not assigned to give reports (listeners). When these same students were tested on a day when there were no class reports, they had almost identical, but relatively low, urinary pH levels (Schachter et al., 1977). These results are shown in Figure 9-3. The relatively low urinary pH levels on the no-report day are reasonable because class participation would normally be expected on such a day, an event that normally elicits a stress response. In the same study, but using a slightly different stressor, Schachter and his colleagues found that as stress increased, so did smoking. Thus they were able to show not only that urinary acidity and smoking are related but that both are increased when people are subjected to a stressful event. To demonstrate that urinary acidity mediates smoking, Schachter, Silverstein, and Perlick (1977) independently manipulated stress and urinary acidity. Their results showed that smoking behavior tracks urinary acidity, not stress.

Smoking increases in a variety of other situations. For example, people often smoke more in social situations. As we noted in Chapter 8, social situations often increase levels of stress. To determine whether the increase in smoking is due to changes in urinary acidity, Silverstein, Kozlowski, and Schachter (1977) measured smoking behavior and urinary acidity at a party. Not only did urinary acidity increase at the party, but smoking increased in a corresponding fashion.

Cannabis (Marijuana, Hashish)
Cannabis produces a number of rather mild physical symptoms, including increased pulse rate, rise in blood pressure, dilation of the pupils, redness of the eyes (due to dilation of the conjunctival blood vessels), and occasionally breathlessness, choking, and some neurological changes reflected in unsteadiness, mus-

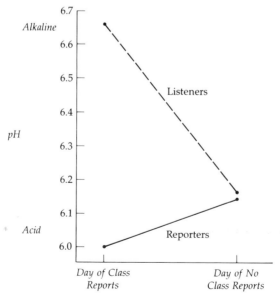

Figure 9-3.   Urinary pH among students assigned to give class reports ("reporters") and among their classmates ("listeners") (Schachter et al., 1977)

cular twitches, tremors of the tongue, and changes in the deep reflexes (Swinson & Eaves, 1978).

Psychologically, cannabis produces a wide variety of reactions. Naive subjects often experience anxiety and apprehension. These reactions, however, may not reflect the action of the drug so much as fear of the unknown. Generally, the effects of the drug are agreeable. Besides a general feeling of euphoria, there are distortions of time and space, together with illusions and even hallucinations. Often there are changes in the body image, together with a feeling of deperson-alization (Joyce, 1970; Paton & Crown, 1972; Swinson & Eaves, 1978).

LSD (Lysergic Acid Diethylamide)

LSD produces a number of changes, including a rise in blood pressure, sweating, dilation of the pupils, increase in muscle tension (sometimes accompanied by nausea), headaches, and lightheadedness (Swinson & Eaves, 1978). These changes are due to the stimulant action of the drug on the reticular activating system. In addition, LSD often produces changes in perceptual processes associated with all sense modalities. The most dramatic changes typically occur in connection with visual perception. Objects appear to change in color, shape, and size. Two-dimensional objects may suddenly appear to be three-dimensional. Under certain conditions, people will experience fully formed hallucinations of objects, events, or even people. There are typically alterations in perception of time or the ability to gauge time. The ability to reason is often disturbed, as is the ability to plan ahead.

LSD produces a number of other effects. However, the direction or nature of these effects is so variable that it is impossible to say they reflect a characteristic action of the drug. For example, whereas some people experience feelings of euphoria, others experience intense anxiety. Thought processes are frequently affected; again, however, there is no unitary pattern. Some people report that they experience a sense of unity and order in themselves and the universe and that the drug improves their ability to concentrate. Others report that the drug disrupts their ability to concentrate and, further, that their thought processes become fragmented. For example, they say that their thought processes are often disrupted by the intrusion of extraneous and irrelevant ideas (a pattern similar to that experienced by schizophrenics). Paranoid or grandiose ideas or delusions and hallucinations are not uncommon. Obviously, people who experience positive feelings and/or enjoy the alterations of their thought processes (whatever the direction) are more likely to use the drug repeatedly. As we shall see shortly, there is evidence that certain types of people tend more than others to use LSD.

There is evidence that LSD acts to depress the activity of the serotonin-containing neurons in the raphe nuclei. According to this explanation, serotonin normally inhibits certain kinds of visual and other activities of the brain. The net effect is that LSD disinhibits activity of the neurons in the visual system, the limbic system (the area of the brain linked to emotions), and other brain areas (Jacobs & Trulson, 1979; Jacobs, 1987). It has been shown that drugs that increase the level of serotonin in the human brain reduce the effects of LSD, while drugs that block serotonin magnify the effect of LSD. It should be noted that psilocybin (the active component of "magic mushrooms") seems to work by the same mechanism.

Amphetamines

Amphetamines are classified as stimulants. They act on the sympathetic part of the autonomic nervous system. Specifically, they appear to stimulate the upper part of the reticular activating system, causing alertness and wakefulness as well as subjective feelings of confidence, security, and control. Amphetamines generally reduce feelings of fatigue while increasing feelings of efficiency, endurance, and perseverance. It is important to note that although people under the influence of amphetamines may experience feelings of reduced fatigue or of greater efficiency, their behavior may not be consistent with those feelings. They may, in fact, behave in a very inefficient manner, and their movements may suggest fatigue rather than energy. Under certain conditions, amphetamines can nevertheless lead to more energetic and efficient behavior. For example, amphetamines have been shown to facilitate such physical and intellectual activities as swimming, running, and cognitive problem-solving tasks. Faster conditioning and decreases in reaction time have also been reported (Barr, 1969; Grinspoon & Hedblom, 1975; Kalant, 1973; Swinson & Eaves, 1978).

Evidence from a variety of sources suggests that whereas small to moderate doses facilitate performance as well as producing pleasant subjective feelings, higher doses often impair performance and produce feelings of restlessness, anxiety, inability to concentrate, and a general deterioration in the ability to think (Swinson & Eaves, 1978). It appears that up to a point, amphetamines facilitate performance; after that point, performance deteriorates. In fact, it appears that the relation between dose and performance follows almost exactly the inverted-U-shaped function proposed by Hebb (1955) to describe the relation between performance and arousal.

Although heroin and cannabis have been reported to induce feelings of euphoria, controlled studies comparing heroin and cannabis with amphetamines have shown that not only do amphetamines more reliably produce euphoria, but the euphoria is far more dramatic (intense) than the euphoria associated with heroin or cannabis (see Grinspoon & Hedblom, 1975).

It has been suggested that the pleasurable effects of amphetamines may be due to the changes in alpha waves that these drugs produce. It has been shown, for example, that amphetamines increase the percentage of alpha waves (Gibbs & Maltby, 1943; Rubin, Malamud, & Hope, 1942) as well as the frequency of the "normal" alpha wave (Gibbs & Maltby, 1943; Lindsley & Henry, 1942). Because alpha waves tend to be correlated with the "highly pleasurable state of relaxed enhanced awareness" (Grinspoon & Hedblom, 1975, p. 71), there is reason to believe that the pleasurable effects of amphetamines are due in part to this state. In addition, amphetamine often enhances ability to control events in one's environment, and this condition may produce pleasurable side effects. Norepinephrine is often elevated by injections of amphetamine, and as we have noted, norepinephrine has been implicated in euphoric or manic states. It has also been shown that amphetamines stimulate the output of dopamine. As Chapter 3 noted, dopamine activates the self-reward systems of the brian. Thus the elation and euphoria produced by amphetamines may be due to the fact that amphetamines indirectly excite the self-reward centers.

Cocaine

Cocaine is a naturally occurring chemical that can be found in significant quantities in the leaves of two species of coca shrub. Cocaine reliably produces positive feelings in many people. Researchers have found that people have difficulty discriminating small doses (less than 10 milligrams) of cocaine from a placebo. At moderate to high levels (25 to 100 milligrams), people who take cocaine intranasally reliably report euphoria within 15 to 30 minutes. Some people may experience anxiety, depression, fatigue, and a desire for more cocaine 45 to 60 minutes after

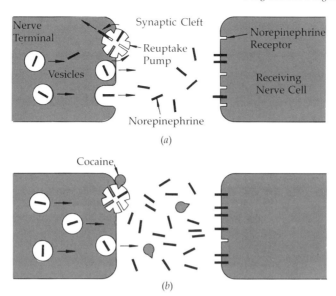

Figure 9-4. Sympathomimetic action of cocaine results when the reuptake of such neurotransmitters as norepinephrine is blocked at synapses of the sympathetic nervous system. (The sympathetic nervous system controls such functions as heart rate and blood pressure.) When the molecules of the neurotransmitter are released from vesicles in the nerve terminal (*a*), the molecules cross the synaptic cleft and stimulate the succeeding nerve cell. Ordinarily some of the neurotransmitter molecules in the cleft are pumped back into the nerve that released them. In the presence of cocaine the action of the reuptake pump is blocked (*b*) and the stimulation by the neurotransmitter molecules increases as their concentration in the synaptic cleft builds up (Van Dyke & Byck, 1982).

taking a 100-milligram dose. There is often a crash period of extreme discomfort after a large amount of cocaine is smoked or injected. This effect is less common when cocaine is taken intranasally. As in the case of many other drugs, it appears that the adverse effects (discomfort or disturbing thoughts) are associated with higher doses (Van Dyke & Byck, 1982).

There is a great deal of evidence that the effects of cocaine are due to its action on the brain. It has been suggested that cocaine produces at least some of its effect by blocking the reuptake of norepinephrine at the synapses (Van Dyke & Byck, 1982). Figure 9-4 shows what happens when cocaine is present in the blood. When cocaine blocks the reuptake pump, concentrations of norepinephrine increase at the synapses. Because we have evidence that an increase in norepinephrine at the synapses is associated with feelings of euphoria and a decrease with feelings of depression, it follows that the feelings of euphoria are probably linked directly to these concentration levels. It should be noted that tricyclic antidepressants also block the reuptake of norepinephrine. In other words, it is believed that tricyclics work because they alter the norepinephrine level in the brain.

It has further been suggested that cocaine blocks the reuptake of dopamine (Bozarth & Wise, 1985). Dopamine, as we shall see shortly, plays an important role in activating the reward centers of the brain. Chronic use of cocaine may also disrupt the balance of the neurotransmitter serotonin. Serotonin normally balances and inhibits norepinephrine. People who use cocaine often become agitated, restless, aggressive, and anxious. These states are thought to result from high levels of norepinephrine that are not properly modulated by the presence of serotonin.

Chronic use of cocaine can cause sleeplessness and loss of appetite—not surprisingly, in view of the fact that cocaine leads to an increase in arousal. As we saw in Chapter 4, a high level of arousal is incompatible with sleep. And as serotonin plays an important role in sleep onset, a disruption of the serotonin level would also account, at least in part, for sleeplessness. As Chapter 5 noted, an increase in the level of norepinephrine in the brain has been shown to reduce feelings of hunger. (Amphetamines, which raise the level of norepinephrine in the brain, were once routinely prescribed by doctors to help people lose weight.) There is some evidence that chronic use may also lead not only to anxiety but to paranoia.

Is cocaine addictive? While it does not produce a tolerance effect or withdrawal symptoms (two of the criteria of a physically addictive drug), there is clear evidence that people can become so psychologically dependent on cocaine that they will go to great lengths to ensure a regular supply. In that sense we say that cocaine is habit-forming, just as we say that nicotine and alcohol are habit-forming.

Death from recreational use of cocaine is rare but not unknown (see Maranto, 1985). In view of the fact that cocaine has been used for over 5,000 years, it is not clear why it has suddenly become so popular. It is difficult to say simply that cocaine is more addictive than other drugs. Any illegal drug that suddenly becomes popular tends to attract a criminal element. That, of course, makes it a political problem. It remains to be seen whether the dangers of cocaine are so much greater than those of alcohol and nicotine as to warrant the attention the media have focused on them.

Heroin and Morphine

Heroin rapidly breaks down to morphine in the body. The most common mood change associated with heroin is euphoria, although panic and anxiety are not uncommon. The maximum effect is reached in about two hours, and the effect begins to wear off in five hours. One of the main medical reasons for administering morphine is to reduce pain. Secondary uses of heroin are for the treatment of diarrhea and the relief of cough. It appears that morphine does not reduce pain (the sensation) so much as it reduces the aversive qualities that people normally report when presented with a painful stimulus (Julien, 1975). Although the exact action of morphine on the brain is still uncertain, it has been established that the brain contains opiate receptors (for example, Fincher, 1979; Snyder, 1977a, 1977b). When these receptors are stimulated by heroin, morphine, or naturally occurring opiates (endorphins), they reduce the aversive quality associated with certain sensations. That is, they reduce pain.

Morphine exerts both excitatory and inhibitory effects on the central nervous system. The main inhibitory, or depressant, effect is observed on respiration. Large doses of morphine frequently lead to respiratory failure. Morphine also suppresses the cough center, which is located in the brainstem. One of the most frequently observed excitatory effects is vomiting. Manic and euphoric effects may be due in part to the excitatory effect of morphine on the central nervous system (Julien, 1975).

At the cortical level, morphine produces EEG patterns similar to those produced by barbiturates. The EEG shifts from one of alertness to one more characteristic of sleep or drowsiness. After repeated use of morphine the EEG returns to a more alert pattern. Thus it appears that the body sets up a resistance to the effects of morphine.

The fact that humans and animals show a marked tolerance to morphine suggests that an opposing metabolic process is at work to counteract the effects of morphine. This opposing process appears to be responsible in some way for the withdrawal symptoms that occur when the effects of an opiate, such as heroin or morphine, have worn off: yawning, secretion of excessive tear fluid, perspiration, runny nose, loss of appetite, gooseflesh, dilated pupils, restlessness, orgasm, increased blood pressure, vomiting, diarrhea, rising body temperature, and insomnia (Stimson, 1973). One theory is that the excitatory effects of the drug outlast the depressant effects and that it is this process that is directly responsible for the withdrawal symptoms. (A more detailed discussion of the theories of withdrawal can be found in Steinberg, 1969 and Wikler, 1961, 1968.)

Exactly what produces the euphoria is not clear. It could be due to the direct action of the drug on the brain, to the increase in norepinephrine that typically follows intake of morphine, to the excitatory action of the drug on the central nervous system, or to the opposing metabolic process. Probably it is some combination of these processes. "Mainliners" (people who inject opiates intravenously) report a "rush" (intense pleasure) shortly after an injection. Either the drug reaches the brain faster than scientists now estimate or the effect is due to the action of the drug on the peripheral nervous system. Until we have more evidence, we must assume that the rush is probably due to the peripheral action of the drug whereas the sustained effects are due to a combination of the factors listed above.

Because heroin will effectively reduce a variety of discomforts, including hunger, fatigue, anxiety, and pain (*Martindale, 1977*), the possibility exists that the heroin addict may have fortuitously learned to use heroin to reduce such discomforts. For example, a person who used heroin at one point to eliminate withdrawal symptoms might learn, through continued use, that heroin is an effective way of coping with anxiety. Nichols (1965) originally suggested this possibility when he pointed out that morphine can short-circuit many biological drives (such as hunger, thirst, and sex). He noted that morphine can reduce the negative state associated with many biological drives. Instead of engaging in appropriate goal-directed behavior, a person might use morphine to reduce the aversive drive stimuli. Reduction of these stimuli would be a sufficient condition for learning, and the person would therefore tend to repeat this behavior whenever the aversive drive stimuli reappeared. It is worth noting that the relapse rate for heroin addicts is 90% (Dole, 1980). This finding is consistent with Nichols' suggestion that heroin use becomes a habit that is probably triggered by a wide variety of stimuli in the environment.

Barbiturates

Barbiturates have generally been used by medical doctors to treat physical and psychosomatic disorders, including anxiety, depressive states, insomnia, and epilepsy (Swinson & Eaves, 1978). The effects of barbiturates are similar to those of alcohol. At low doses they act as cerebral stimulants. At higher doses they produce cerebral depression. Doctors typically prescribe the drug at higher doses to produce the depressant reaction. Barbiturates act mainly on the central nervous system, depressing activity of the reticular activating system. As a consequence, barbiturates generally impair performance on a number of physical and mental tasks.

The psychological effects of barbiturates are very diverse and unpredictable. Single doses can produce excitation, disinhibition, euphoria, and sedation; continued use often produces adverse psychological reactions, including a feeling of loss of control, confusion, unpredictable mood changes, apathy, narrowing of interests, increased suspicion, irritability, and a general deterioration in personal standards of dress, cleanliness, and conduct (Barr, 1969; Claridge, 1970; Swinson & Eaves, 1978).

Humans typically develop a tolerance to barbiturates, requiring that the dose be increased in order to obtain the same effect. Barbiturates affect the enzyme action of the liver, and this process may be responsible for the development of tolerance and the subsequent physical dependence that often occurs. Barbiturates have some toxic side effects, and the increased doses that development of a tolerance requires can result in marked toxic reactions. Such reactions are probably responsible for some of the undesirable psychological and physical reactions to these drugs (Barr, 1969; Claridge, 1970; Swinson & Eaves, 1978).

Until antidepressants were developed, barbiturates were often used in combination with amphetamines to treat depression. Although the mixture of barbiturates and amphetamines is fairly predictable, barbiturates mixed with other drugs often have rather unpredictable and dangerous effects (Swinson & Eaves, 1978).

Summary

Most of the commonly used drugs have one or more reward properties that can explain, at least in part, why a person may tend to use these drugs repeatedly. Alcohol, though a stimulant in small to moderate amounts, is probably best known for its disinhibiting properties. The euphoric effect often associated with alcohol may be due to its ability to stimulate endorphin output. Aversive situations frequently become less aversive after intake of alcohol. Nicotine in small to moderate doses typically acts as a stimulant. In larger doses it can have a calming effect. The fact that smoking often increases in stressful situations suggests that some people smoke to reduce stress. There is very good evidence that urinary acidity mediates the tendency to smoke. Cannabis has stimulant or euphoric properties but is best known for its ability to distort perceptions of time and space. LSD also has stimulant or euphoric properties and, like cannabis, is known for its ability to alter perceptions. Not only are time and space typically altered, but the sense modalities are usually affected—especially vision. Cocaine appears to work by increasing the concentration of norepinephrine (and possibly dopamine) at the synapses. Amphetamines are best known for their ability to produce feelings of euphoria; they can reduce feelings of fatigue and increase feelings of efficiency. They are sometimes used to enhance both physical and mental performance. Heroin and morphine typically produce feelings of euphoria. In addition, heroin and morphine have strong analgesic properties. Barbiturates are frequently prescribed by doctors to treat anxiety, depressive states, insomnia, and epilepsy. Barbiturates typically impair both physical and mental performance. When used with other drugs, barbiturates often have unpredictable and/or dangerous effects. Clearly, drugs are powerful sources of reinforcement. It is not surprising, therefore, that people who find daily life aversive or boring might turn to drugs in order to obtain pleasure.

Biological Theories of Drug Addiction

A number of biological theories have been advanced over the years to account for drug addiction. Some are general theories; others are specific. Specific theories are advanced to account for the effects of one or a few drugs, whereas general theories are assumed to account for the effects of a larger number. Three important theories have been advanced in recent years. One has to do with the effects of drugs on the catecholamines, which in turn affect the operation of self-reward systems. At present, this can be regarded as a more or less general theory. Another has to do with the discovery of opiate receptors and endorphins (natural opiates) in the brains of vertebrates. This is a specific theory to account for opiates' effects. The third theory is Solomon and Corbit's opponent process theory. This is a general theory not only of drug action and drug addiction but of affect in general.

Self-Reward Systems, Catecholamines, and Drugs

More than 30 years ago James Olds discovered that when an electrode was implanted in certain areas of the brain, a rat would bar-press in order to stimulate itself (Olds, 1955, 1956). Certain areas of the brain (such as the medial forebrain bundle) motivated self-stimulation so powerfully that animals would often self-stimulate to the exclusion of eating and mating. Although the existence of these centers has been known for some time, it has not been understood until recently just how they might be involved in the mood changes that often accompany the use of drugs.

Quite independent of the research on self-reward systems, work was being done on the relation of catecholamines to mood (Chapter 7). Norepinephrine and dopamine are two major catecholamines that have been implicated in such moods as elation and euphoria. Many of the commonly used drugs that dramatically affect mood appear to do so by altering catecholamine levels. For example, amphetamine elevates catecholamine levels and produces feelings of euphoria; chlorpromazine blocks the actions of catecholamines and often produces feelings of depression (Akiskal & McKinney, 1973; Routtenberg, 1978).

Recent work has shown that drugs that elevate catecholamines facilitate self-stimulation and drugs that block catecholamines block self-stimulation (Routtenberg, 1978; Wise & Stein, 1969). The direct link between the presence of certain catecholamines and the operation of the self-reward systems suggests that the experience of certain pleasurable moods, such as euphoria, may be due to the activation of one or more of these systems by the catecholamines. Routtenberg has found that dopamine rather than norepinephrine is responsible for increased self-stimulation. Since amphetamine enhances dopamine transmission, the euphoric effect of amphetamine is probably due to the interaction of dopamine and the self-reward systems of the brain.

Catecholamines can be activated in a variety of ways other than by means of drugs. Many natural activities affect catecholamine level. For example, the work of Davis (1973) and Howley (1976) clearly shows that running increases the level of norepinephrine. Zuckerman's work indicates that all forms of sensation-seeking behavior may increase norepinephrine level (Zuckerman, 1978a; Zuckerman, Buchsbaum, & Murphy, 1980).

Although Routtenberg (1978) found that dopamine rather than norepinephrine is responsible for the activation of the reward centers, other researchers have not ruled out the possibility that norepinephrine plays a fundamental role in the phenomenon of self-stimulation (for example, Franklin & Robertson, 1980; Herberg, Stephens, & Franklin, 1976). It may well be, as Herberg and his colleagues have suggested, that dopamine and norepinephrine act jointly to activate these reward centers.

Endorphins: Natural Opiates of the Brain

In 1973 scientists in the United States and Sweden announced almost simultaneously that they had discovered specific receptors for opiates in the brain (Fincher, 1979). Solomon Snyder of Johns Hopkins University located such receptors in the thalamus, the amygdala, and the spinal cord (Snyder, 1977a, 1977b). Assuming that the existence of such sites means that the body produces its own opiate, several scientists began to look for and finally discovered a powerful painkilling molecule, which they called "endorphin" (from *endogenous morphine*). Not only do endorphins kill pain, but they alter mood and remove symptoms of stress. Their more subtle effects are to slow respiration, induce constipation, constrict the pupils, lower body temperature, and alter the functioning of the pituitary (Fincher, 1979).

The discoveries of opiate receptor sites and of endorphins have provided us with a much clearer idea of why people become addicted to opiates, such as morphine, heroin, and methadone. The fact that there are natural opiates (endorphins) suggests that somehow it was necessary for vertebrates to evolve these chemicals—that they were important for survival. (Endorphins are found only in vertebrates and the ancient hagfish.) The strong analgesic qualities of endorphins suggest that they evolved basically as painkillers. It seems reasonable to assume that they evolved to kill the pain that resulted from physical encounters. There are numerous examples of soldiers in battle who fail to experience pain when wounded or athletes who fail to experience pain when injured. The general elevation of mood produced by opiates may also have evolved as an adaptive mechanism. Lionel Tiger (1979), for example, has argued that it is biologically adaptive for an organism to be optimistic. It is important that an individual not give up after being hurt as the result of a physical or psychological encounter. Pain would normally reduce the tendency to engage in future battles, according to the principles of reinforcement; however, if pain is quickly alleviated, this tendency to avoid future encounters will be markedly reduced. Further, if endorphins produce positive affect, the principles of reinforcement suggest that it is likely that the individual will come to seek out situations that stimulate their output. Thus together the analgesic and mood-elevating properties of endorphins ensure that the individual will continue to do battle when the occasion demands. Consequently, when people use opiates, they are short-circuiting a basic survival mechanism. Because the opiate receptor system, like most survival mechanisms, exerts a powerful reinforcing effect, the person is rewarded for using opiates. It is not surprising, therefore, that he or she will tend to continue using opiates even though they might later result in further pain and negative affect. The solution is simple: take more opiates to kill the pain as well as wash away the negative feelings.

The fact that not all people who take opiates become addicts has led Avrom Goldstein (1976) and others to suggest that certain people may be deficient in endorphins. These people, it has been suggested, may take such drugs as heroin to overcome an inborn deficiency, just as a diabetic takes insulin to make up for the inability of the pancreas to secrete adequate amounts of the hormone. Because such people have a biological deficiency, it is suggested, they experience a general malaise. Since use of a drug reduces that aversive condition, the person is predisposed to become addicted to that drug.

Solomon's Opponent Process Theory of Affective Responses

Solomon (Solomon & Corbit, 1974; Solomon, 1980) has noted that whenever a person experiences an increase in positive affect, he or she is likely to experience a sharp increase in negative affect a short time afterward. Similarly, an increase in negative affect is likely to be followed shortly by a sharp increase in positive affect. He argues that the human is designed so that whenever affect departs from a baseline, an opponent process is triggered that returns the person to baseline. He suggests that the opponent process is rather sluggish and requires time to exert its full effect. When it does exert its effect, it produces for a time the affective state opposite to the one that initially triggered it. This sequence is illustrated in Figure 9-5.

Solomon holds that the opponent process is strengthened by use and weakened by disuse. This effect can be viewed as analogous to an immunity reaction in which the presence of a bacterium triggers antibodies to counteract its effects. The increase in antibodies leads to immunity. This means that if the same type of bacterium is introduced into the system a short time later, the antibodies are present in large numbers and therefore can quickly attack the bacterium. If no bacteria are introduced for a period of time, the antibodies tend to diminish in number, and the system is no longer able to counteract the effects of the bacteria as quickly or as strongly as it originally could. Solomon suggests that because the opponent process tends to increase in strength each time it is triggered, the initial affective reaction will be shortened and the opponent affective reaction will get stronger. This change with repeated use is shown in Figures 9-6 and 9-7. Figure 9-6 shows a typical affective reaction to a drug when a person initially uses it. Figure 9-7 shows the reaction after repeated uses. Note that state *A* diminishes in strength while state *B* increases in strength.

Figure 9-8 illustrates, in a slightly different way, what is happening. With repeated stimulations, process *B* occurs more quickly and with greater intensity (panel 2). If the affective reaction is *A* minus *B* (*A* − *B*), then as process *B* increases, the affective reaction decreases, as shown in Figure 9-7.

According to Solomon, this change accompanying repeated use of a drug accounts

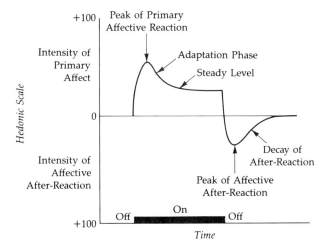

Figure 9-5. The standard pattern of affective dynamics, showing the five distinctive features: the peak of the primary affective reaction, the adaptation phase, the steady level, the peak of the affective after-reaction, and finally the decay of the after-reaction. (The heavy black bar represents the time during which the affect-arousing stimulus is present. The ordinate represents two hedonic scales, each departing from neutrality, one for the primary affect, the other for the affective after-reaction.) (Solomon, 1980)

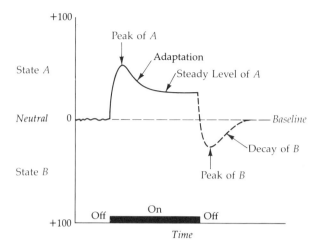

Figure 9-6. The manifest temporal dynamics generated by the opponent process system during the first few stimulations. (The five features of the affective response are labeled.) (Solomon, 1980)

for the tolerance effects often observed when people use opiates, barbiturates, amphetamines, and a number of other drugs. When people take a drug, the body sets up an opponent process that tends to neutralize its effects. As the opponent process strengthens, greater quantities of the drug will be required to provide the same initial reaction. The same process is assumed to be triggered by any stimulus that produces an affective response. If one regularly exposes oneself to a set of stimuli designed to elicit a certain affective response, the intensity of the reaction will weaken, and greater amounts of stimulation will be needed to produce the same initial reaction. The fact that the opponent process is assumed to strengthen

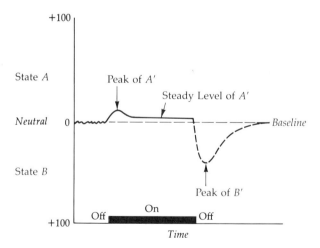

Figure 9-7. The manifest temporal dynamics generated by the opponent process system after many stimulations. (The major features of the modified pattern are labeled.) (Solomon, 1980)

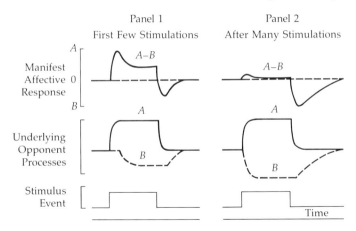

Figure 9-8. The comparison of the effects of *B* processes for relatively novel uncon-
ditioned stimuli and for unconditioned stimuli that are familiar and have frequently
been repeated (Solomon, 1980)

with use has a number of important implications. If a person takes a drug in order
to experience positive affect, he or she will tend to experience greater and greater
negative affect some time after each dosage.

Solomon suggests that the development of tolerance may play a fundamental
role in making a person an addict rather than a casual user. Consider what happens
when someone starts to use an opiate. If the person finds the elation and euphoria
produced by opiates rewarding, he or she will be inclined to use the drug again.
The problem begins to occur, according to Solomon, when the tolerance for the
drug begins to build. At this point the person tends to increase the dose of the
drug in order to experience the same effect and as a result will experience greater
negative aftereffects—pain, fatigue, and depression. If the person should find the
aftereffects intolerable, he or she tends to take the drug in order to reduce or
eliminate the aftereffects. At this point the motivation for using the drug has
shifted. The person is no longer seeking merely to experience a positive affective
state but wants rather to reduce a negative affective state. It is at this point that
the person is gripped by compulsion.

If the person stops taking the drug, then once the opponent process has been
allowed to run its course, the symptoms of withdrawal will also run their course.
The person will no longer be under the influence of the drug and therefore will
no longer be addicted. The problem, however, is that many of the symptoms
produced by the opponent process are very similar to symptoms that occur for
other reasons. People experience pain, fatigue, and depression for a wide variety
of reasons. The principles of learning suggest that if a person has previously
learned to use opiates to reduce or remove those symptoms, he or she will tend
to do so again. Thus former addicts tend to readdict themselves. The prognosis
for an addict is therefore not encouraging. Somehow the person must learn to
deal with such symptoms as pain, fatigue, and depression by means other than
opiates.

Numerous examples demonstrate that the opponent process is not restricted to
drugs (see Solomon, 1980). It is common for people who worked hard to achieve
a goal to report that they experienced a letdown after they attained their goal.

Athletes frequently report a letdown after winning an exciting and hard-fought game. Performers often report that they feel emotionally down or even depressed the day after what they felt was an exciting performance. In contrast, skydivers, who often experience high levels of anxiety before and sometimes during a jump, often talk of the exhilaration that follows a jump. Combat soldiers frequently return from the front lines cheerful and optimistic. After a difficult examination, students will often party into the small hours of the morning. All these examples illustrate that whenever positive affect is triggered, it will be followed more or less automatically by negative affect, and vice versa.

Solomon argues that people can learn to expose themselves to stimuli that elicit an emotion opposite to the one they eventually want to experience. There is good evidence that certain behaviors occur precisely for this reason, although people may not be aware of it. A skydiver, for example, may learn to jump in order to experience the exhilaration that is produced by the opponent process. A person may take on a difficult task in order to experience the positive affect that follows it. The paradox is that humans frequently engage in behaviors that initially produce elation and euphoria but eventually produce more and more negative affect.

Summary

A number of biological theories have been proposed to account for drug addiction. One theory is that certain drugs, such as amphetamines, stimulate the output of catecholamines (mainly dopamine and norepinephrine), which in turn activate the self-reward systems in the brain. Activation of these reward centers has been shown to have powerful reinforcing qualities. This theory suggests that addiction to certain drugs grows out of a desire to experience the pleasure provided by these centers. A second theory is based on the finding that the body contains opiate receptors and, further, that the body manufactures opiates. A person who is deficient in the production of opiates, it is argued, suffers from a general malaise, which heroin or morphine can reduce. Such people tend to become addicted. A third theory, Solomon's opponent process theory, is more general than the other two. It was designed to account for the observation that a marked mood shift, either very positive or very negative, is likely to be followed by the opposite mood. According to Solomon, an opponent process is triggered whenever there is a marked shift in mood. The opponent process is sluggish, but when it does exert its effect, it can be powerful, depending on past experience, and push the mood not only back to baseline but in the opposite direction.

Learned Factors in Addiction

Drugs, Learning, and Dependency

A person who initially uses a drug typically believes her behavior is under her conscious control. She uses the drug and obtains an effect, and presumably that is the end. If, however, the drug produced a strong reinforcing effect (by producing a pleasant feeling or reducing an unpleasant feeling, such as anxiety), there is a strong probability that the person has been subtly changed. Years of research with strong reinforcers have shown that positive reinforcers tend to increase the probability that the same response will occur in the future. Because each subsequent reinforcement tends to produce an additional increase in the probability of repeating that response, a person who begins to use a drug on a regular basis is likely to develop a strong habit of doing so. Once a habit has been established, it is very difficult to break.

That habit plays an important role in drug addiction has been demonstrated by John Nichols (1965). In a series of experiments, Nichols addicted rats by injecting them with morphine every day for 25 days. Half the rats were then trained to perform a response in order to obtain morphine. For example, in one study rats were taught to discriminate between two alternatives, one that provided the opportunity to drink water alone and another that provided the opportunity to drink water plus morphine. Training always took place when the animal would have been experiencing maximum withdrawal (on the third day after the last intake of morphine). In addition, the animals were water-deprived for 24 hours before training. These two conditions, it was assumed, would maximize the reward value of drinking the water/morphine solution. As expected, the animals learned to choose the alternative that led to the water/morphine solution. (It should be noted that rats will not drink water plus morphine unless they are first addicted to morphine.) The other half of the animals served as yoked controls. These animals were not trained to discriminate between the two alternatives but were merely given an injection of morphine equal to the amount drunk by the experimental animal with which they had been paired and were allowed to drink water.

Once training was complete, the animals were not given morphine for the next 14 days. This "drying out" process is complete within 14 days and is generally assumed to free the animal from the aversive symptoms that often accompany morphine use and thereby return the animal to a normal state. Half the experimental and half the control animals were given a choice test after 14 days and half after 49 days. The choice test involved either water alone or water plus morphine. The control animals drank water; however, the experimental animals drank the water/morphine solution, thereby readdicting themselves to morphine. Why did these animals relapse? Nichols argues that they had acquired a habit of drinking the water/morphine solution, which the controls did not acquire. The habit was elicited even though the original motivation for drinking the water/morphine solution was no longer present. As we saw in regard to eating, such habits are fairly common.

Habits appear to be controlled by stimuli. The stimuli governing a habit may be external, internal, or a combination of both. A given habit may be controlled by external stimuli for some people and by internal stimuli for other people. For example, cigarette smoking appears to be governed by internal cues (nicotine levels) in heavy smokers and by external cues in light smokers (Herman, 1974). Herman has shown that light smokers can be made to smoke as much as heavy smokers if the external cues for smoking are made prominent. When a habit produces a reinforcing state of affairs, the person learns to depend on the habit in order to obtain the same reinforcing state of affairs again.

Principles of Associative Learning

According to the principles of classical and instrumental conditioning, if a drug that produces reinforcing effects is used in the presence of certain stimuli, those stimuli will come, over time, to be associated with the internal state that those drugs produce and will come to control drug-taking behavior (S. Siegel, 1979; Wikler, 1980). It has been suggested that the reason some addicts can get a high simply by inserting a needle into their arm (in the absence of any drug effect) is that they associate the insertion of a needle with the euphoric feeling that typically follows an injection of heroin. Associative learning can also explain why many addicts readdict themselves. According to the principles of associative learning, a former addict who returns to the sort of environment in which he originally became addicted is likely to relapse. Shepard Siegel (1983) has noted that Vietnam veterans who relapsed after returning home typically were those who had abused drugs before they went to Asia. In other words, it can be argued that the environment elicited the drug-taking response. If it is assumed that the aversive or noxious state associated with withdrawal is what motivates relapse, principles of associative learning can also account for the readdiction of some Vietnam veterans. According to associative learning theory, if a veteran returned to an environment that bore similarities to the Asian environment in which he became addicted, the similarity of the two situations would be sufficient to trigger a conditioned withdrawal response, and that response would automatically lead to the tendency to take a drug that would reduce those withdrawal symptoms (O'Brien et al., 1980; Wikler, 1980).

State-Dependent Learning

In the 1950s barbiturates were freely prescribed to patients suffering from a number of symptoms, including anxiety, stress, insomnia, and restlessness. People who took barbiturates for such symptoms often reported that they felt better, more relaxed, more confident, less irritable, and better able to cope with daily stress. Many people used barbiturates to help them deal with situations that aroused anxiety and stress—entertaining guests, meeting with the boss, giving a speech. The problem, as it turned out, was that such people soon discovered they were unable to deal effectively with stressful situations without a barbiturate to "calm their nerves." What perplexed scientists was the failure of these people to show any transfer from the drugged to the nondrugged state. If people had learned to perform a skill with the help of a drug, why couldn't they perform the same skill without the drug? Such learning, which could not be transferred from a drugged to a nondrugged state or vice versa, came to be known as state-dependent learning.

One of the clearest demonstrations of state-dependent learning was reported by Donald Overton (1964). Overton injected rats with pentobarbital (a barbiturate) and taught them to turn either right or left in a T maze in order to escape shock. When later tested in a nondrugged state, the rats responded randomly, just like naive animals, sometimes going to the safe arm of the maze and at other times going to the shock arm. When these animals were injected with pentobarbital, they immediately made the correct response. Other animals were trained to turn either right or left in the same T maze while in a nondrugged state. When these animals were tested under pentobarbital, they responded randomly; however, when tested after the drug had worn off, they immediately responded correctly.

This phenomenon is not peculiar to rats; it has been shown to occur in humans as well (for example, Ley et al., 1972). Although state-dependent learning is not associated with all drugs, it has been shown to occur in conjunction with amphetamines, amobarbital, and alcohol, among others (Bustamante et al., 1966; Storm & Caird, 1967; Storm, Caird, & Korbin, 1965; Storm & Smart, 1965). There is some question, however, about the failure of learning to be transferred from a drugged to a nondrugged state in the case of alcohol (Madell, cited in Overton, 1964).

The phenomenon of state-dependent learning shows that habits can be controlled by internal cues. Evidence from a variety of sources indicates that the phenomenon is not restricted to drugs. For example, a variety of "nervous habits," such as nail biting, pulling at one's ear, or tapping one's toes, tend to occur when people experience anxiety, stress, or various other emotional states. Because various emotional states are accompanied by various neurochemical and endocrine changes, there are, in fact, different internal chemical states that accompany a variety of emotions.

What is the significance of state-dependent learning for addiction? The phenomenon of state-dependent learning demonstrates not only that human behavior is often a matter of habit but that habits are controlled by various states of the organism. Many of these states, as I shall discuss later, correspond to common motivational states or conditions. The fact that a behavior is a habit means that it is not under cognitive control. Therefore the person cannot readily alter the behavior merely by determining to do so. Often people are capable of suppressing a behavior by cognitive means; however, if engaging in a certain behavior produces strong reinforcement, there is a good chance that the person will engage in the same behavior again in order to obtain the same reinforcing effect. Anybody who has tried to eliminate a bad habit merely by resolving to stop it can attest to the long-term failure of such an approach.

Exactly why cognitive plans are frequently unsuccessful in eliminating undesirable habits is not altogether clear. It may simply be that humans are basically hedonists—that is, we seek pleasure and avoid pain. As such, we may not be biologically inclined to delay immediate gratification. Many cigarette smokers realize that smoking is bad for their health and may shorten their lives. Nevertheless, they continue to smoke in order to obtain the immediate gratification provided by cigarettes. Research on the principles of learning shows that all animals tend to learn tasks that provide immediate reinforcement. It has been shown also that people who appear to be working toward a long-range goal find that the goal-directed activity provides more positive reinforcement than the attainment of the goal. Drugs, as we know, are powerful reinforcers. Therefore, we should not be surprised that once humans have discovered the reinforcing properties of drugs, the habit of using them persists.

The Learning Model of Addiction: Multiple Determinants of Behavior

The phenomenon of state-dependent learning has provided the impetus to view drug use within a learning model. As we shall see, such a model can account for a number of important findings about both positive and negative addictions.

The learning model recognizes that a single behavior pattern can come to be controlled by a wide range of stimuli, both internal and external. For example, a smoker may tend to light a cigarette whenever one or more of the following conditions occur: a coffee break, seeing another person smoke, boredom, finishing a meal, sitting in a car, experiencing stress, or simply experiencing a lowered arousal level. This fact helps to explain why some people tend to use drugs moderately while others tend to abuse drugs. According to the principles of learning, any time a behavior occurs in the presence of a stimulus, that behavior will tend to come under the control of that stimulus. In other words, an association tends to develop between a stimulus and a behavior. In this way a given behavior can come to be controlled by a wide variety of stimuli. If a person tends to drink alcohol when he is anxious, for example, he will develop the habit of drinking alcohol whenever he feels anxious. Similarly, if he tends to drink with dinner, after a time he will develop a habit of drinking with dinner. If he learns to drink in social situations, a tendency will develop to drink whenever he is part of a social gathering.

The high alcoholism rate in France becomes understandable in the light of this fact. Since France has a good climate for grapes, one of the main industries of France is winemaking. Hence wine is so easily available that it has been customary in many households to drink it throughout the day. Wine is often drunk with breakfast, lunch, and dinner, and between meals too, either to quench thirst or to lubricate social occasions (Swinson & Eaves, 1978). Thus the French tend, from a very early age, to drink wine extensively under a wide variety of stimuli, or cues. As we have noted, alcohol tends to reduce such aversive states as stress and anxiety and to produce feelings of well-being, power, and arousal. The average French citizen has ample opportunity to experience the wide range of reinforcing effects that alcohol produces in various situations, and so to form multiple associations of alcohol intake with internal and external cues.

Italy also has a good climate for grapes and has also developed an extensive wine industry, yet its rate of alcoholism is relatively low (Swinson & Eaves, 1978). The reason for this difference can be found in the fact that most Italians drink wine only with the evening meal. Therefore, drinking is restricted to a particular time and a particular setting. Drunkenness is not condoned. Accordingly, when Italians drink, they tend to drink moderately (Swinson & Eaves, 1978). Since alcoholism usually results from the abuse of alcohol (too much and for the wrong reasons), Italians have less opportunity than the French to learn to associate alcohol with a wide variety of internal and external cues.

Development of an Addiction: A Theoretical Analysis

To understand why one person might become addicted to a drug while another might not, it is necessary to chart a typical addiction pattern. The term *addiction* is used here to refer to the development of a psychological dependency or strong psychological need. In the course of taking a drug, a person can experience a variety of effects, depending on his or her ongoing motivational state. If a person takes morphine when he is tired, for example, one of the main feelings he will experience is a lessening of fatigue. If he takes morphine when he is anxious, he will experience a lessening of anxiety together with a general feeling of well-being. If he should take morphine when he is lonely, he will experience a reduction in loneliness. Because each of these psychological states is more or less distinct, one can learn to use a drug for a wide variety of reasons. Any or all of these states could, therefore, come to control the tendency to use a particular drug.

When people first use drugs, they typically do so under rather well-defined conditions. For example, they may drink alcohol on Friday nights with friends, or they may smoke marijuana late in the evenings, again with friends. When a drug is used under very limited conditions, the person has very limited opportunity to learn the full extent to which the drug can alter various motivational states. Many of the popular drugs have very pervasive effects. Heroin in particular can reduce a number of negative psychological states in addition to producing a general state of euphoria. Over time many people begin to use drugs under a wider range of stimulus conditions. For example, someone might start having a beer after work. Because alcohol in small to moderate amounts is a stimulant, the person might learn to use beer as a means of warding off the fatigue that she experiences after a hard day of work. Because alcohol can reduce feelings of anxiety experienced in social situations, she might also start to use alcohol as an aid to enjoying social gatherings. Thus, as she uses a drug under more and more varied conditions, she has more opportunity to discover that the drug has diverse reinforcing properties.

A person who continues to use a drug under a wide range of conditions is likely to discover that the drug's reinforcing properties are associated with internal states rather than external stimuli. For example, a person might discover that alcohol reduces anxiety in a wide variety of situations or that heroin will reduce a variety of aversive psychological states, including anxiety and depression. We have already seen that many of the commonly used drugs have a variety of effects and are used for a variety of reasons. Presumably each person discovers what property of the drug is reinforcing for him or her as a result of experimenting with it under a variety of conditions. The person slowly learns to use drugs to produce certain internal states. The more the person uses drugs in this way, the more his or her behavior will shift from external to internal control.

Generally people are inhibited from using drugs extensively because of fears for health or social norms. Their behavior therefore remains, at least in part, under external control. A businessman who is concerned that he may be fired if he drinks on the job may restrict his drinking to evenings or weekends. By restricting his drinking to particular times and locations, he is forced to continue exercising coping responses to a number of daily stressors. When a person fails to restrict his intake to particular situations, the stage is set for him to use a given drug in more and more situations and, as a result, to develop a generalized dependency on it.

According to this model of addiction, it is not surprising that high rates of alcoholism are found among people in alcohol-related occupations, such as bartenders. If a person is in a setting where there is little reason to restrict intake, there is a greater opportunity to learn about the extensive reinforcing properties of alcohol.

Constitutional Readiness, Learning, and Addiction

The existence of very general reward systems allows humans to pursue very diverse activities. Presumably these reward systems evolved for precisely this reason. Survival depends on our ability to deal with many varied situations. Our readiness to learn may be a factor in our readiness to become addicted to a wide variety of chemicals and activities. It is not only more difficult to induce an animal to become addicted to a drug—it is often necessary to use rather extreme forms of stress or pain in order to induce addiction (for example, Hadaway et al., 1979). Even then, the addiction is often specific to the stressful situation (for example, Masserman & Yum, 1946). It is interesting to speculate on why certain people are addiction-prone (Nichols, 1972). What is it about the reward systems of these people that makes them susceptible to drugs? Do such people readily develop positive addictions if the circumstances are right? In his book *Moodswing* Ronald Fieve (1975) has noted that many creative people may be susceptible to drug addiction because of their tendency toward periodic depression. If this is so, the tendency toward addiction is clearly not restricted to people who are lacking in skills and talents or people who are mentally incompetent or mentally disturbed. On the contrary, it appears that people who are highly skilled may be just as susceptible.

The Learning Model and the Treatment of Addiction

There has been growing interest in using the principles outlined above to treat addicts, especially alcoholics (Miller & Muñoz, 1976). The basic aim is to teach the person to restrict his drinking to particular situations and then to limit the amount he drinks in those situations. If the person associates with people who drink excessively, he is encouraged to find new friends; if he goes to a place where alcohol is readily available, he is encouraged to seek out places where it is more restricted. In essence, the goal of such programs is to put drinking under external control, as the very nature of alcohol seems to make it difficult for the alcoholic to learn internal control.

Conclusions

According to the above analyses, three factors are responsible for the development of a generalized tendency to use a drug. The first factor is the tendency to use the drug under a wide variety of stimulus conditions. If a person is prevented by social customs or fears from using a drug under a variety of conditions, the person is less likely to develop a generalized habit. Such a person may, however, learn to use a drug extensively under limited stimulus conditions, and there is good evidence that many people do. For example, Ernest Hemingway drank large amounts of alcohol but only under certain conditions (Fieve, 1975). By limiting his drinking to particular times and situations, he was able to continue to write books of high quality. Many businesspeople deliberately do not drink until the end of a workday. They may drink heavily for several hours and then go to bed, ensuring that they will be able to work the next day.

The second factor responsible for a generalized tendency to use a drug is the motivation for using the drug. Motivational states not only vary among people but vary over time for a given person. For example, different people experience anxiety in different amounts and often for different reasons. Similarly, people often experience feelings of euphoria either for no apparent reason (as in mania) or because they have exercised some skill or ability. Thus, regardless of the reason people use a particular drug, there should be differences in the need or tendency to use a drug.

Finally, the third factor may be called simply the availability factor. There is considerable evidence that the availability of a drug plays a very significant role in determining not only whether a person will become addicted but which drugs will form the basis of the addiction (for example, Sheppard et al., 1972; Swinson & Eaves, 1978). It follows from the learning model that if a given society or part of a society condones or even encourages the use of a given drug, then the person will tend not only to use that drug but to discover its reinforcing properties. It is from this perspective that we can understand why various sociological factors tend to be correlated not only with the rate of addiction but with the kind of drug used by various societies, subcultures, or parts of a society. Dole (1980) writes, "In fact, it is the availability of drugs rather than the quality of life that seems to be the most important factor in determining the prevalence of drug use" (p. 140).

Evidence from a wide variety of sources suggests that the motivations to use a drug include curiosity (seeking out new and varied experiences), modeling (following the behavioral example of parents, friends, or a portion of society, such as an ethnic group), group pressure (requirement for admission to a gang, a challenge to prove one is not "chicken"), or medication (prescribed either by a doctor or by oneself). Curiosity, modeling, group pressure, and medication not only are responsible for the tendency to use drugs but often dictate which drug will be used (for example, Roebuck & Kessler, 1972; Sheppard et al., 1972). For example, young people are more likely to use alcohol if their parents or peers do (Braucht et al., 1975; Gorsuch & Butler, 1976). These factors, however, do not tell the whole story. There tend to be large individual differences. The problem is to account for these differences.

Summary

Many habits that humans acquire come to be controlled by internal or external stimuli. As a consequence, certain behaviors are performed in the absence of the motivating state that was originally necessary to establish that habit.

(continued)

Nichols's research shows that even animals will learn to use a drug out of habit. Research on state-dependent learning provides a clear illustration of how this process works. Internal or external stimuli present when a behavior was initially performed come to control that behavior if the behavior occurs repeatedly in the presence of such stimuli. The state-dependent learning research permits us to chart a hypothetical model of why some people use a drug in moderation while others abuse that drug. The difference between the place of wine in the French and Italian cultures provides a good illustration of how the principles of learning can account for differences in drug-abuse (alcoholism) rates between populations. Although the learning model can account for group differences, there are also constitutional differences within groups that make some individuals more likely to acquire an addiction. For example, an anxious person may be susceptible to the reinforcing effects of alcohol and hence may be likely to become an alcoholic. If it is true that learning does play an important role in the addiction process, it should be possible to apply the principles of learning to the treatment of addicts. Considerable work is being done to explore the potential of such an approach.

Cognitive Factors in Drug Use

Beliefs or Expectations about What Drugs Do

People's beliefs about what drugs do play a large role in the process of addiction (Peele, 1985). It has been repeatedly demonstrated, for example, that placebos can be just as effective as an active drug. In one study it was shown that a placebo killed pain as effectively as morphine (Lasagna et al., 1954). Other studies have shown that people become more aggressive and sexually aroused when they erroneously believe that they have been drinking alcohol (Wilson, 1981). Alcoholics even "lose control" when they have been misinformed that they have been drinking alcohol (Engle & Williams, 1972). One of the criteria often used to determine whether a person is an alcoholic is whether the individual can stop drinking after a single drink. The fact that alcoholics lose control in the absence of alcohol intake suggests that it is the belief about what alcohol does when you are addicted (it makes you lose control) rather than the alcohol itself that leads to loss of control. After reviewing studies on the role of expectancy, Hull and Bond (1986) concluded: "Expectancy increases the incidence of illicit social behaviors and has few effects on nonsocial acts. Such a pattern of behavior is consistent with the hypothesis that expectancy provides an attributional excuse to engage in desired but socially prohibited acts" (p. 358).

C. M. Steele (1986) has shown that alcohol has the greatest effects on those behaviors that are under strong inhibitory control. People who experience strong conflict about expressing aggression, for example, are more likely to become aggressive under the influence of alcohol. Similarly, people who inhibit their tendency to offer help to another person, possibly because they fear they will get hurt in the process, tend to rush to the rescue under the influence of alcohol.

Situational Factors

Studies have shown that not only the tendency to use a drug but the amount of a drug that we use and where we use it are governed by situational factors. Situational factors, in this context, are such things as our perceptions of the appropriateness or socially desirability of a behavior in a specific situation. The tendency to develop a drinking problem can be predicted from the amount one's companions drink and the extent to which one's life revolves around drinking (Cahalan & Room, 1974). It has been shown that the tendency to use a narcotic is governed to a very large degree by such things as the appropriateness of the response in a given social situation. Many addicted Vietnam veterans, for example, stopped using heroin for good when they returned to friends and family who did not use it or condone its use (see Robins et al., 1974; Robins, Helzer, & Davis, 1975). Conversely, addicts who had gone through a treatment program but then returned to an environment in which their friends not only condoned the use of drugs but used them themselves tended to show very high readdiction rates (for example, Nichols, 1965, 1972). If drug use were a disease or a biological drive, one could not predict its occurrence on the basis of environmental factors. It has even been shown that the tendency to experience withdrawal symptoms is related to the social acceptability of demonstrating such symptoms. When it is expected that they will occur, they do; when it has been made clear that such symptoms are not only not expected but not acceptable, they do not occur (for example, Zinberg & Robertson, 1972). Such findings have led people to question the whole idea that withdrawal—the pain and discomfort that come when people stop using a drug— is one of the primary reasons that people readdict themselves.

Cultural Factors
Stanton Peele (1984, 1985) has reviewed some of the data on the role of cultural factors in drug use. He points out that the Zuñi and Hopi Indians used alcohol in a ritualistic and regulated manner until the coming of the Spanish, after which they used it in a destructive and generally addictive manner. Peele further points out that the use of alcohol in certain cultures (American Indian, Eskimo, Scandinavian, Eastern European, and United States) leads to antisocial aggressive behaviors but fails to do so in other cultures (Greek, Italian, American Jewish, Chinese, and Japanese). It has been suggested that these and other differences relate to the beliefs that people hold about what drugs do.

Beliefs about Control
Several important implications follow from the idea that cognitions play an important role in addiction. People often have a great deal of information, correct and incorrect, about what happens to people when they become addicted to a drug. Much of this information comes from conversation, newspapers, and television. You may have read, for example, that alcoholics are people who lose control once they start drinking, or have a drink every day, or show a tendency to become aggressive when they drink, or find that it is impossible to quit drinking, or drink progressively more as time goes on. All of these various pieces of information then provide the basis for your belief system. There are two important things to note here. First, few people share precisely the same belief system. Second, two people may have basically the same drinking pattern yet one may fit the criteria of addiction while the other does not.

If belief controls behavior, then it follows that people who come to the conclusion that they are alcoholics will begin to behave in a manner consistent with the label they have applied to themselves. They will tend, that is, to lose control when they drink, or find it virtually impossible to quit drinking, and to exhibit the other behaviors they associate with alcoholism. People who do not label themselves as alcoholics, on the other hand, may drink just as much but manage not to lose control and find it less difficult to quit. Indeed, data suggest that people who do not perceive themselves to be alcoholics (or who perceive themselves as having at least some control) respond much better to rehabilitation programs that involve control of alcohol rather than total abstinence (for example, Skinner, Glaser, & Annis, 1982). Conversely, people who perceive themselves as alcoholics (or as having no control) do not fare well in such programs but do benefit from programs that focus on abstinence (Miller, 1983). That makes sense. If you think you can't control your drinking, then the best solution is not to drink.

It is interesting to note that the program of Alcoholics Anonymous (AA) is based on the principle that certain people can never learn to control their drinking and that if they are ever to live a normal life, they must recognize this fact. The requirement that AA members must openly identify themselves as alcoholics serves to make them admit to themselves that they have lost control. It further reinforces the idea that they can never drink again. The message that they have lost control could be very damaging if they were to generalize it to other parts of their lives. Labeling alcoholism as a "disease," however, helps to reduce the tendency to generalize. At this time there is no clear evidence that alcoholism is a disease. I point this out not because AA is not an effective organization but rather to emphasize AA's message: if you have absolutely no control over your drinking, then your only alternative is abstinence. There is also a danger of relapse for people who label themselves alcoholics. If being an alcoholic means you are unable to control your drinking, then the more you endorse the concept "I am an alcoholic," the more you will tend to lose control when you drink (Heather, Winton, & Rollnick, 1982; Peele, 1985). It is interesting to note that abstinence programs have success rates of only 5 to 10% (Emrick & Hansen, 1983).

Beliefs about Self-Change

There are numerous accounts of people who after drinking heavily for years have suddenly altered their drinking patterns. A father who one day notes that his son is modeling his drinking suddenly stops drinking; a mother who realizes that she is slurring her speech at the dinner table abruptly stops having her usual three or four cocktails before dinner. Peele (1983) has noted that people frequently alter their drinking pattern when it begins to interfere with things that they value. While some people may indeed be unable to control their drinking, it is obvious that many people can. George Vaillant (1983) has presented data that show that alcohol problems regularly reverse themselves without medical intervention. In other words, the inevitable progression that some people say characterizes alcoholics and other drug users does not hold for all people.

Summary

A great many data indicate that cognitive factors play an important role in drug addiction. Beliefs about what drugs do seem to play a large part in determining the effects of drugs. Situational factors, too, such as whether a behavior is perceived to be appropriate, determine to a very large degree the way people behave when they use drugs. As beliefs about the effects of drugs and about appropriate behaviors vary from culture to culture, it is not surprising to find that drugs have quite different effects on people of different cultures. Probably one of the most important factors governing the display of the stereotyped behaviors associated with alcoholism is the drinker's belief about control. It has been found that when people label themselves as alcoholics they have a greater tendency to behave as the stereotyped alcoholic is thought to behave. That is, they show an inability to control their drinking.

(continued)

|||||| The disease model of alcoholism links loss of control directly to the "disease of alcoholism," not to cognitive variables.

An Interaction Model of Addiction

While the biological, learning, and cognitive models can account for some aspects of the addiction process, each has its shortcomings. The list of problems with these models exceeds the scope of this chapter, but they are well presented in Stanton Peele's book *The Meaning of Addiction* (1985).

It should be noted that addiction, as we know it, is a particularly human phenomenon (Peele, 1977). That is, animals do not normally addict themselves. It is possible to addict animals in the laboratory, but often only after an unnatural environment has been created. If rats and other laboratory animals are to become addicted, they must be given very restricted living conditions. A comprehensive research program at Simon Fraser University has shown that rats housed under very restricted conditions (very little space, no social interaction, virtually nothing to explore) are much more inclined to select a morphine solution than animals that have been housed under more natural conditions (more space, opportunity for social interaction, and the availability of objects in the environment to explore) (see Alexander et al., 1985). In one study rats were trained to ingest large amounts of morphine. This technique was devised by Nichols (1965) to produce withdrawal symptoms, one of the conditions that has been hypothesized to motivate drug use. As expected, this technique did produce increased morphine consumption but, interestingly, the effect was much greater in the animals housed under restricted conditions than in those housed under more natural conditions. In other words, the tendency to select morphine, even under conditions of withdrawal, is modified by housing conditions. One interesting finding was that female rats tended more than male rats to prefer morphine under restricted conditions. This effect was magnified after the rats were trained with Nichols' procedure. Why the sex difference? It may, as we shall see, have something to do with the female rat's greater need for social contact and/or opportunity for activity.

Subsequent studies have attempted to separate out the social opportunities of the more natural environment and the opportunity for activity. These studies have shown that it is the combination of space and social contact rather than either space or social contact alone that produces the results.

How can we account for these effects? It has been suggested that the reason rats in the more natural environment fail to use morphine is that morphine interferes with complex rodent activity. If we assume that these activities are rewarding for rodents, it makes sense that rats in an environment that provided those rewards might tend to avoid morphine. Rats' sexual behavior, too, is affected by their environment. If rats are to mate, they need ample space, because their normal procedure consists of a series of chases and mounts. After a female has been mounted, she runs away from the male; he pursues her and mounts her again.

This research has several implications of interest to investigators seeking to understand addiction in humans. It has been suggested that the reason that most of the Vietnam war veterans did not resume taking heroin in the United States was that they returned to an environment that provided them with natural rewards. What about those who did resume using heroin? It has been suggested that many of them were users before they went to Vietnam, and the rest simply did not have or could not find a rewarding environment after their return. As John Falk (1983) has said, drug abuse "depends on what behavior opportunities are available in life's situations, and whether the individual is prepared to exploit those opportunities" (p. 390).

Is There an Addictive Personality?

For some time people have attempted to discover whether there is an addictive personality. That is, is there a constellation of psychological characteristics that make some people more prone to become addicted to all drugs or simply to a single drug, such as alcohol or heroin? Assessment of alcoholics (Vaillant, 1983) and narcotics addicts (Robins et al., 1980) has yielded essentially negative results.

It is important to distinguish between the tendency to use drugs and the tendency to become addicted. There is evidence, for example, that college students drink for a variety of reasons. Some drink to avoid aversive situations, some to socialize, some to satisfy a need for sensation, and some for pure enjoyment. Problem drinkers tend to drink for all of those reasons (McCarty & Kaye, 1984). Various studies have found that people who score high on Zuckerman's sensation-seeking scale (see Chapter 13) are more prone to use drugs than people who score low (Huba, Newcomb, & Bentler, 1981). This does not necessarily mean that these people are more prone to become addicted. At this point there is no evidence to indicate that high sensation seekers are more likely than low sensation seekers to become addicted. Other qualities associated with sensation seeking may, in fact, work against becoming addicted. For example, high sensation seekers perceive themselves as having more control over drugs than low sensation seekers (Franken, Gibson, & Rowland, 1986). As we have seen, belief that one can control one's use of a drug may play an important role in determining whether one becomes addicted. Also, sensation seekers tend to be highly involved in a variety of activities.

Interest in alternative activities has been found to be one of the factors that modulates the tendency to use drugs. In other words, use per se may not be the main factor. As we have noted, Kolb (1962) and others have argued that people who use drugs to escape noxious or aversive situations are more likely to become addicted than people who simply use a drug for recreational purposes.

It is possible that when such traits as sensation seeking are linked to a more maladaptive behavioral style, an individual may be more susceptible to drug abuse and addiction. It has been shown, for example, that sensation seeking contributes to the addiction process when it is part of a more general trait called "antisocial personality." McCarty and Kaye (1984) found a link between sensation seeking and a tendency toward alcohol abuse only when sensation seeking was part of a constellation of factors that included "avoidance."

Factors That Moderate the Use of Drugs

Commitment to other activities. In *The Meaning of Addiction*, Peele (1985) argues that while there is very little evidence for an addictive personality per se, there is considerable evidence that the addiction process is linked to social, cultural, and parental influences, together with a desire to satisfy certain needs. He has argued that lack of commitment to nondrug activities often plays an important role in the process. If drugs interfere with activities that people value, they will limit their drug use or abstain in order to maximize the rewards of the nondrug activity.

Social class. A strong relationship has been found between socioeconomic level and alcohol addiction. Subjects of lower socioeconomic backgrounds are three times more likely to be addicted to alcohol than middle-class subjects (see Vaillant, 1983). The question arises as to the origins of these differences. As we shall see, they may be traceable not to socioeconomic class per se but rather to other characteristics associated with the various classes. The values that one holds, for example, may be the important factor.

Peer and parental influences.   Peers have consistently been found to play an important role in initiating drug use. Research studies have shown that the effect of peer pressure is greatest in regard to marijuana, somewhat less in regard to alcohol, and least in regard to hard drugs (Kandel, Kessler, & Margulies, 1978). While peers may be influential in the initial experimentation with drugs, it is questionable whether peer pressure can account for the tendency of a given individual to abuse drugs. In fact, it has been suggested that peers may provide role models for moderation. It has been found, for example, that groups that encourage controlled use of heroin tend to stress limiting the use of drugs to certain specific occasions while simultaneously encouraging the maintenance of social, scholastic, and professional interests (Jacobson & Zinberg, 1975, cited in Peele, 1985).

Culture and ethnicity.   Membership in a particular ethnic group seems to exert an influence on the likelihood of drug abuse. Several studies in this area point to the fact that cultures or ethnic groups vary widely in the attitudes they foster, and that these attitudes influence drinking patterns. There are wide cultural and ethnic differences in regard to the acceptability of drunkenness, the tolerance of aggression in a drunken person, the idea of drinking as an expression of masculinity, and so forth. Jews as a group tend to be moderate drinkers, whereas the Irish tend to drink to excess (Vaillant, 1983). It has been suggested that this difference is linked to the Jewish tradition of high regard for rationality and self-control (Keller, 1970) and an Irish ethos that is both magical and tragic (see Bales, 1946). The Irish, that is, treat drinking not as something that one may choose to do or not but rather as something that can bring magic into one's life. The Japanese and Chinese tend to be very moderate drinkers, whereas the North American Indians and the Eskimos tend to be excessive drinkers (Klausner, Foulkes, & Moore, 1980). As excessive drinking is incompatible with a commitment to achievement, it has been suggested that this factor may be responsible for the moderate drinking of the Japanese and Chinese (Peele, 1983).

Moderation as a life value.   Drug abuse, it has been suggested, reflects a tendency to excessive behavior (Gilbert, 1981). Conversely, it has been suggested that people for whom moderation is the central organizing principle will be less inclined to develop drug dependence (Peele, 1983). One important factor that may underlie the adoption of the moderation principle is the placing of a high value on health, which may be learned from one's parents or from members of one's social group (Becker, 1974).

Achievement motivation and fear of failure.   There is evidence from a variety of sources that people characterized by strong achievement motivation are less likely to become addicted than people who lack such motivation. People with strong achievement motivation tend to work hard and generally have good opinions of their abilities. People with a strong fear of failure tend to have a low opinion of their abilities, and so tend to avoid situations that may demonstrate their ineptitude. In order to avoid looking bad, they look for easy problems or problems that are so difficult that no one would reasonably expect them to succeed. In short, their lives revolve around attempts to escape the need to perform (to test their skills). One means of escape is to take drugs, often a highly ritualized activity that requires little skill and therefore offers no threat to one's low self-esteem. Birney, Burdick, and Teevan (1969) have suggested that the rise in drug use in the 1960s grew out of this learned fear of failure. Peele (1982) has included this kind of drug use among the coping strategies he calls "magical solutions." While such a coping strategy enables the individual to escape the immediate problem, it has no long-term survival value, for it keeps the individual from facing reality.

Alienation from society. When people become alienated from their society, they have an increased tendency to become addicted. It has been found, for example, that the use of marijuana is associated with alienation from social institutions (Kandel, 1984), for several reasons. When people become alienated from their society, they no longer feel bound by its rules. As a consequence, they see no value in the principle of moderation or the standards by which other people judge the appropriateness of behavior. The lack of activities designed to lead to achievement or other rewards valued by the society makes these people susceptible to the drug experience (Jessor, 1979). It makes sense that when people experience no rewards from the society in which they live, they might look elsewhere for a rewarding experience.

Summary

Rats can be induced to become addicted to morphine if they are subjected to very restricted living conditions. The reason, it has been suggested, is that under restricted living conditions the rats are unable to experience natural rewards. One implication of this research is that people will have a tendency to become addicted or readdicted when they live in an environment that prevents them from experiencing natural rewards.

Researchers have attempted for some time to discover whether there is an addictive personality, but virtually all attempts have yielded negative results. While such personality traits as sensation seeking have from time to time been linked with drug abuse, it appears that such traits by themselves do not necessarily lead to drug abuse or addiction. When sensation seeking is linked with other, antisocial traits, however, or with the fear of failure, it may then lead to addiction.

Several factors moderate the use of drugs. These include commitment to other activities, social class, peer and parental influences, culture and ethnicity, a respect for the value of moderation, the need to achieve, the fear of failure, and degree of alienation from society.

Some Issues Related to Alcohol Use and Abuse

The use of alcohol dates back to biblical days and beyond. Over the centuries people have used and abused alcohol. It is obviously a complex drug that people use for a variety of reasons. Research on alcohol has slowly begun to unravel some of its secrets. In this section I have not tried to separate the biological, learned, and cognitive factors in the use and abuse of alcohol. I think it will become obvious as you read this material that the phenomena I describe represent complex interactions of these three factors working together to produce their effects.

Alcohol and the Need for Power

The extensive consumption of alcoholic beverages throughout the world has made their production and sale a multi-billion-dollar industry. Many governments have come to depend on the extensive revenue generated by several forms of taxes that are collected from the sale of liquor. Even though people find it harder to pay for the necessities of life, let alone luxuries, liquor sales continue to rise. What is in that bottle that won't allow us to leave it alone?

Faced with this fascinating question, McClelland and his associates (1972) set out to determine what, if any, psychological needs are met by alcohol. Armed with the Thematic Apperception Test (TAT), McClelland and his associates asked people to write imaginative stories after consuming various amounts of alcohol. These stories showed that as drinking increased, so did power thoughts—that is, thoughts of having an impact on others, of being aggressive, of sexual conquest, of being strong and influential, and so on. In later work, McClelland found that there are at least two types of power thoughts. One type focuses on personal dominance over others; McClelland called this type "p-Power." The other type focuses on the altruistic use of power—power exercised on behalf of others. This socialized power he called "s-Power." By having men write stories at various states of intoxication, McClelland and his associates were able to determine whether these two kinds of power thoughts were related to the amount of alcohol consumed. Figure 9-9 shows the results of this analysis. After two or three cocktails, the investigators found, s-Power thoughts predominated. As drinking continued, p-Power thoughts tended to replace s-Power thoughts.

To explain this shift, McClelland and his colleagues suggested that after a few drinks, power thoughts have been stimulated, but the drinker is still experiencing a number of inhibiting thoughts. That is, his thought processes are still being influenced by his past training. In short, they are being controlled by the fears and anxieties that normally arise when we think about exercising power over important figures in our lives. Much of the brain acts to inhibit behavior (Eysenck, 1963), and large amounts of alcohol tend to have a depressant effect on the brain. The result is disinhibition. This means that the inhibitions a person normally experiences will weaken or disappear. As a result, thoughts will shift from s-Power to p-Power.

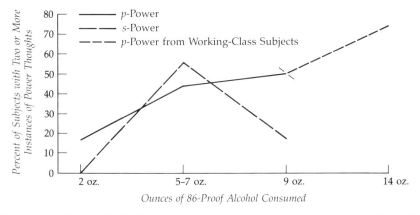

Figure 9-9. Effects of drinking on power thoughts in fraternity men (McClelland, 1971)

McClelland and his colleagues suggest not only that people drink to experience feelings of power but that some people drink more because they have a greater need for power or because society puts greater pressure on them to demonstrate their power. Certain occupations, they argue, accentuate power and influence. A newspaper columnist or army general, for example, not only exercises tremendous power but is expected to do so. These investigators note that such men often become heavy drinkers when they lose their ability to exercise power. A military officer who is forced to retire, a columnist who loses his job, or a government official passed over for an influential position often turns to the bottle to get from it what he has lost in his daily life. Although most people who drink do not become addicted, a large number do, usually those who drink to excess. McClelland and his associates have suggested that people who are unusually concerned about p-Power cannot drink safely. Their excesses cause them to get into fights, accidents, and "personal power actions" that destroy themselves and others (McClelland, 1971, p. 79).

Alcohol and Sexual Arousal

Studies of gender differences in the use of alcohol have consistently found them. While men tend to drink to enhance their feelings of sexual arousal and power, women drink to allay their anxieties about their femininity (Brown et al., 1980; McClelland et al., 1972; Wilsnack, 1976). Even men who only think they have drunk alcohol feel more sexually aroused. This is particularly true of men who have repressed their sexual feelings. Women, in contrast, tend to experience a diminished sex drive with alcohol (Lang et al., 1980), although many of them do associate sexual arousal with the effects of alcohol (Wilson & Lawson, 1978). It has been suggested that alcohol makes men more sexually aggressive and women more accommodating (Wilson, 1981).

These findings make a great deal of sense if we assume that alcohol helps men and women to fulfill their stereotyped sex roles. In our society men are generally expected to be the initiators and women are generally expected to be passive and accommodating. If people are not comfortable with those roles, alcohol can act as a disinhibitor to allow them to carry out their roles more readily.

Alcohol as a Buffer for Stress

"I drink to relax," people often say. But is there empirical support for that idea? One survey found that alcohol consumption does indeed reduce symptoms of stress. Moderate to heavy drinkers, it was found, manifested significantly lower levels of somatic symptoms than did abstainers (Neff, 1984). Another study showed that alcohol reduces not only heart rate but self-reported feelings of anxiety (Sher & Walitzer, 1986). It has been suggested that one reason alcohol reduces stress is that alcohol impairs cognitive processes; thus when alcohol is used in connection with other distracting activities, it blocks out stress-inducing thoughts (Steele, Southwick, & Pagano, 1986). Other studies have questioned the conclusion that alcohol leads to stress reduction and have pointed out that when alcohol is used excessively and chronically to deal with stress, it frequently contributes to an increase in stress (Powers & Kutash, 1985). One important implication is that people who use alcohol to reduce stress must realize that their use of alcohol is at best a short-term solution that may interfere with long-term solutions to the problems that give rise to stress.

A study of two samples of university students found that students tend to use drugs when they feel stressed. These findings support the hypothesis that perceived loss of control and meaninglessness are linked not only to drinking but to substance abuse (Newcomb & Harlow, 1986). In view of McClelland's work, it is probably not surprising that people are more inclined to use drugs when they perceive they have lost control. McClelland's work suggests that alcohol can provide a sense of power or a feeling that one can exert control over events in one's life.

Alcohol and Tension Reduction

One of the most commonly accepted behavioral models of alcohol asserts that alcohol reduces tension. While the tension reduction hypothesis has a great deal of intuitive appeal and has generated a great deal of research since it was originally put forward by Conger (1956), the evidence for the model has not been clear cut. Joseph Volpicelli (1987) has recently challenged the viability of this model and has offered an alternative explanation. Volpicelli argues that people often do not drink in order to reduce tension but rather drink following some event that produces tension or stress.

The evidence for Volpicelli's model comes from the research on controllable versus uncontrollable events. When people are exposed to events that are uncontrollable, they are inclined to experience a great deal of stress—much more than when they are able to make some type of coping response. In the shock avoidance situation, for example, an animal can make some avoidance response. If another animal is given the same pattern of shock (yoked control) but prevented from making an avoidance response, that animal typically experiences a much higher level of stress than the first, as shown by such organic pathology indicators as ulceration (e.g., Weiss, 1971a), decreased resistance to tumors (Visintainer, Volpicelli, & Seligman, 1982), and suppression of the immunological response (Laudenslager et al., 1983). Since the two animals received the same pattern of shocks, the difference has been attributed to the fact that one animal had control while the other did not. What is particularly interesting is that if animals are given an opportunity to drink alcohol, increased alcohol drinking tends to occur *after* aversive events that are uncontrollable (Volpicelli, 1987). According to the tension reduction hypothesis, there would be no motivation for drinking alcohol following the termination of a stressful event.

In addition to the organic indicators of stress, animals in the uncontrollable condition experience greater depletion of central norepinephrine (Weiss et al., 1975) and an increase in plasma beta-endorphin (Rossier et al., 1977). Joseph Volpicelli (1987) has argued that if beta-endorphins are low following a stressful event organisms would be motivated to do something that would return those beta-endorphin levels to their normal resting levels. As noted earlier, Volpicelli has also argued that alcohol has the ability to increase endorphin activity. Any event, therefore, that leads to the depletion of endorphin stores should provide the motivational basis for drinking alcohol, a substance that appears to be capable of inducing increased endorphin activity. Presumably, then, the reinforcement for drinking would be the return of endorphin levels to their normal resting state.

Volpicelli's model (the Endorphin Compensation Hypothesis) can explain such things as why people are inclined to go for a drink after they finish a job that has been particularly stressful, the tendency of students to drink after they have finished exams (Robow & Neuman, 1984), and the tendency of alcoholics to relapse after a negative life event (Marlatt & Gordon, 1980). According to the tension reduction hypothesis, one might expect people to drink in order to reduce the tension that comes with such things as a stressful job, taking exams, or experiencing a negative life event. That is, they would be inclined to drink before rather than after a stressful event. Volpicelli points out that his Endorphin Compensation Hypothesis is not designed to provide an all encompassing explanation as to why people drink, but rather, an explanation as to why people might be inclined to drink after certain kinds of stressful events.

It should be noted that people are often all too aware of the fact that alcohol can interfere with their performance when they are faced with stressful events such as an exam or a negative life event. This knowledge may be one of the factors that prevents people from actually using alcohol when they are experiencing stress. In other words, Volpicelli's hypothesis probably should not be viewed as replacing the tension reduction hypothesis but rather as explaining one facet of drinking that cannot be explained adequately by the tension reduction hypothesis.

Depression and Alcoholism

Researchers have repeatedly found a link between alcohol abuse and depression. Until recently it was concluded that people drink to reduce their depression. In other words, depression somehow leads to drinking. There is now good evidence that the cause/effect relationship is just the reverse. Vaillant (1983) started tracking a group of 600 adolescents before any drinking problems had arisen. He concluded, among other things, that a difficult life was rarely a major reason for developing alcohol dependence. In a *Nova* segment broadcast on public television, Vaillant said, "I found to my surprise [that] alcoholics are depressed because they drink; they don't drink because they are depressed." This finding, of course, is consistent with the observation that alcohol leads to the depletion of norepinephrine and is also consistent with the Endorphin Compensation Hypothesis that was discussed in the previous section.

Genes, Personality, and Alcoholism

While there is little evidence for an addictive personality, there is evidence that one may have a genetic predisposition or vulnerability to alcoholism (see Holden, 1985; Kline, 1985). First, there is considerable evidence that the likelihood of becoming an alcoholic is much greater if one biological parent is an alcoholic and even greater when both biological parents are alcoholics. While 10% of the population are considered alcoholics, for example, 25% of the sons of alcoholic fathers are alcoholics. As the environment obviously contributes to the development of alcoholism, it is important to know whether the child was raised by a biological parent or a foster parent. Comparative studies have shown that the rate of alcoholism is higher among the natural children of alcoholics than among their foster children (Holden, 1985). This finding indicates that while both biological and environmental factors are important, the role of genetic inheritance is greater.

A character disorder called the antisocial personality appears to make certain people susceptible to alcoholism. About 25% of the total alcoholic population are classified as antisocial personalities—a high ratio if you consider that the antisocial personality is found in only about 3% of the general population. The antisocial personality appears early in childhood and is characterized by impulsivity, egocentricity, short attention span, sensation seeking, aggressiveness, and poor socialization. There is good evidence that the antisocial personality is inherited. A study of alcoholics found that when one parent of an alcoholic was an alcoholic antisocial personality, the likelihood that the offspring would also have an antisocial personality was 52%; when both parents were alcoholic antisocial personalities, the rate was 71% (see Holden, 1985).

Evidence for a genetic predisposition also comes from studies of the brain-wave patterns of alcoholics (see Holden, 1985). It has been shown that a brain-wave pattern called the P3 wave is deficient in most chronic alcoholics. A study of the sons of alcoholics, ranging in age from 7 to 13, found that 35% showed a similar deficiency—a rather high figure in view of the fact that it is found in a very small proportion of the general population. This brain-wave pattern has been linked to attention and learning. The fact that these young sons of alcoholics did not drink suggests that it is a genetic predisposition and not simply a result of years of drinking.

It is not yet clear why people who have an antisocial personality and people who are deficient in the P3 wave are particularly vulnerable to alcoholism. Further research is needed to identify the mechanism involved.

Controlled Drinking as a Treatment for Alcoholism

In recent years research has been launched to determine whether people who are abusing alcohol (drinking too much) can learn to cut down on the amount they drink (e.g., Miller and Muñoz, 1976; Sobell & Sobell, 1976). While this research has come under vigorous attack, evidence mounts that some people who have been classified as alcoholics (that is, uncontrolled drinkers) can learn to drink in moderation. In fact, Miller (1983) has reported that 23 of 24 studies on this question have found the reduced drinking technique superior to other treatment techniques for a range of alcohol abuse problems and that no study has shown that abstinence is more effective overall than moderation. It is important to note that we still do not know what determines whether a person can return to a pattern of moderate drinking. Values, beliefs about control, and stress are just some of the factors that need to be explored further in the context of controlled drinking.

Summary

Several issues have been raised by the study of the use and abuse of alcohol. First, McClelland has shown that alcohol stimulates power thoughts. He has suggested that people drink in order to experience the feelings of power that alcohol seems to produce. According to his theory, people who have a strong need for power will drink more when they are unable to satisfy that need by interacting with their environment. There is also evidence that people drink in order to enhance sexual feelings. Interestingly, men become more aggressive and women become more passive or accommodating after drinking alcohol. In view of the fact that alcohol provides feelings of control (power), it is not surprising that people tend to drink when they feel stressed. In order to explain why people often drink more after uncontrollable stressful events than after controllable stressful events, Volpicelli has proposed the Endorphin Compensation Hypothesis. While it has been assumed for some time that depression leads to alcohol abuse, experiments have shown that the relationship may be just the reverse: alcohol abuse leads to depression.

There is growing evidence that alcoholism has a genetic basis. Sons of alcoholic parents are more likely to be alcoholics than sons of nonalcoholic parents. If the alcoholic father also has an antisocial personality, the likelihood of alcoholism in the son is increased, and the son is likely to have the same antisocial personality. Whether it is possible to teach alcoholics to control their drinking has become a very controversial topic. There is reasonably good evidence that some alcoholics can learn to control their drinking.

Main Points

1. Because drug addiction is usually preceded by drug abuse, the current strategy for studying addiction is to identify the factors that lead to drug abuse.
2. Despite the many links between drugs and health disorders, many people use drugs.
3. There is little evidence that drug use will inevitably lead to addiction.
4. There is no clear evidence that "hard" drugs are more likely to produce health disorders than "soft" drugs.
5. The suggestion that the environment is responsible for addiction has received very modest support.
6. There is no clear evidence that only psychologically disturbed people use drugs, even such drugs as heroin.
7. Current models of drug addiction postulate that the tendency to use and abuse drugs is governed jointly by the biochemical properties of a drug, the environment, and personality factors.
8. Most commonly used drugs have reinforcing properties that can account for the tendency to use those drugs repeatedly.
9. The reinforcing properties of drugs tend to vary with environmental conditions.
10. The fact that such drugs as amphetamines activate the self-reward systems of the brain suggests that one reason people take drugs is to experience the positive affect that occurs when such centers are activated.
11. The discovery of opiate receptors in the brain has led researchers to suggest that the use of opiates is a means of tapping into certain naturally occurring reward/survival mechanisms.
12. Solomon's opponent process theory suggests that addiction is due, at least in part, to the strengthening of an opponent process. People need to increase drug intake to overcome the opposing reaction.
13. According to the principles of classical and instrumental conditioning, if a drug that produces reinforcing effects is used in the presence of certain stimuli, those stimuli will come, over time, to be associated with the internal state produced by the drugs.
14. The phenomenon of state-dependent learning suggests that the tendency to use a drug may be triggered by certain internal states, such as stress and anxiety.
15. According to the learning model, a drug habit may be triggered by several different and often unrelated cues. Alcoholism in France can be readily explained by such a model.
16. Constitutional or motivational differences may increase the probability of certain types of learning. Such differences may thus increase the likelihood that a person will acquire a drug habit.
17. Availability of a drug increases the likelihood that a person will discover the drug's reinforcing properties.
18. Beliefs or expectations about what a drug will do have an important influence on the way people behave when they use drugs.
19. The fact that people's reactions to drugs vary with the situation and with the drug taker's culture raises serious questions about the disease model of addiction.
20. Beliefs about both control and self-change play an important role in determining whether a person becomes addicted.
21. According to the interaction model of addiction, the extent of a drug's reinforcing properties depends on environmental conditions. An environment

that is a source of positive reward tends to reduce the reinforcing properties of the drug.

22. There is no clear evidence for an addictive personality.
23. There is evidence, however, that the use of drugs to escape a noxious or aversive situation is more likely to be associated with drug addiction.
24. The use of drugs is moderated by such factors as commitment to other activities, social class, peer and parental influences, culture and ethnicity, adoption of the principle of moderation, a strong need to achieve and a weak need to avoid failure, and commitment to the values of the society in which one lives.
25. Alcohol has been linked to the need for power.
26. Men drink to enhance their feelings of power, whereas women drink to allay their anxieties about their femininity.
27. On a short-term basis, alcohol can reduce feelings of stress.
28. According to the Endorphin Compensation Hypothesis, organisms are more motivated to drink after an uncontrollable stressful event than after a controllable one because an uncontrollable stressful event produces a greater depletion of the endorphin stores. Alcohol is assumed to have the capacity to stimulate endorphin activity and thereby reduce the negative motivation that is associated with decreased concentrations of endorphins.
29. Depression is probably the result of alcohol abuse rather than its cause.
30. There is considerable evidence that genetic inheritance plays an important role in making people vulnerable to alcoholism.
31. There is growing evidence that at least some people who abuse alcohol can learn to control their drinking.

Aggression
and Compliance

Is aggression in our genes?
Are brain structures involved in aggressive behavior?
What is the relation between sex and aggression?
How does our body respond when we become angry?
Do we use aggression to control people in our environment?
Do crowding, heat, erotic stimulation, or other conditions make us more aggressive or less aggressive?
Is there an aggressive personality?
How does early experience affect aggressiveness?
Does television really make people aggressive?
Is it possible to drain off aggressive energy?

The term *aggression* is used to refer to a wide variety of behaviors, of which some are considered socially desirable and some socially undesirable. A person who works long and hard to win a business contract or a person who competes with others to obtain the top position in a large company or an athlete who manages to become the top scorer on the team is typically viewed in our society as being aggressive in a socially acceptable and desirable way. However, a driver who honks his horn at an elderly lady who is being cautious about entering a line of fast-moving traffic or a person who challenges another person to a fight in order to settle an argument is typically regarded as being aggressive in a socially unacceptable or undesirable way. The question is why some forms of aggression are socially acceptable while others are not.

Definitions

Is Aggression Good or Bad?

In general, we make a rather fine distinction between behaviors intended to harm another person and those not intended to harm (see Baron, 1977). The emphasis here is on *intended*, since it is not uncommon in the course of competitive behavior for one person to harm another unintentionally. A person who competes for a top executive position and obtains that position causes others to lose. The very nature of competition means that some will succeed and others will fail. A football player may injure another player while blocking for a teammate. If it was not his intention to injure but rather to provide a needed opening for his teammate, the injury is typically regarded as unintentional. Unintentional harm may occur in a variety of situations. A driver might accidentally hit another car, a clerk might inadvertently short-change a customer, or a professor might err in grading a student's essay, giving a lower grade than the student deserves. The fact that these acts were unintentional means they were not acts of aggression. In contrast, the driver who honks his horn at the elderly lady is directing his behavior specifically at the lady whom he perceives as the source of his immediate problem. His horn honking is intended to prod an obviously unsure person into entering a line of fast-moving traffic. Forcing her to make a bad decision could be fatal.

What if a person wants to harm another person but, for some reason, fails? For example, angered by the taunts of another person, you might swing and miss, or, because the other person ducked, the object you threw did not hit her. Because these acts were intended to harm, even though they didn't, they are acts of aggression.

Although the term *aggression* is used to describe both socially desirable and socially undesirable behaviors, psychologists have, for the most part, focused their research on the socially undesirable aggressive behaviors. Why is it that one human will attempt to harm another? What are the conditions that lead to aggression and violence? In this chapter we will examine some of the research that has to do with humans harming other humans.

Provoked versus Unprovoked Aggression

The public, of course, shares psychologists' interest in the question of why humans harm other humans. Daily our papers are filled with examples of violence. Not only do humans inflict physical harm on other humans, but they vandalize public and private property to the tune of millions of dollars annually. Many people are concerned, as they read about violence of various kinds or hear it reported on the radio and television, that they too might become victims of violence. What alarms people in particular is that there seems to be a great deal of unprovoked violence in our society. Many people are afraid to leave their homes for fear that they will become victims of unprovoked violence in the street or that their property will be vandalized or burglarized in their absence.

Although unprovoked violence may be a very real possibility for most of us at some point in our lives, the actual probability of being a victim of unprovoked violence appears to be relatively low. Most violence can be classified as provoked. By words or actions a person provokes another person to behave aggressively. We are probably all aware that calling someone stupid is likely to elicit anger accompanied by some form of retaliatory aggression. Shoving or elbowing to get to the front of a line is almost certain to provoke a retaliatory shove, a retaliatory elbow, or a sharp verbal rebuff. Imagine what your neighbor might think and feel if you deliberately threw a rock through her window or tripped her as she walked in front of you. Such behavior would be an obvious act of provocation.

Physical versus Verbal Aggression

Although most of us provoke other people in one way or another, rarely do we do anything as extreme as throw a rock through a neighbor's window or trip someone as she passes us. Certain forms of aggression are almost sure to result in severe retaliation. Most people try to avoid doing things that will precipitate physical aggression. Children may resort to physical aggression, but our culture tends systematically to discourage physical aggression. By the time humans have reached their adult years, most aggression is limited to verbal exchanges (Patterson, 1976).

Individual Differences and Aggression

When we consider aggressive behaviors it is important to consider compliant behaviors as well. Whereas some people become aggressive under certain conditions, others become submissive or compliant. For example, one person caught for speeding may become highly abusive to the police officer issuing the ticket; another person may be very polite and apologetic. Why the difference? Is it simply due to differences in learning, or do the two persons perceive the situation quite differently? In this chapter we will examine some of the possible reasons that people react so differently to the same set of cues. Why do some people not become aggressive when it appears they should? Why do others become aggressive when such a response is totally inappropriate? Why do some people escalate aggression when they could just as easily de-escalate it? Why do others become totally submissive in their responses?

Summary

Psychologists typically use the word *aggression* to refer to those behaviors that are intended to harm another person. The word *intended* is the key, because one can accidentally harm another person out of negligence or in the normal course of competitive behavior, as in an athletic contest. Although some acts of aggression are unprovoked, most aggressive acts are provoked. Psychologists have, for the most part, focused their research on provoked aggression. Although children will frequently use physical aggression when provoked, adults tend to avoid physical exchanges and to retaliate verbally to acts of provocation. Wide individual variation has been observed in humans who are provoked. The question arises why this variation exists.

Biological Factors

Although aggressive behavior in humans differs in many respects from aggressive behavior in animals, work with animals has had a great impact on the understanding of human aggressive behavior. The work with animals shows, in a rather pure form, the biological roots of aggressive behaviors. Although humans share these biological roots, cultural influences have modified, to a very large degree, the expression of aggression. In order to appreciate the nature of the biological roots of aggression, we will briefly review some of the work on genetics and some conclusions reached by ethologists from their study of animal behavior.

Genetics and Aggression

There is no doubt that animals can be bred specifically for aggression. There are numerous examples of fighting cocks, fighting dogs, and other animals that have been selectively bred for that characteristic (McLearn, 1969). In a very extensive study of the genetics of aggression, mice were selectively bred for both high and low aggression (Lagerspetz, 1964). Although there are no comparable data for humans, there is some evidence that the expression of aggression in humans is determined in part by genetics. For example, certain chromosomal abnormalities in humans may reduce the tendency to control aggressive impulses. The Klinefelter syndrome (Burnand, Hunter, & Hoggart, 1967) and the XYY syndrome (Kessler & Moos, 1970) have been suggested as two chromosomal conditions that appear to reduce the tendency to control impulses, with a resulting increase in aggressive tendencies.

The ethologists started with the Darwinian assumption that aggressive behavior evolved in order to ensure the survival of the species (Lorenz, 1966). According to this view, aggressive behavior should be viewed not as good or bad but as a factor that contributes to the species' survival. Within the Darwinian framework, an individual's survival is important only insofar as it allows the individual to reproduce and thus ensure the continuation of the species. It is not surprising, therefore, that the early work of the ethologists focused on aggressive behavior patterns that facilitated the animal's opportunity to reproduce. Any animal that did not engage in appropriate aggressive behaviors to ensure its own survival would, of course, not reproduce, and its "nonadaptive" genetic structure would not be passed along to succeeding generations. An animal that had been appropriately aggressive would pass along the appropriate genetic structure.

Territorial behavior. One pattern of behavior that seems to be tied to reproductive activities has come to be called "territorial," or "home range," behaviors (Moyer, 1976). Although territorial behaviors are not limited to mating and reproduction, such behavior seems to be a fundamental aspect of mating and reproduction in a number of species. In many species of birds, for example, the male will select a particular territory and define its boundaries through songs. If another male bird should enter that territory or home range, the "owner" is almost certain to defend its borders. Once the territory has been established (and recognized by others of the species), the bird will attempt to attract a female by displaying his feathers, puffing himself up, or whatever method is characteristic of his species. A similar pattern occurs in other species. Wolves establish territories, often marking the boundaries by urinating at certain points along the border. For our purposes, what is interesting about territorial behavior is the systematic pattern of aggressive and submissive behaviors that tend to occur depending on whether an animal is on its own territory or is on the territory of another member of the species.

In general, animals that are territorial are more likely to stand their ground and fight when they are on their own territory. They are more likely to flee when they are on the territory of another animal. Thus the tendency to fight or to flee is not a stable characteristic of the animal but rather is governed by external cues. It is interesting that this behavior tends to hold irrespective of the animal's size, age, or fighting experience. In general, it can also be said that animals are more likely to win on their own territory. Winning, however, does not mean that one of the animals is killed or mauled. In fact, the confrontation of two animals is typically characterized by a series of threats, counterthreats, and finally some type of submissive response from one of the animals. Typically the invader makes the submissive response and then retreats. The submissive response is usually a highly stereotyped response that is common to all members of the species. It appears to be immediately recognized and can be characterized as innate rather than learned. Figure 10-1 shows a dog with hostile intentions and the same dog in a more humble frame of mind. It has been suggested that the submissive response in dogs and related animals makes the animal look smaller and hides the canine teeth, an important weapon in the dog's arsenal that the dominant dog is quick to display. In many primates the submissive response involves presenting the hindquarters to the aggressor. The sexual overtones of this response have intrigued ethologists for some time. It has been suggested that such a response elicits behaviors that are incompatible with aggression and therefore is effective in stopping aggression. Many a female has learned that she can turn off aggressive responses in males by giving or emphasizing a variety of sexual signals.

It is important to note that the threats, the counterthreats (if any), and the submissive response tend to prevent physical contact that might result in harm to one or both animals. It can be argued, in evolutionary terms, that it is highly adaptive for animals to maintain order without physically harming each other. If aggressive animals tended to fight and kill other aggressive animals of the same species, the aggressive genes would eventually be eliminated from the species. Hence, in order for aggressive behavior patterns to evolve, it was necessary for intraspecies aggression to be kept to a minimum. The stereotyped pattern of threats and counterthreats serves this function while still maintaining a type of order that permits reproduction of the species (Alcock, 1979).

Although humans use physical posturing to show threat and submission, language appears to have replaced physical posturing to a very large degree. By

(a)

(b)

Figure 10-1. (*a*) Dog approaching another dog with hostile intentions; (*b*) the same dog in a humble and affectionate frame of mind (Darwin, 1965)

fighting through language, humans can also avoid physically harming each other. Unfortunately, heated debates can sometimes turn into physical encounters, but this is rare.

Humans constantly exhibit territorial behavior. We live in houses, apartments, condominiums, where the boundaries are defined by walls. If land is attached to the dwelling, it is often carefully fenced or landscaped to define the boundaries. Other people are permitted to enter our territory only if we give them permission to do so. The criminal code not only allows us to defend that territory against intruders (within limits) but sanctions in our homes behaviors that are not permitted everywhere (sex, alcohol consumption, nudity). Offices are often treated as personal territory. We must seek permission to enter someone's office and usually are required to conduct ourselves in certain stereotyped ways that are reminiscent of the submissive behavior displayed by animals when they enter another animal's territory. Automobiles are often treated much like offices. Vans and motor homes, however, are more like extensions of one's residence. People who camp often establish their territory by stringing up clotheslines, parking their cars in certain locations, setting up their chairs in certain places, and even in some circumstances putting up a temporary fence.

The fact that humans are more likely to engage in reproductive behaviors in their own territory gives credence to the ethologists' argument that territorial behavior serves a similar biological function in humans and in animals. The fact that humans engage in analogous behavior does not necessarily mean, of course, that the behavior is necessarily mediated by the same set of variables. It is interesting, nevertheless, to note that humans tend to establish territories and to behave in certain ways within them.

Dominance. Another pattern of behavior that often accompanies reproductive activities is dominance. In a number of species, the members of a group tend to order themselves in terms of dominance, often by a series of threats and physical encounters from which the physically stronger or more capable fighter (perhaps the more cunning) emerges as the winner. In a number of species the most dominant male (often regarded as the most aggressive) is the only one that mates with the females. From an evolutionary point of view, this arrangement ensures that the genes of the more dominant males will be passed along. The assumption is that the characteristics of the dominant males are those characteristics that are most likely to ensure the survival of the species. Since the good fighter may be the most cunning and not necessarily the strongest, this selective breeding process does not necessarily breed strength over intelligence. Rather, the selective breeding process seems to encourage a combination of strength and intelligence (cunning).

Once the dominance hierarchy is established, it tends to remain relatively stable for a time. The more dominant animals threaten the less dominant, who make submissive responses. If a less dominant animal should be so bold as to threaten a more dominant animal, the dominant one typically retaliates at once. Thus the dominance hierarchy serves to maintain the degree of order necessary for survival while keeping physical harm to a minimum (Alcock, 1979).

Because the urge or instinct to mate is very strong, the dominance hierarchy is potentially unstable. As younger males become stronger and gain experience in fighting, they are less likely to remain on the sidelines as other males mate with the females. Eventually they will challenge the hierarchy and in the process alter the hierarchy. This process ensures that the more physically capable and cunning fighter will reach the top of the hierarchy and thus exert control over the gene pool of the species.

The more dominant animal, it appears, does more than contribute to the gene pool. In many instances he provides the leadership required to procure food or fight the enemy. Thus the dominance hierarchy serves to assist in the acquisition of skills as well as in the expression of cooperative social behavior (Alcock, 1979).

It should be noted that the dominance hierarchy described above holds only for certain species (Moyer, 1976). Nevertheless, the pattern is sufficiently prevalent to be regarded as important for the understanding of aggressive behavior in general. The important question from our point of view is whether this pattern of behavior also holds for humans. Although it is true that humans have something analogous to dominance hierarchies (social classes, the executive ladder, bureaucratic hierarchies) and that certain threats and submission patterns exist within these hierarchies, one major difference for humans is that each of us belongs to a variety of hierarchical systems and a single person is likely to occupy different positions within the various systems he or she belongs to. Nevertheless, the dominance hierarchy strongly affects our freedom to express aggression against other members of the hierarchy. Whether these human behavior patterns are biologically determined or culturally conditioned is difficult to determine. At present we can only conclude that these patterns are analogous to those in certain animal species. The analogous behaviors suggest that aggression in humans and in animals may arise from similar biological structures (that is, that the patterns are homologous).

Both territory and dominance have been examined as they pertain to human behavior. The term *territory* in human research refers to those places where individuals perceive themselves as having a relatively high degree of control over access by others (see Altman, 1975; Sundstrom, 1977). *Territorial dominance* refers to the tendency of humans in their own territories to dominate competitive interactions with visitors (Conroy & Sundstrom, 1977). In an experiment to determine some of the conditions in which territorial dominance emerges, pairs of subjects were matched for similarity of opinions. The results indicated that territorial dominance emerges in pairs with dissimilar opinions but hospitality emerges in pairs with similar opinions (Conroy & Sundstrom, 1977). Thus it appears that other factors in addition to territory govern the tendency to dominate in humans.

Kinds of Aggression

The physiological basis of aggression has turned out to be quite complex. Not only have several brain centers been identified as being involved in aggression, but the activity or sensitivity of these systems seems to vary among individuals and in accordance with the levels of certain chemicals circulating in the blood (Moyer, 1976). The complexity can be understood if we recognize that the term *aggression* is used as a broad category covering a number of behaviors that share certain common properties. At least eight types of aggression can be identified (Moyer, 1976):

1. *Predatory*. Attack behavior that an animal directs against its natural prey.
2. *Intermale*. Threat, attack, or submissive behavior by a male in response to a strange male.
3. *Fear-induced*. Aggressive behavior that occurs when an animal is confined. Attack behavior is usually preceded by an attempt to escape.
4. *Territorial*. Threat or attack behavior when an intruder is discovered on home-range territory or submissive and retreat behavior when an animal is confronted while intruding.
5. *Maternal*. Attack or threat directed by the female toward an intruder when her young are present.
6. *Irritable*. Attack or destructive behavior directed toward any object as the result of frustration, pain, deprivation, or any other stressor.
7. *Instrumental*. Aggressive behavior that has previously resulted in some kind of reward.
8. *Sex-related*. Aggressive behavior elicited by the same stimuli that elicit sexual behavior.

Though some of these forms of aggression are more relevant to behavior in animals than in humans, all have at one time or another been treated as aggressive behaviors. Moyer (1976) has pointed out that somewhat different neural systems are involved in each of these types of aggression. A full discussion of the various types of aggression and the neural systems that support them is beyond the scope of this chapter. I will confine my discussion to some of the basic neural systems and the general principles that have emerged from research on such systems.

Neurological Structures and Aggression
Several brain structures have been implicated in various kinds of aggressive behavior (Mark & Ervin, 1970). Figure 10-2 is a cross section of the brain, showing several of the structures that have been implicated in aggressive behavior.

The hypothalamus. The hypothalamus was one of the first brain centers to be implicated in aggressive behaviors. Bard (1928) showed, for example, that the posterior hypothalamus is important for producing a rage response. In the same year Hess (1928) published data showing that another area of the hypothalamus is also implicated in a well-integrated rage response. Still other studies have shown that the hypothalamus is involved in attack or predatory behavior (Egger & Flynn, 1963; Hess & Brugger, 1943) and defensive behaviors (Roberts & Kiess, 1964; Roberts, Steinberg, & Means, 1967). The fact that different areas of the hypothalamus are involved in different types of aggressive behavior provides rather clear evidence that there is no single mechanism for all aggressive behaviors. Rather, it

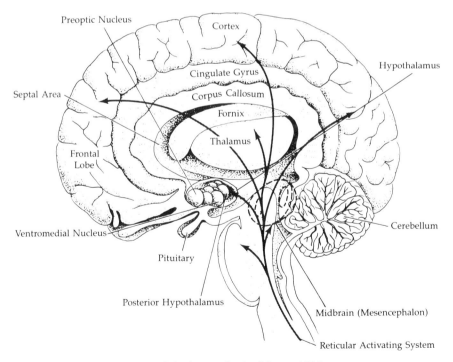

Figure 10-2. Cross section of the human brain (Moyer, 1976)

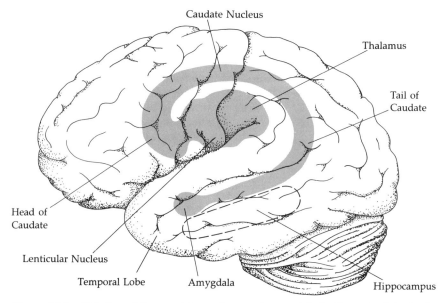

Figure 10-3.   Relation of the caudate nucleus and amygdala to the rest of the brain (Moyer, 1976)

appears that each aggressive behavior must be treated as distinctive, at least at the neurological level.

The limbic system.   The limbic system has also been clearly implicated in aggressive behaviors. Within the limbic system at least three major circuits (hippocampus, amygdala, and septum) have been implicated to some degree in aggressive behaviors (see Figures 10-2 and 10-3). Stimulation of the amygdala and the septum often causes attack and defensive behaviors; lesioning produces a marked calming effect. The septal area seems to be additionally involved in feelings of pleasure, often with sexual overtones (Grossman, 1967).

In reviewing the animal studies on the relation between the amygdala and aggression, Moyer (1976) has concluded that different areas of the amygdala appear to control different types of aggression, even though these areas overlap to some degree. He has noted, for example, that the amygdala contains separate locations for fear-induced, irritable, and predatory aggression. Septal lesions in rats can produce a temporary increase in the tendency to make irritable, as opposed to predatory, attacks on a mouse. Similarly, lesioned rats show an increase in fighting when shocked (Moyer, 1976). This research suggests that the septum may exert an inhibitory function, so that lesioning increases aggressive behavior.

Although lesions in rats have been shown to reduce shock-induced fighting, such lesions have been shown to increase rats' tendency to attack the prod used to shock them (Blanchard, Blanchard, & Fial, 1970). The differences in the reactions suggest that different neural systems mediate responses in these two situations. The role of the limbic system is still not totally understood, but it seems to be important in the instigation and organization of aggressive behaviors that are elicited by a variety of environmental conditions.

The Klüver-Bucy syndrome.   In a now-famous series of studies, Heinrich Klüver and Paul Bucy (1937, 1938, 1939) produced a striking behavioral change by removing the tips of the temporal lobes of normally aggressive rhesus monkeys. The operation removed the amygdala, the anterior hippocampus, and much of the temporal lobe (see Figure 10-3). Monkeys that had been very difficult to manage suddenly became tame, friendly, and easy to handle. They began to approach and explore normally feared objects, such as a snake or a burning match. Further, they showed unusual oral behavior. They would mouth everything within reach, including snakes, a burning match, nails, dirt, and even feces. The male monkeys became hypersexual, masturbating constantly or attempting to copulate with male and female monkeys that were unreceptive or even dogs and cats if they were available. Finally, the monkeys tended to be abnormally restless and active.

Since Klüver and Bucy discovered this unusual pattern of behavior, other research with animals has shown that the fear and anger reduction observed by Klüver and Bucy can be produced by lesioning of the amygdala (for example, Karli & Vergnes, 1965; Siegel & Flynn, 1968). Cutting the tops of the temporal lobes has been shown to control aggressiveness in schizophrenics (Terzian & Ore, 1955) as well as psychopaths (Vallardares & Corbalan, 1959). Most surgical attempts to control aggression in humans, however, have involved selective lesions to the amygdala. The results of this research are unequivocal. Amygdalectomy in humans produces a marked reduction in destructiveness, hostility, aggressiveness, and even excitability (for example, Heimburger, Whitlock, & Kalsbeck, 1966; Narabayashi, 1972). Many patients who had been difficult to manage became model patients after the operation.

Temporal lobe pathology.   One of the most widely publicized cases of extreme hostility that may have resulted from temporal lobe pathology was that of Charles Whitman. He was an introspective young man with no previous history of violence who one night killed his wife and his mother. The next morning he went to the University of Texas administration building, where he killed the receptionist and barricaded himself in the tower. From the top of the tower he used his high-power rifle equipped with a telescopic lens to shoot anyone he could bring into view with his powerful sights. During the next 90 minutes he killed 14 persons and injured another 24. His shooting spree ended only when the police were able to kill him. The autopsy showed a tumor whose exact location was difficult to pinpoint because of the wounds inflicted by police bullets; the evidence seemed to indicate, however, that the tumor was located on the medial part of the temporal lobe.

Whitman's case is particularly interesting because he kept notes on his feelings and had consulted with a psychiatrist about them several months earlier. He revealed to the psychiatrist that he sometimes became so angry that he would like to go to the top of the university tower and start shooting people. The letter he wrote just before he killed his wife and mother provides some insight into his tortured mental state.

> I don't quite understand what it is that compels me to type this letter. Perhaps it is to leave some vague reason for the actions I have recently performed.
>
> I don't really understand myself these days. I am supposed to be an average, reasonable and intelligent young man. However, lately (I can't recall when it started) I have been a victim of many unusual and irrational thoughts. These thoughts constantly recur, and it requires a tremendous mental effort

to concentrate on useful and progressive tasks. In March when my parents made a physical break I noticed a great deal of stress. I consulted a Dr. Cochrum at the University Health Center and asked him to recommend someone that I could consult with about some psychiatric disorders I felt I had. I talked with a doctor once for about two hours and tried to convey to him my fears that I felt overcome (sick) by overwhelming violent impulses. After one session I never saw the doctor again and since then I have been fighting my mental turmoil alone, and seemingly to no avail. After my death I wish that an autopsy would be performed on me to see if there is any visible physical disorder. I have had some tremendous headaches in the past and have consumed two large bottles of Excedrin in the past three months.

It was after much thought that I decided to kill my wife Kathy, tonight after I pick her up from work. . . . I love her dearly, and she has been a fine wife to me as any man could ever hope to have. I cannot rationally pin-point any specific reason for doing this. I don't know whether it is selfishness or if I don't want her to have to face the embarrassment my actions would surely cause her. At this time though, the prominent reason in my mind is that I truly do not consider this world worth living in, and am prepared to die, and I do not want to leave her to suffer alone in it. I intend to kill her as painlessly as possible. . . .

After he had killed his mother and wife, he wrote:

I imagine it appears that I brutally killed both of my loved ones. I was only trying to do a good and thorough job.

If my life insurance policy is valid please see that all the worthless checks I wrote this weekend are made good. Please pay off all my debts. I am 25 years old and have never been financially independent. Donate the rest anonymously to a mental health foundation. Maybe research can prevent further tragedies of this type.*

Other structures involved in aggression.   Lesions in several other structures of the brain have also been found to decrease aggressive behavior. Cingulum ablations (removal of small parts of the cingulum) have been shown to reduce anger, violence, aggression, and agitation (Le Beau, 1952). Lesions in the cingulate gyrus, although they do not eliminate outbursts of anger, have been shown to reduce both the intensity and the duration of such outbursts (for example, Ledesma & Pancagua, 1969; Tow & Whitty, 1953). Lesions in several areas of the thalamus have also been shown to reduce pathological aggression (for example, Poblete et al., 1970; Spiegel et al., 1951). The fact that lesions in various structures of the brain either eliminate or greatly reduce aggressive behaviors emphasizes the point made by Moyer that the expression of aggression is probably controlled by a number of interdependent neural systems, each of which may have a specialized as well as a general role in the expression of aggression. Because a number of structures appear to be involved in the expression of aggression, the question we must deal with next is what factors affect whether or not a particular neural system is active or sensitive.

*From *The Psychobiology of Aggression*, by K. E. Moyer. Copyright © by K. E. Moyer. Reprinted by permission of Harper & Row, Publishers, Inc.

Social Rank and the Expression of Aggression

Although aggressive behaviors may be controlled by a number of neurological structures, it is clear from other research that the tendency to express aggression is also affected by certain social factors. Specifically, social rank seems to be important in determining whether aggression will be inhibited. A study by José Delgado (1967) clearly illustrates this point. An electrode was permanently implanted in the thalamus (nucleus ventralis posterior lateralis) of a monkey called Lina and she was stimulated by means of a radio transmitter when she was low, moderate, or high in dominance. Delgado altered her dominance position by changing the composition of the group of monkeys living with Lina in a large cage. He found that if Lina was stimulated when she was high in the dominance hierarchy, she initiated a relatively large number of attacks; if she was stimulated when she was moderate or low in the hierarchy, however, she initiated very few attacks, as Table 10-1 indicates. Table 10-1 also reveals that Lina was the recipient of many attacks when she was low in the dominance hierarchy and received no attacks when she was high. These results indicate that the social structure plays an important role in determining whether aggressive tendencies are expressed (see also Delgado, 1963, 1966, 1975).

Work by Pribram further illustrates this point (see Pribram, 1976). In one study Pribram and his colleagues set out to determine whether bilateral amygdalectomies would affect fighting and how this might in turn affect the position of a dominant monkey in a colony (Rosvold, Mirsky, & Pribram, 1954). As expected, the lesions resulted in a shift in the dominance hierarchy, as shown in Figures 10-4 and 10-5. The dominant monkey, Dave, became totally submissive. When they subjected the newly dominant monkey, Zeke, to the same operation, he too became submissive, sinking to the bottom of the dominance hierarchy. To their surprise, when they attempted to do this a third time, the newly dominant monkey, Riva, did not become submissive or drop in the hierarchy. This unexpected finding can be understood, Pribram explains, if we note that the number 2 monkey in the dominance hierarchy (Herby) did not challenge Riva. His nonaggressive personality allowed Riva to remain in the top spot. This finding is illustrated in Figures 10-6 and 10-7.

These results show, Pribram (1976) argues, that the amygdala, like other structures that have been implicated in aggression, may have to do not with aggression itself but rather with some brain process that mediates an organism's sensitivity to the social environment. Perhaps the amygdala somehow mediates the way an organism gains or maintains control in the social environment. Therefore, when the amygdala is lesioned in some way, the ability to gain or maintain control is lost or disrupted. If aggressive behavior is a means of gaining control, then it too should be lost or disrupted. Thus when Herby failed to challenge Riva, Riva

Table 10-1. Number of attacks initiated and received by Lina as a function of dominance (Delgado, 1967)

Lina's dominance status	Attacks initiated by Lina	Attacks received by Lina
Low	1	15
Moderate	6	1
High	40	0

Note: Numbers are based on 120 experimental sessions at each dominance level.

Dave 1
Dominant, Self-Assured, Feared

Zeke 2
Aggressive, Attacker

Riva 3
Aggressive, Active

Herby 4
Placid, Unaggressive

Larry 8
Submissive, Cowering,
Frequently Attacked

Shorty 7

Submissive to Others,
Aggressive toward Larry

Arnie 6
Noisy, Eager

Benny 5
Alert, Active Food Getter

Figure 10-4. Dominance hierarchy in a colony of monkeys before any operation (Pribram, 1976)

remained in the top position by default. As we shall see, there is good reason to argue that humans and animals have a need or tendency to control events or other people or animals and that aggression is simply a means of obtaining that control. If this is true, it could be argued that the bilateral amygdala lesions disrupted the means or behavior necessary to gain or maintain control, not the basic motive to control.

Chemical Factors and Aggression

Hormones appear to play a very basic role in modulating the activity of certain neural systems involved in aggression (Moyer, 1976). When certain hormones are present, the individual is more likely to engage in aggressive behavior. When certain other hormones are present, the individual is less likely to engage in aggressive behavior. Whether the individual engages in aggressive behavior, of course, is not determined solely by the activity of certain neural systems. As we have noted, aggressive behavior is often elicited by events in the external environment. The presence or absence of a given hormone will not produce aggressive behavior unless the environmental conditions are appropriate. As I shall discuss shortly, the expression of aggression is also affected by learned and cognitive factors. Hence, even if neural systems for aggression are active and the environmental conditions are appropriate, we will not necessarily observe aggressive behavior. Nevertheless, if neural systems are active because of the presence of a certain hormone, aggressive behavior will be more likely.

Zeke 1
Dominant, Aggressive

Riva 2
Daring, Competes with Zeke

Herby 3

Benny 4

Arnie 5

Larry 7
Dominates and Attacks Dave

Shorty 6

Dave 8
Completely Submissive, Fearful

Figure 10-5.   Dominance hierarchy after bilateral amygdalectomy in Dave, formerly the dominant monkey (Pribram, 1976)

A great deal of research has been done on the relations between sex hormones and aggressive behaviors in animals. This research has clearly indicated that the sex hormones play an important role (for example, Levy & King, 1953). Only recently has it been possible to extend this research to humans. In general, the results with humans seem to parallel the findings with animals. (For a good review of the animal research literature, see Moyer, 1976, pp. 227-274.)

Testosterone and male aggression.   At about age 9, human males show a dramatic increase in testosterone level, which rises about tenfold by age 10-15 (Hamburg, 1971). This increase has been suggested as an explanation for the increase in aggressive behavior that adolescent boys tend to show at this time (Moyer, 1976). Although further research is needed to verify this hypothesis, other research tends to provide some converging evidence that testosterone is, at least in part, responsible for the greater amount of aggressive behavior in young adolescent males.

Though the testosterone level varies widely, it tends to decrease during the twenties. Persky, Smith, and Basu (1971) found that the average testosterone level of a group of men aged 30–66 was half that of a group of men aged 17–28. If testosterone is at least partly responsible for aggression, aggressive behaviors would be expected to decrease somewhat after the twenties. This is exactly what Persky and his colleagues found. Older men were less inclined to be aggressive than younger men, as measured by the Buss-Durkee Hostility Inventory.

Riva 1
Dominant,
Not Threatened by Others

Herby 2

Benny 3

Arnie 4

Zeke 7
Submissive to Others,
Intermittently Aggressive
toward Dave

Shorty 5

Dave 8
Cringes, Avoids Interaction

Larry 6

Figure 10-6.   Dominance hierarchy after bilateral amygdalectomy in Zeke (Pribram, 1976)

Further evidence that androgen (testosterone) plays an important role in aggression has been gained from studies of the effects of castration. Castration has been used primarily to treat sex offenders. Follow-up studies of castrated sex offenders have indicated that castration not only reduces the sex drive but reduces hostility and aggressive tendencies (Bremer, 1959; Hawke, 1950; Sturup, 1961). Injections of testosterone in castrated males have been shown to restore the previous aggressive tendencies (Hawke, 1950). Therefore, the reduction of aggression was very likely due to a decrease in testosterone level, not simply a by-product of the obvious trauma associated with being castrated.

The link between testosterone and acts of aggression and violence has been clearly documented. In a study of a young criminal population, it was found that 10 prisoners with a history of violent and aggressive crimes in adolescence had significantly higher levels of testosterone than a comparable group of 11 prisoners who did not have such a history (Kreuz & Rose, 1972). Similar results have been obtained in two additional studies (Ehrenkranz, Bliss, & Sheard, 1974; Rada, Laws, & Kellner, 1976). A study of hockey players has also found positive correlations between degree of aggression, response to threat, and serum testosterone (Scaramella & Brown, 1978).

Estrogen, antiandrogens, and male aggression.   Stilbestrol, a synthetic drug that has been shown to have the effects of natural estrogen, has often been used

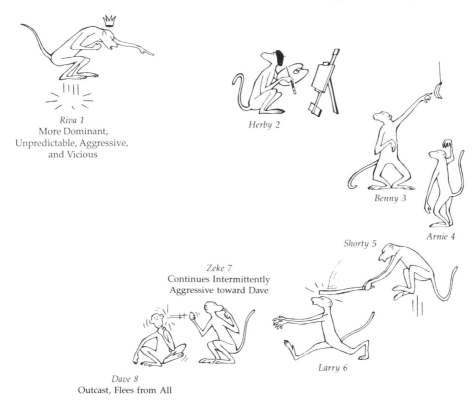

Riva 1
More Dominant,
Unpredictable, Aggressive,
and Vicious

Herby 2

Benny 3

Arnie 4

Shorty 5

Zeke 7
Continues Intermittently
Aggressive toward Dave

Larry 6

Dave 8
Outcast, Flees from All

Figure 10-7.   Dominance hierarchy after bilateral amygdalectomy in Riva (Pribram, 1976)

to control aggressive tendencies of adolescent boys (Foote, 1944; Sands, 1954; Whitaker, 1959). Like estrogen, stilbestrol depresses the anterior-pituitary gonadotropic function. In addition to stilbestrol, there are a number of substances that block androgenic activity and in doing so reduce aggressive behavior.

Estrogen, progesterone, and female aggression.   Just before menstruation and during the initial stage of menstruation, some women experience increased irritability and hostility (see, for example, Ivey & Bardwick, 1968; Shainess, 1961). Not only are they more irritable and hostile, but there is evidence that they tend to act out their feelings and so to get into trouble. For example, one study found that schoolgirls tend to break more rules and as a consequence receive more punishment during their menstruation, while older girls who are responsible for discipline are likely to mete out more punishment during their own menstruation (Dalton, 1960). Women prisoners are also more likely to get into trouble during this phase (Dalton, 1961), and many frequently ask to be isolated because they recognize that their behavior during this phase is likely to get them in trouble (Dalton, 1964). There is further evidence that more crimes are committed during this period (Dalton, 1961; Morton et al., 1953).

There is fairly general agreement that the fall in progesterone level, together with the rise in the ratio of estrogen to progesterone, is associated with these symptoms. Several studies have shown that administration of progesterone will alleviate the symptoms (for example, Dalton, 1964, 1977; Greene & Dalton, 1953; Lloyd, 1964). Katharina Dalton (1977) has done extensive work on the question of using progesterone to alleviate these symptoms and has concluded that progesterone not only will reduce the more common symptoms (irritability and hostility) but will alleviate a number of other symptoms that also increase during this part of the menstruation cycle, including asthma, herpes, tonsillitis, baby battering, epileptic seizures, and alcoholic bouts.

Hypoglycemia and aggression. Hypoglycemia is a state of low blood glucose that has a variety of causes. It is common in children, presumably because their glucose-regulating mechanism is still unstable (Wilder, 1943, 1944), and in middle-aged adults (Kepler & Moersch, 1937). There are several reports of greater aggressive tendencies associated with hypoglycemia—for example, in matrimonial relationships, cruelty toward children, acts of destructiveness, and homicidal threats (Wilder, 1947). One study in particular has demonstrated the close link between hypoglycemia and aggression. Ralph Bolton (1973), an anthropologist, observed that there was a particularly high level of social conflict and hostility among the Qolla people of the Peruvian Andes. He hypothesized that a tendency toward hypoglycemia might be responsible. To test this possibility, he took peer ratings of hostility and measured glucose levels. His results are summarized in Table 10-2. It can be seen that aggression tends to be low when glycemia levels are normal. When hypoglycemia is moderate, the tendency toward aggression abruptly increases. When hypoglycemia is severe, the trend observed under moderate hypoglycemia seems to be reversed. The number of cases observed was small, however, and severe hypoglycemia would be very disruptive; that is, it would be very difficult for a person with severe hypoglycemia to engage in any behavior, let alone an aggressive behavior. In general, the trend is quite clear. Aggression tends to increase when hypoglycemia occurs.

Other sensitizing agents for aggression. There are numerous reports of a relation between a wide variety of allergies and a tendency toward aggression (see Moyer, 1976). Alcohol has also been shown to increase aggression. For example, Kalin, McClelland, and Kahn (1965) found that thoughts of physical aggression were more frequent in subjects who drank heavily (ten drinks). Aggression was higher in a situation designed to evoke aggression after the consumption of alcohol (Mendelson & Mello, 1974; Zeichner & Pihl, 1979). A variety of other drugs have also been implicated. Amphetamines, in particular, seem to precipitate aggression when taken in large amounts (Moyer, 1976). Interestingly, cannabis does not seem to precipitate aggression (Abel, 1977).

Table 10-2. Blood-glucose conditions in the Qolla population, by aggressiveness rankings (Bolton, 1973)

Aggressiveness ranking	Normal glycemia		Moderate hypoglycemia		Severe hypoglycemia	
	Number	Percent	Number	Percent	Number	Percent
1 (High)	1	7.7%	11	84.6%	1	7.7%
2	8	57.2	5	35.7	1	7.1
3	7	50.0	4	28.6	3	21.4
4 (Low)	8	61.5	3	23.1	2	15.4

The finding that so many agents increase the tendency toward aggression is not at all comforting. It appears that the human is easily sensitized by a diverse set of agents—some natural, others synthetic. Thus the whole question of how to control aggression is very complex.

Summary

The fact that animals can be bred for aggression indicates that there is a genetic component for aggression in animals. Work on chromosomal abnormalities has produced evidence that aggression in humans also has a genetic basis. Research on territorial behavior and dominance hierarchies in animals suggests that aggression evolved to ensure the survival of a species. In many respects, territorial behavior and dominance hierarchies facilitate reproductive activities among those animals that possess behaviors important for a species' survival. Although humans engage in territorial behavior and establish dominance hierarchies, their behavior is less stereotyped than animals', suggesting that other factors mediate their behavior.

Moyer has identified eight kinds of aggression, which he argues are mediated by different brain structures or combinations of brain structures. The main structures implicated in aggression are the hypothalamus, the limbic system (hippocampus, amygdala, and septum), and the temporal lobes. The hypothalamus, it has been shown, is involved in the rage response, attack and predatory behavior, and defensive behaviors. The amygdala and septum have been implicated in attack and defensive behaviors. The temporal lobes have been further implicated in acts of hostility and aggression. The behavior of Charles Whitman has been offered as an example of hostility traceable to an abnormality of the temporal lobe. Research on various brain structures implicated in aggression and dominance hierarchies shows that social factors play an important role in modifying (inhibiting) behaviors that have a neurological basis. The question raised by Pribram is whether such structures as the amygdala are specifically structures that mediate aggression or are more general structures that may mediate a more general class of behavior.

A variety of chemicals have been shown to increase aggression: testosterone facilitates male aggression; a change in the ratio of estrogen to progesterone can increase female aggressiveness; hypoglycemia, alcohol, and many allergies can increase aggressiveness. It has been suggested that chemicals exert their influence by activating one or more of the brain structures that are typically involved in an aggressive act.

Psychological States That Evoke Aggression

A number of psychological states evoke aggressive behaviors in humans. Frustration, negative evaluation, and insult are some of the more widely studied of such states.

Frustration

For some time frustration has been held to be one of the main causes of aggression. According to the frustration hypothesis, the tendency to become aggressive increases when goal-directed behavior is blocked (Berkowitz, 1962, 1969; N. E. Miller, 1941). Finding that a favorite restaurant is closed, not being able to find the shoe one wants in the right size, having to wait in line to see a movie, not getting a certain grade on a test—all are examples of everyday events in which goal-directed behavior has been blocked. According to the frustration hypothesis, each of these events might produce frustration, which in turn would increase the tendency to engage in aggressive behavior. Although a fairly large number of studies have obtained results consistent with the frustration hypothesis (for example, Berkowitz & Geen, 1966; Burnstein & Worchel, 1962; Geen, 1968), other studies have failed to find that frustration facilitates the expression of aggression (for example, Buss, 1963, 1966; Kuhn, Madsen, & Becker, 1967; Taylor & Pisano, 1971).

Some limiting conditions.   Robert A. Baron (1977) has carefully examined the conflicting results and has concluded that "frustration can indeed facilitate later aggression" (p. 91). He points out, however, that frustration is likely to produce aggression only when frustration is (1) "quite intense" and (2) "when it is unexpected or arbitrary in nature" (p. 91). Thus having to wait in line may fail to facilitate aggression, because waiting in line is not intense enough. In fact, most of us learn that at times we will have to wait, and as a result of that expectation we often experience little or no frustration. Whether a student's failure to receive the grade he or she expected will facilitate aggression might be affected by the student's perception of whether the grading was fair or arbitrary.

The role of expectancy.   The role of expectancy in a frustrating situation is illustrated in a study carried out by Worchel (1974). Worchel offered students one of three incentives for their participation in an experiment: (1) an hour of experimental credit, (2) $5 in cash, or (3) a bottle of men's cologne. Initially the participants were required to rate these incentives for attractiveness. The rankings allowed the experimenter to manipulate degree of frustration. For example, if a subject was given his first choice, he should experience no frustration; if given his second choice, mild frustration; if given his third choice, the greatest frustration.

To examine the role of expectation, Worchel gave participants different information. A third of the participants were told that after their participation in the experiment the prize they received would be whatever the experimenter's assistant wished to give them. This was called the "no expectancy" condition, because the participants had no idea what they could expect from the assistant. Another third of the subjects were told they would receive the prize they had rated as most attractive. This was called the "expectancy" condition. The final third of the subjects were told they would have the opportunity to choose their prize after participating. This was called the "choice" condition.

After these expectations had been established, the participants were involved in some activities under the supervision of the experimenter's assistant. To determine the effects of frustration, the experimenter had manipulated the distribution of prizes so that some subjects in each condition (no expectancy, expectancy, choice) did not receive or were not allowed to select their favorite prize. Each subject received either his most-preferred, second-most-preferred, or least-preferred object in a manner consistent with the experimental condition. Then the subjects were asked to rate the performance of the experimenter's assistant. The results of interest were their ratings of the assistant. As expected, subjects who were frustrated most (received the least-preferred prize) showed the greatest tendency to aggress verbally toward the experimenter's assistant. This occurred, however, only under the choice and expectancy conditions. When subjects had no expectancy, they did not show greater aggressive tendencies when they failed to receive their most-preferred prize. In other words, frustration alone, at least in this experiment, did not increase the tendency to aggress.

Worchel's study illustrates how cognitive factors affect the expression of aggression. To the degree that we learn not to expect certain consequences, we will not become frustrated. In our society standing in line may or may not be frustrating, depending on whether we are cognitively prepared for this event. There are probably many other potentially frustrating events that, as a result of our daily experiences, fail to elicit feelings of frustration and consequently do not increase the tendency toward aggression.

Negative Evaluation

Being evaluated tends to produce a state of apprehension or anxiety in a large part of the population (Mandler & Sarason, 1952). The physiological changes that accompany this state may be summarized as a mild to moderate stress reaction. Anyone who has faced a difficult examination can attest to the fact that tests can cause increased anxiety, increased heart rate, increased perspiration, and other reactions. Being evaluated does not, by itself, increase aggression. However, when the evaluation appears to be arbitrary, harsh, or negative, anger and aggressive behaviors are increased (for example, Donnerstein & Wilson, 1976; Geen & O'Neal, 1969).

The laboratory procedure for showing the effect of negative evaluation typically involves two steps. First, the participant is asked to write an essay or engage in some other activity that involves submitting to a judgment. Next, the participant is given feedback that his or her essay is poor, silly, or unacceptable. Since participants typically try to cooperate by doing their best, arbitrary or harsh feedback generally angers them (Berkowitz, 1962, 1964). The problem for the psychologist has been to delineate exactly why these procedures evoke anger and, further, why anger leads to aggression.

The research on this question seems to indicate that the perceived intent of the person doing the evaluating may be the main determinant of whether anger is evoked. If the evaluator's actions are perceived as just and fair, there appears to be little anger. However, if the evaluator's actions are perceived to be arbitrary, unfair, or harsh, the participant is likely to become angry and behave aggressively (for example, Greenwell & Dengerink, 1973). In many instances, the participant perceives the evaluator as being deliberately provocative (Greenwell & Dengerink, 1973). In such circumstances humans are inclined to retaliate (for example, O'Leary & Dengerink, 1973; Schuck & Pisor, 1974): they evaluate the evaluator (typically the experimenter's assistant) as harshly as or more harshly than they were evaluated.

Insults

Insults have been used fairly extensively in laboratory research to elicit anger. The experimenter or a confederate will act in a rude manner toward the subject, questioning his or her intelligence, desire to cooperate, or promptness, for example (Ax, 1953; Baron & Bell, 1973; J. Schachter, 1957). Insults, of course, are often used in our society when we are frustrated. When an umpire calls a personal foul on our favorite football player, we might respond with phrases like "Stupid," "Moron," "Are you blind?" When a sales clerk gives us the wrong item, which we must then return, we may (if the clerk is not present) refer to the clerk as "stupid" or "retarded." Such behavior can be provocative. Indeed, most of us are careful not to call a muscular, 300-pound sales clerk "stupid" directly to his face.

Summary

Several psychological events will evoke aggression in humans. Frustration, provided it is quite intense and unexpected or arbitrary, is likely to evoke aggression. Negative evaluation, it has been shown, will often lead to retaliation if an appropriate opportunity is made available. Insults, such as questioning a person's intelligence or his or her willingness to cooperate, have often been used in the laboratory to provoke aggression.

Physiological Correlates of Anger and Aggression

Do feelings of anger play a significant role in the expression of aggression? At the physiological level, what is anger? How does it affect the way people express aggression?

Norepinephrine and Aggression

A rather extensive body of data shows that norepinephrine is associated with anger and aggression whereas epinephrine is related to fear and anxiety (Schildkraut & Kety, 1967). It has been observed, for example, that norepinephrine levels were higher in psychiatric patients during aggressive outbursts and epinephrine levels were higher during staff conferences (Elmadjian, Hope, & Lamson, 1957). In another study (cited in Buck, 1976) it was found that people who responded with anger to a set of conditions in which they were first provoked and then subjected to stress showed increased output of epinephrine.

Injections of norepinephrine and epinephrine produce many similar effects, but there are some essential differences. Norepinephrine produces a large rise in diastolic blood pressure and a fall in heart rate; epinephrine produces a rise in systolic blood pressure and a rise in heart rate. Using these cardiovascular measures, a number of investigators have shown that anger produces a norepinephrine-like physiological response whereas fear and anxiety produce an epinephrine-like pattern (Ax, 1953; Funkenstein, 1955; Funkenstein, King, & Drolette, 1957; J. Schachter, 1957).

In a series of studies Jack Hokanson monitored the rise and subsequent recovery of systolic blood pressure in subjects who were provoked and then either allowed to behave aggressively or not allowed to respond to the instigator. The results of these initial studies clearly showed that heightened blood pressure dropped faster in angered subjects who responded aggressively than in those who did not respond at all (Hokanson & Burgess, 1962a, 1962b; Hokanson, Burgess, & Cohen, 1963; Hokanson & Shetler, 1961).

Sex Differences

When sex was examined in the Hokanson paradigm, however, it was found that this general pattern held only for men (Baker & Schaie, 1969; Gambaro & Rabin, 1969; Holmes, 1966; Vatress & Williams, 1972). In a study designed to examine sex differences, Hokanson and Edelman (1966) introduced a condition in which subjects could also provide a reward to the anger instigator. In this study the subject was seated in one room and his or her partner in another room. Subjects were told the study had to do with interpersonal behavior. The experiment was designed, they were told, to examine how they might behave in a real-life situation if they didn't like someone or didn't like what the person was doing. The subject was led to believe, through instructions, that shocks would come from the partner. In actuality, however, the experimenter delivered the shocks, and the partner was never involved. The experiment was set up so that the partner always responded first. The subject then had the choice of giving the partner a shock, giving the partner a reward, or not responding. Men's responses coincided with those found in previous research; that is, systolic blood pressure dropped faster after an aggressive (shock) response. Women's responses differed considerably: their systolic blood pressure dropped more quickly after they had rewarded their partner.

To explain these and other findings, Hokanson has suggested that men and women have learned different ways of turning off the aggressive behavior of their peers. Men have learned to counter aggression with aggression, while women have learned to behave nonaggressively (Hokanson, 1970). One study designed to examine sex differences (Hokanson, Willers, & Koropsak, 1968) showed that when women are rewarded for behaving like men in order to counter aggression, they tend to show a faster drop in systolic blood pressure when they use aggression as a means of stopping aggression. Similarly, when men are rewarded for behaving like women, they tend to show a faster drop in systolic blood pressure after a nonaggressive response. This study indicates that the normal response styles used by men and women to turn off aggression are probably learned. When given new training, not only will they shift their response style, but the physiological reaction follows the new response style. Thus the differences between men and women are not due to their sex per se but rather to the fact that in our culture the sexes learn to behave differently.

In a study by Frodi (1978), some subjects were required to give a "stream of consciousness" (SOC) report while they responded in an aggression-eliciting competitive task, and others were not required to give a report. Frodi found no sex differences among the subjects not required to give a SOC report but did find the usual sex differences among the subjects required to give one. That is, she found that men were more aggressive than women in the SOC condition. Using the SOC reports, ratings, and other measures, Frodi concluded that men tend to stimulate themselves into more aggression whereas women adopt a nonhostile strategy for coping with stress. Although Frodi monitored both systolic and diastolic blood pressure, only diastolic-blood-pressure responses were consistent with the behavioral measures of anger and aggression. This pattern of results is consistent with the older work of Ax (1953), Funkenstein (1955), and J. Schachter (1957) and with the more recent work of Geen, Stonner, and Shope (1975). In other words, anger and aggression reflect a norepinephrine-like response.

Other studies have also found sex differences in the expression of aggression. One study exploring the use of physical and verbal aggression (based on a learner/teacher paradigm) found that women tended to aggress in the verbal mode whereas men aggressed in both the verbal and physical modes. The teacher/learner paradigm is a commonly used procedure in which the subject is involved in a learning task. Feedback for performance comes in the form of a shock for incorrect responses. Afterward the subject is asked to evaluate the "teacher" either verbally or with shock. The number of aggressive verbal responses or the number of shocks given to the "teacher" is used as a measure of aggression. Using this paradigm, researchers found that men tended to use the physical mode more frequently under two conditions: when the "teacher" was female and the experimenter male and when the "teacher" was male and the experimenter female (Shope, Hedrick, & Geen, 1978). It is likely that men's greater tendency to use physical aggression can be explained by the different social norms for men and women.

Summary

Hokanson has found that men tend to use aggression in response to an anger instigator whereas women in the same situation tend to use rewards. Further, Hokanson found that men's heightened blood pressure dropped faster when they used aggression (as opposed to not responding or using rewards) and that women's heightened blood pressure dropped faster when they used rewards (as opposed to not responding or responding aggressively). The difference in behavior, it appears, is tied to cultural expectations about how men and women should deal with aggression. It is interesting that the same physiological response follows the two different response styles. There is some controversy about whether that response is more epinephrine-like or norepinephrine-like; it appears, at least from the most recent studies, to be norepinephrine-like. This is interesting in view of the fact that various people have concluded that norepinephrine is linked to anger and aggression.

Another Look at the Definition of Aggression

Aggressive Behavior and the Need to Control

There is good reason at this point to question the definition of *aggression* that states that aggression in humans involves the intent to harm. The work of Frodi and Hokanson suggests that aggression may, under certain conditions, represent an attempt to stop aggression by others or, more generally, to regain control of events in the environment. In this sense, aggression may be viewed as basically an adaptive response. It is interesting that women typically rely on rewards to stop aggression. If this is a learned response, as research suggests, it means that aggression may be stopped by a variety of means other than more aggression.

Ethologists have traditionally viewed aggressive behaviors as adaptive. Certain behaviors are required if the animal is to survive. The fact that certain behaviors harm other animals is secondary to the survival instinct. There is no intentional motivation to harm the other animal. According to the ethological position, survival is broadly defined. It has to do with the exercise of the animal's full biological capacities in the ultimate service of the species rather than of the individual member of the species. Reproductive behavior, for example, ultimately is important for the survival of the species. A young male challenging an aging dominant male is exercising his biological capacity, and this behavior is ultimately important for the species. Within this context aggression is neither good nor bad. Rather, aggression is necessary for the survival not only of the individual but of the species.

Humans have for some time been viewed as having certain biological capacities that need to be exercised if they are to experience a basic satisfaction with day-to-day existence (Maslow, 1970). As I have already noted, one of our more basic needs is to be in control of our environment. As we saw in Chapter 8, "Stress, Distress, and Coping," when a person is in control or when the environment is predictable, norepinephrine is secreted, but when the environment is ambiguous or unpredictable, epinephrine tends to be secreted. Norepinephrine, as I pointed out, tends to be associated with positive affect, or mood. It may well be that certain aggressive behaviors represent an attempt to control the environment or make it predictable. If I am threatened in some way, for example, my immediate reaction, according to the control hypothesis, is to regain control. As a man, I may tend to retaliate in kind, especially if I have found that this strategy worked in the past. Because this is my way of exercising control, I will secrete norepinephrine under this condition. A woman, in contrast, may decide to use rewards when she is threatened, especially if she has found that this strategy has worked in the past. Because this is her way of exercising control, she too secretes norepinephrine. Both of us, it follows, experience positive affect for our efforts even though they are quite different. Both of us, in other words, are rewarded for our efforts. Should our strategies begin to fail, we might have to reassess our strategies. If our strategies were not working, we would experience a feeling of loss of control. Presumably our epinephrine levels would rise during this period of ambiguity.

It is not surprising that negative evaluation and insults should evoke the desire to regain control, because they challenge our self-esteem. Frustration results when some goal is blocked. Clearly, inability to attain a goal represents a loss of control or loss of predictability. There are a number of things we might do to regain control. Some of our efforts will obviously be more productive than others. Nevertheless, all of us at one time or another have probably found ourselves kicking some obstacle in our path, hitting a vending machine that just swallowed our last quarter without giving us something in return, or shouting insults at someone who was in our way. These acts, whether productive or not, reflect a desire to right a wrong or simply to reassert our authority over our environment (Allen & Greenberger, 1980).

The Reward Value of Aggression

If aggressive behavior is adaptive, it should also be rewarding. If it is rewarding, it will be repeated. There is, in fact, evidence that it will be, at least under certain conditions. Specifically, it appears that an aggressive act will be repeated if it achieves some desired goal. If aggressive behavior stops the aggressive behavior of an attacker, for example, it is likely that the tendency to engage in similar aggressive acts will increase (Hokanson & Edelman, 1966). Moyer (1976) calls this kind of aggression "instrumental aggression." Severe punishment for aggressive behaviors, however, tends to decrease such behaviors in animals (Ulrich, Wolfe, & Dulaney, 1969), and less severe punishment in the form of "time out" has been used to control severe, long-standing behavior problems in humans (for example, Allison & Allison, 1971; White, Nielsen, & Johnson, 1972). We will further examine the rewarding effects of aggression in the section on development of aggression. For the present, it can be concluded that engaging in aggressive behavior can lead to a reward, which will increase the tendency to be aggressive. The key is whether the aggressive behavior achieves a goal.

Summary

There is reason to argue that many aggressive acts reflect a need to control. It is not surprising that people will often react aggressively when insulted or when given negative evaluations, because both events question whether we are in control. They are threats to our self-esteem. Frustration results when a goal is blocked. Such an event would immediately challenge my perception that I am in control of events in my environment. From what we have learned about the relation between exercising control and secretion of norepinephrine, it is not surprising that strategies designed to gain or regain control should be linked to secretion of norepinephrine.

Factors That Facilitate or Inhibit Ongoing Aggressive Behaviors

Some factors or events that apparently do not by themselves evoke aggression do seem to facilitate or inhibit ongoing aggressive behaviors. Noise, erotic stimuli, crowding, and heat are a few of the factors that have been studied to determine whether or how they affect the expression of aggression.

Noise

Noise is one of the by-products of our technological society that have been found to facilitate interpersonal aggression (Donnerstein & Wilson, 1976; Geen & O'Neal, 1969; Konečni, 1975b). Because noise tends to produce increases in physiological arousal, various investigators have attempted to relate increased aggression to increased arousal (for example, Bandura, 1973). Although there is no definite work on the question, it seems reasonable to assume that arousal probably facilitates aggressive behavior in the same way that arousal has been found to facilitate other behaviors. It is important to note that noise does not seem to evoke aggression by itself. Rather, noise simply facilitates this behavior if it has already been evoked. This point is illustrated by the finding that when subjects were angered (received negative evaluations of essays they had written) and then were exposed to noise, they tended to aggress more in a teacher/learner paradigm than subjects who had been angered and not exposed to noise and more than subjects who had not been angered (Donnerstein and Wilson, 1976). These results, summarized in Figure 10-8, clearly indicate that "noise may facilitate ongoing or later aggression, but only when such behaviors represent a relatively strong or prepotent tendency among potential aggressors" (Baron, 1977, p. 130).

Erotic Stimulation

Exposure to erotic stimuli has been shown both to facilitate aggressive behavior (for example, Donnerstein & Barrett, 1978; Donnerstein & Hallam, 1978; Jaffe et al., 1974; Meyer, 1972; Zillmann, 1971) and to inhibit aggressive behavior (Baron,

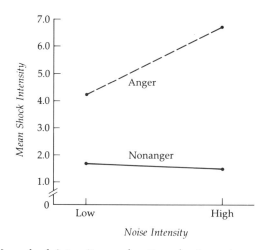

Figure 10-8. Mean shock intensity as a function of noise and anger (Donnerstein & Wilson, 1976)

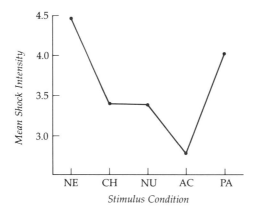

Figure 10-9. Mean intensity of shocks directed against the confederate by subjects exposed to nonerotic stimuli (NE), cheesecake (CH), nudes (NU), sexual acts (AC), or erotic passages (PA) (Baron & Bell, 1977)

1974; Baron & Bell, 1973). After carefully examining the similarities and differences among these studies, Baron and Bell (1977) concluded that mildly erotic materials seem to inhibit aggressive behaviors whereas more arousing erotic materials seem to facilitate them. To check on this hypothesis, Baron and Bell conducted an experiment in which a confederate either praised or insulted the subjects. Then the subjects had the opportunity to examine one of five types of material varying in degree of eroticism. Finally, the subjects participated in a task in which they could physically aggress against the confederate by using shock. The results are summarized in Figure 10-9. The finding of a curvilinear relation between degree of eroticism and aggression accounts for the seemingly contradictory findings reported on this topic.

Although Baron and Bell's (1977) study helps account for the apparently contradictory findings, it does not indicate what psychological mechanism might underlie these results. One possible explanation has been offered by Donnerstein, Donnerstein, and Evans (1975). These investigators have suggested that erotic stimuli have two distinct effects: they increase the level of arousal and they distract the subject from the source of the provocation. Because mildly erotic stimuli have a minimal effect on arousal, their main effect is to distract the person, thereby reducing aggression. As the erotic stimuli become more explicit, their arousing properties come to dominate, thus leading to an increase in aggression. This effect, they argue, would be greatest in a situation in which the person was subjected to strong provocation. As we have noted, strong provocative stimulation is likely to lead to aggression when the person is highly aroused. In a test of their explanation, these investigators used neutral, mildly erotic, and highly erotic stimuli. As expected, they found a U-shaped function. Although subjects could be readily provoked after viewing neutral or highly erotic stimuli, they could not be provoked so readily following the presentation of mildly erotic stimuli. In other words, the mildly erotic stimuli seemed to reduce aggression in an anger-instigated situation. According to Donnerstein and his colleagues, mildly erotic stimuli acted as a distraction. Baron (1979) has obtained further evidence consistent with this hypothesis in a study with female subjects, but Zillman and Sapolsky's (1977) findings do not support this explanation. Further research is required to determine why Zillmann and Sapolsky obtained a different pattern of results.

In a further test of the distraction hypothesis, Baron (1978b) studied the inhibiting effect of sexual humor on aggressive behavior. Two types of sexual humor were identified, exploitive and nonexploitive. Although the distraction hypothesis would predict that both types of humor should reduce aggression, it was found that only exploitive humor did. Baron has suggested that people are more likely to fantasize about exploitive than nonexploitive sexual humor and as a result the impact of exploitive humor would be greater.

Crowding

Although there is evidence from a variety of sources that aggression tends to be greater under conditions of crowding (for example, Hutt & Vaizey, 1966), there is also evidence that crowding may reduce aggression (Loo, 1972) or have no effect on the incidence of aggression (Griffitt & Veitch, 1971). After carefully examining these and other studies, Jonathan Freedman (1975) has concluded that there is no evidence that crowding itself produces aggression. Rather, he suggests that crowding may facilitate aggression provided that the circumstances are such that aggression has already been provoked. That is, crowding may intensify an already-existing behavior pattern. This interpretation is, of course, consistent with a number of other facts. As I have already noted in various contexts, social interactions tend to increase arousal, and this arousal tends to facilitate or intensify ongoing emotional responses (Schachter & Singer, 1962). According to Freedman's interpretation, crowding might facilitate a wide variety of behaviors. Crowding can, for example, increase the pleasure associated with eating or listening to music.

To determine whether crowding can facilitate aggression, a situation was created in which subjects might be expected to express a form of aggression (Freedman et al., 1972). Subjects (either all men or all women) listened to tape recordings of what were purported to be actual criminal trials. Immediately after listening, the subjects were to decide whether the defendant was guilty and, if guilty, to decide on an appropriate length of sentence. In one condition the group listened to the tapes in a small room; in another condition, a large room. Crowding (listening to the tapes in a small room) increased the tendency to give a severe sentence in men but decreased it in women. The unexpected findings for the female subjects might appear, at first glance, to be inconsistent with Freedman's hypothesis. As we have noted, however, women often respond quite differently from men in aggression-related situations. For example, we saw that women will, if given the opportunity, use rewards in a teacher/learner situation, whereas men typically use aggression. If women have a tendency to shy away from aggression, then the findings in regard to women are perfectly consistent with Freedman's hypothesis. To the degree that crowding intensifies ongoing or existing behavioral tendencies, then it would be expected, according to Freedman's hypothesis, that women would be less inclined to punish under conditions of crowding than under uncrowded conditions.

What remains to be explained is why men and women have different response strategies (if they can be called strategies) to deal with aggression. It may simply be that men have been rewarded for aggression while women have not. This hypothesis, of course, is consistent with our society's cultural stereotypes.

Heat

Around 1970 a number of dangerous riots occurred in the United States and in several other countries. Although several factors were identified as possible causes, the media often played heavily on the idea that ambient temperature was a critical factor in precipitating the riots. It was suggested, for example, that high temperatures had shortened tempers and increased irritability, thereby paving the way for rioting.

In a series of laboratory studies, Griffitt and his colleagues (Griffitt, 1970; Griffitt & Veitch, 1971) produced some empirical results consistent with this idea. They found, for example, that people did become more irritable, more negative, and more prone to temper outbursts under uncomfortably hot conditions than under comfortably cool conditions.

More recent research by Baron and his colleagues has shown that the relation between ambient temperature and aggression is far more complex than that initially reported by the press or by Griffitt and his colleagues (Baron, 1972, 1978a; Baron & Bell, 1975, 1976; Baron & Lawton, 1972; Baron & Ransberger, 1978; Bell & Baron, 1976). In the first investigation to study the relation between temperature and aggression, it was found that uncomfortably high temperatures reduced aggression in both angered and nonangered subjects (Baron, 1972). This finding, of course, is inconsistent with the idea that heat increases arousal, which in turn facilitates ongoing aggression (for example, Bandura, 1973). Comments by the subjects in a postexperimental debriefing session indicated that under uncomfortably high temperatures (92–95° F) the subjects deliberately used lower levels of shock in hopes of terminating the experimental session as soon as possible. Further studies have confirmed Baron's initial conclusion that when people are exposed to high ambient temperatures and prior provocation, they will be more strongly motivated to terminate the experiment than to respond to the provocation.

These observations led Baron and his colleagues to speculate that the relation between temperature and aggression might be curvilinear (Figure 10-10). Specifically, they hypothesized that up to some point in temperature aggressive tendencies would increase but beyond that point further increases would decrease aggressive tendencies. They hypothesized that the psychological dimension mediating this relation was level of negative affect (unpleasant feelings). It was hypothesized

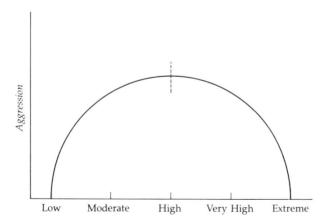

Level of Negative Affect Experienced by Potential Aggressors

Figure 10-10.   Hypothetical relation between negative affect and aggression. At first, aggression increases as negative affect rises. Beyond some determinable point (dashed line), however, further increments in negative affect lead to decreasing aggression (Baron, 1977).

that as temperature increased above the comfortably cool level, people would experience greater and greater negative affect. When negative affect had reached a certain point, the motivation would shift toward reducing the negative affect rather than attacking others even when provocation was great.

In one study Baron and Ransberger (1978) plotted riots as a function of temperature, producing the curvilinear relation that had been predicted. These results, shown in Figure 10-11, not only provide support for the model but attest to the validity of the laboratory studies on the relation between aggression and ambient temperature.

It should be noted that the model may apply to a variety of conditions other than temperature. Any time negative affect reaches an unacceptably high level, there may be a tendency to reduce aggression. Pain, for example, may increase the tendency toward aggression up to some point, after which the tendency toward aggression decreases.

Attribution and Arousal

To examine whether arousal facilitates ongoing aggression, Zillmann and his colleagues have manipulated arousal independent of eliciting aggression (for example, Zillmann, 1971; Zillmann & Bryant, 1974; Zillmann, Johnson, & Day, 1974; Zillmann, Katcher, & Milavsky, 1972). In one study arousal was increased by exercise. Subsequently the subjects were provoked. The results showed that increased arousal led to greater aggression but only in those subjects who were not made aware of the source of their arousal. In other words, when subjects could account for their arousal, it did not facilitate aggression as it did when they were not aware. This result, of course, fits with Schachter and Singer's (1962) position on the interaction of arousal and emotions.

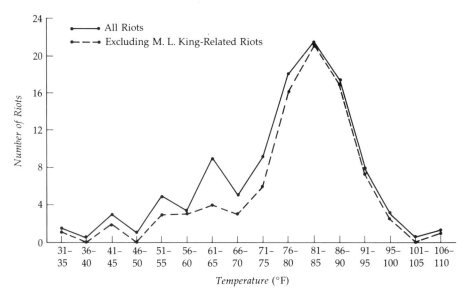

Figure 10-11. Frequency of collective violence (riots) as a function of ambient temperature (Baron & Ransberger, 1978)

Summary

Factors or events that do not themselves provoke aggression may either facilitate or inhibit ongoing aggressive behaviors. Noise, for example, has been shown to facilitate aggression when subjects are angered in a teacher/learner paradigm. Because noise has been shown to increase arousal, it is assumed that the aggression-facilitating effect is mediated by arousal. Erotic stimulation, it has been shown, both increases and decreases provoked aggression. Mildly erotic stimuli tend to decrease aggression; more highly erotic stimuli tend to facilitate it. It has been suggested that mildly erotic stimuli act as a distraction, leading to a decrease in provoked aggression, whereas highly erotic stimuli lead to increases in arousal that facilitate aggression. Crowding, it has been shown, can facilitate provoked aggression. Crowding can lead to increases in arousal, which appears to mediate aggression. Heat can also facilitate aggression. The relation between heat and aggression is an inverted-U-shaped function. Studies that have directly manipulated arousal by such means as exercise have shown that increases in arousal will facilitate aggression provided that the person attributes arousal to provoked aggression, not to the actual (independent) source of arousal.

Development of Aggression

Infants possess one of the most fundamental mechanisms for controlling behavior: they can cry. There seems to be little question that an infant's cry is aversive, although it is not clear whether the aversive effect is unlearned or acquired (Bell, 1971; Bell & Harper, 1977). It has generally been assumed that the infant has been equipped to cry so that he or she is capable of signaling the parent when a biological need exists, such as hunger, thirst, or pain. There is considerable evidence, however, that infants will learn to cry in a number of situations that are not tied so urgently to immediate physical needs (Bell, 1971). For example, children will learn to cry in order to be held or in order to obtain visual stimulation.

As children develop, they acquire a wide variety of responses that enable them to control their environment. Some of these responses are positive, and others are negative or noxious, at least from the parents' viewpoint. For example, one child may learn that she can obtain a glass of milk by saying, "Please, mummy, may I have a glass of milk?" while another child may learn he can obtain a glass of milk by screaming, "Milk!" The two responses are quite different, but each is effective in attaining the desired goal.

It appears that children have a rather marked tendency to use negative or noxious responses in order to control their environment. Laboratory observations have shown that the highest rates of negativistic/disruptive behaviors occur before age 2 (Reynolds, 1928). Although negativistic/disruptive behavior tends to decrease with age, the child acquires a wide variety of other noxious behaviors. Patterson (1976) has suggested that the 3-year-old child has acquired at least 13 noxious behaviors: negative commands, crying, disapproval, dependency, destructiveness, humiliation, ignoring, noncompliance, negativism, negative physical responses, teasing, whining, and yelling. All these noxious behaviors tend to become less frequent as the child develops. There is good reason to believe that the decrease in these behaviors comes about as a result of parental punishment. Most parents systematically punish such noxious behaviors while simultaneously encouraging more positive methods of control (Patterson, 1976).

In a study comparing aggressive and nonproblem boys aged 8–14, Patterson (1976) found that certain noxious behaviors occurred more frequently among the aggressive sample. Specifically, he found that the aggressive boys showed a significantly greater amount of disapproval, destructiveness, negativism, teasing, and yelling. Patterson notes that "the data suggest they manipulate their immediate social environment in a manner characteristic of three- or four-year-old children" (p. 305).

Many parents tend to use violence as a means of control. It may be expected that their children will, as parents, also tend to use violence as a means of control. This is exactly what has been found (Carroll, 1977). In other words, not all children are encouraged to abandon physical means of control.

After reviewing the research literature pertaining to the stability of aggression patterns in males, Olweus (1979) has concluded that marked individual differences in habitual aggression levels manifest themselves at least by age 3. Because individual differences occur at such an early age and, further, because they are relatively stable, Olweus argues that situational factors probably play a much smaller role in later life than one might gather from the research literature on aggression. This does not mean that situational and environmental factors are not important. They obviously account for part of the aggressive behavior patterns that are observed in adults. The consistency of a person's aggression level over time suggests that such patterns are habitual and had their origins early in life.

Summary

There is considerable evidence that children tend to use various noxious behaviors to control their environment. Not all parents are inclined to reduce or eliminate these behaviors. Children who persist in these behaviors are frequently viewed by society as being aggressive. Because aggressive children tend to come from families that condone aggression as a means of control, it has been suggested that aggression is like a habit or strategy that one uses to control events or people.

Physical Aggression and the Hierarchy of Control

The wish or need to exert control over events or people seems to be a fundamental human characteristic (Rotter, 1972). It is not surprising, therefore, that humans develop a wide range of skills for exerting such control. Aggressive behaviors can be viewed as a subclass of control behaviors. Can we specify the conditions under which this subclass of control behaviors is used? Further, can we specify when physical, in contrast to verbal, aggression is used in an attempt to control events and people in the environment?

Hans Toch (1969), who has extensively studied the violent criminal, has pointed out that the violent criminal often lacks the basic social skills that would allow him to control people and events in the environment. Toch has concluded that most violent men are basically "children." He notes that they tend to use force as a means of compensating for their immature and underdeveloped social skills. Physical violence, as I have already noted, is often used by young children but eventually gives way to more socially accepted methods of control (Patterson, 1976). If a person has failed to develop such skills, the only methods of control available to him are these more childlike forms of control. That is, he is prone to use physical aggression. Toch believes that the physically aggressive criminal needs to learn the appropriate social skills for controlling events in the environment. Learning such skills would, he suggests, help eliminate some of the situations that often precipitate acts of assault against others.

When Do Humans Tend to Be Physically Aggressive?

It is relatively easy to produce physical aggression in the laboratory if certain conditions are met. Researchers have often elicited physical aggression by creating some condition that justifies the release of aggression under the guise of punishment, presumably as a means of understanding how punishment can be used to help people. In the teacher/learner paradigm, the participant is led to believe that the shocks he or she is administering may help the recipient learn certain arbitrary associations between words and that this will help science understand how punishment can be used to facilitate learning. In most studies based on this paradigm, the participant is given no chance to use another form of feedback (control) to assist the learner, since the main point of the study is ostensibly to understand how punishment affects learning. As we have seen, some participants, especially women, will choose other forms of feedback if they are given a choice.

The fact that physical aggression is observed under these conditions is probably not surprising. The question is whether these results should be taken as evidence that humans have a high tendency to be physically aggressive, in view of the fact that they have not been given a choice (Baron & Eggleston, 1972). A study by Rule and Nesdale (1974) clearly demonstrates that physical aggression, at least in the laboratory, may not necessarily reflect a desire to harm. Rule and Nesdale used the teacher/learner paradigm with two sets of instructions. One group of subjects was told that higher-intensity shocks would help the learner's performance; another group was told that such shocks would interfere with performance. Another manipulation was to have the partner, who was a confederate of the experimenter, either insult or not insult the subject. Rule and Nesdale reported that subjects who had been told the shocks would interfere with performance chose more intense shocks for the insulting than the neutral confederate. Subjects who had been told the higher-intensity shocks would facilitate learning delivered more intense shocks to the neutral than to the insulting confederate. These findings suggest that the subjects were trying under one condition to assist the confederate and under another condition to disrupt the performance of or even punish an insulting confederate.

Another procedure that effectively elicits physical aggression from participants in the laboratory is initially to administer physical punishment to the subject under the pretext that it is some form of evaluation. For example, a participant may be given a certain number of shocks to indicate the adequacy of his performance on a required essay. The evidence seems to show that the recipient is likely to respond in like kind and number to the punishment if given the chance. That is, if the recipient is given a certain number of shocks, he is likely to return the same number (for example, Borden, Bowen, & Taylor, 1971; Dengerink & Bertilson, 1974; Dengerink & Myers, 1977; Taylor, 1967). Thus, again it is unclear whether such studies show that humans tend to use physical aggression except when provoked to do so.

It is interesting to note that subjects could easily escalate or de-escalate levels of counteraggression by either increasing or decreasing the level of the attack (Borden, Bowen, & Taylor, 1971; Dengerink & Myers, 1977; O'Leary & Dengerink, 1973; Taylor, 1967). Why is it that they return the shock in like kind and number?

It would appear from these and other studies that the counteraggression may serve the function of terminating the aggressive attack. Patterson (1976) has observed that aggressive behavior within the family setting is often used by one member of the family to stop the attacks of another member. He has further observed that when one family member suddenly increases the intensity of the aggressive exchange, the other person is likely to terminate his or her attack. Thus, although gradual escalation of the attack may increase an aggressive exchange, a sharp increase may serve to decrease or stop that exchange. Evidence from other sources is consistent with this observation. For example, when the threat of retaliation for aggressive behavior is high, the tendency to initiate an attack is lowered (Baron, 1973; Dengerink & Levendusky, 1972; Shortell, Epstein, & Taylor, 1970). There is one important exception. It appears that when a person is strongly angered, the threat of retaliation does not reduce the tendency to initiate an attack. Thus, even if the person believes that retaliation not only will be forthcoming but will be severe, he or she will not inhibit an aggressive attack (Baron, 1973).

Being angered is, of course, one of the most fundamental conditions evoking aggressive behavior in humans. Being angered does not, however, necessarily lead to physical aggression. A person may engage in a variety of aggressive verbal behaviors before resorting to physical aggression. It appears that humans often stop short of evoking a physical attack. In diplomatic exchanges, great care is often taken to allow the other party (nation) to "save face" in order to avoid evoking a physical counterattack. The aggressor may escalate the attack to such a high level that the recipient of the attack may feel he or she has no choice but to resort to a physical counterattack. Under these conditions the attacker may be forced to use physical aggression as well.

There is evidence from a variety of sources that humans will often resort to more immature forms of behavior when other behaviors fail. If this idea is applied to aggressive behavior, it suggests that humans will resort to physical aggression if other methods of control fail. Thus physical aggression may be viewed as a last resort (Shortell, Epstein, & Taylor, 1970). For example, a person may try to use positive rewards to control behavior. When these efforts fail, he may move to some form of verbal attack; and finally, if this strategy fails, he may resort to physical aggression.

Zimbardo's Work: The Process of Deindividuation

Philip Zimbardo (1969) has argued that a normal precursor of physical aggression is deindividuation. Deindividuation, according to Festinger, Pepitone, and Newcomb (1952, p. 382), is a state in which the inner restraints are lost when "individuals are not seen or paid attention as individuals." In developing his theory, Zimbardo has stated that deindividuation is characterized by low self-awareness and self-evaluation and a lesser concern for how others evaluate oneself. In other words, when people do not regard themselves in a good light, they are more likely to resort to physical forms of control.

Zimbardo has proposed that anonymity can lead to a state of deindividuation, which in turn will increase the tendency toward physical aggression. Feelings of anonymity occur, Zimbardo has shown, when people perceive that they cannot be identified as distinct individuals. For example, when a person wears a mask or a uniform, his or her identity is often hidden (at least in part) by it. Under such conditions, Zimbardo suggests, people no longer feel constrained by social values and practices. As a result, they are likely to behave in a more primitive, less inhibited fashion. This more primitive or less inhibited behavior is typically characterized by its aggressive qualities. People who experience feelings of anonymity are more likely to give harsh punishment than people who see themselves as distinct and identifiable entities.

In a classic experiment, Zimbardo (1972) simulated a jail to examine the whole question of how humans respond in power-related situations. Paid volunteer university men were randomly assigned to play the role of a guard or a prisoner. To make the situation as real as possible, Zimbardo arranged for the "prisoners" to be picked up and booked by the local police department before being brought to the university, where a makeshift jail had been constructed. Dressed in jail-style uniforms, this group of students began to "serve time" in the improvised jail. The students acting as guards were dressed in appropriate uniforms and carried out the functions normally served by guards in a jail. That is, they transferred prisoners from one section to another and ensured that the rules were obeyed.

To enhance the theme of guard/prisoner subservience, the prisoners were required to engage in various activities designed to emphasize or enhance this theme. For example, at one point they were required to wear bags over their heads while they marched in columns linked by a chain attached to their feet. The guards, of course, were responsible for ensuring that the prisoners carried out this subservient behavior in an organized and proper manner.

Zimbardo found that after six days it was necessary to terminate the experiment. In that short time very dramatic changes had taken place in the behavior of the participants. The students who were acting as guards began to act in a very cruel and debasing fashion toward their fellow participants who had been assigned the role of prisoner. Those students acting as prisoners began to act as very "servile" and "dehumanized robots," "thinking only of escape," "their own survival," and "their hatred for the guards." In short, Zimbardo had to terminate the study because of the growing hatred and aggression that were emerging between guards and prisoners.

Zimbardo's study demonstrates that when humans are given the opportunity to control the behavior of other people, they tend to resort to very basic forms of control: they become aggressive. According to Zimbardo, feelings of anonymity can act as a disinhibitor of behavior. In Zimbardo's study, belonging to a group called "guards" and wearing a uniform symbolizing that group identity were sufficient to provide this sense of anonymity. Under these conditions, Zimbardo argues, a person no longer feels compelled to behave according to his or her personal standards acquired in the process of socialization. Rather, the person tends to resort to more primitive forms of control.

Arousal as a Unifying Concept

Rule and Nesdale (1976a, 1976b) have found that the work on noise, erotic stimuli, crowding, and heat, together with the work of Zillmann and others on arousal, indicates that arousal has a general facilitative effect on aggressive behavior. Further, they suggest that the concept of arousal can help account for the inconsistent relations between anger and aggression that have been reported in the research literature. They note that anger tends to lead to aggression if arousal is high. This effect, however, is tempered by the person's ability to identify the source of arousal. If arousal is perceived to be due to anger, arousal will tend to increase aggression; however, if arousal can be attributed to another source, it may have no effect (see also Konečni, 1975b).

Rule and Nesdale point out that anger may occur in situations in which there is no immediate object to aggress against. For example, certain forms of frustration, such as inability to complete a task, may result in anger. However, since there is nothing to attack there, aggressive behavior may not occur. Thus, in order for arousal to increase aggression, the anger must have a target. That is, there must be something to damage or injure before aggression will be observed.

Rule and Nesdale's explanation of the relation between anger and arousal may help us understand why two quite different responses to aggression lead to a de-escalation of aggression in a competitive or antagonistic situation. Specifically, it has been found that both escalation and de-escalation of shock intensity in response to a competitor will lead to reduction in the shock intensity selected by the competitor (for example, Kimble, Fitz, & Onorad, 1977). From what I have already discussed, it is not surprising that escalation decreases the aggressive behavior of a competitor, since increasing the intensity of an aggressive response appears to be an effective strategy for stopping aggression. It is paradoxical, however, that decreasing the level of shock should also be effective or more effective unless somehow deescalation reduces anger or arousal in the competitor, thereby leading to lowered aggression.

Summary

It appears that aggressive behaviors typically reflect something more than just the desire to harm another person physically. In the case of retaliation, physical aggression may serve the purpose of terminating further attacks. Thus the motivation may more properly be viewed as self-preservation; the fact that another person is harmed is a by-product of the more primary need for self-preservation. There is also evidence that humans often inhibit their aggressive responses when provoked, possibly reflecting an attempt to de-escalate an aggressive exchange. Further, there is evidence that physical aggression occupies a low position on the hierarchy of control behaviors and is used only when the other behaviors have been tried and found ineffective. We need only watch people in the course of a normal day to observe that aggressive verbal exchanges are frequent but that they rarely result in physical aggression. Arousal may be one of the principal underlying factors that mediate aggressive behavior. Although anger does not necessarily lead to aggression, the likelihood that anger will lead to aggression tends to increase as arousal increases. Thus, level of arousal is a critical factor predicting the instigation of aggression.

Personality and Aggression

The fact remains that humans do engage in physical aggression. As we noted in connection with the study by Baron (1973), humans can become so angered that they will engage in physical aggression even if the retaliation is likely to be very severe. Although part of the answer lies in the hierarchy of control, it is also necessary to examine personality traits that somehow affect the tendency toward physical aggression.

Internal versus External Locus of Control

Julian B. Rotter (1972) has suggested that there are two types of people, internals and externals, who differ in their beliefs about their ability to control their own destinies. At one extreme, internals feel they can influence events in their environment; at the other extreme, externals feel powerless to do so. According to Rotter, internals are more likely to respond with aggression than externals if, for example, the aggression will help them to achieve a goal or to remove a barrier or noxious stimulus. In other words, internals are more likely to engage in instrumental aggression than externals.

In an experiment to test this hypothesis (Dengerink, O'Leary, & Kasner, 1975), a large group of male undergraduates—210 subjects—was given Rotter's Internal-External Locus of Control Scale (Rotter, 1966). Two groups of subjects were selected— those scoring high on the scale (externals) and those scoring low (internals). Both groups served in an experiment based on a reaction-time paradigm originally designed by Taylor (1967). In this paradigm, the subject is informed that he will be competing in a reaction-time task with a second subject (in actuality a confederate of the experimenter) and that the person who is slower on any trial will receive a shock that was set by the competitor in advance of that trial. The subject is then made to lose on a predetermined proportion of the trials. Subjects in both groups served in one of three experimental conditions. In the increasing-attack condition, the partner began by setting low shocks and gradually increased the intensity over trials. In the decreasing-attack condition, the partner began by setting high shocks and decreased the intensity over trials. In the constant-attack condition, the partner set a moderate-level shock throughout the experiment.

Dengerink and his colleagues predicted that internals would be more sensitive to the partner's behavior than externals. Specifically, it was predicted that subjects exposed to increasing attacks would become increasingly aggressive, that subjects exposed to decreasing attacks would reduce their level of aggressiveness, and finally that subjects exposed to a constant level would also maintain a constant level of aggression.

Figure 10-12 shows the results. As predicted, internal subjects were far more sensitive to the partner's behavior than externals. Presumably externals are less likely to respond even when strongly provoked because they have a generalized belief that their behavior will have no effect on people or events in the environment. According to Rotter, they feel they are powerless and as a result simply

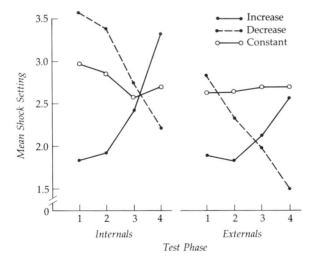

Figure 10-12.   Mean shock settings by internal and external subjects for opponents decreasing, increasing, and not changing shock levels during four blocks of testing (Dengerick, O'Leary, & Kasner, 1975)

accept harsh treatment because they believe they have no ability to control it. As we have noted, people can often stop aggression by escalating the attack. Just why certain people (externals) do not respond in this adaptive way will be examined in the next chapter.

Type A and Type B Personalities

As discussed in Chapter 8, research linking personality and coronary attacks has identified two more or less distinct personality types. The Type A person is the hard-driving achiever who is constantly working under the pressure of time limitations and has been described as "aggressive." The Type B person is more relaxed, less pressured by time, and generally described as less aggressive. There is good evidence now to support the idea that the Type A person is in fact more aggressive. In an experiment by Carver and Glass (1978), half of the Type A and half of the Type B subjects were angered by a confederate who interfered with their performance and then insulted their intelligence. Then all subjects were allowed to aggress, in accordance with the standard teacher/learner paradigm. The results indicated that when Type A subjects were provoked, they gave stronger shocks than Type B subjects. In the absence of provocation, both groups delivered milder shocks.

As we noted earlier, the Type A person appears to have a stronger need to control people and events in the environment. Being provoked would, of course, motivate the Type A person to reassert himself or herself. In this sense Type A people are very similar to internals. Both need to assert themselves, especially in situations that challenge their sense of control.

Anxiety, Fear, and Social Approval

In our society certain forms of aggression, especially physical aggression, are not socially acceptable ways of dealing with people or events in the environment. People who experience a strong need for social approval or people who have anxiety about the use of physical aggression should, therefore, show less tendency toward physical aggression when provoked. Laboratory research has confirmed that in fact people who have greater anxiety (of any kind, not just anxiety about aggression) show less aggression (for example, Dengerink, 1971) as well as people who have a strong need for social approval (for example, Dorsky & Taylor, 1972). In both studies it was found that the tendency of these groups to inhibit aggression lessened as the strength of provocation increased. Under strong provocation, then, people high and low in anxiety tend to be equally aggressive, and people who are high and low in need for social approval are approximately equal in aggression. This finding indicates that as anger increases, personality variables, at least those mentioned, tend to play a less important role in the expression of aggression. This finding is consistent with studies that have shown that the threat of strong retaliation is effective when anger is at a low level but is almost totally ineffective when anger is very strong (Baron, 1973). It makes sense from a survival point of view that a person should retaliate more severely when strongly threatened. It may be desirable for the society to establish prohibitions against aggression, but for the individual it could be fatal, either physically or psychologically, to fail to respond in the face of a strong provocation.

Fitz (1976) has collected data indicating that aggression is more likely to occur if the aggressor can attack a displaced target (for example, someone who is less likely to retaliate than the person who provoked the attack). He further notes that in the course of an attack on a displaced target, the fear of retaliation tends to extinguish. As a result, the threshold for attacking the target tends to decrease, and the aggressor is more inclined to attack the target directly. For example, if an employee is berated (provoked) by his boss, he will be more likely to aggress against the boss's secretary than against the boss herself. After aggressing against the secretary several times, he will, according to Fitz's findings, be more inclined to aggress against the boss.

Guilt

Probably as a result of past conditioning, people often experience guilt after being excessively aggressive (Brock & Buss, 1964; Mosher, 1965). It might be expected, therefore, that such people would inhibit ongoing or possibly future aggressive acts. There is evidence that humans will inhibit aggression when they perceive that another person is suffering pain (Baron, 1971; Buss, 1966), but other evidence indicates that observing pain in the victim can actually facilitate rather than inhibit aggression (Feshbach, Stiles, & Bitter, 1967). Because there are a number of methodological differences between these studies, it is not immediately clear why the findings are discrepant. Dengerink (1976) has concluded that there is no evidence at this time that feelings of guilt are anything more than feelings of social disapproval or anxiety about social disapproval. In other words, the inhibition of aggression is socially controlled—not internally controlled, as the concept of guilt suggests.

Perceived Intent

The expression of aggression is also affected by the way we interpret the events that may elicit aggression. When a person is the recipient of an aggressive attack, for example, there is the question of the intent of that attack. Was it deliberate, was it accidental, was the aggressor simply carrying out an order? In one study (Nickel, 1974) the subject was given a series of high-intensity shocks by a confederate. Before the subject had the opportunity to retaliate, it was explained to the subject that he had received high-intensity shocks because of an error made by the experimenter. As a result of these instructions, the subject counteraggressed with much lower levels of shock than control subjects who were not given these instructions. Clearly, it was not the level of pain or discomfort suffered that determined the level of counteraggression but rather the intent of the attacker.

Horn blowing can be an aggressive act. Anyone who has been the object of an impatient horn-blowing driver can attest that a blast from a horn can readily arouse anger. The intent of the horn blower is, of course, an important factor. For example, if you heard the person behind you blow her horn, you might initially be angered. However, if you discovered that it was a friend greeting you, that anger would quickly subside. There are many situations in which the act itself is not necessarily aggressive. For example, someone may evaluate your behavior unfavorably for constructive rather than destructive reasons. Toch (1969) has noted that the largest category of violent criminals are what he calls "self-image compensators." These people have pronounced feelings of insecurity and low self-esteem. As a result, they feel constantly threatened. Events that would not affect a person with good self-esteem readily provoke these people.

Summary

Personality has been found to mediate the tendency toward aggression. For example, internals, who have a strong need to control, are more likely to act aggressively when provoked than externals. Similarly, Type A's, who also
(continued)

have a strong need to control, are more likely to act aggressively when provoked. People who do not believe that aggression is a socially acceptable way of dealing with aggression and people who have a strong need for social approval typically are less inclined to behave aggressively when provoked. Finally, how a person perceives the intent of another person's behavior plays an important role. People with low self-esteem are more inclined to feel threatened. As a result, they have a greater tendency to behave aggressively.

Issues in Aggression

Aggression as Obedience to Authority

Stanley Milgram (1963, 1974) has shown that under certain conditions people will carry out aggressive behaviors when they are instructed to do so. Milgram told his subjects that he was studying the effects of shock on learning. Each subject was seated in turn in front of a machine that he was told could deliver shocks of up to 450 volts. He was instructed to depress the levers in ascending order when the "learner" in the next room made a mistake, a procedure he was told would deliver progressively more intense shocks.

In actuality, the machine never did shock the other person. The "learner" was a confederate of Milgram and he made errors deliberately, thus requiring the subject to deliver more and more intense shocks. In order to convince the subject that shocks were indeed being delivered and were painful, the confederate cried out in pain as the shock intensity supposedly increased and even pounded on the wall and pleaded with the subject to stop.

Many of the subjects indicated they did want to stop, but Milgram, seated nearby, in an increasingly authoritative voice told them they had no choice, they must continue. Most subjects followed the instructions. In fact, 65% of the subjects administered 450 volts even after the confederate had ceased to respond, giving the impression that the shocks had seriously incapacitated him.

It has been suggested that these results provide evidence that humans will give up personal control or personal morality when they are placed in a situation in which they perceive that another person is in charge and knows what he is doing. The laboratory situation may be considered analogous to war, in which an officer orders soldiers under his command to act in an aggressive manner. The fact that people will obediently carry out acts of aggression ordered by an authoritarian figure has caused a great deal of concern among social scientists. The concern typically involves the potential misuse of authority and the bloodshed that it may precipitate. The problem for the individual is to guard against falling prey to the tendency to obey authority yet at the same time respect the need for authority.

Pornography and Aggression

A great deal of research has focused on the question of whether aggression in pornographic films leads to increasing violence toward women, especially rape (see Donnerstein & Linz, 1986; Malamuth & Donnerstein, 1984). The primary effort of this research has been to distinguish the effects of erotica that involves no violence or force from those of pornography that does portray violence and force. A film showing a woman being raped or tortured, for example, differs substantially from a film depicting two lovers engaged in intercourse. This research has shown that erotica per se does not seem to lead to an increase in male aggression toward women, but that violent pornography, involving scenes of rape, may lead to an increase in the tendency to rape. The reason I use the word *may* is that these studies have not shown that men who have volunteered to participate in them have actually raped as a result of watching scenes of rape; they have shown rather that men who have watched such films tend to develop a somewhat relaxed attitude toward rape. Such men tend to see rape as having no serious or harmful effect on women. A possible reason for this attitude is that pornographic films often portray the rape victim as offering only token resistance before she is swept away by passion for her attacker. Men who fail to understand that rape is a terrifying and traumatic experience for a woman may be misled by these portrayals. In view of the fact that attitudes and information affect our behavior, the finding that violence in pornographic films leads to attitude changes is an important demonstration of the power of pornography. Clearly, such films are not in the best interests of men, of women, or of society at large.

If it is not the depiction of sexual activity that is producing the attitude changes but rather the way women are portrayed in pornographic films, it is important to consider how the media in general portray women. A great deal of violence toward women is shown on television, in films, and in advertising. At this point very little work has been done to evaluate the effects of these portrayals of violence toward women.

Television Violence and Aggression

Does watching television violence promote real violence? Although there has been extensive research on this question, the answer is still not clear. Research has shown that television may increase the tendency for some people to engage in aggressive behaviors, provided they are provoked. This does not mean, however, that television causes aggressive behavior in the absence of provocation. It may be that television acts indirectly to increase aggressiveness (for example, Fenigstein, 1979). At least four explanations have been offered: (1) modeling and imitation of aggression, (2) release, or disinhibition, of aggressive impulses, (3) elicitation of aggressive actions that have been previously learned, and (4) an increase in arousal produced by watching aggressive activities (Bandura, 1973; Geen, 1976).

It has been found that a large proportion of the children who watch violence on television do not show increased aggressiveness, and it is necessary to account for this fact. One important factor is how the parents view violence. If the parents do not endorse violence as a means of settling disputes, achieving goals, and so on, children who watch violence on television tend not to be affected by it (Dominick & Greenberg, 1971). Another factor that needs to be considered is whether a given child prefers violence. Not all children, it appears, like to watch violence. Those who do prefer violence on television also tend to be more aggressive (Eron et al., 1972; Fenigstein, 1979). The fact that viewing television violence is correlated with later aggressiveness is therefore not surprising. The aggressiveness, however, is not necessarily due to TV violence. Rather, it appears to be due to an underlying tendency to be aggressive. Again, parental attitudes may play an important role in facilitating or inhibiting this tendency. Finally, since the tendency toward aggression is mediated by anger, whether a child is angry may play a role in determining whether TV violence will have an effect. As we saw earlier in this chapter, certain environmental factors will increase aggressiveness only if the person is angry. It appears that TV violence can be a very powerful contributor to aggression, at least for a short time, when a person is angry (Doob & Climie, 1972). This finding suggests that TV violence has a general arousal effect that facilitates aggressiveness, as opposed to a specific modeling effect.

Catharsis and the Control of Aggression

Before we leave the topic of aggression, a final comment needs to be made about catharsis. From time to time various people have argued that aggression is the result of aggressive energy that builds up because of frustration. Taking this analogy a step further, some people have suggested that the way to control the expression of aggression is to "drain off" some of the excess energy. This draining off or cleaning out is called "catharsis." From the material already discussed, we know that such a concept is far too simplistic to be considered correct or incorrect. Since arousal can augment aggressive tendencies, however, we might ask whether arousal reduction can reduce the tendency toward aggression. If *catharsis* is thus redefined, there appears to be some affirmative evidence for some type of cathartic process. However, there is ample evidence that aggression often makes the attacker more rather than less anxious, thus increasing arousal. Geen and Quanty (1977, p. 33) have suggested that aggression does not reduce arousal when (1) "the target possesses a higher social status than the attacker," (2) "aggression is a manifestly inappropriate response in the given situation," or (3) "the individual is predisposed to react to aggression with feelings of guilt." Thus, acting on an aggressive "urge" will not necessarily reduce arousal under all conditions. When it does, there appears to be evidence for some type of cathartic process.

Summary

One important issue related to the question of aggression is whether aggression, under certain circumstances, can be induced by the requirement of obedience to authority. Indeed, it can be shown that people can be made to act aggressively when the situation seems "reasonable" and when they have been ordered to do so by an authority figure. While it has been argued that this form of aggression can be an important factor in time of war, the question arises as to how we can guard against being used by authority figures who insist that we behave aggressively in pursuit of the goals they set before us. A second issue related to aggression is whether pornography is responsible for acts of aggression by men against women. The general consensus among social science researchers is that erotica per se does not induce aggressive behavior but that pornography that involves violence toward women does cause aggression. A third issue concerns the larger question of whether the violence portrayed on television increases the likelihood of aggression. The general consensus is that TV violence does not in itself cause aggression but can facilitate it. A fourth issue relates to the question of whether it is possible to drain off aggressive energy in a process of catharsis. While there is some evidence that it is possible to drain off aggressive energy (arousal), there is also evidence that aggressive behavior can increase rather than decrease arousal in some situations.

Main Points

1. Human aggression has frequently been defined as the intent to harm another human. Ethologists do not view aggression as good or bad; rather, they view it as an expression of the self-preservation motive.

2. The fact that it is possible to breed animals for aggressive behavior suggests that aggression in animals is determined in part by genetics. In humans, certain chromosomal abnormalities have been linked to aggression.

3. Both territory and dominance hierarchies govern whether an animal is likely to engage in a fight or a flight response when confronted.

4. Territorial dominance in humans emerges when two persons have dissimilar opinions.

5. Moyer has suggested that there are at least eight kinds of aggression.

6. Several brain structures have been identified as mediating different kinds of aggressive behavior (hypothalamus, amygdala, septum, hippocampus).

7. These brain structures have been shown to interact with social dominance in the expression of aggression.

8. The male sex hormone testosterone has been shown to augment aggression.

9. In women the fall in progesterone level just before menstruation, together with the relative rise in estrogen level, has been associated with aggression.

10. Hypoglycemia (low blood glucose level) and several drugs (including alcohol and amphetamines) have also been shown to increase aggression.

11. Intense and unexpected frustration, negative evaluation, and insult are some of the more common psychological states that evoke aggression.

12. A drop in diastolic blood pressure has been found to be reliably correlated with the expression of aggression.

13. Women are more likely than men to behave in a nonhostile fashion when provoked.

14. Humans appear to have a strong motivation to retaliate in like kind when provoked by an aggressive, degrading, or insulting act.

15. Noise, certain types of erotic stimulation, crowding, and heat are some of the stimuli that have been shown to increase aggression.

16. Studies of the development of aggression suggest that children initially attempt to control their environment by using a number of negative/disruptive responses. Under parental guidance (punishment, modeling, and so on) most children learn more socially acceptable ways of controlling their environments.

17. The tendency to use aggression as a means of control is linked to parental behavior in that the children of parents who use violence as a means of control tend, as adults, also to use violence.

18. Evidence suggests that most humans tend to avoid physical aggression. Physical aggression tends to be used (1) when a person has been provoked by physical aggression and (2) when all other methods of control have failed.

19. Because increases in arousal are typically associated with increases in aggression, arousal has been suggested as one of the many factors that mediate provoked aggression.

20. Most people inhibit the tendency to retaliate physically when provoked. Such inhibition seems to be greatest among people who are sensitive to the evaluations of others and who value an orderly society. It is not surprising, therefore, that people who are alienated in some way from society are more prone to physical violence and destructiveness.

21. People who are angered are less likely to be inhibited by the values of society.

22. Under certain conditions, aggression can be induced by the requirement of obedience to authority.

23. Pornography that portrays violence toward women can alter attitudes or beliefs that may lead to increases in aggression by men against women.

24. There is evidence that watching TV violence is correlated with increased aggression. However, children who are already aggressive are more likely to watch violence on TV.

25. The idea that aggressive energy can be drained off (catharsis) has not been supported. However, there is some evidence that lowering arousal may reduce aggression.

Depression, Controllability, and Assertiveness

How prevalent is depression in our society?

Is there a biological basis for depression?

Do antidepressants cure depression or do they simply remove the symptoms?

When people become depressed, they often feel helpless. Why?

Does depression produce feelings of helplessness or do feelings of helplessness cause depression?

Can people get rid of depressed feelings by changing the way they think?

Do attitudes we hold about ourselves have anything to do with depression?

What is the link between wanting to be in control and feelings of depression?

What forms of therapy are available for people who are suffering from depression?

How Prevalent Is Depression in Our Society?

Some years ago Aaron Beck and J. Young (1978) conducted a survey to determine how prevalent depression was among university students. They found that 78% of the students questioned reported that they had experienced depression at some time during the course of the academic year. Forty-six percent of those who reported depression indicated that their symptoms had been severe enough to warrant psychiatric help. When people are depressed, they frequently entertain thoughts of suicide. A significant number of people actually do kill themselves. Of the 9 to 10 million people who suffer from depression yearly in the United States and Canada, upwards of 150,000 (about 15%) eventually commit suicide (Rosenfeld, 1985). When people are depressed, their motivation typically declines. They often lose their appetites, lose interest in sex and in social interaction generally, have no interest in achieving goals, are unable to concentrate, tire easily and have little energy, and are overwhelmed by feelings of hopelessness, worthlessness, guilt, or self-reproach. In short, they lose the motivation to control their lives.

Beck and Young reported that depression is generally twice as high among university students as in a comparable group of nonuniversity students. Women are two to five times more prone to depression than men. In the past, depression tended to occur more frequently at midlife (the 40s or 50s), but recently it has been occurring earlier. Many people in their 30s, 20s, and even teens are experiencing depression. The elderly, too, are susceptible to depression. Suicide is becoming increasingly common among these groups. Depression hounded many famous figures of history, from Saul and Nebuchadnezzar of biblical times to Abraham Lincoln, Winston Churchill, and Ernest Hemingway.

What is the cause of depression and why is it occurring earlier and earlier? We have no clear answer. Depression is often referred to as a mood disorder. It is certainly a profound mood disorder, but it is much more than that. It involves biological changes in the neurotransmitters and it has been shown that it can be learned. While various researchers have emphasized biological over learned factors or learned over cognitive, it seems obvious that if we are to have a full understanding of depression we will have to understand the interaction of its biological, learned, and cognitive components.

The Biological Component

The catecholamine hypothesis.   After analyzing the relationship between affective disorders and catecholamines, Joseph J. Schildkraut and Seymour Kety (1967) formulated the catecholamine hypothesis of affective disorders. Because drugs that deplete or block norepinephrine produce sedation and depression, whereas drugs that increase norepinephrine relieve depression and produce elation and euphoria, they concluded that norepinephrine is the chemical primarily involved in the mood changes that characterize various affective disorders. According to their hypothesis, excessive amounts of norepinephrine produce the manic state— the high end of the manic-depressive continuum—and that a deficiency of norepinephrine produces the depressive state at the low end.

Electroconvulsive shock treatment.   One of the earliest treatments of depression consisted of electroconvulsive shock therapy, in which the brain is briefly subjected to several hundred volts of electrical current. Doctors who have used this procedure have argued that while electroconvulsive shock may not cure depression and has certain undesirable side effects, such as loss of immediate memory, it can alleviate some of the symptoms and halt the downward spiral that often characterizes depression. Recently we have come to understand why electroconvulsive shock actually works: it stimulates the brain to produce tyrosine hydroxylase, a chemical that is important in the synthesis of norepinephrine. Normally, a low level of norepinephrine triggers the action of tyrosine hydroxylase, and more norepinephrine is synthesized. For some reason, when people become depressed, a low level of norepinephrine fails to produce the expected response by tyrosine hydroxylase, and the norepinephrine level remains low (Weiss, 1982, cited in Turkington, 1982).

The use of drugs to treat depression.   Depression is treated today primarily by drugs. It has been concluded that 60 to 80% of patients treated with drugs experience significant improvement. Tricyclic antidepressants, such as Tofranil and Elavil, are preferred for the initial treatment of symptoms of depression. They take about two weeks to take effect and can have some unpleasant side effects. The tricyclics work the same way that cocaine works: they help to block the reuptake of norepinephrine at the receptors, thereby increasing the concentration of norepinephrine at the receptor sites. Another set of antidepressants that is often used, especially if the tricyclics fail to work or if their side effects are severe, consists of the monoamine oxidase inhibitors (MAOI), such as Narplan, Nardil, and Parnate. Monoamine oxidase is an enzyme that is important in the regulation of such catecholamines as norepinephrine. When the monoamine oxidase level is high, it somehow reduces the level of norepinephrine. As the MAOI inhibits monoamine oxidase, the norepinephrine level rises. In other words, a fairly large body of converging data support Schildkraut and Kety's (1967) contention that depression is closely linked to the norepinephrine level.

Stress and depression.   Numerous studies have found a link between stress and depression. One of the laboratory techniques for inducing stress is to expose humans or animals to uncontrollable shock. When animals are exposed to uncontrollable shock, norepinephrine is released at a high rate from the locus coeruleus, an area in the brainstem that we talked about in connection with sleep and dreams in Chapter 4. Apparently the receptors in the brainstem do not use all of the available norepinephrine, and the unused norepinephrine is reabsorbed by the neuron and destroyed. The store of norepinephrine is then depleted, and as the body cannot synthesize norepinephrine as quickly as it is being released, the norepinephrine level in the locus coeruleus is lowered. This lowered level of norepinephrine is believed to result in feelings of depression (Weiss, 1982, cited in Turkington, 1982).

Depression following drug use.   The depression that often accompanies the use of such drugs as cocaine and the amphetamines can readily be understood in this context. Both cocaine and the amphetamines have been shown to produce feelings of euphoria. Both drugs seem to work by increasing the level of norepinephrine, as we saw in Chapter 9. Once the drug wears off (is metabolized), the level of norepinephrine tends to drop, often dramatically. When that happens, people often experience profound feelings of depression. In this instance the norepinephrine level typically returns to normal fairly quickly. Apparently the drugs exhaust the momentary supply of norepinephrine and the body needs time to rebuild that supply. The depression that we experience after expending a great deal of energy or after concentrating for a long time can be conceptualized in the same way. The difference between these cases and prolonged depression causes us to question why the body sometimes fails to synthesize more norepinephrine when the supply has been reduced or depleted.

Spontaneous remission of depression.   One of the fascinating things about depression is the suddenness with which many depressives spontaneously recover from the affliction without therapy. Can their recovery be traced to a restoration of physiological/neurological functioning or to some cognitive process or to learning? At this point we do not know.

Depression as an Adaptive Mood
The fact that so many people experience depression has led scientists to ask: "Is depression adaptive?" (Costello, 1976). If it is adaptive, the next question is: "What function does depression serve?" The fact that depression often disappears spontaneously suggests that something is happening at some biological level. One possibility is that depression is a protective mechanism that allows the body to rebuild or reprogram itself after one has been exposed to a set of conditions that prevent one from exercising control. Once the rebuilding or reprogramming has taken place (which may take quite a long time), the depressive symptoms disappear. The lack of motivation or simply the lack of initiative that accompanies the mood disorder prevents the individual from engaging in new activities, so that the rebuilding or reprogramming can proceed without interruption.

Another possibility is that depression helps the individual to abandon goals that are unattainable (Klinger, 1975). When people find that events are uncontrollable, they tend to become depressed. When they become depressed, they tend to disengage themselves from ongoing activities. Having abandoned activities that are not adaptive, they can eventually switch to new activities. In the interim they may engage in cognitive activities that will help prepare them to deal again with the environment. The cognitive activities may lead to the setting of new goals or simply to experimentation with new behaviors that eventually lead to the development of new skills. The net effect is an individual who is better prepared to interact with the environment.

What these explanations don't tell us is why people develop self-destructive feelings. Thoughts of suicide hardly seem adaptive for a person in the process of reorganizing for the future or of disengaging from some activity that is causing grief. If we do not view depression as adaptive, however, we are faced with the conclusion that depression somehow represents evolution gone astray, a concept that is difficult to reconcile with other information we have about the adaptive nature of human motivation. Obviously we still have much to learn about this mood disorder.

Summary

Depression is a fairly common mood disorder that has been found to be particularly prevalent among the young, women, and the elderly. There is strong evidence that depression is linked to the catecholamines, especially to norepinephrine. When the norepinephrine level is low, one tends to experience depression; when it is high, one tends to experience euphoria. Data in support of this hypothesis come from two sources: the finding that electroconvulsive shock (often used to treat severe depression) leads to an elevation of the norepinephrine level and the fact that antidepressant drugs elevate the norepinephrine level at the synapses. The link between stress and depression also seems to involve norepinephrine. When we experience prolonged stress, the norepinephrine level declines. The depression that often follows the use of drugs that produce feelings of euphoria may be due to the depletion of norepinephrine. Various people have argued that depression should be viewed as an adaptive mechanism that can be of value to us in our continuing need to deal with a changing environment.

The Learned Component

The main model of learned helplessness has come from the work of Martin E. Seligman and his colleagues. Because his research has occupied such a central place in the research on depression, I will deal with it in some detail.

Seligman's Model of Learned Helplessness

While doing research on the relation between fear conditioning and instrumental learning, Seligman and two colleagues discovered a striking phenomenon that came to be called "learned helplessness" (Overmier & Seligman, 1967; Seligman & Maier, 1967). Initially they restrained dogs in a harness in order to administer moderately painful but not physically damaging shock. Although their original intent had not been to study inescapable shock, that is in fact what they had fortuitously arranged for the dogs. Nothing the dog did could affect the onset, the offset, the duration, or the intensity of the shocks. The shocks were therefore uncontrollable from the perspective of the dog.

The second phase of the experiment was designed to study how these dogs behaved in a shuttle box. The shuttle box (see Figure 8-2) is an apparatus used to study instrumental learning. In the type of shuttle box used with dogs, a barrier divides the space into two areas. The dog can *escape* the shock by jumping over the barrier when the shock comes on. By switching the shock from side to side, the experimenter can make the animal shuttle between the two sides. In order to see whether the animal can learn to *avoid* shock, a light or tone is typically presented before the shock to signal the animal that shock is forthcoming. If the animal jumps over the barrier when the signal is turned on, it indicates the animal has learned to avoid the painful stimulus.

Normally, when naive (untrained) dogs are placed in the shuttle box and the shock is turned on, they frantically jump about the box and accidentally scramble over the barrier to the safe (no shock) side. In a very few trials these dogs learn to jump as soon as the shock begins, thereby drastically limiting the amount of shock they experience at any given trial. Typically it takes several more trials before the dogs will begin to avoid the shock by jumping at the onset of the signal rather than the onset of the shock. They eventually learn this very important adaptive response, which enables them to avoid the painful stimulus altogether.

Much to the surprise of Seligman and his colleagues, the dogs given the inescapable-shock training showed a markedly different pattern of responses to the shock. Initially, they behaved like naive dogs: they frantically ran around the shuttle box when the shock was turned on. After 30 seconds, however, their behavior suddenly changed. They stopped jumping and running, lay down on the shock grid, and whined. When the animals failed to make any further responses for 60 seconds, the shock was turned off. They had, of course, failed to make an escape response. The same pattern of behavior occurred on the next trial. The animal struggled at first and then gave up, passively accepting the shock. On succeeding trials the behavior followed a similar pattern, with increasing passivity toward the shock. On none of the trials did the animal attempt to escape.

To make sure the effects observed were due to lack of control over the shock, not merely to the shock itself, Seligman and his colleagues designed an experiment to isolate the effects of controllability from the effects of shock. The design involved three groups.

The first group of dogs received pretreatment shock that they could control by some response. In one study the dog was able to limit the duration of the shock by pressing a panel with its nose (Seligman & Maier, 1967); in a second study the dog was able to limit the duration of the shock by not moving (Maier, 1970). A second group consisted of yoked controls. These dogs received the same pattern of shock but had no way of controlling it. Thus the second group experienced exactly the same amount of shock as the first without the critical factor of control. In both the first and the second conditions, the animals were restrained by a hammock to prevent them from jumping or running. A third group was given no pretreatment.

After 24 hours the dogs were given escape-avoidance training in a shuttle box. The no-pretreatment group and the group allowed to control the shock during pretreatment readily learned the task. They jumped over the barrier at the onset of shock and then learned to avoid the shock. The group given uncontrollable shock performed much more poorly. Most of the dogs failed to jump the barrier at the onset of shock. These results clearly show that it was not the shock itself that produced the deficit but rather the inability to control the shock. The fact that not moving in Maier's (1970) study was as effective a procedure as nose pressing in Seligman and Maier's (1967) study shows that the important variable was control. Maier's study makes it impossible to argue that the animals were simply learning to be active. In Maier's study the animals were learning not to be active.

Learned Helplessness in Humans

The phenomenon of learned helplessness is by no means restricted to dogs. Learned helplessness has been demonstrated in cats (for example, Thomas & Balter, cited in Seligman, 1975), in fish (for example, Padilla et al., 1970), in rats (for example, Maier, Seligman, & Solomon, 1969; Seligman, Maier, & Solomon, 1971), and in primates (for example, Seligman, 1975). The main interest in learned helplessness, however, has focused on humans.

Numerous studies have been reported on learned helplessness in humans. In one study, Hiroto (1974) used human subjects and replicated almost exactly the findings obtained by Seligman and his colleagues. Subjects in his controllability group were exposed to a loud noise, which they could turn off by pushing a button. His lack-of-controllability group received the same loud noise but could not control it. After this pretreatment, the subjects were tested in a finger-shuttle box that simply required them to move their hand from one side to the other to escape the noise. Just as in the dog experiments, the no-pretreatment and controllability groups quickly learned the escape problem, but the lack-of-controllability group failed to learn it. Most of the subjects in the lack-of-controllability condition sat passively and accepted the noxious noise.

Externals and internals.   Hiroto's study included two additional variables that indicate that the subjects' perceived ability to control the events governed their responses. Half of the subjects in each of the three groups were told their performance in the shuttle box was a test of skill; the remaining half were told their scores were governed by chance. As expected, subjects who received the "chance" instructions tended to respond more helplessly in all the conditions. Hiroto also decided to examine personality differences. He divided his subjects into two groups corresponding to "externals" and "internals," using a personality inventory measure. Externals, according to Rotter (1966), are people who believe that events in their lives are governed to a large degree by chance. Internals believe that events can be controlled and that the application of skills can bring about positive outcomes. As predicted, externals were more inclined to become helpless than internals.

The results of Hiroto's study not only confirm that humans react to lack of control in the same way as animals do but emphasize the cognitive nature of helplessness in humans. This, of course, is consistent with Seligman's suggestion that helplessness reflects a belief about the effectiveness of responding. The helpless person *does not* believe that his or her responses will have any effect on aversive or noxious events, whereas the person who has not learned to be helpless *does* believe that his or her responses will be effective in terminating such events.

Deficits in Learned Helplessness

Seligman has concluded from these and other studies that learned helplessness is characterized by three deficits: (1) failure to initiate responses, (2) failure to learn, and (3) emotional disturbance.

Failure to initiate responses.   Adaptive behavior is generally characterized by repeated attempts to achieve a goal. In the course of initiating responses, the individual typically tries a wide range of responses. Sometimes these behaviors are highly systematic, suggesting that the individual may be systematically testing all possible alternatives in some hierarchy of adaptive responses. Aggressive behavior, as discussed in Chapter 10, may be a class of behaviors that falls within the hierarchy of adaptive responses. That is, aggressive responses may enable the individual to regain control of the environment.

There is evidence indicating that certain adaptive responses are inherited (unlearned) or at least that the predisposition to make these responses is inherited (Bolles, 1970). Other adaptive responses, however, are clearly learned. According to the principles of learning, a response will be repeated if it results in reinforcement. For example, an escape response is learned in the shuttle box because jumping over the barrier reduces the duration of a noxious event, and that is reinforcing. In human terms we might say termination of a noxious event produces relief. We feel relief when we turn off a noxious TV program or when the neighbor's dog stops barking after we yell at the dog or its owner. We know from studies of learning that it is likely that these responses will be repeated because the responses produced a desired effect—relief from the noxious or aversive stimulus.

It can happen that certain aversive events in our environment come and go and we can do nothing about them. For example, our next-door neighbor may play the stereo into the early hours of the morning. We complain, but nothing happens, and then unexpectedly the person moves. A neighbor may have a dog that, despite our pleas, is allowed to bark throughout the night. One day the neighbor sells the dog. In such cases the relief we experience is independent of our responses. According to the principles of learning, the fact that there is no predictable association between a response and the occurrence of a reward means there can be no learning. Seligman has argued, however, that we do in fact learn something. We learn that relief is sometimes independent of our responses. He further suggests that this cognitive set, or belief, can then generalize to other situations. As a result, we may fail to initiate responses in the presence of aversive or noxious stimuli.

Failure to initiate responses of any kind is very nonadaptive. Noxious stimulation not only is aversive but in some cases may threaten our very survival. It is critical, therefore, for us to try to remove or stop the noxious event. We can do so only if we initiate a response, no matter how poor or inappropriate that response may be. Even random behavior may result in termination of the aversive event. Given that most of us have some previous experience dealing with noxious events, we have at our disposal a hierarchy of responses that may help us deal with such events. Failure to initiate responses of any kind reflects, therefore, a loss of basic survival motivation.

Failure to learn.   Another striking characteristic of learned helplessness is inability to learn that one can control certain events in one's environment. In an experiment very similar to that of Hiroto (1974), Miller and Seligman (1975) studied three groups of students who received escapable, inescapable, or no loud noise in the prelearning phase and were then confronted with a task involving skill and a task involving chance. The skill task required subjects to sort 15 cards into ten categories with a time limit of 15 seconds. The experimenter arranged to have them succeed or fail on a given sorting trial by saying the time was up either before or after they had finished. The subjects were unaware that the experimenter was ignoring clock time. At the end of each trial, the subject was asked to estimate his chances of succeeding on the next trial. Subjects who had previously been exposed to the inescapable noise (the helpless condition) showed little change in their expectancy after each new success or failure. The escape group and the no-pretreatment group, in contrast, showed large changes in their expectancy of success after each new success or failure. In other words, the helpless subjects did not perceive that the outcomes were related to their actions, and the escape and no-pretreatment groups did. When the three groups were exposed to a chance task, they showed no difference in expectancy change following success and failure. All three groups responded as though the outcome were independent of their actions—an appropriate way of responding to a chance event. Other studies have replicated this basic finding (for example, Hiroto & Seligman, 1975).

Seligman (1975) has pointed out that evidence from a variety of sources indicates that experiencing two events as independent (noncontingent) makes it very difficult at some later time to learn that they are dependent, or related, when they have been made contingent (for example, Kemler & Shepp, 1971). To explain this fact, Seligman has argued that organisms acquire information about what events are and are not dependent in the environment. He suggests that once two things are perceived as independent, it is just as difficult to alter this perception as it is to alter the idea that two things are dependent. The confirmation either that two things are related or that they are unrelated seems to retard further information processing. As a result, the helpless person fails to learn that two events have become dependent. He or she has, according to Hiroto (1974), become an external type of person. As we shall see, the internal person is like the external in that he or she also fails to respond to certain types of new information. Whereas externals fail to respond to information that their responses are producing changes in the environment, internals fail to respond to information that their responses are not producing changes in the environment.

Emotional disturbance. Numerous studies have shown that lack of controllability produces a variety of emotional responses. As we noted in Chapter 8, uncontrollable shocks are associated with high outputs of epinephrine (for example, Brady, 1967) as well as ulceration (for example, Weiss, 1968, 1971a, 1971b, 1971c). Being in control, in contrast, is associated with high outputs of norepinephrine (Brady, 1967, 1975) and the absence of ulcers (Weiss, 1968, 1971a, 1971b, 1971c). Higher blood pressure has also been found to characterize people who are exposed to uncontrollable situations (for example, Hokanson et al., 1971).

In addition to these and other physiological changes, there are at least two distinct psychological changes. Lack of controllability produces increases in anxiety and depression (Seligman, 1975). Both anxiety and depression are complex psychological states that have been shown to have a very debilitating effect on humans. I will discuss these effects in more detail later. What is clear is that some very basic and important emotional changes are produced when aversive stimulation becomes uncontrollable.

Factors Affecting the Tendency to Become Helpless

There are numerous examples of people who are exposed to uncontrollable events and do not become helpless. Many people who suffer helplessness for a time recover. What is the reason for this difference? Why don't these people, when exposed to uncontrollable events, acquire a cognitive representation that reflects the experience of environmental outcomes independent of responses?

Many people, it appears, are more or less immune to becoming helpless. This is not surprising if we realize that the cognitive representation may reflect a lifetime of experiences. The internal person has come to perceive that his or her responses can alter events in the environment. According to Seligman's theory, this perception could result from a lifetime of experiences in which most of the time responses affect outcomes. The person has come to expect that responses will continue to alter events in the environment, and accordingly he or she continues to emit coping responses. Whether exposure to uncontrollable events will produce helplessness is, according to Seligman, affected by two basic factors: (1) the importance of the event and (2) the similarity between the current uncontrollable situation and other situations that the person may experience in the future.

Importance of the event.   If I were no longer able to do my job or if I could no longer remember the names of my friends or if I found that people could no longer understand me, I would be justifiably distressed and might well become helpless. However, if I found that I was unable to do the latest dance step or if I failed to win a lottery or were not able to remember the name of the producer of a current movie, I probably would not feel very distressed, nor is it likely that I would become helpless. Whether an event affects me is related to how much value I place on that event or how it relates to my self-concept.

Tendency to generalize from a specific event.   Being unable to control a single event does not necessarily produce a general state of helplessness. A person who suddenly finds she cannot effectively deal with rush-hour traffic may simply give up driving in the rush hour and take the bus instead. A person who finds large parties stressful may simply stop going to such parties. Sometimes, however, a given experience will generalize. A person who finds she cannot deal with rush-hour traffic may decide she cannot deal with normal traffic. As a result she may sell her car and avoid going anyplace that requires a car. A person who decides he doesn't like large parties may begin to avoid all social gatherings and eventually become totally withdrawn and antisocial.

Thus, being helpless in one situation may generalize to other situations. How much generalization there will be is not easy to specify. In general, research suggests that the degree of generalization is typically governed by the amount of similarity between the two situations. The greater the perceived similarity, the greater the generalization.

The Reformulated Model of Learned Helplessness

Both the original and reformulated learned helplessness models hypothesize that depression is the result of learning that outcomes are uncontrollable. In the reformulated model, mere exposure to an uncontrollable event is insufficient to produce learned helplessness. To become helpless, the individual actually experiences being helpless and believes he or she will be helpless in the future. When people do develop a feeling of helplessness, they tend to wonder why they are helpless. At this point they begin to make causal attributions about the generality of the experience (whether being helpless in this situation means they will be helpless in other situations) and whether or not the event is likely to be chronic (there is nothing they can do to change the environment or themselves to alter the situation). If they do generalize and accept the belief that nothing will change, they will eventually develop low self-esteem (Abramson, Seligman, & Teasdale, 1978; Miller & Norman, 1979). Note that the key to learned helplessness is the development of expectations of future inability to control events.

Prevention of Learned Helplessness

According to the learned helplessness model, the key to preventing people from developing feelings of helplessness is to help them not to generalize from a single encounter with uncontrollability. Obviously, the tendency to generalize is linked to past experiences. If you have a past history of inability to control events, one more such experience may persuade you that you will never be able to control any event. People whose history has given them confidence in their ability to control events are much less likely to generalize from a single encounter with an uncontrollable event. It follows that giving people experience in mastery will make them more resistant to the effects of uncontrollability. Recent evidence suggests that it may indeed be possible to help people to become resistant to the effects of uncontrollability. In a study with rats, it was shown that if a rat first learned to lever-press to escape shock, it persisted longer in the face of inescapable shock and showed better associative learning (Volpicelli et al., 1983). One of the important things to do when one is confronted with a challenging task (a task that requires one to develop skills that will enable one to control events) is to persist. Persistence can, of course, be maladaptive under some conditions, but generally we think of persistence as a necessary attribute for success.

Some Issues Related to Learned Helplessness

Psychological reactance and helplessness. Wortman and Brehm (1975) have extended reactance theory (Brehm, 1966, 1972) to account for the relation between psychological reactance and helplessness. Reactance theory says that when a person's freedom is threatened or eliminated, the person will be motivated to restore that freedom. In extending this basic idea to helplessness, Wortman and Brehm suggest that a person who is exposed to noncontingency will be motivated to reestablish control, and only after repeated attempts fail will he or she give up and become helpless.

Wortman and Brehm acknowledge that a task must be important if it is to induce a state of helplessness. Given that a task is important, they suggest that a great deal of helplessness training will be required before it is possible to demonstrate helplessness. They suggest that small amounts of helplessness training will simply motivate the person to work harder to reestablish control. Thus their theory predicts that helplessness training may facilitate performance on a subsequent task rather than interfere with it, depending on the amount of helplessness training given.

At least two studies have been reported that are consistent with Wortman and Brehm's prediction (Hanusa & Schulz, 1977; Roth & Kubal, 1975). In Roth and Kubal's study, subjects were trained with noncontingent reinforcement on a concept-formation task. Noncontingent reinforcement involved the administration of a prearranged schedule of "right" and "wrong" answers in response to the subject's performance on each of the trials of the task. Subjects who received 50 trials of training showed a facilitation effect, as Wortman and Brehm had predicted, whereas subjects who received 120 trials showed helplessness. In Hanusa and Schulz's (1977) study, subjects were exposed to the usual helplessness training. This procedure involved noncontingent reinforcement on a concept-formation task. The subjects were divided into four groups. Three groups were given information indicating that their failure at the task was due to either their lack of ability, lack of effort, or the difficulty of the task. The fourth group was given no explanation for its failure. Subjects who were led to believe their failure was due to their lack of ability performed better on a subsequent task involving mazes than all other groups. This finding indicates that information about one's lack of ability facilitates rather than debilitates performance on a later task. This effect, of course, is just the opposite of what would be expected from the helplessness model—namely, that information about one's lack of ability would produce helplessness. The results are, however, consistent with Wortman and Brehm's suggestion that short periods of exposure to information about one's lack of ability would motivate one to try harder in order to reestablish control.

Although Hanusa and Schulz (1977) failed to show that subjects would work harder if they were told their poor performance had been due to task difficulty rather than skill, Tennen and Eller (1977) did show that such information would motivate subjects to work harder. Again, it could be argued that when failure was ascribed to task difficulty, the subjects would try harder on the next task (which was different from the first) in order to convince themselves that they were able to control events in their environment.

Aversive outcomes, uncontrollability, and helplessness.   Before leaving the question of whether subjects in a learned helplessness experiment are motivated solely by the need to reestablish control, we need to examine another issue: whether the need to establish control occurs only in aversive situations (Douglas & Anisman, 1975). Many years ago Alfred Adler asserted that a person who perceives that he or she is lacking in certain skills (skills that others may have) will develop feelings of inferiority. This powerful aversive state, Adler suggested, motivates the person to develop competence. Others have not viewed competence as necessarily motivated by an aversive state. Various critics have argued simply that humans have a need to know about the causes of events (Heider, 1946) or that because humans have a need to interact with the environment, they need to develop skills that will enable them to do so efficiently and successfully (for example, White, 1959).

Although Seligman has suggested that lack of controllability is the main factor responsible for producing learned helplessness, it has been noted that most studies of learned helplessness use tasks on which a failure may be viewed as aversive (Benson & Kennelly, 1976). For example, subjects may perceive their inability to solve a laboratory problem as a reflection on their general intelligence or competence. It may be, therefore, that lack of controllability produces helplessness only when the person is faced with such an aversive outcome. In one study designed to examine this question (Benson & Kennelly, 1976), subjects in the helpless condition were given unsolvable problems (similar to those used by Hiroto & Seligman, 1975) and the usual noncontingent feedback (unsolvable-noncontingent group). Other subjects were given the same unsolvable tasks but were told they were correct on all attempted solutions (always-correct unsolvable-noncontingent group). Thus the latter group was led to believe it was successful. The unsolvable-non-contingent training condition produced the typical learned helplessness phenomenon. The other group, given continual positive feedback, did not show this effect. These results support the idea that lack of controllability will produce learned helplessness only if failure is experienced as aversive. Responses to the attribution questions given at the end of the test phase indicated that both the always-correct and unsolvable-noncontingent groups perceived the feedback to their responses in the pretreatment phase as uncontrollable—that is, external to themselves. Thus, although both groups experienced lack of controllability, only the unsolvable-non-contingent group behaved helplessly.

Other Behavioral Approaches to Depression

One of the things that characterize people who are depressed is failure to be aroused by such basic incentives as food and sex. Eric Klinger (1975) has referred to this process as "disengagement from incentives." Several treatment programs for depression, developed out of the behavioral theories of such people as B. F. Skinner and Albert Bandura, are designed to teach patients to behave in ways that increase rewarding experiences. When people become depressed, they withdraw. In the process of withdrawing, they become lonely, and loneliness deepens their depression. In order to break this downward cycle, people are encouraged to reengage themselves in social activities so that they can experience the pleasure that comes from social interactions.

Assertiveness training, a topic I will cover in some detail at the end of this chapter, is a direct outgrowth of the behavioral approach to depression. Assertiveness training is based on the assumption that people who are depressed often lack the skills that would enable them to control events in their lives. Assertiveness training, in other words, is an attempt to help people to reestablish control.

Summary

According to Seligman's model, feelings of helplessness are learned when a person or animal is exposed to outcomes that are not contingent on responses. Seligman argues that the individual in either a noncontingent or a contingent situation processes the information about the contingency or noncontingency and develops a cognitive representation that can be called learning, expectation, perception, or belief. This cognitive representation then determines whether the individual will make a coping response. The individual who has experienced noncontingency will tend to behave as though no response will be effective. The individual who has experienced contingency will tend to behave as though his or her responses will produce the desired outcome. Although Seligman suggests that noncontingencies are the basis for the cognition called helplessness, not all noncontingencies will necessarily lead to feelings of helplessness. If an event is not regarded as important, failure to control may have little or no effect. Similarly, if an event is not regarded as similar to other events, failure to control that event will probably not generalize to other events.

According to the reformulated model of learned helplessness, the development of helplessness depends on whether one believes that the helplessness one is currently experiencing will be repeated in the future. A person who sees the situation as chronic will eventually develop low self-esteem. The key to preventing the development of helplessness is to help people not to generalize from a single encounter with uncontrollability.

Psychological reactance theory suggests that events that threaten a person's freedom will motivate the person to reestablish control, not produce feelings of helplessness. Some, but not all, research has provided support for this interpretation. Although the motivation to establish control appears to be a fundamental need, this need appears to be greatest when events are aversive. It is probably for this reason that learned helplessness is easier to produce when an aversive event is made uncontrollable.

Behavioral approaches to the treatment of learned helplessness emphasize the need to experience success (rewards) in one's interaction with the environment.

The Cognitive Component

Beck's Theory

Aaron Beck (1967, 1976), a pioneer of cognitive approaches to depression, has proposed that the thinking patterns of depressed people play a critical role not only in initially producing depression but in maintaining it. He has pointed out that depressed people tend to view their current and future situations in negative terms. Such thinking is characterized by three tendencies. First, depressed people tend to view situations as negative even when a positive interpretation is possible. Second, they view interactions with the environment in terms of deprivation and defeat. Third, they tend to tailor facts to fit their negative conclusions. They may even ignore external input that is not consistent with their conclusion that life is essentially bad.

Beck argues that depressed people tend to develop an organized and stable "schema," or representation of themselves, and they process information on the basis of this schema. They screen, differentiate, and code the environment in accordance with the representation they have formed of themselves.

Beck emphasizes that the thinking process of depressed people often leads to "cognitive distortions." Because depressed people have a systematic "bias against the self," so that they compare themselves unfavorably with other people, they develop feelings of deprivation, depreciation, and failure. These cognitive distortions can be viewed as "errors in thinking." One kind of error is the tendency to overgeneralize. If someone points out a mistake that a depressed person has made, for example, the depressed person is likely to view this feedback as evidence that he lacks the skill to perform the task in question. As even highly skilled people can and often do make mistakes, to treat this one piece of feedback as an indication of overall lack of skill is inappropriate. Another kind of error is the tendency to make inferences without consideration of alternative points of view. If someone were to say, "It's taking you longer to finish that job than you planned," the depressed person would interpret the remark to mean "You haven't the ability to do this kind of work"; it would not occur to her that the other person might have meant "That job is tougher than either of us thought it would be."

Other Cognitive Approaches to Depression
While both learned helplessness and Beck's model of depression have enjoyed a great deal of acceptance, a critical appraisal of the two models has led some researchers to conclude that neither model has a great deal of empirical support (Coyne & Gotlib, 1983). The problem is that depression is a very complex syndrome with many and varied characteristics. As a result, it is difficult to develop a parsimonious theory (a theory with a few explanatory concepts) that accounts for all the various characteristics of this syndrome. Several other cognitive approaches to depression have focused on or emphasized other aspects of the process.

Characterological self-blame.   It has been suggested that the attributional models of depression, such as the reformulated model of learned helplessness, ignore the important causal dimension of controllability (Janoff-Bulman, 1979). Besides criticizing their own behavior, depressed people often express self-criticism over the kind of people they are. While people can change their behavior, they cannot change their character, or so we all tend to assume. Obviously, this kind of self-criticism can be devastating because it leads to the conclusion that nothing will ever change, no matter what they do.

Goal setting and standards of performance.   Sometimes people set very high goals or standards for themselves and are very critical of themselves when they fall short of their personal standard of excellence. It has been suggested that when people evaluate themselves and their self-worth against a very high standard, they may be setting themselves up for depression (Carver & Ganellen, 1983). Such people, it has been suggested, may tend to evaluate themselves as worthless on the basis of even a small deviation from their high standards. An "attitudes toward self" (ATS) test, developed to measure some of these qualities, has provided support for the idea that people who set very high goals and hold to very high standards of performance are susceptible to depression (Carver, Ganellen, & Behar-Mitrani, 1985).

Cognitive style, stress, and depression. A study of the links between coping style and depression found that subjects with depressive symptomatology took extraordinary responsibility, responded with more disgust/anger and worry/fear than normal, and were unusually confrontational in their coping style (Folkman & Lazarus, 1986). Such subjects have generally been considered more vulnerable than those who tend to be more accepting and less hostile. In Chapter 8 we noted that people who tend to exert a great deal of energy in connection with loss of control generally tend to be more vulnerable.

We often view stress as something that occurs when we fail to achieve our goals. It has been suggested that the degree to which we are affected by a failure to achieve a goal depends on whether we value achievement over other things, such as interpersonal relationships. While there is general agreement that loss of control in an achievement situation does undermine one's self-concept and so can lead to depression, data support the popular perception that people who stress closeness and intimacy can experience a similar breakdown of their self-concept when they are threatened by loss and rejection (Hammen et al., 1985). Once again, it is the breakdown of one's self-concept that seems to be the critical variable that precipitates feelings of depression.

Cognitive Approaches to Treatment

The cognitive models of depression suggest that one way to treat depression is to make cognitive interventions—that is, somehow alter the way people think about things.

Beck's approach. Beck (1967, 1976) has suggested that people who are depressed have learned inappropriate ways of interpreting their experiences. He has devised a 12-week training program to correct three major thought disorders: seeing themselves as deficient, seeing the world as frustrating rather than a source of fulfillment, and seeing the future as hopeless. Clinical studies have shown that cognitive therapy is more effective than drug therapy (Kovacs et al., 1981).

Interpersonal psychotherapy. Another approach that is promising was developed by Klerman and Weissman (cited in Rosenfeld, 1985). This approach helps patients to strengthen interpersonal relationships. The assumption behind this approach is that when people develop strong interpersonal relationships, their depression will lessen. There is a great deal of evidence that people who have strong interpersonal relationships often experience less stress, presumably because such a relationship helps one to maintain a self-concept as a worthwhile and important person. This approach, like Beck's, assumes that one of the main things that reduces vulnerability to depression is a self-concept that is able to sustain the individual through difficult periods when things are not going well.

Summary

Beck has noted that depressed people tend to view the present and future in negative terms. This negative style of thinking grows out of a stable internal representation, called a "schema." Depressed people, Beck argues, have a "bias against the self" that leads to errors in thinking, such as the tendency to overgeneralize and to make inferences without consideration of alternative points of view.

Other cognitive approaches have stressed different aspects of the cognitive style of depressed individuals. One approach has stressed the importance of characterological blame: depressed people criticize not simply their behavior but the kind of people they are—a form of criticism that is inconsistent with the idea that they may be able to change. Another cognitive approach has stressed the fact that depression sometimes grows out of a tendency to set goals and standards of performance that are too lofty. Finally, still another cognitive approach has examined people's ways of dealing with stress and has concluded that people who are hostile and confrontational tend to be vulnerable to depression. Treatment approaches to depression have stressed the need to correct one's thinking and to develop strong interpersonal relationships; both sorts of changes are believed to be important for the development of a self-concept strong enough to sustain one in times of adversity.

The Interaction of Biological, Learned, and Cognitive Factors

Exactly how do biological, learned, and cognitive factors interact to produce depression? If we accept the proposition that all depression is linked to lowered levels of catecholamines, then we must determine in what way they are linked. In short, what causes what?

Catecholamines and Thought Processes

One possibility is that changes in catecholamines cause changes in thinking. That is, when catecholamine concentrations drop, we have a natural tendency to become more negative, to overgeneralize, to become self-critical and develop a negative self-image. One problem with this model is that it cannot account for the fact that at least some depressions—those classified as reactive depressions—are precipitated by some event in the environment. Research indicates that people are likely to become depressed when they lose control. This model could account for endogenous depression, which seems to occur in the absence of any identifiable precipitating event; but in a study on the relation of stressful life events and depression, Cochran and Hammen (1985) have reported that their data more consistently indicate that depression causes cognitions than the reverse.

Loss of Control and Catecholamines

Another possibility is that loss of control reduces the catecholamine level. It is necessary here to specify exactly what we mean by loss of control. We don't all become depressed when we fail or lose control. The important factor is how we deal with a single experience of losing control. Some people seem to be very resilient after such an experience. They feel depressed, but the depression is very short-lived. We think that one of the main reasons they can bounce back so quickly is that they do not overgeneralize, do not blame their character, do not take a biased view of the situation. There are even some people who seem to show no depression at all. They tend to view loss of control as a challenge.

It is very difficult to specify whether it is the cognition per se or the behavior that follows from positive cognitions that restores the catecholamines. We know that engaging in adaptive behavior is often accompanied by catecholamine output. It has not been demonstrated unequivocally that just thinking positive thoughts produces chemical changes. Perhaps cognitive factors start the process in motion. That is, cognitions prime the catecholamine system, but the real rush of catechol-amines comes from engaging in adaptive behavior. According to this model, one could experience the catecholamine rush without the benefit of cognitions. In other words, we could learn to respond to events automatically. Yet perhaps the making of cognitive plans is what starts the whole process in motion.

A Dual-Process Model of Depression

Still another possibility is that both of the models I have described have elements that are correct. If we view depression as an adaptive process that helps us to reprogram for the future, we should be doing something different during depression than we normally do. If we have failed or if we have lost control, it would be important for us to analyze carefully what went wrong. Beck and others have suggested that we process information differently when we become depressed. When we are optimistic we sometimes ignore or downplay the importance of things we'd rather not think about. We can see a perfect example of this kind of thinking in the failure of the space shuttle *Challenger,* in which several people died: unbridled optimism led administrators to ignore reports that the O-ring seals might fail. When we become depressed, we do not ignore negative messages: we dwell on them. We see what may go wrong rather than what may go right.

This tendency to view things pessimistically appears to occur more or less automatically when the catecholamine level drops. I will call this process A. Process A can generally be viewed as a tendency to dwell on those aspects of the situation that may have led to failure or loss of control. In that sense process A is adaptive. It is adaptive, however, only if it is terminated after an appropriate period of time. One of the things that terminate process A is the release of catecholamines. Cate-cholamines seem to be released more or less automatically when people engage in adaptive behaviors. I will call this process B. One thing that may trigger process B is a plan that will help the individual to regain control.

For many people process A is not followed by process B. One reason that process B may not be triggered is that during process A they focus their attention on the wrong thing. If you focus your attention on a problem, you will probably come up with some reasons why things are not working. Using that information, you can make a new plan. If, however, you focus your attention on such things as flaws in your character or your failure to live up to your high standards, then no plan may occur to you. Instead, you dwell ever more persistently on the flaws in your character. You begin to engage in cognitive distortion, make errors of gen-eralization, and fail to consider alternatives. In other words, you fall into a down-ward spiral. As the downward spiral continues, your sense of self-worth plummets.

According to this model, the thing that differentiates people who recover rapidly from those who do not is the focus of their attention when they become depressed. People who take personal responsibility for their failure tend to focus on their personal shortcomings, whereas people who are less susceptible to depression tend to focus on the task before them. In the second case, depression is brief and beneficial; in the first, it leads to a downward spiral.

It may be possible to train people to think positively, to view potential failure or loss of control as a challenge rather than a threat. Lazarus has pointed out that people who tend to treat situations as challenges rather than as threats are less likely to experience stress, one of the antecedents of depression. People who can develop a positive attitude will be in a good position to take advantage of process A rather than to become its victims.

Many people recover from depression simply as a result of taking antidepressants. According to the dual-process model I have just described, the reason they recover is that the antidepressants restore the depleted catecholamines so that the thinking process can return to normal. For some people, however, it is useful and sometimes necessary to couple antidepressant therapy with cognitive therapy. Cognitive therapy is designed to help people to restructure their thinking, so that when they do encounter failure or loss of control, it does not lead them to focus their attention on themselves or their sense of self-worth rather than on the problem. A person with a good self-concept is able to make plans and engage in adaptive behavior, whereas a person with a low self-concept is not.

Summary
In view of the fact that the catecholamine level is linked to a negative thinking style, the thing to be determined is whether depletion of the catecholamines causes negative thinking or whether negative thinking causes a drop in the catecholamine level. According to the dual-process model, a negative experience causes the catecholamine level to fall, with a resultant negative thinking style (process A). This process can be highly adaptive provided that the individual focuses his or her attention on the problem and not on factors having to do with self-worth. A person who focuses on the problem tends to engage in adaptive behaviors, which trigger the output of catecholamines (process B). With the rise in the catecholamine level, depression lifts.

Some Issues Related to Cognitive Control

The Illusion of Control, or the Value of Being Optimistic
Is it important actually to be in control or is it enough simply to believe that one can gain control? Obviously it is important to be in control. But it is also important to believe that we can attain the control we seek. If we don't believe that we can gain control of a situation, then we are not likely to try very hard. People who are optimistic believe that they can gain control of their situations, often by developing new skills. There is a great deal of evidence that depressed people are more realistic than the nondepressed. Optimism is often unrealistic. Several experiments with nondepressed and depressed college students found the depressed to be more accurate in judging the contingency between their responses and outcomes. This finding led Alloy and Abramson (1979, 1982) to suggest that the sadder are often the wiser. Yet it can be argued that it is good to be optimistic, inasmuch as optimism can lead one to initiate responses that can lead to control. Can we induce depressed individuals to become more optimistic? One recent study has shown that when depressed subjects are required to complete a task in front of others, they perceive themselves to have more personal control (Benassi & Mahler, 1985). This finding is consistent with data suggesting that one of the important moderators of depression is social support. If social support restores a sense of self-worth, as I noted before, it may be the sense of self-worth that leads people to feel that they have personal control. In other words, they are encouraged to act optimistically.

Failure, Controllability, and Aggression

In Chapter 10 I suggested that aggressive behaviors may be viewed as attempts, however socially unacceptable, to gain control over events in the environment. A study by Dengerink and Myers (1977) on the relation between failure and aggression is consistent with this suggestion. Subjects were given either repeated failure or repeated success on a simple anagram task. Each subject was then asked to compete with another person in a reaction-time task. The subjects were given four blocks of trials with six trials per block. At the beginning of each block, the subjects were told to set the shock intensity that each of them wished the other to receive should the other person have the slower reaction time. The two subjects did not in fact compete. Winning or losing and shock intensities were programmed by the experimenter. Shock intensities were increased for each new block of trials. Normally subjects retaliate in like kind to increases in the level of attack. Therefore, it would be expected that shock intensities would increase over blocks.

The results (Figure 11-1) indicate that at lower shock intensities, subjects who had experienced repeated failure on the anagram task selected higher intensities than subjects who had experienced repeated successes. However, because of the tendency of "success" subjects to escalate shocks more in response to stronger provocations, these subjects selected higher shock intensities than "failure" subjects in the final block of trials. These results fit nicely with Seligman's helplessness model. That is, as Seligman's model predicts, subjects given helplessness training (failure subjects) did not respond in an adaptive manner, while success subjects did. Specifically, success subjects escalated aggression, which is a common strategy for dealing with increased provocation because it appears to be an effective way of turning off aggression, but failure subjects did not escalate aggression. As I mentioned in Chapter 10, Patterson (1976) has noted in his studies of aggressive exchanges in families that frequently one party in an aggressive exchange will abruptly increase the level of attack, and this tends to stop all further attacks from the other person. Hokanson, Hillers, and Koropsak (1968) and Knott, Lasater, and

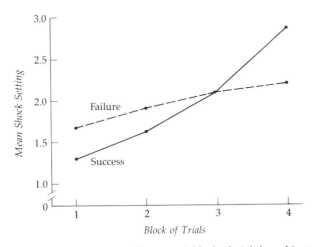

Figure 11-1. Average shock settings during each block of trials by subjects who repeatedly failed or repeatedly succeeded at an anagram task (Dengerink & Meyers, 1977)

Shuman (1974) have also reported that frequency and intensity of aggression will increase if that behavior helps the person avoid further attack from an opponent.

In a further experiment Dengerink and Myers studied the behavior of depressed and nondepressed subjects in the same task as the one described above. If Seligman is correct in asserting that repeated experiences in which consequences are independent of actions will produce the symptoms of depression, then the depressed person should behave like the person exposed to failure experiences in the laboratory setting. In fact, further failure should merely confirm the depressed person's belief that outcomes are independent of actions. The nondepressed person, in contrast, should respond as Wortman and Brehm have suggested—that is, failure should motivate such a person to attempt to reestablish control. Success, according to Seligman, should have relatively little effect on the reactions of a depressed person, because the depressed person tends to have a lowered capacity to learn. Success should also have little effect on the nondepressed person, because this person already believes he or she has control over events in the environment.

The results for depressed and nondepressed subjects after success and failure experiences are shown in Figure 11-2. The results are exactly as expected. Although all subjects in this study escalated shock intensities when given stronger provocation, the nondepressed persons given the failure experiences reacted just as Wortman and Brehm (1975) suggested they would. They dramatically increased their efforts to gain control by sharply escalating the intensity of shock.

Cognitive Control and Stress

Crowding.   Rodin, Solomon, and Metcalf (1978) studied the effects of control on feelings of being crowded in an elevator. When a naive subject entered an elevator, four confederates maneuvered the subject so that the subject was either in front of the panel of floor-selection buttons or on the opposite side of the

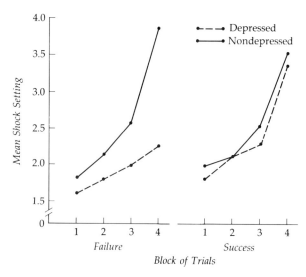

Figure 11-2. Average shock settings during each block of trials by depressed and nondepressed subjects following repeated success or repeated failure (Dengerink & Meyers, 1977)

elevator, far from the floor-selection buttons. When subjects were asked to indicate the degree to which they felt crowded, those who stood in front of the control panel indicated they felt less crowded than those who were maneuvered to the opposite side of the elevator.

In a second study, participants who had agreed to serve in a series of group activities were assigned to a role that gave them no control over the group's activities, control over the onset and administration of the activities, or control over their termination. Half of the subjects in each condition met in a small (high-density) room, the other half in a large (low-density) room. Persons with control reported that they felt less crowded than persons without control. High-density rooms were judged less pleasant and more crowded. Further, there was an interaction of density and control, which suggests that control mediates responses to density and therefore determines to what degree a person will experience crowding.

A number of studies have shown that providing people with information that their arousal level may be independent of other ongoing emotions, or simply that arousal can intensify their feelings, will often give them the cognitive control they need to function effectively in a variety of everyday situations. In one study, subjects were informed about the effects of crowding to determine whether such information reduced the effects of crowding (Langer & Saegert, 1977). Subjects were recruited in a supermarket at crowded and uncrowded times. Half of the subjects were told that people sometimes feel aroused or anxious in crowded situations. All subjects were asked to select the most economical product for each item on a grocery list as well as to provide information about their emotional reactions when they completed the required task. The results showed that information about the effects of crowding not only improved their performance but made them feel more comfortable and less affected by the crowded conditions.

In a review on the relation between crowding and personal control, Schmidt and Keating (1979) argue that crowding can increase arousal if it is perceived that there is a loss of personal control. They further argue that when arousal increases, the person begins to search for an explanation. They suggest that the person may attribute the increased arousal either to its real cause or to something else. Thus, whether or not a person experiences negative affect is related to the attribution process.

Noise.   Noise, as we have noted, reliably produces increases in arousal. It is an irritating by-product of our technological society. Glass and Singer (1972) have stated that "unpredictable and uncontrollable noise should affect aggressiveness, exploitative behavior, liking for others and general irritability in interpersonal relations" (p. 159). In a study to explore the effect of unpredictable and uncontrollable noise on aggressive behavior, Donnerstein and Wilson (1976) found that indeed there is evidence for Glass and Singer's assertion that noise affects the expression of aggression. In their first study (described in Chapter 10), Donnerstein and Wilson (1976) either angered subjects or treated them in a neutral manner and then gave them the opportunity to aggress against another subject in a teacher/learner paradigm while being exposed to either high-intensity (95 dB) or low-intensity (55 dB) noise. Angered subjects selected higher shock intensities than nonangered ones—a common finding in the aggression literature. Further, and more important for our present purposes, noise increased aggression only if the subject had been previously angered. Geen (1978) has further examined this problem and concluded that noise facilitates aggression in angered subjects if the arousal produced by the noise has been attributed to the anger. In other words, as Schach-

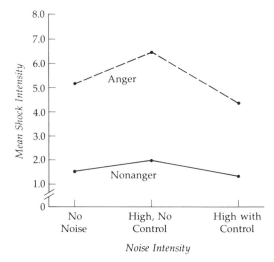

Figure 11-3. Mean shock intensity as a function of noise, control, and anger (Donnerstein & Wilson, 1976)

ter and Singer have argued, arousal will be felt and acted on only if the subject attributes the arousal to the ongoing emotion.

Donnerstein and Wilson (1976) did a second study to examine whether noise would have an effect if subjects were given cognitive control over it. Half of the subjects in the high-noise condition were given control over the noise and half were not. Subjects in the noise-control condition were told they could terminate the noise merely by saying "Terminate" over the intercom. The results are presented in Figure 11-3. This figure shows that angered subjects exposed to high noise selected higher shock intensities than angered subjects in the no-noise condition. Further, opportunity to control the noise eliminated the effects of the noise. Thus perceived control over the noise was a major factor in reducing the tendency to aggress.

Glass and Singer (1972) have noted that people who live in urban centers do not experience the level of stress that might be expected. Noise, crowding, and the threat of violence are all potential stressors. Glass and Singer have argued that people who live in urban centers often perceive they have control over such events. That is, one can avoid these things at any time by rearranging one's daily schedule, staying in one's apartment, leaving the city, or any number of other adaptive behaviors.

In the next section, we will examine how people can learn to gain cognitive as well as behavioral control in situations they cannot currently control.

Summary and Comment

Summary.   One important issue related to cognitive control has to do with the value of optimism over realism in the assessment of personal control. Nondepressed people tend to adopt an optimistic view of personal control; that is, they believe they have greater control than in fact they do.

Another important issue is whether people tend to use aggression, how-
(continued)

ever socially unacceptable, to gain cognitive control. Indeed, evidence consistent with this idea has been obtained. One interesting finding consistent with Seligman's model is that nondepressed people are more likely to retaliate when they are provoked. Aggression can be viewed, as I suggested in Chapter 10, as one means by which some people attempt to regain control.

Being in control can also affect the amount of stress we experience in everyday life. Having access to the floor-button panel in an elevator, for example, can reduce feelings of stress, as can the ability to terminate noise.

Comment. It has been repeatedly suggested that stress in any form, but particularly a life stress such as the loss of a spouse, often causes depression (e.g., Lloyd, 1980). While it is possible to interpret life-events stress as being caused by loss of control, there are many problems with this interpretation. For one thing, depressed people often do not view the loss of a spouse as loss of personal control (Coyne, Aldwin, & Lazarus, 1981). In that case, what is the link between stress and depression? One thing that is important to keep in mind is that stress in any form can reduce catecholamine levels (Sweeney et al., 1980). The reduction in catecholamine not only can lead to a negative mood but can alter the way depressed people think and process information. One study found that depressed people who experienced stressful episodes wanted to have more information before they made decisions (Coyne, Aldwin, & Lazarus, 1981). This finding is consistent with the observation that people tend to seek advice from other people when they are depressed. The question that arises is whether the altered decision-making process these researchers observed may be due to a biochemical change that occurs when people experience stress. It may well be due to what I have referred to as process *A* in the dual-process model of depression. Whenever process *A* occurs, for whatever reason (stress, fatigue, ingested stimulants), we are likely to experience a negative mood and changes in the way we think and process information. In many cases all that may be needed is rest so that the body can rebuild the catecholamine stores. Being able to have a good night's sleep is often important, as we noted in Chapter 4, because it is during sleep that the body often restores the catecholamines. In other words, it may not be appropriate to think of all depression as resulting from something as simple as loss of control. We may experience depression for a variety of reasons, biological, learned, and cognitive.

Depression, Controllability, and Assertiveness

How are depression, controllability, and assertiveness related? People frequently feel inadequate or helpless to alter or control events in their lives. People who feel they cannot control events in their lives are often people who are unable to deal with very ordinary events. For example, they are unable to refuse a request to stay late at work even though they have a previous commitment. They feel that it would be futile to request an adjustment on a bill that overcharged them. They are convinced that it would be impossible for them to exchange a faulty product. They won't ask directions because they believe other people won't help or they are afraid of appearing "stupid." They accept criticism even when it is undeserved. In short, many people fail to assert their rights. They believe that their efforts cannot alter events in any significant way or that they will be punished for asserting their rights. They fear they will lose their job or their credit rating or will be disliked.

Businesses, government agencies, and other institutions often seem designed to frustrate rather than help. A business, for example, may claim that because all products are poorly built today, it cannot assume responsibility for a product that broke or fell apart. To add insult to injury, it is not uncommon for a salesperson to suggest that you probably mishandled the product and therefore it was your fault. A government agency may claim your case is not covered by that department and refer you elsewhere. Eventually you are referred back to the same department. Its personnel refuse to do anything, still insisting it is not their responsibility. And so it goes.

It is not hard to understand why people get discouraged in their attempts to obtain fair and just treatment. Many people come to believe that what happens to them is a matter of luck. Some people are lucky and others are not. Therefore, why try?

Many people do in fact obtain satisfaction when they assert their rights. Because it is often possible to alter events in the environment, people have designed programs to train people to be assertive in dealing with businesses, government agencies, and unreasonable bosses. Not only do they try to give people the skills they need, but they try to change people's expectations about their chances of being treated justly and fairly (Bower & Bower, 1976; Fensterheim & Baer, 1975).

Human happiness involves more than just learning to deal with demanding bosses, bureaucracies, and businesses. To a very large degree human happiness involves satisfying a number of basic needs (love, friendship, appreciation, achievement, respect, self-esteem). Because satisfying many basic human needs is dependent either directly or indirectly on other people, it is important to be able to interact effectively with other people. People who lack the required skills often fail to satisfy some of the basic needs. For example, a person who doesn't know how to make small talk may find it difficult to make friends. A man who fails to tell his boss of his ambitions and abilities may end up in a mundane job with no prospect of promotion. A woman who allows her husband to dominate her life may end up hating him for her failure to pursue a career.

Assertiveness training is currently being used to train people in skills that will help them assert their rights while not hurting others, to teach people that they can achieve their goals, and to teach people that they can express their inner feelings without fear of ridicule, loss of respect, or even loss of love. Assertive behavior has been defined as "the skill to seek, maintain or enhance reinforcement in an interpersonal situation through an expression of feelings or wants when such expression risks loss of reinforcement or even punishment" (Rich & Schroeder, 1976, p. 1082). This definition recognizes that assertive behavior does carry risks. Although the person may fail, he or she may also succeed. If he or she does succeed, the rewards of success will presumably outweigh the risks.

Theory of Assertiveness Training

The theory of assertiveness training is based, for the most part, on principles of conditioning and learning. Most proponents of assertiveness training assume that if people acquire a certain set of skills, they will be able to satisfy their basic needs—or, to put it another way, by acquiring skills a person will be able to achieve those goals that reflect his or her needs. Thus the problem for most people is not that they lack goals but that they don't know how to achieve their goals.

Assertiveness training was introduced by Andrew Salter (1949), who borrowed heavily from Pavlov's ideas about excitation and inhibition. Salter suggested that some people tend to be more action-oriented (have greater amounts of excitation) and others tend to be more neurotic (tend to be dominated by inhibition). According to Salter, the therapist's role is to make people more action-oriented. Salter's patients were encouraged to express their feelings freely in order to achieve greater excitation. Salter viewed greater excitation as a state in which people could realize their full potential both intellectually and emotionally, a state that was both desirable and pleasant. He suggested that many people suffer from the habit of inhibition, which they could eliminate by practicing emotional expression that produced excitation. Eventually the state of excitation would come to balance inhibition. He suggested that the change in behavior would produce a change in the biology of the brain and hence a new personality would emerge, a personality that would make rapid decisions and enjoy responsibility without being plagued by anxiety.

Wolpe and Lazarus are two other major contributors to the development of assertiveness training. They have developed a number of assertiveness-training procedures to help people gain control of events in their lives (Lazarus, 1966, 1971, 1973; Wolpe, 1958, 1969; Wolpe & Lazarus, 1966). For example, Wolpe makes use of role playing to reduce anxiety. Situations that may elicit anxiety in a patient are staged. The patient is then encouraged to respond with anger, affection, or any emotion that may inhibit anxiety. With repeated practice the patient learns to deal with a wide variety of potentially anxiety-producing situations. Eventually, Wolpe says, anxiety will totally disappear. Lazarus believes that people must learn to express their emotions in order to achieve "emotional freedom." He teaches his patients to stand up for their rights. His training involves helping people understand what their legitimate rights are and how they can stand up for their rights and prevent them from being usurped.

Assumptions Underlying Assertiveness Training Therapy
In recent years many people have developed assertiveness training techniques. A review of all these techniques is beyond the scope of this section. All seem to share at least four assumptions.

Skills.   First, and most important, it is assumed that the person must learn that he or she can control events in his or her environment. It is assumed that the best way to come to recognize this fact is to learn the skills required to deal with a number of common, everyday situations. The skills will produce the reinforcement necessary to maintain not only adaptive behaviors but the belief that events are controllable.

Self-concept.   Second, it is assumed that it is important to change the person's self-concept. Studies of high-assertive and low-assertive people have indicated that low-assertive people have a poor self-image (for example, Schwartz & Gottman, 1976). Although learning skills that produce reinforcement may help to alter self-image, various theorists have argued that this may be a very slow way of doing so. For example, if it is assumed that self-image is based on a pool of successes and failures, a few successes in a lifetime of failure should do little to alter a person's self-image (Bower & Bower, 1976). As a result, assertiveness training is often designed to produce a more rapid change in self-image. One technique is to give people positive information about the consequences of having a positive self-image—for example, telling them that they have the secret of a more fulfilling life. *The Power of Positive Thinking*, by Norman Vincent Peale, is a good example of a book designed to show people the dramatic benefits that can result from having a positive self-image. Because a number of low-assertive people tend to have persistent negative thoughts, several assertiveness training programs involve techniques to stop negative "self-talk." One technique is simply to say "Stop" each time a negative thought arises (Fensterheim & Baer, 1975); another is to substitute positive self-talk for negative self-talk (Bower & Bower, 1976). The person is encouraged to say "I can do it," "I have the ability to succeed," and so on.

Pathology.   The third assumption held by most assertiveness training proponents is that pathology (such as anxiety, depression, or shyness) is often the natural and predictable by-product of inability to control events in the environment. Most proponents hold to concepts either similar or identical to those proposed by Seligman (1975). That is, it is generally assumed that being unassertive is more or less equivalent to being helpless. As a result, assertiveness training is directed toward teaching people skills that will put them back in control of their lives. People who suffer from the more specific forms of pathology (such as shyness) are given training to help them satisfy certain basic needs, which, it is assumed, will alleviate the specific symptom.

Personality.   To a greater or lesser degree, all proponents of assertiveness training believe that assertiveness training will produce an assertive personality. In other words, training in specific skills will produce a general change in the way a person thinks and acts. Exactly how this change comes about has received little attention. It is generally assumed that the person abstracts certain principles or response tendencies, which generalize to new situations. It is also generally assumed that as a more positive self-image emerges, the person begins to engage in behaviors appropriate to that self-image. Simply believing that an event is controllable is assumed to be sufficient to produce the appropriate behavior. Therefore, it is not necessary to teach a person all the skills he or she may require.

There is no single approach to assertiveness training. People involved in assertiveness training generally have a very pragmatic view of the training procedure. The procedure must not only teach skills so that people can deal with a variety of everyday situations; the procedure should help change people's attitudes toward themselves. Specifically, the training should help convince people that they will be treated fairly and justly when they assert their rights in a forthright and positive manner.

Benefits of Knowing How to Be Assertive

A number of proponents of assertiveness training believe that learning to be assertive may have benefits other than helping the trainee succeed in situations in which he or she previously failed. One such benefit is greater happiness and better mental health.

It follows from Seligman's work that gaining control of events that were previously regarded as uncontrollable would reduce such symptoms of pathology as depression and anxiety. It seems obvious that a person would be happier if he or she were treated fairly and justly. It has also been suggested that a number of other symptoms may be alleviated by assertiveness training, such as shyness, loneliness, and dependence (Bower & Bower, 1976).

Loneliness, for example, may occur because a person either has failed to seek out friends or has failed to respond to friendly overtures. It is a common characteristic of lonely people that they stay by themselves, making excuses to explain why they are unable to attend a party, share dinner, or meet for a cup of coffee. Often the lonely person feels that other people won't like her once they get to know her, and therefore she avoids many social situations that might allow her to develop friendships. Sometimes a lonely person avoids talking to other people, afraid that she may offend them. As a result of her failure to reciprocate friendly gestures, other people do in fact begin to avoid her. The lonely person then receives confirmation of what she knew all along: people don't like her. And so the vicious, self-defeating circle continues.

It has been suggested that learning to be assertive in everyday situations, such as requesting an adjustment on a bill or exchanging a faulty item, teaches the person something more than just how to deal with a specific situation. It is assumed that the person will learn some more abstract principles, principles that will affect his perception of the world and his self-image.

Low-assertive people are typically very concerned about being disliked and tend to have a poor self-image (Schwartz & Gottman, 1976). Practicing assertiveness, it is assumed, will alter the low-assertive person's self-image and teach him that being assertive will not make people dislike him. For example, when a person obtains fair treatment as a result of being assertive, he should begin to see that he can alter events in the environment. As a result his negative self-image should give way to a more positive one. He will also begin to see that other people don't dislike him for being assertive. In fact, the training is often designed to show the person that people often gain respect for him for being assertive, that people don't necessarily like people who fail to stand up for their rights.

People who have a poor self-image often perceive that their attempts will result in failure. One of the perceived consequences of failure is ridicule. Assertiveness training focuses on getting the person to see that not asserting himself is equivalent to letting another person walk all over him. Not asserting oneself, therefore, is equivalent to failure. By standing up for his rights, a person is at least forcing the other person to defend himself or herself. When the other person cannot defend himself or herself and must hide behind rules and regulations, a partial victory has been won. One has, according to assertiveness theory, indicated to the other person that his or her arguments are unjust, unfair, or irrational. Under these circumstances, the other person is the object of ridicule.

The most general principle that the person learns is that being assertive often does produce results. That is, responding works. Seligman has emphasized the need to initiate responses because without responding the person cannot learn to control events in his or her environment and learn that responding works.

It is clear from a variety of sources that assertiveness training is aimed at changing a person's cognitions. Although most approaches suggest that this can best be done in the context of acquiring skills, others have suggested that it is possible to alter cognitions, such as the person's negative self-image, through purely cognitive means—for example, convincing the person that she is capable of dealing with certain situations or having her practice positive self-talk. Unfortunately, at this time there are no data to show whether such techniques, used by themselves, are effective in making people more assertive.

How does learning these general principles help the person who is lonely or shy? It is assumed that people who are lonely, shy, or timid are low-assertive people. As such, they are people with a negative self-image who are afraid of being disliked. It is assumed that assertiveness training will help such people gain a more positive self-image that will allow them to experience a sense of worth and importance, a self-image not preoccupied with the fear of being disliked. A person who lacks a sense of self-worth has a difficult time believing others could like him. Thus a feeling of self-worth is a necessary first step. It is also important for a person to engage in behaviors that make his wants and intentions known to others. For example, if you want to go to a movie, or if you want to be by yourself, or if you prefer that the stereo be played a little more quietly, at least right now, it is important to let other people know. They may be quite willing to accede to your requests or at least be willing to discuss a compromise. Often people who are lonely perceive (incorrectly) that making their wants and desires known will somehow offend other people. In fact, failure to make one's wishes known often offends. To many people nothing is more frustrating and irritating than trying to talk to a person who expresses no wants or desires or has no opinions or ideas. People are frequently attracted to people because they have different ideas and want to do different things.

Does Assertiveness Training Teach Values?

Assertiveness training often goes beyond just teaching people to assert their rights. Many people have a very hazy idea of what is and what is not their right. During the course of assertiveness training, the person is often instructed in what is right and fair. For example, an assertiveness-training leader may decide to teach someone how to exchange an item no longer covered by a warranty. In effect, the person is being instructed that the warranty system is an unjust system. Sometimes people are taught methods for asserting their rights that usurp other people's rights or just plain hurt other people. A person who learns how to monopolize another person may, in fact, be acting very selfishly. Demanding certain privileges may quickly scuttle a privilege system that benefited a number of people. For example, a boss might be quite willing to allow the company truck to be used on weekends for odd jobs. However, if an employee decided it was his turn no matter what agreements the boss had previously made, and if he decided to assert his "right," he might force the boss to discontinue the courtesy of lending the company truck on weekends.

Assertiveness training is often used for selfish reasons. A company may teach its employees how to be assertive purely to increase sales. A political organization may teach volunteers how to win converts for purely selfish reasons. A religious group may teach assertiveness so that members can better raise money for the church. Clearly, assertiveness training is not necessarily used to help the individual.

Issues in Assertiveness Training

In recent years a number of people have tried to determine whether the claims made by proponents of assertiveness training are true. Two interrelated issues have emerged: is there such a thing as an assertive personality, and does such a person, if he or she exists, respond the same way in all situations?

Is there an assertive personality?   Extensive research has been carried out to identify the assertive personality. Paper-and-pencil tests have been designed to determine how people might respond to a variety of situations in which their rights might be challenged. More recently, subjects have been required to respond behaviorally to role-played situations in an attempt to see whether these two types of measures produce similar results. (See Rich & Schroeder, 1976, for an excellent review of the work done on this problem.) This research indicates that there is, in fact, an assertive personality type.

The research shows that the assertive person differs from the nonassertive in a number of ways. For example, assertive subjects respond faster in a conversation, use louder speech, give longer responses, show more affect in their responses, tend to show much less compliance in their speech and actions, make more requests for new behavior, refuse requests from other people more often, and apologize more after a refusal or a failure to comply (Eisler et al., 1975; Eisler, Miller, & Hersen, 1973; Pitcher & Meikle, 1980; Schwartz & Gottman, 1976). The high-assertive person typically knows the content of an assertive response and has little difficulty making an assertive response in a wide variety of situations. Interestingly, the low-assertive person also knows the content of an assertive response but is either incapable of making such a response or unwilling to make one, even in rather "safe" laboratory settings that involve role playing (Schwartz & Gottman, 1976).

Analysis of self-statements indicates that the low-assertive person often feels inferior to others or feels other people are more important. It appears that one of the major reasons a low-assertive person fails to assert his rights is that he feels he will offend the other person or be disliked by the other person. The high-assertive person, in contrast, is self-confident and does not seem to be concerned about offending another person or having the other dislike him in situations in which the other person is violating or usurping his rights (for example, Pitcher & Meikle, 1980; Schwartz & Gottman, 1976).

Although most of the research on assertion has focused on situations in which a person's rights are somehow being threatened or usurped, there is a growing interest in positive assertion (Eisler et al., 1975; Hersen & Bellack, 1977; Lazarus, 1975; Pitcher & Meikle, 1980). Positive assertion means, for example, giving praise or showing appreciation. One study showed that high-assertive people tend to use more expressions of praise and appreciation than low-assertive people (Pitcher & Meikle, 1980). The fact that high-assertive people tend to be more expressive of their feelings in both positive and negative situations lends support to the idea that there is an assertive personality type.

It appears that both high- and low-assertive subjects engage in a form of self-talk that can generally be classified as assertion-facilitating or assertion-inhibiting. An assertion-facilitating statement for a negative situation might be "I was thinking the other person's behavior was an imposition on me"; an assertion-inhibiting statement might be "I was concerned the other person might think I was being unreasonable." Similarly, an assertion-facilitating statement for a positive situation might be "I was thinking I should let the people know how I was feeling"; an assertion-inhibiting statement might be "I was thinking that the other person might think I was foolish to offer a compliment" (Pitcher & Meikle, 1980). It is clear that high- and low-assertive subjects have very different patterns of self-talk in negative situations.

High-assertive subjects tend to engage in facilitative self-talk to the almost total exclusion of inhibiting self-talk. Low-assertive subjects tend to have a lower level of facilitative self-talk together with a higher level of inhibiting self-talk (Pitcher & Meikle, 1980). These findings are presented in Figure 11-4.

The self-statements of high- and low-assertive subjects related to positive situations predict behavior. Curiously, however, self-statements related to negative situations are not good predictors. This fact raises some question about the relation of self-talk to actual behavior. Will teaching people facilitating self-talk have any effect on behavior? For some time the fact that self-talk and behavior fail to correspond has been a paradox to psychologists. As we know, however, although we may know what we should do, it is sometimes very hard to act on our intentions.

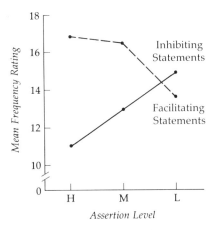

Figure 11-4.   Mean frequency rating of assertion-facilitating and assertion-inhibiting self-statements of high-, moderate-, and low-assertive subjects in negative situations (possible range of scores: 5 to 25) (Pitcher & Meikle, 1980)

Is assertiveness situation-specific?   The second major issue in assertiveness training is whether assertive behavior is situation-specific. That is, are people assertive in some situations and not in others? According to learning theory, learning to be assertive in one situation may show little generalization. Learning theory is based on the assumption that habits are controlled by discriminative stimuli. Unless the habit has been conditioned to a wide variety of cues, it should occur only in the presence of those stimuli that were present at the time of learning or stimuli that are similar to them. There is some evidence that assertive behavior is sometimes situation-specific, but there is also evidence that assertiveness is often a generalized response (for example, Pitcher & Meikle, 1980). If assertiveness is learned, it makes good sense that it would be both situation-specific and general across situations. It takes time for most learned responses to be conditioned to a wide variety of cues. Once a response occurs to a wide variety of cues, it then can be regarded as a trait. That is, it has become a characteristic response of the person.

Summary
People who feel that they cannot control events in their lives are often unable to deal with very ordinary events. They may be unable to refuse a request, ask directions, argue for their rights when they have been overcharged, or respond to any number of other events that challenge their ability to be in control of their lives. Assertiveness training was designed to help people deal more effectively with such daily events. It grows out of the work of Salter and others who believe that failure to assert oneself produces a variety of neurotic symptoms characterized by extreme anxiety. Four basic assumptions underlie assertiveness theory: First, it is important for people to learn the skills that will help them deal with daily events in their lives. Second, it is important for people to develop a positive self-concept. Third, pathology is often the eventual outcome of failure to assert oneself. Fourth, assertiveness training will produce a permanent change in personality.

   Several benefits come from learning the skills necessary to assert oneself.

(continued)

For example, assertiveness training can help people to make friends and thereby escape loneliness, it often helps develop a positive self-image, and it can frequently help people strengthen existing relationships.

Although one can readily defend the position that knowing how to be assertive has many positive consequences for the individual, it must be remembered that people who teach assertiveness to other people may do it for private gain. Businesses, governments, and even churches frequently teach people how to be more assertive so these people will be more successful when they make requests or solicit purchases on behalf of the organization they represent.

Two issues that have arisen with respect to assertiveness training are "Is there an assertive personality?" and "Is assertiveness situation-specific?" Research on these issues suggests that assertiveness training often does produce an assertive personality that is not restricted to the specific situations in which the skills were acquired.

Main Points

1. Depression is very prevalent in our society and is characterized by a lack of motivation.
2. When depression is very severe it leads to thoughts about self-destruction (suicide).
3. It has been suggested that all depression involves a reduction in certain catecholamines, especially norepinephrine.
4. Electroconvulsive shock can be effective in treating some types of depression and appears to work by stimulating the body to produce more norepinephrine.
5. Various drugs that are used in the treatment of depression work by elevating norepinephrine levels.
6. Stress appears to cause depression by lowering norepinephrine levels.
7. It has been suggested that depression is an adaptive mood. Depression may play a role in reprogramming. For example, it may help people abandon goals that are unattainable.
8. Seligman has suggested that depression is learned helplessness, where learned helplessness is defined as "a psychological state that frequently results when events are uncontrollable."
9. Experiments with both animals and humans have shown that exposure to an aversive stimulus event that is both inescapable and uncontrollable is often sufficient to produce learned helplessness.
10. According to Seligman, learned helplessness is characterized by three deficits: (1) failure to initiate responses, (2) failure to learn, and (3) emotional disturbance.
11. Two basic factors affect the tendency to become helpless: (1) the importance of the event and (2) the tendency to generalize.
12. According to the reformulated model of learned helplessness, humans are inclined to make attributions about whether or not a single encounter with helplessness will generalize. When the individual accepts the belief that nothing will change, he or she develops low self-esteem.
13. Helplessness can be prevented by teaching mastery.
14. Wortman and Brehm (extending the theory of psychological reactance) have suggested that people are often motivated to reestablish control when their freedom is threatened and only after repeated failure will they give up and become helpless.

15. According to Beck's theory, depression results from a negative thinking style that alters the way people screen, differentiate, and code the environment. Their "bias against the self" leads to "cognitive distortions" or "errors in thinking."

16. Another model of depression suggests that depression is likely to occur when people blame their character rather than their behavior.

17. Still another model of depression suggests that depression is more likely to occur when people set very high goals or standards for themselves.

18. In a model that attempts to link stress and depression, it is suggested that people who have a more hostile and confrontational cognitive style tend to be vulnerable to depression.

19. Lowered catecholamine levels may be responsible for changes in the way depressed people think.

20. Beliefs about control may lead to adaptive behaviors that trigger catecholamine release.

21. In the dual process model of depression, process *A* (a reduction of catecholamines) is said to produce the altered thinking styles that characterize depressed people. Process *A* is assumed to be triggered by such things as stress, fatigue, and loss of control. Process *B* (an increase in catecholamines) terminates process *A*. Process *B* is assumed to be triggered by adaptive behaviors.

22. Research on the relation between helplessness and aggression indicates that people who feel helpless or depressed fail to retaliate when provoked. This finding is consistent with the interpretation that people who feel they are helpless fail to engage in adaptive behaviors.

23. When people understand that environmental factors, such as crowding and noise, produce arousal, they are less prone to experience the stressful side effects of increased arousal.

24. In recent years there has been a growing interest in teaching people who experience feelings of helplessness how to reestablish control over their environment. The techniques of assertiveness training have developed out of this concern.

25. Low-assertive people appear to be very concerned about being disliked and tend to have a poor self-image; high-assertive people tend to be unconcerned about criticism and enjoy high self-esteem.

26. High-assertive people tend to engage in facilitative "self-talk"; low-assertive people are more prone to engage in self-inhibiting "self-talk."

TWELVE

Motivation for Achievement and Power

Why do people vary in the tendency to achieve goals?

Exactly how do people with a strong tendency to achieve goals differ from those with a weak tendency to achieve goals?

Why are people with a strong tendency to achieve goals more likely to persist than people with a weak tendency to achieve goals?

Why does failure undermine persistence in people with a weak need to achieve but not in those with a strong need to achieve?

Can people develop the motivation to achieve?

Why do people vary in the need for power?

What is the driving force behind people with a strong need for power?

Is it good to have a strong need for power?

Young children are often asked what they are going to be when they grow up. Typical replies are "A fireman," "A bus driver," "A doctor," "A nurse," "An animal trainer," to mention only a few. As children become young adults, their choices typically change. A different set of factors comes to influence their choices. Will the job give me security, money, fame, an exciting life? These factors are further affected by the young adult's perception of his or her ability. Finally, there is the question of willingness to work. Visualizing yourself at the Olympics with a gold medal around your neck, treating a patient in your private clinic, or being elected to a high office is one thing; actually working to achieve such goals is quite another.

In the course of pursuing our goals we receive feedback from time to time about our progress. We may, for example, discover that we are failing to reach our goals. Why? Do I have the ability? Am I working hard enough? The answers will obviously have a great deal to do with my desire to continue. Do I simply need to get motivated? If so, how can I get motivated? If I am failing because I don't have the ability, what should I do? What happens if I fail? What happens if I succeed?

From time to time we have all probably wondered why some people are willing to persist at a task while others are not. Are there personality differences? Do we have to be neurotic to succeed? Do people who succeed have compulsive personalities? Is it possible to become more persistent without becoming compulsive or neurotic? Are there any quick ways of becoming "motivated"?

This chapter will examine some of the theory and research relating to how people make choices and what motivates them to follow through with their choices or let them drop. We will also examine how certain professionals, such as coaches, try to develop persistence and endurance in other people. The question that arises from the work is "Is there a set of principles that can be used to develop persistence and endurance?"

Investigations into Achievement Motivation

The initial impetus for work on achievement motivation came from Henry Murray, who recognized that people vary in their desire or tendency to "overcome obstacles, to exercise power, to strive to do something difficult as well as and as quickly as possible" (Murray, 1938, pp. 80–81). Murray called this tendency the "need to achieve."

It was Murray who devised the Thematic Apperception Test (TAT) to measure variations in human motivation. The test consists of a series of pictures about which people are asked to write stories. The theme of the story is analyzed to obtain a measure of the motives that people have projected into the story. The basic assumption underlying the TAT is that when a particular motive is aroused, people tend to incorporate ideas pertaining to that motive in the stories they write.

McClelland's Contributions

For over four decades David McClelland has been doing research related to the achievement motive. His contributions are so extensive that it is impossible to do justice to them here. His book *Human Motivation* (McClelland, 1985) provides an excellent summary of his work. In order to measure the achievement motive with more precision, McClelland and his colleagues (1953) adapted the TAT and developed a precise method for scoring the achievement motive. A number of studies have been done to assess the validity of the TAT measure they devised. Such studies show that a generalized motive does exist and that it can predict behavior in a wide variety of situations (for example, Atkinson, 1953; French, 1956; Lowell, 1952; Mischel, 1961).

McClelland has not been able to identify an obvious biological link to a brain center or a neurotransmitter. He argues, however, that the achievement motive grows out of a more basic incentive to "do something better"—not to gain approval or any other kind of external reward, but "for its own sake" (McClelland, 1985, p. 228). McClelland points out that the environment plays an important role in the development of this natural incentive. He argues, for example, that parents play an important role, often by providing the kind of environment that allows this motive to develop naturally. Before we look at the role played by parents and society in the development of this motive and the relevance of this motive for our society, let me discuss the model developed by John W. Atkinson, which is linked very closely to the ideas and models that grew out of his collaboration with McClelland.

Atkinson's Theory of Achievement Motivation

One of Atkinson's important contributions to work on achievement motivation was his suggestion that the need to achieve is always tempered by another fundamental need, the need to avoid failure. That is, one cannot set out to achieve a goal without considering the consequences of failure. Atkinson's theory recognizes that people may differ in the strength of these two motives, but in the final analysis, goal-directed behavior is determined by the joint action of the two motives. If the motive to succeed is greater than the motive to avoid failure, it is assumed, the person will strive to attain a particular goal. If the motive to avoid failure is greater than the motive to succeed, it is assumed, the person will select goals that minimize the chance of failure. In other words, fear of failure may alter the goals a person selects. Rather than selecting a goal that would bring the greatest satisfaction, a person may prefer a second-best goal if that goal involves less risk of failure.

It is convenient to discuss the two conflicting motives, the hope of success and the fear of failure, as separate motives. It will then be shown how the two separate motives interact to produce various types of achievement-oriented behaviors. I will start by discussing the first of these two, the hope of success.

Hope of success.　According to Atkinson's theory (1957), hope of success can be expressed as a quantity. Theoretically, hope of success can be calculated for a variety of tasks, so that it is possible to predict which task a person will select.

There are three factors, or values, that need to be determined in order to arrive at this quantity. First, it is necessary to obtain a measure of the general personality disposition that motivates a person to succeed (M_S). As we have noted, the TAT has been adapted for this purpose. Second, it is necessary to determine the difficulty of the task. This can be expressed as the probability of success (P_s). If success if certain, P_s is 1; if failure is certain, P_s is 0. Finally, it is necessary to assess the pleasure or pride that a person may experience following success. This factor has been called the incentive value of success (In_s). For both theoretical and empirical reasons, it is assumed that In_s is simply $1 - P_s$. That is, when the task is difficult (the probability of success is low), the incentive value is high, and when the task is easy (the probability of success is high), the incentive value is low. Atkinson assumes that the three factors operate in a multiplicative fashion according to the following formula:

$$T_s = M_S \times P_s \times In_s$$

where

T_s = tendency to achieve success, or simply hope of success

M_S = motive to achieve success

P_s = perceived probability of success

In_s = incentive value of success ($1 - P_s$)

Fear of failure.   As we have noted, hope of success does not by itself predict final performance. It is assumed that fear of failure, or the tendency to avoid failure (T_{-f}), also plays an important role. It is assumed that fear of failure can also be expressed as a quantity. Again, three factors are assumed to be involved. First, it is assumed that there is a general personality disposition, or motive, to avoid failure (M_F). Atkinson has, for purposes of obtaining a measure of this tendency, used the Test Anxiety Questionnaire (Mandler & Cohen, 1958; Mandler & Sarason, 1952). There is good evidence that situations designed to evaluate performance are likely to arouse this particular motive. Accordingly, the way a person normally responds to tests provides a reasonably good measure of this motive. As in the case of hope of success, task difficulty and incentive are assumed to play important roles in fear of failure. Again, it is assumed that these three factors operate in a multiplicative fashion according to the following formula:

$$T_{-f} = M_F \times P_f \times In_f$$

where

T_{-f} = tendency to avoid failure

M_F = motive to avoid failure

P_f = probability of failure ($1 - P_s$)

In_f = negative incentive value of failure

Resultant achievement motivation.   Whereas success can lead to feelings of pride and satisfaction, failure can lead to feelings of shame. The expectations of success and failure, acting together, lead a person to undertake or not to undertake a given task. Atkinson maintains that these two motives are additive. The way they combine to produce resultant (total) motivation can be expressed as follows:

$$T_s + T_{-f} = (M_S \times P_s \times In_s) + (M_F \times P_f \times In_f)$$

Since In_f is negative, motivation to undertake a task can be positive, negative, or zero, depending on whether hope of success is stronger than fear of failure, fear of failure is stronger than hope of success, or the two are equal. To illustrate this fact, different values have been substituted into the above equation. Table 12-1 shows the outcome when $M_S > M_F$, when $M_F > M_S$, and when $M_S = M_F$.

The important thing to note in Table 12-1 is that when $M_S > M_F$, the maximum motivation is predicted to occur for tasks with a 0.5 difficulty level. These are tasks at which success and failure are equally likely. In contrast, when $M_F > M_S$, the maximum motivation is predicted to occur for tasks with either a 0.1 or 0.9 level of difficulty. Interestingly, the theory predicts that a person in whom $M_F > M_S$ will select either a task at which he is almost sure to succeed or, paradoxically, a task at which he is likely to fail. Atkinson has suggested that this paradoxical prediction can be understood if we consider the psychological consequences of failing at a very difficult task. Failing at a very difficult task does not produce shame to the same degree as failing at an easy task—perhaps none at all. The reason is that no one would expect a person to succeed at a very difficult task. For a person who had played tennis only a few times, losing a tennis match to the current world champion would be no disgrace.

Tests of Atkinson's Theory
Most of the research on Atkinson's theory has been designed to validate the above predictions. Because it is impossible to review all this research, I will discuss

Table 12-1.   Calculations of T_s and T_{-f} for five levels of task difficulty when $M_S > M_F$, when $M_F > M_S$, and when $M_S = M_F$ (Atkinson, 1957)

	Task (P_s)	$(M_S \times P_s \times In_s)$	+	$(M_F \times P_f \times In_f)$	=	$T_s + T_{-f}$
$M_S > M_F$,	A (0.9)	$(5 \times 0.9 \times 0.1)$	+	$(1 \times 0.1 \times -0.9)$	=	0.36
where $M_S = 5$	B (0.7)	$(5 \times 0.7 \times 0.3)$	+	$(1 \times 0.3 \times -0.7)$	=	0.84
and $M_F = 1$	C (0.5)	$(5 \times 0.5 \times 0.5)$	+	$(1 \times 0.5 \times -0.5)$	=	1.00
	D (0.3)	$(5 \times 0.3 \times 0.7)$	+	$(1 \times 0.7 \times -0.3)$	=	0.84
	E (0.1)	$(5 \times 0.1 \times 0.9)$	+	$(1 \times 0.9 \times -0.1)$	=	0.36
$M_F > M_S$,	A (0.9)	$(1 \times 0.9 \times 0.1)$	+	$(3 \times 0.1 \times -0.9)$	=	-0.18
where $M_F = 3$	B (0.7)	$(1 \times 0.7 \times 0.3)$	+	$(3 \times 0.3 \times -0.7)$	=	-0.42
and $M_S = 1$	C (0.5)	$(1 \times 0.5 \times 0.5)$	+	$(3 \times 0.5 \times -0.5)$	=	-0.50
	D (0.3)	$(1 \times 0.3 \times 0.7)$	+	$(3 \times 0.7 \times -0.3)$	=	-0.42
	E (0.1)	$(1 \times 0.1 \times 0.9)$	+	$(3 \times 0.9 \times -0.1)$	=	-0.18
$M_S = M_F$,	A (0.9)	$(5 \times 0.9 \times 0.1)$	+	$(5 \times 0.1 \times -0.9)$	=	0
where $M_S = 5$	B (0.7)	$(5 \times 0.7 \times 0.3)$	+	$(5 \times 0.3 \times -0.7)$	=	0
and $M_F = 5$	C (0.5)	$(5 \times 0.5 \times 0.5)$	+	$(5 \times 0.5 \times -0.5)$	=	0
	D (0.3)	$(5 \times 0.3 \times 0.7)$	+	$(5 \times 0.7 \times -0.3)$	=	0
	E (0.1)	$(5 \times 0.1 \times 0.9)$	+	$(5 \times 0.9 \times -0.1)$	=	0

one experiment that illustrates the type of research that has been carried out to validate the theory.

Franken and Morphy (1970) identified two groups of subjects—those for whom $M_S > M_F$ and those for whom $M_F > M_S$. Both groups were asked to serve in a ring-toss task in which the experimenter could surreptitiously alter the success rate by operating a large electromagnet hidden beneath a 6-inch bull's-eye target. Pretesting showed that, on the average, the magnet improved performance from three hits out of ten attempts to seven hits out of ten attempts when subjects stood at a prescribed distance. In a postexperimental interview, none of the subjects indicated that he had noticed anything unusual or become suspicious. It can therefore be assumed that each subject viewed his particular success pattern as due to his skill.

The participants were told to stand at a given distance that pretesting had shown gave a mean success rate of 0.3. Half of the subjects were tested with the magnet turned on, which gave them a success rate of 0.7. Since Atkinson's theory predicts that a person for whom $M_S > M_F$ will select a difficulty level of 0.5, it was predicted that such subjects in the magnet-on condition would move back when given the choice (making the task more difficult) and that such subjects in the magnet-off condition would move forward (making the task easier). This prediction was confirmed. What about subjects for whom $M_F > M_S$? Because Atkinson's theory predicts that these subjects will select either an easy or a difficult task, it was not possible to predict the exact direction in which these subjects would move, only that they would make the task either easier or harder. As it turned out, the subjects obtaining a hit rate of 0.7 moved toward the target (thus making the task easier), and subjects obtaining a hit rate of only 0.3 moved away from the target (thus making the task even harder). It would appear from these results that these subjects simply followed the path of least resistance by maximizing the outcome that had been arbitrarily arranged for them. To summarize: subjects for whom $M_S > M_F$ changed their position in order to have a task of moderate difficulty, and subjects for whom $M_F > M_S$ changed their position in order to have either a very easy or a very difficult task.

It should be noted that these results were obtained only with men, although both men and women participated in the experiment. The fact that the women did not respond like the men was neither new nor surprising. One of the early and most consistent findings that grew out of the early research was that women responded in a way that could not be explained by Atkinson's theory. I will discuss sex differences in more detail shortly.

Persistence and achievement motivation.   Atkinson's theory predicts the level of task difficulty a person will select. The question arises whether a person will persist at those tasks he initially chooses to work at. The answer is a qualified yes. Norman Feather (1961, 1963) showed, for example, that when the initial P_s was 0.7, subjects in whom $M_S > M_F$ showed greater persistence than subjects in whom $M_F > M_S$. (Recall from Table 12-1 that $M_S > M_F$ subjects should be attracted to such tasks and $M_F > M_S$ subjects should tend to avoid them.) Feather showed further that when the initial P_s was 0.5, persistence was greater among those in whom $M_F > M_S$ than for those in whom $M_S > M_F$. (Again, $M_F > M_S$ subjects are expected to select tasks with a low probability of success.)

An important factor in determining whether a person will continue working is the difficulty level of an alternative activity. The problem in the real world is predicting when the alternative activity will become more desirable than the activity initially selected. It seems reasonable to assume that a person's skill will improve as he works at a given task. As skill increases, the perceived P_s value should increase in direct proportion. This means the person may abandon a task in midstream if an alternative activity becomes available that is nearer his preferred level. This is one explanation of why business executives switch jobs so often. Once they have mastered the operations of one company, they may be motivated by the new challenges offered by another.

Vocational choice and achievement motivation.   The real test of any theory is whether it predicts real-world behavior. One of the obvious challenges to achievement motivation theory is how well it predicts vocational choice. In one very good study of this question, Mahone (1960) predicted that people in whom $M_S > M_F$ should make more realistic vocational choices than people in whom $M_F > M_S$. He reasoned that people in whom $M_S > M_F$ will select goals that are more consistent with their ability, whereas those in whom $M_F > M_S$ are more likely to select goals that are either too easy or too difficult. To test this hypothesis, Mahone asked a group of college students to indicate their vocational goals. Then Mahone had clinical psychologists rate these goals for their degree of realism. In order to make their evaluations, the clinical psychologists were given the students' grade point averages, college entrance examination scores, and other relevant information. Table 12-2 shows the relation between the clinical judgments and the resultant achievement motivation of the subjects. As Mahone predicted, subjects in whom $M_S > M_F$ displayed more realism than those in whom $M_F > M_S$. These results are, of course, consistent with Atkinson's theory. People in whom $M_F > M_S$ tend to select tasks that are either too easy or too difficult.

Mahone also had the students estimate their own ability in relation to other students. These estimates were compared with the objective percentile scores obtained on college entrance exams. Mahone found that students low in resultant achievement motivation were the most inaccurate in estimating their own abilities; students high in resultant achievement motivation were the most accurate. This finding, together with those reported above, indicates that people high in resultant achievement motivation not only have different risk preferences than people low in resultant achievement motivation but have different perceptions of their own abilities. Morris (1966) has also collected evidence that people high in resultant achievement motivation are more likely to select jobs consistent with their ability whereas people low in resultant achievement motivation are more likely to select either overly easy or overly difficult jobs.

Table 12.2.   Clinical judgments of realism of vocational choice in 135 students as a function of need for achievement (*n*Ach) and debilitating anxiety (Mahone, 1960)

		Clinical Judgments (%)	
nAch	*Anxiety*	*Realistic*	*Unrealistic*
High	High	48	52
High	Low	75*	25*
Low	High	39*	61*
Low	Low	68	32

*$\chi^2 = 7.96$, p < 0.003.

Sex Differences in Achievement Motivation

Validity of the TAT for men and women.   While the TAT seems to be able to measure achievement motivation in men, there is a great deal of controversy as to whether or not it measures the same thing in women. The controversy has focused mainly on the question of why women don't produce higher achievement scores when they have been instructed that the test measures IQ or leadership potential. The fact that these instructions have been shown to increase achievement imagery in men has been taken as evidence of the validity of the TAT measure. McClelland and others have argued that if men have a strong underlying achievement motive, this motive should be strongly aroused when they are challenged by the idea that the test they are about to take is a measure of their IQ or their leadership potential rather than some such thing as social desirability. It has been shown, however, that women's achievement imagery increases when they are instructed that the test measures social desirability (see Lesser, 1973). This finding undermines the argument that the TAT measure, as originally validated with men, measures only achievement motivation. In one study it was shown that women at more academically oriented colleges did show the expected increase in achievement imagery after IQ and leadership instructions, whereas women at less academically oriented colleges showed the effect only with social desirability instruction (French & Lesser, 1964). Other studies have obtained similar effects (see Lesser, Krawitz, and Packard, 1962). The net result is that we cannot be sure that a high score on the TAT measure reflects a need to achieve.

Fear of success.   In order to explain why women do not respond in the same ways as men, Martina Horner (1972, 1974a, 1974b) suggested that women have a greater fear of success (FOS) than men. She suggested that fear of success grows out of consideration of the consequences of success. Negative as well as positive things are associated with success. For women, some negative things may be loss of friends, loss of femininity, loss of popularity, and the like. Her suggestions are based on the stories written by male and female students in response to the cue "After first-term finals, Anne [for some subjects "John"] finds herself [himself] at the top of her [his] medical school class." Horner found that 66% of the stories written by women about a female character had themes indicating that success had negative consequences (unpopularity, loneliness, guilt) while only 9% of the stories written by men about a male character had such themes. In attempts to replicate these findings, however, researchers have found that men also show high rates of FOS. For example, Lois W. Hoffman (1974, 1977) attempted to replicate Horner's work and found, like Horner, that FOS occurred in 65% of the women but that it also occurred in either 65% or 77% of men. In other words, FOS either had changed or had increased in men. This failure to replicate Horner's findings was reported by other people as well (for example, Brown, Jennings, & Vanik, 1974; Condry & Dyer, 1976; Tresemer, 1974).

Why have people been unable to replicate Horner's original findings? It appears that sex differences occur only when women get female figures to write about and men get male figures to write about—the procedure Horner used. It is important to recognize also that men and women tell somewhat different stories. Women tend to emphasize their female characters' loss of affiliative relationships as a result of their success, whereas men's stories have a more cynical theme: the male character wonders whether success was worth the effort and sacrifice required to achieve it. In other words, whether or not you get sex differences depends on what you consider to be FOS. Men may not "fear" success in the same way as women, but neither do they embrace it with single-minded enthusiasm. What you get depends somewhat on how you score these tests. If you score them only in terms of the female themes, then you obviously get sex differences. Since her original study, Horner has devised a new scoring method that responds to this criticism.

In addition to the scoring problem is the problem of whether you use multiple-choice questions or some other paper-and-pencil test. One study that used multiple-choice questions about Anne and John found higher FOS in men than in women (Spence, 1974). While some paper-and-pencil tests have shown women to be higher in FOS (Sadd et al., 1978), others have found no sex differences (Ho & Zemaitis, 1981).

The only obvious conclusion that one can draw from all this research is that men and women have different thoughts about the consequences of success. Not surprisingly, women tend more than men to see the loss of affiliative relationships as one of the undesirable outcomes of success.

Fear of success and competitive behavior.   Despite the problems associated with the measurement of FOS, people have pursued the question of whether FOS can predict performance in competitive tasks. Obviously competitive tasks involve the possibility of winning, and in order to win one must perform well. That means, among other things, putting forth effort. There is good evidence that FOS inhibits competitive behavior in women but not in men (Marshall & Karabenick, 1977), and that it inhibits competitive behavior in women when the task is labeled "masculine" (Karabenick, 1977) and when they are competing against a man rather than another woman (Karabenick, Marshall, & Karabenick, 1976). Finally, women who believe in traditional roles for men and women and are high in FOS are less inclined to compete against their boyfriends (Peplau, 1976). This research indicates that FOS cannot be considered apart from other belief systems. That is, FOS is not a general fear that is aroused in all situations but rather is activated only in specific situations.

The Work of J. T. Spence
In recent years Janet Spence and her colleagues have provided a multidimensional view of achievement that has grown out of their work with the Work and Family Orientation (WOFO) Questionnaire. Two main concerns have guided this work. First, how similar are men and women when it comes to achievement motivation? Is achievement motivation structurally the same or structurally different in men and women? Second, what are some of the real-world outlets for the achievement motive? Often women's accomplishments have been dismissed or simply overlooked. Women's achievements as they pertain to the family, for example, have received very little attention. Most research pertaining to achievement motivation has focused on academic and vocational achievement. How does the achievement motive find expression in everyday activities?

Definition of achievement motivation.   Spence and Helmreich (1983, p. 12) suggest that "achievement is task-oriented behavior that allows the individual's performance to be evaluated according to some internally or externally imposed criteria that involve the individual in competing with others, or that otherwise involves some standard of excellence." As they point out, while achievement-oriented individuals often express their achievement in conventional job- and school-related activities, they also find outlets for their achievement striving in other voluntary activities. The *Guinness Book of World Records* is testimony to the fact that humans voluntarily attempt to achieve, master, or compete in a wide range of activities for no other reason than to see if what they have in mind can be done.

The Work and Family Orientation (WOFO) Questionnaire.   The WOFO consists of two parts. The first part consists of items that measure attitudes toward achievement-related activities. The second part consists of items that inquire about people's educational aspirations; the relative importance of work versus marriage as anticipated sources of life satisfaction; and extrinsic and intrinsic goals, such as the desire for pay, prestige, and job advancement (see Helmreich & Spence, 1978).

The first part of the scale focuses on three factors: work, mastery, and competitiveness. The interesting thing about the factor structure is that the same three factors emerge for both men and women—good evidence that the structure of achievement is the same in both sexes.

Results from large samples of university students indicated that men score significantly higher than women on the mastery and competitiveness subscales while women score higher than men on the work subscale. Subsequent studies involving varsity athletes, businesspeople, and academic psychologists obtained the same pattern of results. Though the differences are fairly small, they are significant, and they are found consistently (Spence & Helmreich, 1983).

Ability of WOFO to predict overall GPA.   In order to see whether the scale could predict academic achievement as indicated by a student's cumulative GPA, Spence and Helmreich (1983) administered the WOFO to more than 1,300 students. The results pointed to an interaction of GPA with the three subscales. As work and mastery scores were similarly related to GPA, these two scores were combined into a single work-mastery score. In order to show how the students with higher GPAs differed from those with lower GPAs, the investigators divided each sex into two groups, one consisting of the half with GPAs above the median (high GPA group) and the other of the half with GPAs below the median (the low GPA group). Thus they now had four groups. The results, shown in Figure 12-1, indicate that students with low grades were low in both work-mastery and competitiveness. The finding is not surprising. What was surprising was the finding

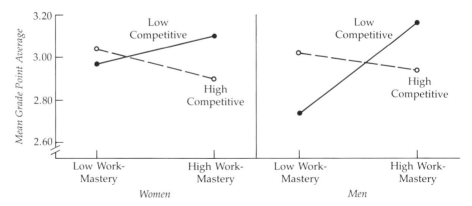

Figure 12-1.   Mean grade point average in the four achievement-motive groups of male and female undergraduates (Spence & Helmreich, 1983)

that the people with high GPAs were high in work-mastery but low in competitiveness. Those who were high in both work-mastery and competitiveness did not do so well academically. Men who were high in work-mastery and high in competitiveness had the lowest GPAs. While it is too early to explain exactly why this should be the case, the findings are obviously very important.

Ability of WOFO to predict annual income. Annual income is often taken as an indication of achievement in the business world. In order to explain the possibility that competitiveness is detrimental not only to academic achievement but to performance in the business world (at least as measured by income), a group of businesspeople were given the WOFO (Saunders, 1978). Businesspeople tend to score relatively high on the competitiveness scale, a finding that is consistent with the idea that in order to survive in the business world, you need to be competitive. If we look at who makes the most money (Figure 12-2), however, we can see that competitiveness has a detrimental effect. People who make the most money are those high in work-mastery and low in competitiveness. Again, while there is no ready explanation for these results, they are obviously important.

Ability of WOFO to predict scientific productivity. If the WOFO scale is a measure of achievement, it follows that it should predict whether or not a person is likely to make a contribution to scientific knowledge. One way of measuring the worth of a scientific contribution is to count the number of times a scientific article has been cited by other scientists in their publications. A count of the number of times a person has been referred to by other scientists is called a citation index.

A study of the citation indexes of academic psychologists suggests that the WOFO can indeed predict scientific attainment (Helmreich et al., 1978, 1980). People who make the most contributions are those who are high in work-mastery and low in competitiveness (Figure 12-3). What makes these findings especially interesting is the fact that they parallel the findings in regard to GPAs and annual salaries. The question that all of these studies raise is why interpersonal competitiveness reduces rather than augments the tendency toward work and mastery. Most of us tend to assume that competitiveness is a kind of energizer. Possibly it is, but rather than helping people to persist (work) and master the tasks before them, it directs behavior in a somewhat different direction.

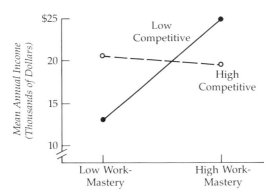

Figure 12-2. Income in four achievement-motive groups of businessmen corrected for years of experience (Spence & Helmreich, 1983)

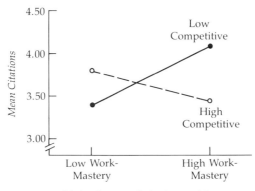

Figure 12-3.   Citations to published research in four achievement-motive groups of male academic scientists (Spence & Helmreich, 1983)

Summary
One of Atkinson's important and fundamental contributions was his suggestion that the need to achieve is always tempered by another fundamental need, the need to avoid failure. According to Atkinson's theory, resultant achievement motivation is determined by two factors, or quantities, referred to as hope of success and fear of failure. Hope of success is made up of three factors, or values: motive to succeed, probability of success, and the incentive value of success. Similarly, fear of failure is made up of three values: motive to avoid failure, probability of failure, and the incentive value of failure. According to the theory, people in whom the motive to succeed is greater than the motive to avoid failure ($M_S > M_F$) will choose tasks with an intermediate (0.5) level of difficulty, while people in whom the motive to avoid failure is greater than the motive to succeed ($M_F > M_S$) will choose tasks that are very easy (0.1) or very difficult (0.9).

Tests of Atkinson's theory with male subjects have generally provided results consistent with the theory. Atkinson's theory has also been shown to predict persistence. In general, people tend to persist at those tasks that they initially selected. Further, there is evidence that people in whom $M_S > M_F$ tend to select jobs consistent with their ability, whereas people in whom $M_F > M_S$ tend to make unrealistic vocational choices.

There has been considerable controversy surrounding the use of the TAT to measure achievement in women. Some studies have shown that instructions stressing social desirability will increase achievement imagery in women. In order to explain why women do not respond in the same way as men, Horner suggested that woman have a greater fear of success (FOS) than men. Subsequent attempts to replicate Horner's original findings have often been unsuccessful. It appears that men also have a relatively strong FOS, but that it inhibits competitive behavior less in men than in women.

Janet Spence and her colleagues have constructed the Work and Family Orientation (WOFO) Questionnaire, which has three subscales: work, mastery, and competitiveness. Men tend to score higher on the mastery and competitiveness subscales while women tend to score higher on the work subscale. The WOFO scale has been successful in predicting a variety of indexes of achievement behavior, such as GPA, annual salary, and scientific
(continued)

productivity. In each of these cases, it has been shown that people who are high in work-mastery and low in competitiveness perform the best. It appears that a high level of interpersonal competitiveness reduces performance.

The Achievement Motive, the Protestant Ethic, and the Rise of Capitalism

In the 1940s Max Weber wrote in *The Protestant Ethic and the Spirit of Capitalism* that the Protestant Reformation in Western Europe had produced a vigorous new type of person. He argued that the new Protestant view encouraged people to work hard and become prosperous, and that this focus on work and prosperity was largely responsible for the development of industrial capitalism. The Calvinist view in particular seemed to encourage this attitude. While Calvinism stressed strict observance of church doctrine, it also stressed that people should work diligently, whatever their station in life. The fact that hard work often brought prosperity was interpreted by the Calvinist as a sign that God was pleased with the individual and that he or she was one of those predestined for salvation. Because strict adherence to the church tenets meant there was little that one could do with one's prosperity except reinvest, Weber concluded, the Calvinist view tended to encourage economic expansion.

Intrigued by the idea that values acquired in childhood might predict later achievement behavior, Winterbottom (1953) examined the attitudes of mothers of boys high and low in need for achievement, or *n*Ach. She found that mothers of boys high in *n*Ach expected their sons to be independent and self-reliant at an earlier age than mothers of boys low in *n*Ach. For example, mothers of boys high in achievement motivation expected their sons to know their way around the city and to do well in competition.

Synthesizing the views of Weber and the findings of Winterbottom, McClelland (1961) suggested that the Protestant view encouraged parents to stress self-reliance and independence at an early age. This parental attitude would tend to produce children with a high need to achieve. As a result, McClelland argued, Protestant societies should have more people with a high need to achieve and should therefore experience greater economic development. To check on this hypothesis, McClelland compared the economic development of countries that are predominantly Catholic and those that are predominantly Protestant. He found modest support for this hypothesis. In general, predominantly Protestant countries showed higher rates of productivity than predominantly Catholic countries.

Encouraged by the modest results of this study, McClelland undertook a number of additional studies to check on the hypothesis that need for achievement determines economic development. In one study McClelland studied economic development in 23 modern societies. To obtain a measure of achievement motivation for each of the societies, McClelland analyzed the content of children's stories at different points in history. McClelland reasoned that if the stories that were being read to children had achievement imagery, children would tend to become achievement-oriented. Further, he reasoned that if society moved away from an achievement orientation, parents would be less inclined to read stories with an achievement theme, or, alternatively, the writers of children's books would be less likely to write books with an achievement orientation. Whatever the exact reason, over time fewer and fewer stories with an achievement theme would be read to children. McClelland found not only that the achievement content of children's stories changed

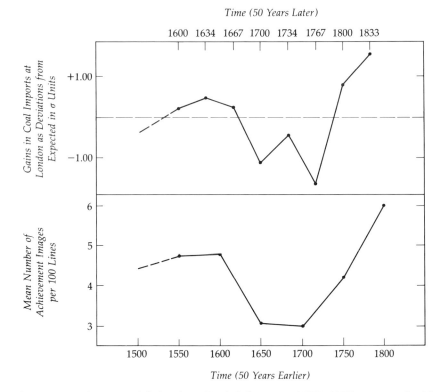

Figure 12-4.   Average *n*Ach levels in English literature (1550–1800) compared with rates of gain in coal imports at London 50 years later (McClelland, 1961)

over time but that it varied from country to country. The important question was whether a change in achievement imagery would precede a change in economic development.

Economic development was measured in several ways, such as electricity use per capita. McClelland predicted that nations with a high level of need for achievement in 1925, as measured in children's stories, would have larger increases in electrical production between 1929 and 1950 than nations low in the need for achievement. This prediction was supported. There was a statistically significant correlation of +0.53 between the level of *n*Ach in 1925 and the 1929–1950 increases in electrical production. Even when a number of analyses were done to control for such things as differences in resources and in war damage, the correlation remained.

McClelland has also attempted to see whether rises and falls in economic development can be predicted. In one study he obtained several measures of *n*Ach from English literature during the period 1550–1800 and compared them with coal imports at London 50 years later. The results of this study, shown in Figure 12-4, indicate that *n*Ach was indeed related to economic level.

Summary

McClelland has collected data showing that achievement imagery at various points in history, as obtained from an analysis of written material, typically
(continued)

correlates with the economic productivity of those periods. More important, his research has shown that a rise in achievement imagery preceded economic growth and that a fall in achievement imagery was followed by a decline in economic growth. This lag suggests that achievement imagery determined the rise and fall of economic productivity and was not simply a by-product of it.

Development of the Achievement Motive

In some recent work on the question of the origins of the achievement motive, McClelland and Pilon (1983) found that parents who put their children on a feeding schedule, demanded early toilet training, and had high standards of neatness were more likely to produce children with strong achievement motivation. These data, McClelland (1985) suggests, indicate that the seeds of achievement motivation are planted very early in life. It may be, he has suggested, that these early demands produce a sense of mastery in very young children. We know from other work that children can be differentiated in terms of achievement by age 3 to $3\frac{1}{2}$ (Heckhausen, 1967). In other words, we have good evidence that this motive is acquired early.

Parents of children high in achievement motivation tend to construct environments that are both strict and permissive. In such environments the child has limits, but within those limits the child has many opportunities to make his or her own choices. It has been suggested that such environments allow the child to develop a sense of mastery or control without being overwhelmed by unlimited freedom. Too much freedom, it has been argued, can so overwhelm a child that he or she becomes anxious and insecure; such conditions are likely to undermine the tendency to develop mastery.

How Do People Respond to Success and Failure?

How do success and failure experiences affect the tendency to achieve? Does failure cause a person to give up, or does it make a person work harder? What about success? Does it make a person want to set new goals, or does it spoil the desire to achieve? These questions are of critical concern in any theory of long-term achievement.

Perceived causes of success and failure.   Some years ago, Bernard Weiner (1972) postulated that success and failure at achievement tasks may be attributed to any of four factors: ability, effort, task difficulty, and luck (see also Weiner et al., 1971). These four factors can be classified along two dimensions: locus of control (internal or external) and stability (stable or unstable). This classification scheme is shown in Table 12-3. Internals believe their successes and failures result from their own actions. Whether they succeed or fail, they attribute the outcome to their ability (or lack of it) or to the effort they did or did not put forth. Externals, in contrast, tend to believe that success or failure is something that happens to them. It is beyond their control. When they succeed, it is because they had an easy task or they were lucky. When they fail, it is because they had a difficult task or had bad luck. Sometimes they win and sometimes they don't.

The stable/unstable classification pertains to the fact that some things are stable over time while others are not. Ability is, for the most part, relatively stable. While it may change over the long run, it typically does not change in the short run.

Table 12-3.   Attributions for success and failure

	Locus of Control	
	Internal	External
Stable	Ability	Task difficulty
Unstable	Effort	Luck

Abilities take time to develop. Effort, in contrast, is not at all stable. Some days we work very hard at a task and on other days we do not. Task difficulty is also stable over time whereas luck is not. If we return to the same task day after day, the difficulty of that task does not change. Luck, on the other hand, is much more capricious. Sometimes things go our way, sometimes they don't. The best we can do with luck is to take advantage of it when it comes. Weiner (1972) has suggested that the following conditions determine the factor to which a person will attribute success or failure.

Ability is inferred from the number, percentage, and pattern of success experiences that a person has had on prior achievement tasks. Whether the successes occurred on difficult or easy tasks is also important. Succeeding at difficult tasks gives rise to greater or stronger feelings of ability than succeeding on easier tasks.

Task difficulty is typically determined by the way others perform at the task (given that they are similar in ability). If few succeed, a task will be judged difficult; if most succeed, the task will be judged easy.

Luck is inferred when the outcome is due to chance rather than skill. Winning a prize after buying a lottery ticket is generally perceived as luck. (It should be noted, however, that people who select a particular ticket sometimes feel their choice has shifted the chances in their favor. Under such conditions, winning may not be perceived as "pure luck.") In general, when the outcome cannot be attributed to skill, it is regarded as a chance outcome.

Effort, we all know from experience, often affects whether we succeed or fail in meeting a goal. Studying hard for a test or working many hours at a project generally produces a more favorable outcome. Consequently, it is common for us to attribute success and failure to effort.

Attribution styles of people high and low in resultant achievement motivation.   Although it is interesting to see how people in general perceive the causes of success and failure, a more interesting question is how people high and low in resultant achievement motivation perceive why they succeed and fail. This is especially interesting in view of the fact that it appears that people high in resultant achievement motivation are motivated by failure whereas people low in resultant achievement motivation are motivated by success.

Weiner and Kukla (1970) found that people high in resultant achievement motivation perceived success as due to ability and effort and failure as due to lack of effort. People low in resultant achievement motivation perceived success as due to task difficulty or luck and failure as due to lack of ability. These rather complicated findings might seem incomprehensible at first glance. They can be readily understood, however, if we consider that people high in resultant achievement motivation see themselves as high in ability whereas people low in resultant achievement motivation perceive themselves as low in ability (Weiner & Potepan, 1970). Weiner (1972) has suggested that because people high in achievement motivation perceive themselves as high in ability, they tend to account for variability in performance as due to effort. Thus, when they fail, they perceive their failure as due to lack of effort. Failure, therefore, motivates them to work harder. (Failure may also challenge their view that they are high in ability and may thereby motivate them to reaffirm this view by trying harder.) Success, curiously, reduces their motivation. Weiner suggests that following success they tend to relax. As a consequence, their performance tends to diminish on subsequent attempts or on subsequent tasks.

Because people low in resultant achievement motivation perceive themselves as low in ability, they easily account for failure. It is simply due to lack of ability. Clearly, it is useless to work harder if one lacks the basic ability. How does such a person account for success? Obviously, if one lacks ability, it would be illogical to attribute success to ability. Because effort is closely linked to ability, it would also be illogical to ascribe success to effort. That is, since effort is the energy for an action while ability provides the direction for that energy, one cannot succeed merely by increasing effort. Success, therefore, must have occurred because the task was easy or the person was lucky.

Why should success motivate the person low in resultant achievement motivation when he perceives that his performance is due to luck? It may simply be that such people want to take advantage of a "run of good luck." This suggestion is consistent with the findings of Weiner and Kukla (1970) that male pupils high in resultant achievement needs are more likely to ascribe success to themselves whereas males low in resultant achievement needs are more likely to ascribe their success to external factors. If success is due to such external factors as luck, then it is important to take advantage of such situations.

Summary

Parents of children who are high in achievement motivation tend to construct environments that are both strict and permissive. It has been suggested that such environments allow the child to develop a sense of mastery without being overwhelmed by freedom of choice.

Weiner has suggested that there are four basic perceived causes of success and failure at achievement tasks: ability, effort, task difficulty, and luck. People who are high and low in resultant achievement motivation respond quite differently to success and failure; the question is how to account for this difference. Weiner and Kukla found that people high in resultant achievement motivation perceived success as due to ability or effort and failure as due to lack of effort, while people low in resultant achievement motivation perceived success as due to task difficulty or luck and failure as due to lack of ability. The key to understanding these findings is that people high in resultant achievement motivation perceive themselves as high in ability whereas people low in resultant achievement motivation see themselves as low in ability.

Setting and Attaining Goals

In our society we encourage people to seek challenges. Reach for the sky, we tell them. Set difficult goals for yourselves. You can have anything you want if you're willing to work for it. That sounds very nice, but as we shall see, several pitfalls await the person who pursues a goal. In this section we will deal with some of those pitfalls.

The Question of Ability

One of the most important variables that determines whether or not people will work toward a goal is their perception of their own ability. As we have seen, one of the reasons that people who are high in resultant achievement motivation tend to put forth great effort is that they perceive themselves to be high in ability.

What exactly do we mean by *ability*? More important, perhaps, how does the average person view the concept of ability? Do we have general ability or do we simply have a number of specific abilities? The average person seems to believe that we have both general and specific abilities. What is general ability? General ability is something that allows us to perform well in a variety of situations. While we often value specific abilities, there is a great deal of evidence that people place higher value on this thing called general ability. We tend to value general ability more because we believe it is important for success. Many people equate general ability with intelligence. It is important not to confuse the average person's notion of intelligence with psychologists' definition of intelligence. Often the two ideas have little in common. The point here is that people generally hold the view that people differ in ability.

Intelligence, ability, and self-esteem.   Humans are very sensitive to the question of ability, especially that more general ability called intelligence. Psychologists have frequently commented on the fact that when they are doing experiments, participants are highly motivated to perform well because they often expect that their performance will reflect on their intelligence. Why are people so sensitive to the question of intelligence? In our society we place a high value on intelligence. Rightly or wrongly, we often see intelligence as the means to success and happiness. Thus to have it is important and not to have it is disastrous. We also tend to judge people's worth on the basis of their intelligence. Again intelligence is an important thing to have. If people perceive that they have abilities that are important, they tend to experience high self-esteem. If they perceive they are lacking in those abilities, their self-esteem tends to be low.

Is intelligence fixed or is it malleable (changeable)? If it is fixed, then there is little one can do but live with what one has. If it is malleable, then one can work to improve one's intelligence. The theory that intelligence is fixed has been called the entity theory, while the theory that it is malleable has been called the incremental theory (Dweck, 1986). The degree to which intelligence is fixed or malleable has never been completely determined. What is important for our present purposes is that some people behave as though they believed in the entity model and some seem to hold to the incremental model.

Consequences of believing in the entity theory.   According to Carol S. Dweck's model, people who believe in the entity theory are motivated to select goals that will indicate they do have ability and to avoid goals that might provide evidence that they lack ability. Consistent with the theory, research indicates that when these people experience failure, they tend to attribute that failure to lack of ability (for example, Elliott & Dweck, 1985, cited in Dweck, 1986). If I believe I lack ability, why should I put forth effort? It makes no sense to put forth effort if I have already come to the conclusion that I lack ability. People who reason in this way have to select their tasks very carefully. Even a single encounter with failure can be damaging because it confirms their lack of ability. After reviewing the research literature on the way children react to success and failure, Dweck has suggested that even a single encounter with failure can make a person helpless.

The important thing to note here is that failure can be devastating to people who hold to the entity theory. For this reason they learn to set their goals with an eye to avoiding failure. In short, they tend to avoid challenges, especially challenges to new ventures in which they cannot be certain of avoiding failure. These people may become low achievers in order to avoid the failure they fear.

Consequences of believing in the incremental theory.   According to Dweck, people who believe in the incremental theory tend to select goals that will enable them to increase their competence (for example, Nicholls, 1984). Since ability (intelligence) is something that you can acquire, it is important to select goals that can maximize learning. Learning, in other words, becomes synonymous with competence and ability. How do you maximize learning? One thing you must be careful not to do is to select goals on the basis of certainty of success. Sometimes you can learn a great deal in situations in which failure is likely. Take the ring-toss task. You can't learn the skills needed to be good at this task by simply standing next to the post and dropping the ring over it. While this may seem obvious, it is not always clear to the person who is obsessed by the need to avoid failure.

Since the development of competence at any task often requires persistence, belief in the incremental theory of ability turns out to be very adaptive in the process of setting and attaining goals. Both rewards and failure simply provide feedback to the individual. Belief in the entity theory is not at all adaptive. To a person who holds to the entity theory, failure is feedback about a lack of competence or ability. When you lack ability, it no longer makes sense to put forth effort. The reason some people do not select challenging goals for themselves, then, is that they view each new task as a potential threat to their self-esteem.

Uncertainty-Reducing Properties of Achievement

It has been suggested that achievement behavior can be understood in the light of its ability to reduce uncertainty (Trope, 1979; Sorrentino & Hewitt, 1984). Some people, it has been suggested, have a greater need for certainty than others. People who have a high need for certainty tend to choose tasks that provide that certainty (an easy outcome leads to success and a hard task leads to failure). People with a low need for certainty, on the other hand, choose a task of intermediate difficulty (P_s = 0.5). Like Dweck's approach, which emphasizes the need to confirm one's ability, this interpretation links achievement-related behaviors to a fundamental need: the need for certainty.

The Self-Serving Bias and Attributions of Success and Failure

Fritz Heider (1976, p. 16) has noted that "one is inclined to attribute to oneself good things but one suffers when one has to attribute to oneself something that is not so good." This tendency has been found repeatedly in the experimental literature. For example, people are more likely to attribute their successes to effort than to ability and their failures to lack of ability rather than lack of effort (Luginbuhl, Crowe, & Kahan, 1975). This asymmetrical assessment of causality, at least according to certain theorists, seems to reflect people's tendency to perceive or show themselves in the best possible light (Bradley, 1978; Miller & Ross, 1975). How does this tendency account for the attributions? One interpretation is that people are more likely to attribute success to factors over which they have control (effort) and failure to factors over which they have no control (ability). In other words, ascribing failure to lack of ability may be a way of deferring personal responsibility, because a person has little immediate control over ability (Luginbuhl, Crowe, & Kahan, 1975).

Several studies have shown that people tend to assume more responsibility for success than for failure (for example, Fitch, 1970; Luginbuhl, Crowe, & Kahan, 1975; Weiner & Kukla, 1970). To see whether this tendency may vary with the importance of success, D. T. Miller (1976) designed a study that manipulated the level of importance of the task. As importance increased, so did the tendency to assume credit for success. This result shows that the tendency to assume credit for success is a motivational tendency rather than a static personality disposition. Had it been a static personality disposition, the manipulation of importance should have had no effect.

Effects on achievement motivation.   As we have noted, people with high resultant achievement motivation tend to perceive that they have high ability, and they tend to perceive that effort produces success. Because the self-serving bias leads people to view success as due to effort, the self-serving bias should facilitate achievement motivation (provided the person is successful) by encouraging the person to view effort as producing success. Unfortunately, because failure tends to be attributed to lack of ability, failure experiences should undermine achievement motivation by undermining the perception of ability. This conclusion, however, fails to consider task difficulty. How do people perceive the causes of success and failure when tasks vary in difficulty?

Task difficulty.   Failures at difficult and at easy tasks generally lead to quite different attributions. A person is more likely to attribute failure at a difficult task to task difficulty and failure at an easy task to lack of ability. Success at easy and difficult tasks is also attributed somewhat differently. Success at an easy task is more likely to be attributed to task difficulty, success at a difficult task to the combination of effort and ability. According to the research on the self-serving bias, success should be attributed mainly to effort. This analysis leads to the prediction that having a difficult task first should enhance achievement motivation (performance) on a second task whereas having a simple task first should undermine achievement motivation (performance) on a second task. That is, because failing at a difficult task would not undermine perceptions of ability whereas succeeding at such a task would contribute to the perception that effort paid off, the tendency to achieve should be enhanced by difficult tasks. Failing at an easy task, in contrast, would tend to undermine perceptions of ability, and success would do nothing to enhance the perception that effort was important.

In a study designed to evaluate whether difficult tasks produce greater increases in performance on subsequent tasks than simple tasks do, it was found that, indeed, working at a difficult task facilitated performance on a later task; having an easy task first was no better or worse than having a task of the same difficulty first (Linsenmeier & Brickman, 1978). It was also found that this effect was stronger for men than for women and for students with high ability than for students with low ability. Why the sex difference? It appears that there may be several reasons.

Sex differences.   In a study by John Nicholls (1975), boys and girls were required to work at a task that involved matching angles in a workbook with a set of standard angles. Nicholls found that boys attributed failure to luck whereas girls attributed failure to lack of skill. The question arises why boys have a defensive reaction to failure and girls have a self-derogatory reaction. The higher expectancies of boys under certain experimental conditions and the tendency of boys to choose more difficult tasks (Nicholls, 1978) suggest that girls may have lower opinions of their ability. This hypothesis is consistent with other findings that girls respond less positively than boys to intellectual challenge (Hoffman, 1972). A study by Feather (1978) suggests that girls may have lower expectations of success at intellectual tasks and, further, that such expectations may be learned from parents and teachers. In studying Australian male and female students, Feather found that boys and girls of high socioeconomic levels responded quite differently from boys and girls of lower socioeconomic levels. Specifically, Feather found a tendency for the affluent students to downgrade, in various ways, the successful girl in relation to the successful boy and the unsuccessful boy in relation to the unsuccessful girl. Feather suggests that this "traditional view" was probably acquired from the parents and reinforced by the private school attended by the affluent students.

Sex differences in competitiveness can also be interpreted as culturally based. Stephan, Rosenfield, and Stephan (1976) studied the attributions of males and females for success and failure in a competitive game. They found that males competing against either sex as well as females competing against females took more credit for success and blamed themselves less for failure. Females competing against males, however, did not show this pattern; they gave more credit to the males for success and blamed themselves more for failure. The investigators suggest that the reaction of the females toward male success was based on the belief that the males were more competent at the "masculine" task than they were.

It has been hypothesized that these differences exist because women tend to avoid skill tasks. This question was examined in a study by Deaux, White, and Farris (1975). Their findings showed that men tend to select games of skill and women tend to select games of luck. Why? Deaux and her colleagues found that, in general, men had a higher expectation of success than women; they interpret this finding as reflecting differences in perceived ability. In other words, their study provides additional evidence that women perceive themselves to have less ability than men at tasks that require physical skills, such as the dart-throwing and ring-toss games typically used in such experiments.

In view of the fact that many of the skill tasks used in such research have a masculine image, it is necessary to study the reactions of men and women to tasks with a more neutral image. Perhaps when women compete at more neutral tasks, their reactions to success and failure will differ little from men's. One of the interesting questions raised by both Nicholls' (1975, 1978) two studies and Feather's (1978) study is whether academic pursuits are viewed as masculine territory. Only recently have women pursued graduate degrees in large numbers. It may be that a large part of society, women as well as men, still perceive intellectual activities as masculine.

Perhaps the fear of success attributed to women is really a perception of lack of the ability required to succeed. This self-perception could account for women's tendency to select tasks that depend on luck rather than skill, to be less persistent than men, to attribute failure in competition with men to lack of ability, and to blame themselves when they fail. Research from a variety of sources suggests that this perception of low ability is learned from parents (especially the mother) and may be reinforced by teachers. There is also evidence that this perception may vary depending on cultural and socioeconomic factors.

In a study of bright junior high students more girls than boys ascribed to an entity theory of intelligence (they saw smartness as a fixed trait) (Leggett, 1985).

This finding is consistent with the finding that girls prefer tasks they know they are good at whereas boys prefer tasks they have to work harder to master (Licht et al., 1984). If you don't believe you can change, it makes sense to work at a task you do well; but if you do think you can change, then it makes sense to select a challenging task. Also consistent with the finding that girls tend more than boys to ascribe to the entity theory is the finding that girls are more inclined to attribute failure to lack of ability (Licht & Shapiro, 1982). As Dweck (1986) points out, it was not that the girls did not perceive themselves to be bright; it had more to do with the way they interpreted failure. Even though they perceived themselves to be bright, their perceptions were readily undermined by a few experiences of failure.

Expectations, Self-Focused Attention, and Reactions to Success and Failure

Self-esteem.   Whether one has a good opinion of oneself (high self-esteem) or a poor opinion of oneself (low self-esteem) has for some time been regarded as a major determinant of such things as achievement behavior. For example, Shrauger (1972) reported that low-self-esteem people do significantly worse in achievement settings than high-self-esteem people. The question arises whether high- and low-self-esteem subjects are differentially affected by success and failure. In a study to examine the reactions of high- and low-self-esteem people, Brockner (1979) found that whereas high-self-esteem people performed equally well following success and failure, low-self-esteem people performed significantly worse following failure (but just as well as high-self-esteem people in the success condition), but only under self-focusing stimulus conditions. That is, when subjects were encouraged to focus on their performance or simply tended to be self-conscious about their performance, low-self-esteem subjects tended to perform poorly if they had previously failed. These findings are consistent with Carver's (1979) model, which suggests that if fear or anxiety cues become salient, they will disrupt performance. According to Carver, when such cues become salient the person is inclined to assess the likelihood of completing the task. Subjects whose expectations are positive (as they are after success) will be motivated to match their behavior against the standard. If they begin to think they will not be able to complete the task, however, they will respond with passivity and withdrawal. Since low-self-esteem subjects tend to have a low opinion of their ability, they will be more inclined to respond to failure with reduced motivation. Tests of this model have shown that positive expectations indeed lead to greater persistence or performance than negative expectations, but only when there is self-focused attention (Carver, Blaney, & Scheier, 1979a, 1979b).

Internals and externals.   Internals tend to believe they can control events in their lives; externals tend to perceive events as outside their control. How do internals and externals respond to success and failure? As might be expected, internals tend to do better than externals after failure but do not differ from externals in response to success (Gregory, 1978). The reduced performance of externals following negative outcomes is consistent with the view that externals do not perceive that events are controllable. Therefore, it would not make sense for externals to react to negative outcomes with increased effort.

Emotional Reactions to Success and Failure
How do people feel after they succeed or fail? Do people experience more intense pride when they believe their success was due to effort? These and other questions

Table 12-4. Attributions and dominant discriminating affect for success and failure (Weiner, 1977)

Attribution	Affect
Success	
Unstable effort	Activation, augmentation
Stable effort	Relaxation
Own personality	Self-enhancement
Other's effort and personality	Gratitude
Luck	Surprise
Failure	
Ability	Incompetence
Unstable effort; stable effort	Guilt (shame)
Personality; intrinsic motivation	Resignation
Other's efforts; other's motivation and personality	Aggression
Luck	Surprise

are of fundamental importance if we are to understand why people react as they do to success and failure. In a study designed to examine whether people respond more intensely to success than to failure or vice versa, Averill, DeWitt, and Zimmer (1978) associated potentially arousing stimuli (such as nudes and corpses) with either failure or success on a problem-solving activity. In their study subjects were given 36 puzzles to solve. After each puzzle the subject was told whether or not he had successfully completed the puzzle and then was shown a photograph for 15 seconds. On completion of the 36 puzzles, subjects were asked to evaluate the photographs. It was found that corpses were judged to be more disturbing and nudes more attractive if they had been associated with failure. The investigators interpret these results as supporting the idea that failure produces greater emotion (arousal) than success. They further suggest that the reason subjects are likely to make a greater emotional attribution after failure than after success is not simply to explain their performance but to excuse it. That is, the self-attribution of emotion may be one way of changing responsibility for negative outcomes. Because this tendency was greater among subjects who perceived the task to be a valid indication of intellectual ability, Averill and his colleagues argue that it is not failure itself that produces the effect but rather the ego involvement of the subject.

Weiner (1977) has offered a general framework for relating emotions to success and failure. Table 12-4 summarizes this conceptual framework. This table indicates that more than simple pride or shame accompanies success or failure, respectively. Failure can result in feelings of incompetence, guilt, resignation, aggression, or surprise, depending on how the person accounts for failure. Similarly, success can produce feelings of activation, relaxation, self-enhancement, gratitude, or surprise (Weiner, Russell, & Lerman, 1978, 1979).

Summary
Humans are very sensitive to the question of what abilities they have or do not have. One ability we value very highly is the ability we sometimes call intelligence. People who believe in the entity model of intelligence are motivated to select goals that will put them in a favorable light. Should they fail, they tend to attribute their failure to lack of ability (intelligence). This perception tends to undermine any future desire to put forth effort. People who

(continued)

hold to the incremental model of intelligence tend to set a goal that will increase their competence. When these people fail, they tend to interpret failure not as lack of ability but as feedback that tells them how well they are performing. They often interpret failure as an indication that they did not put forth the necessary effort, and so they are motivated to work harder.

Research relating the self-serving bias to achievement has shown that people are more likely to assume responsibility for success than for failure. This effect has been found to be more pronounced when the task is regarded as important. Further, subjects are more inclined to take credit for success at a difficult task (they attribute success to effort) but to deny responsibility for failing at a difficult task (they attribute failure to task difficulty). In general, working at difficult tasks is more likely to enhance motivation (effort) than working at simple or intermediate tasks. The sex differences often found in achievement studies seem to be due, at least in part, to women's tendency to perceive themselves as low in ability, especially in skill tasks. Evidence also indicates that women may be more inclined to adopt the entity model of intelligence.

People with high self-esteem are less affected by failure than those with low self-esteem. Further, low-self-esteem people are affected more by self-focusing instructions, a finding that is consistent with Carver's model, which suggests that if fear and anxiety cues are made salient, performance will be disrupted. The finding that internals do better after failure than externals is consistent with the idea that internals are motivated by perceived loss of control whereas externals are not. Although researchers have frequently questioned whether failure produces a greater emotional response than success, only recently have data been collected to answer this question. Indeed, the data suggest that failure frequently has a greater emotional impact than success.

Learning Theory Approaches to Persistence and Endurance

Learning theorists have also attempted to answer the question of why some people persist longer than others at achievement tasks. In addition, learning theorists are interested in identifying the variables that would make it possible to train people to become more persistent. How to become more persistent is a real concern for many people. Attaining a goal often demands that a person persist over long periods of time and in the face of many aversive conditions (fatigue, boredom, heat, cold, hunger, hard work, and so on). The work of the learning theorist, therefore, needs to be considered in some detail.

Amsel's Theory of Persistence

In a period spanning more than 20 years, Abram Amsel (for example, 1958, 1962, 1972) systematically developed a general theory of persistence. This theory has its origins in animal research but readily explains a number of important phenomena relating to human persistence. The theory assumes that persistence is learned in rather specific situations but tends to generalize to other situations that share certain common properties. The basic process or mechanism that is assumed to be responsible for persistence is the counterconditioning of disruptive stimuli.

To illustrate the theory, we will examine some problems associated with a novice swimmer learning to become a competitive swimmer. Let's assume that our swimmer has already learned to swim but has never engaged in competitive swimming. According to Amsel's analysis, when a person exercises a response in the presence of new or different stimuli, it is likely that these stimuli will have a disruptive effect on the response. For example, if a person has never engaged in a competition before, the anticipation of the competition could produce a state of high arousal that might disrupt the response of swimming. Fear of failing might cause anxiety, which could also disrupt performance. Similarly, noise, the presence of spectators, the turbulence of the water, or other aspects of the competition could prove distracting and thereby cause a swimmer to perform poorly.

To perform well, a swimmer must adapt to these stimuli. In learning theory, this process is called "habituation." The best way to learn to ignore or adapt to these stimuli is to exercise the desired response in their presence. A good coach will typically take great care to ensure that an athlete is systematically exposed to all these potentially distracting stimuli prior to any important competition. The coach will, for example, have teammates compete against each other, enter the swimmers in local competitions where spectators and the press are present, make them aware of the importance of winning, and finally introduce them gradually to more and more competitive events.

Amsel suggests that the process of habituation involves counterconditioning. It is assumed that if a person exercises a response in the presence of potentially disrupting stimuli, these stimuli will become conditioned to the response. As a result, the stimuli lose their ability to disrupt the desired response. Further, and more important, Amsel argues, these stimuli come to support the desired response. The idea that disruptive stimuli could become supportive stimuli may not be intuitively obvious. Years of research, however, have shown that this does in fact happen. Not only do the stimuli not disrupt behavior, but in many cases their presence becomes a necessary condition in order for the response to occur—or at least to occur at a very high level. We have probably all heard of athletes who perform better when they begin to lose or an entertainer who performs best when he has a large or hostile audience or a singer who does her best when she is anxious. A famous baseball pitcher, when asked whether it bothered him when he was booed, said that he always did his best when the crowds were hostile. He pointed out that he had learned to pitch under these conditions.

What does this have to do with persistence? According to Amsel's analysis, persistence involves learning to exercise or perform a response in the presence of disruptive cues. As we all know, achieving a goal often involves a great deal of time, effort, and, most of all, frustration. Amsel's theory specifically addresses the question of how people come to deal with frustration.

Amsel (1958, 1962) noted some time ago that when an animal fails to receive a reward for a response that is normally rewarded, the animal becomes highly emotional, a reaction that Amsel labeled frustration. For example, Amsel noted that when laboratory rats failed to receive a reward for a response they had learned, they would urinate and defecate (involuntary responses that have been used as indicators of high emotion in certain animals), become aggressive, and tend to run faster on the next trial. Amsel argued that the faster running on the next trial reflected the increased arousal that normally accompanies frustration. Amsel further noted that if an animal experienced several nonrewards interspersed with rewards, the animal eventually persisted longer in the absence of all rewards than animals that had been continuously rewarded. This is known in the learning literature as the partial reinforcement effect (PRE).

According to Amsel, the reason an animal will persist longer in the absence of all rewards when it has previously experienced nonrewards interspersed with rewards is that it has learned to perform in the presence of frustration cues. Specifically, Amsel has suggested that frustration cues are conditioned to the ongoing response. Thus, rather than disrupting performance, frustration tends to support, or facilitate, performance.

It is important to note that in order to condition frustration cues to the ongoing response, the frustration must never be too great. If frustration becomes too great, it will totally disrupt performance. When this happens, the frustration cues become conditioned to "not responding." A good swimming coach is careful not to push a swimmer into competitions that might totally disrupt the swimmer's ability to perform. Typically a good coach will gradually introduce the athlete to potentially disrupting stimuli in order that such stimuli can be conditioned to the desired response.

One very interesting point that is brought out in Amsel's analysis is that stimuli that can disrupt performance can also energize performance. For example, fear of failing might make a student work harder. Getting a bad review could motivate an entertainer to try harder. Being booed can make an athlete run faster or kick harder. As I mentioned earlier, when an animal fails to get a reward in a situation in which it has previously been rewarded, it typically responds with more vigor (for example, it runs faster) on the next trial. Amsel has suggested that the better performance could become conditioned to the presence of the cue just before the occurrence of that response, provided the response is subsequently rewarded. In other words, not only may frustration lead to improved performance, but the improved performance may become conditioned to frustration. This would explain why an athlete might perform better when booed or why a performer might perform better with a hostile audience or why feelings of anxiety might enhance the quality of a report written by a student.

If persistence involves the conditioning of frustration cues, then it follows, according to Amsel's theory, that greater persistence could be trained by systematic conditioning of more frustration to the desired behavior. A coach, for example, might increase the amount of training time as an athlete becomes more proficient. In the laboratory, the number of nonrewards in relation to rewards might be systematically increased. It has been shown that such a procedure reliably produced increased persistence. Figure 12-5 shows the typical pattern of persistence following training that involved continuous rewards (CRF), training that involved nonrewards interspersed with rewards (PRF), and training that involved a short delay in the delivery of the rewards (PDR).

In summary, Amsel's theory suggests that persistence is acquired over a period of time. It is necessary for a person to be exposed gradually to cues that may disrupt a desired response in order to countercondition those cues. By being exposed to more and more frustrating cues—or any cue, for that matter, that might interfere with performance—the person becomes more or less immune to such disruptive cues. A surgeon working for hours may fail to realize just how tired she has become until she finishes an operation. A long-distance runner may be oblivious of fatigue until she finishes a race. A businessman may skip lunch and not realize until later that he is hungry. These and many more examples can readily be explained by Amsel's theory.

Although Amsel's theory is a very robust theory, it has some limitations. By failing to incorporate the concept of intrinsic motivation, Amsel's theory has difficulty accounting for why an author may continue writing books even though he fails to find a publisher who is willing to publish even one of his manuscripts. The

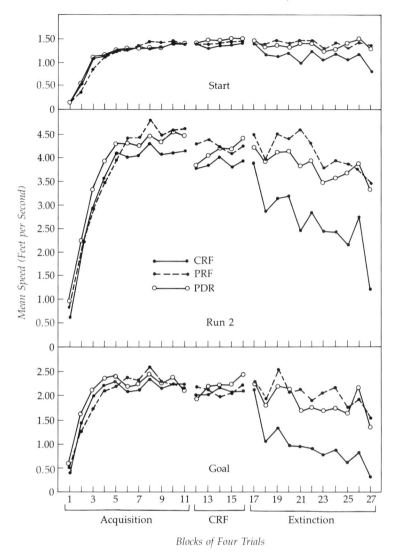

Figure 12-5. Persistence (resistance to extinction) after partial reward and partial delay of reward even after interpolation, between acquisition and extinction, of a block of continuously rewarded trials for all groups and even though the experiment was run at one trial every three days. CRF = continuous reinforcement; PRF = partial reinforcement; PDR = partial delay of reinforcement.

theory also fails to account adequately for the tendency of some people to shift tasks when they become successful or competent at their current task. According to Atkinson's theory, such shifts are very predictable. Nevertheless, Amsel's theory can explain why people often do persist when it appears they should give up in the face of tremendous hardship and frustration.

Practical Application 12-1 explores ways to help people develop the persistence necessary for success at challenging tasks.

Practical Application 12-1
Getting People to Accept Challenges

People with high resultant achievement motivation tend to accept challenges. They will take on difficult tasks, but not ones that are impossible. Once they have committed themselves to a course of action, they persist. The question that many people have asked is how we can get people with low resultant achievement motivation also to accept challenges and take on difficult tasks. In short, how can we motivate people who are not now motivated? At least three approaches have been suggested.

Reducing the Negative Affect Associated with Failure

It has been found repeatedly that people who are high in resultant achievement motivation (success-oriented people) experience pride when they succeed but relatively little shame or guilt when they fail, whereas people low in resultant achievement motivation (fear-oriented people) experience guilt and shame when they fail but relatively little pride when they succeed (Sorrentino & Hewitt, 1984). Rather than pride, fear-oriented people seem to experience something akin to relief. Success means they do not have to deal with the guilt and shame that come with failure.

At this point we do not have a clear understanding of why the affect associated with success and fear is asymmetrical. There are several possibilities. It may simply be that the individual was punished for failure in the past, and therefore shame and guilt have become conditioned rejection or punishment responses. Another possibility grows out of the work of Herbert S. Terrace (1969), who found that when he taught pigeons to make discriminations without errors, they became very emotional when they were transferred to a more difficult task at which they did make errors. Terrace's work has led to the suggestion that people may react to negative feedback (failure) with an unlearned emotional response when they have not previously been exposed to failure. In short, people may become hypersensitive to failure if they have previously known nothing but success.

How do you treat people who are hypersensitive to failure? One obvious procedure is to try to desensitize them. It has been suggested that people who are allowed to fail from time to time in the course of learning automatically become desensitized to failure, and not to failure in that task alone but to failure in general. People who are hypersensitive would have to be introduced to failure under very

(continued)

Summary

Learning theorists who have examined the question of persistence have concluded that the principles of learning can indeed explain why people will often persist in situations in which reward is infrequent or frustration is present. Amsel has argued that when a person performs a response in the presence of frustrating or disrupting cues, those cues become conditioned to the response. As a result, the cues come to support, rather than disrupt,

(continued)

supportive conditions. They then might come to realize that they have nothing to fear when they fail. The idea here is that if people no longer fear failure, they will be more inclined to try difficult or challenging tasks.

Motivating People with Difficult Tasks

A second approach is to require people to work at a difficult task. Give them no choice, in other words: simply tell them to do it. This approach is designed to capitalize on the attributional process that takes place in such situations. When people succeed at difficult tasks, they tend to take credit for their success (the self-serving bias), whereas when they succeed at an easy task, they tend to attribute their success to the fact that the task was not difficult. When the task is difficult, they say to themselves: "Since I did that pretty well, I must be pretty good"; when the task is easy, they say to themselves: "Well, of course I did it well—any fool could have done that." As we have noted, one of the reasons people tend to put forth effort is that they perceive themselves to have ability. It makes no sense, as I have pointed out, for people to work hard at a task for which they think they have no ability.

The second reason for giving people a difficult task lies in the way people respond to failure at easy and difficult tasks. People who fail at a difficult task tend to attribute their failure to the difficulty of the task ("Of course I couldn't do that—I'm not Superman"). A response of this sort, of course, does not undermine their perceptions of their ability. When they fail at an easy task, though, they tend to blame their own lack of ability. Since it takes little or no effort to do an easy task, it is hard to avoid the conclusion that failure can be due to nothing but lack of skill. And of course when people perceive themselves to be lacking in ability, they are reluctant to put forth effort. One variant of this approach is to give people an easy task at which they are likely to succeed and tell them that this task will predict future performance. It has been shown that people then treat that task as providing them with an estimate of their ability (for example, Brickman, Linsenmeier, & McCareins, 1976; Feldman & Bernstein, 1978; Vreven & Nuttin, 1976).

Attributional Retraining

A third approach is to alter people's perceptions of their ability. If people expect to do poorly because of their sex, age, education, race, or whatever, they are not going to put forth effort. The problem here is to change their expectations. It is

(continued)

behavior in those situations. As a result, the person will persist in the presence of cues that would normally disrupt behavior. Withholding a reward for a correct response has also been shown to produce persistence. Amsel argues that the absence of a reward that a person has come to expect normally produces frustration. Performing a response in the presence of the frustration cue of absence of reward will result in the conditioning of this cue to the ongoing behavior. As a result, a person will learn to persist, at least for a time, in the absence of a reward.

important to demonstrate that the factor to which they attribute their failure to perform well, whatever it may be, is not a problem. Often providing examples can help to eliminate the stereotypes to which people cling. If one sees that someone else of the same sex or age or whatever has succeeded, the belief that such factors are important is effectively undermined.

Another important thing to emphasize is the role of effort and persistence (Ostrove, 1978). Sometimes people are simply not aware of the factors that differentiate successful and unsuccessful people. If they can be made aware of those factors, they are more likely to adopt a strategy that will help them to succeed. Once they begin to experience success, they will be more likely to repeat the behaviors that lead to success.

Still another approach is simply to make people aware of the fact that performance is often unstable and not necessarily a good predictor of future performance. In one study college freshmen were given information suggesting that the factors that lead to low grades in the first year are temporary. This suggestion led to improved performance on sample items of the Graduate Record Exam and to improved grades the following semester (Wilson & Linville, 1985). The effects were greater among women than among men, a finding that is consistent with the idea that women have a greater tendency to adopt the entity model of intelligence and ability.

It should be noted that programs designed to provide children with continuous success by giving them relatively easy tasks is not an effective way of producing stable confidence, challenge seeking, and persistence (Relich, 1983). In fact, it has been found that such procedures can backfire and lower children's confidence in their ability (Meyer, 1982). A young child who is always given easy tasks to ensure success may interpret this to mean that the parent or the teacher has no confidence in his or her ability. When people are incompetent, you give them easy things to do. Further, the child may come to the conclusion that it is bad to fail. When people make sure that you avoid something, you are likely to conclude that there must be something bad about that thing you are being protected from. What does this train of thought do for self-esteem? If you have so little ability that you can't be permitted to choose a challenging task for yourself because then you'd fail and feel bad, you're not likely to have much self-esteem left to protect. A major ingredient of self-esteem is the belief that you have ability.

Power

Winter and Stewart (1978) have suggested that Western civilization is characterized by its quest for power. Using their industrial base as a springboard, nations set out to conquer new lands. Empires were established and the people of those empires were given new forms of government and new systems of communication, whether they wanted them or not. Now, as the energy supply for that industrial base becomes threatened, the question arises how to maintain that power. Thus the struggle for power continues.

Definition of the Need for Power

David G. Winter (1973) has suggested that the need for power (as measured by semiprojective techniques) is a stable tendency to seek impact on others, to influence, persuade, or control others, and to gain recognition and acclaim through these forms of behavior. A person with a need for power may attempt to satisfy this motive in a wide variety of ways. Becoming a leader of a small group or organization might be one way. Another way might be to win or earn a position in government, the military, or the church. Still another avenue might be athletic endeavors.

Although the need for power is viewed as a stable tendency, it tends to be aroused only under certain conditions. Table 12-5 presents some of the conditions under which the power motive tends to be aroused. Note that the power motive is aroused when the person is presented with a situation that contains the possibility of controlling other people in some way. The power motive may be perceived as direct, as in the case of hypnosis, or displaced or vicarious, as in the case of viewing a powerful person giving a persuasive or inspirational speech.

The Biological Component

In order to determine whether the power motive has any biological correlates, Robert S. Steele (1973, 1979) had students listen to a tape of an actor reading from famous stirring speeches, such as Winston Churchill's speech after the evacuation of British troops at Dunkirk and Henry V's exhortation of his men on the eve of battle in Shakespeare's *Henry V*, while he measured their epinephrine and nor-

Table 12-5. Experimental situations arousing the need for power (Winter & Stewart, 1978)

Experimental Condition in Which Power Was Aroused	*Neutral Control Condition in Which Power Was Not Aroused*	*Reference*
Candidates for student government offices awaiting the results of voting	Students in an introductory psychology class	Veroff (1957)
Subjects about to enact the role of "psychological experimenter"	Subjects about to participate in a psychological experiment	Uleman (1972)
Students who had just observed a demonstration of hypnosis	Students before observing hypnosis demonstration and unaware of it	Uleman (1966); Stewart & Winter (1976)
Students who had seen a film of John F. Kennedy's inauguration	Students who had seen a film about science demonstration equipment	Winter (1973)
Black students after improvising roles as members of a black action group whose leader had been arrested	Black students before improvising these roles	Watson (1969)
Students after experiencing a multimedia presentation of inspirational speeches (Churchill on Dunkirk, excerpts from *Henry V*, etc.)	Students after experiencing a multimedia presentation of a travelogue	Steele (1973, 1977); Stewart & Winter (1976)

epinephrine levels. The speeches were chosen to arouse the power motive, which they did, in some of the students, as measured by imaginative stories that students wrote in response to pictures. He found not only that the inspirational speeches produced a dramatic increase in power imagery (over stories written by controls who had listened to tape-recorded travel descriptions) but that people who showed the greatest increases in power imagery also showed the greatest increase in epinephrine and norepinephrine. The correlation found between the need for power (n Power) and norepinephrine was 0.66, a highly significant correlation indicating a link between feelings of power and norepinephrine output.

McClelland (1985) also reported some indirect evidence. He found that students who consistently sat to his right (from the students' point of view) so that they had to look to the left to see him were higher in power motivation (66% sat to his right while 25% sat to his left). Looking left has been associated with being right-hemisphere dominant. Since there is evidence that norepinephrine function is concentrated more in the right side of the brain (Oke et al., 1978; Robinson, 1979), it can be argued that when people sit to the right they are attempting to ensure that the right hemisphere is being stimulated. Another way of thinking about this is to remember that when you are sitting to the right, your left ear is more directly in the path of the speaker's voice. Since the left ear sends messages to the right hemisphere, your right hemisphere will be getting more stimulation than your left hemisphere.

A further point to consider is the finding that there is a right-hemisphere advantage in recognizing emotional stimuli (Ley & Bryden, 1982). It has also been shown that people with high n Power scores tend to be better at recognizing the emotional tone of speech when the content of the speech is not recognizable (Rosenthal, 1979). As such an ability would be higher in the right hemisphere, this finding supports the position that the power motive is linked not only to the right hemisphere but to norepinephrine.

Parental permissiveness about sex and aggression.   McClelland and Pilon (1983) found that the mothers of people high in the need for power tended to be permissive about sex and aggression—not permissive about feeding or toilet training or permissive in general, just permissive about sex and aggression. Why should permissiveness in these two areas be linked to the need for power? McClelland (1985) suggests that the link may be the catecholamine arousal system, which has been found to be involved in the power motive. It can be argued that sex and aggression activate the same system, and that early activation of this system may somehow develop or strengthen it. At some later point, the more highly developed catecholamine response that is involved in sympathetic arousal would make it possible for such an individual to experience the rewards that come from engaging in behaviors that activate that system.

This interpretation implies that the child who is prevented from activating the sympathetic arousal system early in life not only will have a lower power motive but will be more inhibited generally. McClelland reports several data that are consistent with this interpretation. Boys who are physically punished, for example, tend not only to be more inhibited but to have a lower power motive. Girls, who typically are discouraged from being aggressive and assertive, tend not only to be more inhibited but to have lower power scores. One way to raise girls' power scores is to encourage them to be more aggressive and assertive.

Summary

Winter has suggested that the need for power is a stable tendency to seek impact on others, to influence, persuade, or control others, and to gain recognition and acclaim through these forms of behavior. Steele has shown that the output of norepinephrine is closely associated with the power motive. Evidence from diverse sources suggests that people with a strong need for power attempt to stimulate the right hemisphere, an area of the brain that seems to have a higher concentration of norepinephrine. McClelland has argued that parental permissiveness in regard to sex and aggression may stimulate the maturation of the biological system (the catecholamine system) that is hypothesized to reward power-related behaviors.

The Learned Component

While the power motive is defined as a need to have impact, control, or influence over another person, McClelland argues that it is the catecholamine system that provides the reward. This hypothesis suggests that the motive may find expression in a wide variety of behaviors.

Aggression.   The power motive is frequently expressed in various forms of aggression. This is not surprising in view of the fact that the power motive seems to have its origins in permissiveness in regard to aggression. Winter (1973) and later McClelland (1975) found that people with strong power needs were more likely to be involved in competitive sports than those with low power needs. McClelland also found that men with a high need for power tended to get into more arguments. In a study that involved the coding of the political speeches of members of the Politburo, the principal policy-making body of the Communist Party of the Soviet Union, it was found that those with a higher power motive favored a more assertive foreign policy toward the United States (Hermann, 1980).

Occupational selection.   Winter (1973) has shown that the power motive is linked to selection of an occupation. People with a strong power motive tend to select occupational fields that offer an opportunity for impact, influence, or control over other people—teaching, psychology, the ministry, business, and journalism, for example, rather than law or medicine. Politics is an obvious outlet for the power motive, and researchers have examined the strength of the power motive in U.S. presidents (see Winter & Stewart, 1978). The overall prestige of a president, together with his assertiveness versus passivity, were found to be strongly and positively related to the need-for-power score and negatively related to the need-for-affiliation score that the researchers derived by scoring motivational imagery in each president's inaugural address (Winter & Stewart, 1978). These results, presented in Table 12-6, show that both Roosevelts, Wilson, Truman, Kennedy, Johnson, and Reagan all had power scores that were relatively higher than their affiliation scores, a pattern that has been associated with effective management (Winter, 1973).

Getting good grades and acquiring prestigious objects.   People with a strong power motive tend to get better grades than people with a weaker power motive. Why should this be the case? Grades not only are a source of recognition but indirectly are a form of power when it comes to gaining access to jobs (Costa & McClelland, 1971). Perhaps more interesting is the finding that a strong power

Table 12-6. Motive scores for twentieth-century U.S. presidents using inaugural addresses (McClelland, 1985)

President	n Achievement	n Affiliation	n Power	n Power less n Affiliation
	Standard-Scored Motives (Mean = 50; Standard Deviation = 10)			
T. Roosevelt	56	45	63	+ 18
Taft	35	39	33	− 6
Wilson	43	41	49	+ 8
Harding	40	48	41	− 7
Coolidge	38	42	38	− 4
Hoover	47	45	38	− 7
F. D. Roosevelt	52	40	54	+ 14
Truman	47	41	59	+ 8
Eisenhower	41	55	43	− 12
Kennedy	58	58	63	+ 5
Johnson	61	45	56	+ 11
Nixon	64	58	48	− 10
Ford	40	80	46	− 34
Carter	63	53	51	− 2
Reagan*	62	50	67	+ 17
Mean score per 1000 words	4.80	3.33	5.53	
Standard deviation	2.53	2.41	2.08	

*Scores provided later by David Winter

need is correlated with the number of prestigious objects one possesses—cars, wine glasses, tape recorders, and the like (Winter, 1973). Credit cards are an obvious symbol of prestige, and it is not surprising that individuals with a high need for power (executives) were found to have more credit cards in their wallets.

The Cognitive Component

The cognitive and symbolic nature of the power motive can be seen to some degree in the research that pertains to the acquisition of grades and prestigious objects, but it can be seen to an even greater degree in the interpersonal behaviors of people who have a strong power motive. It is important to note that data on the role played by cognitive operations in the activation of the catecholamine system support McClelland's hypothesis. In the following discussion, I will be talking about a game that can arouse the power motive. If a game situation can elicit that motive, then it must be the perceptions of the individual that are important in activating that motive.

Interpersonal behaviors.   People with a strong power need like to be in groups of four or five people rather than with only one other person (McAdams, Healey, & Krause, 1982, cited in McClelland, 1985). It has been suggested that the more people present, the better one's opportunity to draw attention to oneself. Consistent with this idea is the finding that when people high in n Power are given the opportunity to select the other members of the group, they tend to pick people who are not particularly well known (Winter, 1973). This strategy, it has been argued, allows them to dominate.

Also consistent with this interpretation is the finding that when people with a strong need for power function in a group, they do not tend to promote group discussion: they dominate the discussion. People low in the need for power are in fact more helpful in promoting group discussion (Fodor & Smith, 1982). It appears that people with a high need for power are more inclined to put their self-interest first. While they are frequently judged to be influential, they are not particularly well liked. Apparently they are too assertive to bring out the good in other people.

As I have indicated, people with a strong need for power are very competitive. How does that competitive nature influence their dealings with other people? A study by Schnackers and Kleinbeck (1975) demonstrates what others have found when they have studied people with a strong need for power. The investigators induced these people, two low in need for power and one high, to participate in a con game that involved throwing dice and using "power cards" of various values that could be multiplied by the score on the dice. The game was designed so that two players could form a coalition, and if they maintained it, they could always defeat the third player. According to the rules, however, a coalition did not have to be maintained; either participant could break it whenever he decided it was to his advantage to do so. The game involved three rounds of play. The left side of Figure 12-6 shows the frequency with which players broke a coalition in each of the three ways it could be broken. These results make it clear that individuals with a high power need are more likely to exploit others in such a situation. Whenever it seems to be to their advantage, they either go it alone, make an offer to the third person, or accept the third person's offer. The right-hand side of the figure shows the points the players won in each of the three rounds.

Social acceptability of the power motive. One of the persistent themes that has emerged from research on the power motive is the question of the social acceptability or social desirability of the power motive. As the discussion so far indicates, people with a strong power motive (especially men) tend not only to exploit other people but generally to act in a self-centered, aggressive fashion, especially in competitive situations. Winter (1982) has pointed out, for example, that men high in the need for power have a tendency to fight, drink, gamble, and

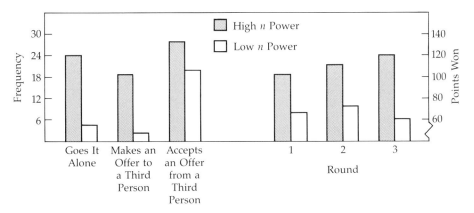

Figure 12-6. Behavior of subjects high and low in *n* Power in a game; (left) frequency of three ways of breaking a coalition; (right) points won in three consecutive rounds (McClelland, 1985)

try to exploit women sexually. Women tend to express the power motive in more socially acceptable ways. This finding could be predicted from what we know about the way boys and girls are raised. While boys are often encouraged to behave aggressively, girls are discouraged from doing so.

Stages in the development of the power motive.   The power motive tends to go through several changes in the course of psychosocial development. Four stages have been identified (McClelland, 1975). We generally conceptualize these changes as resulting from both the socialization process and the resolution of various conflicts that tend to occur as we mature. Stage I has been referred to as the *intake stage* and is characterized by, among other things, an interest in power-oriented material. Stage II has been referred to as the *autonomy stage* and is characterized by a tendency to control anger (probably because the expression of anger is not socially acceptable). Stage III has been referred to as the *assertion stage*. As we develop we tend not only to become more independent but to assert our independence. This stage is characterized in men by a desire to have the freedom to love several women, to drink heavily, and to collect valuable objects; in women, by a tendency to express anger and the desire to travel and try new foods. Stage IV, *generativity/mutuality*, is characterized by membership in many organizations. The important thing to note is that the power motive moves through several phases. Many people never reach stage IV, considered to be the most highly socialized phase.

The leadership motive syndrome.   Considerable attention has focused on stage III, as this stage has been linked to the emergence of leadership. Bear in mind that most of the research on this point has been concerned with men. While assertion is important as far as leadership is concerned, it has been found that it is often important to inhibit what seems to be a natural tendency for high-power people to act aggressively or too assertively. People who have a high need for power but have learned to inhibit their assertiveness have what has been called the leadership motive syndrome (McClelland & Boyatzis, 1982). (It should be noted that men who do not develop the ability to inhibit their assertiveness tend to have poor dating relationships and make poor husbands [McClelland, 1985].)

Some data suggest that parents may play a very active role in producing the leadership syndrome. When parents feel strongly that it is important for their children to be assertive if they are to succeed and survive, they tend to nurture the development of the power motive in their children. A threat to one's status or to one's survival, as in the case of the Jews who were caught in the Holocaust, made many parents more aware of the need to teach their children the importance of being assertive (for example, Heller, 1979, cited in McClelland, 1985). When fathers take an active role in the raising of their sons, the sons too have a strong power motive. It has been suggested that men may have stronger feelings about the need to be assertive if one is to succeed and attempt to pass this belief on to their sons.

What all of this suggests is that, at least to some degree, the power motive not only can be nurtured but can be channeled into socially acceptable forms that make it very productive for both the individual and the society. Yet people who learn to inhibit the more socially unacceptable expressions of the power motive may, as we shall see shortly, create health problems for themselves.

Some Perils Associated with a Strong Need for Power

Loss of objectivity.   It seems reasonable to conclude that people high in the need for power should have the capacity to foster achievement in others. Indeed, this is what has been found. One study found that managers high in power motivation created or fostered an organizational climate conducive to high work performance (McClelland & Burnham, 1976). In an interesting extension of this work, Fodor and Farrow (1979) examined the question of how managers high in power motivation might react to people who tend to be ingratiating. Simulating an industrial situation, Fodor and Farrow studied the reactions of supervisors high and low in power motivation to a person who behaved in an ingratiating manner toward them. Supervisors high in power motivation rated the ingratiator more favorably than supervisors low in power motivation did (Figure 12-7). Fodor and Farrow conclude that although people high in power motivation may be good at influencing people to work, their own needs may interfere with their ability to judge objectively the performance of those they influence. Specifically, the need to be recognized for their power may produce an inflated rating of the ability of those who play to that power motive.

Inhibited power and health.   One of the consequences of inhibited power is high blood pressure (McClelland, 1985). Chronically high blood pressure has been linked to the development of heart disease. It has also been shown that inhibited power is linked to an impaired immune response (McClelland et al., 1980), and

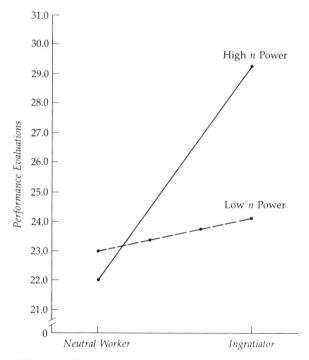

Figure 12-7.   Effects of n Power and ingratiation on performance evaluations by student supervisors (Fodor & Farrow, 1979)

that stress increases the effect (McClelland & Jemmott, 1980). The question that arises out of these findings is why inhibited power leads to a breakdown in the immune response. McClelland argues that the chronic activation of the sympathetic nervous system may produce this effect. McClelland and his colleagues (1980) were able to demonstrate that epinephrine levels are higher in people with the inhibited power syndrome, and further that when epinephrine is high, immunoglobin A in the saliva, a measure of the immune response, is reduced. This research seems to suggest that we inhibit power at our peril. This research also attests to the strength of the power motive in some people and to the effects of inhibiting the assertive quality that is associated with it.

Inhibited power and drinking.   People with a strong need for power tend to consume more alcohol in stage III. In a series of studies McClelland and his associates argued that one of the reasons that people with a strong power motive tend to drink heavily is that drinking produces feelings of power.

If drinking leads to feelings of power, then do people who have a tendency to inhibit power drink less? In order to find the answer, McClelland and his colleagues asked subjects to write stories after they had consumed various amounts of alcohol. They found that alcohol increased power concerns and decreased inhibitory thoughts. When the stories were scored for personal (p) power versus socialized (s) power, they found that people tended to write about s power after a few drinks (moderate level of alcohol consumption) and about p power after several drinks (heavy alcohol consumption). The investigators also measured the amounts drunk by people who did and did not inhibit power, and found that people who did not inhibit power drank more. If we assume that alcohol not only stimulates power feelings but reduces inhibitions, then it is important for the people who inhibit power to restrict their alcohol intake in order to limit the disinhibitory effects that normally accompany alcohol.

The Affiliative Motive and Power

The affiliative motive appears to have a moderating effect on the power motive, which can be useful or detrimental depending on the situation. The affiliative motive has been defined as concern over establishing, maintaining, or restoring positive, affective relationships with other persons (Atkinson, Heyns, & Veroff, 1954). While people with a strong affiliative motive tend to be concerned about the welfare of other people, and therefore their behavior is usually viewed as highly socially acceptable, it can be detrimental in some management situations. At higher levels of management, for example, it is important not only to make individual contributions to the achievement of the organization's goals but to influence others (high need for power) while at the same time not being too concerned about being liked (low in affiliative motivation). People in whom affiliative motivation is high can be poor managers if that motivation interferes with their willingness to make difficult decisions that affect other people. (The role of the affiliative motive is discussed more fully in McClelland, 1985.)

Summary

People apparently can learn to satisfy their power motive in a variety of ways. Such aggressive behaviors as participation in competitive sports and arguing are frequent outlets for people high in the need for power. Selecting an occupation in which you can have impact or influence others is another way of

(continued)

satisfying the power motive. Interestingly, the acquisition of prestigious objects is a prominent means of satisfying a strong need for power.

The interpersonal behavior of people with a strong need for power indicates that such people are highly self-centered. While they are quick to form coalitions that may benefit them, they are just as quick to break those coalitions. This disregard for social conventions can be an important element in the quest for power.

It has been suggested that the power motive goes through four developmental stages: intake, autonomy, assertion, and mutuality. Stage IV can be considered the most highly socialized stage.

The leadership motive syndrome has been linked to stage III. Leaders who are most likely to be promoted are those who learn to inhibit some aspects of their assertiveness so that they do not appear to be too aggressive or simply too insensitive to the needs of other people. McClelland has suggested that parents play an important role in nurturing assertiveness in their children.

There are perils associated with a high need for power. Such men tend not to be liked, to have poor relationships with women before and after marriage, and to overvalue people who are ingratiating. At the same time, inhibition of the power motive can produce a lowered immunological reaction and make people tend to drink too much.

The affiliative motive seems to have a healthy moderating effect on people with a high need for power. It can, however, undermine their ability to make tough decisions that affect other people.

Main Points

1. The need to achieve was originally defined by Murray as the desire or tendency to "overcome obstacles, to exercise power, to strive to do something difficult as well and as quickly as possible."
2. According to Atkinson, resultant achievement motivation is a joint function of the need to achieve and the need to avoid failure.
3. Because the strengths of these two motives appear to vary independently, Atkinson says that the need or motive to achieve may be stronger than the need or motive to avoid failure ($M_S > M_F$), they may be equal ($M_S = M_F$), or the motive to avoid failure may be stronger than the need or motive to succeed ($M_F > M_S$).
4. According to Atkinson's theory, people in whom $M_S > M_F$ tend to select tasks of intermediate difficulty, whereas people in whom $M_F > M_S$ tend to select either very easy or very difficult tasks.
5. Research conducted with male subjects has generally provided support for Atkinson's theory.
6. Subjects in whom $M_S > M_F$ display more realism in regard to vocational choice than subjects in whom $M_F > M_S$.
7. There is a great deal of controversy as to whether the TAT measure of the achievement motive actually measures achievement motivation in women.
8. Horner suggested that one of the reasons women do not perform as well as men is that they have a greater fear of success (FOS) than men. Subsequent studies have found that men are as ambivalent as women about success.
9. FOS inhibits competitiveness in women but not in men.
10. Janet Spence and her colleagues, using the Work and Family Orientation (WOFO)

Questionnaire, have found three aspects or dimensions of achievement: work, mastery, and competitiveness.

11. Men tend to score higher than women on the mastery and competitiveness subscales, whereas women tend to score higher on the work subscale.

12. In a variety of situations it has been found that high levels of achievement are associated with high levels of work and mastery and low levels of competitiveness.

13. McClelland has provided evidence that the level of achievement motivation among members of a society is related to the economic growth of that society.

14. Parents who put their children on a feeding schedule, demand early toilet training, and have high standards of neatness tend to produce children with strong achievement motivation.

15. People attribute success and failure to four factors: ability, effort, task difficulty, and luck.

16. People high in resultant achievement motivation attribute success to ability and effort, failure to lack of effort; people low in resultant achievement motivation attribute success to task difficulty and luck, failure to lack of ability.

17. One of the most important variables that determine whether people will work toward a goal is their perceptions of their own abilities.

18. People who perceive themselves to have ability generally experience good self-esteem.

19. People who believe in the entity theory of intelligence are motivated to set their goals so as to avoid failure, whereas people who believe in the incremental theory are not.

20. People who believe in the incremental theory are more likely to accept challenges.

21. Because humans tend to assume more responsibility for success than for failure, it is said that humans have a self-serving bias.

22. The tendency for women to do poorly in competitive tasks may be due to the fact that women tend to perceive themselves as less skilled than men at a wide variety of tasks.

23. There is some evidence that women tend to believe in the entity theory of intelligence.

24. Studies on self-focused attention indicate that when attention is drawn to failure, it tends to disrupt the performance of subjects low in self-esteem but not of subjects high in self-esteem.

25. Weiner has suggested that a wide variety of emotions accompany success and failure, depending on what the individual thinks caused the success or failure. Success can produce feelings of activation, relaxation, self-enhancement, gratitude, or surprise; failure can produce feelings of incompetence, guilt, resignation, aggression, or surprise.

26. Amsel has suggested that the reason some people persist at a task and others do not lies in the ways they become habituated to disruptive stimulus activities.

27. There have been several suggestions about how to get people to accept challenges. These include reducing the negative affect associated with failure, motivating people with difficult tasks, and attributional retraining.

28. The need for power has been defined as the need to seek impact on others, to influence, persuade, or control others, and to receive recognition for those efforts.

29. The need for power is aroused when the person confronts a situation that presents a possibility of controlling other people in some way.

30. A positive correlation has been found between n Power and norepinephrine output.
31. Parental permissiveness with respect to sex and aggression has been linked to the power motive.
32. People with a strong need for power enjoy such aggressive activities as competitive sports and arguing, tend to select occupations in which they can influence other people, and like to acquire prestigious objects.
33. People with a strong need for power tend to be very self-centered in their interpersonal relationships and are quite willing to exploit others.
34. The power motive goes through four stages: intake, autonomy, assertiveness, and mutuality.
35. The leadership motive syndrome has been linked to the assertive stage.
36. People with a high need for power are very susceptible to ingratiation.
37. Some of the perils associated with an inhibited power need are chronic high blood pressure, a susceptibility to breakdown of the immune system, and a tendency to drink excessively.
38. While the affiliative motive tends to be a moderator of the power motive, it can undermine the ability to make difficult decisions that affect other people.

Curiosity, Exploratory Behavior, Play, and Competence

What motivates people to explore something like a new city?

Is this exploratory behavior learned or unlearned?

Why do people believe that exploratory behavior is motivated by the curiosity drive?

What activates the curiosity drive?

Is the curiosity drive always active, or is it activated only under certain conditions?

Is play a frivolous activity or is it important for learning and development?

What is sensation seeking?

Is the trait of sensation seeking learned or acquired or is it something we are born with?

What is the link between the curiosity drive and the development of competence?

What are some of the factors that are important for the development of competence?

What is the relation of competence to self-esteem?

Exploratory Behavior: Learned or Innate?

Children in particular like to explore their environment. It is common to see young children taking the pots and pans out of the corner cupboard, rummaging through a book of old photos they found in a box in the basement, or to find only the remains of a watch they disassembled but couldn't put back together. Parents often complain that if they left their young children alone, they would empty every cupboard or closet in the house. Many parents find that they must lock certain cupboards, closets, or rooms because children like not only to see and touch but to taste. As our homes are usually filled with all kinds of toxic chemicals, it is necessary to ensure that these chemicals are kept away from children too young to understand that there are dangers associated with exploring the environment.

As children grow up, they begin to explore other areas, such as the neighborhood in which they live. They develop friendships and learn to play games. All of this seems to occur without very much encouragement from their parents. In fact, parents often try to discourage their children from their interest in the contents of closets and cupboards and from wandering too far from home. What motivates this behavior? We often say that such behaviors grow out of a strong curiosity drive. The question that we will deal with in this chapter is what motivates this curiosity drive and what function it ultimately plays in our development. Interestingly, people have not always believed that there is such a thing as a curiosity drive, or that if it did exist, it was very important. Until fairly recently, people tended to view all important behaviors as developing from such basic drives as hunger and sex. That is, they believed that the curiosity drive was learned.

The Behaviorist Explanation

The reinforcement of random behavior. How do we come to learn about our environment? Before the 1950s the behaviorists argued that primary drives, such as hunger, energized the organism to engage in random behavior. When the appropriate goal object was found in the course of such random movements, the drive would be reduced and the behavior that had just preceded the reduction of that drive would be reinforced. The organism would then become more and more efficient at finding the appropriate goal object when a given drive state had been activated. That is, through learning, the organism would come to engage quickly and efficiently in a pattern of movements that would result in the finding of an appropriate goal object.

According to this explanation, exploratory behavior was assumed to be random in the first instance. It became systematic only as a result of learning (reinforcement). Note that according to this explanation, a different pattern of exploratory behavior should occur for each drive state. That is, when you are hungry, you engage in one pattern of responses; when you are thirsty, you engage in another pattern of responses; when you are sexually motivated, you engage in still another pattern of responses; and so forth. In other words, according to the behaviorists of that time, there was no such thing as a generalized curiosity drive. You did not learn for learning's sake. You learned only in order to help you satisfy a more basic (biological) motive system.

The Challenge of the 1950s

Alternation behavior.   The behaviorists' explanation of exploratory behavior was challenged in the 1950s by many studies. One group of studies that challenged this position involved the phenomenon called alternation behavior. If you place a rat in a T-maze and allow the animal to select one of the two arms of the maze, the probability of its selecting either of the two arms of the maze is 50%. If you then remove that animal and immediately give it a second choice, you find that it tends to select the arm of the maze it did not enter on the first trial. This tendency to choose the previously unvisited alternative on the second trial has been referred to as alternation behavior.

The reactive inhibition model.   Clark Hull (a behaviorist) attributed alternation behavior to something he called reactive inhibition. Hull (1943) argued that when organisms make a response, some kind of inhibition to that response builds up. For a time, then (until the inhibition wears off), the animal is unlikely to repeat that response. Thus if an animal made a right-turn response on trial 1, it would not be inclined to make that same response on trial 2. Since the only other response it can make in the T-maze is a left-turn response, it would tend to make that response.

The stimulus satiation model.   An alternative model suggested that on trial 1 the animal became satiated for the stimulus to which it had just been exposed (Glanzer, 1953). Satiation is like inhibition except that the inhibition is not limited to responses. You could become satiated visually or auditorially or olfactorily and so forth. When we're talking about humans, we tend to use the word *bored*. Murray Glanzer demonstrated that if you changed the color of the walls of the arm of the maze that the animal visited on trial 1, the animal tended to repeat a right-turn or left-turn response, as Figure 13-1*a* indicates. The dotted line shows where the animal went on trials 1 and 2.

The stimulus change model.   Were the animals in Glanzer's experiment avoiding a stimulus for which they had become satiated or were they simply approaching a new or different stimulus? William Dember and R. W. Earl (1957) suggested that

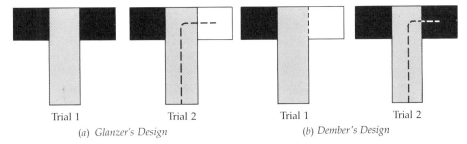

Figure 13-1. (*a*) Glanzer's design to test his stimulus satiation hypothesis; (*b*) Dember's design to test his stimulus change hypothesis

animals are motivated by change or by stimulation that is novel. In order to determine whether this was the case, Dember (1956) designed an ingenious experiment: he made one of the arms of a T-maze white and the other black, and at the entry to each arm he put a glass panel that prevented the animal from entering. As it could turn neither right nor left, it could not develop reactive inhibition. As the animal saw one white arm and one black arm, it would be satiated equally for black and white at the termination of trial 1. As we shall see, this was an important manipulation. After 10 minutes in the maze the animal was removed, the glass panels were removed, and one of the arms was changed so that both arms were now either black or white. On trial 2 Dember watched to see if the animal entered the changed arm or if its behavior was random. According to the reactive inhibition model, since the animal made no response on trial 1, the probability of entering one of the arms on trial 2 should be 50%. According to the satiation model, since the animal was equally satiated to black and white, the probability of entering one of the two arms should also be 50%. According to the stimulus change model, on the other hand, the animal should enter the changed arm. Dember found, as he had predicted, that his animals entered the changed arm (see Figure 13-1*b*).

These studies, as well as others that I discuss shortly, changed forever the way psychologists thought about curiosity and exploratory behaviors. As the animals used in these studies were deprived of neither food nor water, their exploratory behavior had occurred without the activation of some more basic primary drive. The general conclusion that people came to was that these animals explored because it is the nature of organisms to explore. The motivation for this tendency was assumed to be a curiosity drive that motivates organisms to investigate novel things in their environment.

Other studies of the curiosity drive. Many studies have been conducted to investigate the curiosity drive. At the University of Wisconsin, Robert Butler and Harry Harlow did a number of studies that showed that monkeys have a very strong exploratory drive that is motivated by the visual, auditory, and manipulatory properties of the objects they encounter. Harlow (1953) showed, for example, that monkeys will learn to solve various kinds of mechanical puzzles when no motivation is provided other than the presence of the puzzles. Moreover, the monkeys had a persistent tendency to carry out the solution in a flawless manner. Butler (1953) put monkeys in a room with four windows that they could open to see a toy train, various other objects, or other monkeys. These monkeys spent a great deal of time simply looking at things. The monkeys learned which window provided which kind of stimulation. Thus Butler demonstrated that the curiosity drive could reinforce learning—something that is not surprising now but was important to demonstrate at that time because the behaviorists tended to dismiss the curiosity drive as weak, transient, and not very important in the overall functioning of the individual.

The Human Tendency to Seek Out Variety and Novelty

Children in particular like to seek out new and varied stimulation. If a child is presented with an object he has not previously encountered, for example, and he is in a familiar and secure environment, he will tend to approach the object, visually inspect it, and then begin to interact with it by touching it, holding it, picking it up, tapping it, turning it over, and so on. If there are parts that can be moved or removed, the child is almost certain to discover this fact. After the child has thoroughly investigated the object, his interactions with it begin to wane.

Corinne Hutt (1966) gave children a novel object that had a lever connected to a set of counters so that the child could see the numbers change as she moved the lever. In one condition the children could see the counters move; in another condition the counters were covered. Figure 13-2 shows the proportion of time spent by these two groups of children on successive exposures to the object. Note that the proportion of time spent exploring the object decreased with repeated exposure. As expected, when the object provided more stimulation—that is, when the counters were visible—the children found the novel object somewhat more interesting.

When a person stops interacting with a novel object, we say that he or she has become satiated. The term *satiated* implies that the person has had enough, that the object is no longer a source of motivation, that the person has exhausted all the information or entertainment value of the object. Since children often return to objects previously abandoned, it appears that satiation dissipates with time. This is one of the important facts that need to be explained by a theory of curiosity and exploratory behaviors. When children abandon an object, it is usually because

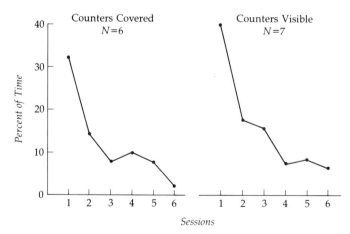

Figure 13-2. Proportions of time children spent exploring a novel object on successive trials when counters were covered and when they were visible. N = number of subjects (Hutt, 1966).

they have shifted their interest and attention to other objects, usually objects that are new or ones they have not encountered for a while. Thus children have a tendency to interact constantly with more and more of the environment.

The emergence of the concept of complexity.   As the studies of the curiosity drive continued, it became very apparent not only that organisms tend to explore things that are novel or different but that they are attracted to things that are complex. One of the important questions that arose out of this research is whether humans are simply attracted to the most complex things in the environment or whether there is some optimal level of complexity that falls short of the greatest complexity possible.

If you assume that organisms are processing the information contained in the stimuli they select, then from an information-processing viewpoint it would make sense for people to attend only to stimuli that provided information they had the cognitive capacity to process. Such an interpretation suggests that children would probably choose less complex stimuli than adults simply because children have had less experience than adults and therefore they do not have the backlog of knowledge, skills, or cognitive structures to deal with very complex stimuli.

The tendency to select increasingly complex stimuli.   One of the first demonstrations of the tendency for humans to respond to increasingly complex stimuli was reported by Robert Earl (1957). He first had children work on block-design puzzles of moderate complexity and then gave them the opportunity to select a new block-design puzzle. The children could choose either more complex or simpler designs. Most selected a design that was somewhat more complex than the design they had just been working on. They did not, for the most part, select either a design that was simpler or a design that was much more complex. This very systematic tendency to select a slightly more complex puzzle indicates that human exploratory behavior is highly systematic. Humans do not, it appears, explore their environment haphazardly. Earl's findings have been duplicated by Richard May (1963). May had preschool children look at checkerboard designs of moderate complexity. Then they were given the opportunity to look at a pile of simpler or more complex checkerboard designs. May found, as did Earl, that most of the children selected the more complex designs. Arkes and Boykin (1971) have further shown that children who participated in a Head Start program came to prefer more complex stimulation. There have been numerous demonstrations that animals also tend to select more complex stimulation after being exposed to moderate complexity. The fact that a wide variety of animals respond in the same way as humans provides evidence that this tendency is a biological characteristic, not a learned behavior pattern.

Age differences in the preference for complexity.   If humans tend to seek out more and more complex stimulation, it follows that older people should prefer more complex stimulation than younger people. To test this hypothesis, various experiments have used geometrical figures that vary in complexity, as defined by the number of angles and sides. Examples of such figures are shown in Figure 13-3. In general, it has been found that older people tend to prefer stimuli of greater complexity (Munsinger & Kessen, 1964; Thomas, 1966).

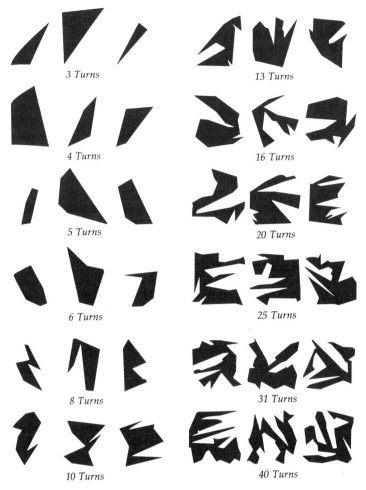

3 Turns

13 Turns

4 Turns

16 Turns

5 Turns

20 Turns

6 Turns

25 Turns

8 Turns

31 Turns

10 Turns

40 Turns

Figure 13-3. The 12 sets of three asymmetrical shapes used by Munsinger and Kessen (1964)

Summary

Research with animals has indicated that the tendency to explore is motivated by novelty or stimulus change. In fact, a great deal of research indicates that animals are motivated by the opportunity to explore the visual, auditory, tactile, and olfactory properties of objects and that they will learn to do things that make it possible for them to experience the stimulation that comes from interacting with various objects. Work with humans indicates that, like animals, we are motivated by the variety and novelty of objects we encounter. There is considerable evidence that animals and humans are motivated by the complexity of objects. It has been shown that children tend to select increasingly complex objects. Apparently as children's ability to handle more complex forms of stimulation increases, they have a natural tendency to select more complex stimuli.

Theories of Exploratory Behavior

Dember and Earl's Theory

The results of the studies that I have just reviewed can be readily accounted for by the Dember and Earl theory. Dember and Earl (1957) assume that organisms are motivated to experience optimal complexity. One special and important feature of their theory is their concept of a pacer stimulus or a pacer range. They suggest that an organism becomes accustomed, or habituated, to a certain level of complexity (called an "adaptation level") and is motivated to explore stimuli that are slightly more complex than this adaptation level. This part of the theory is illustrated in Figure 13-4. The pacer concept is intended to explain why exploratory, curiosity, and play behaviors tend to be systematically directed toward more complex levels of stimulation. Further, the pacer concept is intended to explain why individuals prefer certain stimuli rather than others. The appeal of the theory is its simplicity. It predicts that individuals will always select slightly more complex stimuli (given that they have had time to adapt to a given level of complexity) and that over time individuals will come to prefer more and more complex stimulation.

The measure of any theory, however, is how well it can account for the research findings. Several tests of the theory have shown that, indeed, many forms of stimulation can be ordered in terms of their psychological complexity and, further, that preferences are systematically related to psychological complexity. For example, preference for auditory stimuli appears to be determined by their complexity (Vitz, 1966a, 1966b), as does preference for visual stimuli (for example, Munsinger & Kessen, 1964; Smith & Dorfman, 1975). In addition, a number of studies have

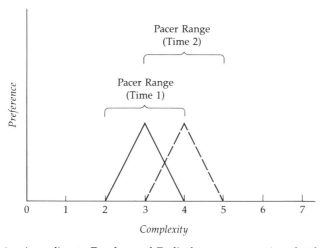

Figure 13-4. According to Dember and Earl's theory, an organism that has adapted to the level of complexity represented by point 2 on the complexity dimension will be inclined to respond only to stimuli enclosed by points 2 and 4, maximum attention being directed toward stimuli at point 3. Interacting with stimuli at point 3 will lead to a new adaptation level corresponding to point 3. As a result, there will be a new pacer range, enclosed by points 3 and 5. Thus, as long as there are stimuli corresponding to those in the pacer range, over time the individual will systematically interact with all stimuli in its environment.

shown that preference for complexity shifts upward as a result of experience with a certain kind of stimulation. For example, Vitz (1966b) found that subjects with greater musical experience rated complex auditory stimuli as more pleasant than other subjects did. Munsinger and Kessen (1964) found that art students preferred more variability than other students. Sackett (1965) found that rhesus monkeys raised in more complex environments preferred more complex stimuli. As I mentioned earlier, Arkes and Boykin (1971) found that children in a Head Start program significantly increased their preference for complexity.

Berlyne's Theory

Probably the most influential of the theories of exploration was proposed by D. E. Berlyne (1960, 1971). Berlyne's theory is based on the assumption that exploration and play are directed toward the processing of information. He suggested that through exploration and play the individual becomes knowledgeable about its environment. Berlyne further theorized, drawing on a large body of data, that such behaviors are highly systematic. Animals as well as humans, he thought, respond systematically to events, especially novel events (Berlyne, 1958). The questions to which Berlyne addressed himself were (1) "What motivates the tendency to process information?" and (2) "What governs the tendency to respond systematically to certain stimuli and not others?"

Berlyne (1960) suggested that the basic mechanism underlying exploratory and play behaviors is level of arousal. He proposed that the relation between arousal and hedonic tone can be described as an inverted-U-shaped function, such that hedonic tone is greatest when arousal is moderate (Figure 13-5). He argued that either very low levels of stimulation or very complex stimulation produces high arousal, and that high arousal is aversive. According to Berlyne's theory, organisms are motivated to seek out positive affect and avoid negative affect. Therefore, a

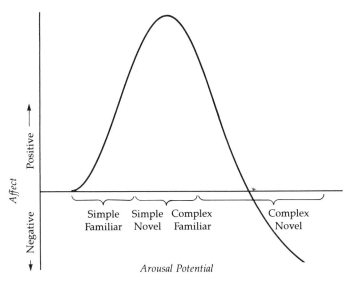

Figure 13-5. The hypothesized relation between affect and the arousal potential of a stimulus as proposed by Berlyne. Note that positive affect is greatest when a stimulus is moderately complex or moderately novel (Berlyne, 1970).

person who is experiencing low arousal (is in a situation that has low arousal potential) will seek out situations that will increase arousal, and a person who is experiencing high arousal (is in a situation that has high arousal potential) will seek out situations that will lower arousal.

Berlyne's theory assumes that arousal comes from interacting with external stimulation or by exercising internal processes, such as imagining, fantasizing, and thinking. Much of Berlyne's research focused on identifying and classifying those forms or characteristics of stimulation that could produce arousal. After carefully analyzing a large body of research, Berlyne suggested there is a class of variables associated with arousal, which he called "collative variables": novelty, degree of change, suddenness of change, surprisingness, incongruity, conflict, complexity, and uncertainty. Figure 13-6 presents examples of stimulus materials illustrating certain collative variables used in Berlyne's research.

Berlyne used the term *collative* to describe these variables because their ability to produce arousal is assumed to depend on the person's comparison of a given stimulus with some "standard" stimulus. Berlyne conceptualized the standard stimulus as some form of memory representation. Berlyne suggested that when a person attends to a stimulus, he or she compares that stimulus with other stimuli represented in memory. If the stimulus departs in some way from other stimuli represented in memory, it should elicit arousal.

How does a standard develop? Berlyne theorized that humans tend to process all the information contained in a stimulus. Processing information, he maintained, is as natural as seeing. He proposed that humans do not simply store a

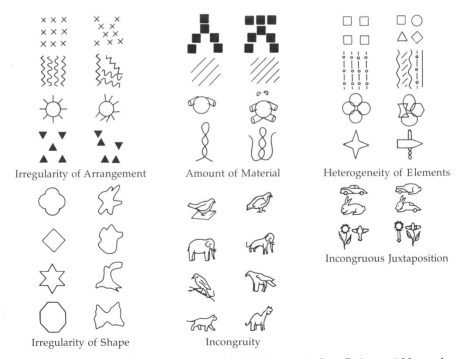

Irregularity of Arrangement   Amount of Material   Heterogeneity of Elements

Incongruous Juxtaposition

Irregularity of Shape   Incongruity

Figure 13-6. Materials of the type used by Berlyne to study collative variables and arousal (Berlyne, 1958)

detailed icon but tend rather to abstract essential features of the stimulus. These essential features make up the "standard." Berlyne argued that once all the essential features have been abstracted, the stimulus loses its ability to elicit further attention. The standard then becomes the backdrop against which all new information is processed. When a person attends to a new stimulus, he or she compares its essential features with those of the standard.

The tendency to process new information is assumed to be governed by the ability of the new stimulus to elicit arousal. When a person encounters a new stimulus that departs in some way from the standard, it is assumed that the discrepancy will elicit arousal. The greater the discrepancy, the greater the arousal. If the discrepancy is moderate, it will elicit moderate arousal, and since moderate arousal is pleasurable, the person will, according to the theory, try to maintain contact with the stimulus. However, because organisms are inclined to process the information contained in a stimulus, it is simply a matter of time before the essential features of the new stimulus will be abstracted. As a result, a novel stimulus becomes familiar, a surprising stimulus will lose its ability to elicit surprise, and an incongruous stimulus will become ordinary and predictable. Because it is assumed that organisms are motivated to maintain moderate arousal, the theory predicts that organisms will be inclined to seek out new stimuli that depart from the standard in order to experience moderate arousal once again. In this way, the organism tends, over time, to learn more and more about different parts of its environment.

According to Berlyne's theory, a stimulus could evoke too much arousal and thus be aversive. Rather than explore such a stimulus, the theory predicts, the individual would tend to terminate contact with the stimulus in order to avoid or reduce negative hedonic tone. This motivational tendency, Berlyne argues, serves an important function. If it is assumed that the ability to process information depends on the existence of certain cognitive structures, certain stimuli may exceed the individual's ability to abstract information they contain. Therefore, until the individual has developed the appropriate structures (presumably as a result of interacting with stimuli that can be processed), there is no point in interacting with such stimuli. In short, it is a waste of the individual's time.

To summarize, Berlyne's theory predicts that people and animals are motivated to explore stimuli that contain a moderate amount of new information (novelty). Such stimuli are defined as having a moderate amount of "arousal potential." If an individual attends to them, they will evoke a moderate amount of arousal, which, according to Berlyne's theory, is the optimal level of arousal for producing positive hedonic tone.

Berlyne recognized that organisms could, for a variety of reasons, experience a chronically high level of arousal. Anxiety, for example, is often characterized by high arousal. Such an individual, according to Berlyne's theory, would be less inclined or not inclined at all to seek out new and different stimulation. In fact, such an individual might be inclined to seek out very common and familiar stimuli to keep arousal from increasing further.

The idea that external stimulation will simply add to the existing arousal level is an intriguing idea that has been subjected to a number of experimental tests. In one experiment, Berlyne, Koenig, and Hirota (1966) initially had rats learn to press a bar in order to experience a certain pattern of light onset/offset. After the animals had become familiar with this pattern, some of them were injected with methamphetamine to increase arousal and some were injected with saline solution (a control condition). In the test phase, the animals had the choice of bar-pressing for the familiar pattern of light onset/offset or for a new pattern. As predicted, the animals given a drug to increase arousal bar-pressed more for the familiar pattern. These results provide excellent support for the idea that external stimulation adds to the pool of existing arousal and can decrease the exploratory tendency.

Arousal and Esthetics

Berlyne (1971) has suggested that esthetics can, in part, be understood within his arousal framework. He pointed out that art often contains elements of novelty, surprise, incongruity, conflict, complexity, and uncertainty. Accordingly, he set out on a program of research designed to analyze esthetic experiences in terms of the collative variables. A large number of studies have tested Berlyne's ideas. The work of Dorfman (1965) and Smith and Dorfman (1975) illustrates how Berlyne's conceptual framework can account for some esthetic preferences.

Dorfman (1965) constructed six visual stimuli that differed in complexity. Each subject was asked to rank all six in order of preference. Although different subjects preferred different levels of complexity, Dorfman found that preferences systematically decreased on each side of the most preferred stimulus. In other words, Dorfman obtained evidence consistent with Berlyne's suggestion of an inverted-U-shaped function. The fact that preferences for stimuli differing in complexity could be related to an inverted-U-shaped function provides support for Berlyne's suggestion that esthetic preferences are mediated by collative variables.

In a somewhat more complex study, Smith and Dorfman (1975) measured liking for visual stimuli as a function of complexity and number of exposures. According to Berlyne's theory, when a person is exposed to a stimulus, he or she is likely to process the information it contains. As a result, his or her liking for that stimulus should decrease. A simple stimulus contains less new information than a complex stimulus, and therefore it should take less time to process all the information a simple stimulus contains. It follows that interest in a simple stimulus should diminish more rapidly with repeated exposures than interest in a complex stimulus. Further, with experience a person might develop the structures necessary to process a complex stimulus. It would be predicted, therefore, that interest in a complex stimulus might increase rather than decrease with repeated exposures. Both of these predictions were confirmed. These results are shown in Figure 13-7. In addition to confirming these two predictions, Smith and Dorfman found that a stimulus of medium complexity initially elicited very little interest or liking. With repeated exposure liking grew and then declined. Presumably, after 20 exposures the subjects had processed the information in the medium-complexity stimulus but still had not exhausted the information in the high-complexity stimulus.

Summary

Dember and Earl argue that organisms are motivated to interact with a level of complexity slightly above their current level. According to Dember and Earl, only a range of stimuli (the pacer range) will be acceptable. Berlyne has suggested that the mechanism underlying exploratory and play behaviors is arousal. He has suggested that when arousal is low, organisms are motivated to increase arousal by interacting with novel stimuli in their environment. Stimuli that can provide optimal arousal will become the objects of attention. According to Berlyne's theory, attention to an object is sufficient to produce information processing. Once all the information has been processed, the individual will be inclined to seek out new stimuli.

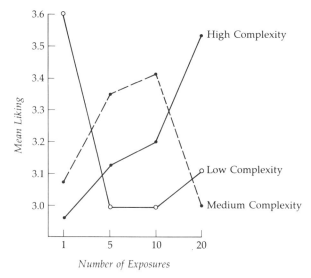

Figure 13-7.   Mean likability ratings at each level of stimulus complexity as a function of number of exposures to the stimulus (Smith & Dorfman, 1975)

Arousal and Exploratory Behavior

Berlyne has argued that organisms are motivated to seek out optimal levels of stimulation. According to Berlyne's theory, arousal produces positive affect (Figure 13-5). Since it is assumed that organisms are motivated to maximize positive affect and to minimize negative affect, the theory assumes that when arousal is high, organisms will not explore. Exploration would lead to further increases in arousal and would be experienced as negative affect.

In one experiment designed to determine whether high levels of arousal will lead to decreased exploratory behavior, Franken and Strain (1974) used a large multiunit maze that permitted certain sections to be changed from white to black or black to white between the two daily trials. Figure 13-8 shows the arrangement of the maze, together with the changes made in it between trials 1 and 2. If exploratory behavior is motivated by the tendency to seek out new stimulation, animals high in that tendency should select and respond to the changed parts of the maze. To determine whether this tendency might decrease when an animal was highly aroused, half of the animals (rats) were injected with methamphetamine (an arousal-producing drug) between the two daily trials, and the other half were injected with saline solution (an inert substance).

As expected, the animals injected with saline solution (low-arousal animals) responded to the changes made in the maze. These animals entered somewhat more cul-de-sacs on trial 2 than on trial 1 even when the cul-de-sacs were not changed, but when they were changed, the animals entered many more of them. The results for the methamphetamine-injected animals (highly aroused) are almost opposite to those of the saline animals but are exactly as predicted by Berlyne's theory. When the cul-de-sacs were changed, the animals tended to avoid them (they entered fewer cul-de-sacs on trial 2 than on trial 1). These results, summarized in Figure 13-9, clearly show that arousal does mediate the tendency to respond

No Change   Cul-de-sacs Changed

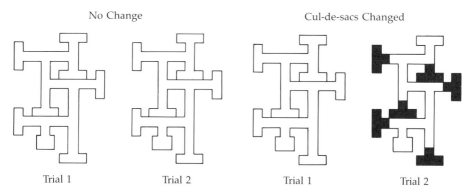

Trial 1   Trial 2   Trial 1   Trial 2

Figure 13-8.   The maze used by Franken and Strain (1974), showing the changes that occurred between trials 1 and 2

to new stimulation. Berlyne has performed similar experiments, manipulating arousal with drugs, and has obtained results that are consistent with his theory (Berlyne, 1969; Berlyne, Koenig, & Hirota, 1966).

The fact that arousal mediates something as basic as exploratory behavior means that arousal indirectly governs what and how much we come to know about our environment. Most developmental psychologists argue that through the process of exploration children come to be knowledgeable about and competent in dealing with their environment (for example, Piaget, 1952; White, 1959).

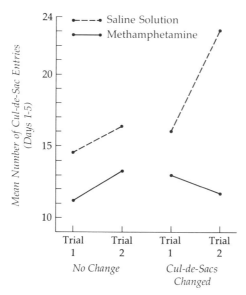

Figure 13-9.   Number of cul-de-sacs entered by rats injected with methamphetamine and by rats injected with saline solution when cul-de-sacs were changed in color between trials and when they were not. Methamphetamine reduced exploration (number of cul-de-sacs entered) as well as the tendency to approach the changed cul-de-sacs on the second trial.

Anxiety, Fear, and Exploration

Fear as the enemy of exploration.   Various researchers have noted that people are less inclined to explore when they are fearful or anxious. White (1959) suggested that fear is the enemy of exploration. People's lack of interest in exploration when they are anxious can be readily explained by Berlyne's theory. According to Berlyne, fear and anxiety produce high levels of arousal. When arousal is high, exploration will be low or nonexistent.

Animals often fail to show exploratory behavior in the laboratory. In order to see if their apathy was due to emotionality (anxiety), experimenters devised procedures to reduce the emotionality of these animals. One procedure that has been used extensively, called "handling" or "taming," calls for the experimenter to spend some time each day playing with the animals (handling them). After a couple of weeks animals that have been treated in this way show much less emotional behavior. It has repeatedly been shown that this taming or handling produces increases in exploratory behavior (Denenberg, 1967).

Implications for facilitating learning.   This research points the way to methods of facilitating learning in children and adults as well. If we expect people to learn by interacting with their environment, then it is important that we make them feel as comfortable and relaxed as possible. An "anxious environment" will simply produce increases in arousal that will get in the way of this kind of learning. Good teachers are typically aware of this fact and work hard to give the environment a relaxed atmosphere.

Individual differences.   Eysenck's (1947) theory predicts that introverts will prefer simpler stimuli and extraverts will prefer more complex stimuli. Although there are some data to support this prediction (Eysenck, 1947), there are also conflicting results (for example, Bryson & Driver, 1972). Because complexity preferences change as a function of contact with stimuli, it is not surprising that the relation between personality and complexity preferences is at best unstable. Munsinger and Kessen (1964) found that art students prefer more complex visual stimuli. This would, of course, be expected, because art students presumably have considerable contact with a wide variety of visual stimuli. Unfortunately, we do not know whether art students are more extraverted than the average person. Further work is needed to determine just how personality affects the tendency to experience complex stimuli. There is good evidence (Thomas, Chess, & Birch, 1970) that children with a relatively stable ("easy") temperament are more receptive to new situations. Children who are less receptive to new experiences ("slow to warm up") will eventually come to respond to new experiences, to explore, and to adapt to new situations once they have become secure in their environment. They are like the anxious person who becomes less anxious or the highly aroused person who experiences a lowering of arousal. When the anxiety and arousal lessen, they readily respond to new and varied stimulation.

We all know from experience that there are times when we are more open to novel and complex stimulation and times when we are less open to it. Presumably these variations are related to whether we are already overloaded with information and therefore are experiencing high levels of arousal.

Cognitive Processes Involved in Information Selection

Although humans are generally motivated to learn about our environment and become competent in dealing with it, we frequently select certain information to process while ignoring other information. Further, we develop certain skills but fail to develop others. The problem, therefore, is to account for what appear on the surface to be lapses in the human's tendency to learn and develop skills.

Probably one of the most important things to understand about humans is that our ability to process information is limited. The very nature of the nervous system makes certain information easier to process than other information. For example, we are blessed with a relatively good visual system, but we have a poor olfactory system. As a consequence we are more likely to use visual information than olfactory information. Even a good sensory system does not allow us to process all the information that impinges on our receptors, and so we are forced to select. Some of the selection is prewired by our nervous system (Hubel & Wiesel, 1979), and some is based on past learning and motivation (Bruner, Matter, & Papanek, 1955). One of the most intriguing findings is that we tend to select information that is consistent with our expectations or beliefs and to reject information that is not.

The need for cognitive consistency.   Humans appear to have a strong need that new information be consistent with existing information. Heider (1946) noted that when two pieces of information are in conflict, a state of imbalance results, and humans have a strong need to reduce this imbalance. He suggested that humans are characterized by a need to obtain a state of "cognitive balance." Festinger (1957) further elaborated this idea, referring to cognitive imbalance as "cognitive dissonance." According to Festinger, cognitive dissonance is an aversive or noxious state that occurs when a person experiences new information that is inconsistent with a behavioral choice. He says that when humans decide on a given course of action, they are inclined to fit or mold new information to match with their decision rather than change the decision. Thus, dissonance theory is about how people process information after they have made a decision. As will be discussed later, this is quite different from the way people process information before making a decision. There appear to be three basic ways in which people deal with cognitive dissonance.

Ways people deal with cognitive dissonance.

1. *Add new cognitions or change existing ones.* Festinger suggests that people may be able to reconcile two pieces of conflicting information by adding new cognitions that make the pieces of information consistent or by changing existing cognitions to make them consistent. For example, a person who experiences feelings of guilt with sexual fantasies about a casual acquaintance might resolve this conflict (dissonance) by adopting an existential point of view. That is, the person might perceive such fantasies as an intellectual exercise necessary to fully understand that humans have the opportunity for determining their destiny. Another person might adopt the view that such fantasies are due to the intrusion of a biological sex drive into conscious thought and are therefore to be ignored.

In the above examples, the guilt feelings might continue; however, the cognitive process might alter the importance attached to the feelings of guilt. Festinger notes that when two pieces of information are given equal cognitive importance, dissonance is greatest. If, however, one piece of information is given greater cognitive importance than the other, dissonance will be reduced. Simply reducing dissonance is rewarding, according to Festinger's theory. Festinger argues that although humans are willing to tolerate small amounts of dissonance, they find high dissonance levels intolerable and will work to reduce them.

2. *Seek information consistent with existing cognitions.* When two pieces of information are in conflict, one way of reducing dissonance is to seek out information that bolsters the validity of one of these pieces of information or, conversely, to seek out information that undermines the other piece of information. For example, if a person bought car X and not car Y and needs to rationalize that decision, he or she might read magazines that have tested both cars. Any information indicating that car X was better than car Y would be processed, and all other information would be ignored or dismissed. In this way the equivalence of the two cars would be dramatically reduced. More important, information about the better quality or desirability of car X versus car Y would be consistent with the person's selection of car X. Thus, there would be little or no dissonance.

Festinger notes that over time dissonance is often reduced. According to Festinger's theory, this happens because humans selectively process information. Usually people tend to make their cognitions consistent with their behavioral decisions. Several studies have been conducted to test this proposition. For example, in one study (Brehm, 1956), female undergraduates were asked to rate the attractiveness of various manufactured products. After giving the ratings, the subjects were told they could select one of the products as a gift for their participation. In one condition the participants were allowed to choose between two gifts that they had rated as equally attractive; in a second condition they were allowed to choose between one attractive and one unattractive gift. After the choice, the participants were required to make a second attractiveness rating. According to cognitive-dissonance theory, once a decision has been made, the person will tend to make all information consistent with that decision. If a person has previously rated two objects as equally attractive and selects one, a state of dissonance should occur. One way of reducing the dissonance would be to alter one's perceptions of the relative attractiveness of the two objects. This could be achieved by perceiving the selected gift as more attractive than before or the nonselected gift as less attractive or both. According to dissonance theory, selecting the more attractive item, as subjects did in the second condition, should not produce any dissonance, and therefore there would be no motivation to alter one's perceptions. These predictions were confirmed. When a subject had two attractive objects from which to choose, attractiveness ratings were altered more than when subjects had had an attractive and an unattractive object. As expected, the selected object was rated as more attractive after it had been selected. However, the shift was greater when the subject had had two attractive objects from which to choose. Brehm has suggested that the reason the shift was greater when there were two attractive objects is that in that condition subjects experienced greater dissonance.

3. *Avoid information inconsistent with existing conditions.* "Don't bother me with the facts, my mind's made up." This phrase does not describe just a few "narrow-minded" people but rather describes most of us after we have made a decision. If I have decided to vote for party X, the best way of avoiding dissonance is to avoid any information that might be inconsistent with that decision. When people are confronted with information that conflicts with their decisions, they frequently attack the credibility of the information. During Watergate many Nixon supporters quickly dismissed any testimony against Nixon as "lies" or "political fabrication."

We have all probably, at one time or another, simply dismissed someone's facts or beliefs as wrong. This process probably represents the most primitive attempt to protect ourselves from having to reanalyze our thinking, our ideas, or our beliefs.

Laboratory studies have shown that people are more likely to reject information if it is inconsistent with their behavior. For example, Festinger (1957) exposed smokers to information that smoking and cancer are linked. The respondents were categorized on the basis of their smoking behavior: nonsmokers, light smokers, medium smokers, and heavy smokers. According to dissonance theory, a heavy smoker would experience greater dissonance than a light smoker and, as a result, would be more highly motivated to reject such information. Subjects' evaluations of the credibility of this information supported the dissonance hypothesis. The proportion of each group reporting they did not believe that the evidence was conclusive was 55%, 68%, 75%, and 86%, respectively.

Summary

There are several things that reduce the tendency to explore. High levels of arousal, such as that produced by drugs, have repeatedly been shown to reduce the tendency to explore. Another thing that reduces the tendency to explore is fear. The reason fear may reduce the tendency to explore is that fear often produces high levels of arousal. Because people often differ in terms of arousal levels and fear, it is not surprising that there are great individual differences associated with the tendency to explore. It may be possible for teachers and parents to increase a child's tendency to explore by creating an environment that is relaxed (low in arousal properties).

The need for cognitive consistency is a factor that has been shown to affect the kinds of information that humans process as well as how much information they process about a given topic. Experimental studies on the need for consistency have shown that when two pieces of information are in conflict people are inclined to do one or more of the following: (1) add new cognitions or change existing ones, (2) seek information consistent with existing cognitions, and (3) avoid information inconsistent with existing cognitions.

Play: Frivolous or Serious?

Exploration appears to be a very serious activity with the obvious function of making the person or animal familiar with the environment; play seems to be less serious. Further, it often appears that play is not systematic. For these reasons, the research on play has been designed to determine whether in fact play serves an important function and, if so, what the function is.

Humans, especially during their so-called formative years, spend a great deal of time engaging in activities collectively called "play." For example, a child may build a tower out of blocks, skip rope with a friend, pretend that he or she is a nurse or doctor, make up a game, draw a picture. Because these activities are quite diverse, it is difficult to decide why they all have come to be called play.

Historically, people have treated certain activities as important and others as frivolous. Work has typically been regarded as important because of its obvious relation to survival needs. School learning has also been regarded as important, at least in certain societies, because it also has a long-term relation to survival needs. Within such a framework, activities that do not have an immediate or future survival function are regarded as frivolous or, in the case of children, as simply playful. They are assumed neither to help nor to hinder preparation for the important activities involved in survival. According to this view, the activity of children during the preschool years is often frivolous. It is assumed that during these years children are simply putting in time until they are ready for the "real" learning that occurs in school.

In recent years we have come to appreciate just how much learning occurs in these early years. Current theories of child development typically regard all forms of play as contributing to the optimal development of the child. Thus play in the formative years is no longer regarded as frivolous. The question remains, of course, whether adult play is frivolous or whether it serves an important function in the physical or psychological well-being of adults. At this point we can only assume that it serves an important function and is not simply a way to pass the time. For the present we will confine our discussion to the play of children and young primates.

A great deal of research on the relation between play and development has been done with monkeys. One advantage of using monkeys for this research is that it is possible to impose a number of experimental controls that would not be possible with humans. Further, since monkeys develop faster than humans, it is possible to study the role of play in development in a relatively short period. Although the results with monkeys may not completely explain the role of play in human development, such research can help indicate the direction that research with humans should take.

The Functions of Social Play

Research by Harry Harlow and his associates has uncovered a number of important relations between play and development. By comparing monkeys that have been raised in various states of isolation and therefore deprived of social play, Harlow has concluded that social play is very important for normal development. A paper by Suomi and Harlow (1971) succinctly summarizes some of these findings:

> We think that play among monkey infants serves two general, but important, functions. First, it provides a behavioral mechanism by which activities appropriate for adult social functioning can be initiated, integrated, and perfected. Play repertoires of monkeys under a year of age contain rudimentary forms of virtually all behaviors that characterize adult social life. Patterns of social grooming, aggression, sex, and dominance are clearly evident in infant monkey play activity. When they first emerge, these patterns are not exhibited at adult levels of competence. Rather, they are clumsy and unsophisticated. It is only after months, even years, of "practice" that the behaviors become truly adult in form. The practice comes through peer play.
>
> It is primarily through play that young monkeys learn to interact in a social world. In the months of early play development the infant progresses from a recognition that social objects differ from the rest of the environment to a state of living with and loving fellow monkeys. Presence of peers is sought, rather than avoided, as with isolate-reared monkeys. Furthermore, the infants pick up social graces, such as how to behave in the presence of a dominant, as opposed to a lower status, peer. Dominance hierarchies established among peers early in life persist, unchanged in form, throughout adulthood. In these respects, the function of play for monkeys closely parallels the role of play among human children.

The second function of play in monkey social development is to mitigate aggression when it emerges in the monkey's behavior repertoire. Aggressive behavior, absent in very young monkeys, seems to manifest itself spontaneously at about seven months of age, independent of rearing conditions. For this reason we believe aggression to be genetically predisposed in the rhesus monkey. All monkeys show aggressive behavior of some form, beginning at seven months of age. However, the situations in which aggressive behavior is exhibited are controlled, not by genetic, but rather by social variables. Monkeys permitted to play exhibit their aggression in their play activity. Because it is part of the play repertoire, it is of relatively mild form. Through play, the control of aggression is achieved [p. 75].*

The Functions of Solitary Play

Harlow's research clearly shows that early social play is important for several related adult behaviors. What about nonsocial—solitary—play? Here again, the research indicates that play serves an important function. In a study by Sylva, Bruner, and Genova (1976), children aged 3–5 were exposed to materials (sticks and clamps) that were involved in a later problem-solving task. The task required the child to retrieve a piece of chalk that could be reached only by joining the shorter sticks together with the clamps. In one condition the child was allowed to play for 10 minutes with the sticks and clamps. In a second condition the child was simply shown how the sticks could be joined together with one of the clamps. In a third condition, a control condition, the child was not given any treatment. Using several indexes to evaluate the children's performance, the investigators concluded that those who played before attempting the solution did better for three reasons: (1) They were more self-initiated in their approach. Self-initiation is, of course, a primary requirement for problem solving. (2) They had learned more about the various ways the sticks could be joined; that is, they had learned alternate ways of solving the problem. (3) They were less frustrated by failure. When one attempt failed, they could modify their approach or start over. Children without the prior play experience were more likely to give up.

These results suggest that play tends to breed intrinsic motivation. Children who experienced prior play seemed to find the process of solving the problem rewarding. They were not preoccupied with finding a solution quickly, nor did they give up when one of their attempts failed. The shift away from goals (success and failure) to the process is, of course, what distinguishes intrinsic and extrinsic motivation.

Summary

Although historically people tended to view play as frivolous, today educators and psychologists take the position that all forms of play are probably important for development. Given this assumption, the question is what function play serves in the developmental process. At this point, there is reason to distinguish between social play and solitary play. Social play in monkeys, according to Suomi and Harlow, serves two important functions: it initiates, integrates, and perfects behaviors important for adult social func-
(continued)

*From "Monkeys at Play," by S. J. Suomi and H. F. Harlow. In *Play: A Natural History Magazine Supplement*. With permission from *Natural History*, December, 1971. Copyright The American Museum of Natural History, 1971.

tioning, and it mitigates aggression when it emerges. Because aggression emerges more or less spontaneously, Suomi and Harlow believe that it may be genetically based, at least in the rhesus monkey. However, aggression is controlled by social variables. It is important that monkeys acquire such control, and play can facilitate this achievement. Solitary play is important in breeding intrinsic motivation.

Extrinsic Motivation—The Enemy of Exploration

In an article titled "Enemies of Exploration: Self-Initiated versus Other-Initiated Learning," John Condry (1977) concludes that in certain contexts, extrinsic incentives not only undermine performance but undermine interest in the activity. Why do extrinsic incentives undermine performance and interest? Before we attempt to answer this question it is important to look briefly at some of the research on this problem.

An obvious extrinsic incentive, or reward, is money. In a series of studies to examine whether money would increase or decrease subsequent interest in a task, Edward L. Deci (1971, 1972) used a game called SOMA®. This game includes a number of blocks that can be arranged into different patterns. Participants in the study were asked to play the game and in different conditions were offered (1) nothing, (2) a monetary reward, or (3) a social reward (praise) for every configuration they produced. In the middle of each of three experimental sessions, the experimenter left the room, and the subjects were viewed surreptitiously to determine whether they continued to play at the game. The amount of time they played with the blocks during these "free sessions" was used as a measure of interest, or intrinsic motivation. Deci found that intrinsic motivation was less when subjects were given an external reward but greater when they were given verbal praise.

The important point about these and other studies is that it is not the receipt of the reward itself that affects subsequent interest but whether the subject undertakes the task in order to receive a monetary reward. For example, if a subject unexpectedly receives a reward, it does not affect his or her performance (for example, Greene & Lepper, 1974; Lepper & Greene, 1975; Lepper, Greene, & Nisbett, 1973). It appears that the promise of a reward alters the person's approach to the task. Several sources (for example, Haddad, McCullers, & Moran, 1976; McGraw & McCullers, 1974, 1975; Miller & Estes, 1961; Spence, 1970) indicate that rewarded children learn less than nonrewarded children. Further, Condry and Chambers (1978) and Maehr and Stallings (1972) have found that rewarded children attempted easier problems and were more answer-oriented. Thus, as Condry (1977) points out, there is evidence that extrinsic motivation leads subjects to adopt different strategies in a learning or problem-solving situation—strategies that do not breed intrinsic motivation.

Facilitating Intrinsic Motivation

What factors facilitate the development of intrinsic motivation? It appears that one of the main factors is being free to learn whatever there is to be learned. To put it another way, it is freedom from constraints, such as having to finish a task quickly, to do it in a certain way, or to please someone else. Before looking at why freedom may lead a person to become intrinsically motivated, let us examine what happens when there is no freedom.

When there are constraints on behavior, such as the need to finish a task quickly or to find a particular solution, behavior is characterized as answer-oriented and shallow (Condry, 1977; Sylva, Bruner, & Genova, 1976). That means the person is not trying to discover the underlying structure or the relation between elements. Rather, the person is simply generating a series of more or less random responses, often in response to external cues, either from the environment or from other people, such as the experimenter. Why does the person not try to understand the nature of the elements and their relation? There are two lines of argument.

According to one line of argument, extrinsic demands increase anxiety or arousal level or simply increase drive level. Increases in anxiety, arousal, or drive, it is argued, alter the way a person processes information. They narrow attention (Bruner, Matter, & Papanek, 1955) or somehow shift attention in some way that interferes with the learner's ability to deal with the more subtle aspects or relations in the situation (Easterbrook, 1959). If learners cannot deal with all the information, they cannot generate a series of systematic responses. They will be forced to respond with only strategies that worked or simply try to proceed on the basis of limited information.

The other line of argument to explain why external constraints lead to stereotyped or trial-and-error behavior is based on the idea that such learning teaches responses and not rules or understanding. The person merely imitates another person's behavior or learns a sequence of responses that somehow works. Although such responding may work in certain situations, it often does not work when the task demands are shifted.

When there is freedom, something quite different happens. A person who has freedom appears to learn about relations between elements. Studies such as that by Sylva and his colleagues (1976) have shown that a person who has had the freedom to interact with the materials to be used in a later problem can generate a wide variety of approaches, suggesting that the person is testing a series of hypotheses. Why should freedom from constraints facilitate intrinsic motivation? Although a complete answer is not possible at this time, several factors are likely to be involved.

First, there is evidence that when people are free from anxiety, emotionality, or any form of excessive arousal, information processing not only is highly motivating but takes a much different form than when people are anxious, emotional, or highly aroused. It appears that when people are free from anxiety, emotionality, or arousal, they are more inclined to explore systematically all the various elements and the relation of those elements. Such learning, it is obvious, would prepare the person to deal with problems based on some or all of the relations contained in that material.

Second, there is considerable evidence that the opportunity to process information is highly motivating for humans as well as animals. Humans, it appears, tend to abstract principles and laws from the information they encounter. This information then becomes the backdrop for the processing of other information. Not only are humans good at fitting together the pieces of a cognitive puzzle, but they find the activity pleasurable. As Leon Festinger (1957) noted some time ago, reducing dissonance is rewarding.

If information processing is rewarding, it follows that activities offering this opportunity will be valued. Further, if exercising one's skill at a task increases one's ability, then a person with more practice will have more opportunity to engage in this highly valued activity. Thus the more one processes information, the more likely this activity is to occur in the future. The key, therefore, is to free the person from the constraints that block or interfere with the natural tendency to process information.

What, then, is the function of extrinsic motivation? Many situations demand the execution of a repetitive task. Extrinsic motivation could serve an important function here. For example, the development of certain skills often requires repetition. Extrinsic motivation could play an important role in sustaining such behavior and thereby facilitate the learning and perfection of important skills.

Individual Differences and Extrinsic Motivation

In view of the fact that achievement motivation is typically regarded as an example of intrinsic motivation, it is interesting to note that subjects high in *n*Ach are more likely to volunteer for difficult tasks when evaluation is internal and for easy tasks when evaluation is external (Maehr & Stallings, 1972). This finding clearly demonstrates that external factors modify the normal tendency of high achievers to select tasks of moderate difficulty. Switzky and Haywood (1974) have also shown that external factors tend to override the natural tendency of intrinsically motivated behavior. Using a personality test to identify intrinsically and extrinsically motivated types (Haywood, 1971), Switzky and Haywood found that under conditions in which a child could reward his or her own performance, intrinsically motivated types maintained their performance longer than extrinsically motivated types. When the rewards were externally administered, extrinsically motivated children maintained their performance longer than intrinsically motivated children.

Summary

Considerable evidence shows that extrinsic motivation not only is the enemy of exploration but leads to incomplete learning or at least a different kind of learning. Extrinsic motivation may alter attentional processes, which in turn affect what is learned. Alternatively, extrinsic motivation may simply teach a series of responses that are not based on an understanding of the task. Intrinsic motivation seems to be tied to the motivation to process information. When a person is free from constraints, he or she is inclined to learn about relations between elements in a given situation. Such learning not only can facilitate later problem solving but can breed intrinsic motivation.

Sensation Seeking

Sensation seeking, according to Marvin Zuckerman (1979), "is a trait defined by the need for varied, novel and complex sensations and experiences and the willingness to take physical and social risks for the sake of such experiences" (p. 10). The important thing to note here is that one of the key elements of sensation seeking is the willingness to take risks. The work on exploratory behavior has typically suggested that organisms tend to avoid exploration (the seeking of new sensations and new experiences) when it entails risks. It has been suggested that risks often arouse fear, and fear is incompatible with exploratory behavior. Several of the theories of exploratory behavior assume that such emotions as fear produce high levels of arousal. Since many of these theories assume that organisms explore in order to increase arousal, it follows that the reason that organisms experiencing fear do not explore is that they are already at an optimal level of arousal. Alternatively, it has been suggested that high arousal tends to shift attention to more survival-related cues (see Chapter 3), behavior that is assumed to be incompatible with exploratory behavior. It is interesting, therefore, that Zuckerman has been able to identify people who are willing to take risks (experience fear) in order to explore. In order to see if you are a high, medium, or low sensation seeker, take the test in Practical Application 13-1.

Origins of the Sensation-Seeking Concept

As we have seen, normally people find restricted environmental stimulation quite aversive. Zuckerman (1979) found in the course of doing work on restricted environmental stimulation that some people are more inclined to volunteer for such experiments and are much more likely to enjoy the effects of environmental stimulation. In order to see if he could actually identify these people, he began to develop a paper-and-pencil test. This test came to be known as the Sensation Seeking Scale (SSS). People who score high on this scale are typically referred to as high sensation seekers, while those who score low are referred to as low sensation seekers or sensation avoiders. (Most people score somewhere in the middle of the scale, and so tend to have characteristics of both the high and the low sensation seeker.)

Zuckerman found that it is the high sensation seekers who are attracted to restricted environmental stimulation. This is not what anyone would expect on the basis of the findings that I reported above. Normally we think that people who prefer change and novelty would prefer more rather than less stimulation. The reason the high sensation seekers said they enjoyed restricted environmental stimulation was that it provided them with a new experience. Under restricted environmental stimulation it is much easier to become aware of bodily functions—the heart beating, the blood rushing through the arteries, food digesting, and so forth. To the sensation seekers, this was a novel experience. If you keep this in mind, together with the idea that these people are willing to take risks in order to have novel experiences, you have two of the basic keys to this personality type. In the following sections I will point out some of the interesting things that characterize sensation seekers. Obviously I can only scratch the surface of this fascinating subject.

SS and Sports

Sensation seekers tend to get involved in sports, especially sports that are thought of as risky. It's the high sensation seekers who climb mountains, hang-glide, scuba-dive, go in for downhill skiing, and so forth. Are the sensation seekers attracted to such activities because they are dangerous? There is no evidence that they are attracted to danger. It appears rather that the sensation seeker does not let risk stand in the way of new experiences. Rowland, Franken, & Harrison (1986) found that high sensation seekers more quickly get bored with a given sport and so try something new. Over a period of time, then, they are likely to participate in more sports than low sensation seekers. If you are constantly trying new sports, you are likely sooner or later to get involved in high-risk sports. Since high sensation seekers are not put off by risk, it is not surprising that more high than low sensation seekers tend to get involved in the more risky sports.

Drugs, Sex, Rock and Roll

In the movie *The Rose* Bette Midler shouts a rhetorical question to her adoring audience: "How do I keep this tired old body in shape?" Without waiting for a reply, she shouts: "Drugs, sex, rock and roll! Drugs, sex, rock and roll! Drugs, sex,

Practical Application 13-1
Are You a High or a Low Sensation Seeker?

To test your own sensation-seeking tendencies, try this shortened version of one of Marvin Zuckerman's earlier scales. For each of the 13 items, circle the choice, A or B, that best describes your likes or dislikes or the way you feel. Instructions for scoring appear at the end of the test.

1. A. I would like a job that requires a lot of traveling.
   B. I would prefer a job in one location.
2. A. I am invigorated by a brisk, cold day.
   B. I can't wait to get indoors on a cold day.
3. A. I get bored seeing the same old faces.
   B. I like the comfortable familiarity of everyday friends.
4. A. I would prefer living in an ideal society in which everyone is safe, secure, and happy.
   B. I would prefer living in the unsettled days of our history.
5. A. Sometimes I like to do things that are a little frightening.
   B. A sensible person avoids activities that are dangerous.
6. A. I would not like to be hypnotized.
   B. I would like to have the experience of being hypnotized.
7. A. The most important goal of life is to live it to the fullest and experience as much as possible.
   B. The most important goal in life is to find peace and happiness.
8. A. I would like to try parachute-jumping.

(continued)

rock and roll!" The audience—sensation seekers all—respond with obvious delight: "Drugs, sex, rock and roll! Drugs, sex, rock and roll!"

There is an abundance of evidence that sensation seekers tend to use alcohol, marijuana, and cocaine (for example, Huba, Newcomb, & Bentler, 1981). It has been suggested that their interest in drugs can be explained by their biological constitution. We shall explore the biological basis of sensation seeking shortly. As far as sex is concerned, an abundance of data indicates that sensation seekers not only like to have sex frequently but like to have a variety of partners (see Zuckerman, 1979). Finally, there is a great deal of evidence that sensation seekers like parties, especially parties that can be called uninhibited. The general picture that emerges is that the sensation seeker likes new experiences, especially ones that involve new people, and likes the feeling of being disinhibited (not bound by the normal constraints of society). The uninhibited party is the perfect place to satisfy such desires.

Thinking Styles and Creativity

It would be not only unfair but incorrect to depict the sensation seeker merely as a jock or a party animal. Sensation seekers often become entrepreneurs, artists, educators, entertainers, scientists, adventurers. They can be found at the leading

B. I would never want to try jumping out of a plane, with or without a parachute.
9. A. I enter cold water gradually, giving myself time to get used to it.
   B. I like to dive or jump right into the ocean or a cold pool.
10. A. When I go on a vacation, I prefer the comfort of a good room and bed.
    B. When I go on vacation, I prefer the change of camping out.
11. A. I prefer people who are emotionally expressive even if they are a bit unstable.
    B. I prefer people who are calm and even-tempered.
12. A. A good painting should shock or jolt the senses.
    B. A good painting should give one a feeling of peace and security.
13. A. People who ride motorcycles must have some kind of unconscious need to hurt themselves.
    B. I would like to drive or ride a motorcycle.

Scoring. Count one point for each of the following items that you have circled: 1A, 2A, 3A, 4B, 5A, 6B, 7A, 8A, 9B, 10B, 11A, 12A, 13B. Add up your total and compare it with the norms below.

    0–3   Very low on sensation seeking
    4–5   Low
    6–9   Average
  10–11 High
  12–13 Very high

edge of many fields. One of the things that enables these people to advance beyond safe boundaries is their creativity, which grows out of their thinking style.

In order to be creative, you need to be able to view things in new ways or from a different perspective. Among other things, you need to be able to generate new possibilities or new alternatives. Tests of creativity measure not only the number of alternatives that people can generate but the uniqueness of those alternatives. The ability to generate alternatives or to see things uniquely does not occur by chance; it is linked to other, more fundamental qualities of thinking, such as flexibility, tolerance of ambiguity or unpredictability, and the enjoyment of things hitherto unknown. Sensation seekers have all of these qualities (Farley, 1986; Franken, 1987), and it is these qualities that enable them to become productive.

Unconventionality and Delinquency

Sensation seekers describe themselves as being open, unconventional, and undependable. If you are going to experience what is new, it is important not to erect barriers between yourself and the new. That means, among other things, that you cannot let what other people think or say interfere with your choice of activities. Sensation seekers indicate that they often do things they know their friends and relatives would not approve of. It is also important that they not let previous decisions prevent them from taking advantage of new experiences. Sensation seekers are quite willing to break a commitment if they find something more interesting to do (Franken, 1987). This tendency not to let the feelings of other people interfere with what they want to do often puts sensation seekers in conflict with authority as well as with convention. Thus the sensation seeker is prone to delinquency (Farley, 1986). If this unconventional way of thinking is channeled into beneficial activities, however, it can lead to creativity and productivity. Being a sensation seeker, in other words, does not make you successful or unsuccessful. Rather, it provides you with qualities that can make you either an idol or an outcast.

Decision-Making Styles and Sensation Seeking

In their book *In Search of Excellence*, Thomas Peters and Robert Waterman (1982) describe the planning and decision-making styles of the top executives of the best-run companies in the United States. They point out that these executives like to make decisions, like to make decisions quickly, can make decisions without having complete information, and are willing to abandon plans that are not working. The general picture that emerges is that these executives have the capacity to stay on the cutting edge of their fields by following their hunches. Sensation seekers tend to behave very much like these executives. That is, they like to make decisions, they like to make them quickly, they can make decisions on the basis of incomplete information, and they can abandon plans that are not working (Franken, in press). Sensation seekers' personality style makes them particularly adept at working in environments where change is a way of life.

The Biological Basis of Sensation Seeking

Monoamine oxidase and sensation seeking.   What is the origin of the sensation-seeking trait? It has been shown that sensation seeking is negatively correlated with monoamine oxidase levels (see Zuckerman, 1979). That is, the level of monoamine oxidase is low in high sensation seekers, high in low sensation seekers. Monoamine oxidase is an enzyme that is important in the regulation and therefore the ultimate availability of such neurotransmitters as norepinephrine. When the monoamine oxidase level is high, little norepinephrine is available; when it is low, norepinephrine is highly available. What makes this fact so important is the additional fact that the level of norepinephrine in the brain is linked to whether or not the "reward centers" of the brain can be activated. One reason that sensation seekers are hypothesized to use such drugs as cocaine is that the effects of these drugs may depend on the activation of these reward centers. If your reward centers are activated or can be activated to a high degree, then it should be possible for you to experience greater pleasure or greater reward as the result of engaging in such activities as using drugs. In other words, it is suggested that high sensation seekers receive more reward value when they use certain drugs and therefore they are more prone to use drugs in the future. Conversely, low sensation seekers are thought to be prevented from experiencing the same level of reward value when they use those drugs and therefore they are less likely to use drugs in the future.

The heritability of monoamine oxidase level.   Where do these differences in monoamine oxidase level come from? Zuckerman (1979, 1983) has argued that these differences are inherited. Twin studies have indeed supported the hypothesis that the monoamine level has a genetic component. Frank Farley (1986) has pointed out, however, that sensation seeking has also been linked to testosterone level. Whatever the exact mechanism, he also endorses the hypothesis that sensation seeking is inherited.

Animal research has shown that exploratory behavior is inherited. Since exploratory behavior has been linked to the need for variety and change, such data provide converging evidence that the sensation-seeking need, or the need to experience novelty and change, may indeed be inherited.

Sex and age differences.   For reasons that are not altogether clear, sex differences have been found in sensation seeking. Men tend to be higher in this trait than women. It has also been shown that the sensation-seeking trait tends to diminish with age.

Summary

Sensation seeking "is a trait defined by the need for varied novel and complex sensations and experiences and the willingness to take physical and social risks for the sake of such experiences." High sensation seekers are inclined to get involved in a variety of sports activities. Their tendency to get involved in risky sports appears to be motivated by their interest in new experiences rather than by an attraction to risk per se. High sensation seekers also tend to use drugs, have a variety of sex partners, and seek out situations, such as parties, at which they can behave in an uninhibited manner.

High sensation seekers tend to be open and unconventional people. This trait can lead to creativity, but if it is not properly channeled it can also lead to delinquency. The tendency to be undependable may grow out of an urge to take advantage of every opportunity for a new experience, even if that means one must break promises or commitments. High sensation seekers like to make decisions, like to make them quickly, and are willing to make decisions with incomplete information. In addition, they are willing to abandon plans that are not working.

Twin studies provide considerable evidence that the sensation-seeking trait may be inherited. Zuckerman has argued that the mechanism that governs sensation seeking is monoamine oxidase. High sensation seekers have low monoamine oxidase levels while low sensation seekers have high monoamine oxidase levels. Farley has suggested that testosterone may play an important role in motivating sensation seeking. Consistent with this interpretation is the finding that men score higher than women on Zuckerman's Sensation Seeking Scale. The sensation-seeking trait, as measured by Zuckerman's scale, has been shown to decline with age.

Theories of Competence

Competence is skill, ability, capacity, proficiency, or fitness. It is something we all have in varying amounts. It is something we strive to attain. It is what parents strive to encourage and develop in their children. The question of interest here is what motivates the development of competence.

Everyone has specific skills that enable him or her to deal with specific situations. We are not particularly interested here in examining such specific skills. Rather, we will examine the broader aspects of competence, the competence that we learn in order to deal with most aspects of our environment.

White's Theory of Competence

One of the most influential articles on the nature of competence was published by Robert White in 1959. White drew heavily on the work of the early 1950s showing that curiosity and exploratory behavior are not tied to such primary drives as hunger, thirst, and sex. He suggested that the tendency to explore is based on a more general motive, which he called *effectance motivation*. This motive, White suggested, is directed toward understanding the nature of the environment and the order inherent in it. *Feelings of efficacy* occur when the individual comes to understand or know that he or she is able to affect the environment. Such feelings, White argues, can act as a reward. An infant who discovers that whenever she kicks her feet, the mobile hanging above her head moves, for example, would experience feelings of efficacy. She might smile, laugh, or show some other outward sign of her internal state. Most important, she would gain a sense of mastery.

White suggests that effectance motivation subsides when the situation has been so thoroughly explored that it no longer presents new possibilities. Thus, unlike primary (biological) rewards, which tend to produce a highly repetitive behavior, feelings of efficacy lead to the persistence of a behavior only so long as that behavior can produce new stimulation or knowledge. This idea is very similar to Berlyne's idea that arousal potential subsides as the individual processes all the information contained in a stimulus and to Dember and Earl's idea that the motivational incentive of a stimulus wanes as the individual's complexity level shifts upward to match that of the pacer stimulus.

White notes that effectance motivation often fails to be aroused when the individual is anxious or when other motive systems are engaged. He suggests that this arrangement is biologically adaptive. It means that when survival motives are engaged, the individual fully attends to the task at hand, and that when survival needs are not pressing, the individual can spend the time that is necessary to explore all the possibilities in the situation. The point to emphasize about effectance motivation is that it does take time to exhaust the possibilities of a situation. The individual must not feel pressured or try to take shortcuts. Doing so would result in incomplete knowledge.

Hunt's Theory of Competence

J. McV. Hunt (1963) says that the processing of information is inherently motivating. Evidence from a variety of sources, he notes, indicates that frustration occurs whenever some obstacle interferes with achieving a goal or a plan. This frustration, he suggests on the basis of Amsel's research, energizes the individual. So, he says, does inability to understand a situation. The lack of congruity in the situation is sufficient to arouse the individual to seek congruity. Incongruity is inherent in any unfamiliar situation. Following the lead of other theorists, Hunt proposes that an individual has an optimal level of incongruity. Incongruity that is too great simply elicits avoidance behavior; incongruity that is too slight is insufficient to motivate the individual to seek congruity.

Examples of how incongruity arouses motivation can be found in daily experience. Probably most of us have at one time or another misread a sign or a headline or misunderstood a passing comment. If you heard "John Quincy is a queer" instead of "John Quincy is a dear," you might respond with surprise or pass it off with a shrug, depending on what you knew about John Quincy. If you read the headline as "Police Applaud Killer" instead of "Police Apprehend Killer," your reaction would likely be surprise rather than relief. Sometimes even the failure to make our arithmetic match our bank statement is enough to drive our blood pressure to new heights. Incongruity is clearly motivating.

Piaget's Theory of Competence

For several decades the Swiss psychologist Jean Piaget wrote about the development of competence (for example, Piaget, 1952; Piaget & Inhelder, 1969). His impact on developmental psychology and education has been enormous. His basic tenet is that competence develops naturally when a child interacts with his or her environment. The environment, Piaget says, forces the child to develop structures that will allow him or her to interact with that environment. This process is called *accommodation*. Equipped with certain cognitive structures, the child is then prepared to integrate the information contained in his or her environment. This process is called *assimilation*. The degree of assimilation is always limited by existing structures. Thus, when the child encounters new information that is discrepant from existing structures, he or she will be unable to process that information adequately. The child is therefore forced to develop new structures, or, in Piagetian terms, to accommodate. Development is characterized by periods of assimilation followed by accommodation followed by further periods of assimilation, and so on. In Dember and Earl's terms, development may be thought of as cognitive adaptation in which the cognitive structures become increasingly complex as the child has contact with stimuli of increasing complexity. Ability to assimilate is limited by the complexity of the child's cognitive structures.

The motivation to develop new structures (to accommodate) is assumed to come from the discrepancy that exists when a child is confronted with a situation that he or she is unable to assimilate adequately. This idea is very similar to Hunt's idea that the motivation to process new information results when we encounter incongruity (when present information deviates from our expectations). Thus Piaget, like Hunt, believes that the motivation for developing competence is inherent or intrinsic. It is not necessary for the parent or the teacher explicitly to reward such behavior.

Implications for Parents and Teachers

What are the implications of this research for parents and teachers? The theories of Berlyne, Dember and Earl, White, Hunt, and Piaget all suggest that children are biologically equipped to develop competence, provided certain conditions are met. First, it is important that a stimulating and varied environment be available. Without such an environment, the motivation to develop competence will be lacking. Children need to be exposed to stimulation that will create moderate incongruity or a moderate discrepancy. Such stimulation, it appears, elicits the intrinsic motivation necessary for developing new cognitive structures, raising the adaptation level, or abstracting new principles. Second, it is important that the child be freed from competing motives. Survival motives (such as hunger and thirst) appear to take precedence over the motivation to develop competence. Anxiety appears to be particularly debilitating. White (1959) has suggested that anxiety is one of the enemies of exploration. Dember and Earl theorize simply that organisms fail to be motivated by a discrepancy between their complexity level and that of the environment when they are anxious. Third, it is important that the child be free to respond as he or she sees fit. Because it is impossible for the parents or teacher to know the exact state of a given cognitive structure, it is best to let the biological process take its natural course. There is good reason to believe that if a child is left to his or her own ways, he or she will eventually exhaust all the possibilities. The fact that children do this in different ways should not be surprising if we remember that the motivation for processing information comes from the environment, which, as we know, is highly varied. Fourth, it is important that a child not be pressured by time. The development of cognitive structures appears to be a complicated process. If we accept the idea that the development of cognitive structures is essentially an abstracting process, then it follows that the child must differentiate relevant from irrelevant information. This can be a very time-consuming process, even for a computer.

Competence and Feelings of Self-Esteem

A frequently asked question is whether competence leads to improved self-esteem, or conversely, whether good self-esteem will lead to improved competence. Weiner (1979) has suggested that self-esteem has to do with the way we feel about ourselves when the locus of control for an event is perceived as internal. Specifically, he notes that internal people are likely to experience feelings not only of pride but of competence when they succeed, and they are likely to experience feelings of shame and of incompetence when they fail. Because these feelings are linked to internal self-attributions (ability and effort), Weiner believes, these feelings have a great deal to do with a person's tendency to persist or not to persist. As we noted previously, people with high *n*Ach not only tend to view themselves as high in ability but tend to persist at tasks that challenge that ability. As we also noted previously, the main factor in changing achievement behavior is to change people's ability or their perceptions of their ability. Apparently, when people have a good opinion of their ability, they are inclined to put forth effort. Once they have put forth effort and succeeded, feelings of self-esteem emerge. Thus esteem feelings become the factor that mediates persistence (Weiner, 1979). To the degree that persistence is a necessary requirement for developing competence, then yes, self-esteem plays an important role in producing competence.

What about the person who holds an external frame of reference? Because, according to Weiner's analysis, such people tend to view success and failure as due to luck or chance, succeeding or failing will not tend to alter their perceptions of their ability or effort. As a result, they will not be inclined to have either a particularly good or a particularly bad view of themselves, nor will they be inclined to persist at a task. To the degree that persistence is an important requirement for developing competence, such people will tend not to become highly competent. In summary, Weiner's position is that when a person has a good opinion of his or her ability (and perceives the environment as essentially controllable), he or she will be inclined to put forth effort. To the degree that effort is fundamental to developing skills, such a person will become competent.

In an extensive study of self-esteem, Stanley Coopersmith (1967) has concluded that people who enjoy high self-esteem (have a good opinion of themselves) differ in a number of important ways from people with low self-esteem. They set higher goals, are less troubled by anxiety, experience less stress together with fewer psychosomatic symptoms, are less sensitive to failure and criticism, experience greater feelings of control (and suffer less from feelings of helplessness), tend to be more enterprising in approaching problems, and tend to explore more (show more curiosity toward themselves and their environment). They are, in a basic sense, intrinsically motivated people who not only tend to be competent but have a positive attitude toward themselves.

What is particularly interesting about Coopersmith's work is his findings concerning the antecedents of self-esteem. Extensive data collected on the parents of high- and low-self-esteem children indicate that parents play a primary role in determining whether a child experiences positive or negative self-esteem. Parents of children who experience high self-esteem are characterized by their total acceptance of and respect for the child, their tendency to set clearly understandable limits on what the child is permitted and not permitted to do, and their tendency to allow the child great latitude to explore and test within those limits. Coopersmith argues that parents of high-self-esteem children create a climate that frees the child from anxiety and doubt. Within such an environment the child can freely explore the environment and in doing so gain competence in dealing with the environment. Coopersmith notes that parents of high-self-esteem children not only encourage the child to become responsible and competent but accept the independence and diversity of expression that often accompany the emergence of such behavior. In other words, the child is informed by the parent (a significant giver of acceptance and love) that he or she is an important individual who can expect to continue being accepted not only by the parents but by society at large even if he or she occasionally fails or if his or her behavior deviates somewhat from the norm. The child reacts to that signal, Coopersmith finds, by continuing to set high goals and to work hard to attain them.

Coopersmith's work indicates that self-esteem may mediate, in part, the tendency to achieve. His work suggests that individual differences in self-esteem are acquired early in life. As we noted earlier, one of the reasons it is difficult to change achievement behavior is that to change achievement it is necessary to change a person's perception of his or her ability. If self-esteem affects one's perception of one's ability (competence), then it becomes necessary to alter self-esteem as well. At this point we run into the chicken-and-egg problem of what to focus on first. The work on changing achievement motivation suggests that we need to focus on both self-esteem and perception of ability so that they can influence each other.

Summary

Competence has to do with skill, ability, capacity, proficiency, or fitness. Several theories have been advanced to explain why some people have more of it than others. White has proposed that competence grows out of curiosity and exploratory behaviors, which are based on a general motive he has called effectance motivation. This motive is directed toward understanding the nature of the environment and the order inherent in it. Feelings of efficacy occur, he suggests, when a person comes to understand or know that he or she is able to affect the environment. Hunt has set forth a theory of competence based on the proposition that information processing is inherently motivating. He has suggested that incongruity arouses the motivation to seek congruity. Piaget has argued that the person is motivated to integrate the information contained in his or her environment. Integration occurs by a process called assimilation. When no structures exist to assimilate information, the person must develop new cognitive structures. This process is called accommodation. Weiner has examined the relation between feelings of self-esteem and competence. He has observed that when people perceive the locus of control as internal, they are more likely to experience feelings of pride and competence when they succeed and to experience feelings of shame and

(continued)

incompetence when they fail. Coopersmith states that people who enjoy high self-esteem set higher goals, are less troubled by anxiety, experience less stress (together with fewer psychosomatic symptoms), are less sensitive to failure, experience greater feelings of control, tend to be more enterprising, and tend to explore more.

Main Points

1. The early behaviorists thought that exploratory behavior was learned.
2. The tendency of animals to alternate in a T-maze has been shown to be motivated by the tendency to respond to change.
3. Research has shown that monkeys are motivated by the visual, auditory, and manipulatory properties of stimulus objects.
4. Humans are motivated to seek out variety and novelty.
5. Various studies have shown that humans are motivated to seek out optimal complexity.
6. According to an information-processing interpretation of curiosity and exploratory behavior, people will be motivated to attend to stimuli that are consistent with their abilities. Consistent with this interpretation, it has been shown that humans prefer increasingly complex stimulation with increasing age.
7. The Dember and Earl theory suggests that all stimulation varies in complexity and that optimal complexity motivates exploration.
8. According to Berlyne's theory, arousal will increase when a person or animal processes new information. Therefore, the environment is always a source of potential arousal.
9. Berlyne suggests that there is a class of variables associated with arousal, which he has labeled "collative variables." These include novelty, degree of change, suddenness of change, surprisingness, incongruity, conflict, complexity, and uncertainty.
10. Berlyne has suggested that esthetics can be partially understood within the arousal framework. Indeed, there is empirical evidence that esthetic preferences are governed by those collative variables that are important in eliciting arousal.
11. A variety of studies have shown that when arousal is too high, organisms are not inclined to explore novelty.
12. Emotionality or anxiety can be considered a state of high arousal that reduces the tendency to explore.
13. One implication of the research on arousal and exploration is that to promote exploratory behavior, it is important to make people relaxed and free from anxiety.
14. Art students tend to prefer more complex forms of stimulation. This preference may reflect their greater experience with collative variables that Berlyne has identified as a source of arousal.
15. The need for consistency governs, in part, what information is processed.
16. There are three primary ways people achieve balance when incoming information produces dissonance: (1) add new cognitions or change existing ones, (2) seek new information that is consistent with existing cognitions, and (3) avoid new information that is not consistent with existing cognitions.
17. In recent years psychologists have begun to appreciate the fact that a great deal of important learning occurs in the course of play.

18. Through play monkeys learn the social skills that are necessary for adult social interactions.
19. Through play monkeys learn to control aggression.
20. Solitary play tends to breed intrinsic motivation.
21. Extrinsic motivation not only reduces the tendency to explore but undermines intrinsic motivation.
22. We can facilitate intrinsic motivation by giving people the freedom to organize tasks as they want and by reducing or eliminating competing motives.
23. High sensation seekers are motivated by a need for novel and complex sensations and experiences.
24. High sensation seekers are willing to take physical and social risks in order to experience varied, novel, and complex sensations and experiences.
25. High sensation seekers tend to be involved in a wide range of sports over a period of time.
26. High sensation seekers tend to use drugs, to have a variety of sex partners, and to like situations that allow them to behave in an uninhibited manner.
27. High sensation seekers tend to have a thinking style that is characterized by flexibility, tolerance of ambiguity, and unpredictability. These qualities of thinking are probably what make the sensation seeker more creative.
28. High sensation seekers' tendency to be open and unconventional can result in delinquency, but if it is properly channeled it can lead to creativity and productivity.
29. High sensation seekers like the responsibility to make decisions, like to make decisions quickly, and are willing to make decisions with incomplete information.
30. High sensation seekers have low monoamine oxidase levels while low sensation seekers have high monoamine oxidase levels.
31. According to White's theory of competence, feelings of efficacy reward the development of competence.
32. J. McV. Hunt maintains that competence grows out of the tendency to process information.
33. Piaget argues that competence develops out of the child's need to interact with his or her environment.
34. Feelings of self-esteem appear to affect the tendency to persist, which may be the basis for developing competency.
35. Acceptance by parents, having limits, and having the opportunity to explore are three factors that appear to be important in the development of self-esteem, which Coopersmith suggests influences a child's tendency to achieve.

Work
Motivation

What makes some people work hard while others work as little as possible?
Why do some people find work satisfying while others do not?
How can management increase the performance of employees?
How important is the pay a person receives?
What role does the work environment play in job satisfaction?

In setting up a new firm, management has several fundamental concerns: What can we offer people that will induce them to take jobs? How much will we have to pay? What benefits will employees want? After they have accepted positions, what is the best type of management structure to keep them happy? What about the work environment? What kind of input can we expect from them? How might we facilitate input? What can we offer in the way of career development? In short, once we have attracted people, how do we keep them?

People seeking jobs today have a wide range of job possibilities. Some jobs offer the possibility for career development, others do not. Some offer the possibility for input, others do not. Some offer job security, others do not. To complicate matters, people differ not only in the skills they offer but also in their desire for such things as job security, possibility for advancement, and input. The field of work motivation is concerned with the question of how to match people to jobs so that both management and employees have a mutually satisfactory arrangement. This is, as we shall see, a complex problem.

Why do people work? The answer, for the most part, is straightforward: most people work in order to get money. Money obviously provides the means for obtaining a wide variety of goods and services. Money not only buys food and shelter but plays an important role in achieving a sense of worth and self-esteem. The question, therefore, is how much money a job seeker wants or needs. There are wide individual differences both in the skills that allow people to make money and in the desire to make money. Some people have skills that allow them to obtain more money than others. In addition, some people are willing to work harder or longer to obtain more money. Work can have several disadvantages, such as risk, stress, and loss of self-esteem; motivation to work at a given job may be related to the negative aspects of the job. If the physical or psychological stress is too great, a person may be less inclined to work. If a person feels the job is degrading, he or she may seek another position.

Although money is generally regarded as the "bottom line" among reasons that people work, the amount of money a person will accept varies greatly. Some people will work long and hard at a job that pays little. What is it about certain jobs that makes such people willing to accept a small return for their efforts? What psychological benefits or rewards do these workers receive in compensation for their monetary loss? In recent years students of work motivation have come to recognize that money is an essential feature, but by no means the only feature, of job satisfaction. Money is, at best, the bottom line. The next question is what is needed above the bottom line.

Job Satisfaction: Four Basic Models

Various models of job satisfaction have been proposed over the years. The assumption underlying these models is that job satisfaction is linked in some fundamental way to performance on the job as well as commitment to the company. The four models discussed here assume somewhat different antecedents of job satisfaction. The *need-fulfillment model* is based on the assumption that humans are born with a basic set of needs that they strive to satisfy. In a sense, this approach might be considered to emphasize the biological side of humans. The *reinforcement model* assumes that job satisfaction is determined by the nature of rewards and reward schedules. This approach is founded in the idea that principles of learning can account not only for job satisfaction but for performance on the job. According to *equity theory,* job satisfaction depends on receiving an equitable return for one's efforts and skills. This approach emphasizes that humans are highly cognitive and have a sense of what is just and equitable. Finally, the *discrepancy model* suggests that people have expectations about what a job should provide in the way of money and psychological rewards. Failure of the job to meet these expectations will result in a discrepancy, which in turn is likely to lead to job dissatisfaction. Because expectations may differ because of learning and social norms, the discrepancy model emphasizes not only the role of cognitive variables but the role of individual differences in the attainment of job satisfaction.

Maslow's Need-Fulfillment Model

Abraham Maslow's (1970) theory of human motivation is unquestionably the best-known and most widely accepted of the need-fulfillment theories. Maslow posits that humans are born with a set of needs that not only energize but direct behavior. He argues that these needs are organized in a hierarchical fashion whereby needs lowest in the hierarchy must be satisfied first. (The hierarchy is upside down in the sense that the needs at the bottom have first priority. Maslow diagrams the need hierarchy as a pyramid in which emergence of "higher," more sophisticated needs, such as esthetic needs, rests on the base provided by fulfillment of "lower" needs, such as hunger and thirst.) These needs dominate the person's attention until they are satisfied. When these "basic" needs have been satisfied, the next set of needs in the hierarchy comes to exert its influence. As before, these needs come to dominate the person's attention. And so the process continues. Eventually, if all the basic needs have been satisfied, the person will reach the top of the hierarchy, a rather lofty position in comparison with most animals. It is a position where we observe many of those behaviors that set us apart from other animals. Let's begin, however, by starting at the bottom of the hierarchy.

Physiological needs.   Humans must satisfy a number of basic physiological needs. For example, they must eat, drink, control their temperature, and ingest certain nutrients in order to live and function normally. Failure to remedy an imbalance in any of these areas would disrupt normal functioning and eventually result in death. Therefore, it is critical for the person to attend to such states of imbalance as soon as possible. From an evolutionary point of view, therefore, it makes good sense that a person should become preoccupied with such need states. That humans do become preoccupied with such physiological need states has been well documented. For example, in Chapter 5, I referred to research that clearly showed that men on semistarvation diets spent much of their waking and sleeping time thinking about food. In a very fundamental sense, all other needs were secondary. These men showed little interest even in such basic motives as sex, let alone improving their cognitive skills.

Safety needs.   Maslow says that once these basic physiological needs have been satisfied, the person comes to focus on another class of needs, "safety needs."

Safety needs, it can be argued, are also basic in that failure to take adequate measures to guard one's safety could result in harm or even death. However, safety needs are secondary to the basic physiological needs. If safety needs took precedence over the physiological needs, we might not venture forth to find the food and water necessary to our survival. For many animals, the satisfaction of physiological needs entails risks. Venturing into unknown territory in pursuit of food or venturing to the watering hole has obvious risk qualities.

For humans, safety comes from knowing about our environment and making it predictable. Although children may look to their parents for their own safety, safety for adults comes from making the environment as orderly, predictable, and lawful as possible. In such an environment one can then pursue one's other needs without constant fear that something or someone will threaten one's safety. Children, Maslow argues, have a strong need for things to be orderly and predictable within their environment. It is within such an environment that they can explore and learn. As we noted in Chapter 13, fear is the enemy of exploration. An afraid or anxious person seeks out the familiar rather than the new. As a result, learning ceases. The person comes to be preoccupied with his or her fear rather than involved in learning about the environment or developing the skills that are necessary to grow and to receive pleasure from the environment.

Neurotic people are in many ways like the fearful child. They are typically anxious, always afraid that something dreadful will happen to them. Because they are preoccupied with the vague feeling that something dreadful will happen, they are preoccupied with making the world safe. It appears that they have adopted a strategy, Maslow argues, of using rigid and often stereotyped behaviors as a means of assuring themselves that the world is indeed orderly and predictable and therefore safe. Because of this preoccupation with safety, they cannot respond to the new or novel in their world. They are "fixated," to use a psychoanalytic term, at the level of satisfying safety needs.

Belongingness and love needs.   If both the physiological and safety needs are fairly well gratified, Maslow says, love, affection, and belongingness needs will emerge. Although there is little scientific information about belongingness needs, they are a common theme in books, poems, songs, and plays. One need only look around to see how many humans gather into groups at coffee breaks or lunchtime. Maslow theorizes that the tendency to join organizations is often motivated by the desire to belong. When people have been separated from other people for some time, they often have a strong need to engage in some type of social exchange. The family unit seems to be held together, in large part, by a need to belong. If that unit is broken by divorce, for example, all members of the unit seem to suffer stress. Bouts of loneliness and depression are common not only for the spouses but for the children as well.

That belongingness needs are not as fundamental as safety and physiological needs has been shown in a variety of contexts. When humans are hungry, their immediate attention is directed toward food, as illustrated by the work on semi-starvation. For example, sex and curiosity drives are reduced. When humans are threatened, their attention typically focuses on flight-or-fight strategies. It is not surprising, therefore, that humans show little tendency to engage in love or belongingness behaviors at such times. People in a burning building are not likely to initiate new friendships. Rather, they are likely to focus all their attention and efforts on finding a safe exit. Once they have reestablished their own safety, they may well share their harrowing experiences with others and may in the process establish new friendships.

Esteem needs.   All people in our society (possibly with a few pathological exceptions) have a need or desire to have a good opinion of themselves. Maslow suggests that there are two subsidiary sets. First, there are the desires for strength, for achievement, for adequacy, for mastery and competence. Second, there is the need for reputation and prestige, status, fame, glory, dominance, recognition, attention, importance, dignity, or appreciation.

Satisfaction of the esteem needs, Maslow argues, leads to feelings of self-confidence, worth, strength, and capacity, together with the feeling of being useful. Failure to satisfy the esteem needs leads to feelings of inferiority, weakness, and helplessness.

Need for self-actualization.   Even if all these needs have been satisfied, Maslow says, we will still experience feelings of discontent and restlessness. Each of us, he argues, is a unique person with unique skills and abilities. To be truly happy, we must do that for which we are uniquely suited. The artist must paint; the musician must make music. Although we may not all be artists, each of us is nevertheless unique. Therefore, Maslow argues, each of us must search for and find that uniqueness so that we may experience satisfaction in knowing and doing that which we as individuals are specially equipped to do.

Implications for job satisfaction.   Maslow's theory has several implications for work motivation. Since we live in a technological society, we can readily satisfy our physiological and safety needs. Further, our technological society gives us the time to belong to many groups. Given that we can satisfy our physiological, safety, and belongingness needs, esteem needs are likely to emerge. The job becomes a vehicle for satisfying the esteem needs. Jobs can provide an opportunity to achieve and to develop competence. Further, a job can give us prestige, status, recognition, and appreciation. It is not surprising, within the context of Maslow's theory, that more and more people should look for jobs that, in addition to giving them money, will allow them to satisfy the esteem needs. The problem for the employer in a technological society is to design a routine job so that it can satisfy the esteem needs. Obviously, this is no easy task.

Current status of Maslow's theory.   For all its appeal, Maslow's theory has not received much scientific support. Theories such as Maslow's are difficult to test, and it is probably for this reason that very few studies can be found demonstrating the validity of the theory (see Salancik & Pfeffer, 1977). Nevertheless, such models continue to guide thinking about the question of job satisfaction. The need models recognize that humans are complex animals. There is no single motive that leads them to work or not to work. Further, these models recognize that motives change. Accordingly, if job satisfaction is to remain high, it is necessary for the job to change or at least to be flexible enough to accommodate the changing person. Maslow's theory is a dynamic one that attempts to capture the dynamic nature of motives. As such, it will continue to play an important role in thinking about work motivation (Alderfer, 1969, 1977).

Reinforcement Theory

The reinforcement model of job satisfaction is based on the work of such reinforcement theorists as B. F. Skinner (1938). The assumptions underlying this model are simple and straightforward. Behavior is governed by rewards and punishments. If a behavior is rewarded, the probability of repeating that behavior is increased. If a behavior is not rewarded, the probability of repeating that behavior will decrease. Punishments are viewed as a form of negative reinforcement. If a punishment always follows a given response, the probability of engaging in that behavior will decrease. Alternatively, if the termination of punishment follows a given response, the probability of repeating that behavior will increase.

Contingencies. If rewards are to be effective, according to the reinforcement model, they must immediately follow the occurrence of the desired behavior. Very simply, rewards are viewed as increasing the probability of the behavior immediately preceding the receipt of a reward, because a contingency between the behavior and the reward has been established. In humans it is not absolutely necessary for rewards to be immediate for them to be effective as long as the person understands that there is a contingency between a given response and the receipt of a reward. A child can learn, for example, that if he mows the lawn, he will be paid by his mother when she arrives home from work. A salesman can learn that at the end of the month he will receive a commission for the appliances he sold during the first half of the month. The important point is that the person have a clear idea of the existence of a contingency.

Applications to the work setting. Applications of the reinforcement model to the work setting usually involve the assumption that workers work only to obtain money. In some jobs the contingency between work and money is made explicit. A commissioned salesperson knows that his or her pay is tied directly to the amount he or she sells. A subcontractor knows that the size of the paycheck is directly related to the number of jobs completed. In many jobs, however, the contingency is not so clear. For example, a receptionist/typist might not know whether it is more important to chat with customers or finish typing an order. A clerk might not know whether he or she is expected to make a sales pitch or simply answer the customer's questions. A factory worker might not know what rate of output is expected or customary. Therefore, in order to achieve the desired behavior, workers must be given feedback telling them when they are doing the correct thing.

The size of one's paycheck can provide some general feedback, but paychecks are typically not an effective way of communicating what is desired or expected. Verbal feedback, usually from an immediate superior, can quickly and effectively provide a worker with information about what he or she should or should not be doing. Employees who want to keep their jobs or get a raise in pay will look to those around them for the feedback they need to do the job properly.

Given that workers tend to look for feedback because they want to keep their jobs, how does management make use of the principles of reinforcement to optimize a worker's performance? W. Clay Hamner (1974) has suggested six rules to follow if one plans to use a contingency approach to increase workers' effectiveness as well as their satisfaction. These rules are summarized in Practical Application 14-1.

Practical Application 14-1
Six Rules for a Contingency Approach to Management

Rule 1: Don't Reward All People the Same

People tend to compare their own performance with that of their peers, and a person who works hard will want to know whether his or her efforts have paid off. According to the reinforcement model, money is what motivates and rewards work behavior. Therefore, although praise may provide momentary feedback, the effectiveness of such secondary rewards must ultimately be tied to the primary reward, which in work situations is assumed to be money. If increased efforts are not translated into money, the worker will, according to the reinforcement model, perceive that his or her efforts have not been rewarded, and he or she will act accordingly.

Rule 2: Failure to Respond Has Reinforcing Consequences

Failure to differentiate the poorer from the better performers will, according to Hamner, affect performance. If the better performers are not given special rewards, the poor performers may interpret this fact as indicating that they are performing at a desired or acceptable level.

Rule 3: Be Sure to Tell a Person What He or She Can Do to Get Reinforced

If workers know the contingencies for obtaining reinforcement, they will have a built-in feedback system for judging the adequacy of their performance. They will also have greater freedom. That is, because they do not have to search for the contingency that leads to reinforcement, they will not have to engage in endless, often random, attempts to discover the nature of the contingency (for example, ingratiation, a positive attitude, loyalty).

Rule 4: Be Sure to Tell a Person What He or She Is Doing Wrong

It must be assumed that people want to do a job right. Therefore, if they are doing it wrong, it probably means they have learned, for whatever reason, to do

(continued)

The Equity Model

The equity model (Adams, 1963, 1965) is based on the assumption that humans want to be paid fairly (equitably) for their services. Job dissatisfaction is assumed to occur whenever a person perceives that he or she is not being paid in an equitable manner.

Factors affecting feelings of equity. Workers perceive that several input factors need to be considered in determining how much they should be paid for a given service. Education, intelligence, experience, training, skills, seniority, age, sex, ethnic background, social status, and effort may all be perceived as relevant. Under certain conditions, attractiveness, health, possession of certain tools, and amount of risk may be considered further relevant factors that contribute to the outcome (service).

it wrong. If a person is simply punished, as by being given lower pay, the punishment may have a generalized effect, decreasing desired behaviors. For example, if an employee is criticized for her slow performance while she is in the process of devising a new and better way of doing a certain job, she will be unlikely to attempt any further changes. As a result, the company may reduce any motivation to devise new and better ideas, which in the long run may be to its own detriment.

Rule 5: Don't Punish in Front of Others
Hamner suggests that punishing (reprimanding) an employee in front of others may have several negative side effects. First, it may damage the worker's self-image, increasing the worker's tendency to retaliate. Second, the work group may misunderstand the reason for the reprimand, so that their respect for the supervisor is undermined. Third, the work group may interpret the reprimand against one of their members as a rebuke of their efforts. A decrease in the output of the entire group could result, especially if the group had been performing at a reasonably acceptable level.

Rule 6: Make the Consequences Equal to the Behavior
If rewards are too great for a given performance or if punishment is too severe for a given omission or error, the employee may perceive that rewards and punishments are not directly contingent on behavior. As a result, the employee may be less inclined to put forth maximum effort. Why should a person work hard if there is not a one-to-one correspondence between performance and reward? It is absolutely critical, if management is to use a contingency system, that the workers be constantly assured that such a system is always in operation. In such a system there can never be favorites who are rewarded for things other than their performance.

Adapted, by permission of the publisher, from "Behavior Modification on the Bottom Line," by W. C. Hamner and E. P. Hamner, *Organizational Dynamics*, Spring 1976, ©1976 by AMACOM, a division of the American Management Associations, pp. 6–8. All rights reserved.

One of the basic areas of conflict between management and workers is the question of which of these factors are important for a given job. Management may be inclined to pay each worker for his or her output, but such a simplistic approach, according to equity theory, is almost certain to lead to feelings of inequity. For example, if two persons are working at essentially the same job, failure to recognize the seniority of one of the workers by giving differential pay may be a source of perceived inequity. Similarly, if two jobs are essentially equal but one involves more risk, failure to recognize this fact by giving differential pay may be a source of perceived inequity.

It sometimes happens that certain workers perceive that their ethnic background or their sex should be recognized as a relevant factor, even though management holds to a policy in which such factors cannot be considered a basis for giving differential pay. Under these conditions, it may be impossible for management ever to be perceived as equitable.

Underpayment and overpayment. The equity model predicts not only that underpayment, as perceived by the worker, will lead to job dissatisfaction but that overpayment, as perceived by the worker, will also lead to job dissatisfaction. This prediction follows from the assumption that workers tend to compare themselves with other workers. When workers are overpaid, they perceive that they are getting more than they deserve. John Thibaut (1950) observed in an experimental setting that when subjects were favored by the experimenter, they displayed "guilty smirks" and "sheepishness." In other words, when subjects receive more than they feel they rightfully deserve, they indicate that the situation is not equitable.

The tendency to compare ourselves with others. The equity model explicitly assumes that all perceptions pertaining to equity arise out of a tendency to compare ourselves with others. Equity is said to exist whenever the ratio of a person's outcomes (performance) to inputs (education, training, skill, and all other factors perceived as relevant) is equal to the ratio of others' outcomes and inputs.

$$\frac{O_p}{I_p} = \frac{O_a}{I_a}$$

Inequity exists whenever the two ratios are unequal.

$$\frac{O_p}{I_p} > \frac{0_a}{I_a} \text{ or } \frac{O_p}{I_p} < \frac{O_a}{I_a}$$

This definition has several interesting and important aspects. First, the conditions necessary to produce equity or inequity are based on the person's *perceptions* of inputs, and outcomes. The objective characteristics, in other words, are less important than the subjective characteristics. Second, inequity is relative to the inputs and outputs of others. That is, inequity does not necessarily occur if a person has high inputs and low outcomes as long as the comparison person or group has a similar ratio. A worker may exhibit job satisfaction when effort is high and payment is low as long as others are in a similar position. Third, inequity is perceived to exist when one's ratio is either greater or smaller than that of the comparison person. It is this aspect of Adams' theory that has generated the most interest, because it suggests that overpayment is a source of difficulty to the person being overpaid. This idea seems counterintuitive, especially if it is assumed that what people like most about their jobs is the pay they receive. Nevertheless, there is evidence that people do in fact respond as the theory predicts (see Mowday, 1979).

Consequences of inequity. J. Stacy Adams (1965, 1979) argues that inequity creates a state of tension, which the person is motivated to reduce. Drawing heavily on Festinger's theory (Festinger, 1957), Adams says there are six basic ways a person can try to reduce this tension.

1. *Altering inputs.* One way of altering feelings of inequity is either to increase or to decrease perceived inputs. According to equity theory, a person is likely to lower inputs when

$$\frac{O_p}{I_p} < \frac{O_a}{I_a} \text{ (case 1)}$$

and to increase inputs when

$$\frac{O_p}{I_p} > \frac{O_a}{I_a} \text{ (case 2)}$$

For example, if someone perceives he is underpaid (case 1) in relation to others, he may reexamine what he thought were relevant factors for the job. He may consider, after such an examination, that his age or his social status is not as important to the job as he initially thought. Thus, by deemphasizing these factors, he reduces the ratio, bringing it more in line with that of others. Similarly, if he feels overpaid (case 2), he may reexamine what he thought were relevant factors for the job. He may reason that his greater education or training accounts for his being paid more. As a consequence, he may include this factor in the input ledger.

One input that people can vary quickly and directly is effort. If underpaid, a person could simply reduce effort and thus reduce the ratio, bringing the person's proportion more in line with that of others. Similarly, when overpaid, a person could increase effort, thus increasing the ratio.

2. *Altering outcomes.* Equity theory says workers will try to increase outcomes in case 1 and decrease outcomes in case 2. Adams maintains that case 1 is more likely to happen than case 2. That is, it is more likely for a person to perceive he or she is underpaid and to ask for a raise than for a person to perceive he or she is overpaid and to offer to return part of the pay. Research shows that people are more likely to experience feelings of inequity in case 1 and therefore more likely to act to reduce this inequity (Adams, 1979).

3. *Cognitively distorting inputs and outcomes.* People who feel underpaid or overpaid may cognitively distort inputs and outputs. For example, a person may reason that because she came from a backwoods college, her degree is not as good as those of her colleagues, or that although she receives less pay than others, it is more than adequate to cover her needs. Adams suggests that for most people such distortions are difficult, simply because most people are heavily influenced by reality. Nevertheless, there is evidence that some people deal with inequity in this manner.

4. *Leaving the field.* One way of dealing with inequity is simply to leave the field. Quitting a job, obtaining a transfer, or staying away from the job are ways of leaving the field. Adams argues that these fairly radical ways of dealing with inequity are more likely to occur when the perceived inequity is large.

5. *Acting on others.* Trying to get others to leave the field is one possible way of reducing inequity. The problem is how to achieve this outcome. One might try to force others out by degrading them or insulting them. Alternatively, one might try to establish equity by altering another person's inputs or outcomes. Adams admits that although forcing others to leave the field is a theoretical possibility, it is probably difficult to realize. Probably the most obvious method used by management to achieve this end is to withhold salary increases and promotions.

6. *Changing the object of one's comparison.* A person may change the object of comparison when inequity occurs. For example, if a person tends to compare himself with person B, but B is beginning to make far more money, he might decide that B is not an appropriate person with whom he should compare himself. Under such circumstances, he may shift his comparison to person C and in doing so reestablish feelings of equity.

Implications for job satisfaction.   Because the equity model was designed to explain the dynamics involved when people perceive they are not being treated equitably, the implications for work motivation are more or less obvious. Workers expect to be treated equitably. When they are not, they experience job dissatisfaction. Quitting the job or simply staying away are possible outcomes. From management's point of view, both of these outcomes are costly. Not only do they affect the smooth running of the organization but they typically affect profits. Since profits are typically the reason for a company's existence, it becomes imperative that management deal with the question of what is equitable.

The Discrepancy Model

According to the discrepancy model of job satisfaction, people have expectations about what a job should provide in the way of money and psychological rewards. Any mismatch between outcomes and expectations is assumed to produce job dissatisfaction. The discrepancy model grows out of what has been called "expectancy/valence theory." Expectancy/valence theory is essentially a cognitive theory of motivation that attempts to incorporate the question of individual differences. That is, the theory acknowledges that people often differ in how confident they are that a reward will come if they meet some desired level of performance or achieve an important goal (expectancy) as well as how highly they value the forthcoming reward (valence). Because the concepts of expectancy and valence are critical to understanding the discrepancy model, I will begin by briefly discussing them.

Expectancy.   The first major component of expectancy/valence theory is expectancy. Two types of expectancy have been identified (Campbell et al., 1970). First, $E \rightarrow P$ expectancy represents a belief that *effort* will lead to a desired outcome. For example, a saleswoman may believe that the more time she spends with a customer, the more likely she is to make a sale. $P \rightarrow O$ expectancy, in contrast, represents a belief about the likelihood that a given *performance* will produce the desired outcome. For example, the saleswoman may be more or less certain that making a sale will result in a bonus or promotion. One could have a high expectation (high $P \rightarrow O$) or a low expectation (low $P \rightarrow O$). Expectancy/valence theory assumes that $E \rightarrow P$ and $P \rightarrow O$ are multiplicative and together represent the expectancy part of the expectancy/valence equation.

Valence.   Valence, the second major component of the expectancy/valence equation, represents the value or preference a person places on a particular outcome. Valences can take on values ranging from $+1.0$ to -1.0. A person could place a high value on a particular outcome ($+1.0$) or a very low—indeed, negative—value on a particular outcome (-1.0).

Performance.   To determine how much effort will be expended (how motivated a person is for a given task), we simply multiply the three values $E \rightarrow P$, $P \rightarrow O$, and valence. Using our saleswoman as an example: Holding a strong belief that time spent with a customer will result in a sale (0.9) and that making a sale will result in a bonus or promotion (0.8) and highly valuing that bonus (0.9) will result in relatively high performance ($0.9 \times 0.8 \times 0.9 = 0.65$). In contrast, if the saleswoman does not believe so strongly that time spent with a customer will result in a sale (0.5) or that making a sale will result in a bonus or promotion (0.4) and does not particularly value a bonus or promotion (0.5), then performance will be lower

(0.5 × 0.4 × 0.5 = 0.10). Even if, in the latter case, she desperately wanted a bonus or promotion (1.0), this factor by itself would not be sufficient to overcome the deficits resulting from holding relatively low $E \rightarrow P$ and $P \rightarrow O$ expectancies.

Expectancy/valence and the discrepancy model. The discrepancy model of job satisfaction assumes that people often come to jobs with expectations, such as "Effort will lead to promotions," "Only 40 hours a week should be necessary to do this job," "The company will promote me if I am loyal," or "It is not important how I dress, only that I do my job well." Such expectations sometimes do not fit with management's expectations. Management may expect an employee to work more than 40 hours, to dress in a certain way, or to be motivated to earn promotions quickly through extra output. Clearly, if the employee's expectations do not fit with the company's, many of the employee's behaviors will not be approved of, let alone rewarded. These outcomes will, it is assumed, have a direct effect on the employee's future expectations. For example, if someone works hard but fails to be recognized through a bonus or promotion because he doesn't follow the company's dress or conduct expectations, he is likely to perceive that effort ($E \rightarrow P$) is not important in this company. To the degree that he has been raised with the belief that effort is important and continues to hold such a belief, he is likely to experience a discrepancy and therefore job dissatisfaction. Similarly, if a person believes that achievement of goals, not personality attributes, should determine promotions (holds a high $P \rightarrow O$ belief about the relation between achievement and promotion), the promotion of a colleague who has achieved less but has strong leadership qualities will represent a discrepancy between the person's belief system and the practices of the company. Such a discrepancy will, it is assumed, result in job dissatisfaction.

The strength of the discrepancy model lies in its recognition that belief systems relating to work and achievement are often fairly stable systems. If an employee holds the belief that leadership qualities should be recognized but finds they are not, she is more likely to search for a new company that does recognize her beliefs than modify such beliefs. If she is unable to find a new job, she will simply perform at some lower level. Therefore, it is critical, from management's perspective, that employees' beliefs are compatible with theirs.

Implications for job satisfaction. How can management ensure that an employee's beliefs are compatible with theirs? One way is to determine carefully whether a person's beliefs are compatible with the organization's before hiring that person. Although this approach has obvious benefits for the person as well as the organization, the question arises whether the conflict produced by employing people who are somewhat incompatible may not be exactly what is needed to keep a company dynamic. Mightn't such people ensure that an organization keep abreast of the times?

Another way of dealing with individual differences in beliefs is to make the company more flexible. Given that the bottom line is some minimal level of performance, allowing for individual differences in dress, how the job is organized, when the employee arrives and leaves, and even rate of promotion or advancement could provide the necessary flexibility. More and more companies are trying to be more flexible, realizing that talented people are often able to find jobs that allow them to work in a manner that is consistent with their value system. In general, it can be said that when there is a shortage of certain skills, people who have those skills can demand more individualized treatment. Companies have less and less chance to force the worker into a mold that suits the needs of management but not the worker.

Summary
There are four basic models of job satisfaction. The need-fulfillment model assumes that humans are born with a set of needs they strive to satisfy. Because our technological society can readily satisfy physiological needs and safety needs, as well as provide for the opportunity to satisfy belongingness needs, people often look to their jobs as an avenue for satisfying esteem needs. The problem is that many jobs in our technological society do not readily lend themselves to satisfying esteem needs. The reinforcement, or reward, model assumes that job satisfaction is determined by rewards and reward schedules. Application of the reward model to the work setting usually involves the assumption that people work only to obtain money. Therefore, according to this model, it is necessary to spell out the exact nature of the contingency between performance and pay. Hamner has suggested six rules management needs to follow if it wants to use a contingency approach. The equity model assumes that workers want to be paid fairly (equitably) for their services. This model predicts that job dissatisfaction will occur when there is inequity among workers. Both underpayment and overpayment, according to this model, are sources of inequity. Finally, the discrepancy model assumes that people have expectations about what a job should provide in the way of money and psychological rewards. Any mismatch between the employee's and employer's expectations may lead to job dissatisfaction. The problem for management is to ensure that an employee's expectations are compatible with its own.

Issues in Work Motivation

The theoretical models discussed above all have something to say about the question of job satisfaction. In the course of examining some of these ideas empirically, researchers have raised certain issues that are important because they bear not only on the validity of various theories but on the day-to-day work setting. We will examine three of these issues: (1) the role of intrinsic motivation, extrinsic rewards, and choice, (2) the relation between performance and job satisfaction, and (3) the relation between performance and job dissatisfaction.

Importance of Intrinsic Motivation
Edward L. Deci (1975) has suggested that intrinsic motivation is tied to a person's need to be competent and self-determining. That is, it reflects the person's need to be in control of events in the environment. Others have argued that intrinsic motivation simply means that a task or activity is enjoyable independent of any external rewards. That is, it is assumed that the nature or structure of the task is sufficient to motivate the person (for example, Kruglanski, Alon, & Lewis, 1972). Because people often work hard at enjoyable (intrinsically motivating) tasks, researchers in the field of work motivation have come to ask whether it is possible to tap this form of motivation in order to improve not only performance but job satisfaction.

Unfortunately, as Deci (1975) points out, research has shown that extrinsic rewards disrupt intrinsic motivation, although intuitively it might be expected that extrinsic reward would simply add to the intrinsic reward and thereby lead to a general increase in motivation. We noted this phenomenon in Chapter 13. Deci argues that external rewards shift the perceived locus of control from internal to external. As a result, the person perceives that the source of reward is extrinsic rather than intrinsic. This perception would, of course, explain why extrinsic rewards disrupt performance on tasks that were initially intrinsically rewarding.

Deci (1975) notes, however, that rewards can also influence intrinsic motivation by affecting perceptions of competence and self-determination. If the rewards assure the person that he or she is competent and in control, they can increase intrinsic motivation. However, rewards can convince the person that he or she is not competent or in control of events and thereby decrease intrinsic motivation. For example, a reduction in pay or simply not receiving an expected increase could lead a person to perceive that he or she was no longer competent or self-determining. In short, any instance of inequity might be sufficient to reduce intrinsic motivation.

The role of choice.   The question arises, therefore, when or whether extrinsic rewards will facilitate performance of tasks that are enjoyable (intrinsically motivating). One hypothesis (Folger, Rosenfield, & Hays, 1978) is that choice determines whether extrinsic rewards will facilitate or disrupt performance of intrinsically motivating tasks. Pay should increase productivity when choice is low and decrease productivity when choice is high. *Low choice* refers to the condition in which a person has little or no choice about working at a task; *high choice* refers to the condition in which a person has the opportunity to refuse. In the real world, employees will sometimes go to a job committed to work but not know what the wages are until the job is finished. This is a low-choice condition. More often, they know what they will be paid and can work or not work, depending on whether they think the returns are sufficient for their perceived efforts (see Deci et al., 1977). To determine exactly how pay and choice interact, the researchers manipulated both choice (high and low) and pay (high and low) in a factorial design. That is, high-choice subjects could receive high or low pay, and low-choice subjects could receive high or low pay. After participants had been exposed to the experimental conditions, they were observed to determine how motivated they were to resume working at a task (a modification of the crossword game Ad Lib®). The dependent measure was the time the subjects took to complete a task-evaluation questionnaire, because the sooner they finished answering this questionnaire, the more time they had to work at the task. The results, shown in Figure 14-1, indicate that choice not only plays a critical role but interacts with level of pay. High-choice/high-pay subjects were less eager to return to the task, indicating that they were less intrinsically motivated. Similarly, low-choice/low-pay subjects were less eager to return to the task.

It should be noted that the design of the study involves insufficient rewards. Insufficient rewards tend to produce cognitive dissonance, which can increase the attractiveness of a task. This effect apparently occurs only when people are well aware that they are working out of choice—that is, are in a high-choice condition (see Cooper & Brehm, 1971). Thus, when people have high choice and high pay, the attractiveness of the task is low. They tend to work only because they are being paid, not because of any dissonance they experience. Indeed, in the present experiment, subjects in the high-choice/high-pay condition failed to finish the questionnaire as rapidly as possible, reflecting a lack of intrinsic motivation. In contrast, subjects in the high-choice/low-pay condition appear to have been intrinsically motivated. The failure of subjects in the low-choice/low-pay condition to finish

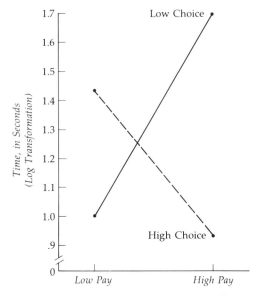

Figure 14-1.   Time spent by subjects playing with the Ad Lib® game when not extrinsically rewarded, as a function of choice and pay (Folger, Rosenfield, & Hays, 1978)

the questionnaire as rapidly as possible simply reflects that no dissonance was created and therefore intrinsic motivation was not altered. In contrast, the tendency of the low-choice/high-pay subjects to work rapidly at finishing the questionnaire reflects that these subjects were motivated by high pay.

Implications for the work setting.   What are the implications for management? It follows that providing minimal compensation will be advantageous for maintaining intrinsic motivation only when a person is in a position to accept or reject the task, as when the person is made a job offer. It must be remembered, however, that people who accept jobs are frequently in a low-choice situation. Such constraints as location, lack of other jobs, and cost involved in not accepting a job immediately can induce a sense of low freedom of choice. Under such conditions, low pay may have disastrous consequences. People who feel they are unfairly paid will perform poorly. The reason higher pay is often needed to sustain interest is that in low-choice situations people generally perceive that they are working only because of pay. Therefore, paying them poorly will merely result in poor performance. Although low pay may be a means of maintaining intrinsic motivation, it must be remembered that low pay seems to have this effect only in a high-choice situation. Many people, obviously, do not have high choice. This means that the ability to use low pay to motivate people is probably, at best, limited.

Performance and Satisfaction
It has generally been assumed that a person who is satisfied with his or her job will perform better. Edward Lawler and Lyman Porter (1967), however, have argued that the causal relation is just the reverse: if a job allows a person to accomplish a goal (perform), he or she will experience satisfaction. Numerous studies supporting this line of argument have been reported. For example, studies have shown

that workers tend to like foremen or supervisors who allow them to fulfill their job goals (Locke, 1970, 1979).

A study of several hundred Air Force officers conducted by Hahn (reported in Locke, 1979) found that when the actions of supervisors were judged to have been responsible for causing a "good day on the job," these actions entailed facilitation of work goals 33% of the time. In contrast, when the actions of supervisors were judged to be responsible for having caused a "bad day on the job," these actions were perceived as having interfered with work-goal attainment 56% of the time. Ned Rosen (1969) found that the best-liked foremen were those who were perceived as being able to "get things for their men" and to "organize the work." These and other studies show that if there are work goals, satisfaction is tied to their accomplishment.

Lawler (1973) has argued that the reason performance leads to satisfaction is that performance is usually perceived not only as a means to obtain intrinsic reward (a feeling of accomplishment) but as indirectly related to extrinsic rewards. That is, people who perform will be rewarded for their efforts. Because extrinsic rewards (pay) are frequently not tied directly to performance, this relation is typically weak. In certain jobs, however, where pay and performance are tied more directly (as in piecework), the relation will be very strong.

Performance and Dissatisfaction

Job dissatisfaction is an important issue because it has been linked to absenteeism, job turnover, and the decision simply not to perform. If other jobs are available, dissatisfaction will often lead to increased turnover. When other jobs are not available, dissatisfaction is likely to lead to absenteeism or simply poor performance. However, the term *dissatisfaction* is typically used to mean something more. It often means the employee is irritated by something in the system. For example, inequity in pay or failure of the organization to provide adequate parking, comfortable places for coffee breaks, opportunity to interact with colleagues, or similar things not directly tied to the job itself can and do lead to dissatisfaction. Figure 14-2 provides a general model of job satisfaction listing some of the important variables that determine whether a worker will experience feelings of satisfaction or dissatisfaction or some other feelings, such as guilt, inequity, or simply discomfort.

Summary

At least three issues in work motivation have arisen in the course of testing various models of job satisfaction. First, the role of intrinsic motivation, external rewards, and choice has received considerable attention in recent years. Although a person may initially find certain jobs intrinsically motivating, Deci argues, external rewards tend to shift the perceived locus of control from internal to external, and as a result external rewards undermine intrinsic motivation. This effect appears to be greatest when external rewards are high. There is evidence that when a person receives low pay under conditions of high choice, external rewards may not undermine intrinsic motivation. Job satisfaction seems to be greatest when a person is allowed to accomplish a goal. Job dissatisfaction frequently occurs when there are irritants in the organization, such as inequity in pay or simply the failure to meet certain expectations, such as adequate parking, places to relax, or the opportunity to interact with associates.

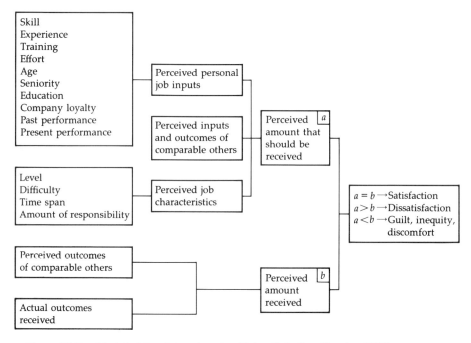

Figure 14-2.   Model of the determinants of job satisfaction (Lawler, 1973)

Attachment to Organizations

Advantages to the Organization
Many organizations have learned that employees who have a sense of attachment, or belonging, not only work harder but are less inclined to be absent or to leave the company. In general, people who have a sense of attachment are more committed to the goals of the company and work harder to achieve those goals (Steers, 1977). It is not surprising, therefore, that organizations try to foster a sense of attachment. It is clearly to their benefit.

Advantages to the Employee
A sense of attachment also has benefits for the worker. It is common for people to want to feel that their job is important. Such a feeling of worth frequently comes from identifying with the more global goals of the company. Even a routine job can take on importance if it is viewed within a larger context (Porter et al., 1974).

To develop a sense of attachment, it is often necessary for the organization to compromise its goals. That is, it must make allowances for individual workers' goals. In return, the worker must realize that his or her own satisfaction is dependent on the health of the organization. If the company does not succeed, then the worker's goals cannot be satisfied. Out of the sense of mutual dependency often develops a familylike atmosphere. Not only is the organization concerned with the problems of the worker, but the worker is concerned with the problems of the organization (Gyllenhammar, 1977).

A Two-Stage Model of Attachment

Steers and Porter (1979) have suggested that organizational attachment can be viewed as a two-stage process, as shown in Figure 14-3. The first stage, called *organizational entry*, refers to the way a person selects a job. What characteristics of the job and of the company influence his or her decision? Although companies often think it is they who select the employee, it must be remembered that selection is a two-way street. In the second stage, called *organizational commitment*, the person must make a decision about the degree of commitment to the organization. To what degree will he or she come to identify with the values of the organization and as a result work toward attainment of its goals? As Figure 14-3 indicates, if organizational commitment is low, the tendency for the person to be absent or leave the job is greater. If commitment is high, the tendency to participate will be greater. Commitment, both attitudinal and behavioral, is synonymous, within this model, with the *decision to participate.*

Organizational entry.   A common model for organizational entry is matching the person and the job. John Wanous (1976, 1977) suggests there are two important "match-ups." First, the person's talents must be matched to organizational needs. Second, the person's needs must be matched to the organizational climate. That is, each person may have somewhat distinctive needs, and these needs must somehow be accommodated by the organization. Within such a model it is generally assumed that the more important match-up is between talent and organizational needs. This match-up probably has the more immediate and powerful effect on job performance. A good match-up is likely to produce good performance (Wanous, 1977). Although this match may be considered more important for performance, a good match between the person's needs and organizational climate is regarded as critical for job satisfaction. Job dissatisfaction, as already noted, can lead to absenteeism or job turnover.

To ensure a good match-up, it is necessary to understand how people select organizations. Most studies indicate that people are attracted to organizations that are rated high on fulfilling an individual's *expectations* and *goals* (for example, Vroom, 1966). Having selected those organizations that are most attractive, the person tries to gain entry into the most attractive one, proceeding from highest to lowest if entry is denied into the organizations considered most attractive (Vroom, 1966).

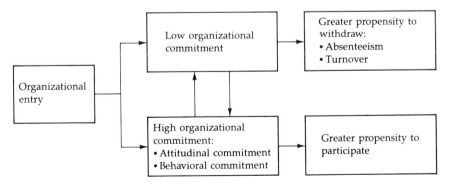

Figure 14-3.   Stages in organizational attachment (Steers & Porter, 1979)

Once entry is gained into a particular organization, the attractiveness of the organization tends to increase in relation to the other organizations on the "most attractive" list (Vroom, 1966). This finding is, of course, to be expected on the basis of cognitive-dissonance theory.

Some time after entry, newcomers often tend to be less satisfied than just before or just after entry (for example, Vroom & Deci, 1971; Wanous, 1977). The important question is why. Wanous (1976) found that prospective employees often have inaccurate information about the nature of the job for which they are applying. Further, he argues that companies either fail to correct such inaccurate information or simply fail to communicate effectively the abstract qualities or characteristics of the job. In a study of telephone employees, he found that expectations about the intrinsic motivational properties of the job declined once the person was "on the inside." That is, once employees experienced the job, they frequently found the job was less than they had originally expected.

If such misperceptions are potential sources of job dissatisfaction, it would seem important for organizations to be more realistic when recruiting newcomers. The problem is, of course, that other companies may present a more glowing description of their jobs and thus entice more and better prospects. A study of M.B.A. students found that recruiters indeed tended to give a glowing rather than balanced description of organizational life (Ward & Athos, 1972). In a series of six experiments, Wanous (1975a, 1975b) studied the effects of realistic job previews on ability to recruit, level of expectation, attitudes of newcomers, and rate of turnover. Wanous's study, as well as others, seems to indicate that more realistic job previews do not adversely affect job recruitment. Realistic job descriptions do lower expectations, but they ultimately produce greater job satisfaction and, more important, reduce turnover. If expectations are brought in line with reality, there will be less discrepancy, a major source of potential job dissatisfaction.

Organizational commitment.   Given that a person has decided to enter an organization, three sets of factors affect whether he or she will develop a sense of commitment: (1) personal characteristics, (2) job characteristics, and (3) work experience (Steers, 1977). The personal characteristics most often found to be related to organizational commitment are age, need for achievement, and education. In general, satisfaction increases with age. For example, when workers are asked how good they feel about their jobs, older workers are more likely to give a positive rating, as shown in Table 14-1. Why does this happen? There are several possible

Table 14-1. Percent of workers expressing a good feeling about their jobs, by age (*Work in America*, 1973)

Age	Percent
20 and under	23
21–29	25
30–44	38
45–64	43
65 and over	53

explanations. It may be simply that as workers have more experience in the work setting, they become more realistic about the types of fulfillment they can expect from work. As a result of this experience they lower their expectations and, as a consequence, tend to view their present job as reasonably close to their expectations. This finding could also reflect the fact that older people have actually found jobs that are more satisfying or, because of achievements and experience, have been promoted into better positions. Whatever the reason, it is a consistent finding that younger people tend not only to be more dissatisfied but to change jobs more often.

The fact that achievement tends to be related to job commitment is not surprising. If a person can gain a sense of satisfaction from achieving goals, being able to work in a setting where such behavior is rewarded should be highly satisfying. The fact that education tends to be related to job satisfaction is also not surprising. People frequently increase their educational qualifications to obtain jobs that are indeed more satisfying. In a study reported in *Work in America* (1973) people in various occupations were asked whether they would choose similar work again. The more educated subjects, who had entered occupations involving achievement, were most likely to say they would choose the same occupation again. When the education requirements were low and the job repetitive, in contrast, very few said they would select the same job again (see Table 14-2).

The job characteristics that have been found to be related to job commitment are job challenge, opportunities for social interaction, task identity, and feedback (Steers, 1977). As we have noted, if given the choice, people are inclined to select jobs that can challenge their skills—especially people with high need for achievement. To the degree that people also experience satisfaction from social interactions, jobs that provide this opportunity are likely to be preferred. If people can see that their job is important if the organization is to function properly and profitably, they will gain a sense of identity from that job, which in turn will lead to a sense of commitment. Further, since people want to know how well they are performing, they want feedback. They want to know whether they are doing their

Table 14-2. Percentages in occupational groups who would choose similar work again (*Work in America,* 1973)

Professional and Lower White-Collar Occupations	Percent	Working-Class Occupations	Percent
Urban university professors	93	Skilled printers	52
Mathematicians	91	Paper workers	42
Physicists	89	Skilled autoworkers	41
Biologists	89	Skilled steelworkers	41
Chemists	86	Textile workers	31
Firm lawyers	85	*Blue-collar workers, cross section*	24
Lawyers	83	Unskilled steelworkers	21
Journalists (Washington correspondents)	82	Unskilled autoworkers	16
Church university professors	77		
Solo lawyers	75		
White-collar workers, cross section	43		

job correctly so they can experience the sense of worth that comes from feeling they are doing an important job for which they will be recognized.

The work experiences that contribute to job commitment are group attitudes toward the organization, organizational dependability, perceived personal importance to the organization, and the extent to which expectations have been met (Steers, 1977). Organizations that recognize individuals' needs and try to allow for the satisfaction of such needs are likely to have employees who feel they are important. Further, it is in such an atmosphere that employees are likely to feel their needs and expectations are being met. It is not surprising that such an atmosphere will engender a positive group attitude toward the organization, together with the feeling that the company is dependable.

Summary

Attachment to organizations has advantages for both the organization and the employee. For the company it usually means higher output and less turnover. For the employee attachment provides a sense of belongingness and an opportunity to identify with the goals of the company. Organizational attachment can be viewed as a two-stage process—*organizational entry* and *organizational commitment*. The first stage has to do with matching the person and the job; the second has to do with the decision to participate in the goals of the organization.

Management Styles for the 1980s and 1990s

Challenge of the 1970s

One of the main themes that concerns many businesses today is the question of how to deal with change. In the 1970s many companies in the United States, Canada, and Western Europe found that they were having a difficult time competing with Japanese firms. Japanese cars were being purchased at ever-increasing rates while large American gas-guzzlers were sitting unsold in the showrooms. Chrysler Corporation was deeply in debt and about to go under. Many companies came to the realization that if they were going to survive this era and deal with the inevitable onslaught of new competition, they would have to change. And they were not going to have to change just a little, they were going to have to make major, even radical changes. For many companies, the 1980s and the 1990s are years of challenge.

While many companies in the 1970s were having difficulty dealing with these new sources of competition, others were not only surviving but expanding. What was the difference? Was it management or was it something else? In their book *In Search of Excellence*, Peters and Waterman (1982) argue that one of the differences between companies that were successful and those that were failing was management style. They came to this conclusion after studying the management styles of the top moneymaking companies of the United States. The managements of those companies had somehow devised a structure that enabled them to become more and more competitive in a world that was and still is characterized by intensive competition.

The ability to deal with change.   One of the key themes that can be found in such books as *In Search of Excellence* and *Megatrends* (Naisbett, 1983) is that companies in the 1980s and 1990s will have to deal with many new forms of competition. This means that many companies will have to devise a strategy for dealing

with almost continual change. Why didn't the North American automobile man-
ufacturers anticipate the fact that people were interested in buying smaller cars?
While the automobile manufacturers said the interest in small cars was linked to
the sudden rise in oil prices, there is a great deal of evidence that this was only
one factor in the trend. Long before the oil crisis many North Americans not only
found it easier to drive smaller cars but had become frustrated by the poor quality
and poor reliability of North American cars.

Why were some companies unable to meet the competition head on? It appears
that many companies had adopted what has been referred to as the rational model
of management, a management style that was not equipped to deal with change
(see Peters & Waterman, 1982).

The Rational Model of Management

Emphasis on analysis. It sounds quite amazing, but many companies in the
1970s and even today make plans on the basis of an analysis of the company's
internal data. They use their present and past data to make predictions about the
future. If oil prices are going up at such-and-such a rate, they simply draw a
straight line to predict where they will be in the future. This was often done with
no regard for the fact that many countries were scrambling to get into the oil
business and that many people were learning how to conserve fuel. As we know,
this approach proved disastrous for many oil companies. The problem is that the
future does not necessarily follow from the past in a rational way. When manage-
ment is predicting future trends, it is often important to look outside the company
to see if other factors may be relevant.

Emphasis on low cost. Many of the companies that adopted the rational model
assumed that the most important thing was to sell a product low in cost. There
was a curious lack of interest in quality. They acted as though they thought the
public did not care about quality, only cost. As it turned out, this assumption was
not altogether correct. Many people began to realize that paying more for quality
would save them money in the long run. As more and more people began to
accept this alternative, more and more people began to abandon products that
failed to measure up to the standards of quality they felt they should be getting.

Decision making. The way you make decisions, according to the rational model,
is to look at the facts. The more facts you have, the better you can make decisions.
All decisions, in other words, were assumed to be rational ones. There was no
room for hunches. Opinions were not important. Everything you wanted to know
was contained in the company records.

Inability to tolerate individual differences. If there is only one way to make
decisions, then there is little room for differences of opinion. And so the offices
of these companies were filled with very similar people, all telling each other that
they were doing the right thing, even as profits declined.

Principles of motivation. The assumptions that govern methods employed to
motivate people within the rational model are very interesting because they pro-
vide us with a glimpse into the way these companies viewed human behavior. If
you start with the assumption that future success depends on analysis of the past,
then the main thing you must do is to make sure you analyze everything. To

accomplish that task you need to make people work long and hard. Remember that you are not interested in creativity, involvement, or anything of the sort. What you want are data that you can analyze.

It is not surprising that one of the main motivational models that emerged from the rational model was concerned with equity. According to the equity model, if you pay people what they deserve, you will get maximum output. Remember that the equity model conceptualizes people as having inputs and outputs and that the performance of a group of people depends on making sure things are equitable.

Many other fascinating things emerged in these companies in regard to motivation. Since production is linked to analysis, the only reason that things can go wrong is that people make mistakes. And so these companies were obsessed with ensuring that people did not make mistakes. This is obviously not the kind of atmosphere in which people offer suggestions. Even if you have carefully thought through as many implications as you can, there is still a possibility of making a mistake. Therefore, it might be better never to make a suggestion.

The New Model for the 1980s and 1990s

It is not altogether correct to talk about this as a new model. The "new model" is new only in the sense that it has incorporated new ideas that have grown out of the work of the social sciences. The model is based on the assumption that if you are going to survive, you need to be able to deal with change.

Listening to the customer.   More and more companies are being forced to recognize that people want changes from time to time and therefore the future will not be like the past. While in the past people may have shopped for the cheapest item, for example, more and more people are now looking for quality. When companies focused entirely on cost, they allowed quality to slip. The net result was a lot of cheap but poor-quality items. For another example we can look again to the auto industry: Detroit was convinced that people still wanted big cars even though millions of people were competing with each other to find quality small cars.

The good companies were and still are listening to their customers. Delta, one of the most successful airlines, works on the philosophy that the customer is central to the survival of the company. Many companies are realizing that only if you listen to the customer will you know when it is time to change. In the past, many companies depended on advertising companies to "shape" public opinion or create a "need." While the idea may still work to some degree, fewer and fewer companies are depending completely on that approach today. They are coming to realize that the consumer is becoming much more discerning and increasingly knowledgeable.

The need for individual differences.   More and more companies are recognizing that any organization needs people with complementary abilities. The rational model leads to one type of decision maker, the rational decision maker. Rational decision makers are able to make decisions only when they have complete information. Sometimes, however, it is necessary to make decisions when information is less than complete. In order to deal with change, it is sometimes necessary to make a decision on the basis of a hunch. In Chapter 13 I pointed out that sensation seekers are people who like to make decisions, like to make them quickly, and like to make them with incomplete information. In other words, some personality types are more suited than others to this new kind of decision making. Such people are not prominent in "rational" companies. They are much in evidence, however, in those companies that have adopted the managerial style of the 1980s.

Abandoning projects that are not working.   One of the things that you must do if you are going to keep up with change is to abandon tasks or projects that are not working. While this may seem obvious, people who operate according to the rational model find it very difficult to abandon tasks that are not working. If something is not working, they are more inclined to go back and check to see if they made any errors in their calculations than to examine their assumptions. One very important characteristic of the new managerial style is that projects are started quickly, often in response to a perceived need or opportunity, and abandoned if they do not work.

New motivation principles.   In order to change, it is necessary to try new things. Companies that did remain competitive in the 1970s and 1980s were those that did try new things. They were innovative. When one tries new things, one is bound to make mistakes. If change is to be possible, then, it is imperative that people not be punished for their mistakes. A basic principle of motivation is that if people are punished for making mistakes, they will work very hard to make sure they don't make mistakes. Since trying new things tends to result in more mistakes than simply doing the same old thing, people learn not to be innovative.

Within this new system, the role of the worker tends to be more highly valued. Managers have come to realize that without the cooperation of the workers they are helpless. Similarly, the workers have to realize that unless they do their job to the very best of their ability, they will not have a job for very long. In other words, what has happened is that everybody, including the customer, is seen as important. Their opinions and ideas are valued, no matter who they are. It has been suggested that the "new" managerial style that Peters and Waterman say is necessary for survival is based on such old values as the importance of hard work, respect for the worker, and, most important, respect for the customer.

Summary

One of the realities that many companies had to face in the 1970s was the fact that there was a whole new group of people, many of them in other countries, who were lean and hungry. They had learned not only how to make quality products but how to make them cheaply. In order to survive, many traditional companies had to face the fact that their managerial structures were incompatible with change.

The "new" managerial style that has emerged and is still emerging is characterized by sensitivity to the needs and desires of the customer. In order to meet the high standards that many people have come to expect, companies have found that it is often necessary not merely to change but to improve their products. To this end workers were given more latitude in their jobs. They were and are being encouraged to try new and different ways of doing things. In this experimental atmosphere there is a greater acceptance of the idea that people are bound to make mistakes. Rather than being punished for their mistakes, people are being told that mistakes are to be expected if they are to make the significant changes that will make them more competitive.

The Work Environment

More and more, it is being recognized that the work environment plays an important role in job satisfaction. Two aspects of the work environment are important: the physical environment and the psychological environment.

The Physical Environment

The physical work environment includes everything from the design of the building to the location of public transportation or parking facilities. If it is difficult to get to the work environment because of poor parking or inadequate public transportation, an employee may arrive irritated and negative. Such feelings can affect one's attitude toward one's job and consequently the quality or quantity of work. Further, if the same problem affects a number of workers, it could lead to low morale. As a consequence, companies have become more concerned about all aspects of the environment that may affect employees' attitudes toward their jobs.

Building design. In the mid-1960s a branch of psychology called environmental psychology emerged to grapple with the question of how the environment affects behavior. One question that has become central to this discipline is how buildings affect work. How can design improve communication, feelings of belongingness, or commitment? Out of this research has developed the horizontal concept of space (Nemcek & Grandjean, 1973). Groups that are expected to communicate are located in adjacent areas, often without walls or doors to separate them. Only partitions are used to designate certain functional groups, such as secretaries, supervisors, and clerks. It has been argued that locating people on different floors of a building tends to break down communication. Walls and doors, it is also argued, break down the natural tendency to communicate. When communication is good, morale should be good, simply because fewer problems should arise in a more open system. What has emerged, therefore, is large, one-story buildings in which the workers and supervisors are on the same floor. They not only can see each other but can communicate with relative ease. In addition, companies have tried to locate these buildings in areas where it is possible to provide good parking together with "green space" (landscaped areas). The end product is a building that not only is pleasant and convenient but provides the worker with a sense of belonging and participation.

Illumination. The question of how illumination affects work has received much attention. Careful research has shown that each job requires a certain level of lighting. Failure to meet this level can cause fatigue, which will be translated into reduced performance.

John E. Flynn (1977) has shown that lighting can affect impressions of *clarity*, *spaciousness*, and *relaxation*. If the main purpose of lighting is clarity, then overhead lighting seems to be best. Interestingly, Flynn found that nonuniform overhead systems that light the central portions more are perceived as providing greater clarity than systems where light level in the central portions is noticeably lower. This holds even for the subjects who are sitting under higher-luminance peripheral areas. To produce feelings of spaciousness and/or relaxation, wall lighting or peripheral lighting is very effective. Nonuniform peripheral lights in combination with warm light tones can significantly increase feelings of relaxation and friendliness. Although cool white fluorescent lighting produces impressions of clarity, warm white produces impressions of relaxation (Flynn & Spencer, 1977). Accordingly, when color is being selected, it must be decided which effect is more desirable.

Noise.   Noise not only is a common cause for complaint in the work setting but, as earlier chapters noted, can be a significant source of arousal. Because noise can increase arousal beyond some optimal level, it can lead to feelings of fatigue and even distress. It is not surprising, therefore, that noise may lead not only to reduced performance but to job dissatisfaction (Kryter, 1970). Periodic rest periods in a quiet location could help return arousal levels to a more normal range, thus helping performance and reducing feelings of dissatisfaction.

If noise levels exceed 95–110 dB for any length of time, they are almost bound to produce a number of physiological changes that could adversely affect one's health. Increased heart rate and blood pressure are two of the changes frequently associated with high noise levels. Hearing loss can result from any intense burst of sound, such as a jet plane taking off (150 dB). Therefore, it is necessary to protect the ears under such conditions.

Music.   A number of offices pipe music to their employees. Even some elevators have piped-in music. Although it has not been shown that music improves work performance, there is evidence that music can make the work environment more pleasant (Grayston, 1974). Generally, music that is piped in is rather innocuous. It is intended to provide a background level of "entertainment" that does not intrude into workers' attention. If it should begin to compete for their attention, it could disrupt performance.

Length and pattern of the work shift.   Although the 40-hour work week has become commonplace, there is a move toward making the work pattern more flexible. Greater freedom in working hours is being tried in a number of organizations. Two common ways of altering the normal 9-to-5 work pattern are to start earlier and quit earlier and to start later and quit later. Many employees find that the early or late pattern allows them to avoid rush hours, take up new hobbies, better arrange for the care of their children, have more time for shopping, and more easily keep appointments. In short, flexible hours provide greater freedom. Although such flexibility may be desirable for the worker, it can cause problems within organizations. It may reduce the opportunity to communicate with other employees or the public and thus cause difficulties in the normal communication system (Evans, 1975).

Four-day workweeks are becoming more and more popular. Employees enjoy the extra day off even if they must work longer days. Management has found that the four-day week can facilitate recruitment, raise morale, lower absenteeism, and even increase production (Poor, 1973).

The Psychological Environment

Boredom.   Two related topics typically appear under the heading of psychological factors of the work environment: boredom and fatigue. Our technological society has produced many jobs that are repetitious. The very nature of these jobs makes them boring; it is virtually impossible to make them interesting or meaningful. The problem for the worker is how to escape boredom. Repetitious jobs frequently lead to absenteeism or some on-job method of escaping boredom, such as consuming alcohol or other drugs. As a consequence, quality of work is often inconsistent or poor. A further problem is safety. Because repetition often decreases arousal level and thereby reduces attention, it is not surprising that repetitious jobs may result in accidents. The use of alcohol or other drugs has obvious implications for safety (Schultz, 1978).

Fatigue.   There are two sources of fatigue: physical exertion and boredom. Research has shown that the level of production closely parallels feelings of fatigue. Therefore, whether fatigue is due to physical or psychological factors, it is necessary for management to attempt to reduce such feelings as much as possible. Periodic total relaxation after a period of physical exertion is necessary to produce good recovery. Hence, if fatigue is due to physical exertion, it is necessary to provide not only rest periods but a place to rest where total relaxation is possible. Rest periods are also important for people experiencing fatigue due to boredom. Change, rather than total relaxation, is the best way to reduce this form of fatigue. As social stimulation can increase arousal levels and thereby reduce feelings of fatigue, opportunity for social contact is desirable (Simonson & Weiser, 1976). Consequently, having a place where social interaction is possible is likely to be a sound investment for any organization.

Summary
Recognition that the work environment can significantly affect job satisfaction has stimulated research on all facets of the work environment. The general layout of work spaces in a building has been shown to affect such things as communication. Illumination has been linked not only to feelings of fatigue but to impressions of clarity, spaciousness, and relaxation. Because noise can directly alter arousal levels, it can improve or retard performance, depending on other characteristics of the task. Music, if properly selected, can facilitate work. Altering the length or pattern of the work shift can frequently lead to not only happier but more productive workers. Both boredom and fatigue are enemies of happiness and productivity. Various things can be done to reduce boredom and fatigue.

Main Points

1. For most jobs there is a minimum amount of money an employee will accept.
2. The need-fulfillment model of job satisfaction is based on the assumption that humans are born with a basic set of needs that they strive to satisfy.
3. Maslow maintains that needs are arranged in a hierarchal fashion, such that as one set of needs is satisfied, another set will emerge.
4. Maslow says humans have five sets of needs: physiological needs, safety needs, belongingness and love needs, esteem needs, and self-actualization needs.
5. Although Maslow's theory is difficult to validate through research, it seems to be an intuitively obvious description of human needs and hence has come to guide thinking about how the structure of a work organization will lead to job satisfaction.
6. The reinforcement model of job satisfaction assumes that people work for extrinsic rewards.
7. According to the reinforcement model, it is necessary for the employee to learn which behaviors are important to the organization so that he or she can engage in those behaviors to obtain the rewards offered by the organization.

8. Although an employee could discover what these contingencies are, it makes a great deal of sense simply to tell the employee the nature of the contingencies.
9. It is important not to punish an employee in front of others because such punishment tends to elicit undesirable behaviors from the employee as well as the group to which he or she belongs.
10. Equity theory says that job satisfaction depends on an employee's receiving an equitable return for his or her services.
11. Workers typically perceive that there are several input factors that need to be considered in determining pay, such as education, intelligence, experience, training, skills, seniority, age, sex, ethnic background, social status, and effort.
12. A basic area of conflict between management and workers is the question of which of these factors are relevant to the job.
13. Under the equity model, job dissatisfaction can result from either overpayment or underpayment. This prediction follows from the assumption that workers tend to compare themselves with others.
14. The equity model assumes that equity exists whenever the ratio of a person's outcomes (performance) to inputs (education, training, skills, and so on) is equal to the ratio of another's outcomes and inputs.
15. Adams theorizes that there are six basic ways in which a worker may try to reduce inequity: (1) alter inputs, (2) alter outcomes, (3) distort inputs or outcomes, (4) leave the field, (5) act on others, and (6) change the object of one's comparison.
16. The discrepancy model of job dissatisfaction assumes that people have expectations about what a job will provide and that any discrepancy from that expectation may cause job dissatisfaction.
17. The discrepancy model is derived from expectancy/valence theory, which assumes that performance is a multiplicative function of $E \rightarrow P$, $P \rightarrow O$, and valence.
18. There is considerable evidence that extrinsic rewards tend to undermine intrinsic motivation.
19. Sometimes people will work for low pay if the job is intrinsically motivating and they have high choice.
20. Job dissatisfaction is due to a number of factors, such as inequity, failure of the organization to meet expectations, or poor working conditions.
21. Attachment to organizations can be viewed as a two-stage process.
22. The first stage, called "organizational entry," affects whether a person will decide to participate.
23. The second stage, called "organizational commitment," affects whether an employee will decide to identify himself or herself with the goals of the organization and hence remain with the company.
24. Three factors determine whether an employee will develop a sense of commitment: personal characteristics, job characteristics, and work experience.
25. Peters and Waterman point out in their book *In Search of Excellence* that successful companies have a management style that equips them to deal actively with change.
26. A model of management that is ill equipped to deal with change has been called the rational model of management. This model focuses on analysis, low cost, a decision style that requires complete information, and the absence of individual differences.
27. The main motivational principle of rational management is avoidance of mistakes.
28. The "new" model of management emphasizes listening to the customer,

accepting and encouraging individual differences, and starting new projects while abandoning those that are not working.

29. Rather than discouraging people from trying new ideas, the new style of management encourages people to try new ideas and permits them to make mistakes.
30. The work environment can play an important role in job satisfaction.
31. Physical characteristics of buildings that promote communication have been found to be a major factor in job satisfaction.
32. Illumination and noise are two other important physical characteristics of the work environment.
33. Varying the length and pattern of the working day is gaining favor as one way of improving work satisfaction.
34. Boredom has been identified as a major determinant of work dissatisfaction.
35. Fatigue resulting from either boredom or physical exertion is a problem that has been handled, in part, by giving workers occasional rest periods.

References

AARONS, L. Sleep-assisted instruction. *Psychological Bulletin*, 1976, *83*, 1–40.

ABEL, E. L. The relationship between cannabis and violence: A review. *Psychological Bulletin*, 1977, *84*, 193–211.

ABELSON, H., COHEN, R., HEATON, E., & SUDER, C. National survey of public attitudes toward and experience with erotic materials. In *Technical Report of the Commission on Obscenity and Pornography* (Vol. 6). Washington, D.C.: Government Printing Office, 1971.

ABRAMSON, L. Y., SELIGMAN, M. E. P., & TEASDALE, J. D. Learned helplessness in humans: Critique and reformulation. *Journal of Abnormal Psychology*, 1978, *87*, 49–74.

ADAMS, D. B., GOLD, A. R., & BURT, A. D. Rise in female-initiated sexual activity at ovulation and its suppression by oral contraceptives. *New England Journal of Medicine*, 1978, *299*(21), 1145–1150.

ADAMS, J. S. Toward an understanding of inequity. *Journal of Abnormal and Social Psychology*, 1963, *67*, 422–436.

ADAMS, J. S. Inequity in social exchange. In L. Berkowitz (Ed.), *Advances in experimental social psychology* (Vol. 2). New York: Academic Press, 1965.

ADAMS, J. S. Inequity in social exchange. In R. M. Steers & L. W. Porter (Eds.), *Motivation and work behavior*. New York: McGraw-Hill, 1979.

ADELSON, S. F. Changes in diets of households, 1955 to 1965. *Journal of Home Economics*, 1968, *60*, 448–455.

ADERMAN, D., & BERKOWITZ, L. Observational set, empathy, and helping. *Journal of Personality and Social Psychology*, 1970, *14*, 141–148.

ÅKERSTEDT, T., TORSVALL, L. & GILLBERG, M. Sleepiness and shift work: Field studies. *Sleep*, 1982, *5*, S95–S106.

AKIL, H., MADDEN, J., IV, PATRICK, R. L., & BARCHAS, J. D. Stress induced increase in endogenous opiate peptides: Concurrent analgesia and its partial reversal by naloxone. In H. W. Kosterlitz (Ed.), *Opiates and endogenous opiate peptides*. Amsterdam: Elsevier North-Holland, 1976.

AKISKAL, H. S., & MCKINNEY, W. T., JR. Psychiatry and pseudopsychiatry. *Archives of General Psychiatry*, 1973, *28*, 367–373.

ALCOCK, J. *Animal behavior: An evolutionary approach.* Sunderland, Mass.: Sinauer, 1979.

ALDERFER, C. P. An empirical test of a new theory of human needs. *Organizational Behavior and Human Performance*, 1969, *4*, 142–175.

ALDERFER, C. P. A critique of Salancik and Pfeffer's examination of need-satisfaction theories. *Administrative Science Quarterly*, 1977, *22*, 658–669.

ALEXANDER, B. K., PEELE, S., HADAWAY, P. F., MORSE, S. J., BRODSKY, A., & BEYERSTEIN, B. L. Adult, infant, and animal addiction. In S. Peele, *The meaning of addiction*. Lexington, Mass.: Lexington Books, 1985.

ALEXANDER, R., & EPSTEIN, S. Reactivity to heteromodal stimulation as a function of stimulus intensity and inner arousal. *Psychophysiology*, 1978, *15*, 387–393.

ALLEN, V. L., & GREENBERGER, D. B. Destruction and perceived control. In A. Baum & J. E. Singer (Eds.), *Advances in environmental psychology* (Vol.

2): *Applications of personal control*. Hillsdale, N.J.: Erlbaum, 1980.

ALLISON, T. S., & ALLISON, S. L. Time-out from reinforcement: Effect on sibling aggression. *Psychological Record*, 1971, *21*, 81–86.

ALLOY, L. B., & ABRAMSON, L. Y. Judgment of contingency in depressed and nondepressed students: Sadder but wiser? *Journal of Experimental Psychology: General*, 1979, *108*, 441–485.

ALLOY, L. B., & ABRAMSON, L. Y. Learned helplessness, depression, and the illusion of control. *Journal of Personality and Social Psychology*, 1982, *42*, 1114–1126.

ALLPORT, G. W. *Personality: A psychological interpretation.* New York: Holt, 1937.

ALTMAN, I. *The environment and social behavior: Privacy, personal space, territory, and crowding.* Pacific Grove, Calif.: Brooks/Cole, 1975.

AMERICAN PSYCHIATRIC ASSOCIATION. *Diagnostic and statistical manual of mental disorders* (3rd ed.). Washington, D.C., 1980.

AMSEL, A. The role of frustrative nonreward in noncontinuous reward situations. *Psychological Bulletin*, 1958, *55*, 102–119.

AMSEL, A. Frustrative nonreward in partial reinforcement and discrimination learning: Some recent history and a theoretical extension. *Psychological Review*, 1962, *69*, 306–328.

AMSEL, A. Behavioral habituation, counterconditioning, and a general theory of persistence. In A. H. Black & W. F. Prokasy (Eds.), *Classical conditioning II: Current research and theory.* New York: Appleton-Century-Crofts, 1972.

ANASTASI, A., & SCHAEFER, C. E. Biographical correlates of artistic and literary creativity in adolescent girls. *Journal of Applied Psychology*, 1969, *53*, 267–273.

APFELBAUM, M. Influence of level of energy intake on energy expenditure in man: Effects of spontaneous intake, experimental starvation, and experimental overeating. In G. A. Bray et al. (Eds.), *Obesity in perspective*, DHEW Publication no. NIH 75–708 (Vol. 2). Washington, D.C.: U.S. Government Printing Office, 1975.

APTER, M. J. *The experience of motivation: Theory of psychological reversals.* New York: Academic Press, 1982.

ARKES, H. R., & BOYKIN, A. W. Analysis of complexity preference in Head Start and nursery school children. *Perceptual and Motor Skills*, 1971, *33*, 1131–1137.

ARKIN, A. M., ANTROBUS, J. S., ELLMAN, S. J., & FARBER, J. Sleep mentation as affected by REMP deprivation. In A. M. Arkin, J. S. Antrobus, & S. J. Ellman (Eds.), *The mind in sleep: Psychology and psychophysiology.* Hillsdale, N.J.: Erlbaum, 1978.

ARMITAGE, A. K., HALL, G. H., & SELLERS, C. M. Effects of nicotine on electrocortical activity and acetylcholine release from the cat cerebral cortex. *British Journal of Pharmacology*, 1969, *35*, 152–160.

ARNOLD, M. B. *Emotion and personality* (2 vols.). New York: Columbia University Press, 1960.

ARNOLD, M. B. Perennial problems in the field of emotions. In M. B. Arnold (Ed.), *Feelings and emotions: The Loyola Symposium.* New York: Academic Press, 1970.

ARONFREED, J. *Conduct and conscience: The socialization of internalized control over behavior.* New York: Academic Press, 1968.

ASCHOFF, J. (ED.) *Circadian clocks.* Amsterdam: North-Holland, 1965.

ASERINSKY, E., & KLEITMAN, N. Regularly occurring periods of eye mobility and concomitant phenomena during sleep. *Science,* 1953, *118,* 273–274.

ASKEVOLD, F. Measuring body image. *Psychotherapy and Psychosomatics,* 1975, *26,* 71–77.

ATHANASIOU, R., SHAVER, P., & TAVRIS, C. Sex. *Psychology Today,* July 1970, pp. 37–52.

ATKINSON, J. W. The achievement motive and recall of interrupted and completed tasks. *Journal of Experimental Psychology,* 1953, *46,* 381–390.

ATKINSON, J. W. Motivational determinants of risk-taking behavior. *Psychological Review,* 1957, *64,* 359–372.

ATKINSON, J. W., HEYNS, R. W., & VEROFF, J. The effect of experimental arousal of the affiliation motive on thematic apperception. *Journal of Abnormal and Social Psychology,* 1954, *49,* 405–410.

AUSTIN, W. Sex differences in bystander intervention in a theft. *Journal of Personality and Social Psychology,* 1979, *37,* 2110–2120.

AUSUBEL, D. P. *Drug addiction: Physiological, psychological, and sociological aspects.* New York: Random House, 1958.

AVERILL, J. R. Personal control over aversive stimuli and its relationship to stress. *Psychological Bulletin,* 1973, *80,* 286–303.

AVERILL, J. R., & BOOTHROYD, P. On falling in love in conformance with the romantic ideal. *Motivation and Emotion,* 1977, *1,* 235–247.

AVERILL, J. R., DEWITT, G. W., & ZIMMER, M. The self-attribution of emotion as a function of success and failure. *Journal of Personality,* 1978, *46,* 323–347.

AX, A. F. The physiological differentiation between fear and anger in humans. *Psychosomatic Medicine,* 1953, *15,* 433–442.

BAEKELAND, F. Exercise deprivation: Sleep and psychological reactions. *Archives of General Psychiatry,* 1970, *22,* 365–369.

BAEKELAND, F., KOULACK, D., & LASKY, R. Effects of a stressful presleep experience on electroencephalograph-recorded sleep. *Psychophysiology,* 1968, *4,* 436–443.

BAEKELAND, F., & LASKY, R. Exercise and sleep patterns in college athletes. *Perceptual and Motor Skills,* 1966, *23,* 1203–1207.

BAKAN, D. *The duality of human existence.* Chicago: Rand McNally, 1966.

BAKER, J. W., II, & SCHAIE, K. W. Effects of aggressing "alone" or "with another" on physiological and psychological arousal. *Journal of Personality and Social Psychology,* 1969, *12,* 80–96.

BALES, R. F. Cultural differences in the rate of alcoholism. *Quarterly Journal of Studies on Alcohol,* 1946, *6,* 380–499.

BANCROFT, J. Human sexual behaviour. In C. R. Austin & R. V. Short (Eds.), *Reproduction in mammals,* vol. 8: *Human sexuality.* Cambridge: Cambridge University Press, 1980.

BANCROFT, J., & SKAKKEBAEK, N. E. Androgens and human sexual behavior. In *Sex hormones and behavior.* Amsterdam: Excerpta Medica, 1979.

BANDURA, A. *Aggression: A social learning analysis.* Englewood Cliffs, N.J.: Prentice-Hall, 1973.

BARASH, D. P. *Sociobiology and behavior.* New York: Elsevier North-Holland, 1977.

BARD, P. A diencephalic mechanism for the expression of rage with special reference to the sympathetic nervous system. *American Journal of Physiology,* 1928, *84,* 490–515.

BARE, J. K. The specific hunger for sodium chloride in normal and adrenalectomized white rats. *Journal of Comparative and Physiological Psychology,* 1949, *42,* 242–253.

BARKER, R. G. *The stream of behavior.* New York: Appleton-Century-Crofts, 1963.

BARLAND, G. H., & RASKIN, D. C. Detection of deception. In W. F. Porkasy and D. C. Raskin (Eds.), *Electrodermal activity in psychological research.* New York: Academic Press, 1973.

BARNES, G. E., MALAMUTH, N. M., & CHECK, J. V. P. Personality and sexuality. *Personality and Individual Differences,* 1984, *5,* 159–172.

BARON, R. A. Aggression as a function of magnitude of victim's pain cues, level of prior anger arousal, and aggressor-victim similarity. *Journal of Personality and Social Psychology,* 1971, *18,* 48–54.

BARON, R. A. Aggression as a function of ambient temperature and prior anger arousal. *Journal of Personality and Social Psychology,* 1972, *21,* 183–189.

BARON, R. A. Threatened retaliation from the victim as an inhibitor of physical aggression. *Journal of Research in Personality,* 1973, *7,* 103–115.

BARON, R. A. The aggression-inhibiting influence of heightened sexual arousal. *Journal of Personality and Social Psychology,* 1974, *3,* 337–339.

BARON, R. A. *Human aggression.* New York: Plenum, 1977.

BARON, R. A. Aggression and heat: The "long hot summer" revisited. In A. Baum, S. Valins, & J. E. Singer (Eds.), *Advances in environmental psychology: The urban environment* (Vol. 1). Hillsdale, N.J.: Erlbaum, 1978. (a)

BARON, R. A. Aggression-inhibiting influence of sexual humor. *Journal of Personality and Social Psychology,* 1978, *36,* 189–197. (b)

BARON, R. A. Heightened sexual arousal and physical aggression: An extension to females. *Journal of Research in Personality,* 1979, *13,* 91–102.

BARON, R. A., & BELL, P. A. Effects of heightened sexual arousal on physical aggression. *Proceedings of the American Psychological Association 81st Annual Convention,* 1973, 171–172.

BARON, R. A., & BELL, P. A. Aggression and heat: Mediating effects of prior provocation and exposure to an aggressive model. *Journal of Personality and Social Psychology,* 1975, *31,* 825–832.

BARON, R. A., & BELL, P. A. Aggression and heat: The influence of ambient temperature, negative affect, and a cooling drink on physical aggression. *Journal of Personality and Social Psychology,* 1976, *33,* 245–255.

BARON, R. A., & BELL, P. A. Sexual arousal and aggression: Effects of type of erotic stimuli and prior provocation. *Journal of Personality and Social Psychology,* 1977, *35,* 79–87.

BARON, R. A., & EGGLESTON, R. J. Performance on the "aggression machine": Motivation to help or harm? *Psychonomic Science,* 1972, *26,* 321–322.

BARON, R. A., & LAWTON, S. F. Environmental influences on aggression: The facilitation of modeling effects by high ambient temperatures. *Psychonomic Science*, 1972, *26*, 80–82.

BARON, R. A., & RANSBERGER, V. M. Ambient temperature and the occurrence of collective violence: The "long, hot summer" revisited. *Journal of Personality and Social Psychology*, 1978, *36*, 351–360.

BARR, T. *Psychopharmacology*. Baltimore: Williams & Wilkins, 1969.

BARRY, H., III, WAGNER, A. R., & MILLER, N. E. Effects of alcohol and amobarbital on performance inhibited by experimental extinction. *Journal of Comparative and Physiological Psychology*, 1962, *55*, 464–468.

BASH, K. W. Contributions to a theory of the hunger drive. *Journal of Comparative Psychology*, 1939, *28*, 137–160.

BAUCOM, D. H., BESCH, P. K., & CALLAHAN, S. Relation between testosterone concentration, sex role identity, and personality among females. *Journal of Personality and Social Psychology*. 1985, *48*, 1218–1226.

BAUM, A., & SINGER, J. E. (EDS.). *Advances in environmental psychology* (Vol. 2): *Applications of personal control*. Hillsdale, N.J.: Erlbaum, 1980.

BEACH, F. A. A review of physiological and psychological studies of sexual behavior in mammals. *Physiological Reviews*, 1947, *27*, 240–307.

BEACH, F. A. Characteristics of masculine "sex drive." In M. R. Jones (Ed.), *Nebraska Symposium on Motivation*. Lincoln: University of Nebraska Press, 1956.

BEACH, F. A. Neural and chemical regulation of behavior. In H. F. Harlow & C. N. Woolsey (Eds.), *Biological and biochemical bases of behavior*. Madison: University of Wisconsin Press, 1958.

BEACH, F. A. *Sex and behavior*. New York: Wiley, 1965.

BEACH, F. A. Cerebral and hormonal control of reflexive mechanisms involved in copulatory behavior. *Physiological Reviews*, 1967, *47*, 289–316.

BEACH, F. A. It's all in your mind. *Psychology Today*, July 1969, pp. 33–35; 60.

BEACH, F. A. Hormonal modification of sexually dimorphic behavior. *Psychoneuroendocrinology*, 1975, *1*, 3–23.

BEACH, F. A. Hormonal control of sex-related behavior. In F. A. Beach (Ed.), *Human sexuality in four perspectives*. Baltimore: Johns Hopkins University Press, 1976.

BEACH, F. A., & FOWLER, H. Individual differences in the response of male rats to androgen. *Journal of Comparative and Physiological Psychology*, 1959, *52*, 50–52.

BEACH, F. A., & LEBOEUF, B. Coital behavior in dogs: I. Preferential mating in the bitch. *Animal Behaviour*, 1967, *15*, 546–558.

BEARY, J. F., BENSON, H., & KLEMCHUK, H. P. A simple psychophysiologic technique which elicits the hypometabolic changes in the relaxation response. *Psychosomatic Medicine*, 1974, *36*, 115–120.

BEAUMASTER, E. J., KNOWLES, J. B., & MACLEAN, A. W. The sleep of skydivers: A study of stress. *Psychophysiology*, 1978, *15*, 209–213.

BECK, A. T. *Depression: Clinical, experimental, and theoretical aspects*. New York: Harper & Row, 1967.

BECK, A. T. *Cognitive theory and emotional disorders*. New York: International Universities Press, 1976.

BECK, A. T., WEISSMAN, A., & KOVACS, M. Alcoholism, hopelessness, and suicidal behavior. *Journal of Studies on Alcohol*, 1976, *37*, 66–77.

BECK, A. T., YOUNG, J. E. College blues. *Psychology Today*, 1978, *12*(4), 80–92.

BECKER, M. (ED.). *The health belief model and personal health behavior*. Thorofare, N.J.: Charles B. Slack, 1974.

BELL, A. P., WEINBERG, M. S., & HAMMERSMITH, S. K. *Sexual preference: Its development in men and women*. Bloomington: Indiana University Press, 1981.

BELL, P. A., & BARON, R. A. Aggression and heat: The mediating role of negative affect. *Journal of Applied and Social Psychology*, 1976, *6*, 18–30.

BELL, P. A., & BYRNE, D. Repression-sensitization. In H. London & J. E. Exner, Jr. (Eds.), *Dimensions of personality*. New York: Wiley, 1978.

BELL, R. Q. Stimulus control of parent or caretaker behavior by offspring. *Developmental Psychology*, 1971, *4*, 63–72.

BELL, R. Q., & HARPER, L. V. *Child effects on adults*. Hillsdale, N.J.: Erlbaum, 1977.

BELLER, A. S. *Fat and thin: A natural history of obesity*. New York: McGraw-Hill, 1978.

BEM, S. L. The measurement of psychological androgyny. *Journal of Consulting and Clinical Psychology*, 1974, *42*, 155–162.

BEMIS, K. M. Current approaches to the etiology and treatment of anorexia nervosa. *Psychological Bulletin*, 1978, *85*, 593–617.

BENASSI, V. A., & MAHLER, H. I. M. Contingency judgments by depressed college students: Sadder but not always wiser. *Journal of Personality and Social Psychology*, 1985, *49*, 1323–1329.

BENSON, H. *The relaxation response*. New York: Morrow, 1975.

BENSON, H., & WALLACE, R. K. Decreased blood pressure in hypertensive subjects who practiced meditation. *Circulation*, 1972, Suppl. 2, 516.

BENSON, J. S., & KENNELLY, K. J. Learned helplessness: The result of uncontrollable reinforcements or uncontrollable aversive stimuli? *Journal of Personality and Social Psychology*, 1976, *34*, 138–145.

BEN-TOVIM, D., WHITEHEAD, J., & CRISP, A. H. A controlled study of the perception of body width in anorexia nervosa. *Journal of Psychosomatic Research*, 1979, *23*, 267–272.

BERKMAN, J. M. Anorexia nervosa, anterior pituitary insufficiency, Simmonds' cachexia, and Sheehan's disease. *Postgraduate Medicine*, 1948, *3*, 237–246.

BERKOWITZ, L. *Aggression: A social psychological analysis*. New York: McGraw-Hill, 1962.

BERKOWITZ, L. Aggressive cues in aggressive behavior and hostility catharsis. *Psychological Review*, 1964, *71*, 104–122.

BERKOWITZ, L. The frustration-aggression hypothesis revised. In L. Berkowitz (Ed.), *Roots of aggression*. New York: Atherton Press, 1969.

BERKOWITZ, L. Social norms, feelings, and other factors affecting helping and altruism. In L. Berkowitz (Ed.), *Advances in experimental social psychology* (Vol. 6). New York: Academic Press, 1972.

BERKOWITZ, L. Reactance and the unwillingness to help others. *Psychological Bulletin*, 1973, *79*, 310–317.

BERKOWITZ, L. Some determinants of impulsive aggression: Role of mediated associations with reinforcements for aggression. *Psychological Review*, 1974, *81*, 165–176.

BERKOWITZ, L., & CONNOR, W. H. Success, failure, and

social responsibility. *Journal of Personality and Social Psychology*, 1966, *4*, 664–669.

BERKOWITZ, L., & DANIELS, L. R. Affecting the salience of the social responsibility norm: Effects of past help on the response of dependency relationships. *Journal of Abnormal and Social Psychology*, 1964, *68*, 275–281.

BERKOWITZ, L., & GEEN, R. G. Film violence and the cue properties of available targets. *Journal of Personality and Social Psychology*, 1966, *3*, 525–530.

BERLYNE, D. E. The influence of complexity and novelty in visual figures on orienting responses. *Journal of Experimental Psychology*, 1958, *55*, 289–296.

BERLYNE, D. E. *Conflict, arousal, and curiosity.* New York: McGraw-Hill, 1960.

BERLYNE, D. E. The reward value of indifferent stimulation. In J. T. Tapp (Ed.), *Reinforcement and behavior.* New York: Academic Press, 1969.

BERLYNE, D. E. Novelty, complexity and hedonic value. *Perception and Psychophysics*, 1970, *8*, 279–286.

BERLYNE, D. E. *Aesthetics and psychobiology.* New York: Appleton-Century-Crofts, 1971.

BERLYNE, D. E., KOENIG, I. D. V., & HIROTA, T. Novelty, arousal, and the reinforcement of diversive exploration in the rat. *Journal of Comparative and Physiological Psychology*, 1966, *62*, 222–226.

BERMANT, G., & DAVIDSON, J. M. *Biological bases of sexual behavior.* New York: Harper & Row, 1974.

BERNSTEIN, A. S. Electrodermal lability and the OR: Reply to O'Gorman and further exposition of the significance hypothesis. *Australian Journal of Psychology*, 1973, *25*, 147–154.

BERNSTEIN, A. S. The orienting response as novelty and significance detector: Reply to O'Gorman. *Psychophysiology*, 1979, *16*, 263.

BERNSTEIN, A. S., TAYLOR, K. W., & WEINSTEIN, E. The phasic electrodermal response as a differentiated complex reflecting stimulus significance. *Psychophysiology*, 1975, *12*, 158–169.

BHANJI, S., & THOMPSON, J. Operant conditioning in the treatment of anorexia nervosa: A review and retrospective study of 11 cases. *British Journal of Psychiatry*, 1974, *124*, 166–172.

BIRNEY, R. C., BURDICK, H., & TEEVAN, R. C. *Fear of failure.* New York: Van Nostrand, 1969.

BIXLER, E. O., KALES, A., SOLDATOS, C. R., VELA-BUENO, A., JACOBY, J. A., & SCARONE, S. Sleep apnea in a normal population. *Research Communications in Chemical Pathology and Pharmacology*, 1982, *36*, 141–152.

BLANCHARD, R. J., BLANCHARD, D. C., & FIAL, R. A. Hippocampal lesions in rats and their effects on activity, avoidance, and aggression. *Journal of Comparative and Physiological Psychology*, 1970, *71*, 92–102.

BLISS, E. L., & BRANCH, C. H. H. *Anorexia nervosa: Its history, psychology, and biology.* New York: Paul Hoeber, 1960.

BLOOM, G., VON EULER, U. S., & FRANKENHAEUSER, M. Catecholamine excretion and personality traits in paratroop trainees. *Acta Physiologica Scandinavica*, 1963, *58*, 77–89.

BLOOMFIELD, H. H., CAIN, M. P., JAFFE, D. T., & KORY, R. B. *TM: Discovering inner energy and overcoming stress.* New York: Dell, 1975.

BLUM, K., HAMILTON, M. L., & WALLACE, J. E. Alcohol and opiates: A review of common neurochemical and behavioral mechanisms. In K. Blum (Ed.), *Alcohol and opiates: Neurochemical and behavioral mechanisms.* New York: Academic Press, 1977.

BOLLES, R. C. Species-specific defense reactions and avoidance learning. *Psychological Review*, 1970, *77*, 32–48.

BOLLES, R. C., & FANSELOW, M. S. Endorphins and behavior. *Annual Review of Psychology*, 1982, *33*, 87–101.

BOLTON, R. Aggression and hypoglycemia among the Qolla: A study in psychobiological anthropology. *Ethnology*, 1973, *12*, 227–257.

BONNET, M. H. Effect of sleep disruption on sleep, performance, and mood. *Sleep*, 1985, *8*, 11–19.

BONVALLET, M., & ALLEN, M. B., JR. Prolonged spontaneous and evoked reticular activation following discrete bulbar lesions. *Electroencephalography and Clinical Neurophysiology*, 1963, *15*, 969–988.

BORDEN, R. J., BOWEN, R., & TAYLOR, S. P. Shock-setting behavior as a function of physical attack and extrinsic reward. *Perceptual and Motor Skills*, 1971, *33*, 563–568.

BORING, E. G. *A history of experimental psychology* (2nd ed.). New York: Appleton-Century-Crofts, 1950.

BOWER, S. A., & BOWER, G. H. *Asserting yourself: A practical guide for positive change.* Reading, Mass.: Addison-Wesley, 1976.

BOZARTH, M. A., & WISE, R. A. Toxicity associated with long-term intravenous heroin and cocaine self-administration in the rat. *Journal of the American Medical Association*, 1985, *253*, 81–83.

BRABAND, J., & LERNER, M. J. "A little time and effort"—Who deserves what from whom? *Personality and Social Psychology Bulletin*, 1975, *1*, 177–181.

BRADLEY, G. W. Self-serving biases in the attribution process: A reexamination of the fact or fiction question. *Journal of Personality and Social Psychology*, 1978, *36*, 56–71.

BRADY, J. V. Emotion and sensitivity of psychoendocrine systems. In D. C. Glass (Ed.), *Neurophysiology and emotion.* New York: Rockefeller University Press, 1967.

BRADY, J. V. Towards a behavioral biology of emotion. In L. Levi (Ed.), *Emotions: Their parameters and measurement.* New York: Raven Press, 1975.

BRAIN, P. F. *Hormones and aggression*, (Vol. 1) Montreal: Eden Press, 1977.

BRAIN, P. F., & NOWELL, N. W. Isolation versus grouping effects on adrenal and gonadal functions in albino mice: I. The male. *General and Comparative Endocrinology*, 1971, *16*, 149–154.

BRAUCHT, G. N., BRAKARSH, D., FOLLINGSTAD, D., & BERRY, K. L. Deviant drug use in adolescence: A review of psychological correlates. *Psychological Bulletin*, 1975, *79*, 92–106.

BREHM, J. W. Postdecision changes in the desirability of alternatives. *Journal of Abnormal and Social Psychology*, 1956, *52*, 384–389.

BREHM, J. W. *A theory of psychological reactance.* New York: Academic Press, 1966.

BREHM, J. W. *Response to loss of freedom: A theory of psychological reactance.* Morristown, N.J.: General Learning Press, Module Series, 1972.

BREMER, J. *Asexualization: A follow-up study of 244 cases.* New York: Macmillan, 1959.

BRICKMAN, P., LINSENMEIER, J. A. W., & MCCAREINS, A. G. Performance enhancement by relevant success and irrelevant failure. *Journal of Personality and Social Psychology*, 1976, *33*, 149–160.

BROADHURST, P. L. Emotionality and the Yerkes-Dodson law. *Journal of Experimental Psychology*, 1957, *54*, 345–352. (a)

BROADHURST, P. L. *Emotionality in the rat: A study of its determinants, inheritance, and relation to some aspects of motivation.* Unpublished doctoral dissertation, University of London, 1957. (b)

BROBECK, J. R. Food and temperature. *Recent Progress in Hormone Research,* 1960, *16,* 439–466.

BROCK, T. C., & BUSS, A. H. Effects of justification for aggression and communication with the victim on post aggression dissonance. *Journal of Abnormal and Social Psychology,* 1964, *68,* 403–412.

BROCKNER, J. The effects of self-esteem, success-failure, and self consciousness on task performance. *Journal of Personality and Social Psychology,* 1979, *37,* 1732–1741.

BROWN, G. M. Endocrine alterations in anorexia nervosa. In P. L. Darby, P. E. Garfinkel, D. M. Garner, & D. V. Coscina, *Anorexia nervosa: Recent developments in research* (pp. 231–247). New York: Alan R. Liss, Inc., 1983.

BROWN, M., JENNINGS, J., & VANIK, V. The motive to avoid success: A further examination. *Journal of Research in Personality,* 1974, *8,* 172–176.

BROWN, S. A., GOLDMAN, M. S., INN, A., & ANDERSON, L. R. Expectations of reinforcement from alcohol: Their domain and relation to drinking patterns. *Journal of Consulting and Clinical Psychology,* 1980, *48,* 419–426.

BROWNMAN, C. P., & TEPAS, D. I. Effects of presleep activity on all-night sleep. *Psychophysiology,* 1976, *13,* 536–540.

BROWNMILLER, S. *Femininity.* New York: Linden Press/Simon & Schuster, 1984.

BRUCH, H. *Eating disorders: Obesity, anorexia nervosa, and the person within.* New York: Basic Books, 1973.

BRUCH, H. How to treat anorexia nervosa. *Roche Report: Frontiers of Psychiatry,* 1975, *5*(8), 1–2; 8.

BRUNER, J. S., MATTER, J., & PAPANEK, M. L. Breadth of learning as a function of drive level and mechanization. *Psychological Review,* 1955, *62,* 1–10.

BRYSON, J. B., & DRIVER, M. J. Cognitive complexity, introversion, and preference for complexity. *Journal of Personality and Social Psychology,* 1972, *23,* 320–327.

BUCHSBAUM, M. S., GERNER, R., & POST, R. M. The effects of sleep deprivation on average evoked potentials in depressed patients and normals. *Biological Psychiatry,* 1981, *16,* 351–363.

BUCK, R. *Human motivation and emotion.* New York: Wiley, 1976.

BURNAM, M. A., PENNEBAKER, J. W., & GLASS, D. C. Time consciousness, achievement striving, and the Type A coronary-prone behavior pattern. *Journal of Abnormal Psychology,* 1975, *84,* 76–79.

BURNAND, G., HUNTER, H., & HOGGART, K. Some psychological test characteristics of Klinefelter's syndrome. *British Journal of Psychiatry,* 1967, *113,* 1019–1096.

BURNSTEIN, E., & WORCHEL, P. Arbitrariness of frustration and its consequences for aggression in a social situation. *Journal of Personality,* 1962, *30,* 528–540.

BUSS, A. H. Physical aggression in relation to different frustrations. *Journal of Abnormal and Social Psychology,* 1963, *67,* 1–7.

BUSS, A. H. The effect of harm on subsequent aggression. *Journal of Experimental Research in Personality,* 1966, *1,* 249–255.

BUSTAMANTE, J. A., ROSSELLO, A., JORDAN, A., PRADERE, E., MARTINEZ, H., & INSUA, A. *Learning and drugs.* Paper presented at the Psychopharmacological and Conduct Regulation Symposium of the 18th International Congress of Psychology, Moscow, 1966.

BUTLER, R. A. Discrimination learning by rhesus monkeys to visual-exploration motivation. *Journal of Comparative and Physiological Psychology,* 1953, *46,* 95–98.

BYRNE, D., FISHER, J. D., LAMBERTH, J., & MITCHELL, H. E. Evaluations of erotica: Facts or feelings? *Journal of Personality and Social Psychology,* 1974, *29,* 111–116.

CAHALAN, D., & ROOM, R. *Problem drinking among American men.* Monograph 7. New Brunswick, N.J.: Rutgers Center of Alcohol Studies, 1974.

CALHOUN, J. B. Population density and social pathology. *Scientific American,* February 1962, pp. 139–148.

CAMPBELL, J. B., & HAWLEY, C. W. Study habits and Eysenck's theory of extraversion-introversion. *Journal of Research in Personality,* 1982, *16,* 139–146.

CAMPBELL, J. P., DUNNETTE, M. D., LAWLER, E. E., III, & WEICK, K. E. *Managerial behavior, performance and effectiveness.* New York: McGraw-Hill, 1970.

CANNON, W. B. The James-Lange theory of emotions: A critical examination and an alternative theory. *American Journal of Psychology,* 1927, *39,* 106–124.

CANTOR, J. R., ZILLMANN, D., & BRYANT, J. Enhancement of experienced sexual arousal in response to erotic stimuli through misattribution of unrelated residual excitation. *Journal of Personality and Social Psychology,* 1975, *32,* 69–75.

CANTWELL, D. P., STURZENBERGER, S., BURROUGHS, J., SALKIN, B., & GREEN, J. K. Anorexia nervosa: An affective disorder? *Archives of General Psychiatry,* 1977, *34,* 1087–1093.

CARLSON, E. R., & COLEMAN, C. E. H. Experiential and motivational determinants of the richness of an induced sexual fantasy. *Journal of Personality,* 1977, *45,* 528–542.

CARLSON, M., & MILLER, N. Explanations of the relation between negative mood and helping. *Psychological Bulletin,* 1987, *102,* 91–108.

CARNEY, A., BANCROFT, J., & MATHEWS, A. Combination of hormonal and psychological treatment for female sexual unresponsiveness: A comparative study. *British Journal of Psychiatry,* 1978, *133,* 339–346.

CARPENTER, J. A. Effects of alcoholic beverages on skin conductance: An exploratory study. *Quarterly Journal of Studies on Alcohol,* 1957, *18,* 1–18.

CARROLL, J. C. The intergenerational transmission of family violence. *Aggressive Behavior,* 1977, *3,* 289–299.

CARRUTHERS, M. E. *The Western way of death: Stress, tension, and heart attacks.* New York: Pantheon, 1974.

CARSKADON, M. A., & DEMENT, W. C. Sleepiness and sleep state on a 90-min schedule. *Psychophysiology,* 1977, *14,* 127–133.

CARSKADON, M. A., & DEMENT, W. C. Cumulative effects of sleep restriction on daytime sleepiness. *Psychophysiology,* 1981, *18,* 107–113.

CARTWRIGHT, R. D., BUTTERS, E., WEINSTEIN, M., & KROEKER, L. The effects of presleep stimuli of different sources and types on REM sleep. *Psychophysiology,* 1977, *14,* 388–392.

CARTWRIGHT, R. D., LLOYD, S., BUTTERS, E., WEINER, L., MCCARTHY, L., & HANCOCK, J. Effects of REM time on what is recalled. *Psychophysiology,* 1975, *12,* 561–568.

CARTWRIGHT, R. D., MONROE, L. J., & PALMER, C. Individual differences in response to REM deprivation. *Archives of General Psychiatry*, 1967, *16*, 297–303.

CARTWRIGHT, R. D., & RATZEL, R. Effects of dream loss on waking behaviors. *Archives of General Psychiatry*, 1972, *27*, 277–280.

CARVER, C. S. A cybernetic model of self-attention processes. *Journal of Personality and Social Psychology*, 1979, *37*, 1251–1281.

CARVER, C. S., BLANEY, P. H., & SCHEIER, M. F. Focus of attention, chronic expectancy, and responses to a feared stimulus. *Journal of Personality and Social Psychology*, 1979, *37*, 1186–1195. (a)

CARVER, C. S., BLANEY, P. H., & SCHEIER, M. F. Reassertion and giving up: The interactive role of self-directed attention and outcome expectancy. *Journal of Personality and Social Psychology*, 1979, *37*, 1859–1870. (b)

CARVER, C. S., & GANELLEN, R. J. Depression and components of self-punishment: High standards, self-criticism, and overgeneralization. *Journal of Abnormal Psychology*, 1983, *92*, 330–337.

CARVER, C. S., GANELLEN, R. J., & BEHAR-MITRANI, V. Depression and cognitive style: Comparisons between measures. *Journal of Personality and Social Psychology*, 1985, *49*, 722–728.

CARVER, C. S., & GLASS, D.C. The coronary prone behavior pattern and interpersonal aggression. *Journal of Personality and Social Psychology*, 1978, *36*, 361–366.

CASTALDO, V., & KRYNICKI, V. Sleep patterns and intelligence in functional mental retardation. *Journal of Mental Deficiency Research*, 1973, *17*, 231–235.

CASTALDO, V., KRYNICKI, V., & GOLDSTEIN, J. Sleep stages and verbal memory. *Perceptual and Motor Skills*, 1974, *39*, 1023–1030.

CAUL, W. F., BUCHANAN, D. C., & HAYS, R. C. Effects of unpredictability of shock on incidence of gastric lesions and heart rate in immobilized rats. *Physiology and Behavior*, 1972, *8*, 669–672.

CAUTHEN, N. R., & PRYMAK, C. A. Meditation versus relaxation: An examination of the physiological effects of relaxation training and of different levels of experience with transcendental meditation. *Journal of Consulting and Clinical Psychology*, 1977, *45*, 496–497.

CHAIKEN, S., & PLINER, P. *Women, but not men, are what they eat: The effect of meal size and gender on perceived femininity and masculinity.* Unpublished manuscript, Vanderbilt University, 1984.

CHAUCHARD, P. Emission and reception of sounds at the level of the central nervous system in vertebrates. In R. G. Busnel (Ed.), *Acoustic behavior in animals.* London: Elsevier, 1963.

CHOMSKY, N. *Language and mind* (Enl. ed.). New York: Harcourt Brace Jovanovich, 1972.

CHRISTIAN, J. J. Effect of population size on the adrenal glands and reproductive organs of male white mice. *American Journal of Physiology*, 1955, *182*, 292-300.

CHRISTIAN, J. J., FLYGER, V., & DAVIS, D. C. Factors in the mass mortality of a herd of Sika deer, *Cervus hippon. Chesapeake Science*, 1960, *1*, 79–95.

CIALDINI, R. B., DARBY, B. L., & VINCENT, J. E. Transgression and altruism: A case for hedonism. *Journal of Experimental Social Psychology*, 1973, *9*, 502–516.

CIALDINI, R. B., & KENRICK, D. T. Altruism as hedonism: A social development perspective on the relationship of negative mood state and helping.

Journal of Personality and Social Psychology, 1976, *34*, 907–914.

CIBA FOUNDATION SYMPOSIUM. *Sex hormones and behavior.* Amsterdam: Excerpta Medica, 1979.

CLARIDGE, G. *Drugs and human behaviour.* London: Penguin, 1970.

CLARK, K. B. Empathy: A neglected topic in psychological research. *American Psychologist*, 1980, *35*, 187–190.

CLARKE, D. H. *Exercise physiology.* Englewood Cliffs, N.J.: Prentice-Hall, 1975.

CLORE, G. L., & BYRNE, D. A. A reinforcement-affect model of attraction. In T. L. Huston (Ed.), *Foundations of interpersonal attraction.* New York: Academic Press, 1974.

COBB, S., & ROSE, R. M. Hypertension, peptic ulcer, and diabetes in air traffic controllers. *Journal of the American Medical Association*, 1973, *224*, 489–492.

COCHRAN, S. D., & HAMMEN, C. L. Perception of stressful life events and depression: A test of attributional models. *Journal of Personality and Social Psychology*, 1985, *48*, 1562–1571.

COHEN, D. B. Neuroticism and dreaming sleep: A case for interactionism in personality research. *British Journal of Social and Clinical Psychology*, 1977, *16*, 153–163.

COHEN, D. B. Dysphoric affect and REM sleep. *Journal of Abnormal Psychology*, 1979, *88*, 73–77.

COLEMAN, M. Serotonin levels in whole blood of hyperactive children. *Journal of Pediatrics*, 1971, *78*, 985–990.

COLEMAN, M., & GANONG, L. H. Love and sex-role stereotypes: Do macho men and feminine women make better lovers? *Journal of Personality and Social Psychology*, 1985, *49*, 170–176.

COLLINS, D. L., BAUM, A., & SINGER, J. E. Coping with chronic stress at Three Mile Island: Psychological and biochemical evidence. *Health Psychology*, 1983, *2*, 149–166.

CONDRY, J. C. Enemies of exploration: Self-initiated versus other-initiated learning. *Journal of Personality and Social Psychology*, 1977, *35*, 459–477.

CONDRY, J. C., & CHAMBERS, J. Intrinsic motivation and the process of learning. In M. R. Lepper & D. Greene (Eds.), *The hidden costs of rewards: New perspectives on the psychology of human motivation.* Hillsdale, N.J.: Erlbaum, 1978.

CONDRY, J., & DYER, S. Fear of success: Attribution of cause to the victim. *Journal of Social Issues*, 1976, *32*, 63–83.

CONGER, J. J. Reinforcement theory and the dynamics of alcoholism. *Quarterly Journal of Studies on Alcohol*, 1956, *17*, 296–305.

CONROY, J., III, & SUNDSTROM, E. Territorial dominance in dyadic conversation as a function of similarity of opinion. *Journal of Personality and Social Psychology*, 1977, *35*, 570–576.

COOPER, J., & BREHM, J. W. Prechoice awareness of relative deprivation as a determinant of cognitive dissonance. *Journal of Experimental Social Psychology*, 1971, *7*, 571–581.

COOPER, J. R., BLOOM, F. E., & ROTH, B. H. *The biochemical basis of neuropharmacology* (4th ed.). New York: Oxford University Press, 1982.

COOPERSMITH, S. *The antecedents of self-esteem.* San Francisco: W. H. Freeman, 1967.

COOVER, G. D., URSIN, H., & LEVINE, S. Plasma-corticosterone levels during active-avoidance learning in rats. *Journal of Comparative and Physiological Psychology*, 1973, *82*, 170–174.

COSCINA, D. V., & DIXON, L. M. Body weight regulation in anorexia nervosa: Insight from an animal model. In P. L. Darby, P. E. Garfinkel, D. M. Garner, & D. V. Coscina (Eds.), *Anorexia nervosa: Recent developments* (pp. 207–220). New York: Alan R. Liss, Inc., 1983.

COSTA, P., & McCLELLAND, D.C. *Predicting rank in class from motivational, social class, and intelligence measures.* Unpublished manuscript, Harvard University, Department of Psychology and Social Relations, 1971.

COSTELLO, C. G. *Anxiety and depression: The adaptive emotions.* Montreal: McGill-Queens University Press, 1976.

COSTELLO, C. G. A critical review of Seligman's laboratory experiments on learned helplessness and depression in humans. *Journal of Abnormal Psychology*, 1978, *87*, 21–31.

COYNE, J. C., ALDWIN, C., & LAZARUS, R. S. Depression and coping in stressful episodes. *Journal of Abnormal Psychology*, 1981, *90*, 439–447.

COYNE, J. C., & GOTLIB, I. H. The role of cognition in depression: A critical review, *Psychological Bulletin*, 1983, *94*, 472–505.

COYNE, J. C., & LAZARUS, R. S. Cognitive style, stress perception, and coping. In I. L. Kutash & L. B. Schlesinger (Eds.), *Handbook on stress and anxiety: Contemporary knowledge, theory, and treatment* (pp. 144–158). San Francisco: Jossey-Bass, 1980.

CRISP, A. H., & KALUCY, R. S. Aspects of the perceptual disorder in anorexia nervosa. *British Journal of Medical Psychology*, 1974, *47*, 349–361.

CROWLEY, W. R., O'DONOHUE, T. L., & JACOBOWITZ, D. M. Changes in catecholamine content in discrete brain nuclei during the estrous cycle of the rat. *Brain Research*, 1978, *147*, 315–326.

CROWTHER, J. H., LINGSWILER, V. M., & STEPHENS, M. A. P. The topology of binge eating. *Addictive Behaviors*, 1984, *9*, 299–303.

CROYLE, R. T., & COOPER, J. Dissonance arousal: Physiological evidence. *Journal of Personality and Social Psychology*, 1983, *45*, 782–791.

CUNNINGHAM, M. R. Weather, mood, and helping behavior: Quasi experiments with the sunshine samaritan. *Journal of Personality and Social Psychology*, 1979, *37*, 1947–1956.

CUTHBERT, B., KRISTELLER, J., SIMONS, R., HODES, R., & LANG, P. J. Strategies of arousal control: Biofeedback, meditation, and motivation. *Journal of Experimental Psychology: General*, 1981, *110*, 518–546.

CZAYA, J., KRAMER, M., & ROTH, T. *Changes in dream quality as a function of time into REM.* Paper presented at the meeting of the Association for the Psychophysiological Study of Sleep, San Diego, 1973.

DALLY, P. J. *Anorexia nervosa.* New York: Grune & Stratton, 1969.

DALTON, K. Schoolgirls' misbehaviour and menstruation. *British Medical Journal*, 1960, *2*, 1647–1649.

DALTON, K. Menstruation and crime. *British Medical Journal*, 1961, *2*, 1752–1753.

DALTON, K. *The pre-menstrual syndrome.* Springfield, Ill.: Charles C Thomas, 1964.

DALTON, K. *The premenstrual syndrome and progesterone therapy.* London: Heinman, 1977.

DALY, E. M., LANCEE, W. J., & POLIVY, J. A canonical model for the taxonomy of emotional experience. *Journal of Personality and Social Psychology*, 1983, *45*, 443–457.

DANOWSKI, T. S., LIVSTONE, E., GONZALES, A. R., JUNG, Y., & KHURANA, R. C. Fractional and partial hypopituitarism in anorexia nervosa. *Hormones*, 1972, *3*, 105–118.

DARLEY, J. M., & LATANÉ, B. Bystander intervention in emergencies: Diffusion of responsibility. *Journal of Personality and Social Psychology*, 1968, *8*, 377–383.

DARWIN, C. *The origin of species.* New York: Modern Library, 1936. (Originally published, 1859.)

DARWIN, C. *The expression of emotions in man and animals.* Chicago: University of Chicago Press, 1965. (Originally published, Philadelphia: R. West, 1873.)

D'ATRI, D. A. Psychophysiological responses to crowding. In S. Saegert (Ed.), *Crowding in real environments.* Beverly Hills, Calif.: Sage Publications, 1976.

DAVIDS, A. An objective instrument for assessing hyperkinesis in children. *Journal of Learning Disabilities*, 1971, *4*, 35–37.

DAVIS, B. *Norepinephrine and epinephrine secretions following rest and exercise in trained and untrained males.* Unpublished doctoral dissertation, University of Illinois at Urbana-Champaign, 1973.

DAVIS, C. M. Self selection of diet by newly weaned infants. *American Journal of Diseases of Children*, 1928, *36*, 651–679.

DAVIS, D. H., GOODWIN, D. W., & ROBINS, L. N. Drinking amid abundant illicit drugs. *Archives of General Psychiatry*, 1975, *32*, 230–233.

DAVIS, V. E., & WALSH, M. J. Alcohol, amines, and alkaloids: A possible biochemical basis for alcohol addiction. *Science*, 1970, *167*, 1005–1007.

DEAUX, K., WHITE, L., & FARRIS, E. Skills versus luck: Field and laboratory studies of male and female preferences. *Journal of Personality and Social Psychology*, 1975, *32*, 629–636.

DECI, E. L. Effects of externally mediated rewards on intrinsic motivation. *Journal of Personality and Social Psychology*, 1972, *22*, 113–120.

DECI, E. L. *Intrinsic motivation.* New York: Plenum, 1975.

DECI, E. L., REIS, H. T., JOHNSON, E. J., & SMITH, R. Toward reconciling equity theory and insufficient justification. *Personality and Social Psychology Bulletin*, 1977, *3*, 224–227.

DE GROEN, J. H. M. Influence of diffuse brain stimulation (DBS) on human sleep: I. Sleep pattern changes. *Electroencephalography and Clinical Neurophysiology*, 1979, *46*, 689–695.

DELGADO, J. M. R. Cerebral heterostimulation in a monkey colony. *Science*, 1963, *141*, 161–163.

DELGADO, J. M. R. Aggressive behavior evoked by radio stimulation in monkey colonies. *American Zoologist*, 1966, *6*, 669–681.

DELGADO, J. M. R. Social rank and radio-stimulated aggressiveness in monkeys. *Journal of Nervous and Mental Disease*, 1967, *144*, 383–390.

DELGADO, J. M. R. Inhibitory systems and emotions. In L. Levi (Ed.), *Emotions: Their parameters and measurement.* New York: Raven Press, 1975.

DELONGIS, A., COYNE, J. C., DAKOF, G., FOLKMAN, S., & LAZARUS, R. S. Relationship of daily hassles, uplifts, and major life events to health status. *Health Psychology*, 1982, *1*, 119–136.

DEMBER, W. N. Response by the rat to environmental change. *Journal of Comparative and Physiological Psychology*, 1956, *49*, 93–95.

DEMBER, W. N., & EARL, R. W. Analysis of exploratory, manipulatory, and curiosity behaviors. *Psychological Review*, 1957, *64*, 91–96.

DEMBROSKI, T. M., MACDOUGALL, J. M., & SHIELDS, J. L. Physiologic reactions to social challenge in persons evidencing the Type A coronary-prone behavior pattern. *Journal of Human Stress*, 1977, *3*(3), 2–9.

DEMENT, W. C. The effect of dream deprivation. *Science*, 1960, *131*, 1705–1707.

DEMENT, W. C. *Some must watch while some must sleep.* San Francisco: W. H. Freeman, 1972.

DEMENT, W. C., & CARSKADON, M. A. Current perspectives on daytime sleepiness. *Sleep*, 1982, *5*, S56–S66.

DEMENT, W. C., & VILLABLANCA, J. Clinical disorders in man and animal model experiments. In O. Petre-Ouadens & J. Schlag (Eds.), *Basic sleep mechanisms*. New York: Academic Press, 1974.

DENENBERG, V. H. Stimulation in infancy, emotional reactivity, and exploratory behavior. In D. C. Glass (Ed.), *Neurophysiology and emotion*. New York: Rockefeller University Press and Russell Sage Foundation, 1967.

DENGERINK, H. A. Anxiety, aggression, and physiological arousal. *Journal of Experimental Research in Personality*, 1971, *5*, 223–232.

DENGERINK, H. A. Personality variables as mediators of attack-instigated aggression. In R. G. Geen & E. C. O'Neal (Eds.), *Perspectives on aggression*. New York: Academic Press, 1976.

DENGERINK, H. A., & BERTILSON, H. S. The reduction of attack instigated aggression. *Journal of Research in Personality*, 1974, *8*, 254–262.

DENGERINK, H. A., & LEVENDUSKY, P. G. Effects of massive retaliation and balance of power on aggression. *Journal of Experimental Research in Personality*, 1972, *6*, 230–236.

DENGERINK, H. A., & MYERS, J. D. The effects of failure and depression on subsequent aggression. *Journal of Personality and Social Psychology*, 1977, *35*, 88–96.

DENGERINK, H. A., O'LEARY, M. R., & KASNER, K. H. Individual differences in aggressive responses to attack: Internal-external locus of control and field dependence-independence. *Journal of Research in Personality*, 1975, *9*, 191–199.

DERMER, M., & PYSZCZYNSKI, T. A. Effects of erotica upon men's loving and liking responses for women they love. *Journal of Personality and Social Psychology*, 1978, *36*, 1302–1309.

DESOR, J. A. Toward a psychological theory of crowding. *Journal of Personality and Social Psychology*, 1972, *21*, 79–83.

DE WIED, D. Inhibitory effects of ACTH and related peptides on extinction of conditioned avoidance behavior in rats. *Proceedings of the Society for Experimental Biology and Medicine*, 1966, *122*, 28–32.

DE WIED, D. Opposite effects of ACTH and glucocorticoids on extinction of conditioned emotional behavior. In L. Martini, F. Fraschini, & M. Motta (Eds.), *Proceedings of the Second International Congress on Hormonal Steroids*. Amsterdam and New York: Excerpta Medica, 1967.

DE WIED, D. Pituitary-adrenal system hormones and behavior. In H. Selye (Ed.), *Selye's guide to stress*

research (Vol. 1). New York: Van Nostrand Reinhold, 1980.

DEY, F. Auditory fatigue and predicted permanent hearing defects from rock-and-roll music. *New England Journal of Medicine*, 1970, *282*, 467–469.

DIAMOND, E. L. The role of anger and hostility in essential hypertension and coronary heart disease. *Psychological Bulletin*, 1982, *92*, 410–433.

DIAMOND, M. C., DOWLING, G. A., & JOHNSON, R. E. Morphologic cerebral cortical asymmetry in male and female rats. *Experimental Neurology*, 1981, *71*, 261–268.

DIGUISTO, E. L., CAIRNCROSS, K., & KING, M. G. Hormonal influences on fear-motivated behavior. *Psychological Bulletin*, 1971, *75*, 432–444.

DOERR, P., PIRKE, K. M., KOCKOTT, G., & DITTMAR, F. Further studies on sex hormones in male homosexuals. *Archives of General Psychiatry*, 1976, *33*, 611–614.

DOLE, V. P. A relation between non-esterified fatty acids in plasma and the metabolism of glucose. *Journal of Clinical Investigations*, 1956, *35*, 150–152.

DOLE, V. P. Addictive behavior. *Scientific American*, 1980, *243*(6), 138–154.

DOMINICK, J. R., & GREENBERG, B. S. Attitudes toward violence: The interaction of television exposure, family attitudes, and social class. In G. A. Comstock & E. A. Rubinstein (Eds.), *Television and social behavior* (Vol. 3): *Television and adolescent aggressiveness*. Washington, D.C.: Government Printing Office, 1971.

DOMINO, G. Creativity and the home environment. *Gifted Child Quarterly*, 1979, *23*, 818–828.

DONNERSTEIN, E., & BARRETT, G. Effects of erotic stimuli on male aggression toward females. *Journal of Personality and Social Psychology*, 1978, *36*, 180–188.

DONNERSTEIN, E., DONNERSTEIN, M., & EVANS, R. Erotic stimuli and aggression: Facilitation or inhibition. *Journal of Personality and Social Psychology*, 1975, *32*, 237–244.

DONNERSTEIN, E., & HALLAM, J. Facilitating effects of erotica on aggression against women. *Journal of Personality and Social Psychology*, 1978, *36*, 1270–1277.

DONNERSTEIN, E., & WILSON, D. W. Effects of noise and perceived control on ongoing and subsequent aggressive behavior. *Journal of Personality and Social Psychology*, 1976, *34*, 774–781.

DONNERSTEIN, E. I., & LINZ, D. G. The question of pornography. *Psychology Today*, 1986, *20*, 56–59.

DOOB, A. N., & CLIMIE, R. J. Delay of measurement and the effects of film violence. *Journal of Experimental Social Psychology*, 1972, *8*, 136–142.

DORFMAN, D. D. Esthetic preference as a function of pattern information. *Psychonomic Science*, 1965, *3*, 85–86.

DÖRNER, G. Hormones and sex-specific brain development. In B. Flérkó, G. Sétáló, & L. Tima (Eds.), *Advances in physiological sciences* (pp. 111–120). New York: Pergamon Press, 1980.(a)

DÖRNER, G. Sex differentiation of the brain. In P. L. Munson, E. Diczfalusy, J. Glover, & R. E. Olson (Eds.), *Vitamins and hormones* (pp. 325–381). New York: Academic Press, 1980.(b)

DÖRNER, G. Sex hormones and neurotransmitters as mediators for sexual differentiation of the brain. *Endokrinologie*, 1981, *78*, 129–137.

DÖRNER, G. Hormone-dependent brain development. *Psychoneuroendocrinology*, 1983, *8*, 205–212.

DÖRNER, G., GEIER, TH., AHRENS, L., KRELL, L., MÜNX, G., SIELER, H., KITTNER, E., & MÜLLER, H. Prenatal stress as possible aetiogenetic factor of homosexuality in human males. *Endokrinologie*, 1980, *75*, 365–368.

DÖRNER, G., GÖTZ, F., & DOCKE, W. D. Prevention of demasculinization and the feminization of the brain in prenatally stressed male rats by perinatal androgen treatment. *Experimental Clinical Endocrinology*, 1982, *81*, 88–90.

DORSKY, F. S., & TAYLOR, S. P. Physical aggression as a function of manifest anxiety. *Psychonomic Science*, 1972, *27*, 103–104.

DOUGLAS, D., & ANISMAN, H. Helplessness or expectation incongruency: Effects of aversive stimulation on subsequent performance. *Journal of Experimental Psychology: Human Perception and Performance*, 1975, *1*, 411–417.

DURDEN-SMITH, J., & DE SIMONE, D. *Sex and the Brain*. New York: Warner, 1983.

DUTTON, D. G., & ARON, A. P. Some evidence for heightened sexual attraction under conditions of high anxiety. *Journal of Personality and Social Psychology*, 1974, *30*, 510–517.

DWECK, C. S. Motivational processes affecting learning. *American Psychologist*, 1986, *41*, 1040–1048.

EARL, R. W. *Problem solving and motor skill behaviors under conditions of free-choice*. Unpublished doctoral dissertation, University of Michigan, 1957.

EASTERBROOK, J. A. The effect of emotion on cue utilization and the organization of behavior. *Psychological Review*, 1959, *66*, 183–201.

EDEN, A. *Growing up thin*. New York: David McKay, 1975.

EGGER, M. D., & FLYNN, J. P. Effects of electrical stimulation of the amygdala on hypothalamically elicited attack behavior in cats. *Journal of Neurophysiology*, 1963, *26*, 705–720.

EHRENKRANZ, J., BLISS, E., & SHEARD, M. H. Plasma testosterone: Correlation with aggressive behavior and social dominance in man. *Psychosomatic Medicine*, 1974, *36*, 469–475.

EHRHARDT, A. A., & MEYER-BAHLBURG, H. F. L. Effects of prenatal sex hormones on gender-related behavior. *Science*, 1981, *211*, 1312–1318.

EIBL-EIBESFELDT, I. *Ethology: The biology of behavior* (2nd ed.). New York: Holt, Rinehart & Winston, 1975.

EISLER, R. M., HERSEN, M., MILLER, P. M., & BLANCHARD, E. B. Situational determinants of assertive behavior. *Journal of Consulting and Clinical Psychology*, 1975, *43*, 330–340.

EISLER, R. M., MILLER, P. M., & HERSEN, M. Components of assertive behavior. *Journal of Clinical Psychology*, 1973, *29*, 295–299.

EKMAN, P., LEVENSON, R. W., & FRIESEN, W. V. Autonomic nervous system activity distinguishes among emotions. *Science*, 1983, *221*, 1208–1210.

ELLIOTT, E., & DWECK, C. S. *Goals: An approach to motivation and achievement*. Unpublished manuscript, 1985.

ELMADJIAN, F., HOPE, J. M., & LAMSON, E. T. Excretion of epinephrine and norepinephrine in various emotional states. *Journal of Clinical Endocrinology*, 1957, *17*, 608–620.

EMRICK, C. D., & HANSEN, J. Assertions regarding effectiveness of treatment of alcoholism: Fact or fantasy. *American Psychologist*, 1983, *38*, 1078–1088.

ENDLER, N. S., & MAGNUSSON, D. (EDS.). *Interactional psychology and personality*. Toronto: Hemisphere, 1976. (a)

ENDLER, N. S., & MAGNUSSON, D. Toward an interactional psychology of personality. *Psychological Bulletin*, 1976, *83*, 956–974. (b)

ENGLE, K. B., & WILLIAMS, T. K. Effect of an ounce of vodka on alcoholics' desire for alcohol. *Quarterly Journal of Studies on Alcohol*, 1972, *33*, 1099–1105.

EPSTEIN, S. The nature of anxiety with emphasis upon its relationship to expectancy. In C. D. Spielberger (Ed.), *Anxiety: Current trends in theory and research*. New York: Academic Press, 1972.

ERDMANN, G., & JANKE, W. Interaction between physiological and cognitive determinants of emotions: Experimental studies on Schachter's theory of emotions. *Biological Psychology*, 1978, *6*, 61–74.

ERON, L. D., HUESMANN, L. R., LEFKOWITZ, M. M., & WALDER, L. Q. Does television violence cause aggression? *American Psychologist*, 1972, *27*, 253–263.

EVANS, M. A longitudinal analysis of the impact of flexible working hours. *Studies in Personnel Psychology*, 1975, *6*, 1–10.

EYSENCK, H. J. *Dimensions of personality*. London: Routledge & Kegan Paul, 1947.

EYSENCK, H. J. Personality and drug effects. In H. J. Eysenck (Ed.), *Experiments with drugs*. Oxford: Pergamon Press, 1963.

EYSENCK, H. J. *The biological basis of personality*. Springfield, Ill.: Charles C Thomas, 1967.

EYSENCK, H. J. Introverts, extraverts, and sex. *Psychology Today*, January 1971, pp. 48–51; 82.

EYSENCK, H. J. Personality and the maintenance of the smoking habit. In W. L. Dunn (Ed.), *Smoking behavior: Motives and incentives*. Washington, D.C.: Winston, 1973.

EYSENCK, H. J. *Sex and personality*. London: Open Books, 1976.

FAIRBORN, C. A cognitive behavioural approach to the treatment of bulimia. *Psychological Medicine*, 1981, *11*, 707–711.

FAIRBORN, C. G. Self-induced vomiting. *Journal of Psychosomatic Research*, 1980, *24*, 193–197.

FAIRBORN, C. G., & COOPER, P. J. Self-induced vomiting and bulimia nervosa: An undetected problem. *British Medical Journal*, 1982, *284*, 1153–1155.

FALK, J. L. Drug dependence: Myth or motive? *Pharmacology Biochemistry and Behavior*, 1983, *19*, 385–391.

FARKAS, G. M., & ROSEN, R. C. Effect of alcohol on elicited male sexual response. *Journal of Studies on Alcohol*, 1976, *37*, 265–272.

FARLEY, F. H. The big T in personality. *Psychology Today*, May 1986, pp. 44–52.

FEATHER, N. T. The relationship of persistence at a task to expectation of success and achievement-related motives. *Journal of Abnormal and Social Psychology*, 1961, *63*, 552–561.

FEATHER, N. T. The relationship of expectation of success to reported probability, task structure, and achievement-related motivation. *Journal of Abnormal and Social Psychology*, 1963, *66*, 231–238.

FEATHER, N. T. Reactions to male and female success and failure at sex-linked occupations: Effects of sex and socio-economic status of respondents. *Australian Journal of Psychology*, 1978, *30*, 21–40.

FEHR, F. S., & SCHULMAN, M. Female self-report and autonomic responses to sexually pleasurable and sexually aversive readings. *Archives of Sexual Behavior,* 1978, *7,* 443–453.

FEINBERG, I., KORESKO, R. L., HELLER, N., & STEINBERG, H. R. Sleep EEG and eye-movement patterns in young and aged normal subjects and in patients with chronic brain syndrome. In W. B. Webb (Ed.), *Sleep: An active process.* Glenview, Ill.: Scott, Foresman, 1973.

FELDMAN, R. S., & BERNSTEIN, A. G. Primacy effects in self-attribution of ability. *Journal of Personality,* 1978, *46,* 732–742.

FENIGSTEIN, A. Does aggression cause a preference for viewing media violence? *Journal of Personality and Social Psychology,* 1979, *37,* 2307–2317.

FENSTERHEIM, H., & BAER, J. *Don't say yes when you want to say no.* New York: Dell, 1975.

FENWICK, P. B., DONALDSON, S., GILLIS, L., BUSHMAN, J., FENTON, G. W., PERRY, I., TILSLEY, C., & SERAFINOWICZ, H. Metabolic and EEG changes during transcendental meditation: An explanation. *Biological Psychology.* 1977, *5,* 101–118.

FENZ, W. D., & EPSTEIN, S. Stress: In the air. *Psychology Today,* September 1969, pp. 28–29; 58–59.

FERN, R. W. Hearing loss caused by amplified pop music. *Journal of Sound and Vibration,* 1976, *46,* 462–464.

FESHBACH, S., STILES, W. B., & BITTER, E. The reinforcing effects of witnessing aggression. *Journal of Experimental Research on Personality,* 1967, *2,* 133–139.

FESTINGER, L. *A theory of cognitive dissonance.* Evanston, Ill.: Row, Peterson, 1957.

FESTINGER, L., & CARLSMITH, J. M. Cognitive consequences of forced compliance. *Journal of Abnormal and Social Psychology,* 1959, *58,* 203–210.

FESTINGER, L., PEPITONE, A., & NEWCOMB, T. Some consequences of de-individuation in a group. *Journal of Abnormal and Social Psychology,* 1952, *47,* 382–389.

FEY, S. G., & LINDHOLM, E. Biofeedback and progressive relaxation: Effects on systolic and diastolic blood pressure and heart rate. *Psychophysiology,* 1978, *15,* 239–247.

FIEVE, R. R. *Moodswing: The third revolution in psychiatry.* New York: Bantam, 1975.

FILTER, T. A., & GROSS, A. E. Effects of public and private deviancy on compliance with a request. *Journal of Experimental Social Psychology,* 1975, *11,* 553–559.

FINCHER, J. Natural opiates in the brain. *Human Behavior,* January 1979, pp. 28–32.

FISHER, C., & DEMENT, W. *Dreams and psychosis.* Paper presented at the meeting of the Western New England Psychoanalytic Society, New Haven, Conn., 1962.

FISHER, W. A., & BYRNE, D. Sex differences in response to erotica? Love versus lust. *Journal of Personality and Social Psychology,* 1978, *36,* 117–125.

FISHMAN, S. M., & SHEEHAN, D. V. Anxiety and panic: Their cause and treatment. *Psychology Today,* April 1985, pp. 26–32.

FITCH, G. Effects of self-esteem, perceived performance, and choice on causal attributions. *Journal of Personality and Social Psychology,* 1970, *16,* 311–315.

FITZ, D. A renewed look at Miller's conflict theory of aggression displacement. *Journal of Personality and Social Psychology,* 1976, *33,* 725–732.

FLYNN, J. E. A study of subjective responses to low energy and nonuniform lighting systems. *Light Design and Application,* 1977, *7*(2), 6–15.

FLYNN, J. E., & SPENCER, T. J. The effects of light source color on user impression and satisfaction. *Journal of the Illuminating Engineering Society,* 1977, 167–179.

FODOR, E. M., & FARROW, D. L. The power motive as an influence in the use of power. *Journal of Personality and Social Psychology,* 1979, *37,* 2091–2097.

FODOR, E. M., & SMITH, T. The power motive as an influence on group decision making. *Journal of Personality and Social Psychology,* 1982, *42,* 178–185.

FOLGER, R., ROSENFIELD, D., & HAYS, R. P. Equity and intrinsic motivation: The role of choice. *Journal of Personality and Social Psychology,* 1978, *36,* 557–564.

FOLKMAN, S. Personal control and stress and coping processes: A theoretical analysis. *Journal of Personality and Social Psychology,* 1984, *46,* 839–852.

FOLKMAN, S., & LAZARUS, R. S. If it changes it must be a process: Study of emotion and coping during three stages of a college examination. *Journal of Personality and Social Psychology,* 1985, *46,* 839–852.

FOLKMAN, S., & LAZARUS, R. S. Stress processes and depressive symptomatology. *Journal of Abnormal Psychology,* 1986, *95,* 107–113.

FOLKMAN, S., LAZARUS, R. S., DUNKEL-SCHETTER, C., DELONGIS, A., & GRUEN, R. J. Dynamics of a stressful encounter: Cognitive appraisal, coping, and encounter outcomes. *Journal of Personality and Social Psychology,* 1986, *50,* 992–1003.

FOLKMAN, S., SCHAEFER, C., & LAZARUS, R. S. Cognitive processes as mediators of stress and coping. In V. Hamilton & D. M. Warburton (Eds.), *Human stress and cognition: An information processing approach* (pp. 265–298). New York: Wiley, 1979.

FOOTE, R. M. Diethylstilbestrol and the management of psychological states in males. *Journal of Nervous and Mental Disease,* 1944, *99,* 928–935.

FORD, C. S., & BEACH, F. A. *Patterns of sexual behavior.* New York: Harper, 1951.

FOULKES, D. Dream reports from different stages of sleep. *Journal of Abnormal and Social Psychology,* 1962, *65,* 14–25.

FOULKES, D. *The psychology of sleep.* New York: Scribner's, 1966.

FOULKES, D., SPEAR, P. S., & SYMONDS, J. D. Individual differences in mental activity at sleep onset. *Journal of Abnormal Psychology,* 1966, *71,* 280–286.

FOULKES, D., & VOGEL, G. Mental activity at sleep onset. *Journal of Abnormal Psychology,* 1965, *70,* 231–243.

FRANKEN, R. E. Sensation seeking, decision styles, and preference for individual responsibility. *Personality and Individual Differences* (in press).

FRANKEN, R. E. *Sensation seeking and beliefs and attitudes.* Unpublished research, 1987.

FRANKEN, R. E., GIBSON, K. J., & ROWLAND, G. L. *Sensation seeking, drug use, and attitudes toward drug use.* Unpublished research, 1987.

FRANKEN, R. E., & MORPHY, D. R. Effects of fortuitous success on goal setting behavior of individuals high and low in achievement motivation. *Perceptual and Motor Skills,* 1970, *30,* 855–864.

FRANKEN, R. E., & STRAIN, A. Effect of increased arousal on response to stimulus change in a complex maze. *Perceptual and Motor Skills,* 1974, *39,* 1076–1078.

FRANKENHAEUSER, M. Experimental approaches to the study of catecholamines and emotion. In L. Levi

(Ed.), *Emotions: Their parameters and measurement.* New York: Raven Press, 1975.

FRANKENHAEUSER, M. Psychoneuroendocrine approaches to the study of stressful person-environment transactions. In H. Selye (Ed.), *Selye's guide to stress research* (Vol. 1). New York: Van Nostrand Reinhold, 1980.

FRANKENHAEUSER, M. The sympathetic-adrenal and pituitary-adrenal response to challenge: Comparison between sexes. In T. M. Dembroski, T. H. Schmidt, & G. Blümchen (Eds.), *Biochemical bases of coronary heart disease* (pp. 99–105). New York: Carger, 1983.

FRANKENHAEUSER, M., & ANDERSSON, K. Note on the interaction between cognitive and endocrine functions. *Perceptual and Motor Skills*, 1974, *38*, 557–558.

FRANKENHAEUSER, M., DUNNE, E., & LUNDBERG, U. Sex differences in sympathetic-adrenal medullary reactions induced by different stressors. *Psychopharmacology*, 1976, *476*, 1–5.

FRANKENHAEUSER, M., & JOHANSSON, G. Task demand as reflected in catecholamine excretion and heart rate. *Journal of Human Stress*, 1976, *2*, 15–23.

FRANKENHAEUSER, M., LUNDBERG, U., & FORSMAN, L. Dissociation between sympathetic-adrenal and pituitary-adrenal responses to an achievement situation characterized by high controllability: Comparison between Type A and Type B males and females. *Biological Psychology*, 1980, *10*, 79–91.

FRANKENHAEUSER, M., NORDHEDEN, B., MYRSTEN, A. L., & POST, B. Psychophysiological reactions to understimulation and overstimulation. *Acta Psychologia*, 1971, *35*, 298–308.

FRANKLIN, K. B. J., & ROBERTSON, A. 5HT blockade and the stimulant effects of d- and l-amphetamine: No interaction in self-stimulation of prefrontal cortex, hypothalamus, or dorsal tegmentum. Unexpected lethality in hippocampal sites. *Pharmacology, Biochemistry, and Behavior*, 1980, *13*(3), 365–370.

FREEDMAN, D. G. *Human sociobiology.* New York: Free Press, 1979.

FREEDMAN, J. L. *Crowding and behavior.* San Francisco: W. H. Freeman, 1975.

FREEDMAN, J. L., LEVY, A. S., BUCHANAN, R. W., & PRICE, J. Crowding and human aggressiveness. *Journal of Experimental Social Psychology*, 1972, *8*, 528-548.

FRENCH, E. G. Motivation as a variable in work-partner selection. *Journal of Abnormal and Social Psychology*, 1956, *53*, 96–99.

FRENCH, E. G., & LESSER, G. S. Some characteristics of the achievement motive in women. *Journal of Abnormal and Social Psychology*, 1964, *68*, 119–128.

FREUD, S. *A general introduction to psychoanalysis.* New York: Washington Square Press, 1934. (Originally published, 1915.)

FREUD, S. The ego and the id. In *The standard edition of the complete psychological works of Sigmund Freud* (Vol. 19). London: Hogarth Press, 1947. (Originally published, 1923.)

FREUD, S. Formulations regarding the two principles of mental functioning. In *Collected papers of Sigmund Freud* (Vol. 4). London: Hogarth Press, 1949. (Originally published, 1911.)

FREUD, S. Instincts and their vicissitudes. In *Collected papers of Sigmund Freud* (Vol. 4.) London: Hogarth Press, 1949. (Originally published, 1915.)

FREUD, S. *The interpretation of dreams.* London: Hogarth Press, 1953. (Originally published, 1900.)

FRIEDMAN, M., BYERS, S. O., DIAMANT, J., & ROSENMAN, R. H. Plasma catecholamine response of coronary-prone subjects (Type A) to a specific challenge. *Metabolism*, 1975, *24*, 201–210.

FRIEDMAN, M., & ROSENMAN, R. H. *Type A behavior and your heart.* New York: Knopf, 1974.

FRIEDMAN, M. I., & STRICKER, E. M. The physiological psychology of hunger: A physiological perspective. *Psychological Review*, 1976, *83*, 409–431.

FRIEDMAN, R. C., & FRANTZ, A. G. Plasma prolactin levels in male homosexuals. *Hormones and Behavior*, 1977, *9*(1), 19–22.

FRIEDMANN, J., GLOBUS, G., HUNTLEY, A., MULLANEY, D., NAITOH, P., & JOHNSON, L. Performance and mood during and after gradual sleep reduction. *Psychophysiology*, 1977, *14*, 245–250.

FRODI, A. Experiential and physiological responses associated with anger and aggression in women and men. *Journal of Research in Personality*, 1978, *12*, 335–349.

FROHMAN, L. A., GOLDMAN, J. K., & BERNARDIS, L. L. Metabolism of intravenously injected 14C-glucose in weanling rats with hypothalamic obesity. *Metabolism: Clinical and Experimental*, 1972, *21*, 799–805.

FROMME, D. K., & O'BRIEN, C. S. A dimensional approach to circular ordering of the emotions. *Motivation and Emotion*, 1982, *6*, 337–363.

FROST, R. O., GOOLKASIAN, G. A., ELY, R. J., & BLANCHARDS, F. A. Depression, restraint, and eating behavior. *Behavioral Research and Therapy*, 1982, *20*, 113–121.

FUNKENSTEIN, D. H. The physiology of fear and anger. *Scientific American*, 1955, *192*(5), 74–80.

FUNKENSTEIN, D. H., KING, S. H., & DROLETTE, M. E. *Mastery of stress.* Cambridge, Mass.: Harvard University Press, 1957.

FUSTER, J. M. Effects of stimulation of brain stem on tachistoscopic perception. *Science*, 1958, *127*, 150.

GAGNON, P., DE KONINCK, J., & BROUGHTON, R. Reappearance of electroencephalogram slow waves in extended sleep with delayed bedtime. *Sleep*, 1985, *8*, 118–128.

GALE, A., COLES, M., & BLAYDON, J. Extraversion-introversion and the EEG. *British Journal of Psychology*, 1969, *60*, 209–223.

GAMBARO, S., & RABIN, A. I. Diastolic blood pressure responses following direct and displaced aggression after anger arousal in high- and low-guilt subjects. *Journal of Personality and Social Psychology*, 1969, *12*, 87–94.

GANELLEN, R. J., & BLANEY, P. H. Hardiness and social support as moderators of the effects of life stress. *Journal of Personality and Social Psychology*, 1984, *47*, 156–163.

GARCIA, J., & KOELLING, R. A. Relation of cue to consequence in avoidance learning. *Psychonomic Science*, 1966, *4*, 123–124.

GARCIA, J., MCGOWAN, B. K., ERVIN, F. R., & KOELLING, R. A. Cues: Their relative effectiveness as a function of the reinforcer. *Science*, 1968, *160*, 794–795.

GARDINER, R. J., MARTIN, F., & JUKIER, L. Anorexia nervosa: Endocrine studies of two distinct clinical populations. In P. L. Darby, P. E. Garfinkel, D. M. Garner, & D. V. Coscina, *Anorexia nervosa: Recent developments in research* (pp. 285–289). New York: Alan R. Liss, Inc., 1983.

GARFINKEL, P. E., & GARNER, D. M. *Anorexia nervosa: A multidimensional perspective.* New York: Brunner/Mazel, 1982.

GARFINKEL, P. E., MOLDOFSKY, H., GARNER, D. M., STANCER, H. C., & COSCINA, D. V. Body awareness in anorexia nervosa: Disturbances in "body image" and "satiety." *Psychosomatic Medicine*, 1978, *40*, 487–498.

GARN, S. M., & CLARK, D. C. Trends in fatness and the origins of obesity. *Pediatrics*. 1976, *57*, 443–455.

GARROW, D. J. S., CRISP, A. H., JORDON, H. A., MEYER, J. E., RUSSELL, G. F. M., SILVERSTONE, T., STUNKARD, A. J., & VAN ITALLIE, T. B. Pathology of eating, group report. In T. Silverstone (Ed.), *Dahlem Konferenzen, Life Sciences Research Report 2.* Berlin, 1975.

GARROW, J. The regulation of energy expenditure. In G. A Bray (Ed.), *Recent Advances in Obesity Research* (Vol. 2). London: Newman, 1978.

GARTRELL, N. K., LORIAUX, L., & CHASE, T. N. Plasma testosterone in homosexual and heterosexual women. *American Journal of Psychiatry*, 1977, *134*, 1117–1119.

GASTOE, J. W. Physiologic reaction of Type A's to objective and subjective challenge. *Journal of Human Stress*, 1981, *7*, 16–20.

GATCHEL, R. J., GAAS, E., KING, J. M., & MCKINNEY, M. E. Effects of arousal level and below-zero habituation training on the spontaneous recovery and dishabituation of the orienting response. *Physiological Psychology*, 1977, *5*, 257–260.

GEBHARD, P. H. Sex differences in sexual responses. *Archives of Sexual Behavior*, 1973, *2*, 201–203.

GEEN, R. G. Effects of frustration, attack, and prior training in aggressiveness upon aggressive behavior. *Journal of Personality and Social Psychology*, 1968, *9*, 316–321.

GEEN, R. G. Observing violence in the mass media: Implications of basic research. In R. G. Geen & E. C. O'Neal (Eds.), *Perspectives on aggression*. New York: Academic Press, 1976.

GEEN, R. G. Effects of attack and uncontrollable noise on aggression. *Journal of Research in Personality*, 1978, *12*, 15–19.

GEEN, R. G. Preferred stimulation levels in introverts and extraverts: Effects on arousal and performance. *Journal of Personality and Social Psychology*, 1984, *46*, 1303–1312.

GEEN, R. G., & O'NEAL, E. C. Activation of cue-elicited aggression by general arousal. *Journal of Personality and Social Psychology*, 1969, *11*, 289–292.

GEEN, R. G., & QUANTY, M. B. The catharsis of aggression: An evaluation of a hypothesis. In L. Berkowitz (Ed.), *Advances in experimental social psychology* (Vol. 10). New York: Academic Press, 1977.

GEEN, R. G., STONNER, D., & SHOPE, G. L. The facilitation of aggression by aggression: Evidence against the catharsis hypothesis. *Journal of Personality and Social Psychology*, 1975, *31*, 721–726.

GEER, J. H., DAVISON, G. C., & GATCHEL, R. J. Reduction of stress in humans through nonveridical perceived control of aversive stimulation. *Journal of Personality and Social Psychology*, 1970, *16*, 731–738.

GEISELMAN, P. J., & NOVIN, D. Sugar infusion can enhance feeding. *Science*, 1982, *218*, 490–491.

GELLER, E., RITVO, E. R., FREEMAN, B. J., & YUWILER, A. Preliminary observations of the effect of flenfluramine on blood serotonin and symptoms in three autistic boys. *New England Journal of Medicine*, 1982, *307*, 165–169.

GERNER, R. H., POST, R. M., GILLIN, J. C., & BUNNEY, W. E. Biological and behavioral effects of one night's sleep deprivation in depressed patients and normals. *Journal of Psychiatric Research*, 1979, *15*, 21.

GESCHWIND, N., & BEHAN, P. Left-handedness: Association with immune disease, migraine, and developmental learning disorder. *Proceedings of the National Academy of Science*, 1982, *79*, 5097–5100.

GIBBS, F. A., & MALTBY, G. L. Effect on the electrical activity of the cortex of certain depressant and stimulant drugs—barbiturates, morphine, caffeine, Benzedrine, and adrenalin. *Journal of Pharmacology and Experimental Therapeutics*, 1943, *78*, 1–10.

GIESE, H., & SCHMIDT, A. *Student sexualität*. Hamburg: Rowohlt, 1968.

GILBERT, D. G. Paradoxical tranquillizing and emotion-reducing effects of nicotine. *Psychological Bulletin*, 1979, *86*, 643–661.

GILBERT, R. M. Drug abuse as an excessive behavior. In H. Shaeffer and M. E. Burglass, *Classic contributions in the addictions*. New York: Brunner/Mazel, 1981.

GILLBERG, M., & AKERSTEDT, T. Body temperature and sleep at different times of day. *Sleep*, 1982, *5*, 378–388.

GILLIN, J. C., & WYATT, R. J. Schizophrenia: Perchance a dream. *International Review of Neurobiology*, 1975, *17*, 297–342.

GLANZER, M. The role of stimulus satiation in spontaneous alternation. *Journal of Experimental Psychology*, 1953, *45*, 387–393.

GLASS, D. C. Stress, competition, and heart attacks. *Psychology Today*, December 1976, pp. 55–57; 134.

GLASS, D. C. *Behavior patterns, stress, and coronary disease*. Hillsdale, N.J.: Erlbaum, 1977. (a)

GLASS, D. C. Stress, behavior patterns, and coronary disease. *American Scientist*, 1977, *65*, 177–187. (b)

GLASS, D. C., & CARVER, C. S. Environmental stress and the Type A response. In A. Baum & J. E. Singer (Eds.), *Advances in environmental psychology* (Vol. 2): *Applications of personal control*. Hillsdale, N.J.: Erlbaum, 1980.

GLASS, D. C., & SINGER, J. E. *Urban stress*. New York: Academic Press, 1972.

GLASSER, W. *Positive addiction*. New York: Harper & Row, 1976.

GLAUBMAN, H., ORBACH, I., AVIRAM, O., FRIEDER, I., FRIEMAN, M., PELLED, O., & GLAUBMAN, R. REM deprivation and divergent thinking. *Psychophysiology*, 1978, *15*, 75–79.

GLAUBMAN, H., ORBACH, I., GROSS, Y., AVIRAM, O., FRIEDER, I., FRIEMAN, M., & PELLED, O. The effect of presleep focal attention load on subsequent sleep patterns. *Psychophysiology*, 1979, *16*, 467–470.

GLICKMAN, S. E., & SCHIFF, B. B. A biological theory of reinforcement. *Psychological Review*, 1967, *74*, 81–109.

GOEBEL, C., & JOVANOVIC, U. J. Effects of acoustic stimuli on motoricity during sleep in humans: Experimental studies on sleep disorders caused by noise. *Waking and Sleeping*, 1977, *1*(2), 181–188.

GOLDFARB, A. I., & BERMAN, S. Alcoholism as a psychosomatic disorder: I. Endocrine pathology of animals and man excessively exposed to alcohol; Its possible relation to behavioral pathology. *Quarterly Journal of Studies on Alcohol*, 1949, *10*, 415–429.

GOLDFOOT, D. A., WESTERBORG-VAN LOON, H., GROENVELD, W., & SLOB, A. K. Behavioral and physiological evidence of sexual climax in the female stump-tailed Macaque (*Macaca arctoides*). *Science*, 1980, *208*, 1477–1479.

GOLDMAN, J. K., SCHNATZ, J. D., BERNARDIS, L. L., & FROHMAN, L. A. Adipose tissue metabolism of weanling rats after destruction of ventromedial hypothalamic nuclei: Effect of hypophysectomy and growth hormone. *Metabolism: Clinical and Experimental*, 1970, *19*, 995–1005.

GOLDMAN, J. K., SCHNATZ, J. D., BERNARDIS, L. L., & FROHMAN, L. A. Effects of ventromedial hypothalamic destruction in rats with preexisting streptozotocin-induced diabetes. *Metabolism: Clinical and Experimental*, 1972, *21*, 132–136. (a)

GOLDMAN, J. K., SCHNATZ, J. D., BERNARDIS, L. L., & FROHMAN, L. A. The *vivo* and *in vitro* metabolism in hypothalamic obesity. *Diabetologia*, 1972, *8*, 160–164. (b)

GOLDMAN, R., JAFFA, M., & SCHACHTER, S. Yom Kippur, Air France, dormitory food, and eating behavior of obese and normal persons. *Journal of Personality and Social Psychology*, 1968, *10*, 117–123.

GOLDMAN, R. F., HAISMAN, M. F., BYNUM, G., HORTON, E. S., & SIMS, E. A. H. Experimental obesity in man: Metabolic rate in relation to dietary intake. In G. A. Bray, G. F. Cahill, E. S. Horton, H. A. Jordan, F. R. McCrumb, Jr., L. B. Salans, & E. A. H. Sims (Eds.), *Obesity in perspective*. Washington, D.C.: Government Printing Office, 1975.

GOLDSTEIN, A. Opioid peptides (endorphins) in pituitary and brain. *Science*, 1976, *193*, 1081–1086.

GOLDWATER, B. C., & LEWIS, J. Effects of arousal on habituation of the electrodermal orienting reflex. *Psychophysiology*, 1978, *15*, 221–225.

GOLEMAN, D. Meditation helps break the stress spiral. *Psychology Today*, February 1976, pp. 82–86; 93.

GOMEZ, J., & DALLY, P. Psychometric ratings in the assessment of progress in anorexia nervosa. *British Journal of Psychiatry*, 1980, *136*, 290–296.

GOOD, R. Frontalis muscle tension and sleep latency. *Psychophysiology*, 1975, *12*, 465–467.

GOODENOUGH, D. R. Field dependence. In H. London & J. E. Exner, Jr. (Eds.), *Dimensions of personality*. New York: Wiley, 1978.

GOODENOUGH, D. R., WITKIN, H. A., KOULACK, D., & COHEN, H. The effects of stress films on dream affect and on respiration and eye-movement activities during rapid-eye-movement sleep. *Psychophysiology*, 1975, *12*, 313–320.

GOODNER, C. J., & RUSSELL, J. A. Pancreas. In T. C. Ruch & H. D. Patton (Eds.), *Physiology and biophysics*. Philadelphia: Saunders, 1965.

GOODSITT, A. Letter: Anorexia nervosa. *Journal of the American Medical Association*, 1974, *230*, 372.

GORSUCH, R. L., & BUTLER, M. C. Initial drug abuse: A review of predisposing social psychological factors. *Psychological Bulletin*, 1976, *83*, 120–137.

GOY, R. W., & McEWEN, B. S. *Sexual differentiation of the brain*. Cambridge, Mass.: M.I.T. Press, 1980.

GRANT, T. N., & DOMINO, G. Masculinity-femininity in fathers of creative male adolescents. *Journal of Genetic Psychology*, 1976, *129*, 19–27.

GRAY, D. S., & GORZALKA, B. B. Adrenal steroid interactions in female sexual behavior: A review. *Psychoneuroendocrinology*, 1980, *5*, 157–175.

GRAY, S. W., & KLAUS, R. A. An experimental preschool program for culturally deprived children. *Child Development*, 1965, *36*, 887–898.

GRAY, S. W., & KLAUS, R. A. The Early Training Project and its general rationale. In R. D. Hess & R. M.

Bear (Eds.), *Early education: Current theory, research, and action*. Chicago: Aldine, 1968.

GRAY, S. W., & KLAUS, R. A. The Early Training Project: A seventh year report. *Child Development*, 1970, *41*, 909–924.

GRAYSTON, D. Music while you work. *Industrial Management*, 1974, *4*, 38–39.

GREEN, R. Variant forms of human sexual behavior. In C. R. Austin & R. V. Short (Eds.), *Reproduction in mammals* (Vol. 8: *Human sexuality*). Cambridge: Cambridge University Press, 1980.

GREENBERG, R., & PEARLMAN, C. A. Cutting the REM nerve: An approach to the adaptive role of REM sleep. *Perspectives in Biology and Medicine*, 1974, *17*, 513–521.

GREENBERG, R., PILLARD, R., & PEARLMAN, C. The effect of dream (stage REM) deprivation on adaptation to stress. *Psychosomatic Medicine*, 1972, *34*, 257–262.

GREENE, D., & LEPPER, M. R. Effects of extrinsic rewards on children's subsequent intrinsic interest. *Child Development*, 1974, *45*, 1141–1145.

GREENE, R., & DALTON, K. The premenstrual syndrome. *British Medical Journal*, 1953, *1*, 1007–1014.

GREENOUGH, W. T., VOLKMAR, F. R., & JURASKA, J. M. Effects of rearing complexity on dendritic branching in frontolateral and temporal cortex of the rat. *Experimental Neurology*, 1973, *41*, 371–378.

GREENOUGH, W. T., WEST, R. W., & DEVOOGD, T. J. Subsynaptic plate perforations: Changes with age and experience in the rat. *Science*, 1978, *202*, 1096–1098.

GREENWELL, J., & DENGERINK, H. A. The role of perceived versus actual attack in human physical aggression. *Journal of Personality and Social Psychology*, 1973, *26*, 66–71.

GREGORY, W. L. Locus of control for positive and negative outcomes. *Journal of Personality and Social Psychology*, 1978, *36*, 840–849.

GREISER, C., GREENBERG, R., & HARRISON, R. H. The adaptive function of sleep: The differential effects of sleep and dreaming on recall. *Journal of Abnormal Psychology*, 1972, *80*, 280–286.

GREIST, J. H., KLEIN, M. H., EISCHENS, R. R., FARIS, J., GURMAN, A. S., & MORGAN, W. P. Running as treatment for depression. *Comprehensive Psychiatry*, 1979, *20*, 41–54.

GRESHAM, S. C., AGNEW, H. W., JR., & WILLIAMS, R. L. The sleep of depressed patients. *Archives of General Psychiatry*, 1965, *13*, 503–507.

GRIFFIN, S. J., & TRINDER, J. Physical fitness, exercise, and human sleep. *Psychophysiology*, 1978, *15*, 447–450.

GRIFFITT, W. Environmental effects on interpersonal affective behavior: Ambient effective temperature and attraction. *Journal of Personality and Social Psychology*, 1970, *15*, 240–244.

GRIFFITT, W., & KAISER, D. L. Affect, sex guilt, gender, and the reward-punishing effects of erotic stimuli. *Journal of Personality and Social Psychology*, 1978, *36*, 850–858.

GRIFFITT, W., MAY, J., & VEITCH, R. Sexual stimulation and interpersonal behavior: Heterosexual evaluative responses, visual behavior, and physical proximity. *Journal of Personality and Social Psychology*, 1974, *30*, 367–377.

GRIFFITT, W., & VEITCH, R. Hot and crowded: Influence of population density and temperature on interpersonal affective behavior. *Journal of Personality and Social Psychology*, 1971, *17*, 92–98.

GRINSPOON, L., & HEDBLOM, P. *The speed culture: Amphetamine use and abuse in America.* Cambridge, Mass.: Harvard University Press, 1975.

GROSSMAN, S. P. *A textbook of physiological psychology.* New York: Wiley, 1967.

GROSVENOR, A., & LACK, L. C. The effect of sleep before or after learning on memory. *Sleep,* 1984, 7, 155–167.

GUY, R. F., RANKIN, B. A., & NORVELL, M. J. The relation of sex-role stereotyping to body image. *Journal of Psychology,* 1980, 105, 167–173.

GYLLENHAMMAR, P. G. How Volvo adapts work to people. *Harvard Business Review,* July-August 1977, pp. 102–113.

HADAWAY, P. F., ALEXANDER, B. K., COAMBS, R. B., & BEYERSTEIN, B. The effect of housing and gender on preference for morphine-sucrose solution in rats. *Psychopharmacology,* 1979, 66, 87–91.

HADDAD, N. F., McCULLERS, J. C., & MORAN, J. D. Satiation and the detrimental effects of material rewards. *Child Development,* 1976, 47, 547–551.

HAESSLER, H. A., & CRAWFORD, J. D. Fatty acid composition and metabolic activity of depot fat in experimental obesity. *American Journal of Physiology,* 1967, 213, 255–261.

HALL, J. B., & BROWN, D. A. Plasma glucose and lactic acid alterations in response to a stressful exam. *Biological Psychology,* 1979, 8, 179–188.

HALMI, K. A. Anorexia nervosa: Demographic and clinical features in 94 cases. *Psychosomatic Medicine,* 1974, 36, 18–25.

HALMI, K. A., DEKIRMENJIAN, H., DAVIS, J. M., CASPER, R., & GOLDBERG, S. Catecholamine metabolism in anorexia nervosa. *Archives of General Psychiatry,* 1978, 35, 458–460.

HALMI, K. A., FALK, J. R., & SCHWARTZ, E. Binge eating and vomiting: A survey of a college population. *Psychological Medicine,* 1981, 11, 697–706.

HALMI, K. A., POWERS, P., & CUNNINGHAM, S. Treatment of anorexia nervosa with behavior modification. *Archives of General Psychiatry,* 1975, 32, 93–96.

HAMBURG, D. A. Recent research on hormonal factors relevant to human aggressiveness. *International Social Science Journal,* 1971, 23, 36–47.

HAMILTON, P., HOCKEY, B., & REJMAN, M. The place of the concept of activation in human information processing theory: An integrative approach. In S. Dornič (Ed.), *Attention and performance VI.* Hillsdale, N.J.: Erlbaum, 1977.

HAMILTON, W. D. The genetic theory of social behavior: I and II. *Journal of Theoretical Biology,* 1964, 7, 1–52.

HAMMEN, C., MARKS, T., MAYOL, A., & DE MAYO, R. Depressive self-schemas, life stress, and vulnerability to depression. *Journal of Abnormal Psychology,* 1985, 94, 308–319.

HAMNER, W. C. Reinforcement theory and contingency management in organizational settings. In H. L. Tosi & W. C. Hamner (Eds.), *Organizational behavior and management: A contingency approach.* Chicago: St. Clair Press, 1974.

HAMNER, W. C., & HAMNER, E. P. Behavior modification on the bottom line. *Organizational Dynamics,* Spring 1976, pp. 6–8.

HANSEN, J. R., STOA, K. F., BLIX, A. S., & URSIN, H. Urinary levels of epinephrine and norepinephrine in parachutist trainees. In H. Ursin, E. Baade, and S. Levine (Eds.), *Psychobiology of stress: A study of coping men.* New York: Academic Press, 1978.

HANUSA, B. H., & SCHULZ, R. Attributional mediators of learned helplessness. *Journal of Personality and Social Psychology,* 1977, 35, 602–611.

HARLOW, H. F. Mice, monkeys, men, and motives. *Psychological Review,* 1953, 60, 23–32.

HARLOW, H. F. Heterosexual affectional systems in monkeys. *American Psychologist,* 1962, 17, 1–9.

HARLOW, H. F., & HARLOW, M. K. Social deprivation in monkeys. *Scientific American,* November 1962, pp. 137–146.

HARLOW, H. F., & HARLOW, M. K. Effects of various mother-infant relationships on rhesus monkey behaviors. In B. M. Foss (Ed.), *Determinants of infant behavior* (Vol. 4). London: Methuen, 1969.

HARMON, D. K., MASUDA, M., & HOLMES, T. H. The Social Readjustment Rating Scale: A cross-cultural study of Western Europeans and Americans. *Journal of Psychosomatic Research,* 1970, 14, 391–400.

HARRIMAN, A. E. The effect of a preoperative preference for sugar over salt upon compensatory salt selection by adrenalectomized rats. *Journal of Nutrition,* 1955, 57, 271–276.

HARRINGTON, D. M., & ANDERSEN, S. M. Creativity, masculinity, femininity, and three models of psychological androgyny. *Journal of Personality and Social Psychology,* 1981, 41, 744–757.

HARTMANN, E. L. *The functions of sleep.* New Haven, Conn.: Yale University Press, 1973.

HARTMANN, E. L. The functions of sleep. *Annual of Psychoanalysis,* 1974, 2, 271–289.

HARTMANN, E. L., BAEKELAND, F., & ZWILLING, G. R. Psychological differences between long and short sleepers. *Archives of General Psychiatry,* 1972, 26, 463–468.

HARTMANN, E. L., & STERN, W. C. Desynchronized sleep deprivation: Learning deficit and its reversal by increased catecholamines. *Physiology and Behavior,* 1972, 8, 585–587.

HARTSE, K. M., ROTH, T., & ZORICK, F. J. Daytime sleepiness and daytime wakefulness: The effect of instruction. *Sleep,* 1982, 5, S107–S118.

HASELTINE, F. P., & OHNO, S. Mechanisms of gonadal differentiation. *Science,* 1981, 211, 1272–1278.

HASHIM, S. A., & VAN ITALLIE, T. B. Studies in normal and obese subjects with a monitored food dispensory device. *Annals of the New York Academy of Science,* 1965, 131, 654–661.

HAWKE, C. C. Castration and sex crimes. *American Journal of Mental Deficiency,* 1950, 55, 220–226.

HAWKINS, R. C., & CLEMENTS, P. F. Development and construct validation of a self-report measure of binge eating tendencies. *Addictive Behaviors,* 1980, 5, 219–226.

HAWKINS, R. C., JR., TURELL, S., & JACKSON, L. J. Desirable and undesirable masculine and feminine traits in relation to students' dietary tendencies and body image dissatisfaction. *Sex Roles,* 1983, 9, 705–724.

HAYWOOD, H. C. Individual difference in motivational orientations: A trait approach. In H. Day, D. E. Berlyne, & D. E. Hunt (Eds.), *Intrinsic motivation: A new direction in education.* Toronto: Holt, Rinehart & Winston, 1971.

HEATH, R. G. Electrical self-stimulation of the brain in man. *American Journal of Psychiatry,* 1963, 120, 571–577.

HEATHER, N., WINTON, M., & ROLLNICK, S. An empirical test of "a cultural delusion of alcoholics." *Psychological Reports,* 1982, 50, 379–382.

HEBB, D. O. *The organization of behavior.* New York: Wiley, 1949.

HEBB, D. O. Drive and the C.N.S. (conceptual nervous system). *Psychological Review*, 1955, *62*, 243–254.

HECKHAUSEN, H. *The anatomy of achievement motivation.* New York: Academic Press, 1967.

HEIDER, F. Attitudes and cognitive organization. *Journal of Psychology*, 1946, *21*, 107–112.

HEIDER, F. *The psychology of interpersonal relations.* New York: Wiley, 1958.

HEIDER, F. A conversation with Fritz Heider. In J. H. Harvey, W. J. Ickes, & R. F. Kidd (Eds.), *New directions in attribution research* (Vol. 1). Hillsdale, N.J.: Erlbaum, 1976.

HEILBRUN, A. B., JR. Measurement of masculine and feminine sex role identities as independent dimensions. *Journal of Consulting and Clinical Psychology*, 1976, *44*, 183–190.

HEILMAN, M. E., & SARUWATARI, L. R. When beauty is beastly: The effects of appearance and sex on evaluations of job applicants for managerial and non-managerial jobs. *Organizational Behavior and Human Performance*, 1979, *23*, 360–372.

HEIMAN, J. R. Women's sexual arousal. *Psychology Today*, April 1975, pp. 91–94.

HEIMAN, J. R. A psychophysiological exploration of sexual arousal patterns in females and males. *Psychophysiology*, 1977, *14*, 266–274.

HEIMBURGER, R. F., WHITLOCK, C. C., & KALSBECK, J. E. Stereotaxic amygdalotomy for epilepsy with aggressive behavior. *Journal of the American Medical Association*, 1966, *198*, 165–169.

HELLER, D. *Children of holocaust survivors: The second generation effect.* Unpublished Bachelor of Arts thesis, Harvard College, Department of Psychology and Social Relations, 1979.

HELLER, J. F., GROFF, B. D., & SOLOMON, S. H. Toward an understanding of crowding: The role of physical interaction. *Journal of Personality and Social Psychology*, 1977, *35*, 183–190.

HELMREICH, R. L., BEANE, W. E., LUCKER, G. W., & SPENCE, J. T. Achievement motivation and scientific attainment. *Personality and Social Psychology Bulletin*, 1978, *4*, 222–226.

HELMREICH, R. L., & SPENCE, J. T. The Work and Family Orientation Questionnaire: An objective instrument to assess components of achievement motivation and attitudes toward family and career. *JSAS Catalog of Selected Documents in Psychology*, 1978, *8*, 35.

HELMREICH, R. L., SPENCE, J. T., BEANE, W. E., LUCKER, G. W., & MATTHEWS, K. A. Making it in academic psychology: Demographic and personality correlates of attainment. *Journal of Personality and Social Psychology*, 1980, *39*, 896–908.

HELMREICH, R., STAPP, J., & ERVIN, C. The Texas Social Behavior Inventory (TSBI): An objective measure of self-esteem or social competence. *JSAS Catalog of Selected Documents in Psychology*, 1974, *4*, 79.

HELSON, R. Personality of women with imaginative and artistic interests: The role of masculinity, originality, and other characteristics in their creativity. *Journal of Personality*, 1966, *34*, 1–25.

HELSON, R. Women mathematicians and the creative personality. *Journal of Consulting and Clinical Psychology*, 1971, *36*, 210–220.

HELSON, R. Creativity in women. In J. Sherman & F. Denmark (Eds.), *The psychology of women: Future directions in research.* New York: Psychological Dimensions, 1978.

HERBERG, L. J., STEPHENS, D. N., & FRANKLIN, K. B. J. Catecholamines and self-stimulation: Evidence suggesting a reinforcing role for noradrenaline and a motivating role for dopamine. *Pharmacology, Biochemistry, and Behavior*, 1976, *4*, 575–582.

HERMAN, C. P. External and internal cues as determinants of smoking behavior of light and heavy smokers. *Journal of Personality and Social Psychology*, 1974, *30*, 664–672.

HERMAN, C. P., & MACK, D. Restrained and unrestrained eating. *Journal of Personality*, 1975, *43*, 646–660.

HERMAN, C. P., & POLIVY, J. *Breaking the diet habit.* New York: Basic Books, 1983.

HERMAN, C. P., & POLIVY, J. A boundary model for the regulation of eating. In A. J. Stunkard & E. Stellar (Eds.), *Eating and its disorders.* New York: Raven Press, 1984.

HERMANN, M. G. Assessing the personalities of Soviet Politburo members. *Personality and Social Psychology Bulletin*, 1980, *6*, 332–352.

HERRENKOHL, L. Prenatal stress reduces fertility and fecundity in female offspring. *Science*, 1979, *206*, 1097–1099.

HERSEN, M., & BELLACK, A. S. Assessment of social skills. In A. R. Ciminero, K. S. Calhoun, & H. E. Adams (Eds.), *Handbook of behavioral assessment.* New York: Wiley, 1977.

HERTZ, M. M., PAULSON, O. B., BARRY, D. I., ET AL. Insulin increases transfer across the blood/brain barrier in man. *Journal of Clinical Investigation*, 1981, *67*, 595–604.

HERZOG, D. B. Bulimia: The secretive syndrome. *Psychosomatics*, 1982, *23*, 481–487. (a)

HERZOG, D. B. Bulimia in the adolescent. *American Journal of Diseases of Children*, 1982, *136*, 985–989. (b)

HESS, W. R. Stammganglien-reizversuche. *Berichte über die Gesamte Physiologie und Experimentelle Pharmakologie*, 1928, *42*, 554.

HESS, W. R., & BRUGGER, M. Das subkortikale zentrum der afektiven abwehrreaktion. *Helvetica Physiologica et Pharmacologia Acta*, 1943, *1*, 33–52.

HINDE, R. A., & STEVENSON-HINDE, J. (EDS.). *Constraints on learning.* New York: Academic Press, 1973.

HINES, M. Prenatal gonadal hormones and sex differences in human behavior. *Psychological Bulletin*, 1982, *92*, 56–80.

HIROTO, D. S. Locus of control and learned helplessness. *Journal of Experimental Psychology*, 1974, *102*, 187–193.

HIROTO, D. S., & SELIGMAN, M. E. P. Generality of learned helplessness in man. *Journal of Personality and Social Psychology*, 1975, *31*, 311–327.

HIRSCH, J., KNITTLE, J. L., & SALANS, L. B. Cell lipid content and cell number in obese and nonobese human adipose tissue. *Journal of Clinical Investigation*, 1966, *45*, 1023.

HIRSCHMAN, R., & HAWK, G. Emotional responsivity to nonveridical heart rate feedback. *Journal of Research in Personality*, 1978, *12*, 235–242.

HO, R., & ZEMAITIS, R. Concern over the negative consequences of success. *Australian Journal of Psychology*, 1981, *33*, 19–28.

HOCKEY, G. R. J., DAVIES, S., & GRAY, M. M. Forgetting as a function of sleep at different times of day. *Quarterly Journal of Experimental Psychology*, 1972, *24*, 386–393.

HOFFMAN, L. W. Early childhood experiences and women's achievement motives. *Journal of Social Issues*, 1972, *28*, 129–155.

HOFFMAN, L. W. Fear of success in males and females:

1965 and 1971. *Journal of Consulting and Clinical Psychology,* 1974, *42,* 353–358.

HOFFMAN, L. W. Fear of success in 1965 and 1974: A follow-up study. *Journal of Consulting and Clinical Psychology,* 1977, *45,* 310–321.

HOFFMAN, M. Homosexual. *Psychology Today,* July 1969, pp. 43–45; 70.

HOFFMAN, M. Homosexuality. In F. A. Beach (Ed.), *Human sexuality in four perspectives.* Baltimore: Johns Hopkins University Press, 1976.

HOFFMAN, M. L. Developmental synthesis of affect and cognition and its implications for altruistic motivation. *Developmental Psychology,* 1975, *11,* 607–622.

HOKANSON, J. E. Psychophysiological evaluation of the catharsis hypothesis. In E. I. Megargee & J. E. Hokanson (Eds.), *The dynamics of aggression: Individual, group and international analyses.* New York: Harper & Row, 1970.

HOKANSON, J. E., & BURGESS, M. The effects of three types of aggression on vascular processes. *Journal of Abnormal and Social Psychology,* 1962, *64,* 446–449. (a)

HOKANSON, J. E., & BURGESS, M. The effects of status, type of frustration, and aggression on vascular processes. *Journal of Abnormal and Social Psychology,* 1962, *65,* 232–237. (b)

HOKANSON, J. E., BURGESS, M., & COHEN, M. F. Effects of displaced aggression on systolic blood pressure. *Journal of Abnormal and Social Psychology,* 1963, *67,* 214–218.

HOKANSON, J. E., DEGOOD, D. E., FORREST, M. S., & BRITTAIN, T. M. Availability of avoidance behaviors in modulating vascular-stress responses. *Journal of Personality and Social Psychology,* 1971, *19,* 60–68.

HOKANSON, J. E., & EDELMAN, R. Effects of three social responses on vascular processes. *Journal of Personality and Social Psychology,* 1966, *3,* 442–447.

HOKANSON, J. E., & SHETLER, S. The effect of overt aggression on physiological arousal. *Journal of Abnormal and Social Psychology,* 1961, *63,* 446–448.

HOKANSON, J. E., WILLERS, K. R., & KOROPSAK, E. The modification of autonomic responses during aggressive interchange. *Journal of Personality,* 1968, *36,* 386–404.

HOLDEN, C. Genes, personality, and alcoholism. *Psychology Today,* January 1985, 38–44.

HOLMES, D. S. Effects of overt aggression on level of physiological arousal. *Journal of Personality and Social Psychology,* 1966, *4,* 189–194.

HOLMES, D. S. Meditation and somatic arousal reduction. *American Psychologist,* 1984, *39,* 1–10.

HOLMES, J. G., MILLER, D. T., & LERNER, M. J. Symbolic threats in helping situations: The *"exchange fiction."* Unpublished manuscript, University of Waterloo, 1974.

HOLMES, T. H., & RAHE, R. H. The Social Readjustment Rating Scale. *Journal of Psychosomatic Research,* 1967, *11,* 213–218.

HOOKER, E. The adjustment of the male overt homosexual. *Journal of Projective Techniques,* 1957, *21,* 18–31.

HOON, P. W., WINCZE, J. P., & HOON, E. F. Physiological assessment of sexual arousal in women. *Psychophysiology,* 1976, *13,* 196–204.

HOON, P. W., WINCZE, J. P., & HOON, E. F. A test of reciprocal inhibition: Are anxiety and sexual arousal in women mutually inhibitory? *Journal of Abnormal Psychology,* 1977, *86,* 65–74.

HORNE, J. A. The effects of exercise upon sleep: A critical review. *Biological Psychology,* 1981, *12,* 241–290.

HORNE, J. A., & WALMSLEY, B. Daytime visual load and the effects upon human sleep. *Psychophysiology,* 1976, *13,* 115–120.

HORNER, M. S. Toward an understanding of achievement-related conflicts in women. *Journal of Social Issues,* 1972, *28,* 157–175.

HORNER, M. S. The measurement and behavioral implications of fear of success in women. In J. W. Atkinson & J. O. Raynor (Eds.), *Motivation and achievement.* New York: Wiley, 1974. (a)

HORNER, M. S. Performance of men in noncompetitive and interpersonal competitive achievement-oriented situations. In J. W. Atkinson & J. O. Raynor (Eds.), *Motivation and achievement.* New York: Wiley, 1974. (b)

HOROWITZ, M. J. Psychological response to serious life events. In V. Hamilton & D. Warburton (Eds.), *Human stress and cognition: An information processing approach.* New York: Wiley, 1979.

HORVATH, F. S. The effect of selected variables on interpretation of polygraph records. *Journal of Applied Psychology,* 1977, *62,* 127–136.

HOWLEY, E. T. The effect of different intensities of exercise on the excretion of epinephrine and norepinephrine. *Medicine and Science in Sports,* 1976, *8,* 219–222.

HOYENGA, K. B., & HOYENGA, K. T. *The question of sex differences: Psychological, cultural, and biological issues.* Boston: Little, Brown, 1979.

HOYT, M. F., & SINGER, J. L. Psychological effects of REM ("dream") deprivation upon waking mentation. In A. M. Arkin, J. S. Antrobus, & S. J. Ellman (Eds.), *The mind in sleep: Psychology and psychophysiology.* Hillsdale, N.J.: Erlbaum, 1978.

HUBA, G. J., NEWCOMB, M. D., & BENTLER, P. M. Comparison of canonical correlation and interbattery factor analysis on sensation seeking and drug use domains. *Applied Psychological Measurement,* 1981, *5,* 291–306.

HUBEL, D. H. The visual cortex of normal and deprived monkeys. *American Scientist,* 1979, *67,* 532–543.

HUBEL, D. H., & WIESEL, T. N. Brain mechanisms of vision. *Scientific American,* September 1979, pp. 150–162.

HUGDAHL, K., FREDRIKSON, M., & ÖHMAN, A. "Preparedness" and "arousability" as determinants of electrodermal conditioning. *Behavior Research and Therapy,* 1977, *15*(4), 345–353.

HULL, C. L. *Principles of behavior.* New York: Appleton-Century-Crofts, 1943.

HULL, J. G., & BOND, C. F. Social and behavioral consequences of alcohol consumption and expectancy: A meta-analysis. *Psychological Bulletin,* 1986, *99,* 347–360.

HUMPHRIES, C., CARVER, C. S., & NEUMANN, P. G. Cognitive characteristics of the Type A coronary-prone behavior pattern. *Journal of Personality and Social Psychology,* 1983, *44,* 177–187.

HUNT, J. McV. Motivation inherent in information processing and action. In O. J. Harvey (Ed.), *Motivation and social interaction: Cognitive determinants.* New York: Ronald Press, 1963.

HUTT, C. Exploration and play in children. In P. A. Jewell & C. Loizos (Eds.), *Play, exploration, and territory in mammals.* Symposia of the Zoological

Society of London, No. 18. New York: Academic Press, 1966.

HUTT, C., & VAIZEY, M. Differential effects of group density on social behavior. *Nature*, 1966, *209*, 1371–1372.

HUXLEY, J. S. *Evolution: The modern synthesis*. London: Allen & Unwin, 1942.

ICKES, W. J., & KIDD, R. F. An attributional analysis of helping behavior. In J. H. Harvey, W. J. Ickes, & R. F. Kidd (Eds.), *New directions in attributional research* (Vol. 1). Hillsdale, N.J.: Erlbaum, 1976.

ISEN, A. M. Success, failure, attention, and reaction to others: The warm glow of success. *Journal of Personality and Social Psychology*, 1970, *15*, 294–301.

ISEN, A. M., HORN, N., & ROSENHAN, D. L. Effects of success and failure on children's generosity. *Journal of Personality and Social Psychology*, 1973, *27*, 239–247.

ISRAEL, N. R. Leveling-sharpening and anticipatory cardiac response. *Psychosomatic Medicine*, 1969, *31*, 499–509.

IVEY, M. E., & BARDWICK, J. M. Patterns of affective fluctuation in the menstrual cycle. *Psychosomatic Medicine*, 1968, *30*, 336–345.

IZARD, C. E. &. TOMKINS, S. S. Affect and behavior: Anxiety as negative affect. In C. D. Spielberger (Ed.), *Anxiety and behavior*. New York: Academic Press, 1966.

JACOBS, B. L. How hallucinogenic drugs work. *American Scientist*, 1987, *75*, 386–392.

JACOBS, B. L., & TRULSON, M. E. Mechanisms of action of LSD. *American Scientist*, 1979, *67*, 396–404.

JACOBSON, R. C., & ZINBERG, N. E. *The social basis of drug prevention*. Publication SS-5. Washington, D.C.: Drug Abuse Council, 1975.

JAFFE, Y., MALAMUTH, N., FEINGOLD, J., & FESHBACH, S. Sexual arousal and behavioral aggression. *Journal of Personality and Social Psychology*, 1974, *30*, 759–764.

JAMES, W. What is an emotion? *Mind*, 1884, *9*, 188–205.

JANOFF-BULMAN, R. Characterological versus behavioral self-blame: Inquiries into depression and rape. *Journal of Personality and Social Psychology*, 1979, *37*, 1798–1809.

JASPER, H. H. Electroencephalography. In W. Penfield & T. C. Erickson (Eds.), *Epilepsy and cerebral localization*. Springfield, Ill.: Charles C Thomas, 1941.

JEFFREY, D. B., & KATZ, R. G. *Take it off and keep it off*. Englewood Cliffs, N.J.: Prentice-Hall, 1977.

JESSOR, R. Marijuana: A review of recent psychosocial research. In R. L. Dupont, A. Goldstein, & J. O'Donnell (Eds.), *Handbook on drug abuse*. Rockville, Md.: National Institute on Drug Abuse, 1979.

JEVNING, R., WILSON, A. F., & DAVIDSON, J. M. Adrenocortical activity during meditation. *Hormones and Behavior*, 1978, *10*, 54–60.

JOHANSSON, G., COLLINS, A., & COLLINS, V. P. Male and female psychoneuroendocrine response to examination stress: A case report. *Motivation and Emotion*, 1983, *7*, 1–9.

JOHNSON, J. H., & SARASON, I. G. Life stress, depression, and anxiety: Internal-external control as a moderator variable. *Journal of Psychosomatic Research*, 1978, *22*, 205–208.

JOHNSON, J. H., & SARASON, I. G. Moderator variables in life stress research. In I. Sarason and C. Spielberger (Eds.), *Stress and anxiety* (Vol. 6, pp. 151–167). New York: Halstead, 1979.

JOHNSON, L. C., TOWNSEND, R. E., & WILSON, M. R. Habituation during sleeping and waking. *Psychophysiology*, 1975, *12*, 574–584.

JOUVET, M. The states of sleep. *Scientific American*, February 1967, pp. 62–72.

JOYCE, C. R. B. Cannabis. *British Journal of Hospital Medicine*, 1970, *4*, 162–166.

JULIEN, R. M. *A primer of drug action*. San Francisco: W. H. Freeman, 1975.

KAGAN, J. Psychology of sex differences. In F. A. Beach (Ed.), *Human sexuality in four perspectives*. Baltimore: Johns Hopkins University Press, 1976.

KAHN, R. L. Stress: From 9 to 5. *Psychology Today*, September 1969, pp. 34–38.

KAHN, R. L., WOLFE, D. M., QUINN, R. P., SNOEK, J. D., & ROSENTHAL, R. A. *Organizational stress: Studies in role conflict and ambiguity*. New York: Wiley, 1964.

KAHNEMAN, D. *Attention and effort*. Englewood Cliffs, N.J.: Prentice-Hall, 1973.

KALANT, O. J. *The amphetamines: Toxicity and addiction* (2nd ed.). Toronto: University of Toronto Press, 1973.

KALES, A., BIXLER, E. O., SOLDATOS, C. R., VELA-BUENO, A., CALDWELL, A. B., & CADIEUX, R. J. Role of sleep apnea and nocturnal myoclonus. *Psychosomatics*, 1982, *23*, 589–595, 600.

KALIN, R., McCLELLAND, D. C., & KAHN, M. The effects of male social drinking on fantasy. *Journal of Personality and Social Psychology*, 1965, *1*, 441–452.

KALLMANN, F. J. A. A comparative twin study on the genetic aspects of male homosexuality. *Journal of Nervous and Mental Disease*, 1952, *115*, 283–298.

KANDEL, D. B. Marijuana users in young adulthood. *Archives of General Psychiatry*, 1984, *41*, 200–209.

KANDEL, D. B., KESSLER, R. C., & MARGULIES, R. Z. Antecedents of adolescent initiation into stages of drug use: A developmental analysis. In D. B. Kandel (Ed.), *Longitudinal research on drug abuse*. Washington, D.C.: Hemisphere, 1978

KANFER, F. H. Personal control, social control, and altruism. *American Psychologist*, 1979, *34*, 231–239.

KARABENICK, S. A. Fear of success, achievement and affiliation dispositions and the performance of men and women under individual and competitive conditions. *Journal of Personality*, 1977, *45*, 117–149.

KARABENICK, S. A., MARSHALL, J. M., & KARABENICK, J. D. Effects of fear of success, fear of failure, type of opponent, and feedback on female achievement performance. *Journal of Research in Personality*, 1976, *10*, 369–385.

KARLI, P., & VERGNES, M. Rôle des différentes composantes du complexe nucléaire amygdalien dans la facilitation de l'aggressivité interspécifique du rat. *Comptes Rendus des Séances de la Société de Biologie*, 1965, *159*, 754.

KATZ, J. Hormonal abnormality found in patients with anorexia nervosa. *Journal of the American Medical Association*, 1975, *232*, 9–11.

KAZDIN, A. E. *History of behavior modification: Experimental foundations of contemporary research*. Baltimore: University Park Press, 1978.

KEESEY, R. E., & POWLEY, T. L. Hypothalamic regulation of body weight. *American Scientist*, 1975, *63*, 558–565.

KELLER, M. The great Jewish drink mystery. *British Journal of Addiction.* 1970, *64*, 287–295.

KELLY, J. A., & WORRELL, L. Parent behaviors related to masculine, feminine, and androgynous sex role orientations. *Journal of Consulting and Clinical Psychology*, 1976, *44*, 843–851.

KEMLER, D., & SHEPP, B. The learning and transfer of dimensional relevance and irrelevance in children. *Journal of Experimental Psychology*, 1971, *90*, 120–127.

KENRICK, D. T., BAUMANN, D. J., & CIALDINI, R. B. A step in the socialization of altruism as hedonism: Effects of negative mood on children's generosity under public and private conditions. *Journal of Personality and Social Psychology*, 1979, *37*, 747–755.

KENRICK, D. T., & CIALDINI, R. B. Romantic attraction: Misattribution versus reinforcement explanations. *Journal of Personality and Social Psychology*, 1977, *35*, 381–391.

KENRICK, D. T., & JOHNSON, G. A. Interpersonal attraction in aversive environments: A problem for the classical conditioning paradigm? *Journal of Personality and Social Psychology*, 1979, *37*, 572–579.

KEPLER, E. J., & MOERSCH, F. P. The psychiatric manifestations of hypoglycemia. *American Journal of Psychiatry*, 1937, *94*, 89–110.

KERBER, K. W., & COLES, M. G. H. The role of perceived physiological activity in affective judgments. *Journal of Experimental Social Psychology*, 1978, *14*, 419–433.

KESSLER, S., & MOOS, R. H. The XYY karyotype and criminality: A review. *Journal of Psychiatric Research*, 1970, *7*, 153–170.

KEYS, A. B., BROZEK, J., HENSCHEL, A., MICHELSEN, O., & TAYLOR, H. L. *The biology of human starvation.* Minneapolis: University of Minnesota Press, 1950.

KIDD, R. F., & BERKOWITZ, L. Effect of dissonance arousal on helpfulness. *Journal of Personality and Social Psychology*, 1976, *33*, 613–622.

KIESLER, C. A., & PALLAK, M. S. Arousal properties of dissonance manipulations. *Psychological Bulletin*, 1976, *83*, 1014–1025.

KIMBLE, C. E., FITZ, D., & ONORAD, J. R. Effectiveness of counteraggression strategies in reducing interactive aggression by males. *Journal of Personality and Social Psychology*, 1977, *35*, 272–278.

KINSEY, A. C., POMEROY, W. B., & MARTIN, C. E. *Sexual behavior in the human male.* Philadelphia: Saunders, 1948.

KINSEY, A. C., POMEROY, W. B., & MARTIN, C. E. *Sexual behavior in the human female.* Philadelphia: Saunders, 1953.

KLAUSNER, S. Z. The intermingling of pain and pleasure: The stress-seeking personality in its social context. In S. Z. Klausner (Ed.), *Why man takes chances: Studies in stress-seeking.* Garden City, N.Y.: Anchor Books (Doubleday), 1968.

KLAUSNER, S. Z., FOULKES, E. F., & MOORE, M. H. *The Inupiat: Economics and alcohol on the Alaskan North Slope.* Philadelphia: Center for Research on the Acts of Man, University of Pennsylvania, 1980.

KLECK, R. E., & RUBENSTEIN, C. Physical attractiveness, perceived attitude similarity, and interpersonal attraction in an opposite-sex encounter. *Journal of Personality and Social Psychology*, 1975, *31*, 107–114.

KLEIN, R., & ARMITAGE, R. Rhythms in human performance: 1½ hour oscillation in cognitive style. *Science*, 1979, *204*, 1326–1328.

KLEIN, R. F., BOGDONOFF, M. D., ESTES, E. H., JR., & SHAW, D. M. Analysis of the factors affecting the resting FAA level in normal man. *Circulation*, 1960, *20*, 772.

KLEINGINNA, P. R., JR., & KLEINGINNA, A. M. A categorized list of motivation definitions, with suggestions for a consensual definition. *Motivation and Emotion*, 1981, *5*, 263–291. (a)

KLEINGINNA, P. R., JR., & KLEINGINNA, A. M. A categorized list of emotion definitions, with suggestions for a consensual definition. *Motivation and Emotion*, 1981, *5*, 345–379. (b)

KLINE, D. The anatomy of addiction. *Equinox*, September/October 1985, pp. 77–86.

KLINGER, E. Consequences of commitment to and disengagement from incentives. *Psychological Review*, 1975, *82*, 1–25.

KLOPFER, P. Mother love: What turns it on. *American Scientist*, 1971, *59*, 404–407.

KLÜVER, H., & BUCY, P. C. Psychic blindness and other symptoms following bilateral temporal lobectomy in rhesus monkeys. *American Journal of Physiology*, 1937, *119*, 352–353.

KLÜVER, H., & BUCY, P. C. An analysis of certain effects of bilateral temporal lobectomy in the rhesus monkey with special reference to "psychic blindness." *Journal of Psychology*, 1938, *5*, 33–54.

KLÜVER, H., & BUCY, P. C. Preliminary analysis of the function of the temporal lobe in monkeys. *Archives of Neurology and Psychiatry*, 1939, *42*, 979–1000.

KNOTT, P. D., LASATER, L., & SHUMAN, R. Aggression-guilt and conditionability for aggressiveness. *Journal of Personality*, 1974, *42*, 332–344.

KOBASA, S. C. Stressful life events, personality, and health: An inquiry into hardiness. *Journal of Personality and Social Psychology*, 1979, *37*, 1–11. (a)

KOBASA, S. C. Personality and resistance to illness. *American Journal of Community Psychology*, 1979, *7*, 413–423. (b)

KOBASA, S. C. Commitment and coping in stress among lawyers. *Journal of Personality and Social Psychology*, 1982, *42*, 707–717.

KOBASA, S. C., MADDI, S. R., & KAHN, S. Hardiness and health: A prospective study. *Journal of Personality and Social Psychology*, 1982, *42*, 168–177.

KOBASA, S. C., & PUCCETTI, M. C. Personality and social resources in stress-resistance. *Journal of Personality and Social Psychology*, 1983, *45*, 839–850.

KOLATA, G. Brain receptors for appetite discovered. *Science*, 1982, *218*, 460–461.

KOLB, L. *Drug addiction, a medical problem.* Springfield, Ill.: Charles C Thomas, 1962.

KONEČNI, V. J. Annoyance, type and duration of postannoyance activity, and aggression: The cathartic effect. *Journal of Experimental Psychology: General*, 1975, *104*, 76–102. (a)

KONEČNI, V. J. The mediation of aggressive behavior: Arousal level versus anger and cognitive labeling. *Journal of Personality and Social Psychology*, 1975, *32*, 706–712. (b)

KOOPMANS, H. S. Satiety signals from the gastrointestinal tract. *American Journal of Clinical Nutrition*, 1985, *42*, 1044–1049.

KOULACK, D., PREVOST, F., & DE KONINCK, J. Sleep, dreaming, and adaptation to a stressful intellectual activity. *Sleep*, 1985, *8*, 244–253.

KOVACS, M., RUSH, A. J., BECK, A. T., & HOLLON, S. D. Depressed outpatients treated with cognitive therapy or pharmacotherapy. *Archives of Psychiatry*, 1981, *38*, 33–39.

KRAINES, S. H. *Mental depressives and their treatment.* New York: Macmillan, 1957.

KRAMER, M., CZAYA, J., ARAND, D., & ROTH, T. *The development of psychological content across the REMP.* Paper presented at the meeting of the Association for the Psychophysiological Study of Sleep, Jackson Hole, Wyo., 1974.

KRANTZ, D. S., & MANUCK, S. B. Acute psychophysiologic reactivity and risk of cardiovascular disease. *Psychological Bulletin*, 1984, *96*, 435–464.

KRANTZ, D. S., & SCHULZ, R. A model of life crisis, control, and health outcomes: Cardiac rehabilitation and relocation of the elderly. In A. Baum & J. E. Singer (Eds.), *Advances in environmental psychology* (Vol. 2: *Applications of personal control.*) Hillsdale, N.J.: Erlbaum, 1980.

KREBS, D. L. Altruism—An examination of the concept and a review of the literature. *Psychological Bulletin*, 1970, *73*, 258–302.

KRECH, D., ROSENZWEIG, M., & BENNETT, E. Environmental impoverishment, social isolation, and changes in brain chemistry and anatomy. *Physiology and Behavior*, 1966, *1*, 99–104.

KREUZ, L. E., & ROSE, R. M. Assessment of aggressive behavior and plasma testosterone in a young criminal population. *Psychosomatic Medicine*, 1972, *34*, 321–332.

KRUGLANSKI, A. W., ALON, S., & LEWIS, T. Retrospective misattribution and task enjoyment. *Journal of Experimental Social Psychology*, 1972, *8*, 493–501.

KRYTER, K. D. *The effects of noise on man.* New York: Academic Press, 1970.

KUHN, D. Z., MADSEN, C. H., & BECKER. W. C. Effects of exposure to an aggressive model and "frustration" on children's aggressive behavior. *Child Development*, 1967, *38*, 739–745.

LACEY, B. C., & LACEY, J. I. Two-way communication between the heart and the brain: Significance of time within the cardiac cycle. *American Psychologist*, 1978, *33*, 99–113.

LACEY, J. I., KAGAN, J., LACEY, B. C., & MOSS, H. A. The visceral level: Situational determinants and behavioral correlates of autonomic response. In P. Knapp (Ed.), *Expression of the emotions in man.* New York: International Universities Press, 1963.

LACEY, J. I., & LACEY, B. C. Some autonomic-central nervous system interrelationships. In P. Black (Ed.), *Physiological correlates of emotion.* New York: Academic Press, 1970.

LAFERLA, J. J., ANDERSON, D. L., & SCHALCH, D. S. Psychoendocrine response to sexual arousal in human males. *Psychosomatic Medicine*, 1978, *40*, 166–172.

LAGERSPETZ, K. Studies on the aggressive behavior of mice. *Annales Academiae Scientiarum Fennicae*, Series B, 1964, *131*, 1–131.

LANG, A. R., SEARLES, J., LAUERMAN, R., & ADESSO, V. Expectancy, alcohol, and sex guilt as determinants of interest in and reaction to sexual stimuli. *Journal of Abnormal Psychology*, 1980, *89*, 644–653.

LANGE, C. *The emotions.* Baltimore: Williams & Wilkins, 1922. (Originally published, 1885.)

LANGE, J. D., BROWN, W. A., WINCZE, J. P., & ZWICK, W. Serum testosterone concentration and penile tumescence changes in men. *Hormones and Behavior*, 1980, *14*, 267–270.

LANGER, E. J., & SAEGERT, S. Crowding and cognitive control. *Journal of Personality and Social Psychology*, 1977, *35*, 175–182.

LARSON, L. A., & MICHELMAN, H. *International guide to fitness and health: A world survey of experiments in science and medicine applied to daily living.* New York: Crown, 1973.

LASAGNA, L., MOSTELLER, F., VON FELSINGER, J. M., & BEECHER, H. K. A study of the placebo response. *American Journal of Medicine*, 1954, *16*, 770–779.

LATANÉ, B., & DABBS, J. M., JR. Sex, group size, and helping in three cities. *Sociometry*, 1975, *38*, 180–194.

LATANÉ, B., & DARLEY, J. M. Group inhibition of bystander intervention in emergencies. *Journal of Personality and Social Psychology*, 1968, *10*, 215–221.

LAUDENSLAGER, M. A., RYAN, S. M., DRUGAN, R. C., HYSON, R. L., & MAIER, S. E. Coping and immunosuppression, inescapable but not escapable shock suppresses lymphocyte proliferation. *Science*, 1983, *221*, 568–570.

LAWLER, E. E., III. *Motivation in work organizations.* Pacific Grove, Calif.: Brooks/Cole, 1973.

LAWLER, E. E., III, & PORTER, L. W. The effect of performance on job satisfaction. *Industrial Relations*, 1967, *7*, 20–28.

LAZARUS, A. A. Behavioral rehearsal vs. non-directive therapy vs. advice in effective behavior change. *Behavior Research and Therapy*, 1966, *4*, 95–97.

LAZARUS, A. A. *Behavior therapy and beyond.* New York: McGraw-Hill, 1971.

LAZARUS, A. A. On assertive behavior: A brief note. *Behavior Therapy*, 1973, *4*, 697–699.

LAZARUS, R. S. The self-regulation of emotion. In L. Levi (Ed.), *Emotions: Their parameters and measurement.* New York: Raven Press, 1975.

LAZARUS, R. S. The stress and coping paradigm. In C. Eisdorfer, D. Cohen, A. Kleinman, & P. Maxim (Eds.), *Models for clinical psychopathology* (pp. 177–214). New York: Spectrum, 1981.

LAZARUS, R. S., & LAUNIER, R. Stress-related transactions between person and environment. In L. A. Pervin & M. Lewis (Eds.), *Perspectives in interactional psychology.* New York: Plenum, 1978.

LE BEAU, J. The cingular and precingular areas in psychosurgery (agitated behaviour, obsessive compulsive states, epilepsy). *Acta Psychiatrica et Neurologica, København*, 1952, *27*, 205–316.

LEDESMA, J. A., & PANCAGUA, J. L. Circunvolución del cíngulo y agresividad. *Actas Luso-Españolas de Neurología y Psiquiatría*, 1969, *28*, 289–298.

LEDWIDGE, B. Run for your mind: Aerobic exercise as a means of alleviating anxiety and depression. *Canadian Journal of Behavioural Science*, 1980, *12*, 126–140.

LEFCOURT, H. M., MARTIN, R. A. & SALEH, W. E. Locus of control and social support: Interactive moderator of stress. *Journal of Personality and Social Psychology*, 1984, *47*, 378–389.

LEFCOURT, H. M., MILLER, R. S., WARE, E. E., & SHERK, D. Locus of control as a modifier of the relationship between stressors and moods. *Journal of Personality and Social Psychology*, 1981, *41*, 357–369.

LEGGETT, E. *Children's entity and incremental theories of intelligence: Relationships to achievement behavior.* Paper presented at meeting of Eastern Psychological Association, Boston, March 1985.

LEIBOWITZ, S. F. Hypothalamic catecholamine systems controlling eating behavior: A potential model for anorexia nervosa. In P. L. Darby, P. E. Garfinkel, D. M. Garner, & D. V. Coscina, *Anorexia nervosa: Recent developments in research* (pp. 221–229). New York: Alan R. Liss, Inc., 1983.

LEON, G. R. Current directions in the treatment of obesity. *Psychological Bulletin*, 1976, *83*, 557–578.

LEPPER, M. R., & GREENE, D. Turning play into work: Effects of adult surveillance and extrinsic rewards on children's intrinsic motivation. *Journal of Personality and Social Psychology*, 1975, *31*, 479–486.

LEPPER, M. R., GREENE, D., & NISBETT, R. E. Undermining children's intrinsic interest with extrinsic reward: A test of the "overjustification" hypothesis. *Journal of Personality and Social Psychology*, 1973, *28*, 129–137.

LERNER, M. J. The desire for justice and reactions to victims. In J. Macaulay & L. Berkowitz (Eds.), *Altruism and helping behavior.* New York: Academic Press, 1970.

LERNER, M. J. The justice motive: Some hypotheses as to its origin and forms. *Journal of Personality*, 1977, *45*, 1–52.

LERNER, M. J., & MILLER, D. T. Just world research and the attribution process: Looking back and ahead. *Psychological Bulletin*, 1978, *85*, 1030–1051.

LERNER, M. J., & SIMMONS, C. H. Observers' reaction to the "innocent victim": Compassion or rejection? *Journal of Personality and Social Psychology*, 1966, *4*, 203–210.

LESSER, G. S. Achievement motivation in women. In D. C. McClelland, & R. S. Steele (Eds.), *Human motivation: A book of readings.* Morristown, N. J.: General Learning Press, 1973.

LESSER, G. S., KRAWITZ, R. N., & PACKARD, R. Experimental arousal of achievement motivation in adolescent girls. *Journal of Abnormal and Social Psychology*, 1962, *66*, 59–66.

LESTER, J. T. Stress: On Mount Everest. *Psychology Today*, September 1969, pp. 30–32; 62.

LEVI, L., & KAGAN, A. Psychosocially-induced stress and disease—Problems, research strategies, and results. In H. Selye (Ed.), *Selye's guide to stress research* (Vol. 1). New York: Van Nostrand Reinhold, 1980.

LEVINE, S. Stimulation in infancy. *Scientific American*, May 1960, pp. 80–86.

LEVINE, S. Stress and behavior. *Scientific American*, January 1971, pp. 26–31.

LEVINSON, D. J. *The seasons of a man's life.* New York: Ballantine, 1978.

LEVY, J. Lateral differences in the human brain in cognition and behavioral control. In P. Buser (Ed.), *Cerebral correlates of conscious experience.* New York: North-Holland, 1978.

LEVY, J. V., & KING, J. A. The effects of testosterone propionate on fighting behavior in young male C57BL/10 mice. *Anatomical Record*, 1953, *117*, 562–563.

LEWIN, I., & GLAUBMAN, H. The effect of REM deprivation: Is it detrimental, beneficial, or neutral? *Psychophysiology*, 1975, *12*, 349–353.

LEY, P., SWINSON, R. P., JAIN, V. K., EAVES, D., BRADSHAW, P. W., KINCEY, J. A., CROWDER, R., & ABBISS, S. A state-dependent learning effect produced by amylobarbitone sodium. *British Journal of Psychiatry*, 1972, *120*, 511–515.

LEY, R. G., & BRYDEN, M.P. A dissociation of right and left hemispheric effects for recognizing emotional tone and verbal content. *Brain and Cognition*, 1982, *1*, 3–9.

LICHT, B. G., LINDEN, T. A., BROWN, D. A., & SEXTON, M. A. *Sex differences in achievement orientation: An "A" student phenomenon?* Paper presented at meeting of American Psychological Association, Toronto, August 1984.

LICHT, B. G., & SHAPIRO, S. H. *Sex differences in attributions among high achievers.* Paper presented at meeting of American Psychological Association, Washington, D.C., August 1982.

LIEBHART, E. H. Effects of false heart rate feedback and task instructions on information search, attributions, and stimulus ratings. *Psychological Research*, 1977, *39*, 185–202.

LIEBMAN, R., MINUCHIN, S., & BAKER, L. An integrated treatment program for anorexia nervosa. *American Journal of Psychiatry*, 1974, *131*, 432–435.

LIENERT, G. A., & TRAXEL, W. The effects of meprobamate and alcohol on galvanic skin response. *Journal of Psychology*, 1959, *48*, 329–334.

LINDSLEY, D. B. Psychological phenomena and the electroencephalogram. *Electroencephalography and Clinical Neurophysiology*, 1952, *4*, 443–456.

LINDSLEY, D. B. Attention, consciousness, sleep, and wakefulness. In J. Field (Ed.), *Handbook of physiology: Neurophysiology* (Vol. 3). Baltimore: Williams & Wilkins, 1960.

LINDSLEY, D. B., & HENRY, C. E. The effect of drugs on behavior and the electroencephalograms of children with behavior disorders. *Psychosomatic Medicine*, 1942, *4*, 140–149.

LINSENMEIER, J. A. W., & BRICKMAN, P. Advantages of difficult tasks. *Journal of Personality*, 1978, *46*, 96–112.

LLOYD, C. Life events and depressive disorder reviewed. II. Events as precipitating factors. *Archives of General Psychiatry*, 1980, *37*, 541–548.

LLOYD, C. W. Problems associated with the menstrual cycle. In C. W. Lloyd (Ed.), *Human reproduction and sexual behavior.* Philadelphia: Lea & Febiger, 1964.

LLOYD, R. W., JR., & SALZBERG, H. C. Controlled social drinking: An alternative to abstinence as a treatment goal for some alcohol abusers. *Psychological Bulletin*, 1975, *82*, 815–842.

LOCKE, E. A. Studies of the relationship between satisfaction, goal-setting, and performance. *Organizational Behavior and Human Performance*, 1970, *5*, 135–158.

LOCKE, E. A. The supervisor as a "motivator": His influence on employee performance and satisfaction. In R. M. Steers & L. W. Porter (Eds.), *Motivation and work behavior.* New York: McGraw-Hill, 1979.

LOCKSLEY, A., & COLTEN, M. E. Psychological androgyny: A case of mistaken identity. *Journal of Personality and Social Psychology*, 1979, *37*, 1017–1031.

LONG, G. T., & LERNER, M. J. Deserving, the "personal contract" and altruistic behavior by children. *Journal of Personality and Social Psychology*, 1974, *29*, 551–556.

LOO, C. M. The effects of spatial density on the social behavior of children. *Journal of Applied Social Psychology*, 1972, *2*, 372–381.

LORENZ, K. Z. *On aggression.* London: Methuen, 1966.

LORENZ, K. Z. Innate bases of learning. In K. H. Pribram (Ed.), *On the biology of learning*. New York: Harcourt, Brace & World, 1969.

LORO, A. D., & ORLEANS, C. S. Binge eating in society: Preliminary findings and guidelines for behavioral analysis and treatment. *Addictive Behaviors*, 1981, *6*, 155–166.

LOVEJOY, C. O. The origin of man. *Science*, 1981, *211*, 341–350.

LOWELL, E. L. The effect of need for achievement on learning and spread of performance. *Journal of Psychology*, 1952, *33*, 31–40.

LOWTHER, W. Marriage running down. *Maclean's*, August 6, 1979, p. 43.

LUCE, S. *Insomnia: The guide for troubled sleepers*. Garden City, N. Y.: Doubleday, 1969.

LUCKHARDT, A. B., & CARLSON, A. J. Contributions to the physiology of the stomach: XVII. On the chemical control of the gastric hunger mechanism. *American Journal of Physiology*, 1915, *36*, 37–46.

LUGINBUHL, J. E. R., CROWE, D. H., & KAHAN, J. P. Causal attributions for success and failure. *Journal of Personality and Social Psychology*, 1975, *31*, 86–93.

LUNDBERG, O., & WALINDER, J. Anorexia nervosa and signs of brain damage. *International Journal of Neuropsychiatry*, 1967, *3*, 167–173.

LUNDBERG, U. Urban commuting: Crowdedness and catecholamine excretion. *Journal of Human Stress*, 1976, *2*, 26–32.

LUNDBERG, U., & FRANKENHAEUSER, M. Psychophysiological reactions to noise as modified by personal control over noise intensity. *Biological Psychology*, 1978, *6*, 51–59.

LYNN, R. *Attention, arousal, and the orientation reaction*. Oxford: Pergamon Press, 1966.

MACANDREW, C., & EDGERTON, R. B. *Drunken comportment: A social explanation*. London: Nelson, 1970.

MACCOBY, E. E., & JACKLIN, C. N. *The psychology of sex differences*. Stanford: Stanford University Press, 1974.

MACKWORTH, N. H. The breakdown of vigilance during prolonged visual search. *Quarterly Journal of Experimental Psychology*, 1948, *1*, 6–21.

MACLEAN, P. D. *A triune concept of the brain and behavior*. Toronto: University of Toronto Press, 1973.

MACLEAN, P. D. Sensory and perceptive factors in emotional functions of the triune brain. In L. Levi (Ed.), *Emotions: Their parameters and measurement*. New York: Raven Press, 1975.

MAEHR, M. L., & STALLINGS, W. M. Freedom from external evaluation. *Child Development*, 1972, *43*, 177–185.

MAHONE, C. H. Fear of failure and unrealistic vocational aspiration. *Journal of Abnormal and Social Psychology*, 1960, *60*, 253–261.

MAHONEY, M. J., & MAHONEY, K. *Permanent weight control*. New York: W. W. Norton, 1976.

MAIER, S. F. Failure to escape traumatic shock: Incompatible skeletal motor responses or learned helplessness? *Learning and Motivation*, 1970, *1*, 157–170.

MAIER, S.F., & LAUDENSLAGER, M. Stress and health: Exploring the links. *Psychology Today*, 1985, *19*, 44–49.

MAIER, S. F., SELIGMAN, M. E. P., & SOLOMON, R. L. Pavlovian fear conditioning and learned helplessness. In B. A. Campbell & R. M. Church (Eds.), *Punishment*. New York: Appleton-Century-Crofts, 1969.

MAKARA, G. B., PALKOVITS, M., & SZENTAGOTHAI, J. The endocrine hypothalamus and the hormonal response to stress. In H. Selye (Ed.), *Selye's guide to stress research* (Vol. 1). New York: Van Nostrand Reinhold, 1980.

MALAMUTH, N. M., & DONNERSTEIN, E. *Pornography and sexual aggression*. New York: Academic Press, 1984.

MALTZMAN, I. Orienting reflexes and significance: A reply to O'Gorman. *Psychophysiology*, 1979, *16*, 274–282.

MANDLER, G., & COHEN, J. E. Test anxiety questionnaires. *Journal of Consulting Psychology*, 1958, *22*, 228–229.

MANDLER, G., & SARASON, S. B. A study of anxiety and learning. *Journal of Abnormal and Social Psychology*, 1952, *47*, 166–173.

MANUCK, S. B., CRAFT, S., & GOLD, K. J. Coronary-prone behavior pattern and cardiovascular response. *Psychophysiology*, 1978, *15*, 403–411.

MARANTO, G. Coke: The random killer. *Discover*, March 1985, 16–21.

MARGULES, D. L. Beta-endorphin and endoloxone: Hormones of the autonomic nervous system for the conservation or expenditure of bodily resources and energy in anticipation of famine or feast. *Neuroscience and Biochemical Reviews*, 1979, *3*, 155–162.

MARGULES, D. L., MOISSET, B., LEWIS, M. J., SHIBUYA, H., & PERT, C. B. Beta-endorphin is associated with overeating in genetically obese mice (ob/ob) and rats (fa/fa). *Science*, 1978, *202*, 988–991.

MARK, V. H., & ERVIN, F. R. *Violence and the brain*. New York: Harper & Row, 1970.

MARLATT, G. A., & GORDON, J. R. Determinants of relapse: Implications for the maintenance of behavior change. In P. O. Davidson, & S. M. Davidson (Eds.). *Behavioral medicine: Changing lifestyles*. New York: Brunner/Mazel, 1980.

MARSHALL, G. D., & ZIMBARDO, P. G. Affective consequence of inadequately explaining physiological arousal. *Journal of Personality and Social Psychology*, 1979, *37*, 970–988.

MARSHALL, J. M., & KARABENICK, S. A. Validity of an empirically derived projective measure of fear of success. *Journal of Consulting and Clinical Psychology*, 1977, *45*, 564–574.

MARTIN, R. A., & LEFCOURT, H. M. The sense of humor as a moderator of the relation between stressors and moods. *Journal of Personality and Social Psychology*, 1983, *45*, 1313–1324.

Martindale: The extra pharmacopoeia (A. Wade & J. E. F. Reynolds, Eds.). London: Pharmaceutical Press, 1977.

MASLACH, C. Negative emotional biasing of unexplained arousal. *Journal of Personality and Social Psychology*, 1979, *37*, 953–969.

MASLOW, A. H. *Motivation and personality* (2nd ed.). New York: Harper & Row, 1970.

MASON, J. W. Psychological influences on the pituitary-adrenal cortical system. *Recent Progress in Hormone Research*, 1959, *15*, 345–389.

MASON, J. W. Emotions as reflected in patterns of endocrine integration. In L. Levi (Ed.), *Emotions: Their parameters and measurement*. New York: Raven Press, 1975.

MASON, J. W., BRADY, J. V., & SIDMAN, M. Plasma 17-hydroxycorticosteroid levels and conditioned behavior in the rhesus monkey. *Endocrinology*, 1957, *60*, 741–752.

MASON, J. W., BRADY, J. V., & TOLSON, W. W. Behavioral adaptations and endocrine activity. In R. Levine (Ed.), *Endocrines and the central nervous system: Proceedings of the Association for Research in Nervous and Mental Diseases.* Baltimore: Williams & Wilkins, 1966.

MASON, J. W., MAHER, J. T., HARTLEY, L. H., MOUGEY, E. H., PERLOW, M. J., & JONES, L. G. Selectivity of corticosteroid and catecholamine responses to various natural stimuli. In G. Serban (Ed.), *Psychopathology of human adaptation.* New York: Plenum, 1976.

MASSERMAN, J. H., & YUM, K. S. An analysis of the influence of alcohol on experimental neuroses in cats. *Psychosomatic Medicine*, 1946, *8*, 36–52.

MASTERS, W. H., & JOHNSON, V. E. *Human sexual response.* Boston: Little, Brown, 1966.

MASTERS, W. H., & JOHNSON, V. E. *Human sexual inadequacy.* Boston: Little, Brown, 1970.

MASTERS, W. H., & JOHNSON, V. E. *The pleasure bond: A new look at sexuality and commitment.* Boston: Little, Brown, 1975.

MASTERS, W. H., & JOHNSON, V. E. *Homosexuality in perspective.* Boston: Little, Brown, 1979.

MASUDA, M., & HOLMES, T. H. Life events: Perceptions and frequencies. *Psychosomatic Medicine*, 1978, *40*, 236–261.

MATTHEWS, K. A. Psychological perspectives on the Type A behavior pattern. *Psychological Bulletin*, 1982, *91*, 293–320.

MATTHEWS, K. A., & BRUNSON, B. I. Allocation of attention and the Type A coronary-prone behavior pattern. *Journal of Personality and Social Psychology*, 1979, *37*, 2081–2090.

MATTHEWS, K. A., & SAAL, F. E. Relationship of the Type A coronary-prone behavior pattern to achievement, power, and affiliation motives. *Psychosomatic Medicine*, 1978, *40*, 631–636.

MAY, R. *The meaning of anxiety.* New York: Norton, 1983.

MAY, R. B. Stimulus selection of preschool children under conditions of free choice. *Perceptual and Motor Skills*, 1963, *16*, 203–206.

MAYER, J. Regulation of energy intake and the body weight: The glucostatic theory and lipostatic hypothesis. *Annals of the New York Academy of Sciences*, 1955, *63*, 15–43.

MAYNARD-SMITH, J. Group selection and kin selection. *Nature*, 1964, *201*, 1145–1147.

MAYR, E. Behavior programs and evolutionary strategies. *American Scientist*, 1974, *62*, 650–659.

McADAMS, D. P., HEALEY, S., & KRAUSE, S. *Relationships between social motives and patterns of friendship.* Unpublished manuscript, Loyola University, Department of Psychology, 1982.

McCARTY, D., & KAYE, M. Reasons for drinking: Motivational patterns and alcohol use among college students. *Addictive Behaviors*, 1984, *9*, 185–188.

McCLELLAND, D. C. *The achieving society.* Princeton, N.J.: Van Nostrand, 1961.

McCLELLAND, D. C. The power of positive drinking. *Psychology Today*, January 1971, pp. 40–41; 78–79.

McCLELLAND, D. C. *Power: The inner experience.* New York: Irvington, 1975.

McCLELLAND, D. C. *Human motivation.* Glenview, Ill.: Scott, Foresman, 1985.

McCLELLAND, D. C., ATKINSON, J. W., CLARK, R. A., & LOWELL, E. L. *The achievement motive.* New York: Appleton-Century-Crofts, 1953.

McCLELLAND, D. C., & BOYATZIS, R. E. The leadership motive pattern and long-term success in management. *Journal of Applied Psychology*, 1982, *67*, 737–743.

McCLELLAND, D. C., & BURNHAM, D. H. Power is the great motivator. *Harvard Business Review*, March-April 1976, pp. 100–110.

McCLELLAND, D. C., DAVIDSON, R. J., FLOOR, E., & SARASON, C. Stressed power motivation, sympathetic activation, immune function, and illness. *Journal of Human Stress*, 1980, *6*, 11–19.

McCLELLAND, D. C., DAVIS, W. N., KALIN, R., & WANNER, E. *The drinking man.* New York: Free Press, 1972.

McCLELLAND, D. C., & JEMMOTT, J. B., III. Power motivation, stress, and physical illness. *Journal of Human Stress*, 1980, *6*, 6–15.

McCLELLAND, D. C., & PILON, D. Sources of adult motives in patterns of parent behavior in early childhood. *Journal of Personality and Social Psychology*, 1983, *44*, 564–574.

McCLELLAND, D. C., ROSS, G., & PATEL, V. The effect of an academic examination on salivary norepinephrine and immunoglobulin levels. *Journal of Human Stress*, 1985, *11*, 52–59.

McDOUGALL, W. *An introduction to social psychology* (30th ed.). London: Methuen, 1950. (Originally published, 1908.)

McEWEN, B. S. Neural gonadal steroid actions. *Science*, 1981, *211*, 1303–1311.

McGRATH, M. J., & COHEN, D. B. REM sleep facilitation of adaptive waking behavior: A review of the literature. *Psychological Bulletin*, 1978, *85*, 24–57.

McGRAW, K. O., & McCULLERS, J. C. The distracting effect of material reward: An alternative explanation for superior performance of reward groups in probability learning. *Journal of Experimental Child Psychology*, 1974, *18*, 149–158.

McGRAW, K. O., & McCULLERS, J. C. *Some detrimental effects of reward on laboratory task performance.* Paper presented at the meeting of the American Psychological Association, Chicago, September 1975.

McGUINNESS, D. *When children don't learn: Understanding the biology and psychology of learning disabilities.* New York: Basic Books, 1985.

McLEARN, G. E. Biological bases of social behavior with particular reference to violent behavior. In D. J. Mulvihill, M. M. Tumin, & L. A. Curtis (Eds.), *Crimes of violence* (Vol. 13). Staff report submitted to the National Commission on the Causes and Prevention of Violence. Washington, D. C.: Government Printing Office, 1969.

McPARTLAND, R. J., & KUPFER, D. J. Rapid eye movement sleep cycle, clock time, and sleep onset. *Electroencephalography and Clinical Neurophysiology*, 1978, *45*, 178–185.

MECKLENBURG, R. S., LORIAUX, D. L., THOMPSON, R. H., ANDERSON, A. E., & LIPSETT, M. B. Hypothalamic dysfunction in patients with anorexia nervosa. *Medicine*, 1974, *53*, 147–159.

MENDELSON, J., & MELLO, N. K. Alcohol, aggression, and androgens. In "Aggression." *Association for Research in Nervous and Mental Disease*, 1974, *52*, 225–247.

MEYER, T. P. The effect of sexually arousing and violent films on aggressive behavior. *Journal of Sex Research*, 1972, *8*, 324–333.

MEYER, W. U. Indirect communications about perceived ability estimates. *Journal of Educational Psychology*, 1982, *74*, 888–897.

MEYER-BAHLBURG, H. F. Sex hormones and male homosexuality in comparative perspective. *Archives of Sexual Behavior, 1977, 6,* 297–325.

MEYER-BAHLBURG, H. F. L., & EHRHARDT, A. A. Prenatal sex hormones and human aggression: A review, and new data on progestogen effects. *Aggressive Behavior, 1982, 8,* 39–62.

MEYERS, W. U. Indirect communications about perceived ability estimates. *Journal of Educational Psychology, 1982, 74,* 888–897.

MILGRAM, S. Behavioral study of obedience. *Journal of Abnormal and Social Psychology, 1963, 67,* 371–378.

MILGRAM, S. *Obedience to authority.* New York: Harper & Row, 1974.

MILLER, D. G., GROSSMAN, Z. D., RICHARDSON, R. L., WISTOW, B. W., & THOMAS, F. D. Effect of signaled versus unsignaled stress on rat myocardium. *Psychosomatic Medicine, 1978, 40,* 432–434.

MILLER, D. T. Ego involvement and attributions for success and failure. *Journal of Personality and Social Psychology, 1976, 34,* 901–906.

MILLER, D. T. Personal deserving versus justice for others: An exploration of the justice motive. *Journal of Experimental Social Psychology, 1977, 13,* 1–13.

MILLER, D. T., & ROSS, M. Self-serving biases in the attribution of causality: Fact or fiction? *Psychological Bulletin, 1975, 82,* 213–225.

MILLER, G. A. The magical number seven, plus or minus two: Some limits on our capacity for processing information. *Psychological Review, 1956, 63,* 81–97.

MILLER, G. A., GALANTER, E., & PRIBRAM, K. H. *Plans and structure of behavior.* New York: Holt, 1960.

MILLER, I. W., III, & NORMAN, W. H. Learned helplessness in humans: A review and attribution-theory model. *Psychological Bulletin, 1979, 86,* 93–118.

MILLER, L. B., & ESTES, B. W. Monetary reward and motivation in discrimination learning. *Journal of Experimental Psychology, 1961, 61,* 501–504.

MILLER, N. E. The frustration-aggression hypothesis. *Psychological Review, 1941, 48,* 337–342.

MILLER, N. E. Learnable drives and rewards. In S. S. Stevens (Ed.), *Handbook of experimental psychology* (pp. 435–472). New York: Wiley, 1951.

MILLER, N. E. Learning resistance to pain and fear: Effects of overlearning, exposure, and rewarded exposure in context. *Journal of Experimental Psychology, 1960, 60,* 137–145.

MILLER, N. E. Effects of learning on physical symptoms produced by psychological stress. In H. Selye (Ed.), *Selye's guide to stress research* (Vol. 1). New York: Van Nostrand Reinhold, 1980.

MILLER, S. M., LACK, E. R., & ASROFF, S. Preference for control and the coronary-prone behavior pattern: "I'd rather do it myself." *Journal of Personality and Social Psychology, 1985, 49,* 492–499.

MILLER, W. R. Controlled drinking: A history and critical review. *Journal of Studies on Alcohol, 1983, 44,* 68–83.

MILLER, W. R., & MUÑOZ, R. F. *How to control your drinking.* Englewood Cliffs, N.J.: Prentice-Hall, 1976.

MILLER, W. R., & SELIGMAN, M. E. P. Depression and learned helplessness in man. *Journal of Abnormal Psychology, 1975, 84,* 228–238.

MILLS, J. H. Noise and children: A review of literature. *Journal of Acoustical Society of America, 1975, 58,* 767–779.

MILLS, J. H. Effects of noise on young and old people. In D. M. Lipscomb (Ed.), *Noise and audiology.* Baltimore: University Park Press, 1978.

MILSTEIN, R. M. Responsiveness in newborn infants of overweight and normal weight parents. *Appetite, 1980, 1,* 65–74.

MINUCHIN, S. *Families and family therapy: A structural approach.* Cambridge, Mass.: Harvard University Press, 1974.

MINUCHIN, S., ROSMAN, L. B., BAKER, L., & LIEBMAN, R. *Psychosomatic families: Anorexia nervosa in context.* Cambridge, Mass.: Harvard University Press, 1978.

MISCHEL, W. Delay of gratification, need for achievement, and acquiescence in another culture. *Journal of Abnormal and Social Psychology, 1961, 62,* 543–552.

MISCHEL, W. Processes in delay of gratification. In L. Berkowitz (Ed.), *Advances in experimental social psychology* (Vol. 7). New York: Academic Press, 1973.

MOISEEVA, N. I. The significance of different sleep states for the regulation of electrical brain activity in man. *Electroencephalography and Clinical Neurophysiology, 1979, 46,* 371–381.

MOLDOFSKY, H., & GARFINKEL, P. E. Problems of treatment of anorexia nervosa. *Canadian Psychiatric Association Journal, 1974, 19,* 169–175.

MOLTZ, H. Some mechanisms governing the induction, maintenance, and synchrony of maternal behavior in the laboratory rat. In W. Montagna & W. A. Sadler (Eds.), *Reproductive behavior.* New York: Plenum, 1974.

MONEY, J. Sex hormones and other variables in human eroticism. In W. C. Young (Ed.), *Sex and internal secretions.* Baltimore: Williams & Wilkins, 1961.

MONEY, J. Endocrine influences and psychosexual status spanning the life cycle. In H. M. Van Praag, M. H. Lader, O. J. Rafaelsen, & E. J. Sachar (Eds.), *Handbook of Biological Psychiatry, pt. 3, Brain mechanisms and abnormal behavior—Genetics and neuroendocrinology.* New York: Dekker, 1980.

MONEY, J. Sin, sickness, or status: Homosexual gender identity and psychoneuroendocrinology. *American Psychologist, 1987, 42,* 384–399.

MONEY, J., & EHRHARDT, A. A. *Man and woman, boy and girl: The differentiation and dimorphism of gender identity from conception to maturity.* Baltimore: Johns Hopkins University Press, 1972.

MOOK, D. G. Oral and postingestional determinants of the intake of various solutions in rats with esophageal fistulas. *Journal of Comparative and Physiological Psychology, 1963, 56,* 645–659.

MOORE, B. S., UNDERWOOD, B., & ROSENHAN, D. L. Affect and altruism. *Developmental Psychology, 1973, 8,* 99–104.

MORGAN, C. J. Bystander intervention: Experimental test of a former model. *Journal of Personality and Social Psychology, 1978, 36,* 43–55.

MORGAN, E. *The descent of woman.* New York: Stein and Day/Bantam, 1972.

MORGAN, W. P., & HORSTMAN, D. H. Anxiety reduction following acute physical activity. *Medicine and Science in Sports, 1976, 8,* 62.

MORGANE, P. J., & STERN, W. C. The role of serotonin and norepinephrine in sleep-waking activity. *National Institute on Drug Abuse, Research Monograph Series, 1975, No. 3,* 37–61.

MORRIS, D. *The naked ape.* New York: Dell, 1969.

MORRIS, J. L. Propensity for risk taking as a determinant of vocational choice: An extension of the theory of achievement motivation. *Journal of Personality and Social Psychology*, 1966, *3*, 328–335.

MORRISON, A. R. A window on the sleeping brain. *Scientific American*, 1983, *248*, 94–102.

MORSE, D. R., MARTIN, J. S., FURST, M. L., & DUBIN, L. L. A physiological and subjective evaluation of meditation, hypnosis, and relaxation. *Psychosomatic Medicine*, 1977, *39*, 304–324.

MORTON, J. H., ADDITION, H., ADDISON, R. G., HUNT, L., & SULLIVAN, J. J. A clinical study of premenstrual tension. *American Journal of Obstetrics and Gynecology*, 1953, *65*, 1182–1191.

MORUZZI, G., & MAGOUN, H. W. Brain stem reticular formation and activation of the EEG. *Electroencephalography and Clinical Neurophysiology*, 1949, *1*, 455–473.

MOSES, J. M., JOHNSON, L. C., NAITOH, P., & LUBIN, A. Sleep stage deprivation and total sleep loss: Effects on sleep behavior. *Psychophysiology*, 1975, *12*, 141–146.

MOSES, J. M., LUBIN, A., NAITOH, P., & JOHNSON, L. C. Circadian variation in performance, subjective sleepiness, sleep, and oral temperature during an altered sleep-wake schedule. *Biological Psychology*, 1978, *6*, 301–308.

MOSES, J. M., NAITOH, P., & JOHNSON, L. C. The REM cycle in altered sleep/wake schedules. *Psychophysiology*, 1978, *15*, 569–575.

MOSHER, D. L. Interaction of fear and guilt in inhibiting unacceptable behavior. *Journal of Consulting Psychology*, 1965, *29*, 161–167.

MOSHER, D. L. The development of multitrait-multimethod matrix analysis of three measures of three aspects of guilt. *Journal of Consulting and Clinical Psychology*, 1966, *30*, 25–29.

MOSHER, D. L., & ABRAMSON, P. R. Subjective sexual arousal to films of masturbation. *Journal of Consulting and Clinical Psychology*, 1977, *45*, 796–807.

MOUNT, G. R., WALTERS, S. R., ROWLAND, R. W., BARNES, P. R., & PAYTON, T. I. The effects of relaxation techniques on normal blood pressure. *Behavioral Engineering*, 1978, *5*(1), 1–4.

MOWDAY, R. T. Equity theory predictions of behavior in organizations. In R. M. Steers & L. W. Porter (Eds.), *Motivation and work behavior.* New York: McGraw-Hill, 1979.

MOWRER, O. H. A stimulus-response analysis of anxiety and its role as a reinforcing agent. *Psychological Review*, 1939, *46*, 553–565.

MOYER, J. A., HERRENKOHL, L. R., & JACOBWITZ, D. M. Stress during pregnancy: Effects on catecholamines in discrete brain regions of offspring as adults. *Brain Research*, 1978, *144*, 173–178.

MOYER, K. E. *The psychobiology of aggression.* New York: Harper & Row, 1976.

MOYER, K. E., & BRUNELL, B. N. Effects of injected adrenaline on an avoidance response in the rat. *Journal of Genetic Psychology*, 1958, *92*, 247–251.

MOYER, K. E., & KORN, J. H. Effect of adrenalectomy and adrenal demedullation on the retention of an avoidance response in the rat. *Psychonomic Science*, 1965, *2*, 77–78.

MULLANEY, D. J., JOHNSON, L. C., NAITOH, P., FRIEDMANN, J. K., & GLOBUS, G. G. Sleep during and after gradual sleep reduction. *Psychophysiology*, 1977, *14*, 237–244.

MUNSINGER, H., & KESSEN, W. Uncertainty, structure, and preference. *Psychological Monographs*, 1964, *78* (9, Whole No. 586).

MURRAY, A. D. Infant crying as an elicitor of parental behavior: An examination of two models. *Psychological Bulletin*, 1979, *86*, 191–215.

MURRAY, H. A. *Explorations in personality.* New York: Oxford University Press, 1938.

MYERS, R. Neurology and social communication in primates. In H. O. Hofer (Ed.), *Neurology, physiology, and infectious diseases* (Vol. 3). *Proceedings of the Second International Congress of Primatology*, 1968, *3*, 1–9.

NACHMAN, M. Learned taste and temperature aversions due to lithium chloride sickness after temporal delays. *Journal of Comparative and Physiological Psychology*, 1970, *73*, 22–30.

NAISBETT, J. *Megatrends: Ten new directions transforming our lives.* New York: Warner Books, 1983.

NAKAZAWA, Y., KOTORII, M., KOTORII, T., TACHIBANA, H., & NAKANO, T. Individual differences in compensatory rebound of REM sleep with particular reference to their relationship to personality and behavioral characteristics. *Journal of Nervous and Mental Disease*, 1975, *161*, 18–25.

NARABAYASHI, H. Stereotaxic amygdalectomy. In B. Eleftheriou (Ed.), *The neurobiology of the amygdala.* New York: Plenum, 1972.

NASH, S. C. Sex role as a mediator of intellectual functioning. In M. A. Wittag & A. C. Petersen (Eds.), *Sex-related differences in cognitive functioning* (pp. 263–302). New York: Academic Press, 1979.

NATHAN, P. E., & LISMAN, S. A. Behavioral and motivational patterns of chronic alcoholics. In R. E. Tarter & A. A. Sugerman (Eds.), *Alcoholism: Interdisciplinary approaches to an enduring problem.* Reading, Mass.: Addison-Wesley, 1976.

NEFF, J. A. The stress-buffering role of alcohol consumption: The importance of symptom dimension. *Journal of Human Stress*, 1984, *10*, 35–42.

NEMCEK, J., & GRANDJEAN, E. Results of an ergonomic investigation of large-space offices. *Human Factors*, 1973, *15*, 111–124.

NEWCOMB, M. D., & HARLOW, L. L. Life events and substance use among adolescents: Mediating effects of perceived loss of control and meaninglessness in life. *Journal of Personality and Social Psychology*, 1986, *51*, 564–577.

NICHOLLS, J. G. Causal attributions and other achievement-related cognitions: Effects of task outcome, attainment value, and sex. *Journal of Personality and Social Psychology*, 1975, *31*, 379–389.

NICHOLLS, J. G. The development of the concepts of effort and ability, perception of academic attainment, and the understanding that difficult tasks require more ability. *Child Development*, 1978, *49*, 800–814.

NICHOLLS, J. G. Conceptions of ability and achievement motivation. In R. Ames & C. Ames (Eds.), *Research on motivation in education* (Vol. 1). New York: Academic Press, 1984.

NICHOLS, J. R. How opiates change behavior. *Scientific American*, 1965, *212*(2), 80–88.

NICHOLS, J. R. The children of drug addicts: What do they inherit? *Annals of the New York Academy of Science*, 1972, *197*, 60–65.

NICKEL, T. W. The attribution of intention as a critical factor in the relation between frustration and aggression. *Journal of Personality*, 1974, *42*, 482–492.

NISBETT, R. E. Taste, deprivation, and weight determinants of eating behavior. *Journal of Personality and Social Psychology*, 1968, *10*, 107–116.

NISBETT, R. E. Hunger, obesity, and the ventromedial hypothalamus. *Psychological Review*, 1972, *79*, 433–453.

NISBETT, R. E., & SCHACHTER, S. Cognitive manipulation of pain. *Journal of Experimental Social Psychology*, 1966, *2*, 227–236.

NISHIHARA, K., MORI, K., ENDO, S., OHTA, T., & KENSHIRO, O. Relationship between sleep efficiency and urinary excretions of catecholamines in bed-rested humans. *Sleep*, 1985, *8*, 110–117.

NOTTEBOHM, F., & ARNOLD, A. P. Sexual dimorphism in vocal control areas of the songbird brain. *Science*, 1976, *194*, 211–213.

O'BRIEN, C. P., NACE, E. P., MINTZ, J., MEYERS, A. L., & REAM, N. Follow-up of Vietnam veterans. I. Relapse to drug use after Vietnam service. *Drug and Alcohol Dependence*, 1980, *5*, 333–340.

OKE, A., KELLER, R., MEFFORD, I., & ADAMS, R. N. Lateralization of norepinephrine in human thalamus. *Science*, 1978, *200*, 1411–1413.

OLDS, J. Physiological mechanisms of reward. In M. R. Jones (Ed.), *Nebraska Symposium on Motivation* (Vol. 3). Lincoln: University of Nebraska Press, 1955.

OLDS, J. Pleasure centers in the brain. *Scientific American*, October 1956, pp. 105–116.

OLDS, J., & MILNER, P. Positive reinforcement produced by electrical stimulation of the septal area and other regions of the rat brain. *Journal of Comparative and Physiological Psychology*, 1954, *47*, 419–427.

O'LEARY, M. R., & DENGERINK, H. A. Aggression as a function of the intensity and pattern of attack. *Journal of Experimental Research in Personality*, 1973, *7*, 61–70.

OLMSTED, M. P., & GARNER, D. M. *The significance of self-induced vomiting as a weight control method among college women*. Unpublished manuscript. Clarke Institute of Psychiatry, Toronto, 1982.

OLWEUS, D. Stability of aggressive reaction patterns in males: A review. *Psychological Bulletin*, 1979, *86*, 852–875.

OSBORN, C. A., & POLLACK, R. H. The effects of two types of erotic literature on physiological and verbal measures of female sexual arousal. *Journal of Sex Research*, 1977, *13*, 250–256.

OSTROVE, N. Expectations for success on effort-determined tasks as a function of incentive and performance feedback. *Journal of Personality and Social Psychology*, 1978, *36*, 909–916.

OSTWALD, P. *Soundmaking: The acoustic communication of emotion*. Springfield, Ill.: Charles C Thomas, 1963.

OSTWALD, P. The sounds of infancy. *Developmental Medicine and Child Neurology*, 1972, *14*, 350–361.

OVERMIER, J. B., & SELIGMAN, M. E. P. Effects of inescapable shock on subsequent escape and avoidance responding. *Journal of Comparative and Physiological Psychology*, 1967, *63*, 28–33.

OVERTON, D. A. State-dependent or "dissociated" learning produced with pentobarbital. *Journal of Comparative and Physiological Psychology*, 1964, *57*, 3–12.

PADILLA, A. M., PADILLA, C., KETTERER, T., & GIACALONE, D. Inescapable shocks and subsequent escape/avoidance conditioning in goldfish *(Carassius auratus)*. *Psychonomic Science*, 1970, *20*, 295–296.

PARKES, K. R. Locus of control, cognitive appraisal, and coping in stressful episodes. *Journal of Personality and Social Psychology*, 1984, *46*, 655–668.

PARMEGGIANI, P. L. Interaction between sleep and thermoregulation. *Waking and Sleeping*, 1977, *1*(2), 123–132.

PATON, W. D. M., & CROWN, J. (EDS.). *Cannabis and its derivatives: Pharmacology and experimental psychology—Symposium proceedings*. London: Oxford University Press, 1972.

PATTERSON, G. R. The aggressive child: Victim and architect of a coercive system. In E. J. Mash, L. A. Hamerlynck, & L. C. Handy (Eds.), *Behavior modification and families*. New York: Brunner/Mazel, 1976.

PAVLOV, I. P. *Conditioned reflexes* (G. V. Anrep, trans.). New York: Dover, 1927.

PAXTON, S. J., TRINDER, J., & MONTGOMERY, I. Does aerobic fitness affect sleep? *Psychophysiology*, 1983, *20*, 320–324.

PEELE, S. Redefining addiction. I: Making addiction a scientifically and socially useful concept. *International Journal of Health Services*, 1977, *7*, 103–124.

PEELE, S. Love, sex, drugs and other magical solutions to life. *Journal of Psychoactive Drugs*, 1982, *14*, 125–131.

PEELE, S. Out of the habit trap. *American Health*, September/October 1983, 42–47.

PEELE, S. The cultural context of psychological approaches to alcoholism. *American Psychologist*, 1984, *39*, 1337–1351.

PEELE, S. *The meaning of addiction*. Lexington, Mass.: Lexington Books, 1985.

PEPLAU, L. A. Impact of fear of success and sex-role attitudes on women's competitive achievement. *Journal of Personality and Social Psychology*, 1976, *34*, 561–568.

PERSKY, H., LIEF, H. I., STRAUSS, D., MILLER, W. R., & O'BRIEN, C. P. Plasma testosterone level and sexual behavior of couples. *Archives of Sexual Behavior*, 1978, *7*, 157–173.

PERSKY, H., SMITH, K. D., & BASU, G. K. Relation of psychologic measures of aggression and hostility to testosterone production in man. *Psychosomatic Medicine*, 1971, *33*, 265–277.

PETERS, T. J., & WATERMAN, R. H. *In search of excellence*. New York: Warner, 1982.

PHILLIP, J. D., JR., & BOONE, D. C. Effects of adrenaline supplement on the production of stress induced ulcers in adrenal sympathectomized male rats. *Proceedings of the 76th Annual Convention of the American Psychological Association*, 1968, *3*, 261–262 (Summary).

PIAGET, J. *The origins of intelligence in children*. New York: International Universities Press, 1952.

PIAGET, J. Piaget's theory. In P. H. Mussen (Ed.), *Carmichael's manual of child psychology* (Vol. 1, 3rd ed.). New York: Wiley, 1970.

PIAGET, J., & INHELDER, B. *The psychology of the child*. New York: Basic Books, 1969.

PILIAVIN, I. M., RODIN, J., & PILIAVIN, J. A. Good samaritanism: An underground phenomenon? *Journal of Personality and Social Psychology*, 1969, *13*, 289–299.

PILIAVIN, J. A., & PILIAVIN, I. M. Effect of blood on reactions to a victim. *Journal of Personality and Social Psychology,* 1972, 23, 353–361.

PITCHER, S. W., & MEIKLE, S. The topography of assertive behavior in positive and negative situations. *Behavior Therapy,* 1980, 11, 532–547.

PITTS, F. N., JR. The biochemistry of anxiety. *Scientific American,* 1969, 220(2), 69–75.

PIVIK, T., & FOULKES, D. "Dream deprivation": Effects on dream content. *Science,* 1966, 153, 1282–1284.

PLOTKIN, W. B. Long-term eyes-closed alpha-enhancement training: Effects on alpha amplitudes and on experiential state. *Psychophysiology,* 1978, 15, 40–52.

POBLETE, M. M., PALESTINI, M., FIGUEROA, E., GALLARDO, R., ROJAS, J., COVARRUBIAS, M. I., & DOYHARCABAL, Y. Stereotaxic thalamotomy (lamella medialis) in aggressive psychiatric patients. *Confinia Neurológia,* 1970, 32, 326–331.

POLIVY, J. Perception of calories and regulation of intake in restrained and unrestrained subjects. *Addictive Behavior,* 1976, 1, 237–243.

POLIVY, J., & HERMAN, C. P. *Breaking the diet habit: The natural weight alternative.* New York: Basic Books, 1983.

POLIVY, J., & HERMAN, C. P. Dieting and binging: A causal analysis. *American Psychologist,* 1985, 40, 193–201.

POLIVY, J., HERMAN, C. P., HACKETT, R., & KULESHNYK, I. The effects of self-attention and public attention on eating in restrained and unrestrained subjects. *Journal of Personality and Social Psychology,* 1986, 50, 1253–1260.

POLIVY, J., SCHUENEMAN, A. L., & CARLSON, K. Alcohol and tension reduction: Cognitive and physiological effects. *Journal of Abnormal Psychology,* 1976, 85, 595–600.

POOR, R. *4 days, 40 hours: Reporting a revolution on work and leisure* (rev. ed.). Cambridge, Mass.: Bursk & Poor, 1973.

PORTER, L. W., STEERS, R. M., MOWDAY, R. T., & BOULIAN, P. V. Organizational commitment, job satisfaction, and turnover among psychiatric technicians. *Journal of Applied Psychology,* 1974, 59, 603–609.

POST, R. M., LAKE, C. R., JIMERSON, D. C., BUNNEY, W. E., WOOD, J. H., ZIEGLER, M. G., & GOODWIN, F. K. Cerebrospinal fluid norepinephrine in affective illness. *American Journal of Psychiatry,* 1978, 135, 907–912.

POWELL, L. F. The effect of extra stimulation and maternal involvement on the development of low-birth-weight infants and on maternal behavior. *Child Development,* 1974, 45, 106–113.

POWERS, P. S. Obesity: Psychosomatic illness review: No. 2. *Psychosomatics,* 1982, 23, 1027–1039.

POWERS, R. J., & KUTASH, I. L. Stress and alcohol. *International Journal of Addictions,* 1985, 20, 461–482.

PRIBRAM, K. H. Self-consciousness and intentionality. In G. E. Schwartz & D. Shapiro (Eds.), *Consciousness and self-regulation: Advances in research* (Vol. 1). New York: Plenum, 1976.

PRIBRAM, K. H., & McGUINNESS, D. Arousal, activation, and effort in the control of attention. *Psychological Review,* 1975, 82, 116–149.

QUAY, H. C. Psychopathic behavior: Reflection on its nature, origins and treatment. In F. Weizman & I. Uzfiris (Eds.), *The structure of experience.* New York: Plenum, 1977.

QUIRCE, C. M., ODIO, M., & SOLANO, J. M. The effects of predictable and unpredictable schedules of physical restraint upon rats. *Life Sciences,* 1981, 28, 1897–1902.

RABINOWITZ, D., & ZIERLER, K. L. Forearm metabolism in obesity and its response to intra-arterial insulin: Characterization of insulin resistance and evidence for adaptive hyperinsulinism. *Journal of Clinical Investigation,* 1962, 41, 2173–2181.

RADA, R. T., LAWS, D. R., & KELLNER, R. Plasma testosterone levels in the rapist. *Psychosomatic Medicine,* 1976, 38, 257–268.

RADLOFF, R., & HELMREICH, R. Stress: Under the sea. *Psychology Today,* 1969, 3(4), 28–29.

RAHE, R. H., HERVIG, L., & ROSENMAN, R. H. Heritability of Type A behavior. *Psychosomatic Medicine,* 1978, 40, 478–486.

RAHE, R. H., McKEAN, J. D., & ARTHUR, R. J. A longitudinal study of life-change and illness patterns. *Journal of Psychosomatic Research,* 1967, 10, 355–366.

REINBERG, A., & LAGOGUEY, M. Circadian and circannual rhythms in sexual activity and plasma hormones (FSH, LH, testosterone) of five human males. *Archives of Sexual Behavior,* 1978, 7, 13–30.

REISENZEIN, R. The Schachter theory of emotions: Two decades later. *Psychological Bulletin,* 1983, 94, 239–264.

RELICH, J. D. *Attribution and its relation to other affective variables in predicting and inducing arithmetic achievement.* Unpublished doctoral dissertation, University of Sydney (Australia), 1983.

REYNOLDS, M. M. *Negativism of preschool children: An observational and experimental study.* Contributions to Education, No. 288. New York: Teachers College Press, Columbia University, 1928.

RICE, R. D. Neurophysiological development in premature infants following stimulation. *Developmental Psychology,* 1977, 13, 69–76.

RICH, A. R., & SCHROEDER, H. E. Research issues in assertiveness training. *Psychological Bulletin,* 1976, 83, 1081–1096.

RICHARDSON, G. S., CARSKADON, M. A., ORAV, E. J. & DEMENT, W. C. Circadian variations in elderly and young adult subjects. *Sleep,* 1982, 5, S82–S94.

ROBERTS, W. W., & KIESS, H. O. Motivational properties of hypothalamic aggression in cats. *Journal of Comparative and Physiological Psychology,* 1964, 58, 187–193.

ROBERTS, W. W., STEINBERG, M. L., & MEANS, L. W. Hypothalamic mechanisms for sexual, aggressive, and other motivated behaviors in the opossum (*Didelphis virginiana*). *Journal of Comparative and Physiological Psychology,* 1967, 64, 1–15.

ROBINS, L. N., DAVIS, D. H., & GOODWIN, D. W. Drug use by U.S. Army enlisted men in Vietnam: A follow-up on their return home. *American Journal of Epidemiology,* 1974, 99, 235–249.

ROBINS, L. N., HELZER, J. E., & DAVIS, D. H. Narcotics use in Southeast Asia and afterward. *Archives of General Psychiatry,* 1975, 32, 955–961.

ROBINS, L. N., HELZER, J. E., HESSELBROCK, M., & WISH, E. Vietnam veterans three years after Vietnam: How our study changed our view of heroin. In L. Brill & C. Winick (Eds.), *The yearbook of substance use and abuse* (Vol. 2). New York: Human Sciences Press, 1980.

ROBINSON, R. G. Differential behavioral and biochemical effects of right and left hemispheric cerebral infarction in the rat. *Science,* 1979, 105, 707–710.

ROBOW, J., & NEUMAN, C. A. Saturday night live: Chronicity of alcohol consumption among college students. *Substance and Alcohol Actions/Misuse,* 1984, *5,* 1–7.

RODGERS, D. A., & THIESSEN, D. D. Effects of population density on adrenal size, behavioral arousal, and alcohol preferences of inbred mice. *Quarterly Journal of Studies on Alcohol,* 1964, *25,* 240–247.

RODGERS, W. L. Specificity of specific hungers. *Journal of Comparative and Physiological Psychology,* 1967, *64,* 49–58.

RODIN, J. *Obesity theory and behavior therapy: An uneasy couple.* Unpublished manuscript, 1980.

RODIN, J. Current status of the internal-external hypothesis for obesity. *American Psychologist,* 1981, *36,* 361–372.

RODIN, J. Effects of food choice on amount of food eaten in a subsequent meal: Implications for weight gain. In J. Hirsch and T. B. Van Itallie (Eds.), *Recent advances in obesity research* (Vol. 4). Lancaster, Penn.: Technomic, 1984.

RODIN, J., & LANGER, E. J. Long-term effects of a control-relevant intervention with the institutionalized aged. *Journal of Personality and Social Psychology,* 1977, *35,* 897–902.

RODIN, J., RENNERT, K., & SOLOMON, S. K. Intrinsic motivation for control: Fact or fiction. In A. Baum & J. E. Singer (Eds.), *Advances in environmental psychology* (Vol. 2: *Applications of personal control*). Hillsdale, N. J.: Erlbaum, 1980.

RODIN, J., & SLOCHOWER, J. Externality in the nonobese: Effects of environmental responsiveness on weight. *Journal of Personality and Social Psychology,* 1976, *33,* 338–344.

RODIN, J., SLOCHOWER, J., & FLEMING, B. Effects of degree of obesity, age of onset, and weight loss on responsiveness to sensory and external stimuli. *Journal of Comparative and Physiological Psychology,* 1977, *91,* 586–597.

RODIN, J., SOLOMON, S. K., & METCALF, J. Role of control in mediating perceptions of density. *Journal of Personality and Social Psychology,* 1978, *36,* 988–999.

RODIN, J., WACK, J., FERRANNINI, E., & DEFRONZO, R. A. Effect of insulin and glucose on feeding behavior. *Metabolism,* 1985, *34,* 826–831.

ROEBUCK, J. B., & KESSLER, R. G. *The etiology of alcoholics: Constitutional, psychological, and sociological approaches.* Springfield, Ill.: Charles C Thomas, 1972.

ROGERS, C. R. A theory of therapy, personality, and interpersonal relationships, as developed in the client-centered framework. In S. Koch (Ed.), *Psychology: A study of a science. Study 1: Conceptual and systematic* (Vol. 3: *Formulations of the person and the social context*). New York: McGraw-Hill, 1959.

ROHDE, W., STAHL, F., & DÖRNER, G. Plasma basal levels of FSH, LH, and testosterone in homosexual men. *Endokrinologie,* 1977, *70,* 241–248.

ROSE, G. A., & WILLIAMS, R. T. Metabolic studies on large and small eaters. *British Journal of Nutrition,* 1961, *15,* 1–9.

ROSEN, J. C., & LEITENBERG, H. Bulimia nervosa: Treatment with exposure and response prevention. *Behavior Therapy,* 1982, *13,* 117–124.

ROSEN, N. A. *Leadership change and work-group dynamics.* Ithaca, N.Y.: Cornell University Press, 1969.

ROSENFELD, A. H. Depression: Dispelling despair. *Psychology Today,* 1985, *18,* 29–34.

ROSENHAN, D. L. Learning theory and prosocial behavior. *Journal of Social Issues,* 1972, *28,* 151–164.

ROSENMAN, R. H., BRAND, R. J., JENKINS, C. D., FRIEDMAN, M., STRAUS, R., & WURM, M. Coronary heart disease in the Western Collaborative Group Study: Final follow-up experience of 8½ years. *Journal of the American Medical Association,* 1975, *233,* 872–877.

ROSENMAN, R. H., FRIEDMAN, M., STRAUS, R., JENKINS, C. D., ZYZANSKI, S. J., & WURM, M. Coronary heart disease in the Western Collaborative Group Study: A follow-up experience of 4½ years. *Journal of Chronic Disease,* 1970, *23,* 173–190.

ROSENMAN, R. H., FRIEDMAN, M., STRAUS, R., WURM, M., JENKINS, D., & MESSINGER, H. B. Coronary heart disease in the Western Collaborative Group Study: A follow-up experience of two years. *Journal of the American Medical Association,* 1966, *195,* 86–92.

ROSENTHAL, A. M. *Thirty-eight witnesses.* New York: McGraw-Hill, 1964.

ROSENTHAL, R. (ED.) *Skills in nonverbal communication.* Cambridge, Mass.: Oelgeschlager, 1979.

ROSENTHAL, R. H., & ALLEN, T. W. An examination of attention, arousal, and learning dysfunctions of hyperkinetic children. *Psychological Bulletin,* 1978, *85,* 689–715.

ROSMAN, B. L., MINUCHIN, S., & LIEBMAN, R. Family lunch session: An introduction to family therapy in anorexia nervosa. *American Journal of Orthopsychiatry,* 1975, *45,* 846–853.

ROSMAN, B. L., MINUCHIN, S., LIEBMAN, R., & BAKER, L. Input and outcome of family therapy in anorexia nervosa. In *Adolescent psychiatry* (Vol. 5). New York: Jason Aronson, 1977.

ROSSIER, J., BLOOM, F. E., & GUILLEMIN, R. Endorphins and stress. In H. Selye (Ed.), *Selye's guide to stress research* (Vol. 1). New York: Van Nostrand Reinhold, 1980.

ROSSIER, J., FRENCH, E. D., RIVIER, C., LING, N., GUILLEMIN, R., & BLOOM, F. E. Foot-shock induced stress increases beta-endorphin levels in blood but not brain. *Nature,* 1977, *270,* 618–620.

ROSVOLD, H. E., MIRSKY, A. F., & PRIBRAM, K. H. Influence of amygdalectomy on social behavior in monkeys. *Journal of Comparative and Physiological Psychology,* 1954, *47,* 173–178.

ROTH, S., & KUBAL, L. Effects of noncontingent reinforcement on tasks of differing importance: Facilitation and learned helplessness. *Journal of Personality and Social Psychology,* 1975, *32,* 680–691.

ROTH, T., KRAMER, M., & LUTZ, T. The effects of sleep deprivation on mood. *Psychiatric Journal of the University of Ottawa,* 1976, *1,* 136–139.

ROTTER, J. B. Generalized expectancies for internal versus external control of reinforcement. *Psychological Monographs,* 1966, *80*(1, Whole No. 609).

ROTTER, J. B. An introduction to social learning theory. In J. B. Rotter, J. E. Chance, & E. J. Phares (Eds.), *Applications of a social learning theory of personality.* New York: Holt, Rinehart & Winston, 1972.

ROUTTENBERG, A. The two-arousal hypothesis: Reticular formation and limbic system. *Psychological Review,* 1968, *75,* 51–80.

ROUTTENBERG, A. The reward system of the brain. *Scientific American,* November 1978, 154–164.

ROWLAND, G. L., FRANKEN, R. E., & HARRISON, K. Sensation seeking and participation in sporting activities. *Journal of Sports Psychology*, 1986, *8*, 212–220.

ROZIN, P. Specific hunger for thiamine: Recovery from deficiency and thiamine preference. *Journal of Comparative and Physiological Psychology*, 1965, *59*, 98–101.

ROZIN, P. Specific aversions as a component of specific hungers. *Journal of Comparative and Physiological Psychology*, 1967, *64*, 237–242.

RUBENSTEIN, J. Maternal attentiveness and subsequent exploratory behavior in the infant. *Child Development*, 1967, *38*, 1089–1100.

RUBIN, M. A., MALAMUD, W., & HOPE, J. M. The electroencephalogram and psychopathological manifestations in schizophrenia as influenced by drugs. *Psychosomatic Medicine*, 1942, *4*, 355–361.

RUBIN, R. T., REINISCH, J. M., & HASKETT, R. F. Postnatal gonadal steroid effects on human behavior. *Science*, 1981, *211*, 1318–1324.

RUCH, L. O., & HOLMES, T. H. Scaling of life change: Comparison of direct and indirect methods. *Journal of Psychosomatic Research*, 1971, *15*, 221–227.

RUDERMAN, A. J. Dietary restraint: A theoretical and empirical review. *Psychological Bulletin*, 1986, *99*, 247–262.

RULE, B. G., & NESDALE, A. R. Differing functions of aggression. *Journal of Personality*, 1974, *42*, 467–481.

RULE, B. G., & NESDALE, A. R. Emotional arousal and aggressive behavior. *Psychological Bulletin*, 1976, *83*, 851–863. (a)

RULE, B. G., & NESDALE, A. R. Environmental stressors, emotional arousal, and aggression. In I. G. Sarason & C. D. Spielberger (Eds.), *Stress and anxiety* (Vol. 3). New York: Wiley, 1976. (b)

RUSSEK, M. Participation of hepatic glucoreceptors in the control of food. *Nature*, 1963, *197*, 79–80.

RUSSELL, J. A. & STEIGER, J. H. The structure in persons' implicit taxonomy of emotions. *Journal of Research in Personality*, 1982, *16*, 447–469.

SACKETT, G. P. Effects of rearing conditions upon the behavior of rhesus monkeys *(Macaca mulata). Child Development*, 1965, *36*, 855–868.

SADAVA, S. W. Research approaches in illicit drug use: A critical review. *Genetic Psychology Monographs*, 1975, *91*, 3–59.

SADAVA, S. W. Etiology, personality, and alcoholism. *Canadian Psychological Review*, 1978, *19*, 198–214.

SADAVA, S. W. Towards a molar interactional psychology. *Canadian Journal of Behavioral Science*, 1980, *12*, 33–51.

SADD, S., LENAUER, M., SHAVER, P., & DUNIVANT, N. Objective measurement of fear of success and fear of failure: A factor analytic approach. *Journal of Consulting and Clinical Psychology*, 1978, *46*, 405–416.

SALANCIK, G. R., & PFEFFER, J. An examination of need-satisfaction models of job attitudes. *Administrative Science Quarterly*, 1977, *22*, 427–456.

SALTER, A. *Conditioned reflex therapy.* New York: Farrar, Straus, 1949.

SANDS, D. E. Further studies on endocrine treatment in adolescence and early-adult life. *Journal of Mental Science*, 1954, *100*, 211–219.

SARASON, I. G. Stress, anxiety, and cognitive interference: Reactions to tests. *Journal of*

Personality and Social Psychology, 1984, *46*, 929–938.

SAUNDERS, D. *The relationship of attitude variables and explanations of perceived and actual career attainment in male and female businesspersons.* Unpublished doctoral dissertation, University of Texas at Austin, 1978.

SCARAMELLA, T. J., & BROWN, W. A. Serum testosterone and aggressiveness in hockey players. *Psychosomatic Medicine*, 1978, *40*, 262–265.

SCARR-SALAPATEK, S., & WILLIAMS, M. L. The effects of early stimulation on low-birth-weight infants. *Child Development*, 1973, *44*, 94–101.

SCHACHTER, J. Pain, fear, and anger in hypertensives and normotensives. *Psychosomatic Medicine*, 1957, *19*, 17–29.

SCHACHTER, S. The interaction of cognitive and physiological determinants of emotional state. In P. H. Leiderman & D. Shapiro (Eds.), *Psychobiological approaches to social behavior.* Stanford, Calif.: Stanford University Press, 1964. Also in L. Berkowitz (Ed.), *Advances in experimental social psychology* (Vol. 1). New York: Academic Press, 1964.

SCHACHTER, S. *Emotion, obesity, and crime.* New York: Academic Press, 1971. (a)

SCHACHTER, S. Some extraordinary facts about obese humans and rats. *American Psychologist*, 1971, *26*, 129–144. (b)

SCHACHTER, S. Nicotine regulation in heavy and light smokers. *Journal of Experimental Psychology: General*, 1977, *106*, 5–12.

SCHACHTER, S., GOLDMAN, R., & GORDON, A. Effects of fear, food deprivation, and obesity on eating. *Journal of Personality and Social Psychology*, 1968, *10*, 91–97.

SCHACHTER, S., & GROSS, L. P. Manipulated time and eating behavior. *Journal of Personality and Psychology*, 1968, *10*, 98–106.

SCHACHTER, S., KOZLOWSKI, L. T., & SILVERSTEIN, B. Effects of urinary pH on cigarette smoking. *Journal of Experimental Psychology: General*, 1977, *106*, 13–19.

SCHACHTER, S., SILVERSTEIN, B., KOZLOWSKI, L. T., HERMAN, C. P., & LIEBLING, B. Effects of stress on cigarette smoking and urinary pH. *Journal of Experimental Psychology: General*, 1977, *106*, 24–30.

SCHACHTER, S., SILVERSTEIN, B., KOZLOWSKI, L. T., PERLICK, D., HERMAN, C. P., & LIEBLING, B. Studies of the interaction of psychological and pharmacological determinants of smoking. *Journal of Experimental Psychology: General*, 1977, *106*, 3–4.

SCHACHTER, S., SILVERSTEIN, B., & PERLICK, D. Psychological and pharmacological explanations of smoking under stress. *Journal of Experimental Psychology: General*, 1977, *106*, 31–40.

SCHACHTER, S., & SINGER, J. E. Cognitive, social, and physiological determinants of emotional states. *Psychological Review*, 1962, *69*, 379–399.

SCHACHTER, S., & SINGER, J. E. Comments on the Maslach and Marshall-Zimbardo experiments. *Journal of Personality and Social Psychology*, 1979, *37*, 989–995.

SCHACHTER, S., & WHEELER, L. Epinephrine, chlorpromazine, and amusement. *Journal of Abnormal and Social Psychology*, 1962, *65*, 121–128.

SCHAEFER, C., COYNE, J. C., & LAZARUS, R. S. The health-related functions of social support. *Journal of Behavioral Medicine*, 1981, *4*, 381–406.

SCHAEFER, H. H., & COLGAN, A. H. The effect of pornography on penile tumescence as a function of reinforcement and novelty. *Behavior Therapy,* 1977, *8,* 938–946.

SCHILDKRAUT, J. J., & KETY, S. S. Biogenic amines and emotion. *Science,* 1967, *156,* 21–30.

SCHLEISER-STROPP, B. Bulimia: A review of the literature. *Psychological Bulletin,* 1984, *95,* 247–257.

SCHMIDT, D. E., & KEATING, J. P. Human crowding and personal control: An integration of the research. *Psychological Bulletin,* 1979, *86,* 680–700.

SCHNACKERS, U., & KLEINBECK, U. Machtmotiv und machtthematisches Verhalten in einem Verhandlungsspiel. *Archiv für Psychologie,* 1975, *127,* 300–319.

SCHUBERT, D. S. P. Alertness and clear thinking as characteristics of highy naturally occurring autonomic nervous system arousal. *Journal of General Psychology,* 1977, *97,* 179–184.

SCHUCK, J., & PISOR, K. Evaluating an aggression experiment by use of simulating subjects. *Journal of Personality and Social Psychology,* 1974, *29,* 181–186.

SCHULTZ, D. P. *Psychology and industry today* (2nd ed.). New York: Macmillan, 1978.

SCHWARTZ, G. E. The facts of transcendental meditation: Part II. TM relaxes some people and makes them feel better. *Psychology Today,* April 1974, pp. 39–44.

SCHWARTZ, G. E., DAVIDSON, R. J., & GOLEMAN, D. J. Patterning of cognitive and somatic processes in the self-regulation of anxiety: Effects of meditation versus exercise. *Psychosomatic Medicine,* 1978, *40,* 321–328.

SCHWARTZ, R. M., & GOTTMAN, J. M. Toward a task analysis of assertive behavior. *Journal of Consulting and Clinical Psychology,* 1976, *44,* 910–920.

SCHWARTZ, S. Normative influences on altruism. In L. Berkowitz (Ed.), *Advances in experimental social psychology* (Vol. 10). New York: Academic Press, 1977.

SCHWARTZ, S. H., & CLAUSEN, G. T. Responsibility, norms, and helping in an emergency. *Journal of Personality and Social Psychology,* 1970, *16,* 299–310.

SCRIMA, L. Isolated REM sleep facilitates recall of complex associative information. *Psychophysiology,* 1982, *19,* 252–259.

SCRIMA, L., BROUDY, M., NAY, K. N., & COHN, M. A. Increased severity of obstructive sleep apnea after bedtime alcohol ingestion: Diagnostic potential and proposed mechanism of action. *Sleep,* 1982, *5,* 318–328.

SELIGMAN, M. E. P. *Helplessness: On depression, development, and death.* San Francisco: W. H. Freeman, 1975.

SELIGMAN, M. E. P., & MAIER, S. F. Failure to escape shock. *Journal of Experimental Psychology,* 1967, *74,* 1–9.

SELIGMAN, M. E. P., MAIER, S. F., & SOLOMON, R. L. Unpredictable and uncontrollable aversive events. In F. R. Brush (Ed.), *Aversive conditioning and learning.* New York: Academic Press, 1971.

SELYE, H. Stress: It's a G.A.S. *Psychology Today,* September 1969, pp. 25–26; 56.

SELYE, H. *Stress without distress.* Philadelphia: Lippincott, 1974.

SELYE, H. *The stress of life* (Rev. ed.). New York: McGraw-Hill, 1976.

SELYE, H. On the real benefits of eustress. *Psychology Today.* March 1978, pp. 60–63; 69–70.

SENNECKER, P., & HENDRICK, C. Androgyny and helping behavior. *Journal of Personality and Social Psychology,* 1983, *45,* 916–925.

SHAINESS, N. A. A reevaluation of some aspects of femininity through a study of menstruation: A preliminary report. *Comprehensive Psychiatry,* 1961, *2,* 20–26.

SHEPPARD, C., FRACCHIA, J., RICCA, E., & MERLIS, S. Indications of psychopathology in male narcotic abusers, their effects and relation to treatment effectiveness. *Journal of Psychology,* 1972, *81,* 351–360.

SHER, K. J., & WALITZER, K. S. Individual difference in the stress-response-dampening effect of alcohol: A dose-response study. *Journal of Abnormal Psychology,* 1986, *95,* 159–167.

SHOPE, G. L., HEDRICK, T. E., & GEEN, R. G. Physical/verbal aggression: Sex differences in style. *Journal of Personality,* 1978, *46,* 23–42.

SHORT, R. V. The origins of human sexuality. In C. R. Austin & R. V. Short (Eds.), *Reproduction in mammals,* vol 8: *Human sexuality.* Cambridge: Cambridge University Press, 1980.

SHORTELL, J., EPSTEIN, S., & TAYLOR, S. P. Instigation to aggression as a function of degree of defeat and capacity for massive retaliation. *Journal of Personality,* 1970, *38,* 313–328.

SHOTLAND, R. L., & HUSTON, T. L. Emergencies: What are they and do they influence bystanders to intervene? *Journal of Personality and Social Psychology,* 1979, *37,* 1822–1834.

SHOTLAND, R. L., & JOHNSON, M. P. Bystander behavior and kinesics: The interaction between helper and victim. *Environmental Psychology and Nonverbal Behavior,* 1978, *2,* 181–190.

SHRAUGER, J. S. Self-esteem and reactions to being observed by others. *Journal of Personality and Social Psychology,* 1972, *23,* 192–200.

SIEGEL, A., & FLYNN, J. P. Differential effects of electrical stimulation and lesions of the hippocampus and adjacent regions upon attack behavior in cats. *Brain Research,* 1968, *7,* 252–267.

SIEGEL, J. M. Reticular formation activity and REM sleep. In R. Drucker-Colin, M. Shkurovich, & M. B. Sterman (Eds.), *The functions of sleep.* New York: Academic Press, 1979.

SIEGEL, S. The role of conditioning in drug tolerance and addiction. In J. D. Keehn (Ed.), *Psychopathology in animals: Research and clinical implications.* New York: Academic Press, 1979.

SIEGEL, S. Classical conditioning, drug tolerance, and drug dependence. In R. G. Smart, F. B. Glasser, Y. Israel, H. Kalant, R. E. Popham, and W. Schmidt (Eds.), *Research advances in alcohol and drug problems.* New York: Plenum, 1983.

SIGNORELLA, M. L., & JAMISON, W. Masculinity, femininity, androgyny, and cognitive performance: A meta-analysis. *Psychological Bulletin,* 1986, *100,* 207–228.

SILVERSTEIN, B., KOZLOWSKI, L. T., & SCHACHTER, S. Social life, cigarette smoking, and urinary pH. *Journal of Experimental Psychology: General,* 1977, *106,* 20–23.

SIM, F. H., & SPENCE, J. T. Gender-related traits and helping behaviors. *Journal of Personality and Social Psychology,* 1986, *51,* 615–621.

SIMON, W., & GAGNON, J. H. Psychosexual development. In W. Simon & J. H. Gagnon (Eds.), *The sexual scene.* Chicago: Trans/Action Books, 1970.

SIMONS, C. W., & PILIAVIN, J. A. Effect of deception on reactions to a victim. *Journal of Personality and Social Psychology,* 1972, *21,* 56–60.

SIMONSON, E., & WEISER, P. C. *Psychological aspects and physiological correlates of work and fatigue.* Springfield, Ill.: Charles C Thomas, 1976.

SIMPSON, M. T., OLEWINE, D. A., JENKINS, C. D., RAMSEY, F. H., ZYZANSKI, S. J., THOMAS, G., & HAMES, C. G. Exercise-induced catecholamines and platelet aggregation in the coronary-prone behavior pattern. *Psychosomatic Medicine,* 1974, *36,* 476–487.

SIMS, E. A. H., GOLDMAN, R. F., GLUCK, C. M., HORTON, E. S., KELLEHER, P. C., & ROWE, D. W. Experimental obesity in man. *Transcripts of the Association of American Physicians,* 1968, *81,* 153–170.

SINGER, J. E., LUNDBERG, U., & FRANKENHAEUSER, M. Stress on the train: A study of urban commuting. In A. Baum, J. E. Singer, & S. Valins (Eds.), *Advances in environmental psychology* (Vol. 1). Hillsdale, N.J.: Erlbaum, 1978.

SJÖSTROM, L. Fat cells and body weight. In A. J. Stunkard (Ed.), *Obesity.* Philadelphia: Saunders, 1980, pp. 72–100.

SKINNER, B. F. *The behavior of organisms: An experimental analysis.* New York: Appleton-Century-Crofts, 1938.

SKINNER, H. A., GLASER, F. B., & ANNIS, H. M. Crossing the threshold: Factors in self-identification as an alcoholic. *British Journal of Addiction,* 1982, *77,* 51–64.

SLADE, P. D., & RUSSELL, G. F. M. Awareness of body dimensions in anorexia nervosa: Cross-sectional and longitudinal studies. *Psychological Medicine,* 1973, *3,* 188–199.

SMART, R. G. Effects of alcohol on conflict and avoidance behavior. *Quarterly Journal of Studies on Alcohol,* 1965, *26,* 187–205.

SMITH, G. F., & DORFMAN, D. D. The effect of stimulus uncertainty on the relationship between frequency of exposure and liking. *Journal of Personality and Social Psychology,* 1975, *31,* 150–155.

SMITH, J. E., CO, C., FREEMAN, M. E., SANDS, M. P., & LANE, J. D. Neurotransmitter turnover in rat striatum is correlated with morphine self-administration. *Nature,* 1980, *287,* 152–154.

SMITH, R. P., JR. Frontalis muscle tension and personality. *Psychophysiology,* 1973, *10,* 311–312.

SMITH, T. W., HOUSTON, B. K., & STUCKY, R. J. Type A behavior, irritability, and cardiovascular response. *Motivation and Emotion,* 1984, *8,* 221–230.

SNYDER, F., SCOTT, J., KARACAN, I., & ANDERSON, D. Presumptive evidence on REMS deprivation in depressive illness. *Psychophysiology,* 1968, *4,* 382.

SNYDER, M., SIMPSON, J. A., & GANGESTAD, S. Personality and sexual relations. *Journal of Personality and Social Psychology,* 1986, *51,* 181–190.

SNYDER, S. The brain's own opiates. *Chemical and Engineering News,* 1977, *55*(48), 26–35; 266–271.(a)

SNYDER, S. Opiate receptors and internal opiates. *Scientific American,* 1977, *236*(3), 44–56. (b)

SOBELL, M. B., & SOBELL, L. C. Second year treatment outcome of alcoholics treated by individualized behavior therapy: Results. *Behavior Research Therapy,* 1976, *14,* 195–215.

SOLOMON, R. L. The opponent-process theory of acquired motivation: The costs of pleasure and the benefits of pain. *American Psychologist,* 1980, *35,* 691–712.

SOLOMON, R. L., & CORBIT, J. D. An opponent process theory of motivation: I. Temporal dynamics of affect. *Psychological Review,* 1974, *81,* 119–145.

SOLOMON, R. L., & WYNNE, L. C. Traumatic avoidance learning: The principles of anxiety conservation and partial irreversibility. *Psychological Review,* 1954, *61,* 353–385.

SORRENTINO, R. M., & HEWITT, E. C. The uncertainty-reducing properties of achievement tasks revisited. *Journal of Personality and Social Psychology,* 1984, *47,* 884–899.

SOURS, J. A. The anorexia nervosa syndrome. *International Journal of Psycho-Analysis,* 1974, *55,* 567–576.

SPENCE, J. T. The distracting effects of material reinforcers in the discrimination learning of lower- and middle-class children. *Child Development,* 1970, *41,* 103–111.

SPENCE, J. T. The Thematic Apperception Test and attitudes towards achievement in women: A new look at the motive to avoid success and a new method of measurement. *Journal of Consulting and Clinical Psychology,* 1974, *42,* 427–437.

SPENCE, J. T. Masculinity, femininity, and gender-related traits: A conceptual analysis and critique of current literature. In B. A. Maher and W. B. Maher (Eds.), *Progress in experimental personality research* (vol. 13, pp. 1–97). New York: Academic Press, 1984.

SPENCE, J. T., & HELMREICH, R. L. *Masculinity and femininity: Their psychological dimensions, correlates, and antecedents.* Austin: University of Texas Press, 1978.

SPENCE, J. T., & HELMREICH, R. L. Achievement-related motives and behavior. In J. T. Spence, *Achievement and achievement motives.* San Francisco: W. H. Freeman, 1983.

SPENCE, J. T., HELMREICH, R. L., & STAPP, J. A. A short version of the Attitudes Towards Women Scale (AWS). *Bulletin of the Psychonomic Society,* 1973, *2,* 219–220.

SPERRY, R. W. The great cerebral commissure. *Scientific American,* 1964, *210*(1), 42–52.

SPIEGEL, E. A., WYCIS, H. T., FREED, H., & ORCHINIK, C. The central mechanism of the emotions. *American Journal of Psychiatry,* 1951, *108,* 426–432.

SPINKS, J. A., BLOWERS, G. H., & SHEK, D. T. L. The role of the orienting response in the anticipation of information: A skin conductance response study. *Psychophysiology,* 1985, *22,* 385–394.

STANGLER, R. S., & PRINTZ, A. M. DSM-III: Psychiatric diagnosis in a university population. *American Journal of Psychiatry,* 1980, *26,* 391–398.

STARKÁ, L., ŠIPOVÁ, I., & HYNIE, J. Plasma testosterone in male transsexuals and homosexuals. *Journal of Sex Research,* 1975, *11,* 134–138.

STAUB, E. *Positive social behavior: Social and personal influences* (Vol. 1). New York: Academic Press, 1978.

STEELE, C. I. Weight loss among teenage girls: An adolescent crisis. *Adolescence,* 1980, *15,* 823–829.

STEELE, C. M. What happens when you drink too much? *Psychology Today,* January 1986, pp. 48–52.

STEELE, C. M., SOUTHWICK, L., & PAGANO, R. Drinking your troubles away: The role of activity in mediating alcohol's reduction of psychological stress. *Journal of Abnormal Psychology*, 1986, 95, 173–180.

STEELE, R. S. *The physiological concomitants of psychogenic motive arousal in college males*. Unpublished doctoral thesis, Harvard University, 1973.

STEELE, R. S. Power motivation, activation, and inspirational speeches. *Journal of Personality*, 1977, 45, 53–64.

STEELE, R. S. Psychoanalysis and hermeneutics. *International Review of Psychoanalysis*, 1979, 6, 389–411.

STEERS, R. M. Antecedents and outcomes of organizational commitment. *Administrative Science Quarterly*, 1977, 22, 46–56.

STEERS, R. M., & PORTER, L. W. Attachment to organizations. In R. M. Steers & L. W. Porter (Eds.), *Motivation and work behavior* (2nd ed.). New York: McGraw-Hill, 1979.

STEIN, L. The chemistry of reward. In A. Routtenberg (Ed.), *Biology of reinforcement: Facets of brain stimulation reward*. New York: Academic Press, 1980.

STEINBERG, H. (ED.). *The scientific basis of drug dependence*. London: Churchill, 1969.

STELLAR, E. The physiology of motivation. *Psychological Review*, 1954, 61, 5–22.

STEPANSKI, E., LAMPHERE, J., BADIA, P., ZORICK, F., & ROTH, T. Sleep fragmentation and daytime sleepiness. *Sleep*, 1984, 7, 18–26.

STEPHAN, W. G., ROSENFIELD, D., & STEPHAN, C. Egotism in males and females. *Journal of Personality and Social Psychology*, 1976, 34, 1161–1167.

STEWART, A. J., & WINTER, D. G. Arousal of power motive in women. *Journal of Consulting and Clinical Psychology*, 1976, 44, 495–496.

STIMSON, G. V. *Heroin and behaviour: Diversity among addicts attending London clinics*. New York: Wiley, 1973.

STORM, T., & CAIRD, W. K. The effects of alcohol on serial verbal learning in chronic alcoholics. *Psychonomic Science*, 1967, 9, 43–44.

STORM, T., CAIRD, W. K., & KORBIN, E. The effects of alcohol on rote verbal learning and retention. Paper presented at the meeting of the Canadian Psychological Association, Vancouver, B.C., 1965.

STORM, T., & SMART, R. G. Dissociation: A possible explanation for some features of alcoholism and implications for its treatment. *Quarterly Journal of Studies on Alcohol*, 1965, 26, 111–115.

STRIEGEL-MOORE, R. H., SILBERSTEIN, L. R., & RODIN, J. Toward an understanding of risk factors for bulimia. *American Psychologist*, 1986, 41, 246–263.

STRUBE, M. J., BERRY, J. M., & MOERGEN, S. Relinquishment of control and the Type A behavior pattern: The role of performance evaluation. *Journal of Personality and Social Psychology*, 1985, 49, 831–849.

STRUBE, M. J., TURNER, C. W., CERRO, D., STEVENS, J., & HINCHEY, F. Interpersonal aggression and the Type A coronary-prone behavior pattern: A theoretical distinction. *Journal of Personality and Social Psychology*, 1984, 47, 839–847.

STRUBE, M. J., & WERNER, C. Relinquishment of control and the Type A behavior pattern. *Journal of Personality and Social Psychology*, 1985, 48, 688–701.

STUART, R. B. *Act thin, stay thin*. New York: Norton, 1978.

STUNKARD, A. J. Obesity and the denial of hunger. *Psychosomatic Medicine*, 1959, 21, 281–289.

STUNKARD, A. J., FOCH, T. T., & HRUBEC, Z. *A twin study of human obesity*. Unpublished manuscript, University of Pennsylvania, Philadelphia, 1985.

STUNKARD, A. J., SORENSON, T. I. A., HANIS, C., TEASDALE, T. W., CHAKRABORTY, R., SCHULL, W. J., & SCHULSINGER, F. *An adoption study of human obesity*. Unpublished manuscript. University of Pennsylvania, 1985.

STURUP, G. K. Correctional treatment and the criminal sexual offender. *Canadian Journal of Corrections*, 1961, 3, 250–265.

SUEDFELD, P. The benefits of boredom: Sensory deprivation reconsidered. *American Scientist*, 1975, 63, 60–69.

SUEDFELD, P., & KRISTELLER, J. L. Stimulus reduction as a technique in health psychology. *Health Psychology*, 1982, 1, 337–357.

SUGIYAMA, Y. Social organization of hanuman langurs. In S. Altmann (Ed.), *Social communication among primates*. Chicago: University of Chicago Press, 1967.

SUINN, R. M. The cardiac stress program for Type A patients. *Cardiac Rehabilitation*, 1975, 5, 13–15.

SUINN, R. M. How to break the vicious cycle of stress. *Psychology Today*, December 1976, pp. 59–60.

SUINN, R. M., BROCK, L., & EDIE, C. Behavior therapy for Type A patients. *American Journal of Cardiology*, 1975, 36, 269–270.

SUNDSTROM, E. Interpersonal behavior and physical environment. In L. Wrightsman (Ed.), *Social psychology in the seventies* (2nd ed.). Pacific Grove, Calif.: Brooks/Cole, 1977.

SUOMI, S. J., & HARLOW, H. F. Monkeys at play. *Play, A Natural History Magazine Supplement*, December 1971, pp. 72–77.

SVEBAK, S., & MURGATROYD, S. Metamotivational dominance: A multimethod validation of reversal theory constructs. *Personality and Social Psychology*, 1985, 48, 107–116.

SWEENEY, D. R., GOLD, M. S., POTTASH, A. L. C., & DAVIES, R. K. Neurobiological theories. In I. L. Kutash et al., *Handbook on stress and anxiety* (pp. 112–126). San Francisco: Jossey-Bass, 1980.

SWINSON, R. P., & EAVES, D. *Alcoholism and addiction*. Estover, Plymouth, England: MacDonald and Evans, 1978.

SWITZKY, H. N., & HAYWOOD, H. C. Motivational orientation and the relative efficacy of self-monitored and externally imposed reinforcement systems in children. *Journal of Personality and Social Psychology*, 1974, 30, 360–366.

SYLVA, K., BRUNER, J. S., & GENOVA, P. The role of play in the problem-solving of children 3–5 years old. In J. S. Bruner, A. Jolly, & K. Sylva (Eds.), *Play: Its role in development and evolution*. New York: Penguin, 1976.

SYMONS, D. *The evolution of human sexuality*. New York: Oxford University Press, 1979.

TAGGART, P., & CARRUTHERS, M. E. Endogenous hyperlipidaemia induced by emotional stress of racing driving. *Lancet*, 1971, 1, 363–366.

TAGGART, P., CARRUTHERS, M. E., & SOMERVILLE, W. Electrocardiogram, plasma catecholamines and lipids, and their modification by oxprenolol when speaking before an audience. *Lancet*, 1973, 2, 341–346.

TAKASAWA, N. Change in the amount of performance and change of physiological activity level. *Journal of Child Development*, 1978, 14, 1–15.

TALLMAN, J. F., PAUL, S.M., SKOLNICK, P., & GALLAGER, D. W. Receptors for the age of anxiety: Pharmacology of the benzodiazepines. *Science*, 1980, *207*, 274–281.

TANNER, O. *Stress*. New York: Time-Life, 1976.

TARLER-BENLOLO, L. The role of relaxation in biofeedback training: A critical review of the literature. *Psychological Bulletin*, 1978, *85*, 727–755.

TAUB, J. M. Behavioral and psychological correlates of a difference in chronic sleep duration. *Biological Psychology*, 1977, *5*, 29–45.

TAUB, J. M., HAWKINS, D. R., & VAN DE CASTLE, R. L. Personality characteristics associated with sustained variations in the adult human sleep/wakefulness rhythm. *Waking and Sleeping*, 1978, *2*(1), 7–15.

TAYLOR, S. E. Adjustment to threatening events: A theory of cognitive adaptation. *American Psychologist*, 1983, *38*, 1161–1173.

TAYLOR, S. P. Aggressive behavior and physiological arousal as a function of provocation and the tendency to inhibit aggression. *Journal of Personality*, 1967, *35*, 297–310.

TAYLOR, S. P., & PISANO, R. Physical aggression as a function of frustration and physical attack. *Journal of Social Psychology*, 1971, *84*, 261–267.

TEITELBAUM, P. Disturbances in feeding and drinking behavior after hypothalamic lesions. In M. R. Jones (Ed.), *Nebraska Symposium on Motivation* (Vol. 9). Lincoln: University of Nebraska Press, 1961.

TEMPLER, D. I. Anorexic humans and rats. *American Psychologist*, 1971, *26*, 935.

TEMPLETON, R. D., & QUIGLEY, J. P. The action of insulin on the motility of the gastrointestinal tract. *American Journal of Physiology*, 1930, *91*, 467–474.

TENNEN, H., & ELLER, S. J. Attributional components of learned helplessness and facilitation. *Journal of Personality and Social Psychology*, 1977, *35*, 265–271.

TERRACE, H. S. Extinction of a discriminative operant following discrimination learning with and without errors. *Journal of the Experimental Analysis of Behavior*, 1969, *12*, 571–582.

TERZIAN, H., & ORE, G. D. Syndrome of Klüver and Bucy: Reproduced in man by bilateral removal of the temporal lobes. *Neurology*, 1955, *5*, 373–380.

TESSER, A., & PAULHUS, D. L. Toward a causal model of love. *Journal of Personality and Social Psychology*, 1976, *34*, 1095–1105.

THARP, G. D. The role of glucocorticoids in exercise. *Medicine and Science in Sports*, 1975, *7*, 6–11.

THIBAUT, J. An experimental study of the cohesiveness of underprivileged groups. *Human Relations*, 1950, *3*, 251–278.

THOMAS, A., CHESS, S., & BIRCH, H. G. The origins of personality. *Scientific American*, August 1970, pp. 102–109.

THOMAS, H. Preference for random shapes: Ages six through nineteen years. *Child Development*, 1966, *37*, 843–859.

TIENARI, P. Psychiatric illness in identical twins. *Acta Psychiatrica Scandinavica*, 1963, *39*, Suppl. No. 171, 1–195.

TIGER, L. *Optimism: The biology of hope*. New York: Simon & Schuster, 1979.

TILLEY, A. J. Recovery sleep at different times of the night following loss of the last four hours of sleep. *Sleep*, 1985, *8*, 129–136.

TOCH, H. *Violent men*. Chicago: Aldine, 1969.

TOW, P. M., & WHITTY, C. W. Personality changes after operations on the cingulate gyrus in man. *Journal of Neurology, Neurosurgery, and Psychiatry*, 1953, *16*, 186–193.

TRACY, R. L., & TRACY, L. N. Reports of mental activity from sleep stages 2 and 4. *Perceptual and Motor Skills*, 1974, *38*, 647–648.

TRAVAGLINI, P., BECK-PECCOZ, P., FERRARI, C., AMBROSI, B., PARACCHI, A., SEVERGNINI, A., SPADA, A., & FAGLIA, G. Some aspects of hypothalamic-pituitary function in patients with anorexia nervosa. *Acta Endocrinologica*, 1976, *81*, 252–262.

TRESEMER, D. Fear of success: Popular but unproven. *Psychology Today*, March 1974, pp. 82–85.

TRINDER, J., BRUCK, D., PAXTON, S. J., MONTGOMERY, L., & BOWLING, A. Physical fitness, exercise, age, and human sleep. *Australian Journal of Psychology*, 1982, *34*, 131–138.

TROPE, Y. Uncertainty-reducing properties of achievement tasks. *Journal of Personality and Social Psychology*, 1979, *37*, 1505–1518.

TSUDA, A., & HIRAI, H. Effects of the amount of required coping response tasks on gastrointestinal lesions in rats. *Japanese Psychological Research*, 1975, *17*, 119–132.

TURKINGTON, C. Depression seen induced by decline in NE levels. *APA Monitor*, 1982, *13*, 11.

ULEMAN, J. S. *A new TAT measure of the need for power*. Unpublished doctoral dissertation. Harvard University, 1966.

ULEMAN, J. S. The need for influence: Development and validation of a measure, in comparison with a need for power. *Genetic Psychology Monographs*, 1972, *85*, 157–214.

ULRICH, R. E., WOLFE, M., & DULANEY, S. Punishment of shock-induced aggression. *Journal of Experimental Analysis of Behavior*, 1969, *12*, 1009–1015.

UNGER, R. K. Personal appearance and social control. In M. Safir, M. Mednick, I. Dafna, & J. Bernard (Eds.), *Women's worlds: From the new scholarship* (pp. 142–151). New York: Praeger, 1985.

UPHOUSE, L. *In vitro* RNA synthesis by chromatin from three brain regions of differentially reared rats. *Behavioral Biology*, 1978, *22*, 39–49.

UPHOUSE, L. Reevaluation of mechanisms that mediate brain differences between enriched and impoverished animals. *Psychological Bulletin*, 1980, *88*, 215–232.

UPHOUSE, L., & MOORE, R. Effect of rearing condition on *in vitro* RNA synthesis by brain chromatin. *Behavioral Biology*, 1978, *22*, 23–28.

URSIN, H., COOVER, G. D., KØHLER, C., DERYCK, M., SAGVOLDEN, T., & LEVINE, S. Limbic structures and behavior: Endocrine correlates. In W. H. Gispen, Tj. B. van Wimersma Greidanus, B. Bohus, & D. de Wied (Eds.), *Hormones, homeostasis, and the brain. Progress in Brain Research*. Amsterdam: Elsevier, 1975.

VAILLANT, G. E. *The natural history of alcoholism*. Cambridge: Harvard University Press, 1983.

VALENSTEIN, E. S., COX, V. C., & KAKOLEWSKI, J. W. Reexamination of the role of the hypothalamus in motivation. *Psychological Review*, 1970, *77*, 16–31.

VALINS, S. Cognitive effects of false heart-rate feedback. *Journal of Personality and Social Psychology*, 1966, *4*, 400–408.

VALINS, S. Emotionality and information concerning internal reactions. *Journal of Personality and Social Psychology*, 1967, *6*, 458–463.

VALINS, S., & NISBETT, R. E. Attribution processes in the development and treatment of emotional disorders. In E. Jones, D. Kanouse, H. Kelley, R. E. Nisbett, S. Valins, & B. Weiner (Eds.), *Attribution: Perceiving the causes of behavior.* Morristown, N.J.: General Learning Press, 1972.

VALLARDARES, H., & CORBALAN, V. Temporal lobe and human behavior. 1st International Congress, *Neurological Science*, 1959, 201–203.

VAN DYKE, C., & BYCK, R. Cocaine. *Scientific American*, 1982, *246*, 128–141.

VANTRESS, F. E., & WILLIAMS, C. B. The effect of the presence of the provocator and the opportunity to counteraggress on systolic blood pressure. *Journal of General Psychology*, 1972, *86*, 63–68.

VEREBY, V., & BLUM, K. Alcohol euphoria, possible mediation via endorphinergic mechanisms. *Journal of Psychedelic Drugs*, 1979, *11*, 305–311.

VERNIKOS-DANELLIS, J., & HEYBACH, J. P. Psycho-physiologic mechanisms regulating the hypothalamic-pituitary-adrenal response to stress. In H. Selye (Ed.), *Selye's guide to stress research* (Vol. 1). New York: Van Nostrand Reinhold, 1980.

VEROFF, J. Development and validation of a projective measure of power motivation. *Journal of Abnormal and Social Psychology*, 1957, *54*, 1–8.

VISINTAINER, M. A., VOLPICELLI, J. R., & SELIGMAN, M. E. P. Tumor rejection in rats after inescapable or escapable shock. *Science*, 1982, *216*, 437–439.

VITZ, P. Affect as a function of stimulus variation. *Journal of Experimental Psychology*, 1966, *71*, 74–79. (a)

VITZ, P. Preference for different amounts of stimulus complexity. *Behavioral Science*, 1966, *11*, 105–114. (b)

VOGEL, G. W. A review of REM sleep deprivation. *Archives of General Psychiatry*, 1975, *32*, 749–761.

VOGEL, G. W. Sleep-onset mentation. In A. M. Arkin, J. S. Antrobus, & S. J. Ellman (Eds.), *The mind in sleep: Psychology and psychophysiology.* Hillsdale, N.J.: Erlbaum, 1978.

VOGEL, G. W. A motivational function of REM sleep. In R. Drucker-Colin, M. Shkurovich, & M. B. Sterman (Eds.), *The functions of sleep.* New York: Academic Press, 1979.

VOLPICELLI, J. R. Uncontrollable events and alcohol drinking. *British Journal of Addiction*, 1987, *82*, 385–396.

VOLPICELLI, J. R., ULM, R. R., ALTENOR, A., & SELIGMAN, M. E. P. Learned mastery in the rat. *Learning and Motivation*, 1983, *14*, 204–222.

VON EULER, U. S. *Noradrenaline.* Springfield, Ill.: Charles C Thomas, 1956.

VOSSEL, G., & LAUX, L. The impact of stress experience on heart rate and task performance in the presence of a novel stressor. *Biological Psychology*, 1978, *6*, 193–201.

VREVEN, R., & NUTTIN, J. R. Frequency perception of successes as a function of results previously obtained by others and by oneself. *Journal of Personality and Social Psychology*, 1976, *34*, 734–745.

VROOM, V. H. Organizational choice: A study of pre- and post-decision processes. *Organizational Behavior and Human Performance*, 1966, *1*, 212–225.

VROOM, V. H., & DECI, E. L. The stability of post-decision dissonance: A follow-up study of the job attitudes of business school graduates. *Organizational Behavior and Human Performance*, 1971, *6*, 36–49.

WAID, W. M., & ORNE, M. T. The physiological detection of deception. *American Scientist*, 1982, *70*, 402–409.

WALKER, E. L. *Psychological complexity and aesthetics, or the hedgehog as an aesthetic mediator (HAM).* Invited address to American Psychological Association convention, New Orleans, September 1974.

WALKER, E. L. *Psychological complexity and preference: A hedgehog theory of behavior.* Pacific Grove, Calif.: Brooks/Cole, 1980.

WALLACE, R. K., & BENSON, H. The physiology of meditation. *Scientific American*, February 1972, pp. 84–90.

WALLACE, R. K., BENSON, H., & WILSON, A. F. A wakeful hypometabolic physiologic state. *American Journal of Physiology*, 1971, *221*, 795–799.

WALSH, B. T., KATZ, J. L., LEVIN, J., KREAM, J., FUKUSHIMA, D. K., HELLMAN, L. D., WEINER, H., & ZUMOFF, B. Adrenal activity in anorexia nervosa. *Psychosomatic Medicine*, 1978, *40*, 499–506.

WALSTER, W., & WALSTER, G. W. *A new look at love.* Reading, Mass.: Addison-Wesley, 1978.

WALTERS, J., APTER, M. J., & SVEBAK, S. Color preference, arousal, and the theory of psychological reversals. *Motivation and Emotion*, 1982, *6*, 193–215.

WANOUS, J. P. A job preview makes recruiting more effective. *Harvard Business Review*, 1975, *53*(5), 16; 166–168. (a)

WANOUS, J. P. Tell it like it is at realistic job previews. *Personnel*, 1975, *52*(4), 50–60. (b)

WANOUS, J. P. Organizational entry: From naive expectations to realistic beliefs. *Journal of Applied Psychology*, 1976, *61*, 22–29.

WANOUS, J. P. Organizational entry: The individual's viewpoint. In J. R. Hackman, E. E. Lawler III, & L. W. Porter (Eds.), *Perspectives on behavior in organizations.* New York: McGraw-Hill, 1977.

WARD, J. L. Exogenous androgen activates female behavior in non-copulating, prenatally stressed male rats. *Journal of Comparative and Physiological Psychology*, 1977, *91*, 465–471.

WARD, L. B., & ATHOS, A. G. *Student expectations of corporate life.* Boston: Division of Research, Graduate School of Business Administration, Harvard University, 1972.

WARM, J. S., & DEMBER, W. N. Awake at the switch. *Psychology Today*, April 1986, pp. 46–53.

WARREN, M. P., & VANDEWIELE, R. L. Clinical and metabolic features of anorexia nervosa. *American Journal of Obstetrics and Gynecology*, 1973, *117*, 435–449.

WATERS, W. F., McDONALD, D. G., & KORESKO, R. L. Habituation of the orienting response: A gating mechanism subserving selective attention. *Psychophysiology*, 1977, *14*, 228–236.

WATSON, D., & CLARK, L. A. Negative affectivity: The disposition to experience aversive emotional states. *Psychological Bulletin*, 1984, *96*, 465–490.

WATSON, J. B., & MORGAN, J. J. B. Emotional reactions and psychological experimentation. *American Journal of Psychology*, 1917, *28*, 163–174.

WATSON, R. I. *Motivation and role induction.* Unpub-lished honors thesis, Wesleyan University, 1969.

WEBB, W. B. *Sleep: The gentle tyrant*. Englewood Cliffs, N. J.: Prentice-Hall, 1975.

WEBB, W. B. Theories of sleep functions and some clinical implications. In R. Drucker-Colin, M. Shkurovich, & M. B. Sterman (Eds.), *The functions of sleep*. New York: Academic Press, 1979.

WEBB, W. B. A further analysis of age and sleep deprivation effects. *Psychophysiology*, 1985, *22*, 156–161.

WEBB, W. B., & AGNEW, H. W., JR. Are we chronically sleep deprived? *Bulletin of the Psychonomic Society*, 1975, *6*, 47–48. (a)

WEBB, W. B., & AGNEW, H. W., JR. Sleep efficiency for sleep-wake cycles of varied length. *Psychophysiology*, 1975, *12*, 637–641. (b)

WEBB, W. B., & AGNEW, H. W., JR. Analysis of the sleep stages in sleep-wakefulness regimens of varied length. *Psychophysiology*, 1977, *14*, 445–450.

WEBB, W. B., & FRIEL, J. Sleep stage and personality characteristics of "natural" long and short sleepers. *Science*, 1971, *171*, 587–588.

WEBB, W. B., & LEVY, C. M. Age, sleep deprivation, and performance. *Psychophysiology*, 1982, *19*, 272–276.

WEBER, M. *The Protestant ethic and the spirt of capitalism* (T. Parsons, trans.). New York: University of Nebraska Press, 1964.

WEINER, B. *Theories of motivation: From mechanism to cognition*. Chicago: Markham, 1972.

WEINER, B. Attribution and affect: Comment on Sohn's critique. *Journal of Educational Psychology*, 1977, *69*, 506–511.

WEINER, B. A theory of motivation for some classroom experiences. *Journal of Educational Psychology*, 1979, *71*, 3–25.

WEINER, B. A cognitive (attribution)-emotion-action model of motivated behavior: An analysis of judgments of help-giving. *Journal of Personality and Social Psychology*, 1980, *39*, 186–200.

WEINER, B., FRIEZE, I., KUKLA, A., REED, L., REST, S., & ROSENBAUM, R. M. Perceiving the causes of success and failure. In E. E. Jones, D. E. Kanouse, H. H. Kelly, R. E. Nisbett, S. Valins, & B. Weiner (Eds.), *Attribution: Perceiving the causes of behavior*. Morristown, N.J.: General Learning Press, 1971.

WEINER, B., & KUKLA, A. An attributional analysis of achievement motivation. *Journal of Personality and Social Psychology*, 1970, *15*, 1–20.

WEINER, B., & POTEPAN, P. A. Personality characteristics and affective reactions towards exams of superior and failing college students. *Journal of Educational Psychology*, 1970, *61*, 144–151.

WEINER, B., RUSSELL, D., & LERMAN, D. Affective consequences of causal ascriptions. In J. H. Harvey, W. J. Ickes, & R. F. Kidd (Eds.), *New directions in attribution research* (Vol. 2). Hillsdale, N.J.: Erlbaum, 1978.

WEINER, B., RUSSELL, D., & LERMAN, D. The cognitive-emotional process in achievement-related contexts. *Journal of Personality and Social Psychology*, 1979, *37*, 1211–1220.

WEINER, H., & KATZ, J. L. The hypothalamic–pituitary–adrenal axis in anorexia nervosa: A reassessment. In P. L. Darby, P. E. Garfinkel, D. M. Garner, & D. V. Coscina, *Anorexia nervosa: Recent developments in research* (pp. 249–270). New York: Alan R. Liss, Inc., 1983.

WEISS, J. M. Effects of coping responses on stress. *Journal of Comparative and Physiological Psychology*, 1968, *65*, 251–260.

WEISS, J. M. Somatic effects of predictable and unpredictable shock. *Psychosomatic Medicine*, 1970, *32*, 397–408.

WEISS, J. M. Effects of coping behavior in different warning signal conditions on stress pathology in rats. *Journal of Comparative and Physiological Psychology*, 1971, *77*, 1–13. (a)

WEISS, J. M. Effects of punishing the coping response (conflict) on stress pathology in rats. *Journal of Comparative and Physiological Psychology*, 1971, *77*, 14–21. (b)

WEISS, J. M. Effects of coping behavior with and without a feedback signal on stress pathology in rats. *Journal of Comparative and Physiological Psychology*, 1971, *77*, 22–30. (c)

WEISS, J. M., GLAZER, H. I., & POHORECKY, L. A. Coping behavior and neurochemical changes: An alternative explanation of the original "learned helplessness" experiments. In G. Serban & A. Kling (Eds.), *Animal models in human psychobiology*. New York: Plenum, 1976.

WEISS, J. M., GLAZER, H. I., POHORECKY, L. A., BRICK, J., & MILLER, N. E. Effects of chronic exposure to stressors on avoidance-escape behavior and on brain norepinephrine. *Psychosomatic Medicine*, 1975, *37*, 522–534.

WEISS, J. M., STONE, E. A., & HARRELL, N. W. Coping behavior and brain norepinephrine level in rats. *Journal of Comparative and Physiological Psychology*, 1970, *72*, 153–160.

WEISS, J. M. Alcohol as a depressant of psychological conflict in rats. *Quarterly Journal of Studies on Alcohol*, 1958, *19*, 226–237.

WESTON, J. The pathology of child abuse. In R. Helfer & L. Kempe (Eds.), *The battered child*. Chicago: University of Chicago Press, 1968.

WHALEN, R. E. Brain mechanisms controlling sexual behavior. In F. A. Beach (Ed.), *Human sexuality in four perspectives*. Baltimore: Johns Hopkins University Press, 1976.

WHITAKER, L. H. Oestrogen and psychosexual disorders. *Medical Journal of Australia*, 1959, *2*, 547–549.

WHITE, A., HANDLER, P., & SMITH, E. L. *Principles of biochemistry* (3rd ed.). New York: McGraw-Hill, 1964.

WHITE, G. D., NIELSEN, G., & JOHNSON, S. M. Timeout duration and the suppression of deviant behavior in children. *Journal of Applied Behavior Analysis*, 1972, *5*, 111–120.

WHITE, J. A., ISMAIL, A. H., & BOTTOMS, G. D. Effects of physical fitness on the adrenocortical response to exercise stress. *Medicine and Science in Sports*, 1976, *8*, 113–118.

WHITE, R. W. Motivation reconsidered: The concept of competence. *Psychological Review*, 1959, *66*, 297–333.

WHITLEY, B. E., JR. Sex-role orientation and self-esteem: A critical meta-analytic review. *Journal of Personality and Social Psychology*, 1983, *44*, 765–778.

WIEDEKING, C., LAKE, R., ZIEGLER, M., KOWARSKI, A. A., & MONEY, J. Plasma noradrenaline and dopamine-beta-hydroxylase during sexual activity. *Psychosomatic Medicine*, 1977, *39*, 143–148.

WIKLER, A. On the nature of addiction and habituation. *British Journal of Addiction*, 1961, *57*, 73–79.

WIKLER, A. *Opioid dependence.* New York: Plenum, 1980.

WIKLER, A. (ED). *The addictive states.* Baltimore: Williams & Wilkins, 1968.

WILCOXIN, H. C., DRAGOIN, W. B., & KRAL, P. A. Illness-induced aversions in rat and quail: Relative salience of visual and gustatory cues. *Science,* 1971, *171,* 826–828.

WILDER, J. Psychological problems in hypoglycemia. *American Journal of Digestive Diseases,* 1943, *10,* 428–435.

WILDER, J. Malnutrition and mental deficiency. *Nervous Child,* 1944, *3,* 174–186.

WILDER, J. Sugar metabolism in its relation to criminology. In S. Lindner & B. J. Seliger (Eds.), *Handbook of correctional psychology.* New York: Philosophical Library, 1947.

WILLIAMS, R. H. Hypoglycemosis. In R. H. Williams (Ed.), *Diabetes.* New York: Hoeber, 1960.

WILM, E. C. *The theories of instinct: A study of the history of psychology.* New Haven, Conn.: Yale University Press, 1925.

WILSNACK, S. C. The impact of sex roles on women's alcohol use and abuse. In M. Greenblatt, & M. A. Schuckit (Eds.), *Alcoholism problems in women and children.* New York: Grune & Stratton, 1976.

WILSON, E. O. *Sociobiology, the new synthesis.* Cambridge, Mass.: Harvard University Press, 1975.

WILSON, G. T. The effect of alcohol on human sexual behavior. In N. Mello (Ed.), *Advances in substance abuse: Behavioral and biological research.* Greenwich, Conn.: JAI Press, 1981.

WILSON, G. T., & LAWSON, D. M. Expectancies, alcohol, and sexual arousal in women. *Journal of Abnormal Psychology,* 1978, *87,* 358–367.

WILSON, J. D., GEORGE, F. W., GRIFFIN, J. E., ET AL. The hormonal control of sexual development. *Science,* 1981, *211,* 1285–1294.

WILSON, T. D., & LINVILLE, P. W. Improving the performance of college freshmen with attributional techniques. *Journal of Personality and Social Psychology,* 1985, *49,* 287–293.

WING, L. *Autistic children: A guide for parents.* London: Constable, 1971.

WINGATE, B. A., & CHRISTIE, M. J. Ego strength and body image in anorexia nervosa. *Journal of Psychosomatic Research,* 1978, *22,* 201–204.

WINTER, D. G. *The power motive.* New York: Free Press, 1973.

WINTER, D. G. *The power motive in women.* Unpublished manuscript. Wesleyan University, Department of Psychology, 1982.

WINTER, D. G., & STEWART, A. J. The power motive. In H. London & J. E. Exner, Jr. (Eds.), *Dimensions of personality.* New York: Wiley, 1978.

WINTERBOTTOM, M. T. *The relation of childhood training in independence to achievement motivation.* Unpublished doctoral dissertation, University of Michigan, 1953.

WISE, C. D., & STEIN, L. Facilitation of brain self-stimulation by central administration of norepinephrine. *Science,* 1969, *163,* 299–301.

WOLFF, M., & STEIN, A. Head Start six months later. *Phi Delta Kappan,* 1967, *48,* 349–350.

WOLPE, J. *Psychotherapy by reciprocal inhibition.* Stanford, Calif.: Stanford University Press, 1958.

WOLPE, J. *The practice of behavior therapy.* New York: Pergamon Press, 1969.

WOLPE, J., & LAZARUS, A. A. *Behavior therapy techniques.* New York: Pergamon Press, 1966.

WOODS, S. C., VASSELLI, J. R., KAESTNER, E., SZAKMARY, G. A., MILBURN, P., & VITIELLO, M. V. Conditioned insulin secretion and meal feeding in rats. *Journal of Comparative and Physiological Psychology,* 1977, *91,* 128–133.

WOOLEY, S. C., WOOLEY, O. W., & DYRENFORTH, S. R. Theoretical, practical, and applied social issues in behavioral treatments of obesity. *Journal of Applied Behavioral Analysis,* 1979, *12,* 3–25.

WORCHEL, P. The effect of three types of arbitrary thwarting on the instigation to aggression. *Journal of Personality,* 1974, *42,* 301–318.

WORICK, W. W., & SCHALLER, W. E. *Alcohol, tobacco, and drugs: Their uses and abuses.* Englewood Cliffs, N.J.: Prentice-Hall, 1977.

Work in America: Report of a special task force to the U.S. Department of Health, Education, and Welfare. Cambridge, Mass.: MIT Press, 1973.

WORTMAN, C. B., & BREHM, J. W. Responses to uncontrollable outcomes: An integration of reactance theory and the learned helplessness model. In L. Berkowitz (Ed.), *Advances in experimental social psychology* (Vol. 8). New York: Academic Press, 1975.

WRIGHT, R. A., TOI, M., & BREHM, J. W. Difficulty and interpersonal attraction. *Motivation and Emotion,* 1984, *8,* 327–341.

WURTMAN, R. J. Nutrients that modify brain function. *Scientific American,* 1982, *246,* 50–59.

WYLER, A. R., MASUDA, M., & HOLMES, T. H. Magnitude of life events and seriousness of illness. *Psychosomatic Medicine,* 1971, *33,* 115–122.

WYNNE, L. C., & SOLOMON, R. L. Traumatic avoidance learning: Acquisition and extinction of dogs deprived of normal peripheral autonomic function. *Genetic Psychology Monographs,* 1955, *52,* 241–284.

WYNNE-EDWARDS, V. C. *Animal dispersion in relation to social behavior.* New York: Hafner, 1962.

YARROW, L. J., RUBENSTEIN, J. L., PEDERSEN, F. A., & JANKOWSKI, J. J. Dimensions of early stimulation and their differential effects on infant development. *Merrill-Palmer Quarterly,* 1972, *18,* 205–218.

YOUNG, P. T., & CHAPLIN, J. P. Studies of food preference, appetite, and dietary habit: III. Palatability and appetite in relation to body need. *Comparative Psychology Monographs,* 1945, *18*(3), 1–45.

ZEICHNER, A., & PIHL, R. O. Effects of alcohol and behavior contingencies on human aggression. *Journal of Abnormal Psychology,* 1979, *88,* 153–160.

ZENTALL, S. S., & ZENTALL, T. R. Optimal stimulation: A model of disordered activity and performance in normal and deviant children. *Psychological Bulletin,* 1983, *94,* 446–471.

ZIKA, S., & CHAMBERLAIN, K. Relation of hassles and personality to subjective well-being. *Journal of Personality and Social Psychology,* 1987, *53,* 155–162.

ZILLMANN, D. Excitation transfer in communication—mediated aggressive behavior. *Journal of Experimental Social Psychology,* 1971, *7,* 419–434.

ZILLMANN, D., & BRYANT, J. Effect of residual excitation on the emotional response to provocation and delayed aggressive behavior. *Journal of Personality and Social Psychology,* 1974, *30,* 782–791.

ZILLMANN, D., JOHNSON, R. C., & DAY, K. D. Attribution of apparent arousal and proficiency of recovery from sympathetic activation affecting excitation transfer to aggressive behavior. *Journal of Experimental Social Psychology,* 1974, *10,* 503–515.

ZILLMANN, D., KATCHER, A. H., & MILAVSKY, B. Excitation transfer from physical exercise to subsequent aggressive behavior. *Journal of Experimental Social Psychology,* 1972, *8,* 247–259.

ZILLMANN, D., & SAPOLSKY, B. S. What mediates the effect of mild erotica on annoyance and hostile behavior in males? *Journal of Personality and Social Psychology,* 1977, *35,* 587–596.

ZIMBARDO, P. G. The human choice: Individuation, reason, and order versus deindividuation, impulse, and chaos. In W. J. Arnold & D. Levine (Eds.), *Nebraska Symposium on Motivation* (Vol. 17). Lincoln: University of Nebraska Press, 1969.

ZIMBARDO, P. G. Pathology of imprisonment. *Society,* 1972, *9,* 4–8.

ZINBERG, N. E., & ROBERTSON, J. A. *Drugs and the public.* New York: Simon & Schuster, 1972.

ZUCKERMAN, M. The search for high sensation. *Psychology Today,* February 1978, pp. 38–46; 96–99. (a)

ZUCKERMAN, M. Sensation seeking. In H. London & J. E. Exner, Jr. (Eds.), *Dimensions of personality.* New York: Wiley, 1978. (b)

ZUCKERMAN, M. *Sensation seeking: Beyond the optimal level of arousal.* Hillsdale, N.J.: Erlbaum, 1979.

ZUCKERMAN, M. *Biological bases of sensation seeking, impulsivity, and anxiety.* Hillsdale, N.J.: Erlbaum, 1983.

ZUCKERMAN, M., BUCHSBAUM, M. S., & MURPHY, D. L. Sensation-seeking and its biological correlates. *Psychological Bulletin,* 1980, *88,* 187–214.

Author Index

Subject Index

Credits

These pages constitute an extension of the copyright page.
We have made every effort to trace the ownership of all copyrighted material and to secure permission from copyright holders. In the event that any question arises as to the use of any material, we will be pleased to make the necessary corrections in future printings.

Photo Credits

Chapter 1: 1, Maureen Fennelli, Photo Researchers **2,** Ellis Herwig, Stock, Boston **8,** The Bettmann Archive **11,** Photo Researchers, Inc. **14,** Photo Researchers, Inc;

Chapter 2: 21, Cary Wolinsky, Stock, Boston **41,** Mike Mazzaschi, Stock, Boston **45,** Ed Buryn, Jeroboam;

Chapter 3: 48, Ellis Harwig, Stock, Boston;

Chapter 4: 74, Deborah Kahn-Kalas, Stock, Boston;

Chapter 5: 102, Peter Menzel, Stock, Boston;

Chapter 6: 137, Christopher Brown, Stock, Boston;

Chapter 7: 184, J. Howard, Stock, Boston;

Chapter 8: 222, Evan Johnson, Jeroboam;

Chapter 9: 264, Charles Gatewood, Jeroboam;

Chapter 10: 307, Lebo, Jeroboam;

Chapter 11: 351, Robert Foothorap, Jeroboam;

Chapter 12: 383, Michael Hayman, Stock, Boston;

Chapter 13: 424, Joseph Schuyler, Stock, Boston;

Chapter 14: 458, Christopher Morrow, Stock, Boston.

Other Credits

Chapter 3: 50, Figure 3-1 from *Handbook of Physiology: Neurophysiology,* by D. B. Lindsley, Vol. 3, 1960. Copyright 1960 by the American Physiological Society. Reprinted with permission. **52,** Figure 3-2 from "Electroencephalography," by H. H. Jasper. In *Epilepsy and Cerebral Localization,* by W. Penfield and T. C. Erickson (Eds.). Copyright 1941 by Charles C Thomas, Publishers. **53,** Figure 3-3 from "Sex Differences in the Brain," by

1966, *43*, 227–248. Copyright 1966 by the Association for Research in Nervous and Mental Diseases. Reprinted with permission. **196,** Figure 7-5 from "Valium/GABA Receptor," by S. M. Fishman and D. V. Sheehan, *Psychology Today.* Reprinted from *Psychology Today Magazine.* Copyright © 1985 American Psychological Association. **201,** Quote from *Why Man Takes Chances: Studies in Stress-Seeking,* by S. Z. Klausner (Ed.). Copyright 1968 by the Bureau of Social Science Research. This and all other quotations from the same source are reprinted with permission. **202,** Figure 7-6 from "Stress in the Air," by W. D. Fenz and S. Epstein, *Psychology Today,* September, 1969, 3(4), 58–59. Reprinted from *Psychology Today Magazine.* Copyright © 1969 American Psychological Association. **211,** Figure 7-7 from "Altruism as Hedonism: A Social Development Perspective on the Relationship of Negative Mood State and Helping," by R. P. Cialdini and D. T. Kenrick, *Journal of Personality and Social Psychology,* 1976, *34,* pp. 907–914. Copyright 1976 by the American Psychological Association. Reprinted with permission. **217,** Table 7-1 from "A Theory of Motivation," by B. Weiner, *Journal of Educational Psychology,* 1979, *71, 3–25.* Copyright 1979 by the American Psychological Association. Reprinted with permission.

Chapter 8: 226, 228, and 232, Figures 8-1, 8-2, and 8-3 from "Stress and Behavior," by S. Levine, *Scientific American,* January, 1971, 26–31. Copyright © 1971 by Scientific American, Inc. All rights reserved. **227,** Table 8-1 from "Hormonal Influences on Fear-Motivated Behavior," by E. L. Di Giusto, K. Cairncross, and M. G. King, *Psychological Bulletin,* 1971, *75,* 432–444. Copyright 1971 by the American Psychological Association. Reprinted with permission. **235 and 236,** Figures 8-4 and 8-5 from "Somatic Effects of Predictable and Unpredictable Shock," by J. M. Weiss, *Psychosomatic Medicine,* 1970, *32*(4), 397–408. Copyright 1970 by Elsevier North-Holland, Inc. Reprinted with permission. **243,** Table 8-2 from *Organizational Stress: Studies in Role Conflict and Ambiguity,* by R. L. Kahn, D. M. Wolfe, R. P. Quinn, J. D. Snoek, and R. A. Rosenthal. Copyright 1964 by John Wiley and Sons, Inc. Reprinted with permission. **247,** Table 8-3 from "Scaling of Life Change: Comparison of Direct and Indirect Methods," by L. O. Ruch and T. H. Holmes, *Journal of Psychosomatic Research,* 1971, *15,* 221–227. Copyright © 1971 by Pergamon Press, Inc. Reprinted with permission. **258,** Figure 8-6 from "The Physiology of Meditation" by R. K. Wallace and H. Benson, *Scientific American,* February 1972, pp. 84–90. Copyright © 1972 by Scientific American, Inc. All rights reserved.

Chapter 9: 266, Figure 9-1 based on *Alcoholism and Addiction,* by R. P. Swinson and D. Eaves. Copyright 1978 by Macdonald and Evans, Ltd., Estover, Plymouth. **274,** Figure 9-3 from "Effects of Stress on Cigarette Smoking and Urinary pH," by S. Schachter, B. Silverstein, L. T. Kozlowski, C. P. Herman, and B. Leibling, *Journal of Experimental Psychology: General,* 1977, *106,* 24–30. Copyright 1977 by the American Psychological Association. Reprinted with permission. **277,** Figure 9-4 from "Cocaine," by C. VanDyke and R. Byck, *Scientific American,* 1982, *246,* 128–141. Copyright © 1982 by Scientific American, Inc. All rights reserved. **283, 284, and 285,** Figures 9-5 through 9-8 from "An Opponent-Process Theory of Motivation: 1. Temporal Dynamics of Affect," by R. L. Solomon and J. D. Corbit, *Psychological Review,* 1974, *81,* 119–145. Copyright 1974 by the American Psychological Association. Reprinted with permission. **300,** Figure 9-9 from "The Power of Positive Drinking," by D. C. McClelland, *Psychology Today,* January 1971, *4,* 40–41. Reprinted from *Psychology Today Magazine.* Copyright © 1971 American Psychological Association.

Chapter 10: 312, Figure 10-1 from *The Expression of Emotions in Man and Animals,* by Charles Darwin. Copyright 1873 by R. West, Philadelphia. Reprinted from *The Expression of Emotions in Man and Animals,* by Charles Darwin, by permission of The University of Chicago Press, copyright 1965. **315 and 316,** Figures 10-2 and 10-3 from *The Psychobiology of Aggression,* by K. E. Moyer. Copyright © 1976 by K. E. Moyer. Reprinted with permission of Harper & Row, Publishers, Inc. **319,** Table 10-1 adapted from "Social Rank and Radio-Stimulated Aggressiveness in Monkeys," by J. M. R. Delgado, *The Journal of Nervous and Mental Diseases,* 1967, *144,* pp. 383–390. Copyright © 1967 by The Williams and Wilkins Co., Baltimore. Reprinted with permission. **320–323,** Figures 10-4 through 10-7 from "Self-Consciousness and Intentionality," by K. Pribram. In G. E. Schwartz and D. Shapiro (Eds.), *Consciousness and Self-Regulation: Advances in Research* (Vol. 1). **324,** Table 10-2 from "Aggression and Hypoglycemia among the Qolla. A Study in Psychobiological Anthropology," by R. Bolton, *Ethnology,* 1973, *12,* 227–257. Copyright 1973 by *Ethnology.* Reprinted with the permission of the publisher and author. **332,** Figure 10-8 from "Effects of Noise and Perceived Control on Ongoing and Subsequent Aggressive Behavior," by E. Donnerstein and D. W. Wilson, *Journal of Personality and Social Psychology,* 1976, *34,* 774–781. Copyright 1976 by the American Psychological Association. Reprinted with permission. **333,** Figure 10-9 from "Sexual Arousal and Aggression by Males: Effects of Type of Erotic Stimuli and Prior Provocation," by R. A. Baron and P. A. Bell, *Journal of Personality and Social Psychology,* 1977, *35,* 79–87. Copyright 1977 by the American Psychological Association. Reprinted with permission. **335,** Figure 10-10 from *Human Aggression,* by R. A. Baron. Copyright 1977 by Plenum Publishing Corporation. Reprinted with permission. **336,** Figure 10-11 from "Ambient Temperature and the Occurrence of Collective Violence: The 'Long Hot Summer' Revisited," by R. A. Baron and V. M. Ransberger, *Journal of Personality and Social Psychology,* 1978, *36,* 351–360. Copyright 1978 by the American Psychological Association. Reprinted with permission. **343,** Figure 10-12 from "Individual Differences in Aggressive Responses to Attack: Internal-External Locus of Control and Field Dependence-Independence," by H. A. Dengerink, M. R. O'Leary, and K. H. Kasner, *Journal of Research in Personality,* 1975, *9,* 191–199. Copyright 1975 by Academic Press. Reprinted with permission.

Chapter 11: 369 and 370, Figures 11-1 and 11-2 from "The Effects of Failure and Depression on Subsequent Aggression," by H. A. Dengerink and J. D. Myers, *Journal of Personality and Social Psychology,* 1977, *35,* 88–96. Copyright 1977 by the American Psychological Association. Reprinted with permission. **372,** Figure 11-3 from "Effects of Noise and Perceived Control on Ongoing and Subsequent Aggressive Behavior," by E. Donnerstein and D. W. Wilson, *Journal of Personality and Social Psychology,* 1976, *34,* 774–781. Copyright 1976 by the American Psychological Association. Reprinted with permission. **380,** Figure 11-4 from "The Topology of Assertive Behavior in Positive and Negative Situations," by S. W. Pitcher and S. Meikle, *Behavior Therapy,* 1980, *11,* 532–547. Copyright 1980 by the Association for Advancement of Behavior Therapy. Reprinted with permission.

Chapter 12: 387, Table 12-1 from "Motivational Determinants of Risk-Taking Behavior," by J. W. Atkinson, *Psychological Review,* 1957, *64,* 359–372. Copyright 1957 by the American Psychological Association. Reprinted by permission. **389,** Table 12-2 from "Fear of Unrealistic Vocational Aspiration," by C. H. Mahone, *Journal of Abnormal and Social Psychology,* 1960, *60,* 253–261. Copyright 1961 by the American Psychological Association. Reprinted with permission. **392, 393, and 394,** Figures 12-1, 12-2, and 12-3 from "Achievement-Related Motives and Behavior," by J. T. Spence and R. L. Helmreich, in Janet T. Spence (Ed.), *Achievement and Achievement Motives.* Copyright 1983 by W. H. Freeman. Reprinted with permission. **396,** Figure 12-4 from *The Achieving Society,* by D. C. McClelland. Copyright 1961 by D. Van Nostrand Co. Reprinted with permission.

405, Table 12-4 from "Attribution and Affect: Comment on Sohn's Critique," by B. Weiner, *Journal of Educational Psychology,* 1977, *69,* 506–511. Copyright 1977 by the American Psychological Association. Reprinted with permission. **409,** Figure 12-5 from "Partial Reinforcement and Partial Delay of Reinforcement Effects with 72-Hour Intertrial Intervals and Interpolated Continuous Reinforcement," by M. E. Rashotte and C. T. Surridge, *Journal of Experimental Psychology,* May 1969, *21,* 156–161. Copyright 1969 by the Journal of Experimental Psychology and the authors. Reprinted with permission. **413,** Table 12-5 from "The Power Motive," by D. G. Winter and A. J. Stewart. In H. London and J. E. Exner, Jr. (Eds.), *Dimensions of Personality.* Copyright 1978 by John Wiley & Sons, Inc. Reprinted with permission. **416 and 417,** Table 12-6 and Figure 12-6 from *Human Motivation,* by David C. McClelland. Copyright 1985 by Scott, Foresman and Company. Reprinted by permission. (Figure based on Heckhausen, H., *Motiv und Handen,* Springer Verlag, 1980, and Kleinbeck, U., and Schnackers, U., *Archiv für Psychologie,* 1975, No. 127, pp. 300–319). **419,** Figure 12-7 from "The Power Motive as an Influence on Use of Power," by E. M. Fodor and D. L. Farrow, *Journal of Personality and Social Psychology,* 1979, *37,* 2091–2097. Copyright 1979 by the American Psychological Association. Reprinted with permission.

Chapter 13: 428, Figure 13-2 adapted from "Exploration and Play in Children," by C. Hutt, *Symposium of the Zoological Society of London,* No. 18, 61–81. Copyright 1966 by the Zoological Society of London. Reprinted with permission. **430,** Figure 13-3 from "Uncertainty, Structure and Preference," by H. Munsinger and W. Kessen, *Psychological Monographs,* 1964, *78,* 1–23. Copyright 1964 by the American Psychological Association. Reprinted with permission. **432,** Figure 13-5 from "Novelty, Complexity and Hedonic Value," by D. E. Berlyne, *Perception and Psychophysics,* 1970, p. 283. Copyright 1970 by the Psychonomic Society, Inc. Reprinted with permission. **433,** Figure 13-6 from "The Influence of Complexity and Novelty in Visual Figures on Orienting Responses," by D. E. Berlyne, *Journal of Experimental Psychology,* 1958, *55,* 289–296. Copyright 1958 by the American Psychological Association. Reprinted by permission. **436,** Figure 13-7 from "The Effect of Stimulus Uncertainty on the Relationship between Frequency of Exposure and Liking," by G. F. Smith and D. D. Dorfman, *Journal of Personality and Social Psychology,* 1975, *31,* 150–155. Copyright 1975 by the American Psychological Association. Reprinted with permission. **437,** Figures 13-8 and 13-9 reprinted with the permission of the publisher from: Franken, R. E., & Strain, A., "Effect of Increased Arousal on Response to Stimulus Change in a Complex Maze." *Perceptual and Motor Skills,* 1974, *39,* 1076–1078. Fig. 1. **448 and 449,** Practical Application 13-1 from "The Search for High Sensation," by M. Zuckerman, *Psychology Today,* February, 1978, *11*(9), 38–46. Reprinted from *Psychology Today Magazine.* Copyright 1978 American Psychological Association.

Chapter 14: 472, Figure 14-1 from "Equity and Intrinsic Motivation: The Role of Choice," by R. Folger, D. Rosenfield, and R. P. Hays, *Journal of Personality and Social Psychology,* 1978, *36,* 557–564. Copyright 1978 by the American Psychological Association. Reprinted with permission. **474,** Figure 14-2 from *Motivation in Work Organizations,* by E. E. Lawler. Copyright © 1973 by Wadsworth, Inc. Reprinted with the permission of Brooks/Cole Publishing Company, Pacific Grove, California 93950. **475,** Figure 14-3 from *Motivation and Work Behavior,* by R. M. Steers and L. W. Porter. Copyright © 1979 by McGraw-Hill, Inc. Used with the permission of the McGraw-Hill Book Company. **476 and 477,** Tables 14-1 and 14-2 adapted from *Work in America: Report of a Special Task Force to the U.S. Department of Health, Education and Welfare* by permission of The MIT Press, Cambridge, Massachusetts. Copyright 1973 by The MIT Press.